Organizational Behavior for School Leadership

Organizational Behavior for School Leadership provides a theoretical and practical framework to help emerging leaders build the mental models they need to be effective. Presenting traditional, modern, and contemporary perspectives, each chapter offers opportunities for readers to reflect on the ideas and apply their leadership perspective and skills to their own work settings. In this way, this important book helps graduate students in educational leadership understand organizational situations and circumstances, an essential step in making appropriate decisions about people, school operations, and the community that generate improved student and teacher outcomes.

Special features include:

- *Guiding questions*—chapter openers to initiate student thinking.
- *Case studies and companion rubrics*—engage students in applying content to real-life school scenarios with guiding rubrics to help think through answers.
- *Reflections and relevance*—interactive learning activities, simulations, and graphic assignments deepen readers' understanding.
- *PSEL Standards*—each chapter aligns with the 2015 Professional Standards for Educational Leaders.
- *Companion website*—includes case studies and rubrics, supplementary materials, additional readings, and PowerPoint slides for instructors.

Leslie S. Kaplan is a retired school administrator, a full-time education writer, and an Adjunct Research Professor at Old Dominion University, USA.

William A. Owings is Professor of Educational Leadership at Old Dominion University, USA.

Organizational Behavior for School Leadership

Leveraging Your School for Success

Leslie S. Kaplan and
William A. Owings

Routledge
Taylor & Francis Group

NEW YORK AND LONDON

First published 2017
by Routledge
711 Third Avenue, New York, NY 10017

and by Routledge
2 Park Square, Milton Park, Abingdon, Oxon, OX14 4RN

Routledge is an imprint of the Taylor & Francis Group, an informa business

© 2017 Taylor & Francis

The right of Leslie S. Kaplan and William A. Owings to be identified as the authors
of this part of the work has been asserted by them in accordance with sections 77 and 78
of the Copyright, Designs and Patents Act 1988.

Library of Congress Cataloging in Publication Data
Names: Kaplan, Leslie S., author. | Owings, William A., 1952– author.
Title: Organizational behavior for school leadership : leveraging your school for success /
by Leslie S. Kaplan and William A. Owings.
Description: New York, NY : Routledge, 2017.
Identifiers: LCCN 2016044279| ISBN 9781138948693 (hardback) |
ISBN 9781138948709 (pbk.) | ISBN 9781315669502 (master ebook) |
ISBN 9781317364290 (mobi/kindle)
Subjects: LCSH: School management and organization. | Organizational behavior. |
Organizational change. | Educational leadership. | Communication in education.
Classification: LCC LB2805 .K364 2017 | DDC 371.2—dc23
LC record available at https://lccn.loc.gov/2016044279

ISBN: 978-1-138-94869-3 (hbk)
ISBN: 978-1-138-94870-9 (pbk)
ISBN: 978-1-315-66950-2 (ebk)

Typeset in Sabon and Helvetica Neue
by Florence Production Ltd, Stoodleigh, Devon, UK

Visit the companion website: www.routledge.com/cw/kaplan

Printed and bound in Great Britain by
TJ International Ltd, Padstow, Cornwall

Contents

Detailed Contents

About the Authors

Leslie S. Kaplan, Ed.D., a retired school administrator in Newport News, VA is a full-time education writer. She has provided middle and high school instructional and school improvement leadership as an assistant principal for instruction as well as central office leadership as a director of program development. Before becoming a school administrator, she was a middle and high school counselor, and these insights continue to infuse her leadership perspective. Her professional interests focus on principal quality, teacher quality, school culture, school finance, and educational foundations and their relationship to school improvement and increasing student achievement. She has co-authored several books and monographs with William Owings including *Introduction to the Principalship: Theory to Practice*; *Culture Re-Boot: Reinvigorating School Culture to Improve Student Outcomes*; *American Public School Finance* (2nd edition); *Educational Foundations* (2nd edition); *Leadership and Organizational Behavior in Education: Theory into Practice*; *The Effective Schools Movement: History, Analysis, and Application*; *Teacher Quality, Teaching Quality, and School Improvement*; *Best Practices, Best Thinking, and Emerging Issues in School Leadership*; and *Enhancing Teacher and Teaching Quality*. Kaplan's scholarly publications, co-authored with Owings, appear in numerous peer-reviewed national and international professional journals. Kaplan serves on the National Association of Secondary School Principals' (NASSP) *Bulletin* Editorial Advisory Board. She is a past president of the Virginia Counselors' Association and the Virginia Association for Supervision and Curriculum Development and recently served as Board Secretary of Voices for Virginia's Children.

William A. Owings, Ed.D., is currently a professor of educational leadership at Old Dominion University in Norfolk, VA. Owings has worked as a public school teacher, an elementary and high school principal, assistant superintendent, and superintendent of schools. His professional interests are in school finance, principal quality, and teacher quality as they relate to school improvement and student achievement. In addition, his scholarly publications co-authored with Leslie Kaplan include articles in *NASSP Bulletin, Journal of School Leadership, Journal of Education Finance, Journal of Effective School*s, *Phi Delta Kappan*, the *Teachers College Record,* the *Eurasian Journal of Business and Economics*, and *The European Journal of Economic and Political Studies*. Owings has served on the state and international board of the

Association for Supervision and Curriculum Development (ASCD) and serves on the *Journal of Education Finance* Editorial Advisory Board.

Kaplan and Owings are frequent presenters at state and national conferences on topics including educational leadership, school finance, school culture, and instructional improvement. Owings and Kaplan share the 2008 Virginia Educational Research Association Charles Edgar Clear Research Award for Consistent and Substantial Contributions to Educational Research and Scholarship. They were each named in 2014 as Distinguished Fellows of Research & Practice by the National Education Finance Academy.

Preface

Schools are highly complex organizations. More than brick-and-mortar buildings, schools are people working together in structured ways to achieve a common purpose. The number of interdependent tasks and people needed to provide a high-quality learning environment is almost overwhelming. Yet most leadership and organizational behavior texts that graduate students study don't ready them to be school leaders. This one does.

Your authors ought to know. Between us, Leslie Kaplan and Bill Owings, we have spent more than 60 years working in PreK-12 public schools as teachers, counselor, department chair, assistant principal, principal, central office leaders, and district superintendent. We know how schools work and how leaders work in schools. We know first-hand the stress of juggling dozens of responsibilities at the same time; the tensions between meeting deadlines and meeting with the many people who deserve our attention; and the constant surprises that rip our focus from the important to the urgent.

In our experiences, graduate leadership preparation coursework may present a semester's worth of *topics*—chapters on leadership history and theories, school governance, motivation, conflict, decision making, and so on—that we needed to know. We "aced" those courses. But knowing "the facts" did not mean we knew how to use them to *make sense of*—and hopefully, *to shape*—the events happening in our schools.

How is this book different? First, we have selected what we believe—*and research shows*—to be the *essential* traditional and contemporary leadership and organizational behavior ideas for school leaders. These range from scientific management to complexity leadership theory and from rationalistic to sensemaking theories. Second, we build this book on sound pedagogy. After major concepts, *Organizational Behavior for School Leadership* offers opportunities for graduate students to reflect on these ideas, apply them to their work settings, and discuss them with classmates and professors. In the process, students create personal meaning and workplace relevance, gaining deepened understanding and increasing retention. And by helping graduate students develop accurate mental models of organizational (school) leadership and a theory of practice to guide their perspectives, thoughts, and actions, they transfer their learning about organizational leadership from the university classroom to the schoolhouse or district office. In short, *Organizational Behavior for School Leadership* prepares readers to see, think, and (as opportunities present themselves) act as school leaders now. So when your time comes, you will not just be available and certified as school leaders: *you* will be *ready*.

FEATURES OF *ORGANIZATIONAL BEHAVIOR FOR SCHOOL LEADERSHIP: LEVERAGING YOUR SCHOOL FOR SUCCESS*

This book intends to help novice school leaders understand the essentials of traditional and contemporary leadership and organizational behavior theories in ways that prepare them to be effective school leaders in their current and future roles. First-rate content and pedagogically sound features *presented in innovative ways* support this goal.

- *Guiding questions.* Each chapter begins with guiding questions that identify the concepts readers will be able to analyze, assess, define, describe, discuss, explain, or summarize after reading. These tend to be "big picture" issues. For example, after reading Chapter 1, "Leading Organizations: Evolving Perspectives," readers will be able to discuss how expectations for school leadership have evolved along with changing societal expectations for children's education.
- *Case studies and rubrics.* Problems that school leaders face tend to be poorly structured, complex, dynamic, and abstract. So are our case studies. Each chapter has two case study scenarios with companion rubrics. One introduces the chapter; the second appears on the book's website. The first rubric—*that your authors have already completed*—is akin to "thinking out loud" with a successful principal about what the situation presents and how to address it. The rubrics help readers view the situation from varied frames of reference, make reasonable assumptions, prompt informed decisions about how to proceed, and consider *how this situation might have been prevented.* The second case study and rubric on the book's website asks readers to apply what they learned in the chapter to construct their own responses (using the first case study rubric as a model). A discussion of how to use the case studies and rubrics appears below.
- *Mental models and theories of practice.* Just as travelers use up-to-date road "apps" to help them visualize and plan trips, educational leaders can use conceptual maps—*mental models* and *theories of practice*—to guide what they look at and shape their perceptions so they can better anticipate events, explain what is happening, predict future occurrences under specific conditions, and consider how to control a situation or influence an outcome. Each chapter contains selected relevant theories to help readers begin constructing and applying these conceptual tools to help them make sense of their schools and become effective leaders within their organizations.
- *Educational and school examples. Organizational Behavior for School Leadership* is anchored in PreK-12 school realities. It answers "So what use is this?" by connecting theory with practice. Theory without relevant application lacks meaning. Application without relevant theory is random. To this end, we deliberately chose content for its fidelity to established and current knowledge of leadership and organizational behavior *germane to schools.* Frequent examples show how each

concept looks in practice. And each chapter ends with "Implications for Educational Leaders" which highlights the key "take-aways" that readers can bring with them into their workplaces now.

- *Reflections and Relevance.* After each major concept, reflection and engagement activities invite readers to apply the new perspective to themselves as leaders and to their own schools as organizations. Individual reflections, paired and small group conversations, graphic exercises, and whole class simulations and discussions reinforce the content and give it deeper and personal meaning. Being prompted to make pertinent links between the content, themselves, and their worksites further increases student learning and the probability of transfer into practice. This socially mediated learning also strengthens collegiality and makes professional networking more likely. Of course, professors can revise and adapt these activities to meet their instructional goals.

- *Professional Standards for Educational Leaders (PSEL).* Since the New England "schoolmaster," school leaders' roles and responsibilities have shifted along with the evolution of American society and public schools. The 2015 Professional Standards for Educational Leaders (PSEL) describe what educational leaders should know and be able to do to ensure *each and every* student's academic success and wellbeing. Underscoring the holistic and systemic nature of school leaders' work, PSEL standards highlight setting mission, vision, and core values; enacting ethical and professional behavior; developing the professional staff's capacity; emphasizing leadership for school improvement, cultural responsiveness, and equity; providing high-quality curriculum, instruction, and assessment; ensuring accountable operations and management; and focusing on creating a community of care for faculty and staff. Each chapter begins by identifying the relevant PSEL standards in that chapter. Chapter 1 introduces the PSEL standards and explains the research that supports these benchmarks for effective professional practice. PSEL standards, their rationale, and links between educational leadership and student learning are available at: www.ccsso.org/Documents/2015/ProfessionalStandardsforEducational Leaders2015forNPBEAFINAL.pdf

- *Companion website.* This book has a companion website that includes a set of PowerPoint slides, a second case study and rubric for each chapter, and additional theorists, topics, and learning activities. Each chapter also has at least six videos (mainly TED-Ed and YouTube) with web addresses, and six documents. All have accompanying curricular activities to intensify and extend students' understanding of the chapter's contents.

LEARNING WITH THE CASE STUDIES

Case studies are complex learning experiences—essentially, *virtual simulations* of situations schools leaders actually face. Each chapter contains two case studies with accompanying *rubrics*—a coherent set of criteria to guide thinking and decision making. The first case study introduces the chapter; the second appears on the book's website listed under that chapter. Every scenario comes from the authors' combined 60 years of PreK-12 experiences as school leaders. Since the case relates to the chapter's content—that readers have not yet read—your authors have completed Case Study 1's rubric in each chapter for you. In this way, readers can follow the authors' "thinking out loud" about the case's circumstances and how to address them.

The rubrics provide three questions to guide the readers' thinking in problem solving. Across the top, the rubric asks:

What are the factors at play in this case?
What steps should be considered in solving the problem?
What could have been done to avoid this dilemma?

Presented down the left-hand column, the rubric presents several conceptual lenses or context factors to consider in decision making:[1]

Situational context: the task, personal abilities, and school environment
Organizational context: goals, values, policies, and culture
People context: individual needs, beliefs, goals, and relationships
Political context: individuals or groups competing for power, influence, and resources
Traditional context: school culture, rituals, meaning, and heroes

These situation-specific as well as larger context factors recognize schools as open systems with many influences, stakeholders, and competing interests that impact decision making.

Although we walk students through the thought process for each chapter's first case study, students construct answers for the second case on the companion website using what they learned in the chapter. This second case study presents a different situation but uses the same rubric. Engaging with the case studies and rubrics is a *formative* activity. The further students progress through the book and the more they learn, the more complete and accurate their rubric answers should become. Professors can determine the quality of students' performance on this second case study rubric according to their course expectations.

STEPS FOR USING THE CASE STUDIES

1. **Read the case study.** Once readers understand the situation presented, they can address each of the three rubric questions (across the top) in relation to the context factors to be considered in decision making (in the left column) and construct meaningful responses (in the boxes where the questions intersect the context).
2. **Read the questions across the rubric's top and apply each conceptual lens (context) in the left hand column to construct an answer.**
   - Question 1: "What factors are at play in this case?" The first step in problem solving is to identify the key facts. Concisely summarize the state of affairs.

What is happening? Who is involved? What do they want? The scenario either clearly states or suggests these answers.

Consider this question as it relates to the situation-specific factors: the *task* at hand, the *personal abilities* of those involved, and the overall *school environment*. What does the case study say or suggest about these factors and how might they influence solving the protagonist's problem?

- **Question 2: "What steps should be considered in solving the problem?"** What various actions should the school leader take in solving the problem?

  Consider this question as it relates to the situation-specific factors: the *task* at hand, the *personal abilities* of those involved, and the overall *school environment*. What does the case study say or suggest about these factors and how might they influence solving the protagonist's problem?

- **Question 3: "What could have been done to avoid this dilemma?"** This question helps readers think proactively and learn from their experiences. Unless leaders are proactive, they risk having the same issues coming up time and time again (a situation to avoid).

  Consider this question as it relates to the situation-specific factors: the *task* at hand, the *personal abilities* of those involved, and the overall *school environment*. What does the case study say or suggest about these factors and how might they influence solving the protagonist's problem?

3. **Examine the whole case scenario from the organizational, people, political, and tradition contexts.** Examine the issue from an *organizational lens*—the goals, values, policies, and beliefs prominent in the scenario's school and district. Second, look from a *people lens*—the individuals in the situation and their personal or professional needs, beliefs, goals, and the relationships with each other and within the school. Third, examine the *political lens*—the competing needs for power, influence, and resources. Finally, examine the *school's or district's tradition lens*— its culture, rituals, mascots, what the school stands for, and who they celebrate as heroes. Not each of these contexts will be applicable; the case study information is limited. But if the scenario does not give this information, *imagine* context factors that *might* influence decision making—and *how*. Happy thinking!

With this unique case study and rubric process, we give readers a system—a mental model—for approaching, understanding, interpreting, and resolving complex situations that can bring effective and sustainable solutions. In this way, graduate students can practice the thinking that goes into solving poorly structured, complex, dynamic, and abstract problems that they will face as school leaders in a way that transfers to their worksites.

NOTE

1   We thank leadership theorists discussed in this book and Lee G. Bolman and Terrence E. Deal for inspiring us to consider varied lenses—*contexts*—for making decisions in organizations. See: Bolman, L.G. & Deal, T.E. (2013). *Reframing organizations* (5th ed.). San Francisco, CA: Jossey-Bass.

Acknowledgments

Throughout writing and production, Heather Jarrow, our Routledge development editor, continues to be our valued companion, guiding us with her intelligence, encouragement, flexibility, and practical suggestions. Sincere thanks to Rebecca Collazo, our Routledge Editorial Assistant, who has the talent to spot and *effectively resolve* potential problems before bringing them to our attention. Thanks, too, to Hannah Slater, our Routledge Production Editor and to Victoria Brown, our copy editor from Production Editorial Services, for their excellent support during the production process. "Thank you"s also go to the rest of the Routledge team.

CHAPTER 1

Leading Organizations: Evolving Perspectives

GUIDING QUESTIONS

1.1 Explain how mental models and a theory of practice can influence a school leader's real world performance.

1.2 Define systems thinking and describe how it can help future school leaders successfully transition from the classroom to the principalship.

1.3 Describe how the cultural, social, economic, and organizational changes from the Industrial Era and the Knowledge Era led to the need for different organizational leadership skills.

1.4 Analyze the differences in the relationship between the individual leader and the group in entity and collectivist leadership theories.

1.5 Explain the differences in traditions, practices, and limitations between rationalistic and sensemaking theories.

1.6 Discuss how expectations for school leadership have evolved along with changing societal expectations for children's education.

1.7 Identify the essential leadership and organizational concepts underlying the 2015 Professional Standards for Educational Leaders.

1.8 Summarize the cautions for educational leadership students in studying leadership and organizational theories.

2015 PROFESSIONAL STANDARDS FOR EDUCATIONAL LEADERS (PSEL):
1, 2, 3, 4, 5, 6, 7, 8, 9, 10

CASE STUDY 1.1

Watching the Parade through a Knothole in a Fence or Seeing the Entire Parade from the Grandstand

Franklin Ford High School (FFHS) is located in a traditionally rural area of the state and houses 2,200 students. Jerry Edwards, now 55 years old, has been the Assistant Principal for Operations (APO) since entering the assistant principalship after working five years as a business teacher. He has been awarded state honors for the efficient manner in which he keeps the buses rolling and textbooks and supplies ordered, his consistent by-the-book discipline practices, his accounting prowess and inventory control, and student locker management skills.

Bill Smith has been the beloved principal at FFHS for the last 20 years. While Bill and Jerry are not close friends, Bill admires Jerry for how he keeps the school operating like a "well-oiled machine." This allows Bill to concentrate on the other tasks that require his attention—working with the school leadership teams, mentoring new teachers and assistant principals, providing instructional leadership, and dealing with community issues—"big picture issues" as Bill calls it. The other three assistant principals are all relatively new with tenures of 1, 3, and 4 years. FFHS assistant principals frequently tend to move on to their own principalships after several years of working closely with Bill. In fact, the two most senior assistant principals announced in February that they are leaving in June to become principals in nearby school systems.

At the end of April, Bill Smith told the Superintendent he would be retiring at the end of the year. Secretly, Jerry wanted to be the principal for some time and thought he would be a better principal than Bill. Jerry considered that all Bill did was to meet with teachers and community members while Jerry was the real leader and organizer of the school. The Superintendent, Bill, and Jerry met in May to discuss the leadership transition. Bill recommended that Jerry become the principal for continuity and for the fact that there would be two new APs and the returning one would have only one year of experience. The Superintendent agreed, and the School Board announced at the June 1st Board meeting that Jerry would succeed Bill next year.

Over the summer and the first semester, Jerry continued to concentrate on the operations side. He assigned each grade level 9–12 to one of the assistant principals, three of whom are new, to do what he thought Bill had done: observe the teachers, coordinate curriculum decisions, and deal with parents and community concerns. By November, tensions grew within and across grade levels about substantial curriculum, personnel, and communication problems. Each assistant principal was acting independently. At a December faculty meeting, tempers flared and more than half the faculty walked out in protest of unresolved issues. What is Jerry to do?

RUBRIC 1.1

Lens and/or factors to be considered in decision making	What are the factors at play in this case?	What steps should be considered in solving the problem?	What could have been done to avoid this dilemma?
The situation			
• The task	Faculty leadership and coordination issues not resolved following transition.	Meet with faculty (in departments or grade levels) and leadership teams to define the problem and listen to suggested solutions.	Superintendent and Jerry clarify the principal and AP roles and responsibilities in the FFHS transition.
• Personal abilities	Jerry's mental model of leadership did not see the principal's overall role clearly. He failed to make the conceptual and behavioral transition from AP to principal.	Assessment of Jerry's ability to lead as the principal; professional development for new APs; mentoring and monitoring by central office.	Professional development for the new FFHS administrative team from Central Office; Keeping Bill Smith on for the transition.
• The school environment	Negative work climate; Faltering morale and frustrated faculty due to lack of coordination.	Meet with faculty after defining the problem and share the resolution plan asking for further comments.	Transition team planning meetings with retiring Bill, Jerry, new APs, and central office coordinator.
Look Wider			
Organizational (goals, values, policies, culture)	A once well-run school has had a leadership change that resulted in faculty frustration.	Meeting with the faculty to get input about the issue and meeting with them again to share ideas for improved communication.	Jerry needed to understand the culture, norms, and expectations that Bill built and how he achieved it.
People (individuals with needs, beliefs, goals, relationships)	Bill saw the value of the combined leadership of the team. Jerry continued operating as the AP he had been before.	Jerry and the APs need to meet ASAP and discuss the problem. Central office may need to assess Jerry's ability to continue as the principal.	Jerry needed to understand that his role was not to continue doing what he had always done. His role needed to change. Did he have the skills needed?
Competing Interests (for power, influence, and resources)	N/A	N/A	N/A
Tradition (school culture, rituals, meaning, heroes)	N/A	N/A	N/A

OVERVIEW: WHY CONSIDER AN ORGANIZATIONAL PERSPECTIVE ON LEADERSHIP?

According to *Global Human Capital Trends 2014*, leadership is still the No. 1 talent issue facing organizations everywhere. In their survey of over 2,500 business and human resource leaders in 94 countries, 86 percent of respondents rated developing "leaders at all levels" as "urgent" or "important." And, in a world where knowledge doubles each year and skills stay current 2.5 to 5 years, leaders need to continuously learn if they are to understand the rapidly changing technologies, disciplines, and realities in their fields.[1] Organizations of all kinds have ongoing needs to develop leaders to meet the changing workforce expectations, responsibilities for meeting clients' requests, and advance their institution's interests. The capability gap between the *urgency* of what organizations require to thrive and their *readiness* to address these concerns is huge. Effective leadership is essential if organizations are to survive and prosper.

In our complex world, organizations carry out much of life's daily business. Organizations—such as schools, businesses, industries, military services, and government—are not brick-and-mortar buildings. They cannot be air conditioned, painted, or locked down every evening. Rather, organizations are people working together in structured ways to meet a need or to produce specific goods, services, or other outcomes. They are social systems that bring people together for a common purpose. And because organizations tend to be big and multifaceted, they depend on effective leaders who can energize and direct competent followers to make their enterprises work.

At every level of organizations, leaders provide clear focus and direction. They have a deep understanding of the organization's central mission and its core knowledge and skill sets. They have the capacity to set direction, innovate, and inspire others to perform at their best. They have the ability to lead in uncertain situations. Flexible and collaborative, leaders are strong at developing relationships and effective teams. They create and sustain the climates that support employees' efforts, tapping into their motives to help them invest in their work, continue learning, and increase their skills. Leaders guide colleagues through frequent improvement changes. They ensure that problems in their organizations are quickly identified, ethically decided, and effectively resolved. Conflict is well managed. Accountability for performance is clear, fair, and public. No wonder finding leadership talent is such a vital need. In fact, business consultants conclude that the quality of leaders is declining and suggest that organizations "re-examine and redesign" their leadership development programs.[2] What it took to be a leader several decades ago is not sufficient to be a successful leader today.

As organizations, schools need robust and effective leaders—not only in the superintendents' or principals' office but also at every grade level, in every department, and in every classroom—if students are to learn what they need for civic responsibility, meaningful, well-compensated employment, and life-long education. But leadership does not happen in a vacuum. It can only occur in interactions with others in a particular context as individuals become groups working for a common purpose. Thus, to learn how to be a highly successful leader—and administrator, to make the endeavor operate effectively—one must learn how to function skillfully within organizations. Accordingly, understanding both leadership and organization disciplines—and their interactions—become essential topics for professional study.

CONCEPTUAL TOOLS TO UNDERSTAND LEADERSHIP IN ORGANIZATIONS

Education is a very complicated endeavor. Lenay Dunn, an Arizona State University educational researcher and evaluator, observes that education involves inputs educators cannot control (such as family resources, parent education, children with different cultures, languages, and learning needs); variables they can't easily measure (such as classroom culture, peer influence, teacher beliefs and biases, and principal leadership); and outcomes they cannot predict or easily assess (including emotional intelligence, practical intelligence, creativity, persistence, and resilience).[3] Similarly, the late Kenneth E. Boulding, a Nobel Prize-nominee in both Peace and Economics, wryly noted that if physical systems were as complex as social systems, "we would creep hesitantly out of bed each morning, not knowing whether we were about to crash to the floor or float to the ceiling."[4] It is no wonder that principals often feel overwhelmed, as if they are responsible for everything that happens in their buildings over which they have only indirect (if any) control.

Most future principals were once highly effective classroom teachers. Many have found that moving from classroom teacher to assistant principal or principal can be a real culture shock. Although teachers and principals are both educators, they actually represent two different professions within education, each with its own body of knowledge and skills, professional norms, and mental models. Classroom expertise, although central to teaching effectiveness, is only part of the knowledge, skills, and mind sets that principals need to be successful school leaders. Each profession holds its own conceptual frameworks that influence how its practitioners think, interpret events, and act.

Teachers and principals see and act differently in the school. While teachers lead learning in their classrooms, principals orchestrate the school's entire educational program and the performance of everyone within it according to district and state standards. Teachers manage their course materials and meet their grade level expectations for student learning. Principals navigate improvement efforts with all academic departments in a context of ambiguity and competing demands from inside and outside the school and district. While teachers have predictable daily schedules organized by ringing bells and moving students, principals tend to arrive early, stay late (especially if they work in middle or high schools that have sports teams), and see their plans frequently interrupted by "urgent" rather than "important" issues. Teachers' time frame focuses on the week, the marking period, or the semester. Principals' strategic and school improvement planning spans days to years. Teachers consult with colleagues and with students and parents, usually one-on-one or in small groups. Principals consult with a wide array of adults in the school community in formats ranging from individuals to small and auditorium-sized groups.

Accordingly, a good place to begin thinking about leadership in schools—and where this chapter begins—is with a larger lens. We begin with a look at mental models, theories of practice, and a conceptual model for understanding organizational leadership. We then move to evolving perspectives on leadership and organizations, including systems thinking. We conclude with a look at the changing principalship, the 2015 Professional Standards for Educational Leaders (PSEL), and the implications for education leaders. Our examples will focus on schools. In this way, future education leaders can begin to build the conceptual schema to make sense of the array of organizational leadership viewpoints before studying their individual elements. The shift in thinking from whole to parts with a practical application in schools will inform emerging leaders' perspective and give them increased agency in the real world situations they will face.

DEVELOPING MENTAL MODELS

Just as travelers use up-to-date road maps to help them visualize and plan trips, educational leaders can use conceptual maps—or *mental models*—to help them anticipate, plan for, and conduct school leadership activities. Having the best maps, reading them correctly, and making adjustments when needed help leaders select the most appropriate routes to their destinations. Similarly, we all carry in our heads small scale images—or models—that represent our understanding of external reality. In fact, one might persuasively argue that thinking of organizations as systems of interacting elements is, itself, a mental model.

Peter Senge, a management expert, defines *mental models* as deeply ingrained assumptions, generalizations, or images that shape how we understand the world and how we take action.[5] Mental models act as *conceptual lenses*—cognitive frames of reference used to focus thinking about a particular topic, a unifying factor that ties ideas together and permits a deeper understanding of the subject under review.[6] Because they shape our perceptions, mental models serve as guides to what we see and how we should interpret, consider, and act in different situations. At the same time, they may limit us to our familiar ways of thinking and acting. When our mental models no longer work to accurately interpret the world and we feel off kilter, we construct new ones. Since mental models may exist unseen, beyond our conscious awareness, yet influencing how we interpret and act on events, managing our mental models is important. To do this, we can make our mental models conscious, tacit, available for review scrutiny, and reflection. Only once we challenge the limitations in our current ways of knowing can we remedy our views with more complete and accurate insights.

For example, schools' leaders may hold the following mental models:

- A leader's power comes from developing strong, trusting relationships with others in the environment whose growth and empowerment are keys to organizational success.
- Learning is successful when the *students* find the content the teacher presents as relevant, intellectually rigorous, and personally meaningful.
- Receiving high quality, constructive feedback is an essential component of professional and organizational growth.

- Collaboration between teachers and administrators—and between teachers and other teachers—improves student outcomes.
- No problem exists in isolation. Factors in the issue, the environment, and the individuals all influence effective decision making and must be considered.

All models are simplifications. Thus, it is not so much a matter of whether our mental models are "right" or "wrong." Rather, it is important that we know what they are. When they are conscious, they become available for examination to ensure they are accurate, appropriate, and complete. Unexamined mental models remain unchanged. They prevent learning. And, the gap between how we see and understand our world and the realities of what the world actually is can grow larger. As this happens, our thoughts and actions become increasingly counterproductive. In contrast, as individuals open their mental models to examination, revise outdated or incorrect assumptions, and develop accurate ones, mental models can support and accelerate learning. When this happens, thoughts and actions become more productive; and our relationships and organizations benefit. In fact, contemporary research shows that most of our mental models are flawed: they miss critical feedback relationships, misjudge time delays, or concentrate on visible or salient variables rather than on those with high influence.[7]

As Senge observes, traditional leaders in organizations abide by the creed of managing, organizing, and controlling. In today's organizations, however, the new creed is vision, values, and mental models.[8] Organizations that thrive will be those that can systematically bring people together to develop the most effective mental models for addressing any situation they may face.

Most of us have mental models about what effective school leadership looks like, and we use this image to decide not only where to look but also how to interpret what we see. For instance, we may walk in on a high school faculty meeting in which small groups of teachers are actively talking together, and the principal is walking around. Do we see a mass of teachers boisterously off task, or do we see teachers from every academic department working together in small groups for a common purpose? Do we quickly decide that the principal is a poor leader whose teachers are "out of control," or do we think that the principal is an excellent motivator who wants to engage teachers in identifying and solving problems that affect them and their students? What details we look for and the conclusions we draw depend on what mental model we hold for principal leadership.

Likewise, school improvement depends on changing behaviors—and often, on changing teachers' mental models. New insights and practices often fail to get put into practice—or are not sustainable—because they conflict with teachers' and parents' deeply held internal images of what schools are and should do to advance student learning. Since mental models impact how people think and act, school leaders benefit when they help teachers uncover and express their mental models, test them for completeness and accuracy, and expand or revise how they see and interpret the events in their schools. Unless this occurs, teachers may *comply* with their principals' requests but they will not *commit* themselves to making the necessary changes in a way that will be sustained once the principal moves on.

DEVELOPING A THEORY OF PRACTICE

If principals don't succeed in transitioning from classroom to organizational leadership, it is sometimes because they lack the appropriate mental models—or theory of practice— for how to enact this new role with its new sets of expectations and skills. Many fledgling school leaders know what works "on paper" but cannot translate these ideas and skills into real world performance. Transitioning from graduate student to school leader, they have difficulties knowing how to move their ideas for school improvement from concept to actuality.

Theory is systematically organized knowledge and thought used to explain observed phenomena.[9] Theory is not a guess or a hunch. Nor is it an ivory tower thesis that professors dream up to make themselves feel smarter than their colleagues or their students. Good theory is based on research. All theories are situational, based on an underlying set of values, beliefs, and assumptions that frame how an individual perceives the world, including assumptions about desirable results for an array of circumstances.[10] Theories are useful when they can offer a foundation for thinking systematically about complex issues—such as the organizational characteristics that need attention if leaders are to generate the best outcomes or the qualities and conditions that contribute to effective leadership. Having a well-grounded theory allows individuals to explain what is happening, predict future occurrences under specific conditions, and consider ways to control a situation or influence an outcome. Good theories give direction for how to take appropriate action in a fast-paced, dynamic environment where most problems are complicated, time is always less than one would prefer, and any decision usually leads to additional ones. In short, good theories are enormously practical and can help school leaders hit the targets in their efforts to move schools forward.

A *theory of practice* is an integrated set of interrelated theories of action rooted in problems that occur in a professional's specific work setting and guide an individual's professional behavior. Individuals construct their theories of practice by synthesizing learned facts and personal experiences into a coherent set of related concepts for making sense of the school leadership role. Describing routines, procedures, and specific practices for dealing with common problems at work,[11] theories of practice are an individual's personal understanding of causal relationships. They help individuals make sense of the varied influences that affect the way they perform a particular role. One's theory of practice provides the intellectual footings that influence school leaders' daily decisions and long-term strategies.[12]

An *educational leadership theory of practice* includes the cognitive structures, processes, and behaviors that make up effective instructional leadership in schools.[13] Educational leadership students develop a theory of practice when they integrate an array of related theories with their professional experiences into a unified, consistent understanding of how leadership works in schools. For instance, instructional leaders might draw from their own classroom experiences and their graduate coursework to construct a theory of practice affirming that inviting teacher participation in making school decisions promotes more workable solutions, teachers' increased job satisfaction, and increased student achievement. Some suggest that theories of practice can also help school leaders reflect on their own actions in ways that enhance their professional effectiveness, bridging the gap between theory and practice.[14]

To develop a theory of practice for educational leadership, it is essential to understand three key concepts (that this book will address):[15]

- How adults working in organizations (particularly in schools) think and act. This aspect of organizational theory explores what motivates individuals at work, how they continue learning and improving their work performance and relationships, and how they make decisions and solve problems related to their professional performance.
- How organizational contexts influence people at work. This feature of organizational theory considers how leaders plan, structure, and organize work for individuals who must engage cooperatively with others to produce desired outcomes—and how environmental factors impact decision making and behaviors in schools.
- How leaders in organizations think and act. This aspect of organizational theory explains how leaders interface with people in their organization in ways that create a positive work climate and culture, communicate effectively, motivate employees, lead change, manage conflict, build capacity, think and act ethically, and provide resources in an effective and efficient manner.

Developing a theory of practice requires deep and extended learning, a mix of hands-on experiences, formal education, and intensive reflection on what it means to lead a group in a common endeavor. Once constructed, the leader can clearly express his or her theory of practice in words and deeds. It becomes a frame of reference for making sense out of leadership in schools. It also provides teachers with a sense of the leader's predictability. After several interactions, teachers soon understand what their leader believes and how their leader acts. This consistency and coherence boosts the leader's credibility and trustworthiness with others. And although one theory of practice in educational leadership may resemble others, its mooring in one's own experiences, readings, and interpretations make it uniquely one's own.

REFLECTIONS AND RELEVANCE 1.1

Developing a Theory of Practice

An educational leadership theory of practice is the individuals' personal understanding of the causal relationships that make up effective school leadership.

Begin to articulate your tentative theory of practice for school leadership. Make sure that each cluster web has at least one group addressing it. Using the section above to get ideas and working along, identify two cause and effect relationships about this concept that school leaders should know if they are to be effective in their leadership role and write them on the cluster web on page 10.

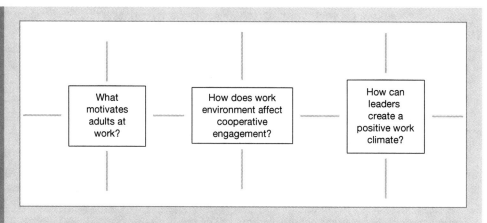

What motivates adults at work?	How does work environment affect cooperative engagement?	How can leaders create a positive work climate?

After 5 minutes, collaborate with two classmates to get additional ideas. When your small group has finished, discuss your findings as a class. You might want to return to these "mind maps" as you read this book to see what adjustments you want to make to more accurately depict your evolving theory of practice.

A CONCEPTUAL LENS FOR UNDERSTANDING ORGANIZATIONAL LEADERSHIP

With the big picture in mind, Figure 1.1 illustrates a set of four related conceptual lenses helpful for studying leadership in organizations: a view of systems, historical time frame, view of leadership, and ways of engaging with the environment. As with any *conceptual lens,* it is a unifying factor that ties ideas together and permits a deeper understanding of the subject under review.

Like eyeglasses, the conceptual lenses in Figure 1.1 have a right and a left eyepiece separated by a nose bridge. They depict two contrasting ideas—such as Industrial Era and Knowledge Era. Yet in eyeglasses, the nose bridge not only separates the two lenses; it also connects them, in a continuum. Just as the conceptual lenses and eyes see images separately, our minds (and we) learn—with more information—to see the images as whole. And rather than one separate phenomena in each lens, the continuum (the arrow line connecting the alternative across the horizontal) allows for flexible boundaries and overlap. Aspects of each dimension may appear at the same time to accomplish different purposes. For instance, entity and collectivist leader behaviors may both occur in the same school, the former for organizing lockers and the latter for school improvement. Readers may want to refer back to this figure as they continue this chapter and book.

EVOLVING PERSPECTIVES ON LEADERSHIP AND ORGANIZATIONS

Over the centuries, our understanding of leadership has grown. The original definition of *lead* comes from the Old English *laedan,* meaning "take with one" to "show the way," an individual who safely guides others along their journey.[16] Before recorded history,

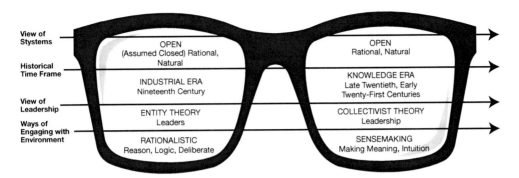

FIGURE 1.1 Conceptual Lenses: Evolving Perspectives in Leadership and Organizations
Source: Leslie S. Kaplan and William A. Owings, 2017

leaders were literally essential for the group's survival. They were the tribes' strongest and fastest hunters, the best fighters; they could feed group members and protect them from wild beasts or marauding outsiders. They were the guides, the path blazers, and pathfinders. In calmer hours, those who could organize others to find shelter, grow food, or make sense of their seemingly random world became natural leaders. Over time, civilization grew, and survival became less tentative. Brute force as a key leadership trait made way for other essential qualities—intelligence, integrity, self-discipline, the ability to identify and solve problems, and the ability to work well with others.

As our society and daily life have become more complex, our concept of leadership has matured, evolving to meet these new realities. Today, although leadership has hundreds of definitions,[17] they share many commonalities. Jerry Patterson, a leadership studies professor and former PreK-12 principal and district superintendent, defined *leadership* simply as, "the process of influencing others to achieve mutually agreed upon purposes for the organization."[18] In this view, leadership is a purposeful process based in relationships that uses influence to accomplish goals that both the employees and the organization share. Despite competing viewpoints on leaders and leadership processes, all share these core elements.

Likewise, our conception of organizations has also shifted over the years, along with changes in society and technology. Changing ideas about systems thinking, the historical eras, views of leadership, and ways to engage with the environment all play key roles in how we understand leadership in today's organizations. We will begin with the largest lens and then focus to more detail.

DEVELOPING SYSTEMS THINKING

Despite their leaders' genius or their employees' skills, organizations often break down because they are not able to integrate their various functions and talents into a coherent, productive whole. Experts in organizational minutiae often miss the "big picture." Addressing issues piecemeal or incrementally, not assimilating solution ideas, dealing with issues one academic discipline at a time, and thinking within the existing "way things are" contribute to education's failure to adapt to changing societal expectations and economic realities.[19] A more holistic approach, systems thinking, highlights the whole (not only the parts), and integrates rather than differentiates.[20]

Understanding systems thinking is a first step in understanding how to lead in organizations. In his book, *The Challenge of School Change* (1997),[21] Michael Fullan observed that understanding interrelationships (rather than cause-and-effect links) and recognizing processes of change (rather than point-in-time snapshots) provide real leverage for improving organizations. Likewise, Peter Senge asserts that systems thinking—looking for interrelationships within an organization—is the discipline that integrates all the other leadership aspects into a coherent whole.[22]

A *system* is a set of two or more elements that function as a whole to achieve a common purpose.[23] Elements work together in subsystems whose interrelationships and interdependence work to keep the larger system in balance.[24] Since the elements' behaviors are interrelated and interdependent, the behavior of the parts affects the behavior of the whole. Neither the system—nor its elements—can work without the other. Finally, systems are synergistic: the whole (system) is greater than the sum of its parts (elements).[25] Thus, considering the whole—*the system*—can help the leader make sense of the complexity that cannot happen when looking at the separate elements, one-by-one.[26] A new-model automobile has 15,000–20,000 separate parts, but unless all of them function properly together, in synergy as a system, the car won't go.

Systems thinking is a conceptual framework developed in the mid-twentieth century to help individuals recognize the complete patterns—the wholes and interrelationships rather than single-event snapshots—of events that affect us. It is a discipline for seeing the structures that undergird complex situations. Senge compares systems thinking to a rainstorm. When one sees the sky darken, the clouds gather, and leaves turn upward, we suspect that rain is coming. After the storm, the sky will clear, and the runoff will feed into groundwater miles away. Even though all these events are separate in time and space, they are connected within the same hydrologic cycle. Each influences the rest, although the ties are not always visible. As one can only understand the system of a rainstorm by considering the whole web of relationships (rather than concentrating on a single raindrop), so too, are businesses, schools, and other human activities systems connected by interrelated actions that lie outside visible awareness.

Since we as individuals are part of the pattern, we cannot always see the complete picture from our unique vantage points. But when we think in systems terms, we can better understand the factors that affect us. In this way, we gain more insight and leverage into how to create positive, innovative, and lasting change in our organizations.[27] For instance, a principal might solve a particular problem for the social studies department, but unless the decision making also considers preventing this solution from adversely affecting every other department's teachers and students—and all the other relevant variables at play—the social studies department may get its wish, but more problems elsewhere are likely to emerge. Similarly, helping a 7th grade math teacher solve his classroom management problems might require looking for solutions not only with the teacher's instructional practices (individual level) but also at factors in the school climate (school level), supportive structures (team, school, and district levels), and teachers' (unrealistic) expectations for appropriate student conduct (school levels).

Systems theory includes different types of systems—open or closed—and different types of open systems—rational and natural. Understanding these variations offers a clearer view of organizational functioning in schools.

Open Systems Theory

If organizations are to remain viable, their design and management practices must shift in accord with societal and technological changes. Scholars suggest different models to describe organizations' relation to their external environment. Open and closed-system models are one way to understand types of organizational functioning.

First appearing during the Industrial Revolution to efficiently organize workers for the new manufacturing, *closed systems theory* is typically known as classical or traditional organizational theory. Closed system theory considers the external environment (such as technology improvements, societal culture, demographics, legal and governmental actions) to be steady, foreseeable, and not interfering with an organization's operations. Instead, organizations rely mainly on internal organizational processes and dynamics to explain organizational, group, and individual actions. Scientific management, administrative management, and bureaucratic management are examples of closed systems theory. Rational and natural systems theories each began as parts of closed system model. Untested, these closed system theories made inaccurate assumptions.[28] In today's highly complex environment, closed system models appear unrealistic.[29]

In contrast, *open systems theory* sees organizations as both influenced by—and dependent on—outside forces. Outside factors (such as competition, available resources, cultural values, economic conditions, political pressures, and the quality of employees' education and training) as well as inside factors (including worker motivation, informal social networks, quality and quantity of professional development) impact an organization's internal workings. Contingency theories (that argue that organizations are structured in ways that best fit their environments) and institutional theories (that view organizations as a means by which societal values and beliefs are embedded in organizational structure and expressed in organizational change) share the open systems perspective: the organization's survival depends on its relationship and interaction with its environment.[30] Today, we believe that all organizations are open systems. Figure 1.2 illustrates an open system.

In Figure 1.2, organizations take in specific inputs (people, materials, funds) from the environment, transform them, and produce outputs (products, services, knowledge). Feedback from outputs helps revise or enhance the transformation process to make it more effective. Organizations have formal and informal structures, planned and unplanned features, and rational and irrational characteristics. In all organizations, both rational and natural elements coexist within a system that is open to its environment.

Chester Barnard (1938), Herbert Simon (1957), Max Weber (1947), and Talcott Parsons (1960) all contributed to the open systems perspective.[31] As the Bell Telephone Company of New Jersey's President, Barnard developed a comprehensive theory of cooperative behavior in formal organizations and explained how industry and society could interact for the public good. Simon, a Nobel Prize-winning American social scientist, extended Barnard's work and developed a formal theory of work motivation, viewing the organization as an exchange system which offers employees incentives (such as salary, advancement, recognition) in exchange for work. Weber, a German economist,

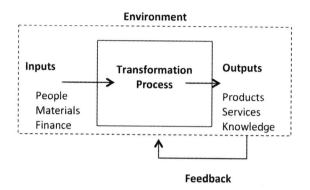

FIGURE 1.2 An Open System with Feedback Loop

Source: Adapted from Hoy, W.K. & Miskel, C.G. (2013). *Educational administration. Theory, research, and practice.* (9th ed.) (p. 19). New York, NY: McGraw-Hill.

viewed organizations as social systems that interact with—and are dependent on—their environments. Further advancing this view, Parsons, an American sociologist, emphasized the influence of the environment on the organization.

Schools are open systems, taking inputs (resources such as educators, students, and material resources) and (ideally) transforming them into increasingly knowledgeable and literate students and experienced educators. Feedback (data) from the outputs—including graduation rates, achievement test scores, attendance records, college acceptances, scholarship amounts, and employment histories—flow back to the transformation process (the school improvement process) to refine or revise current practices. Schools face both rational and natural limitations that adapt as the environment forces change.

The criticism of open systems theory is small bore. Some critics insist that organizations must either be open, natural systems or open, rational systems, each adapted to different types of environments.[32] Other critics reject the open systems theory's vagueness and its lack of guidance about various aspects of organizational functioning and survival.[33] These critiques are akin to tinkering around the edges of a widely accepted viewpoint.

REFLECTIONS AND RELEVANCE 1.2

Working in Open Systems

Open systems theory sees organizations as both influenced by—and dependent upon—outside forces.

In groups of four, identify at least five external influences on public education and on your school in particular. Discuss how each one's particular "agenda" affects the inputs, transformations, and outcomes in your (or other) schools. When your group has completed this task, the class as a whole will create a combined list of outside influences and discuss the ways these influences impact your school and you as a teacher or administrator and the outcomes.

Rational Systems Theory

Rational systems theory sees organizations as structural arrangements designed to achieve specific organizational goals. *Rationality* is the degree to which a series of actions is logically organized and implemented to achieve preset goals with maximum efficiency.[34] Today, rational systems are understood to be open systems affected by their environments.

Briefly, rational systems models have their early origins in late nineteenth century traditional organizational thought. The beliefs: organizations could be made effective and efficient by using clearly defined decisions and reasonably ordered processes. Worker behaviors could be purposeful, disciplined, and practical. Frederick Taylor and his scientific managers considered rational systems to be closed. Their concept of organization was a machine model: humans at work were most productive when they could be "programmed" (taught and supervised) to perform as efficient machines (and organizations could be built according to a blueprint, as one would construct a bridge).[35] A clear division of labor was the foundational principle; the more each task could be separated into its components, the more specialized the work, and the more effective and efficient the workers. Work could be standardized. Tasks were grouped into jobs, jobs collected into departments. Bureaucratic organization kept rules clear and precise, ensuring organizational stability.

Later, Henri Fayol applied—and Max Weber expanded—the rational systems approach to administration. They applied rationality to the organizational structure, not necessarily to its people. They assigned leadership and management a series of defined structures, functions, and procedures, including a bureaucratic hierarchy responsible for planning, organizing, staffing, directing, coordinating, controlling, reporting, and budgeting. Similarly in education, school administrators looked at organizational behavior from a job analysis perspective, identifying the specific tasks to be performed and the most effective ways to do them.[36]

Today, rational systems theorists' guiding principles continue to include division of labor, specialization and expertise, top-down hierarchy of authority, narrow span of control, formalized rules and regulations, compliance, coordination, and goal specificity.[37] Superiors deal with exceptional situations that the rules don't discuss. Jobs are codified, standardized, and regulated. Specific goals guide decision making, direct resource allotments, and structure architectural design decisions. Relationships are formalized, promoting discipline and fact-based (rather than emotion-based) decision making. Departing individuals can be routinely replaced with minimal disruption to the whole. In school districts, for example, practices that affect educators' routines, such as job descriptions, employee handbooks, graduation requirements, and student discipline policies keep the organization predictable and stable, each member knowing what to expect from themselves and others in their work setting.

Critics of rational systems call it dehumanizing because of its focus on organizational structure rather than on people, with management practices that stress control over creativity and initiative.[38] Others conclude that rational systems theory's biggest weakness is believing and acting as if logically precise planning and control inside the organization could withstand (or prevent) outside influences from interfering with internal processes.[39] In fact, events outside the organization can seriously affect it.

A severe economic downturn will alter the monies the district receives to support school staffing and instructional resources. A war that suddenly relocates military parents to overseas posts will disrupt their children's focus for learning during their absence. Likewise, imperfectly coordinated events inside the rationally organized structure can have negative impacts. For instance, if the class and lunch schedules are not perfectly synched and too many students are in the halls at the same time, student supervision and safety may become compromised. In short, a leader's actual "control" of the rationally structured organization is illusionary.

REFLECTIONS AND RELEVANCE 1.3

Working in Rational Systems

Rational systems theory sees organizations as structural arrangements designed to achieve specific organizational goals using logically organized and implemented actions with maximum efficiency.

In small groups, name each person/title who has formal authority over teachers. Give specific examples of the ways in which they exercise their authority. Describe the division of labor and specialization within your school. Describe the extent to which the boundaries between administrators and teachers are rigid or flexible when it comes to decision making and school improvement. Give examples to illustrate how fixed or flexible the instructional practices and curricula in your school are. Report back to the class, and as a class, discuss the extent to which your schools are rational systems.

Natural Systems Theory

Originated in the 1930s, the natural systems theory—or human relations approach— was a reaction against the scientific management and rational systems models. Natural systems theory focuses on informal organization, people, and human needs (rather than the formal organization, structure, and organizational demands). From a natural systems perspective, formal organizations are not only a means to achieve specific outcomes; they are also vehicles by which individuals can satisfy their human needs. Once considered a closed system, natural systems now reflect an open systems viewpoint.

The Hawthorne studies at the Western Electric Company in Chicago during the late 1920s and early 1930s are credited with developing the human relations approach. Investigators conducted several experiments to alter working conditions (such as improving lighting, letting employees choose their own coworkers, and using employee suggestions to upgrade work practices) to assess their impact on worker productivity. Researchers Elton Mayo and Fritz Roethlisberger found that informal organization with its own unofficial social structure, informal norms, friendships, values, emotions, and communication patterns—rather than job specifications—affected workers' interactions and productivity. The work group enforced respect for the informal norms by exerting pressure on those who don't follow them. Although formal structures exist, informal structures also regulate organizational behavior, transforming the formal system.

Similarly, American social worker and management theorist, Mary Parker Follett pioneered the idea that human relations are as important as operations to organizational management. She saw organizations as group networks rather than as hierarchical structures and thought good group human relations improved organizational outcomes. By working together, face-to-face, management and workers could cooperatively achieve common goals, and members fulfilled themselves through the process of the group's development. Thus, organizations' basic challenge was to develop and maintain amicable relationships among employees. Follett's ideas were forerunners of the learning organization, and ahead of mainstream management thinking in the 1930s and 1940s.[40]

Of course, the natural systems/human relations approach has its critics. Some claim that it oversimplified the complexities of organizational life.[41] Others argue that the human relations movement's concern for workers was not genuine caring but rather a management strategy to manipulate workers.[42] It is true, however, that the human relations approach did reduce scientific management's emphasis on organizational structure as it added a new focus on employee motivation, satisfaction, and group morale. In schools, the human relations approach led to an emphasis on a more people-sensitive administration, supervision, teaching, and decision making.[43]

REFLECTIONS AND RELEVANCE 1.4

Working in Natural Systems

Natural systems see formal organizations as not only a means to achieve specific outcomes but also as vehicles by which individuals can satisfy their human needs.

In groups of four, identify persons in your school who have informal power but not formal authority. Explain the type of influence this person has and why. Describe the key informal norms that your school faculty holds. Describe the relationship between those who hold formal power and those who hold informal power in your school. Identify areas of conflict between them—and give examples. What insights can you draw from this discussion? Discuss your findings with the entire class.

THE INDUSTRIAL ERA AND THE KNOWLEDGE ERA

The past two centuries have seen important shifts in our understanding of leadership and organizations. From the early nineteenth to the late twentieth century, the Industrial

Era transitioned into the Knowledge Era. The Industrial Era saw the rise of factories as manufacturing moved production from family farms and local workshops to large urban settings. Raw materials were core commodities. With thousands of workers coming together in large facilities to produce goods on a mass scale, industrial leaders created bureaucracies to direct and control operations. A leader in position of authority was in charge to direct a hierarchy of managers who coordinated the movement of raw materials to semiskilled workers. Other managers organized, directed, and controlled the workers' efforts and the physical assets they generated. Change occurred slowly. Problems were technical: mainly, coordinating the resources to—and the products from—employees. These could be addressed with the available knowledge, processes, and proven solutions.

In contrast, the Knowledge Era exists in a very different social, political, and economic context. Knowledge is a core commodity. Organizational accomplishments depend on its employees' social and intellectual assets—its "corporate IQ"—as its raw materials to effectively meet emerging events. To keep their competitive edge in a fast-paced, high-tech, interconnected world, organizations need speed, flexibility, and adaptability to survive. Given these realities, the traditional view of leadership as a position and authority—of administrative edicts and standard operating procedures—is no longer sufficient to meet today's marketplace demands. In the Knowledge Era, leadership becomes an *emergent, interactive dynamic*—a complex interplay of people, ideas, and systems that generates a collective incentive for action and change. As a result, the leadership challenge is to create an environment in which knowledge is widespread, accumulated, and shared at low cost rather than relying on the "limited intelligence of a few brains" in the corner office.[44]

In short, whereas the Industrial Age depended on *leaders* (individuals who act with position and authority to keep the organization functioning), the Knowledge Era depends on *leadership* (involving the complex dynamics of interacting, interdependent groups, systems, and processes throughout the organization). And, rather than leading for the Industrial Era's efficiency and control, organizational leaders in the Knowledge Era are steering for adaptability, knowledge, and continuous learning.[45]

Accordingly, today's leadership scholars have reframed and expanded views on leadership and systems to include new models. Entity versus collectivist leadership theories and rationalistic versus sensemaking theories bring more nuanced ways of understanding leadership and leadership behaviors in organizations.

ENTITY AND COLLECTIVIST THEORIES OF LEADERSHIP

The Industrial Age's transition to the Knowledge Era brought cultural and organizational changes that prompted scholars to reconsider the essential nature of leadership. But since humans and organizations are highly complex phenomena, entity and collectivist theories of leadership cannot be neatly divided into two discrete categories. Overlap exists. Today's leaders need aspects of both theories.

Entity Leadership Theories

To *entity leadership theorists*, leaders are those specific individuals in organizations who are responsible for getting others to make things happen. This traditional view perceives the leader as a unique *individual* with a special set of traits or skills—such as physical strength, self-confident personality, intelligence, ability to get things done, strategic thinking, and astute people skills—who helps a larger group continue and advance their shared interests. In organizations, leaders are visionaries, planners, and decision makers who work within top-down, bureaucratic models of authority to coordinate and control raw materials and workers. Leaders' characteristics, their behaviors, and the situational factors interact to determine their effectiveness. For leaders, work occurs in a particular location—the workshop, factory, and city. Workers have clearly defined, specialized skill sets that will likely serve them well for many years on the job. Decision making is deliberate, rational, and logical.

Examples of Entity Theories

Entity theories of leadership include the "Great Man" Theory and Evolutionary Leadership Theory. In prehistory, leaders were those individuals who ensured their group's survival and prosperity. The Great Man Theory of Leadership, popularized by Thomas Carlyle, the nineteenth century Scottish philosopher, posits that leaders are born, not made. One either is a natural born leader or one isn't. Alexander the Great, Genghis Khan, and Napoleon were military heroes who increased their group's power by invading and conquering their neighbors' lands. George Washington, Abraham Lincoln, and Mahatma Gandhi offer other examples of great men who seemed to come from nowhere and yet altered the course of their respective nation's history.

Challenging this idea, we now know that environmental factors such as social culture, education, experiences, and personalities also contribute to a person's leadership abilities. Social environments and individuals shape each other, reciprocally. And as sociologist Herbert Spencer, a Victorian philosopher and sociologist, suggested, leaders are the products of the society in which they live: "Before he can remake his society, his society must make him."[46]

Applying the principles of evolutionary biology and behavioral ecology[47] to better understand human psychology, Evolutionary Leadership Theory (ELT) proposes that leadership evolved to solve important problems in group living. Basically, ELT assumes that the human mind—our thinking, feeling, and doing—is the product of innate psychological mechanisms that evolved via natural selection over thousands of years, shaped by experiences and genetics, to better adapt to its environment. During its evolution, the human mind developed many specialized psychological mechanisms (brain modules) —including "if-then" decision rules related to actions such as foraging, self-protection, mating, parenting, collaborating, and resolving conflicts. These skills enabled early humans to solve recurring problems that threatened their survival. But since biological evolution is a very gradual process, decision rules that worked successfully in simpler contexts may not produce adaptive outcomes in more complex environments. This mismatch highlights many difficulties in contemporary leadership.[48] Clearly, ELT is leader-centered. Although ancestral leadership was fluid, distributed, and situational, the individual most qualified for the task at hand had the biggest influence on the group's action and wellbeing.[49]

The array of entity theories of leadership does not end here. Entity leadership theories also include Frederick Taylor's Scientific Management Theory, Henri Fayol's Administrative Management Theory, Max Weber's Bureaucratic Organizational Theory, Ralph Stogdill's Leadership Trait Theory, Contingency Theories, Human Relations Theory, and LMX (Leader-Member Exchange theory). These approaches focus on leaders as individuals managing tasks, people, and situations—in increasingly sophisticated ways—that benefit their organizations. Later chapters will consider these theories in more detail.[50]

Criticism of ELT is vigorous, pointing to the difficulty of testing its hypotheses empirically, its vagueness about its evolutionary assumptions, and the lack of emphasis on non-genetic and not-adaptive explanations as well as political and ethical issues (such as appearing to justify existing social hierarchies and work against social justice).[51] Cognitive scientists cite the growing neurological evidence of brain plasticity and changes in neural networks in response to personal experiences and environmental stimuli.[52] Others assert that many human traits considered universal by ELT advocates are actually dependent on particular cultural and historical contexts.[53]

Collectivist Leadership Theories

In contrast to entity theories—and in response to the Knowledge Economy expectations—collectivists study *leadership:* the social interactions and interdependencies between leaders, followers, and organizational elements (such as policies or physical structures) that produce employee learning and beneficial organizational outcomes. Accordingly, leadership can only be understood in the context of group dynamics, a cooperative practice of leaders and followers working together to add to others' learning or pursue changes to cope with adaptive challenges. Leadership and management occur through collaboration and teamwork.[54] Leaders are individuals who act in ways that influence these interactions, interdependences, and outcomes among people who work together.

Collectivists and entity theorists also perceive the work setting and human capital differently. Entity theorists tend to see leaders as place-bound, working in specific settings. In contrast, in the Knowledge Economy—with globalization, technology, interconnectivity, flexibility, and lots of high quality information as its mainstays—a person with the right knowledge, critical thinking, teamwork and communication skills, adaptability, and capacity to learn can be a "subcontractor," work anywhere in the world, and never leave home (as long as a computer and an internet connection are available). Work settings for collectivists include the nature of interactions and interdependences among people, ideas, and other factors inside and outside the organization. In the Knowledge Economy, leadership models include both a position and authority *and* a complex, interactive, and adaptive dynamic—a view that may be more appropriate to its larger context than considering only hierarchical and control structures within one facility.[55] Accordingly, collectivist leadership theorists believe that organizational life is nuanced and often based on personal and relational experiences that contribute to collaboratively constructed meaning not often discussed in entity-based theories.[56]

Examples of Collectivist Leadership Theories

Whereas entity leadership theories stress the individual leader characteristics and behaviors interacting with situational factors that result in organizational effectiveness, collectivist leadership theories stress that leadership can only be understood as leader-follower interactions and group dynamics. In a way, entity and collectivist leadership perspectives resemble the differences between psychology and sociology: the former views leadership as an individual attribute that may be affected by the situation while the latter focuses on the social structure, the group in which leadership occurs. Complexity Leadership Theory and Institutional Leadership Theory illustrate this collectivist perspective.[57]

Complexity Leadership Theory (CLT) is an outgrowth of Complexity Theory, a perspective born of the Knowledge Economy where information flows in large amounts, change is constant, surprises frequent, and market competition fierce. This high-demand environment is too much for one person or a small group to make sense of or act upon appropriately. Instead, leaders need many perspectives if they are to explore, understand, and adapt to emerging problems. In this rapidly shifting environment, entity leadership theories' rigidity and complicated structures fall short.

Thus, CLT assumes that leadership is a systems function, not centered in the individual. Organizations are clusters of interactive, interdependent, and inter-influencing agents. Leadership is collaborative: decision making, initiative, and leadership are distributed throughout the organization. As such, semi-autonomous individuals can engage in unified collective action to adapt, innovate, and successfully perform organizational functions in a rapidly changing, information-rich environment. Good ideas for organizational improvement come from the bottom-up as well as the top-down. As a result, leadership acts *within*, more than *on*, the organization, and learning occurs throughout.[58]

While affirming the useful aspects of studying leaders' traits, behaviors, and situational influences, Institutional Leadership Theory (ILT) focuses more on the character of the society's shared normative ties and "legitimizing principles" about the "proper" ways of organizing social relations. ILT views organizations as socially constructed meaning patterns, reflecting their society's institutionalized system of beliefs and values (influenced by tradition, laws, and possibly a charismatic leader's vision). Organization members adopt practices, positions, and structural arrangements that reflect taken-for-granted understandings and ideas of "what is appropriate" and what will advance the organization's values (without reference to efficiency or profit).[59]

Within this context, leadership is an interactional process related to the social structures in which it is found. Leaders are credible to others in their organizations—and their strategies only understood—to the extent of their willingness to uphold the norms of the society in which they are embedded.[60] For example, Martin Luther King, Jr. based his leadership strategy in the American civil rights movement on nonviolent disobedience. He relied on U.S. laws and ideologies (individualistic, egalitarian, and self-governing) to increase and mobilize popular sentiment to support his goals. King's strategy would not have worked in a dictatorship or monarchy where societal values rested in an undemocratic past or a present that did not value individual rights. In ILT, leadership does not reflect what someone is; rather, leadership is what is performed in their relationship with others.

Critics of entity and collectivist theories assert that creating this either-or separation fosters the mistaken assumption that entity and collectivist theories are 180-degree opposites.[61] Since leadership involves characteristics of *both* entity and collectivist theories—the individual leaders' characteristics as well as the social interactions and interdependencies between leaders and followers—entity versus collectivist thinking is simplistic and does not make sense in the real world.[62] As with many false dichotomies, what one sees depends on where one stands.

Rationalist and Sensemaking Theories of Leadership

Entity and collectivist theorists also differ on how individuals and leaders understand and engage with their environments. In this domain, entity theorists tend to be rationalists while collectivist theorists tend to be sensemakers. Rationalist and sensemaking theories closely reflect their origins in the Industrial or Knowledge Eras, respectively.

Rationalist theories posit that understanding and interacting with one's environment rely on a highly cognitive, deliberate, and extensive reasoning process. Reality is consensual. Everyone agrees on what the situation at hand means. For instance, individuals recognize a circumstance requiring a decision. They gather and assess relevant information, logically evaluate the data, make choices, and test them with actions to generate feedback about their effectiveness. Human emotion and intuition may appear during the process, but rationalists view these as "primitive cognitions" and "poor guides for action."[63] A useful model for relatively stable environments (and that continues to be useful today), rationalist theory has thrived in our science-oriented, "if, then" culture.

In contrast, *sensemaking theories* assume that knowledge is constructed: reality is how we perceive it, what we define it to be, how we interpret it, and how we make our experiences meaningful to ourselves.[64] Truths are relative, even temporal. Accordingly, sensemaking theories explain how leaders (and others) cognitively structure the unknown in their organizations so they can act on it. Leader and follower behaviors, therefore, are products of *collective sensemaking*[65]—the process by which a group of individuals give meaning to their experiences in order to guide their thoughts and actions. Extensive social interactions among leaders and followers contribute to the shared sensemaking.

Sensemaking is, literally, "making sense" of the fluid, ambiguous situations in which individuals find themselves.[66] Like cartographers,[67] sensemakers try to map an unfamiliar situation, looking for a unifying order by framing and "structuring the unknown."[68] Alternating between intuition and reasoning, emotions and logic, leaders cognitively construct a plausible meaning to an unfamiliar circumstance based on the available clues as filtered through their prior experiences, personal biases, mental maps, and feelings with similar situations.[69] In the process, individuals turn confusing occurrences into ones they can understand, express clearly in words, and act upon.[70] With the mental maps they construct from sensemaking, leaders can engage in other leadership activities such as visioning, relating, and inventing. Once they have constructed a likely explanation, leaders must be able to engage others in their organizations in the sensemaking process—sharing interpretations of events, testing hypotheses with action, reviewing the evidence, and refining—or jettisoning—their mental maps in favor of more accurate and credible understandings. When independent people interact and become interdependent, they develop common understandings. Similarly, when speed is important, plausibility may be more important than accuracy; it allows the problem solving process to move forward despite an elusive and changing reality, inviting people to discuss and share ideas and test them through action.[71]

Rationalism and sensemaking each have their critics. Although the idea that individuals' logical reasoning powers could free them from captivity to their immediate sensual or murderous desires goes back to Greek philosophers, rationalism has its limitations. When used exclusively as the means for understanding and acting in the world, rationalism can reduce the individual's awareness of non-rational but essential information (from emotions, intuition, or the environment) that if unaddressed, could have negative social, personal, or health implications.[72] Rationalist approaches also fail to recognize the uncertainty and ambiguity that make understanding a situation difficult, deny the limits of individuals' cognitive capacities to handle large amounts of information, and reject the possibility of individuals using intuition to make decisions and rationalizing them as justifications after the fact.[73]

In turn, sensemaking critics claim that it neglects the role of larger social, historical, and institutional contexts in making present conditions meaningful; making sense is not context free.[74] Finding fault with both approaches, critical theorists note that rationalism and sensemaking each focus on reproducing the socially learned existing ideas of organization rather than using new ideas to understand (and promote) social change.[75] Others suggest that these theories may give individuals a false sense of control by not recognizing the way each theory restricts the ways of viewing the world.[76]

REFLECTIONS AND RELEVANCE 1.5

Using Evolving Perspectives on Leadership in Organizations

How we understand leadership and organizations has changed along with shifts in the larger culture and society.

Working in pairs, from the perspective of future school leaders, identify the strengths and weaknesses of the entity and collectivist leadership theories and the rationalist and sensemaking theories of engaging the environment. Which concepts are you already using in your professional practice? Give examples. Which concept do you believe will be most helpful to you in comprehending the principal leadership role and why? Discuss findings as a class.

TODAY'S PRINCIPALS AND ORGANIZATIONAL LEADERSHIP

Even as perspectives on leadership and organizations have changed, so too have conceptions of school leadership. The shifts in skill sets, roles, and responsibilities from New England "schoolmaster" to twenty-first century principal follow the evolution of American society and public schools. The 2015 Professional Standards for Educational Leaders (PSEL) describe what educational leaders, in schools and in the central office, should know and be able to do to ensure each student's academic success. It provides another useful lens with which to better assess the practical merits and limitations in leadership and organizational theories discussed in later chapters.

THE EVOLVING ROLE OF THE AMERICAN SCHOOL PRINCIPAL

Throughout our national history, schools have been a powerful agency to socialize diverse communities into the American mainstream. During colonial times, the first teachers in New England town schools were male. These "schoolmasters" were educated men, most preparing themselves for the ministry or other professions who agreed to teach the local town's children as a way to support themselves while completing college. Other men became teachers to repay debts owed from their trips from Europe to North America. In the late seventeenth century, the few women ("school dames") employed as teachers were only assistants to the schoolmaster.[77] Given the cultural norms of the time, women were not permitted to be full-fledged teachers in their own right. Yet because ongoing labor shortages opened other career options for talented schoolmasters, teacher turnover was high; the best teachers left the schoolhouse for higher paying and higher status occupations. Eventually, the schoolmasters' jobs went to itinerant teachers and college students in the winters and to female teachers in the summers.[78]

By 1870, however, women outnumbered men as teachers, and men largely served as school administrators. Teaching was becoming a gendered profession. For many generations, female teacher turnover (young women leaving to have families) was a typical aspect of school culture. Since women teachers left and male administrators stayed, men came to see themselves as education professionals: school-based managers who supervised day-to-day school operations, trained teachers, implemented state and local policies and provided oversight and stability to schools. During the nineteenth and most of the twentieth centuries, principals were school managers. They had less to do with student learning and more to do with maintaining the bureaucracy and responding to public pressures. Schools reserved the rigorous curriculum and high academic standards for college-bound students planning to enter the professions. Others received a less rigorous curriculum until they either graduated or dropped out.

Today, the community holds high academic expectations for all students so they can eventually compete successfully in the high knowledge/skill economy and become responsible citizens. Likewise, communities hold high expectations for the principals to help their children reach this goal. Accordingly, principals have become their schools' instructional leaders, responsible for creating the school climate and conditions that result in every student learning.

More than 40 years of research supports the principal's central importance as an instructional leader who affects school climate and student achievement.[79] According to Philip Hallinger and Ronald Heck's (2000) national analysis of 15 years of research on school leadership, an outstanding principal exercises a "measurable though indirect effect" on school effectiveness and student achievement.[80] Kenneth Leithwood and his colleagues (2004) find that leadership is second only to classroom instruction among all school-related factors that influence student outcomes. They report that direct and indirect leadership effects account for about one-quarter of total school effects on student learning.[81] Similarly, Robert Marzano, Timothy Waters and Brian McNulty's (2005) meta-analysis on 30 years of research on the effects of principals' practices on student achievement finds a significant, positive correlation of 0.25 between effective school leadership and student achievement. For an average school, having an effective leader can mean the difference between scoring at the 50th percentile or the 60th percentile on a given achievement test.[82] Finally, Anthony S. Bryk and colleagues conducted a 15-year longitudinal study of hundreds of Chicago elementary schools. Schools that made sustainable improvements in student learning were led by principals who drove the change by building trust, sharing leadership, and enacting several integrated, mutually reinforcing practices to actively support improved teaching and learning.[83]

2015 PROFESSIONAL STANDARDS FOR EDUCATIONAL LEADERS

The Professional Standards for Educational Leaders (PSEL), formerly called the Interstate School Leaders Licensure Consortium (ISLLC) Standards, takes a holistic view of what education leaders should know and be able to do to advance every student's learning, achievement, development, and wellbeing.[84] First published in 1996 and modestly updated in 2008 based on the empirical research at the time, the 2015 PSEL Standards reflect the changing demands of educational leaders' jobs. Drawing extensively from the expanding empirical and best practices knowledge bases, PSEL incorporates what we now know about how educational leaders' influence student achievement— by providing challenging academic rigor along with caring environments to support each student's learning.[85] The Standards apply to all levels of educational leadership: principals, assistant principals, teacher leaders, and district leaders.

As compared with earlier versions, the 2015 PSEL Standards make explicit what was previously implicit, elaborating and clarifying key leadership themes that make them easier to enact in schools. Placing a stronger emphasis on meeting *each* student's academic success and wellbeing (rather than *all* students as a group), the Standards also highlight ethics; stress developing the professional staff's capacity; emphasize leadership for school improvement and leaders' cultural responsiveness and equity; focus on creating a community of care for faculty and staff; and underscore the holistic and systemic nature of school leaders' work. Aspirational as well as practical, the 2015

Standards seek to ensure that *each and every* child is well educated and prepared for the twenty-first century. They also aim to inspire accomplished leadership practice, encourage educational leaders to continue growing so they may reach a level of excellence in practice wherever they may be in their careers. And they reflect the importance of cultivating leadership capacity in others.[86] PSEL Standards provide a roadmap by which education leaders can grow their professional, interpersonal, cultural, and ethical skills. Each chapter in this book begins by indicating the relevant PSEL Standards it addresses.

Earlier PSEL Standards (previously called Interstate School Leaders Licensure Consortium Standards, or ISLLC) had their critics. Concerns included: the lack of direct connection between the leadership standards and student achievement gains,[87] the omission of special areas such as school technology leadership,[88] vague criteria for standards,[89] lack of attention to leadership context,[90] assumption that leadership is provided by a single individual,[91] and failure to identify the empirical data upon which the standards are based.[92] In response, ISLLC advocates countered, explained, or justified these Standards.[93] By attending to these weaknesses and deliberately reconciling the gaps between the 2008 Standards, school leaders' daily work, and expected future demands, the 2015 PSEL Standards appear to remedy these earlier concerns.

REFLECTIONS AND RELEVANCE 1.6

Making Sense of Evolving Leadership

A local school board hires you and three colleagues as leadership consultants to help educate them about what to think about and look for in hiring new principals for three unaccredited schools in their economically diverse community. Most students are not performing well on standard achievement measures; even high-achieving students' scores are flat and modest. Over the past 10 years, the board has hired a dozen mature principals who come in with attractive school improvement ideas, tell teachers to put these plans into action, but leave their schools within three years. The constant principal turnover is roiling their schools and the district.

As leadership consultants, develop a 3 to 5-minute oral presentation with at least one graphic to orient the school board about the changes in how they might understand school leadership for twenty-first century schools, and what to look for in a principal who can actually make a difference. Use insights from at least three of the following—Industrial and Knowledge Era leadership needs, entity and collectivist theories, rationalist and sensemaking theories, open systems thinking, and PSEL Standards—without being pedantic—to help board members rethink the leadership their schools need. Present your presentations to the class as a whole and discuss which perspectives or lenses discussed in this chapter will help you make sense of—and find useful insights from—this book.

IMPLICATIONS FOR EDUCATIONAL LEADERS

Organizations are not brick and mortar. They are people, social systems, working together in structured ways for common purposes. By their size and complexity, organizations need leaders at every level to set clear direction, energize, and direct employees to make the enterprise work. Given the massive changes in our technologies, social norms, and culture over the past 50 years, the knowledge and skills needed to be an effective leader then are not enough to be an effective leader in today's organizations.

Educational leadership students don't typically involve themselves in academic debates. They don't care whether entity or collectivist leadership scholars score more points or whether rationalist or sensemaking scholars have the last word. Practitioners' concern is what works on the ground. The pioneering industrial engineers and organization leaders did not label themselves *rationalists* or *entity leadership theorists* who worked in *closed systems*. They simply tried to design the structures and processes and organize the workers in ways that would help their nascent businesses meet their goals. Only after two centuries, did contemporary theorists look back at the many changes in society, culture, and manufacture between then and now and consciously label the "before-and-after" in eras, organizations, leadership, and thinking. They wanted a systematic framework to more scientifically identify and understand what had happened to their culture and to leadership in organizations.

In academia, defining one's conceptual "turf" occasionally means striking well-defined (if artificial) boundaries between different perspectives to establish superiority of one viewpoint over the other. In fact, the boundaries between theoretical viewpoints are often permeable: much overlap and interaction exist. Few are the scholars like Herbert Simon, a Nobel Prize-winning economist, psychologist, and sociologist whose broad knowledge helped him see theoretical boundaries as porous and integrate both the rational and the irrational (or actual) in organizational life. Simon's Theory of Bounded Rationality advances the idea that most people making decisions "satisfice" (stop at a "good enough" solution) rather than "maximize" (or search for the best possible solution). Inventorying all possible choices available at a given time and weighing their pros and cons simply isn't worth the time or expense. And it ignores the reality that asking ordinary people to mentally hold and manipulate large amounts of information is beyond their cognitive capacities.[94] When academic theory "hits the wall" of actual human behavior, it makes sense to challenge and modify the theory to better reflect reality. In this book, both the authors and the readers will want to do the same.

Similarly, aspects of contrasting theories make sense. Contemporary organizational leaders cannot simply ignore the traditional (Industrial Age) strategies of directing organizing, and controlling aspects of their roles. These are essential practices to coordinate functions and employees in businesses (and schools). Rather, present-day leaders recognize that these processes may be *necessary* but *not sufficient* for twenty-first century (Knowledge Age) organizational survival. Traditional processes must be refined and connected with other technologies, such as flexibility, adaptability, critical thinking, networking, interacting and interdependent teams, and widely spread and continually increased knowledge throughout the organization. Both leaders (entity theory) and leadership (collectivist theory) are needed.

Lastly, a full and accurate understanding of leadership in organizations may include aspects of several theories. Leadership and organizations are complex phenomena. Complex phenomena do not always fit neatly into carefully labeled categories. Any complex behavior requires several steps. It is possible that entity and collectivist leadership theories, for example, as well as rationalist and sensemaking theories all hold insights about enacting certain facets of leadership in organizations. This is especially true when a perspective comes with substantial and credible empirical support. In ethical decision making, for example, rationalist and sensemaking theories are complementary, working together on different aspects of the situation: "both-and" not "either-or." On occasion, theorists like Simon will put the seemingly conflicting elements together to make sense; sometimes, the practitioners will. Educational leadership students are cautioned to appreciate every theory in this book for its historical relevance, challenge its appropriateness for contemporary worksites, and find those elements from varied viewpoints that make sense to them as they construct their own theory of practice.

Leadership and organizational theories—representing an array of viewpoints—are legitimate topics that can help educational leaders leverage their knowledge of organizational behavior to create successful schools. Whatever useful perspectives can inform future school leaders as they develop the mental models and theory of practice to better understand their people, their discipline, their organizations, and the factors and interactions that influence them, the more effective the leaders will be. And the more our children will benefit.

NOTES

1   Schwartz, J., Bersin, J. & Pelser, B. (2014). Global human capital trends 2014 survey. Top 10 findings. pp. 7–23. In *Global human capital trends 2014. Engaging the 21st-century workforce.* Westlake, TX: Deloitte University Press. Retrieved from: http://dupress.com/wp-content/uploads/2014/04/GlobalHumanCapitalTrends_2014.pdf.

2   Canwell, A., Dongrie, V., Neveras, N. & Stockton, H. (2014, May 7). Leaders at all levels. Close the gap between hype and readiness. *Global human capital trends 2014* (pp. 26–33). Westlake, TX: Deloitte University Press. Retrieved from: http://dupress.com/wp-content/uploads/2014/04/GlobalHumanCapitalTrends_2014.pdf.

3   Berliner, D.C., Glass, G.V. & Associates (2014). *50 myths and lies that threaten America's pubic schools.* New York. NY: Teachers College Press.

4   Berliner, D.C. & Glass, G.V. (2015). Trust but verify. *Educational Leadership, 72* (5), 10–14, p. 12.

5   Senge, P. M. (1990). *The fifth discipline. The art and practice of the learning organization.* New York, NY: Doubleday.

6   We will use the terms mental models and conceptual lenses interchangeably.

7   Senge (1990). Op. cit., p. 203.

8   Hanover Insurance Company's CEO Bill O'Brien as cited in Senge (1990). Op. cit., p. 181.

9   Owens, R.G. & Valesky, R.C. (2015). *Organizational behavior in education,* 11th ed. New York, NY: Pearson, p. 2.

10 Argyris, C. & Schön, D. (1974). *Theory in practice: Increasing professional effectiveness.* San Francisco, CA: Jossey-Bass.

11 Argyris & Schön (1974). Ibid.

12 Owens & Valesky (2015). Op. cit.
13 Houchens, G.W. & Keedy, J.L. (2009). Theories of practice: Understanding the practice of educational leadership. *Journal of Thought, 44* (3–4), 49–61.
14 Keedy, J.L. (2005). Reconciling the theory and practice schism in education administration through practitioner-developed theories in practice. *Journal of Educational Administration, 43* (2), 134–153.
15 Owens & Valesky (2015). Op. cit.
16 Hoad, T.F. (Ed.) (1988). *The concise Oxford dictionary of English etymology*, Oxford, UK: Oxford University Press.
17 Warren Bennis and Burt Nanus identified 350 different definitions of leadership from thousands of studies. See: Bennis, W. & Nanus, B. (1985). *Leaders: The strategies for taking charge*. New York, NY: Harper-Collins.
18 Patterson, J.L. (1993). *Leadership for tomorrow's schools*. Alexandria, VA: ASCD, p. 3.
19 Banathy, B.H. (1991). *Systems design of education: A journey to create the future*. Englewood Cliffs, NJ: Educational Technology Publications.
20 Betts, F. (1992). How systems thinking applies to education. *Educational Leadership, 50* (3), 38–41.
21 Fullan, M. (1997). *The challenge of school change*. Thousand Oaks, CA: Sage, pp. 33–56.
22 Senge (1990). Op. cit.
23 Betts, F. (1992). How systems thinking applies to education. *Educational Leadership, 50* (3), 38–41.
24 Steele, 2003, p. 2; Martinelli, D.P. (2001). Systems hierarchies and management. *Systems Research and Behavioral Science, 18* (1), 69–82.
25 Betts, F. (1992). How systems thinking applies to education. *Educational Leadership, 50* (3), 38–41.
26 Betts (1992). Ibid.
27 Senge (1990). Ibid. pp. 6–7.
28 March, J. & Simon, H. (2009). Organizations. In H.L. Tosi (Ed.), *Theories of organization*. (pp. 93–102). Thousand Oaks, CA: Sage.
29 Allen, J.M. & Sawhney, R. (2009). *Administration and management in criminal justice*. Thousand Oaks, CA: Sage. Retrieved from: www.sagepub.com/upm-data/33001_2.pdf.
30 Contingency theories appear in Chapter 2 and institutional theories appear in Chapter 3.
31 Barnard, C.I. (1938). *Functions of the executive*. Cambridge, MA: Harvard University Press; Parsons, T. (1960). *Structure and process in modern societies*. Glencoe, IL: Free Press; Simon, H. (1957). *Models of man*. New York, NY: Wiley; Weber, M. (1947). *The theory of social and economic organizations*. In T. Parsons (Ed.), A.M. Henderson & T. Parsons (Trans.), New York, NY: Free Press.
32 Lawrence, P.R. & Lorch, J.W. (1967). *Organization and environment: Managing differentiation and integration*. Boston, MA: Graduate School of Business Administration, Harvard University.
33 Yoon, S. & Kuchinke, K.P. (2005). Systems theory and echnology. Lenses to analyze an organization. *Performance Improvement, 44* (4), 15–20; Castells, M. (1996). The network enterprise: the culture, institutions, and organizations of the informational economy. In M. Castells (Ed.), *The rise of the network society* (pp. 151–200). Oxford, UK: Blackwell; Clippinger, J. III. (1999). Order from the bottom up: complex adaptive systems and their management. In J. Clippinger (Ed.), *The biology of business: Decoding the natural laws of enterprise* (pp. 1–30). San Francisco: Jossey Bass.
34 Scott, W.R. (1992). *Organizations: Rational, natural, and open*, 3rd ed. Englewood Cliffs, NJ: Prentice Hall.
35 Worthy, J.C. (1950). Factors influencing employee morale. *Harvard Business Review, 29* (1), 61–73.
36 Campbell, R., Fleming, T., Newell, L.J. & Bennion, J.W. (1987). *A history of thought and practice in educational administration*. New York, NY: Teachers College Press.

37 Scott (1998, 2007). Op. cit.

38 Jex, S.M. (2002). *Organizational psychology: A scientist-practitioner approach*. New York, NY: John Wiley & Sons.

39 March, J.G. & Simon, H. (1958). *Organizations*. New York, NY: John Wiley & Sons.

40 Smith, M.K. (2002) Mary Parker Follett: Community, creative experience and education. *The encyclopedia of informal education*. London, UK: YMCA George Williams College. Retrieved from: http://infed.org/mobi/mary-parker-follett-community-creative-experience-and-education.

41 Etzioni, A. (1964). *Modern organizations*. Englewood Cliffs, NJ: Prentice Hall.

42 Clark, D.L., Astuto, T.A., Foster, W.P., Gaynor, A.K. & Hart, A.W. (1994). Organizational studies: Taxonomy and overview. In W.K. Hoy, T.A. Astuto & P.B. Forsyth (Eds), *Educational administration: The UCEA document base*. New York, NY: McGraw-Hill; Scott, W.R. (1998). *Organizations: rational, natural, and open systems*, 4th ed. Englewood Cliffs, NJ: Prentice Hall.

43 Hoy, W.K. & Miskel, C.G. (2013). *Educational administration. Theory, research, and practice*, 9th ed. New York, NY: McGraw-Hill.

44 Uhl-Bien, M., Marion, R. & McKelvey, B. (2007). Complexity leadership theory: Shifting leadership from the industrial age to the knowledge era. *The Leadership Quarterly*, 18 (4), 298–318.

45 Uhl-Bien, Marion & McKelvey (2007). Ibid.

46 Spencer, H. (1873). Herbert Spencer's critique of "Great Man Theory" from *The study of sociology*. Furman University. Retrieved from: http://history.furman.edu/benson/fywbio/fywbio_spencer_excerpts.htm. Spencer, as other nineteenth century (and earlier) thinkers, considered leadership as a male prerogative, hence the gender pronouns. Authors of this book will keep pronouns gender neutral or give both male and female pronouns when needed.

47 *Behavioral ecology* is the study of how evolution has changed animal—including human—behavior.

48 Vugt, von M. & Ronay, R. (2014). The evolutionary psychology of leadership. Theory, review, and roadmap. *Organizational Psychology Review*, 4 (1), 74–95.

49 Vugt & Ronay (2014). Ibid.

50 All entity theories mentioned here appear in more detail in Chapter 2 except Leader-Member Exchange Theory appears in Chapter 3.

51 Plotkin, H. (2004). *Evolutionary thought in psychology: A brief history*. Malden, MA: Blackwell, p. 150; Rose, H. & Rose, S. (2000). Introduction. *Alas, Poor Darwin: Arguments against evolutionary psychology* (pp. 1–13). New York, NY: Harmony Books.

52 Hamilton, R. (2008). The Darwinian cage: Evolutionary psychology as moral science. *Theory Culture and Society* 25 (2): 105–125; Ward, C. (2012). Evolutionary psychology and the problem of neural plasticity. In K.S. Plaisance & A.C. Reydon (Eds), *Philosophy of behavioral biology* (pp. 235–254). Dordrecht, Netherlands: Springer.

53 Paulson, W.R. (2001). *Literary culture in a world transformed. A future for the humanities* (p. 83). Ithaca, NY: Cornell University Press; Davies, S. (2012). *The artful species. Aesthetics, art, and evolution*. Oxford, UK: Oxford University Press, p. 142.

54 Anacona, D. (2012). Sensemaking. Framing and acting in the unknown. In S. Shnook, N. Nohria & R. Khurana, (Eds), *The handbook for teaching leadership*. Chapter 1. (pp. 3–19). Thousand Oaks, CA: Sage.

55 Uhl-Bien, Marion & McKelvey (2007). Op. cit.

56 Marion & Gonzales (2014). Op. cit., p. 183.

57 Complexity Leadership Theory and Institutional Leadership Theory will be discussed in Chapter 3.

58 Marion, R. & Gonzales, L.D. (2014). *Leadership in education. Organizational theory for the practitioner*, 2nd ed. Long Grove, IL: Waveland Press.

59 Biggart, N.W. & Hamilton, G.G. (1987). An institutional theory of leadership. *Journal of Applied Behavioral Sciences*, 23 (4), 429–441.

60 Biggart & Hamilton (1987). Ibid.
61 Schwartz, S.H. (1990). Individualism-collectivism. Critique and proposed refinements. *Journal of Cross-Cultural Psychology, 21* (2), 139–157; Omi, Y. (2012). Collectivistic and individualism: Transcending a traditional opposition. *Culture and Psychology, 18* (3), 403–416.
62 Omi (2012). Ibid.
63 Rest, J.R. (1986). *Moral development: Advances in research and theory.* Minneapolis, MN: University of Minnesota Press.
64 Haidt, J. (2001). The emotional dog and its rational tail: A social intuitionist approach to moral judgment. *Psychology Review, 108* (4), 814–834; Marion & Gonzales (2014). Op. cit., p. 216.
65 O'Meara, K. & Bloomgarden, A. (2011). The pursuit of prestige: The experience of institutional striving from a faculty perspective. *The Journal of the Professoriate, 4* (1), 39–72; Weick, K.E. (2009). *Making sense of the organization: The impermanent organization.* West Sussex, UK: John Wiley & Sons.
66 Weick, K.E. (1995). *Sensemaking in organizations* (p. 4).Thousand Oaks, CA: Sage.
67 Weick, K.E. (2001). *Making sense of the organization.* Oxford, UK: Blackwell.
68 Waterman, R.H. Jr. (1990). *Adhocracy: The power to change* (p. 41). Memphis, TN: Whittle Direct Books.
69 Sonenshein S. (2007). The role of construction, intuition, and justification in responding to ethical issues at work: The sensemaking-intuition model. *Academy of Management Review, 32* (4), 1022–1040.
70 Weick, K.E., Sutcliffe, K.M. & Obstfeld, D. (2005). Organizing and the process of sensemaking and organizing. *Organization Science, 16* (4), 409–421.
71 Weick (1995). Op. cit.
72 Rosen, M. (2004). Against rationalism. *Scholar.* Cambridge, MA: Harvard University. Retrieved from: http://scholar.harvard.edu/files/michaelrosen/files/against_rationalism.pdf.
73 Sonenshein, S (2007). Op. Cit.
74 Weber, K. & Glynn, M.A. (2006). Making sense with institutions: Context, thought and action in Karl Weick's theory. *Organization Studies, 27* (11), 1639–1660.
75 Mills (2008). Op. cit.; Holt, R. & Cornelissen, J. (2014). Sensemaking revisited. *Management Learning, 45* (5), 525–539.
76 Holt & Cornelissen (2014). Ibid.
77 Preston, J.A. (2003, September). "He lives as a Master": Seventeenth century masculinity, gendered teaching, and careers of New England schoolmasters. *History of Education Quarterly, 43* (3), 360–371.
78 Sklar, K.K. (2003, September). The schooling of girls and changing community values in Massachusetts towns, 1750–1820. *History of Education Quarterly, 33* (4), 511–542.
79 See: Hallinger, P. & Heck, R. (2000, October). Exploring the principal's contribution to school effectiveness, 1980–1995. In *Leadership for Student Learning: Reinventing School Leadership for the 21st Century.* Washington, D.C.: The Institute for Educational Leadership; Heck, R.H., Larsen, T.J. & Marcoulides, G.A. (1990). Instructional leadership and school achievement: Validation of a casual model. *Educational Administration Quarterly, 26* (2), 94–125; Leithwood, K., Harris, A. & Hopkins, D. (2008). Seven strong claims about successful school leaders. *School Leadership and Management, 28* (1), 27–42; Leithwood, K, Louis, K.S., Anderson, S. & Wahlstrom, E. (2004). *How leadership influences student learning.* New York, NY: The Wallace Foundation; Marzano, R.J., Waters, T. & McNulty, B.A. (2005). *School leadership that works. From research to results.* Alexandria, VA: Association for Supervision and Curriculum Development.
80 Hallinger & Heck (2000). Op. cit.
81 Leithwood et al. (2004) Op. cit.
82 Marzano, Waters & McNulty (2005). Op. cit.

83 Bryk, A.S., Sebring, P.B., Allensworth, E., Luppescu, S. & Easton, J.Q. (2010). *Organizing schools for improvement: Lessons from Chicago*. Chicago, IL: University of Chicago Press; Bryk, A.S. (2010). Organizing schools for improvement. *Phi Delta Kappan, 91* (7), 23–30.

84 National Policy Board for Educational Administration (2015). *Professional Standards for Educational Leaders 2015*. Reston, VA. Retrieved from: www.ccsso.org/Documents/2015/ ProfessionalStandardsforEducationalLeaders2015forNPBEAFINAL.pdf.

85 Murphy, J. (2014, December 11). Standards for school leaders. ISLLC 2015. National Association of Secondary School Principals Webinar. Hosted by Pete Reed. Retrieved from YouTube (May 4, 2015) from: www.youtube.com/watch?v=W8QakXv9QZk.

86 National Policy Board for Educational Administration (2015). Op. cit.

87 Davis, S., Darling-Hammond, L., LaPointe, M. & Meyerson, D. (2005). Review of leadership: School leadership study—Developing successful principals. Stanford, CA: Stanford Educational Leadership Institute; Gronn, P. (2003). *The new work of educational leaders: Changing leadership practice in an era of school reform*. Thousand Oaks, CA: Sage.

88 Canole, M. & Young, M. (2013). *Standards for educational leaders: An analysis*. ISLLC Analysis Report. Washington, DC: Council of Chief State School Officers. Retrieved from: www.ccsso.org/Documents/Analysis%20of%20Leadership%20Standards-Final-070913-RGB.pdf.

89 Keeler, C.M. (2002). Exploring the validity of standards for school administration preparation. *Journal of School Leadership, 12* (5), 579–602; Leithwood, K. & Steinbach, R. (2005). Toward a second generation of school leadership standards. In P. Hallinger (Ed.), *Global trends in school leadership preparation*. Netherlands: Swets & Zeitlinger.

90 English, F. (2003). Cookie-cutter leaders for cookie-cutter schools: The teleology of standardization and the de-legitimization of the university in educational leadership preparation. *Leadership and Policy in Schools, 2* (1), 27–47; Gronn (2003). Op. cit.

91 Pitre, P. & Smith, W. (2004). ISLLC standards and school leadership: Who's leading this band? *Teachers College Record, 10–10–2004*. Available from www.tcrecord.org.

92 Achilles, C. & Price, W.J. (2001). What is missing in the current debate about educational administration? *The AASA Professor, 24* (1), 8–13; Hess, F.M. (2003, January). *A license to lead? A new leadership agenda for America's schools*. Washington, DC: Progressive Policy Institute; Waters, T. & Grubb, S. (2004). *The leadership we need: Using research to strengthen the use of standards for administrator preparation and licensure programs*. Aurora, CO: McREL.

93 Canole & Young (2013). Op. cit.; Murphy, J. (1999). *The quest for a center: Notes on the state of the profession of educational leadership*. Columbia, MO: University Council for Educational Administration; Murphy, J. (2002). Reculturing the profession of educational leadership: New blueprints. *Educational Administration Quarterly, 38* (2), 176–191; Murphy, J. (2005). Unpacking the foundations of ISLLC standards and addressing concerns in the academic community. *Educational Administration Quarterly, 41* (1), 154–191; Murphy, J., Yff, J. & Shipman, N.J. (2000). Implementation of the interstate school leaders licensure consortium standards. *International Journal of Leadership in Education, 31* (1), 17–39.

94 More about Herbert Simon and his ideas in Chapter 2.

2

Leadership Theory: Managing Tasks and People (late Nineteenth to late Twentieth Centuries)

GUIDING QUESTIONS

2.1   Explain why "scientific management" is an appropriate term to describe Frederick Taylor's approach to increasing organizational efficiency and fairness among workers and administrators.

2.2   Discuss the ways in which Henri Fayol's administrative management theory expands both management practices and respect for workers.

2.3   Describe the strengths and limitations of Max Weber's "ideal" bureaucracy in theory and in practice.

2.4   Summarize Mary Parker Follett's holistic views of organizations and the people in them.

2.5   Trace how Elton Mayo's attention to the workplace's informal organization eventually helped shape the organizational leadership profession.

2.6   Explain Chester Barnard's view that organizations' leadership's challenge is to balance the inherent tension between the needs of individuals inside and outside the organization with the organization's goals.

2.7   Describe how Herbert Simon applied his interest in human decision making and problem solving processes to understanding organizational functioning.

2.8   Summarize the contributions of leader trait, leader behavior, and situational leadership theories to our understanding of leadership theory.

2015 PROFESSIONAL STANDARDS FOR EDUCATIONAL LEADERS:
2, 3, 4, 5, 6, 7, 8, 9

CASE STUDY 2.1

An Abrupt Culture Change

Two weeks before school started, Ginny Khan received an appointment as principal of Fairhaven Elementary, a school that had improved greatly during the last 6 years under Mary Love's principalship. Under Mary's leadership, student test scores increased, good teaching was celebrated, and weak teachers either got better or left. The faculty knew Mary cared about the students and the teachers—and she would not allow bad teaching to continue. Based on Fairhaven's noteworthy academic progress and their caring, inclusive, and professional community, the neighboring school system recruited Mary to become assistant superintendent and lead their instructional program. Yet in spite of the significant improvement, student achievement still fell short of meeting all state standards, and Fairhaven was perilously close to receiving state sanctions.

At her first faculty meeting, Ginny told the faculty that she was here to get student test scores up and not to make friends. She added that she expected each teacher's student test scores to meet or exceed state standards. She would move for dismissal of each teacher whose students did not "meet her mark" with no exceptions. She announced that teachers would start using a new math curriculum. Khan ended the meeting with, "Now get to work" as she left a stunned faculty, without answering any questions.

Khan's first meeting with the PTA was equally ill received. She told the parents that she was appointed principal to make sure student achievement increased and exceeded state expectations. Khan noted, "You are their first teachers, and many of you have not done a good enough job helping with your children's development. You need to support your child's teachers and make sure homework is done well. If you don't, you will be supporting your children financially much longer than you want." She then dismissed the parents to go to their children's teachers' classrooms. The parents' stunned silence turned into an audible gasp as Khan left the room. That evening, school board members received numerous parental calls.

Many of the teachers wrongly thought this harsh leadership behavior would not continue. Six teachers, with whom Love had worked and improved to an "excellent" rating, resigned after their first lesson observation in September. By October, all six grade level chairs had left their leadership positions. Khan was left with no one willing to take the leadership spots. Her faculty meetings were terse and filled with threats. The October benchmark tests indicated that student growth would fall very short of her goals for the students.

After two meetings with the assistant superintendent, in spite of Ginny's promises to change her approach, complaints from teachers and parents continued unreduced. On November 5, the worried district superintendent asked Khan to meet. An incredulous Khan told the superintendent, "You are firing me for being laser focused on increasing student achievement? That's what you told me to do when I accepted the job. You will be talking with my lawyers!" She truly wondered how this could have happened to her.

RUBRIC 2.1			
Lens and/or factors to be considered in decision making	What are the factors at play in this case?	What steps should be considered in solving the problem?	What could have been done to avoid this dilemma?
The situation			
• The task	The previous principal, Love, had shown active concern for the task *and* the people. Improved student achievement resulted. Khan showed concern only for the task.	Khan's dismissal resolves the issue for now, but the student achievement issue remains. A new principal will be hired and central office personnel will need to help heal the wounds, mentor the new principal on school culture and teacher needs, and get improvement back on track.	More guidance and communication from central office about what was working well at Fairhaven and what practices Khan would be advised to continue. A transition meeting between Love and Khan about how best to motivate Fairhaven teachers may have been helpful.
• Personal abilities	Khan's immaturity as a leader has hampered her effectiveness with the organization by failing to recognize the human part of schooling.	Khan's task orientation with no concern for motivating and developing people needs to change, but it may be too late.	An orientation for the new principal, close monitoring and consultations, and an earlier central office intervention should have occurred to support Khan's leadership as well as improve test scores.
• The school environment	Plummeting morale.	Since two meetings with the assistant superintendent have not worked—principal replacement appears to be the only solution.	Some clearer expectations from the superintendent could have helped. The environment went from high concern for task and people to task only.
Look		**Wider**	
Organizational (i.e., the organizational goals, values, policies, culture)	The organization had changed from a leader who persuaded and developed teachers to one who commanded.	The problem has gotten so out of hand that Ginny has been fired.	Ginny needed a better understanding of the established school culture—as a human enterprise—and to behave accordingly.
People (i.e., individuals with needs, beliefs, goals, relationships)	The faculty's zone of indifference was decreased due to the new leader's behavior.	Ginny had the wrong mental model entering the job.	Ginny needed a better understanding of the good culture that Love had established and the behaviors that supported it.

continued . . .

Competing Interests			
(i.e., competing interests for power, influence, and resources)	Ginny's focus on increasing test scores vies with need to motivate and support teachers.	Ginny's leadership needs to enact both task and people functions.	Central office leaders could have prepared and mentored their new principal more effectively.
Tradition			
(i.e., school culture, rituals, meaning, heroes)	Fairhaven's culture of a balanced concern for task and people was shattered.	Teacher leaders could meet with their new principal to suggest ways she can adjust her leadership actions to better motivate and support teachers in ways that will improve students' achievement.	Central office orientation and oversight should have been more rigorous. Ginny needed to understand the school's culture and enact a balance between task and relationship behaviors.

OVERVIEW: EARLY TO MODERN VIEWS OF LEADING ORGANIZATIONS

Organizations are concepts; they are what we define them to be. As our culture, society, and technology change, so does our understanding of what organizations are and how to best lead them.

Organizations—including school systems—consist of four key interacting components: people (the employees, their knowledge, skills, and actions), tasks (the work and goals), technology (tools that aid in completing the work), and structure (the hierarchy, relationships, communication and coordination patterns throughout the organization).[1] These four factors are interdependent; any change in one of these components will prompt changes in all the others. As variables, they differ over time and from organization to organization. Their interactions determine whether an organization thrives—or fails. Organizational theorists attempt to account for these four components.

This chapter will consider the early to modern organizational and leadership theorists and their views about organizations and how to best lead them. Frederick Taylor, Henri Fayol, Max Weber, Mary Parker Follett, Elton Mayo, Chester Barnard, Herbert Simon, and others would contribute to an increasingly complex and sophisticated understanding of organizations. Leader trait theorists, leader behavior theorists, and situational leadership theorists would each contribute facets to understanding organizational leadership. Across these years, the concept and practice of organizations would transition from a machine-centered environment that neglected or minimized individual differences to a social context where individuals' needs and motives could find expression and satisfaction as they met organizational goals. Attaining an appropriate balance between organizational goals, employees' needs, and the fluctuating internal and external environments would come to define contemporary organizational leadership.

TRADITIONAL (CLASSICAL) ORGANIZATIONAL THEORY

As the nineteenth century was ending, business and industry leaders in the United States and Europe were looking to increase industrial profits. They wanted to lower their assembly lines' per-unit costs. In their view, the organization was a rational machine that could provide precision, speed, clarity, continuity, and knowledge. Leaders and managers were specific persons,[2] entities with specific technical and administrative skills essential to get the job done. Workers were "a given" rather than an essential variable in the system, no more than an "inert instrument performing the tasks assigned."[3] Rationality and predictability were paramount. Clear lines of authority, careful planning, and well-defined structures made the work process efficient and effective. And if, despite the rigorous planning and execution, something went wrong, it was likely due to human error or engineering defects. Industrial engineers, chief executives, public officials, and sociologists would design complementary approaches of how to best lead organizations to the utmost efficiency and effectiveness.

Frederick W. Taylor's scientific management theory intended to engineer the maximum worker productivity, starting at the shop floor. Henri Fayol's administrative management theory would efficiently structure and control the general processes common to all organizations and recognize the importance of managers with a talent for working with people, organizing, and adapting to changing circumstance. Max Weber's bureaucratic management theory would give rationality, rules, and stability to large public organizations. Although these three theorists held varying beliefs about people and control within the organization, all three tried to connect theory with practice; and many of their ideas continue to influence organizational thinking and methods today.

Frederick W. Taylor: Managing Tasks

A mechanical engineer by training, Frederick Winslow Taylor (1856–1915) became a top engineering consultant to American business and industry. He initiated the concept of *scientific management*, the rational defining of purpose and the intelligent organization and use of manpower, technology, and other means to accomplish organizational goals.[4] Scientific management practices intended to end waste in human energy, equipment, and machine power through standardization and specialization. In trying to solve practical production problems in American factories, Taylor arguably originated the concept of "work smarter, not harder."[5] With his ideas holding sway from approximately 1910 to 1935, Taylor began the era of modern management. His book, *Principles of Scientific Management* (1911) had widespread international appeal.

To increase worker productivity, Taylor focused his attention on the shop floor where the actual labor occurred. At a time of massive industrial expansion, workers were largely uneducated; many were recent immigrants who lacked English literacy. Even lower level supervisors had an average of 3 years formal schooling.[6] Taylor believed that most workers were lazy, preferring to do as little work as they could without getting fired.[7] Since cheap labor was available and workers not protected by unions, Taylor believed that he could increase productivity by exerting intensive control over the workplace. In his view, neither workers nor their supervisors, each with low education levels and questionable work habits, were qualified to plan how the work should be done.

At its core, scientific management is a rational scientific-engineering based approach designed to increase workers' productivity through the systematic analyses of work in painstaking detail. Taylor intended to remove workplace inconsistencies by logically breaking each complex production step into a sequence of simple repetitive subtasks. To do this, he observed the inefficiencies in craftsmen's efforts that resulted from dealing with variations in their machinery, materials, and "rules of thumb."[8] Investigating why workers used traditional procedures, Taylor conducted time-and-motion studies to determine the optimal speed that each step in the procedure should take. Then, he connected the most efficient parts of each procedure into a single, faster, and easier standard practice. To synthesize his findings, Taylor developed his four principles of scientific management:[9]

1. **Scientific job analysis.** End the guesswork of "rule of thumb" methods to deciding how each worker should do a job. Instead, use scientific measurement to separate a job into a series of small, related tasks.
2. **Selection of personnel.** Use more scientific, systematic methods of selecting workers and training them for specific jobs. Don't allow workers to choose their own tasks and train themselves as best they can.
3. **Management cooperation.** Develop congenial workers and management relations to ensure that workers understand the job task and are properly trained to perform it according to scientifically devised procedures.
4. **Functional supervision.** Establish a clear division of responsibility between management and workers. Management sets the goals, plans, and supervises. Workers perform the required tasks.

To facilitate this arrangement, Taylor separated industrial planning from actual production. He created planning departments staffed by engineers to develop the work methods, establish the production goals and the rewards systems, and train personnel in how to use the scientifically designed methods to reach these ends. He advocated for clear lines of authority and responsibility, hierarchical relationships, and well-defined rules for running the enterprise. Taylor believed that the true long-term interests of both management and workers depended on prosperity for both.

Although Taylor initially focused on the shop floor, his ideas included basic administrative practices and employee wellbeing in the larger organization. He saw scientific management bringing justice to managers and workers, a promising first step in making the workplace more democratic.[10] Work was to be almost equally shared between the two groups, each group responsible for the tasks for which it was best suited. Management would do the science and instruction; workers would perform the labor. Salaries were pay-based incentives, closely tied to the job difficulty and actual work quality and quantity. This would increase fairness and provide incentives for greater effort and improved outcomes. Managers only intervened when their subordinates did not meet their performance standards.

Worker development was also essential. Supervisors were expected to study each worker's character, nature, and performance; identify the workers' limitations and possibilities for individual development; and then systematically train, help, and teach this worker the skills needed. When possible, managers could provide opportunities for capable workers' advancement. In this way, otherwise unskilled workers could improve their productivity enough to raise their pay nearly to that of skilled labor; workers could earn middle-class wages, giving them greater purchasing power, and a higher living standard.[11]

Taylor's advances were evident in the fields of industrial engineering, personnel, and quality control. And scientific management's popularity in the early twentieth century rested on its measurable increases in workplace productivity.[12]

Taylor's approach did not come without criticism. Although scientific management is to be credited with increasing production efficiency by replacing guesswork with rational coordination and standardization, many managers abused its practices. They applied Taylor's techniques without his philosophy of close manager-worker cooperation or the benefits of developing human capital.[13] As a result, critics pointed to its "stopwatch" mentality as "dehumanizing" and "exploitive" to workers, making them into "a 'simple appendage' of machinery,"[14] pressured to work faster to increase the organization's productivity and the employer's profits without giving them a share in the earnings. Detractors also claim that it ignored the human need for interesting and satisfying work,[15] using money as the only incentive.[16] Likewise, critics note that separating planning from doing, brainwork from muscle work (managers responsibility for "thinking" and employees responsibility for "doing"), removing workers from the decision-making process, and stressing individual over group performance are self-defeating practices.[17] Necessary improvements could be made on the spot.[18] Some accuse Taylor of provoking industrial unrest and conflict, higher employee turnover and absenteeism, industrial sabotage, low employee morale, and other managerial problems.[19]

What might be technically efficient in the short-term could be highly inefficient over the long-term. Over time, strictly separating mental work from physical work; using rigid standardization to remove individual workers' initiative, judgment, choice, creativity, and responsibility; and management's lack of flexibility in the face of changing conditions would prove scientific management theory to be counter-productive.

REFLECTIONS AND RELEVANCE 2.1

Scientific Management in Schools

In the early 1900s, educators identified superficial parallels between schools and factory work, adapting Taylor's ideas to the school as a workplace.

Working in groups of four, identify today's school practices that reflect their origins in scientific management thinking. Consider daily scheduling, student placement by age and grade; curriculum, lesson plans, academic programs, instruction and assessment; school administrators' views of themselves, teachers, students, and parents; and central office staff. As a class, discuss, "How do scientific management practices often affect the relationships between administrators and teachers? Between teachers and students? How do these practices affect slower-learning students?"

Henri Fayol: Managing Tasks and People

While Taylor approached the study of management from the workshop or technical level and up the hierarchy, Jules Henri Fayol (1841–1925), a French manager-engineer, viewed management from the CEO's office and down. Although both are considered traditionalists and were virtual contemporaries, their professional experiences and perspectives on organizational functioning differed profoundly. With his executive background, Fayol tried to improve management thought and practice and laid the foundations for contemporary management theory. His ideas were largely unfamiliar to English speakers until the translation of his *General and Industrial Management* in 1949.[20]

Educated as a mining engineer, Fayol's innovative advances in fighting underground coal fires led to his promotion to manager, and his people-managing skills later led him to become chief executive officer. As general manager, Fayol realized that overseeing ten thousand employees in many separate locations required administrators who did more than devise systems and methods for increasing output. Instead, successful management involved all the activities connected with producing, distributing, and selling a product, organizing plant and equipment, and working with people—a job that required knowledge and skills not taught in engineering school. Likewise, he observed that a company's performance depended more on its leaders' managerial abilities—their talents for working with people, organizing, and adapting to changing circumstances—than on their technical abilities (not that technical knowledge was unimportant). Believing that all employees, from foremen to superintendents, needed some management training, Fayol assumed that schools and universities did not offer it because no management theory yet existed. So Fayol created one. In his retirement, he set up a Centre for Administrative Studies where he became a management philosopher, writer, and teacher.[21]

From 50 years of mining administration experience, Fayol began to construct his own ideas about management.[22] He identified and described the five elements or functions of management:[23]

- **Planning**—forecasting, examining the future and identifying short- and long-term actions to be taken.
- **Organizing**—defining the lines of authority and responsibility.
- **Commanding**—putting the plans into action.
- **Coordinating**—defining the timing and sequencing of activities; connecting and harmonizing them all.
- **Controlling**—monitoring and adjusting, ensuring conformity with rules, and evaluating results.

Fayol also saw the value of what would later be called "participatory management," calling for contributions from all department heads in formulating plans. He valued initiative from both managers and workers, seeing it as a potent motivator of individuals and a benefit to the organization.[24] He learned that communication skills were essential. Notably, Fayol recognized it was people, not structure, that made the difference between the success of two otherwise similar firms.[25]

In *General and Industrial Administration* (1916), the first formal paper on management theories,[26] Fayol proposed fourteen flexible principles based on the knowledge he found most useful in his own career. Table 2.1 presents these. When linked with intelligence, experience, decision, and proportion (a combination of tact and experience), these principles could guide managers to effective thought and practice. Clearly, Fayol conceived of the organization as an open, rational, and natural system.[27]

Fayol saw his ideas as generic, holistic, flexible, and universal; every organization needed management.[28] He knew that data collection and theory building were ongoing and interdependent activities that could be compared to other analyses. He believed that many of his ideas and Taylor's ideas were complementary.[29] Table 2.2 compares these two early organizational theorists. Considering Taylor and Fayol as "traditional" or "classical" more accurately reflects the fact that they were virtual contemporaries rather than that they shared similar ideas about organizational management. Fayol's comprehensive theories and flexible principles anticipated more present-day approaches and remain relevant to today's organizational leadership.

Contemporary views on Fayol are mixed. Some insist that his management theories remain meaningful and relevant in the modern world.[30] His ideas anticipate the human relations movement, systems and contingency theories, and participatory decision making.[31] Some discount Fayol because his conclusions don't match findings from contemporary research.[32] Several critics (some with competing theories)[33] complain that his practitioner experiences biased his observations about management theory, and his ideas lacked research rigor.[34] Other critics appear to simplify and misunderstand his views[35] or argue about what Fayol actually meant.[36] In rebuttal, one defender compares Fayol critics to "academics fighting scholastic wars" who misread Fayol's work as they seek to assert their own originality—only to discover that their "different generalizations . . . are often the same fundamental truths in different words."[37]

Fayol's principles were not meant to be exhaustive in scope or rigidly applied. Management was to adapt to a firm's environment and balance worker autonomy with corporate efficiency. Many of these practices were already in use, but Fayol was the

TABLE 2.1 Fayol's Fourteen Principles of Management

Principle	Description
Division of work	Assigning separate tasks to individual specialists (by worker's abilities and preferences) focuses their attention, produces better work, and increases productivity with same effort but less boredom from monotony.
Authority (and responsibility)	The right to give orders and expect obedience, but personal authority and responsibility go with it.
Discipline	Respect for authority and obedience to established rules and managerial direction between a firm and its employees are needed for smooth functioning.
Unity of command	For any action, an employee should receive instruction from only one supervisor.
Unity of direction	One leader and one plan for a group of activities having the same objective coordinates efforts for unity of action.
Subordination of individual interests to the general interest	The interests of individuals and groups within the organization should not take priority over the interests of the organization as a whole.
Remuneration	Pay should be fair to both the workers and the firm. Nonfinancial incentives should be available to reward successful performance.
Centralization	Managers retain final responsibility but they should give subordinates enough authority to make decisions that will successfully complete their tasks. The appropriate degree of centralization varies in proportion to the business conditions and personnel quality.
Scalar chain	The line of authority from top to bottom of the organization should be clear and followed. Lateral communications through the shortest path (for instance, to have foremen talk directly to each other) may be needed to prevent delays.
Order	People and materials should be coordinated to be at the right place at the right time to avoid wasting either.
Equity	Managers should use kindliness and fairness towards subordinates to build loyalty.
Stability of tenure of personnel	High employee turnover is inefficient. Successful organizations need a stable workforce. Management should provide orderly personnel planning and ensure that qualified replacements are available to fill vacancies. Settling into a new job takes time.
Initiative	Within the limits of authority and discipline, all levels of staff should be encouraged to show initiative—to suggest new ideas, think out, and execute a plan (even if some mistakes occur). This will motivate workers and generate enthusiasm and energy in their work.
Esprit de corps	Managers should promote and maintain teamwork, team spirit, and morale to build harmony and unity within a firm, using each person's abilities and rewarding each one's merit without arousing jealousies.

Sources: Based on Fayol, H. (1949). *General and industrial administration.* (pp. 20–41). New York, NY: Pitman. Originally published in 1916 in French, titled *Administration industrielle et général*; Fayol, H. *General and industrial management*, trans. Constance Storrs. London, United Kingdom: Sir Isaac Pitman and Sons; Cole, G. (2004). *Management theory and practice*. 6th ed. London, United Kingdom: Cengage Learning, p. 15.

TABLE 2.2 Comparing Frederick Taylor and Henri Fayol

Criteria	Taylor	Fayol
View of organization	From the shop floor and actual production, up to the CEO's office. A foreman's perspective. CEO, managers control all decisions.	From the CEO's office, down to the shop floor. An executive's perspective. All organization members should participate in its management.
Focus of attention	The task. Specialization and standardization of production processes. Congenial manager—worker relations.	Management and workers. Administration elements and principles are common to all organizations. Vertical integration of organization. Interpersonal relations are important.
View of workers	Lazy, uneducated, needing specific directions, supervision; motivated by wages. May develop more skills, more interesting work with managerial encouragement.	Educate managers. Motivate workers by paying them fairly, giving occasions to suggest ideas, use initiative to plan, enact innovations. Treat equitably. Teamwork and esprit de corps valued.
Managers' needs	Technical skills are paramount. Need to enforce rules, standards strictly.	Interpersonal, communication, flexibility, and organizational leadership skills, and administrative knowledge from formal education and experience—are more important than technical skills, alone.[a]
Organizing principles	Mechanistic, well defined, all-inclusive. "One best way" to perform a task efficiently. Management thinking only for management cadre.[b]	Flexible, holistic, open to be new ideas, adaptable to changing circumstances, learning from mistakes.[c] Everyone in organization should understand and use some management concepts.

a Technical skills are still important to managers. Fayol, a mining engineer, had them. But in managing organizations, management skills were *more* important.

b Parker, L.D. & Ritson, P. (2005a). Fads, stereotypes, and management gurus: Fayol & Follett today. *Management Decision, 43* (10), 1135–1357.

c Parker & Ritson (2005a). Op. cit.; Lamond, Parker & Ritson. (2005) Op. cit.

Source: Kaplan & Owings, 2017

first person to express them as a holistic set of general management principles. These ideas continue to influence management thinking and practice.

Max Weber: Structuring the Organization with Bureaucracy

Karl Emil Maximilian "Max" Weber (1864–1920), a German economist, sociologist, and contemporary of both Taylor and Fayol, proposed ideas about how organizations should be structured. Manufacturing was evolving from small stores and owner-managed firms to large companies that spanned continents with their communication, transportation, and products. Government was expanding, too. Organizational complexity increased but lacked a structural and procedural roadmap. Weber saw the need for a rational and efficient organizational structure and expert administration to keep these burgeoning enterprises coherent and productive. Bureaucratic organizational theory would logically coordinate these processes.[38]

In Weber's time, businesses were typically led and managed by individuals, often well born. They frequently hired relatives and friends (or sold the offices) to manage their firms. Nepotism and other types of favoritism, corruption, and coercion characterized these pre-modern administrative systems. Decision making was unpredictable and self-serving. Managers exploited workers. Organizational leaders relied on tradition and charisma to give them authority to plan operations and direct employees. In Weber's view, this mismanagement reduced organizational efficiency and wasted human resources.

Organizational authority based on an individual's charisma or on traditional power could be arbitrary, irrational, and unstable. As a remedy, Weber proposed a *bureaucracy* —a set of rules rather than people, competence rather than favoritism, and a hierarchy of positions rather than persons that are to be respected as management.[39] In his view, bureaucracy transitioned an unstable, unpredictable structure of authority into a more stable, rational, predictable, and legal one. Bureaucracy embodied a concept of Western society's justice: equal application of the law.[40] In bureaucracy, *legal authority* comes from reasonably designed written rules and regulations based on systematic knowledge that governs activities in pursuit of specific goals. Bureaucrats were to be impartial administrators with the legal authority to interpret and enforce these rules. In turn, employees owed obedience to the impersonal office of manager, not to the individual person of the manager. In this way, authority outlasted the individual's tenure in office— as with the military, politically elected offices, colleges and universities. And the organization's clients would receive expert, impartial, and unbiased service in their— rather than the managers'—best interests.

Characteristics and Advantages of Bureaucracy

Weber identified the essential characteristics of his "ideal" bureaucracy to clearly define responsibility and authority; increase individual expertise, accountability, and organizational efficiency; improve communications; reward merit; and increase fairness and rationality. These included:[41]

- **Division of labor and specialization.** A variety of knowledgeable and expert individuals, hired for their technical qualifications, handle large, complex tasks. (In schools, teachers are state licensed, based on their college transcripts and earned degrees, to teach a specific subject or grade. Administrators earn a different license based on their transcripts and degrees.)
- **Managerial hierarchy of authority.** Each office or position is controlled and supervised by a higher one. The organizational chart illustrates these vertical relationships. (In local school districts, school boards and superintendents are at the top; principals, teachers, and students are lower on the hierarchy.)
- **Formal rules and regulations.** All employees have written rules and standard operating procedures to base their decisions on and direct how they perform their

responsibilities. (School district or school level employee handbooks provide these rules to educators.)

- **Formal selection.** Employee appointment and promotion are based on merit and technical competence (and, at times, on seniority) rather than personal or political connections. (School districts must post and advertise job openings with specified candidate requirements to ensure a wide array of applicants.)
- **Impersonal social relations.** Organization rules and controls are applied impersonally and uniformly in all cases. Employees make decisions based on facts and rules, not emotions. (Ideally, this holds true for schools.)
- **Career orientation.** Most employees are career professionals (rather than political appointees), who work for fixed salaries, receive promotions by seniority or achievement, and pursue occupations within their respective fields. (Teachers typically gain salary increases according to a posted step scale based on years working in the district and with a specified sum added for completing additional academic degrees.)

In recognition of his constructing the ideas of bureaucracy, Weber is known as the "Father of Organization Theory."

Notably, Weber's bureaucracy was an idealized concept, a "pure case" that did not exist in reality; he did not intend it to be a working model.[42] He assumed that the organization deals with predictable, uniform, recurring events and relies on traditional knowledge rather than on social skills. His goal was systemization, not perfection, moving managerial practice and organizational design to a more rational way of functioning.[43] Likewise, Weber assumed that organization problems were standard, unsurprising, and occurred in a very slowly changing environment. He also recognized the limitations inherent in this organizational model. While celebrating its efficiency, bureaucracy could limit individual freedom and cause them to lose sight of their own activities in relation to the organization as a whole. In addition, *bureaucratization* had the capacity to create an "iron cage" of rigidity and mindless routines and mechanization.[44]

Others also recognize bureaucratic organization theory's limitations, disadvantages, and unintended consequences.[45] For one thing, organizations are open systems, and what appears to be functional on paper may be irrational and inefficient in the "real world."[46] Administrators become overly focused on enforcing the rules and "formalized procedures" (the means) rather than on the organization's aims (the ends). This attitude and practice leads to behavioral rigidity, an inability to adjust to new realities, an unwillingness to give a client personal consideration, and may encourage a lack of individual responsibility. Ultimately, bureaucratic inflexibility harms clients.

Critics also point to Weber's theory's internal contradictions. For example, it is unclear whether bureaucratic authority is based on technical competence or on legal powers and discipline.[47] The esprit de corps and *informal organization*—the system of interpersonal relations that form naturally within all formal organizations and that shapes individuals' behaviors—creates subgroups, cliques, and "in-groups" that often prefer to defend their established interests rather than assist "out-group" colleagues and clients.[48] In addition, contemporary critics observe that Weber's theory neglects to address gender issues,[49] and comment on his difficult writing style.[50] All in all, bureaucracy's emphasis on "rules for rules' sake" without regard for the organization's goals carries "the seeds of its own destruction."[51]

When assessing traditional organizational theory, historical context matters. Weber intended his model to be a starting point for further study, a concept to be evaluated as useful or not, rather than as a blueprint for organizational design.[52] The focus of both respect and controversy, Weber saw bureaucracy as a rational way to structure authority in organizations so as to deliver justice and equal application of law. For its strengths—and despite its limitations—bureaucracies have become a key feature in contemporary organizations.

REFLECTIONS AND RELEVANCE 2.2

Administrative Management Theory and Bureaucracy Theory in Today's Schools

Fayol's Administrative Management Theory and Weber's Bureaucracy Theory created rational structures by which to arrange and conduct organizational business, and many of their ideas continue to influence organizational practice to this day.

Working in pairs for 10 minutes—with half the pairs working with Fayol's ideas and the other half working with Weber's—identify the school practices in effect today that likely reflect their origins in Fayol's administrative management theory or in Weber's bureaucracy theory. Consider factors including the managerial hierarchy, division of labor, authority and responsibility, subordination of individual's interest to the general wellbeing, initiative, esprit de corps, formal rules and regulations, formal selection for position, impersonal social relations, career orientation, communication throughout the organization, the ability to work well with people, and management flexibility to meet changing circumstances. As a class, discuss "What aspects of administrative management and bureaucracy theory remain in today's schools?" How do these practices often affect the relationships between administrators and teachers? Between teachers and students? How do these organizational structures and processes affect students and parents? Which aspects of each are—and are not—serving the purposes for which they were originally intended?

MODERN (TWENTIETH CENTURY) ORGANIZATIONAL THEORY: LEADING PEOPLE AND TASKS

Although Taylor's scientific management theory, Fayol's administrative management theory, and Weber's bureaucratic organization theory all found expression in the early twentieth century (Fayol's and Weber's ideas mostly in Europe until translated into English around midcentury), they focused mainly on organizational structures and practices. Only indirectly did they address the people who worked there. Later theories would expand and mature (or discard) these earlier viewpoints to better match the shifting social, psychological, political, and technological cultures. Ideas about human relations in organizations and organizational leadership were about to appear. Mary Parker Follett, Elton Mayo, Chester Barnard, Herbert Simon, and others added perspectives about the relationships between leaders, workers, and meeting organizational goals that would further shape our understanding and experiences in organizations.

MARY PARKER FOLLETT: A HOLISTIC VIEW OF ORGANIZATIONS

Mary Parker Follett (1868–1933), an administration management theorist, focused on the human side of the person-machine relationship. Working during the era when Taylor's and Fayol's theories were gaining substantial business and public interest, Follett was, according to some, "a prophet in the management wilderness."[53] Although her writings and unique viewpoint garnered limited attention in her day, she provided new thinking that would transition organizational theory from scientific management to behavioral science.[54] Both idealistic and pragmatic, Follett believed that administration was a necessary process that integrated individuals into an organization for two purposes: to complete their individual potential and to effectively accomplish the organization's goals.[55] Employees could use their work to help fully develop and express their innate interests and talents while the organization could socialize employees to become efficient means to achieve organizational ends. Her holistic perspective focused on the interrelationships among the organization's parts. Not until the 1960s and 1970s, and again in the 1980s and 1990s did her ideas gain momentum in the United States.

Unlike Taylor, Fayol and Weber, Follett was a social worker and sociologist; she never led a for-profit company. Well-educated—with a *summa cum laude* from Radcliffe and postgraduate study at Cambridge University and in Paris—readings in politics, economics, sociology, law, biology, psychology, and philosophy influenced her ideas. Later, in Boston, she gained prominence by managing an innovative education and recreation program, founding evening centers for community use, working with community groups at all levels, and serving on the Boston Placement Bureau. As a Massachusetts Minimum Wage Board member, she met regularly with representatives of employers and employees. An active writer and speaker, she became an authority on business administration with farsighted ideas about leadership theory. In her view, authority and control were horizontal and situational (not only hierarchical), and organizational conflict could be constructive.

Follett viewed organizations holistically. Businesses have social as well as economic dimensions. Administrators were responsible for the whole product, not only their narrow specialty within the division of labor. Organizing businesses so managers would feel this responsibility for the functional whole generates a sense of collective responsibility that enriches workers and dignifies their labor. Similarly, as citizens and as members of the business profession, managers have a social and "corporate" responsibility to maintain professional standards and to educate the public about these norms. Extending the holistic view, Follett pioneered the idea of including *stakeholders*, interdependent groups or individuals (such as creditors, stockholders, clients, competitors, suppliers, and the community) who affect or are affected by business decisions; they are key interest groups for managers to consider when making decisions and with whom to keep positive relations.[56]

Follett also viewed people in organizations holistically. Less interested in specific management techniques than with their sociological and psychological foundations, she concluded that human relations are basic to effective management of organizations.[57] Believing that the technical and human aspects of organizations can never be completely separated, she argued that organizational managers must account for both production and personnel. Organizations needed to allow more flexibility than Taylor's system permitted.[58] Moreover, since employees were complex persons with many roles—a father, mother, a religious believer, and citizen—organizations should deal with workers as whole people with other interests, abilities, and persuasions rather than simply as interchangeable cogs in the machine. Given this, managers should educate rather than blame when faced with a subordinate's shortcomings.[59] Well-run businesses in which managers treat employees appropriately would improve the organization, society in general, and individuals' lives.

Likewise, Follett believed the informal organization held much influence, with group power more important than personal power. Groups of workers had the ability to control themselves (as a group and as individuals) and develop their own ideals and norms rather than have management try to control them. In addition, she asserted, real leadership was facilitating, not commanding.[60] Of three types of leadership—position, personality, and function—functional leadership was the most important—because this leader understood the whole evolving situation and the interrelation of all the parts.[61]

Accordingly, Follett advocated that organizational authority and control be less hierarchical, more cooperative, and influenced by the situation.[62] She understood *control* as an ongoing, dynamic, holistic process of continuous adjustment and coordination.[63] Likewise, *organizational control* is the group and group members' exercise of power *with* one another—not power *over* one another. She believed that since workers have the capacity to make good decisions, executives, managers, and workers could share organizational control, distributing responsibility, power, and authority throughout the organizational ranks. Genuine power is "coactive" (power *with*), not "coercive" (power *over*); power sharing in organizations advanced democratic as well as organizational interests.[64] With shared authority, workers and managers would be able to influence each other, and the organization would achieve greater efficiency.

Presciently, Follett recognized that aspects of the environment influenced decision making. Her "law of the situation" expected workers to take their cues from the requirements of the specific circumstances rather than only from the organization's hierarchy of authority.[65] Using lateral communication to coordinate activities, Follett proposed that workers at the same level talk directly to each other and integrate their views rather than strictly following the chain of command.[66] She believed that direct, ongoing interaction with each other to achieve common goals helped members fulfill themselves as they developed the organization. But although coordination *provided* control, employees interacting *was* control.[67] All these approaches reduced the "power over" aspects of administration and further flattened the power hierarchy.

Follett saw constructive organizational conflict as a way to reduce the *power-over* situation. She identified three ways of handling conflict: dominate, compromise, or integrate. *Domination* presents a win-lose orientation: someone wins at the other's expense. *Compromise* requires each side to give up part of their original interest in exchange for an agreement. *Integration* looks for a new and better solution where both parties have a stake and neither side sacrifices anything. Identifying and meeting each party's underlying and often compatible needs could accomplish integration. In her view, only "win-win" integration stabilizes the organization, although this is not always a possible outcome.[68] Moving beyond the "either/or" of false choices in settling a dispute, Follett was first to coin the phrase, "conflict resolution."[69]

Critics point to Follett's inability to reconcile organizational idealism with pragmatism (that is, explain how enlightened administration can benefit both the individual and the organization), claiming that she opportunistically put a "veneer" of pragmatism on to her idealistic training in order to find popular American readership. This dualism blinded Follett to the downsides of organizations.[70] Others challenge her notions that modern organizations could save democracy (when, in fact, organizations could stifle individuality, pluralism, and diversity)[71] or that conflict could be reconciled harmoniously.[72] A few critics chide her for suggesting complex—rather than simple and easily implemented—solutions to management problems.[73] Follett's social welfare background, her gender, and her lack of a university post may have also swayed critics to discount her ideas.[74]

Although Follett's ideas were largely ignored until their rediscovery in the mid-and later twentieth century, her views predated later emerging schools of organizational leadership thought and practice. With her humanistic approach to workers, her views on facilitative leadership, worker empowerment, distributed organizational control, constructive conflict, effective teamwork, and the importance of considering stakeholders and work contexts in decision making, Follett anticipated the systems theory and many management ideas and practices that have resonance today.

ELTON MAYO: THE HAWTHORNE STUDIES AND HUMAN RELATIONS

George Elton Mayo (1880–1949), an industrial psychologist at Harvard Business School, was curious about how workers responded to their work environments. Writing at a time of escalating social, economic, and political unrest (especially conflicts between management and labor) between World War I and the New Deal, he focused his research and writings on the interpersonal and social needs of factory workers in industrial production. Mayo was among the first to apply psychology to managerial and organizational contexts.[75] With his proposed solutions to the problems of industrial discord, Mayo is credited with highlighting the importance of workers as social people and initiating the human relations movement in organizational management.

From 1924 to 1927, the National Research Council conducted a series of studies at the Western Electric Company's Hawthorne plant in Cicero, Illinois to determine the optimum level of lighting in a workshop for maximum production efficiency. The results were "inconclusive and puzzling"[76]—confounding the expectation that favorable lighting would improve productivity. In response, Western Electric's management instituted its own studies from 1927 to 1933 and invited Mayo and his Harvard colleague, F.J. Roethlisberger, to join as consultants. The studies consisted of experiments and interviews with 21,126 Western Electric workers to learn what employees liked and disliked about their work environment. Investigators examined the workplace's physical and environmental influences (including changes in the brightness of lights at stated intervals, humidity, and managers' behaviors) and their psychological aspects (such as work breaks, group pressure, working hours, and managerial leadership) on two groups of workers. Researchers then measured and analyzed changes in the two groups' productivity. Regardless of the changes, productivity in both control and experimental groups increased, even when the situation worsened.

Mayo and Roethlisberger concluded that employees' needs for recognition, security, a sense of belonging, and effective management are more essential in determining workers' morale and productivity than the physical conditions under which they work. Organizations had a human-social element: an *informal organization* operated in the workplace that affected job performance. Mayo surmised that the workers enjoyed having the researchers' attention—known as the "novelty effect" (now also known as the Hawthorne effect). Their recommendation: to increase organizational productivity, managers needed to grant workers an active and significant voice in making management decisions. Group collaboration must be planned and developed.

Authorized to write the official account of the Hawthorne studies,[77] Mayo became the research group's most effective spokesperson, popularizing its findings. He is credited with founding the Human Relations Movement (HRM), an orientation exploring how to humanize the workplace (as compared with Taylor's mechanistic and technical focus). The HRM's key theoretical contribution was its focus on the *informal organization*—an unofficial social structure of relationships and interactions with unofficial leaders, norms, values, and communication patterns based on and expressed through emotions, viewed as non-rational—as compared with formal management, hierarchy, and rationality. The Human Relations Movement attempted to move beyond the simplistic models of human nature and interactions in organizations. Scholars have assessed Mayo's contributions as central to the formation of the disciplines of organizational behavior and industrial relations,[78] organizational development,[79] and personnel policies and practices.[80]

It would be incorrect to view Mayo as the workers' advocate, however. As this chapter has discussed, he was not the first to consider the "human problems of industry." Even before the Hawthorne experiments, the term "human relations" was used frequently.[81] In addition, Mayo came to the Hawthorne studies with his views on the psychology of workers' behaviors already well formed.[82] He concluded that counter-productive work behaviors—anything from daydreaming to labor unrest—stemmed from the workers' inability (and unconscious disorientation and "irrationality") to adapt to the conditions of industrial life.[83] He asserted the importance of a managerial elite who should be in control,[84] recommended that experts in psychology study labor unrest,[85] and proposed that psychological theories and techniques—such as clinical interviews—be used in the workplace to reduce worker dissatisfaction (and quiet labor unrest).[86] Nonetheless, by applying psychology to business and management and his active popularization of how understanding human behavior in the work setting increased industrial productivity, Mayo helped shape the organizational leadership profession.

Mayo's critics question his credibility, his views, and his place in management history. Some argue that his interpretation of the Hawthorne studies reflected his original biases (about politics, psychology, and industry) rather than the actual empirical findings.[87] Critics also assert that he crossed the line from analyzing data into advocacy.[88] Likewise, critics claim that Mayo built the Human Relations School as a set of psychological theories and psychotherapeutic techniques for managers to control workers through their thoughts and emotions,[89] an undemocratic innovation to give the conservative business community a humanistic and academically-supported language and a "technology of social control"[90] to take back their "right to manage" that they believed the New Deal had challenged. Others see Mayo's real agenda as promoting human relations theory to help the fledgling Harvard Business School win corporate and academic support as an elite school to prepare business leaders.[91] Likewise, critics observe that with much of Mayo's research, writings, and Harvard Business School salary directly funded by the Rockefeller Foundation,[92] his rhetoric and conclusions may have been geared to please his patron.

Controversial as his place in organizational theory might be, Mayo's ideas about the informal organization and providing worker incentives enhancing their workplace performance gained widespread acceptance. A managerial leadership style stressing interpersonal relations, listening, communication, and social and human skills could help workers be happier and more productive at their jobs.

CHESTER BARNARD: ORGANIZATIONAL MANAGEMENT THEORY

Chester I. Barnard (1886–1961) laid the foundation for management and organizational theory as its exists today.[93] A successful corporate executive and a strong theorist on the nature of corporate organizations, Barnard believed that people working collectively and systematically, linked by effective communications to reinforce organizational growth and complexity, would advance organizational goals. He theorized that an organization's survival depends on its ability to sustain a balance with its ever-changing external environment by readjusting its internal processes to match environmental factors. And organization's leadership challenge is to reconcile and balance the inherent tension between individual employees' needs with the organization's goals in an ever-shifting milieu.

Barnard was not an academic; his theories came from decades of first-hand organizational experience, eclectic readings, and reflection. Growing up in a working class intellectual family, Barnard apprenticed as a piano tuner to learn a trade to help him pay his way through prep school. With a scholarship, he attended Harvard (but left before graduation for lack of funds). At age 23, he became a statistician with the American Telephone and Telegraph Company (AT&T) in Boston. At age 41, he became the first president of New Jersey Bell Telephone, a position he held for 21 years. During the 1930s, Barnard served as state director of the New Jersey Relief Administration. The Harvard Circle of American management theorists (including Elton Mayo) invited Barnard to join their group as they were developing a new conceptual model to explain the behavior of workers in modern organizations. Through their encouragement, Barnard wrote two seminal books on company organization and human relations, integrating his own executive experiences with the Harvard group's new schema. After his retirement from Bell, he became president of the Rockefeller Foundation.

Barnard believed that management's central challenge was balancing both the formal organization's requirements with its social and human dimensions. For Barnard, employees were not *"objects* to be *manipulated"* but *"subjects* to be *satisfied."*[94] In *Functions of the Executive* (1938), Barnard analyzed organizations as "cooperative systems," open ended, natural, dynamic systems of mutual effort that survived only if they met two conditions: they must be effective *and* efficient. To do this, firms must meet their organizational objectives and also gain the cooperation of their individual contributors, inside and outside the organization. This required a balanced leadership approach that executives could implement by formulating and communicating a common organizational purpose (to give meaning and unifying principle to the rest of the environment), accounting for individual motives (that the organization had to satisfy in order to gain the individual's efforts), and providing a communication process (clear oral and written language) to bring these two opposite entities into a dynamic equilibrium.

Barnard was one of the first management scholars to investigate the links between companies and their external environments. External environments include customers, competitors, government regulations, and labor unions—in short, stakeholders whose behaviors affected the organization. In *The Functions of the Executive* (1938), Barnard examined the impact of environmental uncertainty on organizational strategies. He believed that the physical environment was inherently unstable, and managers' inability to comprehend all the information available in a given situation created ambiguity during the decision-making process. A company's strategic uncertainty resulted. Herbert Simon and James G. March would expand Barnard's work with their concept of "bounded rationality," acknowledging that managers and firms in complex environments are forced to make decisions without complete information about their strategic options.[95]

Barnard's view of authority has been a subject of considerable debate. Many scholars saw authority as management's formally given right to lead within the organization's hierarchy and power structure. In contrast, Barnard saw authority as depending on the consent of subordinates, authority coming from the bottom-up (from the cooperation of work groups) rather than from the top-down. Managers cannot coerce appropriate employee behavior. Because the workers have chosen to enter the organization, they are free to accept or reject their supervisors' directive if that employee believes the actions are not in the organization's best interests. Rather, organizational leaders' authority rests in their ability to persuade rather than to command. Barnard asserted that when leaders use authority of leadership (that comes from the respect and confidence that others have for that individual's superior ability) rather than of authority of position (that comes strictly from a person's rank or title, without regard to their expertise), they are more able to gain workers' consent and cooperation.[96] The executive's job was to create the conditions that increased the workers' acceptance of leadership's authority.

Barnard also theorized that people have a "zone of indifference" within which they will accept orders without questioning the giver's authority. When organizational leaders can combine both authority of position and leadership—and offer workers personal incentives or inducements (such as increased power or prestige, opportunities for increased participation, or more desirable physical conditions)—leaders can enlarge workers' "zone of indifference," making them more willing to accept authority.[97]

An organization's informal organization was also important to Barnard. He saw the formal and informal organization as interdependent, with the informal organization providing such essential functions as communication, cohesion, and protecting the individuals' integrity against certain aspects of the formal organization that tended to disregard individuals. He recognized the influence of what is now called "corporate culture" and the executives' role in maintaining the informal organization by using intangible influence to shape values and promote cooperation and self-discipline. Further, Barnard speculated that employees are more willing to accept authority when they believe that their actions will contribute to the shared organizational goal.

Critics complain of Barnard's labored writing style: his abstract, theoretical discussions and "invented" terminology often make his prose hard to follow.[98] Some contend that Barnard's views represented the interest group in power: white, well-born, Anglo-Saxon men[99] or that Barnard's definition of organization—the conscious coordination of activities or forces of two or more persons—is inadequate.[100] Others point to his omissions, such as the lack of discussion about relations between an organization and its customers or how the executive interacts with the board of directors or stockholders.[101] Also, critics comment that his views on diversity are "unenlightened" by today's standards.[102]

Barnard focused his ideas on the organization as a system and on the social and informal aspects of organizations. Considering management as an art and a science,[103] his was likely the first balanced approach to the management process.[104] Many organizational theory scholars—such as Herbert A. Simon—would build upon Barnard's ideas.

HERBERT A. SIMON: ADMINISTRATIVE BEHAVIOR THEORY

Herbert A. Simon (1916–2001), a 1978 Nobel Prize winning economist and professor at Carnegie Mellon University, was a social scientist who made pivotal contributions in academic fields including psychology, administration, economics, and operations research. In all these areas, his interest centered on human decision making and problem solving processes and their implications for social institutions. His empirical study of organizations introduced an array of organizational arrangements and the subtle forces operating within them. He believed in theory building based on empirically validated hypotheses of how organizations actually functioned.[105]

Simon came by his eclectic interests honestly. His father was an electrical engineer, inventor, and patent lawyer, and his mother an accomplished pianist-turned-home-maker. Simon grew to become a widely read intellectual and a skilled pianist (who used his piano playing as thinking time). A lover of the outdoors, he climbed the Alps for his 65th birthday.[106] Throughout his career, he used the knowledge and tools of varied disciplines to understand decision making and problem solving by individuals and organizations.

In his ground breaking *Administrative Behavior* (1947),[107] Simon used Chester Barnard's earlier work as a springboard to precisely describe how an administrative organization looks and works. Barnard and Simon used sociological methods to examine the organization as an interactive social system and as a system of exchange. In Simon's view, whether or not an organization continues to exist depends on the balance of contributions and inducements for employee participation.[108] In other words, both the employees and the organization cooperate on goals as long as the organization continues to meet employees' needs. Like Barnard, Simon saw the organization was a human enterprise seeking internal and external equilibrium, trying to balance its goals, the needs of the individuals working within it, and environmental inputs. Therefore, the employee must be appreciated as a desirable and active individual with *limited* knowledge, potential to learn, and ability to solve problems. With this book, Simon became a contributor to generic organizational theory.[109]

Decision making was Simon's central focus, and he challenged key aspects of the neoclassical view of rationality.[110] For Simon, "The central concern of administrative theory is with the boundary between the rational and the non-rational aspects of human social behavior."[111] Principally, he argued that an organization could be understood by studying its decision processes in a way that permits scientific analysis. He posited that humans make decisions within real world constraints, and, as a result, the "administrative man" makes "satisfactory" rather than "optimal" decisions. He emphasized the power and authority of rules is based on the employees' agreement and the importance of cooperation and delegating authority.

In his book with co-author, James March, *Organizations*, Simon reviewed scientific management theory and administrative management theory.[112] Although Frederick Taylor and Henri Fayol, and others, were generally concerned with finding the most effective way to organize tasks to achieve organizational goals, their theories remained untested. Neither did they consider the human factor nor the complexities of organizations. Recognizing these limitations, Simon and March expanded ideas about the influence processes: decision making in the human and goal interactions and their intended and unintended consequences in organizational functioning.[113]

In describing organizational functioning, Simon and March go to a level of detail not seen before in organizational theories. For example, in organizations, the individual faces two different decisions, each with diverse factors: the decision to participate (whether or not to stay with the organization) and the decision to produce (whether or not to work hard and smart). Individuals base their decision to participate on the concept of organizational equilibrium, the balance of organizational incentives relative to their work contributions. Their concepts underlying organizational equilibrium are:[114]

- The organization is a system of interrelated social behavior of participants.
- The organization gives each participant and group incentives for their contributions.
- The individual participates as long as the incentives he/she receives are greater than his/her contribution. The individual makes this evaluation measured in terms of his/her own values; these may include gains other than economic (such as satisfaction with the organization, identification with group members, and other noneconomic beliefs).
- Various groups make contributions that become sources from which the organization creates incentives to pay others.
- Equilibrium (or solvency) occurs when the organization can keep providing incentives to members to obtain their contributions.

When the person has high job satisfaction—that is, if the job suits the individual's life style, the work is personally meaningful, fits with the self-concept, and work relationships are supportive—the individual may decide to stay (participate) and work (produce). By contrast, if the individual is not satisfied with the job, he or she may consider transferring to a different position within the organization—or leave it. The employee's decision to participate and produce may be motivated by "semiconscious" factors, and the incentives/contributions balance allows some flexibility in how the individual finds his/her equilibrium. But, should one person or group leave or change its nature, it disturbs the balance, and the organization must seek a new level of equilibrium.

Simon has a sophisticated and detailed understanding of organizational dynamics, especially noting the many decision points and processes in human-organization interactions. Simon also advanced thinking about organizational and leadership issues including rational decision making,[115] a formal theory of the employment relationship,[116] organizational strategy,[117] and goals.[118]

Many of Simon's critics, also scholars, debate the finer points of social psychology or administration that would seem esoteric and irrelevant to educational leadership students. Some academics argue past each other in an "artificial debate."[119] Generally, some critics see Simon's use of social psychology's decision theory as insufficient to explain the whole of organization, noting that his explanations are too "rational" and narrow in focus to account for the ambiguities and uncertainties contained in organizational life and the larger society.[120] Others write that a science of organizations is impossible due to cultural differences among organizations.[121]

Throughout Simon's 40 years of work, his thinking continued to evolve. His contributions to the concept of organization, organizational theory, the study of administrative behavior, and organizational communication are significant and extensive. They continue to influence our thinking about organizations.

REFLECTIONS AND RELEVANCE 2.3

Comparing and Contrasting Taylor, Fayol, Weber, Follett, Mayo, Barnard, and Simon (See Table 2.3 and Above)

Frederick Taylor, Henri Fayol, Max Weber, Mary Parker Follett, Elton Mayo, Chester Barnard, and Herbert Simon made significant contributions to understanding organizational leadership. Working in small groups of six to eight (with a leader, a note taker, and a reporter), each group will identify areas of agreement and disagreement for any four of the seven theorists on *one* of the following topics and then discuss their findings as a class:

- The use of sociology and psychology to understand employee behavior in organizations.
- The organization as a human enterprise.
- The relationships between an organization's social and informal dynamics and how successfully it achieves its goals.
- Whether the administrative hierarchy or collaborative work groups offers the most efficient and effective way for organizations to solve problems and make decisions.
- How organizational leaders use incentives to find the balance between meeting the organization's goals and meeting employees' needs.
- How to distribute authority, responsibility, and power in the organization to best achieve organizational goals.
- How situational factors inside and outside the organization influenced planning and achieving organizational goals.

LEADERSHIP: TRAIT, BEHAVIOR, AND SITUATIONAL THEORIES

Until the mid-1950s, schools of education had minimal contact with the scholarly thought and research in business or behavioral science. Former school superintendents tended to teach educational administration courses, using their own experiences to give a practical, how-to approach to the subject. But by midcentury, educational administration recognized a new concept—schools, as organizations, were social systems. Behavioral sciences—leadership, motivation, decision making, organizational climate and culture, organizational change—began to influence the study of school leadership along with traditional courses in finance, law, and school plant and facilities. Theories about leadership characteristics, leadership behavior, and the extent to which leaders addressed the organizational tasks, the people who accomplished the tasks, and the situations in which all occurred would increasingly influence education leaders' preparation.

TABLE 2.3 From the Traditional to Modern Era in Organizational Leadership Theory

Person Professional Background Theory Years of Major Influence	View of Organizations	View of Workers
Focus on Organizational Structures and Practices		
Industrial Era **Frederick W. Taylor** Engineer Scientific Management 1911–1935	A rational machine to manage tasks, end waste through standardization; separate mental from physical work.	Generally lazy, needed direction, training, cooperative relations with managers.
Henri Fayol Engineer and CEO Administrative Management Theory 1916–1949	Complex, shared features. Managers needed training.	Welcomed employees initiative, participation in management decisions; treat workers fairly, kindly.
Max Weber Economist, Sociologist Bureaucratic Organization Theory 1910 to present	Stable, needed rational rules, hierarchy to structure activities, authority, and accountability.	Employees are specialized, should follow written rules, be treated fairly, promotions based on merit.
Focus on Leading People and Tasks to Meet Organizational Goals		
Modern Era **Mary Parker Follett** Social Worker, Consultant Modern Management Theory 1960s to present	Organizations are social and economic (holistic). Authority and control are horizontal and situational. Conflict can be constructive.	Individuals can meet own potentials as they fulfill organization's goals. Human relations are basic to effective management. Educate, don't blame.
Elton Mayo Industrial Psychologist Human Relations Movement 1930s to present	Organizations have informal social groups that affect workers' job performance.	Workers are social people with interpersonal (irrational) needs.
Chester Barnard Corporate Executive Organizational Management Theory Late 1930s to present	Organizations as cooperative open systems that must adapt to their complex external environments.	Leaders needed to balance individual employees' needs with organization's goals. Employees as subjects to be satisfied.
Herbert Simon Economist, Social Scientist Administrative Behavior Theory Late 1940s to present	Organizations as interactive social and exchange, rational and irrational systems.	Organization and its employees cooperate on balancing goals and needs with environmental inputs.

Source: Kaplan & Owings, 2017

Unlike earlier organization and administration theorists like Taylor, Fayol, Weber, Follett, Mayo, Barnard, or Simon whose ideas would become popular and influence the field for decades, mid-twentieth century leadership theory and research was marked by a disparity of approaches, a narrow research focus, questionable methodologies, and a lack of broad theories to integrate the findings. Research in trait theory, leader behavior theory, and situational theory attempted to refine and expand our understanding of how organizational leadership worked but seldom included leadership components from other perspectives. As a result, no one theorist dominates the field. Nevertheless, sets of variables from different approaches can be seen as part of a larger network, related in meaningful ways to leadership effectiveness.[122] Together, they helped expand our understanding of leadership from entity to collectivist theories and from the Industrial Era to the Knowledge Era. Leader trait theories, leader behavior theories, situational leadership theories, and an integrated approach all merit attention.

Leader Trait Theories

For centuries, folk wisdom held that great leaders are born to take charge of a situation and lead their people to safety or success. So-called "Great Man" theories of leadership had been popular since the 1840s when historian Thomas Carlyle wrote that "the history of the world is but the biography of great men,"[123] divinely inspired extraordinary leaders who had the personal charisma, intelligence, wisdom, and political skills to influence others in ways that had decisive impact. Inverting this view, in 1860, sociologist Herbert Spencer argued instead that great men are products of their societies, their ideas and behaviors merely outcomes of their social environments.[124] Society shaped these individuals. Spencer's views influenced leadership study throughout the next century—and still do.

Hundreds of trait studies conducted in the 1930s and 1940s failed to find any traits that would guarantee leadership success.[125] After World War II, the studies to identify the traits or characteristics that differentiated leaders from their followers continued. Often examined traits included physical characteristics (height, weight, energy and activity levels) and personality factors (intelligence, charisma, personal needs and values, task and interpersonal skills). Eventually, researchers recognized that learning and environmental factors—as well as inheritance—affected traits.

Ralph Stogdill at Ohio State University reviewed 124 trait studies of leadership completed between 1904 and 1947 and classified the personal factors associated with leadership into five general categories: capacity, achievement, responsibility, participation, and status.[126] Although Stogdill found that traits such as above average intelligence, dependability, participation, and status consistently separated leaders from nonleaders, the trait approach, alone, had unclear and insignificant findings. No traits guaranteed leadership success. Plus, the impact of traits varied, depending on the circumstances. Later, Stogdill added a sixth leadership factor—situational components—that would influence researchers for decades. Subsequent investigators agreed.[127]

The trait theory approach had many conceptual and methodological limitations. Because so few of the traits clearly separated leaders from followers, they cannot be used reliably in leadership selection. Additionally, the theories erroneously assumed that traits are stable and unchanging regardless of the circumstance. The traits also tended to reflect male leaders, a subjective bias reflecting the absence of female leaders. As a result, the trait approach lost its influence in place of behavioral and situational leadership theories.[128]

A second generation of trait theory studies, using improved measurement procedures, focused on the relationship between leader traits and leader effectiveness. It has produced a more consistent set of findings. Namely, possessing certain traits–aspects of personality (self-confidence, stress tolerance, integrity, and emotional maturity), motivation (power and achievement needs, expectations, self-efficacy), and skills (technical, interpersonal, and cognitive)—increases the likelihood that a leader will be effective while acknowledging that traits, situations, and organizational contexts influence leadership behaviors.[129] Critics still noted that leadership characteristics are not organized in a meaningful conceptual construction, don't consider how their complex relationships connect with outcomes, ignore the situation's impact, and lack a systematic conceptual framework.[130] Eventually, studies would find leaders' traits, behaviors, and situational variables all influenced leadership effectiveness.

Leader Behavioral Theories

Since World War II, behavioral science has investigated the relationship between what an organization's leader does and the organization's success. In 1945, scholars at Ohio State University worked on developing an instrument for describing leadership behavior.

Initiating Structure and Consideration

Using factor analysis on leadership data, Andrew W. Halpin and B.J. Winer isolated two basic leadership behaviors in formal organizations: initiating structure and consideration.[131] *Initiating structure* (or task-oriented behaviors) is the degree to which a leader defines and organizes roles or relationships and establishes clearly defined patterns of communication and organization aimed at getting the job done. A high score here suggests a person who actively directs group activities through planning, communicating, scheduling, and trying out new ideas. *Consideration* (or people-oriented behaviors) is the degree to which a leader shows concern and respect for followers and their ideas, looks out for their wellbeing, and expresses appreciation and support. A high score here indicates a climate of good rapport and two-way communication. Investigators also determined that the most effective leaders integrate both high initiating structure and high consideration: they have both high task and high people skills.[132]

Although scholars have criticized the leadership behavior concepts, methodology, and usefulness,[133] many studies have confirmed a moderately strong relationship between initiating structure, consideration, and leadership outcomes. Consideration correlates more strongly with employee satisfaction and initiating structure ties more strongly with performance or effectiveness.[134] As a result, these two features "have proven to be among the most robust leadership concepts" in leadership research,[135] and they have been adapted into a popular format used for management training.[136]

Situational (Contingency) Leadership Theories

The situational approach to leadership theory stresses the importance of contextual factors. These include the leader's authority and discretion, the nature of the work performed by the leader's unit, subordinates' characteristics, the particular circumstances, and the nature of the external environment. Situational theories operate on the assumption that different behavior patterns will be effective in different situations, and the same behavior pattern may not be best in all circumstances.

LPC Contingency Theory

In 1967, Fred E. Fiedler constructed the first major theory whose research was able to document a complex interaction of leader behavior, situational (contingency) factors, and effectiveness. In this theory, a leader's effectiveness was a function of their leadership style and the moderating influences of the situational components (i.e., the leader's personal relations with group members, the position's power and authority, and the degree of structure in the assigned task).[137] Leaders' effectiveness, therefore, is contingent on matching the appropriate leadership style with the particular situation. The model's usefulness is problematic, however. Many studies testing the model had mixed findings;[138] methodological problems make any findings questionable, and the model's serious conceptual deficiencies limit its usefulness for explaining leadership effectiveness.[139]

Path-Goal Theory

One of the 1970s and 1980s most popular leadership theories looks at the organizational factors that affect the leader's use of initiating structure and consideration.[140] Robert J. House's Path-Goal Theory advanced the idea that leaders motivate higher performance by acting in ways that influence subordinates to believe that they can gain valued outcomes by making a serious effort to do their assigned work.[141] Elements in the situation—such as the type of task, the work environment, and workers' attitudes and skills—determine the optimal amount of each type of leader behavior for improving workers' job satisfaction and performance. Reviews of this research support certain parts of the theory,[142] but the theory has conceptual limitations, while its research has methodological ones.[143]

Other situational leadership theories, including Paul Hersey and Kenneth Blanchard's Situational Leadership Theory (suggesting that the optimal amount of task and relations behavior between the organization leader and employees depends on the employee's maturity),[144] and Victor Vroom and Phillip Yetton's Normal Decision Theory (that identifies decision rules to use in certain situations)[145] also found popularity in management circles; but neither has fully stood up to empirical or conceptual scrutiny.[146]

An Integrated View

Gary Yukl, a business leadership professor from State University of New York at Albany, studied these early leadership effectiveness theories and their related research and criticism. By the late 1980s, he concluded that the initially fragmented ideas were gradually converging into a larger, meaningful framework of interacting variables that addressed leadership effectiveness. Organizational effectiveness, as judged by final outcomes, is mediated by a core set of intervening variables. Leaders can directly or indirectly influence employee behaviors toward organizational goals by using leaders' position and personal power. Or, the leader's influence may be swayed (or overwhelmed) by stronger situational factors and by leader traits and values, role expectations, and interpretation of what is occurring. Yukl also found themes repeated from the 1960s: developing human potential and a sense of ownership; an emphasis on power sharing, mutual trust, and participatory decision making; activating higher order needs in service to the organization; and awareness of political and symbolic processes and organizational culture that conferred meaning, both shaping the organization and being shaped by them.[147]

In addition, Yukl saw leadership theory becoming more balanced, with two trends emerging. First, leaders can have high concern for both the task and the people—as well as act differently in different situations. Second, the scholarly focus was moving away from individual leaders toward concepts of leadership as a shared process embedded in social systems, moving from the entity perspective to the collective perspective. Yukl concluded that leadership study needed new theories to describe the interactive leadership processes that occur over time in social systems.[148] Chapter 3 will consider many of these new theories.

REFLECTIONS AND RELEVANCE 2.4

Leadership Traits, Behaviors, and Situational Theories

Leadership theory and research soared in the mid- to late-twentieth century with their focus, variably, on leadership traits, behaviors, and situational influences.

In groups of three (with a facilitator, recorder, and reporter), identify the five most important ideas (supported by research) from these leadership theories. Then, as a class, discuss your findings, reach consensus on the class's top five ideas, and speculate on where the next generation of leadership theories might go.

IMPLICATIONS FOR EDUCATIONAL LEADERS

Schools are complex organizations, and the community has very high expectations for what they want their schools—and their school leaders—to accomplish. This chapter contains several ideas that help aspiring school leaders begin to build the conceptual framework to enact this role successfully: the organization as an interacting system of many parts; the organization as a human enterprise; the need for leaders to develop people and task-oriented skills. Plus, school leaders must recognize and navigate effectively the traditional scientific management, administrative, and bureaucratic thinking and practices still operating in today's schools.

Schools as Interacting Systems

School systems, as all organizations, consist of four key interacting components: people, tasks, technology, and structure. These components are interdependent; what happens in one area will impact functioning in the others. Principals are responsible for making them work in synch to achieve the school's goals. Most likely, school leaders will want to delegate daily management oversight for aspects of these components to assistant principals, department heads, or others. But since principals remain responsible for every school goal, practice, and outcome, they must continually monitor activities, practices, and progress in each area. Checking in frequently with assistant principals or department heads—regularly and often sitting together at the same meetings to ensure the necessary coordination of interdependent activities—is essential. These discussions help leaders assess ongoing developments and learn if any unforeseen issues are arising that may interfere with meeting the organization's goals. The oversight frequency will depend on the delegatee's maturity and experience in the assigned roles and the time urgency. For instance, building the master schedule in June, July, and August may require daily contact, while supervising grounds maintenance may only occur every few weeks. But since "the buck stops" at the principal's desk, learning how to delegate wisely and supervise effectively are essential leadership skills that keep the complex enterprise of schooling functioning smoothly.

Schools are Human Enterprises

Above all, organizations are human enterprises. People are individuals, not interchangeable cogs in the larger machine. People can be knowledgeable, diligent, responsible, innovative, and tireless workers, and they can also be unpredictable, self-serving, and "irrational." How well the organization achieves its goals depends, to a large extent, on the relationships between the organization's formal and informal dynamics. Workgroups, friendship networks, and cliques can help leaders get the job done—or they can openly or covertly refuse to accept the leaders' direction. Knowing and caring about employees as individuals—and showing it in ways that matter to them—allow employees to feel valued, respected, inspired, and encouraged to commit their best efforts to the school's goals. A people-friendly school is welcoming to all and creates a positive learning climate for both adults and children.

Key Leadership Needs: Task *and* People Skills

Schools generate so much work to do, so many tasks to perform, at such a rapid pace. Given the pressure to complete one task and move on to the next, school leaders often give short shrift to the people doing them. It is very tempting to shut the office door and complete the task at hand. Stopping to talk to a teacher, student, or parent risks not getting the job done on time. But thinking this way hurts the school and its students.

The need for aspiring school leaders to develop both deep, extensive professional knowledge about organizational leadership *and* strong, active people skills cannot be overstated. Given organizations' formal and informal dynamics, research suggests that effective leaders have high skills in initiating structure (task-oriented behaviors) *and* consideration (people-oriented behaviors). Inclusive, caring, and ethical professional environments that engage meaningfully with their students, parents, and communities to promote each child's academic success and wellbeing do not just happen. They are deliberately constructed and attentively maintained by investing time in speaking with each other, getting to know colleagues as individuals, and learning what they value and need to be effective in their jobs. Even a brief daily greeting and exchange of "How's it going today?" at their classroom doors will strengthen the ties between school leaders and teachers. Having conversations with others in school is not a distraction from the main event: it *is* the main event.

Déjà Vu All Over Again

Managing the people and tasks while mediating inputs from the situation and the environment is not simple. Developing organizational leadership skills takes time, experience, quality feedback, and intensive reflection. And all this must occur within the many traditional Industrial Age structures of hierarchy, control, planning, and other functions essential to keep the organization intact. Many of Taylor, Fayol, and Weber's concepts continue in contemporary organizational thinking and practices. School leaders must learn to identify where these practices are facilitating the school's goals and where they are limiting them. When traditional thinking or practices become obstacles to teacher or student learning, school leaders work with other district leaders to revise or replace them.

NOTES

1 Leavitt, H. (1965). Applied organizational change in industry: Structural, technological, and humanistic approaches. In J.G. March (Ed.), *Handbook of organizations*. Chicago, IL: Rand McNally.
2 This text will use the terms *leaders* and *managers* interchangeably.
3 March, J.G. & Simon. H.A. (1993). *Organizations*, 2nd ed. (p. 48). Cambridge, MA: Blackwell.
4 Van Riper, P.P. (1995). Luther Gulick on Frederick Taylor and scientific management. *Journal of Management History*, *1* (21), 6–7.
5 Drucker, P. (1991). The new productivity challenge. *Harvard Business Review*, *69* (6), 69–79.
6 Davis, E. (1980). Individuals and the organization. *California Management Review*, *22* (2), 5–14.
7 Taylor F.W. (1911). *The principles of scientific management* (pp. 36–37). Elibron Classics. New York, NY: Harper & Brothers. Republished (1964). New York, NY: Adamant Media.
8 *Rules of thumb* are informal procedures based on experience rather than on a specific scientific calculation, such as literally using one's thumb as a convenient measuring tool.

9 Taylor (1911/1964). Op. cit., pp. 36–37.

10 Ralston, S.J. (2014). Doing versus thinking: John Dewey's forgotten critique of scientific management. *Southwest Philosophy Review*, *30* (1), 205–217.

11 Bedeian, A. (1998). Exploring the past. *Journal of Management History*, *4* (1), 4–15; Drucker, P.F. (1968). *The age of discontinuity*. New York, NY: Harper & Row.

12 Lamond, D., Parker, L.D. & Ritson, P. (2005). Fads, stereotypes, and management gurus: Fayol and Follett today. *Management Decision*, *43* (10), 1335–1357.

13 Gray, K. (1993). Why we lost: Taylorism in American schools. *Phi Delta Kappan*, *69* (1), 9–16.

14 Caldari, K.L. (2007). Alfred Marshall's critical analysis of scientific management. *European Journal of History of Economic Thought*, *14* (1), 55–78.

15 Caldari (2007). Ibid.

16 Sandrone, V. (1997). *F. W. Taylor and scientific management*. Sydney, AU: University of Technology. Retrieved from: www.skymark.com/resources/leaders/taylor.asp.

17 Morgan, G. (1986), *Images of organization* (p. 30). Newbury Park, CA: Sage.

18 Caldari (2007). Op. cit.; Kanigel, R. (1997). *The one best way: Frederick Winslow Taylor and the enigma of efficiency*. New York, NY: Viking Penguin; Morgan, G. (1997). *Images of organization*, 2nd ed. Thousand Oaks, CA: Sage.

19 Sewell, G. & Wilkinson, B. (1992), Someone to watch over me: Surveillance, discipline and the just-in-time labor process. *Sociology*, *26* (2), 271–289.

20 Fayol, H. (1949). *General and industrial management*. (C. Storrs, Trans.) London, UK: Pitman.

21 Parker, D. & Ritson, P.A. (2005). Revisiting Fayol: Anticipating contemporary management, *British Journal of Management*, *16* (3), 175–193.

22 Wren, D.A. (1995). Henri Fayol: Learning from experience. *Journal of Management History*, *1* (1), 5–12.

23 Fells, M. (2000). Fayol stands the test of time. *Journal of Management History*, *6* (8), 345–360.

24 Fayol (1949). Op. cit., p. xi;

25 Wren, D.A. & Bedeian, A.G. (2009). *The evaluation of management thought*, 6th ed. New York, NY: Wiley.

26 Fayol, H. (1930) *Industrial and general administration*. (J.A. Coubrough, Trans.) Geneva: International Management Institute; and Fayol (1949). Op. cit.

27 Wren (1995). Op. cit.

28 Wren (1995). Op. cit.; Fells (2000). Op. cit.

29 Fells (2000). Op. cit.

30 See: Archer, E.R. (1990). Towards a revival of the principles of management. *Industrial Management*, *32* (1), 19–22; Fells (2000). Op. cit.; Hales, C.P. (1986). What do managers do? A critical review of the evidence. *Journal of Management Studies*, *23* (1), 88–115.

31 Parker, D. & Ritson, R.A. (2005b). Revisiting Fayol: Anticipating contemporary management. *British Journal of Management*, *16* (3), 175–194.

32 Rolph, P. & Bartram, P. (1992). *How to choose and use an executive information system*, London, UK: Mercury Books; Secretan, L.H.K. (1986). *Managerial moxie*, Toronto, CA: Macmillan of Canada.

33 Reid, D. (1995). Reading Fayol with 3D glasses. *Journal of Management History*, *1* (3), 634–671.

34 Wren (1995). Op. cit.; Kotter, J.P. (1982). *The General Managers*. New York, NY: The Free Press, Macmillan.

35 Crainer, S. (1996). *Key management ideas*. London, UK: Prentice-Hall; Davidson, P. & Griffin, R.W. (2000). *Management: Australia in a global context*. Milton, Queensland, AU: John Wiley & Sons; George C.S. (1972). *The history of management thought*. Englewood Cliffs, NJ: Prentice-Hall.

36 See: Cole, G.A. (2004). *Management: Theory and practice*, 6th ed. London, UK: Cengage Learning; Dessler, G. (1977). *Management fundamentals: A framework*. Reston, VA: Reston Publishing; Holt, D.H. (1993). *Management: Principles and practices*, 3rd ed. Englewood Cliffs, NJ: Prentice-Hall.

37 Koontz, H. (1961). The management theory jungle. *Journal of the Academy of Management*, 4 (3), 175–187. (p. 184).

38 Hartley, N.T. (2006). Management history: An umbrella model. *Journal of Management History*, 12 (3), 278–292.

39 Hartley (2006). Ibid., p. 284.

40 Fry, B.R. & Raadschelders, J.C.N. (2014). *Mastering public administration: From Max Weber to Dwight Waldo* (pp. 22–51). Los Angeles, CA: Sage.

41 Litwak, E. (1961). Models of bureaucracy which permit conflict. *American Journal of Sociology*, 67 (2), 177–184; Wren & Bedeian (2009). Op. cit.

42 Fry & Raadschelders (2014). Op. cit., p. 51.

43 Wren & Bedeian (2009). Op. cit.

44 Ritzer, G. (1974–1975). Professionalization, bureaucratization, and rationalization: The views of Max Weber. *Social Forces*, 53 (4), 627–634: Fry & Raadschelders (2014). Op. cit.; Merton, R.K. (1940). Bureaucracy, structure, and personality. *Social Forces*, 18 (4), 560–565.

45 Wren & Bedeian (2009). Op. cit., pp. 232–233.

46 Fry & Raadschelders (2014). Op. cit., p. 50.

47 Gouldner, A. (1954). *Patterns of industrial bureaucracy*. New York, NY: Free Press; Parsons T. (1947). *Max Weber: The theory of social and economic organization*. (pp. 3–86). In A.M. Henderson & T. Parsons (Trans.). New York, NY: Free Press.

48 Merton (1940). Op. cit.

49 Martin, J. & Knopoff, K. (1999). The gendered implications of apparently gender-neutral theory: Rereading Weber. In E. Freeman & A. Larson (Eds) *Business ethics and women's studies*, (pp. 30–49). Ruffin lectures series. Vol. 3. Oxford, UK: Oxford University Press.

50 Fry & Raadschelder (2014). Op. cit.

51 Robert Merton as cited in Fry & Raadschelder (2014). Op. cit., p. 51.

52 Freund, J. (1972). *The sociology of Max Weber*. Hammondworth, UK: Penguin.

53 George, C.S. Jr. (1972). *The history of management thought*, 2nd ed., Englewood Cliffs, N.J.: Prentice-Hall, p. 139.

54 Graham, P. (1996). *Mary Parker Follett prophet of management*. Boston, MA: Harvard Business School Press; Parker, L.D. (1984). Control in organizational life: The contribution of Mary Parker Follett. *Academy of Management*, 9 (4), 736–745.

55 Stever, J.A. (1986). Mary Parker Follett and the quest for pragmatic administration. *Administration & Society*, 18 (2), 159–177.

56 Follett, M. P. (1940). *Dynamic administration. The collected papers of Mary Parker Follett*. Henry C. Metcalf and L. Urwick (Eds). New York, NY: Harper & Brothers, pp. 80–81, 93, 136; Wren, D.A. (1979). The *evolution of management thought*, 2nd ed. New York, NY: Wiley.

57 Metcalf, H.C. & Urwick, L. (Eds) (1941). *Dynamic administration: The collected papers of Mary Parker Follett*. London: Sir Isaac Pitman & Sons Ltd.; Massie, J.L. (1965). Management theory. In J.G. March (Ed.), *Handbook of organizations* (pp. 387–421). Chicago: Rand McNally.

58 Follett, M.P. (1941). How must business management development in order to possess the essentials of a profession. In H.C. Metcalf & L. Urwick (Eds), *Dynamic administration: The collected Papers of Mary Parker Follett* (pp. 117–145). London: Sir Isaac Pitman & Sons Ltd.

59 Follett, M.P. (1918). The new state: Group organization—The solution of popular government. New York, NY: Longmans Green.

60 Lamond, Parker & Ritson (2005). Op. cit.

61 Humphreys, J.H. & Einstein, W.O. (2003). Nothing new under the sun: Transformational leadership from a historical perspective. *Management Decision*, 40 (1/2), 85–95.

62 Metcalf & Urwick (1941). Op. cit.

63 Follett, M.P. (1937). The process of control. In L. Gulick & L. Urwick (Eds), *Papers on the science of administration.* (pp. 161–169). New York, NY: Institute of Public Administration; Follett, M.P. (1973a) The illusion of final authority. In E.M. Fox & L. Urwick (Eds) *Dynamic administration: The collected papers of Mary Parker Follett,* 2nd ed. (pp. 117—131). London, UK: Pitman.

64 Follett, M.P. (1924/2001). *Creative experience.* Bristol, UK: Thoemmes, p. 187.

65 Livingstone, J.L. (1965). Management controls and organizational performance. *Personnel Administration, 28* (1), 37–43.

66 Follett, M.P. (1918). The new state: Group organization—the solution of popular government. New York, NY: Longmans Green.

67 Follett, M.P. (1973b). The psychology of control. In E.M. Fox & L. Urwick (Eds) *Dynamic administration: The collected papers of Mary Parker Follett,* 2nd ed. (pp. 148–174). London, UK: Pitman.

68 Follett (1949). Op. cit., pp. 35–36.

69 (2013). Mary Parker Follett. *New World Encyclopedia.* Retrieved from: www.newworld encyclopedia.org/entry/Mary_Parker_Follett.

70 Stever, J.A. (1986). Mary Parker Follett and the quest for pragmatic administration. *Administration & Society, 18* (2), 159–177.

71 Scott, W.G. & Hart, D.K. (1973). Administrative crisis: The neglect of metaphysical speculation. *Public Administration Review, 33* (September/October), 415–422; Chackerian, R. & Abcarian, G. (1984). *Bureaucratic power in society.* Chicago: Nelson-Hall.

72 Kariel, H. (1955). The new order of Mary Parker Follett. *Western Politics Quarterly, 8* (September), 425–440; Schilling, M.A. (2000). Decades ahead of her time: Advancing stakeholder theory though the ideas of Mary Parker Follett. *Journal of Management History,* 6 (5), 224–242.

73 Lamond, Parker & Ritson (2005). Op. cit.

74 Wren (1979). Op. cit.; Kanter, R.M. (1995). Preface. In P. Graham (Ed.), *Mary Parker Follett—prophet of management,* (pp. xii–xix). Boston, MA: Harvard Business School Press; Parker, L.D. (1999). Fayol and Follett: Messages for contemporary management and accounting. *Accounting, Accountability & Performance, 5* (2), 41–67.

75 O'Connor, E. (1999a). Minding the workers: The meaning of "human" and "human relations" in Elton Mayo. *Organization. 6* (2), 223–246.

76 Smith (2000). Ibid., p. xv.

77 Bruce, K. & Nyland. C. (2011). Elton Mayo and the deification of human relations. *Organization Studies, 32* (3), 383–405.

78 See: Clegg, S. & Bailey, J.R. (Eds). (2008). Human relations school. *International Encyclopedia of Organization Studies* (pp. 610–613). Los Angeles, CA: Sage; Roethlisberger, F. (1977). *The elusive phenomena: An autobiographical account of my work in the field of organizational behavior at the Harvard Business School.* Cambridge, MA: Harvard University Press.

79 Woodworth, W., Meyer, G. & Smallwood, N. (1982). Organization development: A closer scrutiny. *Human Relations, 35* (4), 307–319.

80 Whitsett, D.A. & Yorks, L. (1983). *From management theory to business sense: The myths and realities of people at work.* New York, NY: Amacom.

81 Bruce & Nyland (2011). Op. cit.

82 Mayo earned a BA and an MA in psychology from the University of Queensland, Australia where he taught psychology, studied the nature of nervous breakdown from working with a Brisbane physician treating patients with shell shock psychoanalytically, and believed that industrial unrest had psychological causes. See: Bourke, H. (1986). Mayo, George Elton (1880–1949). *Australian Dictionary of Biography, 10.* Retrieved from: http://adb.anu.edu.au/biography/mayo-george-elton-7541.

83 Mayo, E. (1923). Recovery and industrial fatigue. *Journal of Personnel Research, 3,* 273–259.

84 O'Connor, E.S. (1999b). The politics of management thought: A case study of the Harvard Business School and the Human Relations School. *Academy of Management Review, 24* (1), 117–131; Trahair, H. (1984). *The humanist temper: The life and work of Elton Mayo.* New Brunswick, NJ: Transaction Books.

85 Mayo (1923). Ibid. 120–121.

86 O'Connor (1999b). Op. cit.

87 Carey, A. (1967). The Hawthorne studies: A radical criticism. *American Sociological Review, 32* (3), 403–416; Smith, J.H. (1998). The enduring legacy of Elton Mayo. *Human Relations, 51* (3), 221–249; Wren D. & Greenwood, R. (1998). *Management innovators: The people and ideas that have shaped modern business.* New York, NY: Oxford University Press.

88 Trahair, R.C.S. (1984). *The humanist temper: The life and work of Elton Mayo.* New Brunswick, NJ: Transaction Books.

89 Deetz, S. (2003). Disciplinary power, conflict suppression and HRM. In M. Alvesson & H. Willmott (Eds), *Studying management critically.* London, UK: Sage; Rose, M. (1978). *Industrial behaviour: Theoretical developments since Taylor.* Harmondsworth, UK: Penguin; Townley, B. (1993). Foucault, power/knowledge, and its relevance for human resource management. *Academy of Management Review, 183* (3), 518–545.

90 Gillespie, R. (1991). *Manufacturing knowledge: A history of the Hawthorne experiments.* Cambridge, UK: Cambridge University Press, pp. 112–113.

91 O'Connor (1999b). Op. cit.

92 John D. Rockefeller, Jr.'s interest in industrial relations increased after the 7-month strike at a Rockefeller-owned Ludlow mine that ended in the "massacre" of 10 men, 2 women, and 12 children. Rockefeller wanted to support employee representation in decision making without ceding management authority. See: O'Connor (1999a), p. 120; Clegg & Bailey (2008). Op. cit.

93 Andrews, K.R. (1968). Introduction to the thirtieth anniversary edition of *The functions of the executive.* Cambridge, MA: Harvard University Press; Wolf, W. (1974). *The basic Barnard: An introduction to Chester I. Barnard and his theories of organization and management.* New York, NY: ILR Press, Cornell University.

94 Barnard, C. (1938). *The functions of the executive.* Cambridge, MA: Harvard University Press, p. 40.

95 Simon, H.A. (1957). *Models of man, social and rational.* New York, NY: John Wiley & Sons; March, J.G. & Simon, H.A. (1958). *Organizations.* New York, NY: McGraw-Hill.

96 Barnard (1938). Op. cit.

97 Barnard (1938). Op. cit.

98 Chandran, J.P. (2014). The relevance of Chester Barnard for today's manager. Retrieved from: www.telelavoro.rassegna.it/fad/socorg03/l4/barnard.pdfl; Wolf (1974). Op. cit.; Gabor & Mahoney (2013). Op. cit.

99 Scott, W.G. (1994). Chester I. Barnard and the other antecedents of the present management order. *International Journal of Public Administration, 17* (6), 1093–1106.

100 Rainey, H.G. (1991). *Understanding and managing public organizations.* San Francisco, CA: Jossey-Bass.

101 Keon, T.L. (1986). *The functions of the executive* by Chester I. Barnard. *Academy of Management Review, 11* (2), 456–459.

102 Wolf, W.B. (1973). *Conversations with Chester I. Barnard.* Ithaca, NY: New York State School of Industrial and Labor Relations, Cornell University.

103 Mahoney, J.R. (2002). The relevance of Chester U. Barnard's teachings to contemporary management education: Communicating the aesthetics of management. *Internal Journal of Organizational Theory & Behavior, 5* (1/2), 159–172.

104 Peters, T.J. & Waterman, R.H. (1982). *In search of excellence.* New York, NY: Harper & Row.

105 Frank, K.S. (n.d.). *Herbert A. Simon: A family memory.* Pittsburgh, PA: Carnegie Mellon School of Computer Science. Retrieved from: www.cs.cmu.edu/simon/kfrank.html; Simon, H.A. (1991). Organizations and markets. *The Journal of Economic Perspectives, 5* (2), 25–44.

106 Frank (n.d.). Op. cit.

107 Simon, H.A. (1947). Administrative behavior: A study of decision-making processes in administrative organization. New York, NY: Macmillan.

108 Peng, W-S. (1992). A critique on H.A. Simon's administrative behavior theory. *Public Administration Quarterly, 16* (2), 254–264.

109 Sherwood, F.P. (1990). The half-century's 'great books' in public administration. *Public Administration Review, 50* (2), 249–264.

110 Augier, M. & March, J.A (2002). A model scholar: Herbert A. Simon. *Journal of Economic Behavior and Organization, 49* (1), 1–17.

111 Simon (1947). Ibid., p. xxviii.

112 March, J.G. & Simon, H.A. (1958). *Organizations.* New York, NY: Wiley.

113 Tosi, H.L. (2009). James March and Herbert Simon, organizations. In H.L. Tosi (Ed.), *Theories of organization.* (pp. 93–102). Thousand Oaks, CA: Sage.

114 Tosi (2009). Op. cit., p. 95.

115 See: Simon, H.A. (1979). Rational decision making in business organizations. *The American Economic Review, 68* (4), 493–513; Simon, H.A. (1991). Bounded rationality and organizational learning. *Organization Science, 2* (1), 125–154.

116 Simon, H.A. (1951). A formal theory of the employment relationship. *Econometrica, 19* (3), 293–305.

117 Simon, H.A. (1993). Strategy and organization evolution. *Strategic Management Journal, 14* (52), 131–142.

118 Simon, H.A. (1964). On the concept of organizational goal. *Administrative Science Quarterly, 9* (1), 1–22.

119 Golembiewski, R.T. (1988). Nobel laureate Simon 'looks back': A low-frequency mode. *Public Administration Quarterly, 12* (3): 275–300; Smith, G. & May, D. (1980). The artificial debate between rationalist and incrementalist models of decision making. In Hill, M. (Ed.) (1997). *The policy process: A reader.* 2nd ed. New York, NY: Prentice Hall.

120 Peng (1992). Op. cit.; Lindblom, C. (1959). The science of muddling through. *Public Administration Review, 19* (2), 78–88.

121 Golembiewski, R.T. (1988). Perspectives on Simon's Administrative Behavior: Stock-taking on the fortieth Anniversary—Part I. *Public Administration Quarterly, 12* (3), 259–382.

122 Yukl, G. (1989b). Managerial leadership: A review of theory and research. *Journal of Management, 15* (2), 251–289.

123 Carlyle, T. (1840). *On heroes, hero-worship, and the heroic in history.* Retrieved from: http://history.furman.edu/benson/fywbio/carlyle_great_man.htm.

124 Spencer, H. (1896). *The principles of sociology.* New York, NY: Appleton.

125 Stogdill, R.M. (1974). *Handbook of leadership: A survey of the literature.* New York, NY: Free Press.

126 Stogdill, R.M. (1948). Personal factors associated with leadership: A survey of the literature. *Journal of Psychology, 25* (1), 35–71.

127 Mann, R.D. (1959). A review of the relationships between personality and performance. *Psychological Bulletin, 56* (4), 241–270.

128 Pervin, L.A. (1994). A critical analysis of current trait theory. *Psychological Inquiry, 5* (2), 103–113; Yukl (1989). Op. cit.

129 Yukl, G.A. (2002). *Leadership in organizations,* 5th ed. Upper Saddle River, NJ: Prentice Hall; Yukl (1989b). Op. cit.

130 Yukl, G.A. (2006). *Leadership in organizations,* 6th ed. Upper Saddle River, NJ: Pearson Prentice Hall; Zaccaro, S.J. (2007). Trait-based perspectives of leadership. *American Psychologist, 62* (1), 6–16.

131 Halpin, A.W. & Winer, J. (1957). A factorial study of the leader behavior description questionnaire. In R.M. Stogdill and A.E. Coons (Eds), *Leader behavior: Its description and measurement*. (Research Monograph No. 88). (pp. 39–51). Columbus, OH: Bureau of Business Research, the Ohio State University.

132 Halpin, A.W. (1966). *Theory and research in administration*. New York, NY: Macmillan.

133 See: Fleishman, E.A. (1995). Consideration and structure: Another look at their role in leadership research. In F. Dansereau & F.H. Yammarino (Eds), *Leadership: The multiple-level approaches* (pp. 51–60). Stamford, CT: JAI Press; Judge, T.A., Piccolo, R.F. & Ilies, R. (2004). The forgotten ones? The validity of consideration and initiating structure in leadership research. *Journal of Applied Psychology*, 89 (1), 36–51.

134 Judge, Piccolo & Ilies (2004). Op. cit.

135 Fleishman (1995). Op. cit., p. 51.

136 Blake, R.R. & Mouton, J.S. (1964). *The managerial grid*. Houston, TX: Gulf Publishing. A discussion of Blake and Mouton's Management Grid is available on the companion website.

137 Fiedler, F.E. (1967). *A theory of leadership effectiveness*. New York, NY: McGraw-Hill.

138 Strube, M.J. & Garcia, J.E. (1981). A meta-analytic investigation of Fiedler's contingency model of leadership effectiveness. *Psychological Bulletin*, 90, (2), 307–321; Peters, L.H., Hartke, D.D. & Pohlman, J.T. (1985). Fiedler's contingency theory of leadership: An application of the meta-analysis procedures of Schmidt and Hunter. *Psychological Bulletin*, 97, (2), 274–285.

139 Vecchio (1983). Op. cit.; Yukl (1989a). Op. cit.

140 Judge, Piccolo & Ilies (2004). Op. cit.

141 See: Evans, M.G. (1970). The effects of supervisory behavior on the path-goal relationship. *Organizational Behavior and Human Performance*, 5 (3), 277–298; House, R.J. (1971). A path-goal theory of leader effectiveness. *Administrative Science Quarterly*, 16 (3), 321–339. House, R.J. & Mitchell, T.R. (1974). Path-goal theory of leadership. *Contemporary Business*, 3 (4), 81–98.

142 Indvik, J. (1986). Path-goal theory of leadership: A meta-analysis. In *Proceedings of the Academy of Management Meetings*, 189–192.

143 Yukl (1989b). Op. cit.

144 Hersey, P. & Blanchard, K.H. (1969). Life cycle theory of leadership. *Training and Development Journal*, 23 (2), 26–34; Hersey, P. & Blanchard, K.H. (1988). *Management of organizational behavior*, 5th ed. Englewood Cliffs, NJ: Prentice-Hall.

145 Vroom, V.H. & Yetton, P.W. (1973). *Leadership and decision making*. Pittsburgh, PA: University of Pittsburgh Press.

146 See: Graeff, C.L. (1983). The situational leadership theory: A critical review. *Academy of Management Review*, 8 (3), 285–296; Vecchio, R.P. (1987). Situational leadership theory: An examination of a prescriptive theory, *Journal of Applied Psychology*, 72, (3). 444–451.

147 Yukl (1989b). Op. cit.

148 Yukl (1989b). Op. cit.

CHAPTER 3

Contemporary Theories: Leadership as a Shared Process

GUIDING QUESTIONS

3.1 Explain how Getzels and Guba's model of organization sees the leaders' role as integrating conflicting demands between the institutional and people dimensions in ways that satisfy both and the styles by which leaders do so.

3.2 Compare and contrast transactional and transformational leadership on the nature of leader-follower relationships, the exchanges made, and the outcomes.

3.3 Discuss the conditions under which distributed leadership can be most effective and describe the leader's role in making this happen.

3.4 Summarize the Leader Member Exchange (LMX) Theory and identify the benefits (the exchanges) it brings to leaders and members.

3.5 Describe how Complexity Leadership Theory (CLT) addresses issues of organizational leadership in a context of uncertainty and unpredictability in a rapidly changing world.

**2015 PROFESSIONAL STANDARDS FOR EDUCATIONAL LEADERS:
1, 2, 5, 6, 7, 9, 10**

CASE STUDY 3.1

What Has Happened Here?!

Susan Johnson had just finished her tenth year as Pines Middle School principal. She had been a teacher and assistant principal at the high school before receiving her current appointment. On the last day of school, the faculty threw a party for her tenth anniversary. Everyone felt proud of the school's progress and their common vision for the school's child-centered culture focused upon each student's academic success and wellbeing as well as teacher leadership.

The next week, in a power play among the five school board members, the board fired the superintendent and assistant superintendent. Three of the five board members wanted to "overhaul" the high school with a better vision for students and to "shake up" the many "unsatisfactory" teachers. They appointed the Director of Secondary Education as the new superintendent. The high school faculty had always had deep internal problems with varying factions and philosophical differences among members.

The following week, the Human Resources Department announced a massive personnel transfer. Susan was shocked at the transfers from and to her school. Half of her best teachers were going to the high school, and many of the "difficult" high school teachers were replacing them at Pines Middle. Over the summer, Susan met with all her new and returning faculty members. With faculty input, she made all the committee assignments and teaching teams. She established the school improvement team (SIT) and the leadership teams (LT), mingling the new and returning faculty. Susan thought that having some of the high school folks help on the SIT and LT would be a healthy way of inducting them into the Pines's culture.

The summer rolled by quickly, and the faculty returned for the pre-school meetings. At the general faculty meeting, Susan sensed a disturbing amount of bickering. The reconstituted faculty was not agreeing or as cooperative as the previous Pines faculty. The SIT and LT meetings were a disaster. All the progress made over the last 10 years seemed to be slipping way as new faculty members argued, "That's not the way we should approach working with the students" and "We never did it that way before. This is not good for students or us!" Defending their school culture and vision they loved and knew worked, the veteran middle school teachers quickly became as confrontational as their new colleagues.

For the past 5 years, Susan had run these two committees as an ex officio member. But she quickly saw that unless she took control, the school climate and culture would be devastated. The impact would harm teachers' morale and students' learning. She quickly announced that the teams' roles would be advisory, not decision making. The returning teachers were offended that Susan did not appear to value their decisions. The new teachers saw Susan as a power-hungry autocrat.

That evening, Susan left the building distraught. She wondered what had happened, what was she to do, and what could have been done differently to sustain the climate and save the culture.

RUBRIC 3.1

Lens and/or factors to be considered in decision making	What are the factors at play in this case?	What steps should be considered in solving the problem?	What could have been done to avoid this dilemma?
The situation			
• The task	A sudden district leadership change has resulted in many faculty transfers. As a result, the school climate has changed and its culture is at risk. Susan gave the new faculty roles on the SIT and the LT, but the new teachers are undermining the climate and culture.	Susan has already told the SIT and the LT team that their role would be advisory. This gives her the chance to educate and acculturate the new faculty and reassure the returning ones that operations will return to normal.	Susan should have placed faculty on the SIT and LT who knew and shared the Pines culture. She should have met with the teams before school started to establish ground rules. Meeting with the new teachers and orienting them to the Pines culture may have helped.
• Personal abilities	Faculty members new to Pines were seen as "problems" at their previous schools. If they felt abused by the transfer, they may direct their anger at their new school's personnel.	Professional development about the middle school concept should be considered for the new faculty.	The new superintendent should have been made aware of the mass transfers' potential damage to Pines at the expense of improving the high school.
• The school environment	The collaborative climate and culture of Pines has changed.	The new teachers need a culture reboot.	The Pines' principal could have been invited to participate in selecting (and rejecting) potential transfers.
Look		**Wider**	
Organizational			
(i.e., the organizational goals, values, policies, culture)	School board members did not value constructive problem solving nor did they see district schools as an interactive system and the harm a mass transfer would do.	Organizationally, the one school should not have to absorb so many of the high school's "difficult" personnel.	The superintendent can hold a board retreat to understand school districts as a system and have members experience effective interpersonal problem solving. Involve principals in decisions about involuntary transfers to their schools.
People			
(i.e., individuals with needs, beliefs, goals, relationships)	Transferred teachers, Pines principal, and teachers all feel	The Pines principal and teacher leaders should meet with new teachers	School board should work out problems constructively. The high

continued . . .

	disrespected and frustrated at their treatment. Pines personnel want to protect their successful vision and practices.	(in small groups) to learn their educational views, let them vent, and introduce Pines' vision and practices in words and deeds.	school principal should take responsibility and accountability for addressing the high school's problems. Invite principals who will receive transfers to have a say in school assignment decisions.
Competing Interests (i.e., competing interests for power, influence, and resources)	School board members met their own needs at the district's expense and helped the high school at the middle school's expense.	Pines principal and all teachers should revisit their vision and practices (with evidence of its impact on student learning) with new faculty, discuss other views, build buy-in and collaborative culture.	School board members work out their differences constructively without undue influence or manipulation.
Tradition (i.e., school culture, rituals, meaning, heroes)	Angry, involuntary transferees are challenging Pines Middle School practices, culture, and climate.	Provide safe occasions for all Pines teachers to express their education values and work towards developing common aims and practices.	The Pines principal and teacher leaders could have met with transferring-in teachers (in small groups) during the summer and fall to listen to their concerns and educational views and begin inducting them into the Pines culture.

OVERVIEW: LEADERSHIP AS A SOCIAL AND RELATIONAL PROCESS

Twenty-first century organizational leadership is about shaping and enabling individuals and groups to accomplish shared aims and to adapt and thrive in a changing environment. Through the late nineteenth and early to mid-twentieth century, organizational theory evolved from a focus on structure and function to a focus on the interactions between leaders, workers, and environments in meeting organizational goals. Theorists began to see organizations as human enterprises whose informal dynamics could profoundly influence how and how well organizations operated. In the early 1950s, psychology (particularly social psychology) and sociology illustrated the importance of simultaneously meeting the needs of both institutions and individuals. Situational and environmental issues became important factors in organizational problem solving. Likewise, during these years, leadership moved beyond individuals in formal roles to include leadership as shared, dyadic, and a complex social dynamic able to adapt to rapidly changing environments to ensure their organizations survived.

By mid-twentieth century, organizational scholars were reaching several conclusions. Organizational effectiveness, as judged by final outcomes, depended on developing employees' human potential and a sense of ownership; power sharing, mutual trust and participatory decision making; activating employees' higher order needs in service to the organization; and awareness of how political and symbolic processes and organizational culture conferred meaning on activities. Likewise, leadership scholars were developing two key concepts. First, effective leaders have high concern for the task, the people, and the situational awareness to act appropriately for different circumstances. Second, individual leaders are important but leadership is also a shared process embedded in social systems.[1] These trends would find fuller expression in the years ahead, as this chapter will describe.

NEW PARADIGMS FOR UNDERSTANDING ORGANIZATIONS

At mid-twentieth century, education leaders wanting to understand organizations usually had to read the public administration, business administration, or social science literature and apply their models to education. Since then, educational administration theory has been maturing,[2] and new ways of understanding organizational leadership emerging.

Leadership would be seen as more than transactions with bosses using power over employees to give them rewards in exchange for work. Rather, organizational leaders would look for their employees' potential motives and attempt to satisfy their higher needs as they did their assigned tasks and met their organizational goals. Scholars would begin to see leadership as a shared process that allows organizations enough structure and control to set direction and meet goals *plus* the flexibility and creativity to adapt rapidly and appropriately to unforeseen problems in their environment. Organizational theory would move from Industrial to Knowledge Era, from entity to collectivist, from assumed closed to recognized open systems, and from rationalistic to sensemaking in its problem solving orientation.

Jacob Getzels and Egon Guba would propose an organizational theory of social behavior relevant to educators that spanned the gap between entity and collectivist perspectives. James MacGregor Burns and Bernard Bass would propose transformational leadership theory in contrast to exchange-based transactional leadership. Distributed, shared, and collective leadership, Leader-Member-Exchange Theory, and Complexity Leadership Theory would propose models to show how organizational leadership could be most effective in a fast-moving, knowledge-rich culture. Several theories would offer direct relevance for educational leaders, others were more nuanced. Each helps provide a fuller understanding of how organizational leadership works in an era of constant change and the need to quickly adapt—or fail.

THE GETZELS-GUBA MODEL OF ORGANIZATION

Jacob Getzels (1912–2001) and Egon Guba (1924–2008) brought organization theory into an educational context. They conceptualized a general theoretical model of administration as an interactive social process between individual and institution in any healthy organization.[3] In their view, role and personality interacted to influence the individual and the organization. The first to differentiate the organizational expectations for meeting its goals from the needs of individuals who achieve them,[4] Getzel and Guba's theory became a classic model of social behavior and the administrative process.[5]

Jacob W. Getzels, Professor of Education and Psychology at the University of Chicago and Egon G. Guba, Professor of Education at Indiana University, each came to the United States as children of immigrant parents. With Getzels first working alone, and then in collaboration with Guba (who was one of Getzels's first doctoral students at the University of Chicago),[6] they designed an open systems model of organizations that bridges the span between the entity perspectives (that people interpret reality as individuals) and constructivist perspectives (humans create their reality by interacting with others to interpret their shared experiences of reality).[7]

According to Getzels and Guba, institutions have five characteristics: they are purposive (they are established to carry out certain ends); peopled (organizations contain actors with functions to perform), structured (rules organize actors), normative (actors' roles have expected modes of behavior), and sanction bearing (have the positive and negative capacity to enforce the norms). Together, the institution's purposes, actors, structures, norms, and sanctions produce an array of organizational roles. Each role contains a behavior continuum from "required" to "prohibited." Between the "absolutely required" behaviors (such as teachers using effective pedagogy to enable their students to learn) and the totally "forbidden" behaviors (such as teachers developing sexual relationships with their students) lie many other permissible behaviors that make the roles relatively flexible, allowing different people with their unique personalities to all hold the same position, feel comfortable, and be effective. Moreover, the roles are interdependent and complementary, each deriving its meaning in relation to other roles in the institution. As a result, two or more roles can become a coherent, interactive unit. For instance, a middle school team of English, math, social studies, and science teachers, an assistant principal, and a school counselor, each with a different set of personalities and overlapping responsibilities, can together provide learners with a full array of information and skills needed to support student success.

Getzels and Guba saw people in organizations as a social system that involves two main types of independent and interdependent phenomena: the institutional (the nomothetic dimension) and the individual (the idiographic dimension). The *institutional dimension* specifies employees' roles and expectations structured to meet the organization's goals. The *individual dimension* includes personalities, personal needs, and dispositions. Interactions between the institution and employees' personalities determine organizational behavior. The nature of the organization, the particular job, and the unique individuals who "people" it determine how much influence the role expectations and the individuals' personalities and needs express themselves in social behavior. In schools, for example, teachers and administrators take on certain roles and expectations that will help them achieve the organization's goals. At the same time, their unique personalities and dispositions also affect how they do their jobs. Friendly and gregarious assistant principals walking down the classroom halls each morning generate responses from teachers and students that differ from their reactions to A.P.s

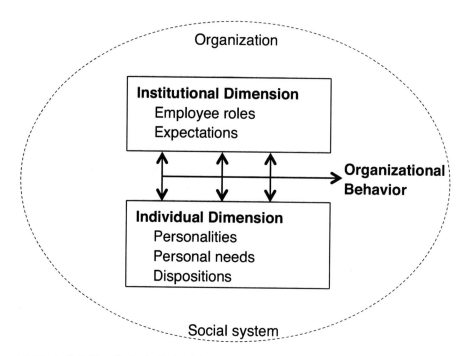

FIGURE 3.1 The Getzels-Guba Model of Social Behavior in Organizations

Source: Based on Getzels, J.W. & Guba, E.G. (1957). Social behavior and the administrative process. *The School Review*, 65 (4), 423–441.

who typically stomp and scowl. Interactions between institutional and people dimensions create social behavior. Any given act, therefore, simultaneously reflects the individual and institutional dimensions, as illustrated in Figure 3.1.[8]

Naturally, tensions (conflict) likely will arise between personal and collective interests (between the nomothetic and ideographic dimensions). Conflict includes occasions when the role expectations might not match the role holder's needs or interests (i.e., a teacher is expected to attend Back to School Night but prefers to stay home with his or her family). The role itself may require contradictory, mutually exclusive, or inconsistent behaviors so that to do one makes it impossible to do the others (i.e., principals want a good relationship with students but will have to call parents to inform them about inappropriate behaviors). Or the role holder may hold opposing needs and dispositions (i.e., teachers want to support students' learning but will not work with them after school if they do not come prepared for class that day). Thus, leadership's task is to integrate the institutional demands and the staff members' demands—and reconcile differing interests—in a way that satisfies both the organization's need to be productive and its employees' needs to feel fulfilled. When role incumbents can meet both their situational expectations and personal needs, they are assumed to gain maximum satisfaction.

Given this view of institutional and personality interactions, Getzels and Guba believed that organizational leadership-followership takes one of three distinct styles:

institutional, individual, or transactional. The *institutional style* leader goes "by the book" (and, typically, the leader "writes the book") and expects subordinates to act in strict conformity with the organization's rules and procedures. If employees are technically competent, leaders can expect the desired outcomes. For institutional style, the leadership excellence standard is institutional adjustment and effectiveness, not individual integration and efficiency.

Next, the *individual style* stresses the individual, personal, and need/disposition requirements rather than the institutional ones. Although sharing the same goals as the institutional style, the individual style leader sees the most effective path to the goal is having each person contribute what is most relevant and meaningful to that person rather than rigorously enforcing defined roles. Leaders expect employees to work things out for themselves and behave in ways that meet their personal needs. The saying, "the best government is the one that governs least" applies here. In this style, the leadership standard for excellence is individual integration and efficiency, not institutional adjustment and effectiveness.

Lastly, in the *transactional style*, leaders develop a thorough awareness of the individual's and institution's limits and resources and intelligently adapt the people and the organization to meet the demands of a particular situation. Transactional leadership behavior highlights accomplishing organizational goals in an environment of individual fulfillment. The proportion of role and personality factors that determine behavior varies with the specific act, the specific role, and the specific personality involved. Leadership excellence in this style is individual integration and efficiency, satisfaction, and institutional adjustment and effectiveness. This transactional leadership style describes the most frequent leadership behavior in schools.

In the early years, the Getzels-Guba model assumed schools to be a closed system model.[9] Over time, they modified their model of behavior in social systems to posit three dimensions: the individual (idiographic or psychological), the organizational (organizational nomothetic or sociological), and the context (cultural or ethnographic).[10] Further, Getzels, James Lipham and Roald Campbell extended the model for school administrators. Their composite model sees the school as a social system with educational administration as a social process. In their view, culture, climate, and values held by individuals in the school and school system explain much social behavior. In addition, any social system—whether the classroom, the school, or the district—operates within a larger environment.[11]

Although Getzels and Guba's model found modest research support,[12] their conceptualization of educational administration as a field appropriate for scientific investigation, use of theory (as a set of assumptions to be tested against real-world observations), operationalizing their concept for objective investigation, and use of hypotheses (mostly by reasonable deduction and intuition) to guide their studies had a noteworthy impact on theory and research in educational administration for its time.[13] Occurring when the scientific thinking in their profession was best described as "intellectual provincialism and naiveté,"[14] Getzels and Guba's empirical approach presented a meaningful shift in scholarship about educational administration. Nonetheless, the instruments used were psychological tests filled with their own theoretical concepts that weakened and confused their results.[15]

Critics of Getzels and Guba's theory of a school as a social organization call it "rationalistic," bureaucratic, and "sterile" with little relevance to administrative practice in actual schools.[16] Some argue that their model lacks accuracy because it considers only the male perspective and ignores the possible conflicts that women experience in leadership.[17] Debating the finer points of logic, one education philosophy theorist censures Getzels and Guba for inappropriately using the mathematical term, *function*, to describe the interaction between role and personality because this word presents an "unwarranted" certainty that prevents other possibilities of interaction.[18] The same detractor faults the pair for developing a model that is vague, ambiguous, and has internal inconsistencies.[19]

In contrast, educational administration scholars consider Getzels to be a senior member of the movement to use behavioral sciences to connect theory, research, and practice in educational administration,[20] giving the discipline a "scientific" base.[21] Importantly, Getzels and Guba's ideas stitched together the interface between entity and collectivist viewpoints and brought the complexity of organizational leadership into the study of leadership in schools.

REFLECTIONS AND RELEVANCE 3.1

Getzels and Guba's Model

Organizational leaders reconcile competing demands of the institution and its members. Considering Getzels and Guba's three leadership styles— institutional, individual, and transactional—and working in small groups of three, discuss the following questions. When you are finished, discuss your insights and conclusions with the class.

1. Identify the specific behaviors you might observe or hear from principals or administrators using each of the three leadership styles.
2. Which leadership styles have you experienced as an employee? Describe your response to each.
3. Under which leadership style/s do you most—or least—enjoy working? Explain.
4. Which leadership style best—and least—reflects the way you handle your own leadership responsibilities? Explain with an example.

TRANSACTIONAL AND TRANSFORMATIONAL LEADERSHIP THEORIES

The late 1970s introduced a new leadership paradigm. The concept of *contingent reward*—giving "this-for-that," offering compensation or return in exchange for a desired behavior—had psychological and economic support and worked reasonably well under most conditions.[22] Nevertheless, historians and social scientists had long recognized that leadership goes beyond simple exchanges. Early organizational theorists, including Frederick Taylor,[23] Henry Fayol,[24] Mary Parker Follett,[25] and Chester Barnard[26] had suggested the possibilities of leader-follower working together. Elton Mayo saw the need for leadership, supported by social and human skills, which could influence the informal organization. Max Weber's study of charismatic leaders (and the need for an objective bureaucracy to overcome these leaders' limitations) pointed to affective qualities of the leader-follower relationship that was more than simple exchange. Stepping beyond traditional theories' emphasis on rational processes, theories of transformational leadership would emphasize emotions and values, the influence of symbolic behaviors, and the leader's role in making events meaningful for followers.[27]

In the late twentieth century, leadership scholars James MacGregor Burns and Bernard Bass conceived of organizational leadership that went beyond day-to-day social exchanges of work-for-rewards. Burns first popularized, and Bass expanded, the theory of transformational leadership.[28] They theorized that transformational leaders would offer followers a purpose that meets their higher order intrinsic needs, inspires employees to commit to a shared vision and goals for an organization (or a subunit), and stimulates them to be inventive problem solvers and develop their own leadership capacities. By providing individually meaningful incentives and linking employees' identity to the project and organization, transformational leaders would motivate employees to do more than they originally intended to do—indeed, more than they thought was possible. Higher performance, higher productivity, and higher worker satisfaction would result.[29]

James MacGregor Burns

As a historian and political science professor at Williams College in Massachusetts, James MacGregor Burns (1918–2014) enjoyed analyzing great leaders' ideas and wondered about the personal, environmental, and psychological forces that shaped their actions. One day, in a colleague's office, Burns noticed a book by Abraham Maslow whose theory of human wants and needs seemed to hold potential for understanding leadership and change. As a Pulitzer Prize-winning biographer of Franklin D. Roosevelt, Burns concluded that political figures who engage daily in give-and-take transactional behaviors may also have the qualities that enable them to "transcend and even transform [difficult situations], transforming the people they lead in the process."[30]

In his 1978 book, *Leadership*,[31] Burns conceptualized leadership as either transactional or transformational. *Transactional* leaders are those who lead through social exchange of "this-for-that." The leader discusses with others what is required, and spells out the conditions and rewards they will receive if they fulfill those requirements. A *transaction*, or exchange of one valued thing for another, then occurs: salary for work, higher salary for more responsibility at work, stock options for institution-wide productivity, or votes for campaign contributions. Each party bargains consciously and recognizes the other as a person with related purposes. But the relationships do not go beyond the exchange process.

In contrast, *transformational* leaders are those who invigorate and inspire followers to achieve exceptional results and, by doing so, grow their own—and their followers'—

leadership capacities. Transformational leaders have deeply held value systems that include justice and integrity that motivate their actions. Through the force of their vision and personality, transformational leaders can inspire (and persuade) followers to change their perceptions, expectations, and motivation to work toward common, meaningful, challenging goals that align with the organization's goals. Burns asserted that *transformation* means basic alterations—qualitative changes—in the entire systems. The key feature of transformational change is the *nature* of the change, not the *degree* of change.[32] Ultimately, Burns proposed, transforming leadership becomes moral: it raises human behavior and the ethical aspirations of both leader and follower.

To Burns, transactional and transformational leadership are opposite ends of a continuum. They are not two completely separate factors.[33]

Burns believed in the importance of individual leaders. He observed that by the 1990s, almost all leadership scholars stressed the role of followers, but some went further. They advocated that leaders and followers merge in interdependent collectivities in which it was hard to separate the two, essentially denying a distinct leadership function. Burns disagreed. He argued that leaders take the initiative in mobilizing people to join in the change process, encouraging a sense of group identity and group efficacy by empowering followers, inspiring and animating them (rather than by exercising power over them) to rise above narrow interests and work together for worthy goals. In his view, this was a capacity that collective leadership did not have.

Bernard M. Bass

A contemporary of Burns, Bernard M. Bass (1925–2007) was an internationally renowned leadership scholar at the State University of New York at Binghamton and founding editor of *The Leadership Quarterly Journal*. Bass first acquired the idea of studying transformational leadership in 1979: a former graduate student recommended he read "Jim" Burns's good book on leadership. Bass's major interest became the research and application of transformational leadership theory to management development. After investigating leadership in organizations in at least 20 countries, Bass found more similarities than differences in what makes a good leader.[34]

Extending Burns's work, Bass explained the psychological factors that undergird transformational leadership, explained how transformational leadership could be measured, and showed how it influenced followers' motivation and behaviors. Unlike Burns the political scientist and presidential biographer (who derived his theory of leadership by intensively analyzing the lives of specific leaders), Bass the leadership scholar studied leadership empirically, looking for its implications for more effective organizational management. To do this, Bass operationalized transformational leadership into specific behaviors and attitudes managers could learn and use to enhance their professional leadership effectiveness. He developed the Multifactor Leadership Questionnaire (MLQ) for subordinates to rate how frequently their leader uses either a transactional or transformational type of behavior.[35] Using surveys of corporate leaders and clinical and case evidence, Bass enlarged and refined the transformational theory of leadership.

In Bass's view, *transactional leadership*—initializing and organizing work and showing consideration for employees; getting things done by making and fulfilling promises of recognition, increased salaries, and promotions for highly performing employees while penalizing poor performers—can be effective. But it can also lead to mediocrity, eliciting employees' compliance for completing assigned tasks rather than their commitment to meeting larger organizational goals. In addition, not all managers have the authority to influence salary, promotions, or penalties, Bass argued. Contract provisions, organizational politics, and scarce resources also affect what can happen in an organization. Instead, leaders can perform in outstanding ways—become *transformational*—when they broaden and raise their employees' interests, build awareness and acceptance of the group's purpose and mission, and arouse employees to look past immediate self-interest and toward the group's wellbeing.[36] Unlike Burns, who conceived transactional and transformational leadership as occupying opposite ends of a continuum, Bass viewed them as separate concepts.[37] Bass asserted that the best leadership is both transactional and transformational, with the latter strengthening —not replacing—the former.[38]

Bass identified ways that transformational leaders motivate others to achieve "great things" by committing extra effort: by influencing and inspiring others; by intellectually stimulating them, and/or by meeting employees' individual needs. Sometimes called "the four I's," transformational leaders behave in ways that achieve outstanding results by using one or more of the following:[39]

Idealized Influence

Transformational leaders articulate an appealing vision for a better future, explain how to attain it, and act in ways that generates followers' admiration, trust, and respect. Leaders use emotionally laden values and symbols to emphasize their message. In turn, followers see their leaders as having exceptional skills, high standards, persistence, predictability, and determination. Identifying with their leaders, followers see them as role models to emulate. Idealized influence, therefore, includes both leaders' actions as well as followers' emotions and actions in response. This quality is sometimes called *charisma*.[40]

Inspirational Motivation

Transformational leaders act in ways that arouse and influence followers by providing high standards, challenge, and meaning to their work. Leaders appeal to followers' own interests to the extent possible or persuade them to go beyond their immediate gratification for the benefit of the group or organization. The leaders' enthusiasm and optimism help generate positive team spirit. Leaders clearly communicate their expectations that followers want to meet and show commitment to their shared vision and goals.

Intellectual Stimulation

Transformational leaders excite others into new ways of thinking and acting. They encourage followers' critical thinking, sharing knowledge, creativity, risk taking, and innovation by questioning old assumptions and ways of doing things. Including followers in identifying problems and finding answers, leaders invite their fresh ideas, innovative solutions, and novel approaches—without public criticism or punishment for individual members' errors, or mistakes (even if their ideas differ from the leaders' ideas).

Individual Consideration

Transformational leaders personalize their interactions with followers. Acting as teacher, mentor, or coach, leaders pay attention to each individual, recognize and accept individual differences, and respond appropriately (giving more support, more autonomy, firmer standards, or increased task structure as needed) to support the employee's needs for achievement and growth. By seeing each individual as a whole person and by providing new and individualized learning opportunities in a supportive climate, leaders develop their colleagues and followers to increasingly higher levels of potential and performance.

Empirical work has confirmed these four factors.[41] Bass also asserted that transformational leaders have better relationships with their supervisors and make a more substantial contribution to their organizations than do transactional leaders. What is more, employees tell that they put forth more effort on behalf of managers who they perceive to be transformational leaders. Studies also find that transactional leadership can work "reasonably well" if leaders are able to provide rewards that followers value.[42] Table 3.1 compares transactional and transformational leadership.

Bass admitted that transformational leadership is not a cure-all: it is not appropriate for every organizational situation. If the markets, workforce, technology, and environment are stable, day-to-day transactional managers can keep things going by promising and delivering rewards to employees for completing their assignments; managers can take corrective action when needed. Clearly understood and accepted rules and regulations can even sidestep the need for leadership in certain situations. But when an organization finds itself in rapidly changing internal and external environments and the "givens" become uncertain, Bass claimed that transformational leaders at all levels can generate the flexibility to understand the circumstances and meet new demands. Bass also believed that transformational leadership can be learned. It is an art and a science that can be part of leadership training and development.[43]

A large and growing body of research supports the effectiveness of transformational leadership over transactional and other forms of leadership at the organizational,[44] industrial,[45] and national[46] levels. Most studies support the distinction between transformation and transactional behavior,[47] although some inconsistencies appear.[48] Meta-analytic reviews of 39 studies suggest that transformational leadership can generate more committed, loyal, and satisfied followers, and it is positively correlated with subordinate satisfaction and performance.[49] Research also suggests that transformational leader behavior generates an augmentation effect—performance, effort, and satisfaction that are higher than those derived by transactional leadership behavior.[50] Studies find the four transformational leadership components to be the most important factors in leaders' effectiveness, followed by the social exchange practices (contingent reward); laissez faire leadership appears to be the least effective leadership approach.[51] Descriptive studies based on interviews and observation suggest that transformational leadership

TABLE 3.1 Comparison of Transactional and Transformational Leadership

	Transactional Leadership	Transformational Leadership
Leader–Employee Interaction	Simple exchange: "this-for-that"; employee gives effort to complete specified work in return for salary, promotion.	Complex exchange: includes completing work and the nature of leader–employee relationship and interactions.
Nature of Leader–Employee Relationship	A social and rational process of using power to give reward or apply punishment to achieve an organizational goal.	Relationship includes shared emotions, values, and symbolic behaviors, and commitment to organization's goals and values.
Leadership Behaviors	Initiates, organizes work; shows consideration; makes and fulfills promises to employees; expects compliance; intervenes only if standards not met.	Articulates an appealing vision, mission for a better future and how to attain it; inspires with clear, high expectations, and makes work meaningful; promotes critical thinking, problem solving, and skill development; personalizes interactions with followers about their needs, concerns, and motives.
Nature of Rewards	Extrinsic: salary, bonuses, vacations, promotions.	Intrinsic: work has meaning and purpose; organization and work become linked with employees' identities.
Employee Commitment to the Organization	Minimal, compliance.	High, commitment.
Organizational Outcomes	No substantial change in employee behavior or attitudes; potential for mediocre outcomes.	Enhanced employee respect, trust, loyalty, and satisfaction; more effort, higher performance, and productivity; potential for abuse of power.

Source: Original table by Leslie Kaplan and William Owings, 2017.

is effective in an array of situations,[52] and research evidence worldwide suggests that transformational leadership qualities are valued in all countries.[53]

As critics have noted, transformational leadership theory has its shortcomings. The most frequent critiques: the theory's preference for the "great men" leadership stereotype,[54] its potentials for abuse of power,[55] and its possibility to be antidemocratic.[56] In response to these questions about morality or abuse potential, Bass separated *transformational leaders* who are ethical from *pseudo-transformational leadership* who are unethical (like the Pied Piper who lured children to follow him to their own harm).[57] Adolf Hitler and Joseph Stalin are examples of pseudo-transformational leaders with initial appeal but whose autocratic and antidemocratic behaviors led to extremely disastrous outcomes. Similarly, followers' "blind trust" may lead them to fulfill their leader's vision regardless of its merit, clarity, or practicality.[58] Yet Bass did not specify how to identify pseudo-transformational leaders who pretend to be transformational.[59]

In addition, critics note the theory's lack of conceptual clarity: Bass's four components have substantial overlap.[60] This leads to doubt about their construct validity and ambiguity in measuring and explaining transformational leadership's effectiveness. Nor has Bass explained how leaders can use transformational leadership's four components.[61]

Despite its limitations, transformational leadership theories help explain the exceptional influence that some leaders have on their followers. Certain leader behaviors motivate followers to perform better. Research supports transformational leadership as essential to organizational success. Nonetheless, most versions of transformational leadership theory have influence moving in one direction: from leaders to followers.[62] It does not describe a reciprocal influence process or shared leadership. Alternative leadership theories would depict leadership as a shared process of strengthening the individual and collective capacities of employees to effectively enact their work roles.

REFLECTIONS AND RELEVANCE 3.2

Transactional and Transformational Leadership

Both transactional and transformational leadership can have effective outcomes. Working in groups of four, complete the graphic organizers below by noting the behaviors and words that a transactional and a transformational leader might use.

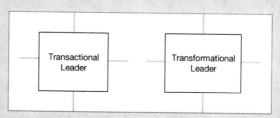

- Next, in your groups, identify one transactional and one transformational (if any) principal or assistant principal with whom you have worked—and describe this administrator's actions and words that make him/her transactional or transformational. As an employee, how did you respond to each approach?
- Discuss whether you as an employee have ever experienced one of the following transformational leadership behaviors—idealized influence, inspirational motivation, intellectual stimulation, or individual consideration—and how did that affect your attitude, behavior, and work outcomes?
- Which of these transformational leadership behaviors do you believe you are already using with colleagues? Which of these behaviors would you like to develop more fully—and how to do you plan to do this?
- Discuss your findings as a class.

DISTRIBUTED LEADERSHIP

Given contemporary organizations' complexity, information intensity, and fast pace, no single person would seem to have the knowledge, expertise, energy, or time to be firmly "in charge" in every situation. To meet this reality, leaders disperse tasks—along with power and authority—across many roles and individuals. In schools, these include the central office personnel, school building administrators, teachers, counselors, bookkeepers, custodians, parents, students, and outside consultants. Although the concept of distributed leadership has been discussed since the mid-1920s and explicitly termed in the 1950s, it became widely considered in the mid-1990s and 2000s when the culture became ready to accept this allegedly "radical" view of leadership.[63]

Distributed leadership (DL)—in which multiple individuals and groups substitute or share leadership responsibilities that traditionally had been one person's purview—became a popular and pragmatic antidote to "heroic leadership."[64] Sometimes called "shared leadership," "collective leadership," "collaborative leadership," "co-leadership," or "emergent leadership," organizations with DL have multiple sources of leadership and influence across the organization to guide and complete the many tasks that need completing. In schools, shared duties may vary from simple, recurring, and routine events (such as attending staff meetings or supervising school sports events) to multifaceted, broad scope actions (such as leading the change process, sustaining a vision for change, altering existing practices, monitoring progress, and handling emergencies).

Distributed leadership collaborations may be spontaneous (where groups or individuals with unique knowledge, skills, and capacities come together on their own to complete a task or project) or planned (where, after consultation, resources and responsibilities are distributed to individuals and/or groups best positioned to lead the specific task or function). Long-lasting working groups may become institutionalized as a regular part of the operations. In contrast, collaborations also may be misaligned (where leadership distribution is unplanned or where leaders pursue their own goals independently, leading to conflict).[65] Clearly, DL takes many forms, practices, and outcomes.

Although the professional literature depicts DL in several variations, most share three basic ideas. First, leadership is a nascent characteristic of a group or network of interacting individuals. Second, the leadership boundaries are open. Third, different types of expertise are spread widely, among many people.[66] Some DL approaches include the situation as part of the collective interactions among leaders and followers.[67] But despite their overlap, not all DL concepts have equal merit.[68] Likewise, scholars dispel four common misunderstandings of DL: it is *not* a blueprint for leadership and management; it does *not* negate the role of CEOs (or school principals); *not* everyone is a leader; and it does *not* only refer to collaborative situations.[69] Instead, DL sees both formal and informal kinds of leadership practice as different parts of leadership performance, reflecting the reciprocal interdependences that shape it.[70] DL is a "yes/and" not an "either/or" approach.

Notably, DL is more of a systemic perspective on leadership than a distinct leadership theory. What is important is not *that* leadership is distributed but *how* leadership is distributed. Some patterns of DL are more likely to contribute to positive organizational change than others. Specifically, tasks that are highly interdependent require much creativity, and those that are highly complex are those most likely to benefit from distributed leadership.[71] Likewise, formal leadership plays a key role in creating the structures and conditions—the cultural, development, and reward systems that create the environment—where shared leadership is valued, nurtured, and focused in purposeful actions.

Most of the research on DL occurs within the field of school leadership.[72] Findings are mixed. To begin, studies suggest that "distributing" leadership, by itself, does not necessarily benefit an organization: what matters is *how* the leadership is distributed.[73] A number of studies show a positive relationship between DL and organizational change,[74] teacher leadership,[75] and professional learning communities.[76] Although studies find no strong link between DL and school improvement or leadership development,[77] data suggest a positive—if indirect—relationship between leadership distribution and student learning outcomes[78] and improved organizational outcomes.[79] Largely, this link reflects DL's positive correlation to staff morale, and enhanced teacher efficacy and motivation,[80] which, in turn, positively influence student behavior and learning outcomes.[81] In addition, study findings reinforce the view that without the active, full support of persons in formal school leadership positions, DL is not likely to be effective or sustained.[82] In contrast, evidence also suggests that distributing leadership can have a negative effect on team performance, including "dispersion" of responsibility,[83] a reduced sense of stability and security,[84] and boundary management issues (i.e., "That's not MY job!").[85] Outside education, evidence suggests that getting and sustaining high performing organizations in sports and business, use DL leadership in well-managed and strategic ways. Again, how organizations enact DL influences its outcome.[86] In sum, the research on DL and organizational development is encouraging but unsettled. A more nuanced appreciation for the variations in DL—and how leaders' specific behaviors influence their effectiveness—is needed.[87]

Distributed leadership does not lack for controversy or criticism. Some question leaders' motives, suggesting that DL is a superficially attractive way of encouraging naïve teachers to do more work (and an undemocratic way of delivering top-down policies).[88] Those with a critical theory perspective see DL as "inclusion lite," a new way to "maintain the status quo of power."[89] Critics also note that the DL perspective does not include other essential contextual factors that influence leadership effectiveness in organizations,[90] such as the dynamics of power and influence (while leadership is distributed, power may not be),[91] and its lack of attention to gender,[92] race,[93] or cross- and multicultural[94] participation. Additional critiques note that DL's focus on collective leadership slights "everyday heroes and heroines"[95] and the "sacred" character of leaders' work.[96] Given these limitations, one reviewer called DL an "adolescent" concept.[97]

Although not appropriate for every situation, DL concepts represent an important shift away from leaders as solitary individuals with position, authority, and specific characteristics and behaviors. Although DL does not replace one-person leadership, it does suggest a basic change in how formal leaders understand and enact their role: actively negotiating, enabling, and supporting the leadership of others. It moves leadership understanding and practice away from traditional, trait, situational, and transformational leadership (entity) theories—to a more collective, integrated, and systemic view of leadership as an interactive social process.[98] Leadership becomes a group activity that works through and within relationships, rather than relying solely on individual action. In this light, leadership becomes fluid and emergent instead of a rigid fact.[99] Finally, the question is not "vertical *vs.* shared leadership"? Rather, the questions are: *When, why,* and *how* do organizational leaders leverage both vertical and shared leadership to most effectively utilize workers' capabilities to reach organizational goals? DL's positive potential can occur only under the right conditions; and the goal is not one of increasing the numbers of leaders but of increasing leadership quality and competence.

REFLECTIONS AND RELEVANCE 3.3

Distributed Leadership

As a class, discuss the following:

1. Explain the meaning of the statement: "What is important about distributed leadership is not *that* leadership is distributed but *how* it is distributed." Give examples to support your ideas.
2. What are leaders' responsibilities for ensuring effective DL practices in schools?
3. What leadership practices might undermine the effectiveness of DL practices in schools?
4. If research supports the view that shared leadership practices are best for situations where tasks are highly interdependent, highly complex, and require creativity, identify situations in schools where DL may be—or may not be— appropriately used?

LEADER–MEMBER EXCHANGE THEORY (LMX)

Through the years, leadership scholars continue to ask what leadership is and how to achieve it. In the late twentieth century, scholars suggested a *process* approach that focuses on the dynamic interactions between a leader and his/her subordinates. The leader-member exchange (LMX) theory is one such approach.

Originated in the 1970s and modified since, LMX is an entity theory that examines the *quality* of the social exchange relationship between leader-member dyads and the consequences of high- or low-quality exchange relationships in subordinates' attitudes and behaviors at individual, group, and organizational levels. LMX assumes that leaders do not interact with all subordinates in the same way; no "average" leadership style exists.[100] Further, LMX assumes that time and resource limits press the leader to develop a cadre of valued assistants to help meet organizational goals. Therefore, leaders develop differentiated relationships with a few of their direct reports, built on trust, respect, loyalty, liking, and support.[101] In the process, they informally categorize workers as either cadres (in-group, with intensive cooperation and communication) or hired hands (out-group with only superficial contact). These two-way interactions affect their work relationships as well as the organizational outcomes.

In the LMX view, leadership occurs when leaders and followers are able to develop and sustain effective, mature dyadic relationships (partnerships) that result in a strong *incremental influence* (a leader's ability to get subordinates to perform above that required by compliance with routine directives).[102] When this occurs, leaders and members gain access to the many benefits—the exchange—that these relationships bring.[103] Members' gains include mutual respect, trust, special attention, recognition, information sharing, resources (such as being assigned attractive tasks and offered training opportunities), and emotional and career support.[104] Leaders' gains include highly engaged employees and successfully accomplished tasks. When organizations have many high-quality relationships—that is, the more high quality teams, clusters, and networks of "partnership" dyads—organizational outcomes improve.[105] These dyadic "partner" relationships also can occur in and between organizations.[106]

At the base of the LMX construct lie three dimensions—respect, trust, and obligation. Theorists speculate that an offer to become partners will not be made—and will not be accepted—without the mutual respect for the other's professional abilities, anticipation of an increasing reciprocal confidence, and expectation that the interactions will grow over time as career-oriented social exchanges strengthen into a partnership. Notably, the LMX builds on characteristics of the working relationship, not a personal or friendship relationship.[107]

Over time, LMX theory has developed a four-stage model of how high quality leader-follower relationships may develop and mature. In the "stranger" phase (Stage 1), individuals who hold interdependent organizational roles, a superior and a subordinate, meet as unknowns. Their interactions are formal, a basic contractual exchange. Leaders give members what they need to do their job, and members act only as required to complete their assigned tasks. During this stage, the leader assesses the new member's competence and performance through several tryouts.[108] Studies stress the importance of first impressions and first experiences in developing high- and low-quality working relationships, mutual expectations, and assessments during the first days of the dyadic relationship for predicting how the relationship will develop.[109]

Next, in the "acquaintance" stage (Stage 2), either party can make and accept an "offer" for an improved working relationship through a career-oriented social exchange. At this point, more social exchanges beyond the contractual occur between members. In a limited way, they begin to share more personal and work-related information and resources. They test the work relationship by equitably returning favors over a certain time period.

When the relationships grow to the next level, they become a "mature partnership" (Stage 3). Now, members' exchanges are highly developed, reciprocated "in kind," and occur over a long time span. During this stage, leaders may offer the member occasions for giving input and decision making and receiving information, feedback, respect, recognition, rewards, attractive work assignments, and career opportunities. In exchange, subordinates may offer loyalty, commitment, and extra effort for the leader personally and for the work unit and organization overall.[110] The dyad comes to depend on each other, and their influence over each other grows to very high levels.

Lastly, recognizing that leadership in complex organizations typically has leaders working together with multiple members in interdependent dyadic relationships, LMX offers a "systems-level" perspective (Stage 4) in which mature two-person relationships combine to form larger groups and networks. Emerging from how organizational members enact their roles, these network assemblies make up the organization's pattern of leadership relationships among individuals across workgroups, functional, divisional, and even organizational boundaries. More effective leadership relationships among participants affect how well the tasks will be completed. Given the nature of the work, however, certain relationships tend to be more critical to influencing success or failure of work activities than others.[111]

Depending on the stage, LMX Theory can be either transactional or transformational.[112] According to LMX, Stages 1 (stranger, low LMX) and 2 (acquaintance, medium LMX) align with transactional leadership as Bass (1985)[113] defines it. Here, the exchange is based on the persons' formal organizational roles, hierarchical status, and followers' motivation to satisfy their own self-interests without regard for the group or organization. The dyad meets the employment contract at its most basic level. LMX theorists see this type of exchange as "management" or "supervision," not leadership. By contrast, mature dyads in Stage 3 (partnership, high-LMX) share a large array and depth of exchange. Within the relationship, mutual respect, trust, and obligation continue to increase. Stage 3 aligns to Bass's transformational leadership. Each member feels empowered and motivated to expand beyond the formalized work contract roles and into a partnership based on mutual reciprocal influence. They look beyond their own self-interests to larger mutual interests, gaining the support and resources from their "partnership" to take on extra responsibilities within the organization.

Despite the conceptual and methodological difficulties,[114] studies have found that, to a large extent, LMX theory accurately reflects real world assessment of high-quality working relationships. Having a high-quality relationship with one's supervisor can affect the entire work experience positively. A 1987 meta-analytic study suggests significant relationships between LMX and job performance ratings (both as perceived by the employee and objectively assessed by the supervisor),[115] satisfaction (supervisory and overall), role clarity, organizational commitment, and turnover intentions (less intent to leave the job).[116] Enhanced subordinate career outcomes have also been found to result from high-quality LMX relationships.[117] Additionally, LMX appears to operate mainly at the two-person (superior and subordinate dyad) level; it is most strongly related to performance and shows the strongest effects when superior and subordinate agree about their working relationship and values.[118] Other research finds that higher-quality LMX relationships also predict organizational citizenship behaviors.[119]

LMX critics point to theoretical weaknesses, including varying operational definitions of its terms;[120] lack of clarity about the components of the leader-member working relationship itself;[121] absence of specifics as to how it operates;[122] lack of adequate explanation for changes or the theory underlying them;[123] and problems with the instruments used to measure them.[124] Much of this critique stems from the continual modifications of theory, measurement, and instruments.[125] As a result, it is difficult to make comparisons across studies, replicate findings, and make sense of them.[126] In addition, most of the research is correlational and not causational.[127] Critics also note that LMX theory and research do not consider that leader-member relationships occur within a system of other relationships.[128] Others complain of LMX's lack of attention to issues of fairness, equity, justice,[129] group dynamics,[130] or diversity or cultural issues.[131] Some assert that the theory potentially legitimizes inequalities between in-group and out-group members.[132] As a theory with practical application to organizational leadership, LMX appears to be a work in progress.[133]

LMX theory provides a closer look at the relationship quality between leader and member and its implications for human and organizational outcomes. As a theory, LMX has been receptive to constructive criticism and has incorporated needed changes over the years.[134] It continues to extend its scope. Many leadership scholars believe that LMX has meaningfully contributed to deepening their understanding of the basic leadership process.

REFLECTIONS AND RELEVANCE 3.4

LMX Theory

LMX is an entity theory that examines the *quality* of the social exchange relationship between leader-member dyads and the consequences of high- or low-quality exchange relationships in subordinates' attitudes and behaviors at the individual, group, and organizational levels.

First working in groups of three for 10 minutes, describe your work experiences (identify your work site, your position, and your leader's position) in each of the applicable LMX Stages (Stage 1, stranger; Stage 2, acquaintance; Stage 3, mature partnership; Stage 4, systemic). Describe the type of exchanges you experienced at each stage in your LMX dyad: what exchanges did you receive and what exchanges did you give? Explain the roles of mutual respect, trust, and obligation as you experience them at each stage.

As a class, compile four lists on the board or chart paper, one list for each LMX stage, and have members give examples of the exchanges they experienced at each stage. Discuss the findings. Consider, what types of exchanges are necessary between leaders and members if they are to increase mutual respect, trust, and obligation—and what types of behaviors are likely to undermine the maturation of these factors.

COMPLEXITY LEADERSHIP THEORY

During the late twentieth century, the very concept of organization shifted from an Industrial Age bureaucracy with clear boundaries and defined areas of authority to a Knowledge Era milieu with fluid and flexible internal and external boundaries.[135] In keeping with this evolution, organizational leadership models moved from their traditional emphasis on top-down bureaucratic paradigm (appropriate to study an economy based on physical production in a closed system) to leadership in settings of complex behavior (more aligned with an economy where knowledge is a core commodity and speed, flexibility, and adaptability are basic to organizational survival).[136] Contemporary organizations see their success as resting more with their people assets than with their physical assets. Complexity science (a concept originated in the physical sciences and that social sciences adopted) suggests a framework befitting a world in which boundaries are not fixed but interpenetrate.[137] In this context, organizations must increase their complexity to the level of the environment complexity—"using complexity to deal with complexity"[138]—if they are to find innovative solutions to unforeseen problems.

Simply expressed, *Complexity Leadership Theory* (CLT) moves away from linear, mechanistic views of the world of simple cause-and-effect solutions to a perspective of the world as nonlinear and organic, typified by uncertainty and unpredictability.[139] CLT sees organizations as complex adaptive systems composed of diverse agents who interact, mutually affect one another, and generate novel behavior for the system as a whole.

At its most basic unit, CLT begins with complex adaptive systems (CAS): neural-like networks of informally interacting, interdependent agents, ideas, and events linked by shared goals, outlooks, and needs that emerge naturally in social systems.[140] These agents jostle into each other somewhat erratically in a process that allows the organization to adapt quickly and creatively to internal or environmental pressures.[141] The CAS adapt by diversifying their behaviors and strategies—including using counter-moves, modified or new approaches, learning and new knowledge, work-around changes, combining stratagems, experimentation, finding new allies, and new technologies. Although imperfect and messy, the process does find solutions that individuals, regardless of their expertise or position, could not find alone. Changes in complex adaptive systems occur organically, nonlinearly, and in unanticipated locations; their history of how they happened cannot be revisited.[142]

Next, CLT asserts that leadership is not a person but rather a set of interpersonal dynamics. Leadership is *emergent*—a nonlinear suddenness that describes change in complex systems.[143] Similarly, leadership's informal interactive, interdependent processes are considered *informal emergence*.[144] Accordingly, CLT concentrates on identifying and exploring the strategies and actions that enable knowledge-producing organizations and their subunits to learn, create, and adapt when necessary. It recognizes that its social assets and rapid learning are essential to keeping its competitive advantage. Most notably, CLT's leadership framework includes *both* the innovation and creativity that arises from small interacting and interdependent work groups *and* the formal organizations' structures to coordinate and produce outcomes aligned with the organization's vision and mission. The challenge for leadership is to maintain this balance, integrating complexity dynamics and bureaucracy. In short, organizational leadership is "connective, distributed, dynamic, and contextual."[145]

Complex adaptive systems differ from *complicated* systems: complicated systems can be described by their individual parts whereas complex systems contain such a variety of parts, environments, and interactions that one cannot fully understand the whole simply by analyzing its parts.[146] For example, sending a rocket to the moon is complicated; raising a child is complex.[147]

CLT places complex adaptive systems into an overarching framework that describes how they operate within a bureaucratic organization. The theory rests on four key ideas. First, events occur in a context,[148] a climate that generates a given system's persona, its traditions, its interactions, and interdependencies among agents (such as people and ideas), its hierarchical divisions, organizations, and environments. In and from this context, CAS and leadership are *socially constructed*.[149] The people in workgroups or larger organizations jointly form their understanding of who they and their leaders are by observing their actions, influence on organizational functioning, and outcomes. Typically, they use sensemaking rather than job titles to organize their perceptions and understandings of events around them.

Second, CLT separates *leadership* and *leaders*. In this original view, *leadership* is an emergent, interactive dynamic that produces adaptive outcomes, whereas *leaders* are individuals who act in ways that influence this dynamic and its outcomes. Leadership relates to actions and consequences, not necessarily with individuals or positions. CLT leaders may lead indirectly, without authority, temporarily, in tandem or in rotation with others. They might be unaware of their role but simply arise with a given situation.

Third, CLT viewpoint distinguishes *leadership* (the process) from *management* (the bureaucratic positions or "offices"). Organizational leaders whose influence and behaviors make good outcomes happen do not necessarily hold formal positions or titles.

Fourth, complexity leadership arises when faced with *adaptive challenges*, problems that require new learning, innovation, and fresh styles of behavior (as befits the Knowledge Era); these are not technical problems that can be solved with already existing knowledge and standard operating practices (as befits the Industrial Era).[150] One might think of this distinction as the difference between management and leadership development: management development involves applying proven solutions to known problems whereas leadership development looks to circumstances in which groups must learn their way out of problems that they never saw coming.[151]

To clarify leadership roles in organizations, and to accommodate organizations' needs for both structure and innovation, CLT recognizes three broad types of leadership functions: administrative, adaptive, and enabling leadership.[152]

- *Administrative leadership* refers to the actions of individuals and groups in formal managerial roles who plan and coordinate organizational activities so as to efficiently and effectively achieve designated outcomes. Administrative leaders reflect the organization's hierarchical and bureaucratic functions. These leaders build vision, direct organizational strategy, plan and structure tasks, allocate resources to achieve goals, and manage crises and conflicts. They structure the conditions in which adaptive leadership occurs. CLT advises administrative leadership to think about the organization's need for creativity and flexibility. For instance, stressing efficiency at the expense of adaptive capacity could limit the organization's ability to thrive.
- *Adaptive leadership* refers to the CAS's informal, emergent, interacting dynamic that produces learning and creative outcomes in response to unfamiliar organizational or environmental problems. Adaptive leadership begins in the conceptual struggles

among agents and groups over conflicting needs, ideas, or preferences. It ends in seeing beyond original assumptions, gaining new knowledge, and generating creative ideas, lessons, or adjustments. Adaptive leadership is not a person (although it involves people) and is not an act of authority (although it is related to it). Adaptive behaviors can occur in line employees' workgroups or in boardrooms.

- *Enabling leadership* minimizes the organization's bureaucratic constraints, enhances employees' potential for flexibility and innovation, and facilitates the movement of knowledge and creativity from adaptive structures into administrative structures. This leadership creates both access and resources to help the organization thrive. Enabling behaviors include: creating the general structure of complex networks that encourage interaction and interdependence; infusing useful conceptual (not interpersonal) tension to help motivate and coordinate the interactions; enlarging personal networks; staying up-to-date about one's organization and field; and monitoring the environments to understand the stressors it is experiencing.

Enabling, administrative, and adaptive leadership work in tandem and each benefits from the others. Since the leadership functions are intertwined, adaptive leadership gains strategic direction and structure while administrative leadership gains innovative and appropriate solutions to meet organizational needs. Enabling leadership occurs at all organizational levels, but its character varies with the hierarchical level and position. At times, enabling leadership overlaps with administrative or adaptive leadership; the same person may perform either role "by changing hats" as needed.

Research in complexity leadership theory tends to use complicated models rather than statistical analysis to follow interaction among agents and variables over time. It also tends to address *mechanisms*—processes such as catalysis and aggregation over time—more than variables. As a result, methodologies include qualitative research, computer simulations, non-linear differential equations, and observation protocols.[153] Given its intricacy, its idiosyncratic terms, and its measurement challenges, however, complexity leadership theory lacks a substantial research base to help move from theory to practice.[154]

Critics note that complexity leadership theorists present their ideas with invented phrases and terms that may "confuse more than clarify."[155] Some argue that the theory has not developed implications for leadership practice,[156] that it lends itself to "mysticism and obfuscation,"[157] and risks becoming a fad.[158] Others point to the unforeseen and potentially destructive consequences inherent in leadership that stems from "emergent events" that are unpredictable, claiming that they offer no guarantee of beneficial or successful results.[159] In addition, critics decry the absence of studies on the psychological effects of the emergence process.[160] As a result, the usefulness of CLT cannot yet be determined.[161]

Complexity Leadership Theory suggests that leaders must create the environments and conditions necessary for innovation—opportunities for interdependence and interaction—rather isolating or controlling related work groups or creating the innovation, itself. Although CLT is more an idea than a guide to practical leadership actions, seeing leadership as informal, formative, and enabling organizational effectiveness as well as administrative, it is a concept that broadens our understanding and practice of leadership.

REFLECTIONS AND RELEVANCE 3.5

Complexity Leadership Theory (CLT)

Complexity Leadership Theory addresses issues of organizational leadership in a context of uncertainty and unpredictability in a rapidly changing world.

Working first in groups of three and then as a class, answer the following questions:

1. Describe the *complex adaptive system* (CAS, the informal, interacting, and interdependent agents, ideas, and events) of which you are a part at work. Identify the other members, their positions, and roles. Give examples of how your CAS has adapted to changes in your environment. Mention the internal and external pressures to which your CAS must adapt. Describe how leadership in your CAS is emergent (or not).
2. Complexity Leadership Theory proposes three broad types of leadership functions: administrative, adaptive, and enabling. Identify the individuals (and their positions) in your school, at your grade level, and/or on your team who typically enact each of these roles. In which of these leadership functions do you feel most comfortable at this point in your career? In which areas do you want to develop more skills and confidence? How will you do this?

IMPLICATIONS FOR EDUCATIONAL LEADERS

As this chapter describes, contemporary views of organizational leadership are changing. Evolving views consider organizations as both rational and irrational; leadership is a shared dynamic; organizational leadership facilitates tasks, relationships, and change; and organizational leaders respond to internal and external environments.

Organizations as Rational and Irrational

Organizations—including schools—are both a formal system of hierarchy, rules, and authority and an adaptive and social system of interacting individuals. They have both rational and non-rational dimensions in their formal structure and in their people, respectively; each of these will strongly influence how the organization performs (i.e., Getzels and Guba). Thus, schools are defined by the tensions between their stated formal rational goals and non-rational pressures that come from individual employees (who have personalities, ideas, needs, values, and other idiosyncratic variables that affect how they do their jobs) and the environmental pressures of funding, community expectations, and educational accountability (i.e., Getzels and Guba). If schools are to continue to educate our community's children, they must adapt successfully to their environment's influences and constraints (i.e., Getzels and Guba, complexity leadership theory).

Leadership as a Shared Dynamic

Similarly, leadership as a concept and practice has moved beyond individuals in formal roles to now include leadership as a shared, interactive, and complex social dynamic (i.e., Getzels and Guba, transformational leadership theory, distributed leadership, leader-member-exchange theory, complexity leadership theory). In modern life—the amount and intensity of available information, the variety of tasks, the environmental pressures, and the rapid pace—no single formal "leader" can have the knowledge, energy, time, or expertise to be firmly "in charge" in every situation. Schools have a range of tasks, relationships, change, and external elements—all occurring within specific circumstances—with which leaders must deal (i.e., LMX Theory, CLT). To address these responsibilities, today's leadership is enacted *formally* and *informally*, *individually* and *shared*. To meet this reality, school leaders (typically, district superintendents and principals) accept that although they have certain responsibilities and tasks that only they must do, they also need to disperse tasks and responsibilities—along with power and authority—across many roles and individuals (i.e., distributed leadership, LMX Theory, CLT) if the work of educating children is to be accomplished successfully.

Organizational Leadership Facilitates Tasks, Relationships, and Change

Despite the assorted terms used to describe similar functions, theorists suggest several types of leadership functions related to task, relationships, change, and environments that occur in schools.[162] First, leaders use task-oriented (i.e., transactional theory, CLT's administrative leadership) behaviors to ensure efficient use of people, equipment, and other resources to accomplish the group's or organization's mission. As with any organization, schools need individuals with formal position and authority (typically principals, assistant principals, and department heads) to take the initiative to prepare and organize work; set direction; and plan, coordinate, and align resources, people, and activities to achieve the school's desired outcomes. Task-oriented leadership also solves problems that interfere with the organization's operations (i.e., CLT's adaptive and enabling leadership) and fulfills the basic contractual obligations between employer and employee (i.e., transactional leadership). As they prepare for their role, future principals will want to see who in their present work setting are fulfilling these leadership functions and how the formal leadership is supporting, monitoring, and rewarding them for achieving successful outcomes.

Second, leadership is about building relationships—the work-focused social interactions between a leader and an individual member multiplied across dyads, small groups, and systems across and beyond the organization (i.e., LMX, CLT's administrative, adaptive, and enabling leadership, transactional and transformational leadership). Leaders use relations-oriented behaviors—what they *do* even more than what they *say*—to strengthen their professional ties. Building upon mutual respect, trust, and obligation, leaders can help develop shared beliefs in each others' intentions, competence, and working partnerships. Would-be leaders needs to refine, extend, and monitor their people skills as an essential asset in their leadership work.

TABLE 3.2 Knowledge Era Leadership as a Shared Process

Theory	Principal Theorists	View of Leadership in Organizations
General theoretical model of administration	Jacob W. Getzels Egon G. Guba	Administration is an interactive social process between individual (role and personality), institution, and context. Organizational roles are interdependent and complementary. Leaders integrate institutional and members' demands.
Transformational Leadership	James MacGregor Burns	Conceptualized the difference between transactional and transformational leaders. Transformational leaders inspire followers to achieve common goals with exceptional results through vision, personality, and values.
	Bernard M. Bass	Operationalized transformational leadership into specific behaviors and attitudes to enhance leadership effectiveness: idealized influence, inspirational motivation, intellectual stimulation, individual consideration. Best leadership is both transactional and transformational.
Distributed Leadership		Multiple individuals and groups share leadership and influence across the organization. Leadership is a nascent characteristic of interacting individuals, leadership boundaries are open, and different types of expertise spread widely among many people. Situations also influence.
Leader-Member Exchange Theory (LMX)	George B. Graen Robert C. Liden	Leadership is a process of dynamic interactions between a leader and subordinates. The quality of the social exchange work relationship in leader-subordinate dyads (respect, trust, obligation) has consequences in subordinates' attitudes and behaviors and in organization outcomes.
Complexity Leadership Theory	Mary Uhl-Bien Russ Marion Bill McKelvey	Organizations, with fluid, flexible boundaries, must be complex, adaptive systems if they are to rapidly innovate in response to unforeseen problems. Leadership is a set of socially constructed interpersonal dynamics that permits administrative (formal), adaptive (informal), enabling (facilitates knowledge movement and relationships) functions.

Source: Original table by Leslie Kaplan and William Owings, 2017.

Third, in an era of rapid change, change-oriented leadership functions (i.e., transformational leadership, CLT's adaptive and enabling leadership) are essential to keep the school and district adjusting appropriately to its shifting environments. Today's school leaders—principals, A.P.s, department and committee chairs—create the work climate and conditions that allow colleagues to engage flexibly and productively with others. They express an inspiring vision of why a certain change is needed and what it looks like as they facilitate organizational learning. These change-oriented actions encourage a sense of group identity and efficacy; build awareness and acceptance of the group's purpose; and energize teachers and staff to look past immediate self-interest for the group's wellbeing. Future school leaders will want to identify and observe the "who," "how," and "why" of change-oriented leadership in their present schools and decide how they can build and apply these skills.

Organizational Leaders Respond to Internal and External Environments

Fourth, although a minor topic in this chapter, leaders respond to both internal and external environments. External leadership behaviors provide relevant information about events and ideas outside the organization. Networking with others who can provide information, resources, and political support (as noted in LMX Stage 4, CLT's enabling leadership), external monitoring (securing and analyzing information for relevant events and changes, identifying threats and opportunities), and representing (acting for their team or school in transactions with superiors, peers, and outsiders) are constructive leadership responses to environmental presses. Future principals will want to identify how their school is conducting their internal and external leadership functions and start maturing their relevant skills by participating in them.

NOTES

1 Yukl, G. (1989). Managerial leadership: A review of theory and research. *Journal of Management*, 15 (2), 251–289.
2 Halpin, A.W. (1958). *Administrative theory in education*. New York, NY: Macmillan; Griffiths, D.E. (1959). *Administrative theory*. New York, NY: Appleton-Century-Crafts.
3 Getzels, J.W. & Guba, E.G. (1957). Social behavior and the administrative process. *The School Review*, 65 (4), 423–441.
4 Hoy, W.K. & Miskel, C.G. (1987). *Educational administration: Theory, research, and practice*. New York, NY: Random House.
5 Stronge, J.H. (1995). Balancing individual and institutional goals in educational personnel evaluation: A conceptual framework. *Studies in Educational Evaluation*, 21 (2), 131–151.
6 Marion, R. & Gonzales, L. (2014). *Leadership in education: Organizational theory for the practitioner*. Long Grove, IL: Waveland Press, pp. 84–85
7 Marion & Gonzales (2014). Ibid., p. 85.
8 Getzels modified this model several times over the next 20 years, but its essential framework remained.
9 Griffiths, D.E. (1983). Evolutional research and theory: A study of prominent researchers. *Educational Administration Quarterly*, 19 (3), 201–221.
10 Getzels & Guba (1957). Op. cit.; Getzels, J., Lipham, J. & Campbell, R. (1968), *Educational administration as a social process*. New York, NY: Harper & Row.

11 Getzels, J., Lipham, J. & Campbell, R. (1968). *Educational administration as a social process: Theory, research and practice.* New York, NY: Harper & Row.

12 Getzels, J.W. & Guba, E.G. (1955). Role conflict and personality. *Journal of Personality*, 24 (1), 74–85; Guba, E.G. & Getzels, J.W. (1955). Personality and teacher effectiveness: A problem in theoretical research. *Journal of Educational Psychology*, 46 (6), 330–344; Jackson, S.E. & Schuler, R.S. (1985). A meta-analysis and conceptual critique of research on role ambiguity and role conflict in work settings. *Organizational Behavior and Human Decision Processes*, 36 (1), 16–78.

13 Griffiths (1983). Op. cit., p. 204.

14 Griffiths (1983). Op. cit., p. 202.

15 Griffiths (1983). Op. cit.

16 Owens, R.G. & Shakeshaft, C. (1992). The new revolution in administrative theory. *Journal of Educational Administration*, 30 (2), 4–17.

17 Shakeshaft, C. & Nowell, I. (1984). *Issues in Education*, 2 (3), 186–203.

18 Rozycki, E.G. (1999). *Traditions of ideology in administrative theory.* New Foundations.com. Retrieved from: www.newfoundations.com/EGR/AdminIdeology.html.

19 Rozyckik (1999). Ibid.

20 Oplatka, I. (2010). *The legacy of educational administration: A historical analysis of an academic field.* Frankfurt am Main, Germany: Peter Lang; Scribner, J. (1967). Halpin, A.W. Theory and research in administration. Reviews. *American Educational Research Journal*, 4 (1), 74–76.

21 Mulford, B. (2012). Tinkering towards a utopia: Trying to make sense of my contribution to the field. *Journal of Educational Administration*, 50 (1), 98–124.

22 Podsakoff, P.M. & Schriescheim, C.A. (1985). Leader reward and punishment behavior: A methodological and substantive review. In B. Staw & L.L. Cummings (Eds), *Research in organizational behavior.* San Francisco, CA: Jossey-Bass.

23 Drucker, P.F. (1976). The coming rediscovery of scientific management. *The Conference Board Record*, 13 (6), 23–27; Wren, D.A. (1994). *The evolution of management thought.* New York, NY: John Wiley & Sons.

24 Wren (1994). Ibid.

25 Follett, M.P. (1933). *The essentials of leadership.* Lecture delivered at Department of Business Administration, London School of Economics and Political Science. January. Reprinted from L. Urwick (Ed.), *Freedom and Coordination*, Chapter 4 (pp. 47–60). London, UK: Management Publication Trust; Graham. P. (1996). *Mary Parker Follett prophet of management.* Boston, MA: Harvard Business School.

26 Barnard, C. (1938). *The functions of the executive.* Cambridge, MA: Harvard University Press.

27 Yukl, G. (1999). An evaluation of conceptual weaknesses in transformational and charismatic leadership theories. *The Leadership Quarterly*, 10 (2), 285–305.

28 Although Burns originated the transformational leadership concept, today, the theory is referred to as Bass's Transformational Leadership Theory.

29 Bass, B.M. & Riggio, R.E. (2006). The transformational model of leadership. In B.M. Bass & R.E. Riggio (Eds), *Transformational leadership*, 2nd ed. (pp. 3–16). Mahwah, NJ: Lawrence Erlbaum Associates.

30 Burns, J.M. (1978). *Leadership.* New York, NY: HarperCollins.

31 Burns (1978). Ibid.

32 Burns, J.M. (1998). Transactional and transforming leadership. In G.R. Hickman (Ed.), *Leading Organizations.* (pp. 133–134). Los Angeles, CA: Sage.

33 Hay, I. (n.d.). Transformational leadership: Characteristics and criticisms. leadingtoday.org. Retrieved from: www.leadingtoday.org/weleadinlearning/transformationalleadership.htm.

34 Bergstrom, A. (2003). An interview with Dr. Bernard M. Bass. Kravis Leadership Institute, *Leadership Review.* Retrieved from: www.leadershipreview.org/2003winter/article3_winter_2003.asp.

35 Bass, B.M. (1996). *A new paradigm of leadership: An inquiry into transformational leadership.* Alexandria, VA: U.S. Army Research Institute for the Behavioral and Social Sciences; Bass, B.M. & Avolio, B.J. (1990). *Multifactor leadership questionnaire.* Palo Alto, CA: Consulting Psychologists Press.

36 Bass, B.M. (1991). From transactional to transformational leadership: Learning to share the vision. *Organizational Dynamics, 18* (3), 19–31.

37 Judge, T.A. & Piccolo, R.F. (2004). Transformational and transactional leadership: A meta-analytic test of their relative validity. *Journal of Applied Psychology, 89* (5), 755–768.

38 Bass, B.M. & Steidlmeier, P. (1999). Ethics, character, and authentic transformational leadership behavior. *Leadership Quarterly, 10* (2), 181–218; Waldman, D.A., Bass, B.M. & Yammarino, F.J. (1990). Adding to contingent-reward behavior: The augmenting effect of charismatic leadership. *Group & Organizational Studies, 15,* 381–394; Kanungo, R.N. & Mendonca, M. (1996). *Ethical dimensions in leadership.* Beverly Hills, CA: Sage.

39 Bass, B.M. & Avolio, B.J. (1994). *Organizational effectiveness through transformational leadership.* Thousand Oaks, CA: Sage; Bass, B.M. & Riggio, R.E. (2006). The transformational model of leadership. In B.M. Bass & R.E. Riggio (Eds), *Transformational leadership,* 2nd ed. (pp. 3–16). Mahwah, NJ: Lawrence Erlbaum.

40 Bass uses the term *charisma* in 1991 but calls it *idealized influence* in 1994. Gary Yukl (1999) and other leadership scholars believe that charismatic leadership and transformational leadership are *not* equivalent but their processes do partially overlap. Conceptual ambiguity and inconsistent use of terms makes it difficult to accurately compare the two concepts.

41 See, for example: Bass, B.M., Avolio, B.J., Jung, D.I. & Berson, Y. (2003). Predicting unit performance by assessing transformational and transactional leadership. *Journal of Applied Psychology, 88* (2), 207–218.

42 Bass (1991). Op. cit.

43 Bass (1991). Op. cit.

44 See: García-Morales, V.J.; Jiménez-Barrionuevo, M.M. & Gutiérrez-Gutiérrez, L. (2012), Transformational leadership influence on organizational performance through organizational learning and innovation. *Journal of Business Research, 65* (7), 1040–1050; Liao, H. & Chuang, A. (2007). Transforming service employees and climate: A multilevel, multisource examination of transformational leadership in building long-term service relationships. *Journal of Applied Psychology, 92* (4), 1006–1019.

45 See: García-Morales, Jiménez-Barrionuevo & Gutiérrez-Gutiérrez (2012). Op. cit.; Howell. M. & Avolio, B.J. (1993). Transformational leadership, transactional leadership, locus of control, and support for innovation: Key predictors of consolidated-business-unit performance. *Journal of Applied Psychology, 78* (6), 891–902; Liao & Chuang (2007). Op cit.

46 Howell & Avolio (1993). Op. cit.; Jung, D., Wu, A. & Chow, C.W. (2008). Towards understanding the direct and indirect effects of CEOs' transformational leadership on firm innovation. *Leadership Quarterly, 19* (5), 582–594; Walumbwa, F.O., Orwa, B., Wang, P. & Lawler, J.J. (2005). Transformational leadership, organizational commitment, and job satisfaction: A comparative study of Kenyan and U.S. financial firms. *Human Resource Development Quarterly, 16* (2), 235–256.

47 Bass (1996). Op. cit.

48 Yukl (1999). Op. cit.

49 Bass (1996). Op. cit.; Lowe, K.B., Kroeck, K.G. & Sivasubramaniam, N. (1996). Effectiveness correlates of transformational and transactional leadership: A meta-analytic review of the MLQ literature. *Leadership Quarterly, 7* (3), 385–425.

50 See: Geyer, A.L.J. & Steyrer, J.M. (1998). Transformational leadership and objective performance in banks. *Applied Psychology: An International Review, 47* (3), 397–420; Hater, J.J. & Bass, B.M. (1988). Superiors' evaluations and subordinates' perceptions of transformational and transactional leadership. *Journal of Applied Psychology, 73* (4), 695–702; Yammarino, F.J. & Bass, B.M. (1990). Transformational leadership and multiple levels of analysis, *Human Relations, 43* (10), 975–995.

51 Bass, B.M. & Riggio, R.E. (2006). The transformational model of leadership. In B.M. Bass & R.E. Riggio (Eds), *Transformational leadership*. 2nd ed. (pp. 3–16). Mahwah, NJ: Lawrence Erlbaum Associates.

52 See: Bennis, W.G. & Nanus, B. (1985). *Leaders: The strategies for taking charge*. New York, NY: Harper & Row; Tichy, N.M. & Devanna, M.A. (1986). *The transformational leader*. New York, NY: Wiley.

53 See: Bass, B.M. (1997). Does the transactional-transformational leadership paradigm transcend organization and national boundaries? *American Psychologist*, 52 (2), 130–139; Den Hartog, D.N., House, R.J., Hanges, P.J., Ruiz-Quintajilla, S.A. & Dorfman, P.W. (1999). Culture specific and cross-cultural generalizable implicit leadership theories: Are attributes of charismatic/transformational leadership universally endorsed? *The Leadership Quarterly*, 10 (2), 219–256.

54 Yukl (1999). Op. cit.; Tourish, D. & Pinnington, A. (2002). Transformational leadership, corporate cultism and the spirituality paradigm: An unholy trinity in the workplace. *Human Relations*, 55 (2), 147–172.

55 Yukl (1999). Op. cit.

56 Northouse, P.G. (2013). *Leadership: Theory and practice*. Thousand Oaks, CA: Sage.

57 Bass, B.M. (1999), Two decades of research and development in transformational leadership. *European Journal of Work and Organisational Psychology*, 8 (1), 9–32; Lee, M. (2014). Transformational leadership: Is it time for a recall? *International Journal of Management and Applied Research*, 1 (1), 17–29.

58 Northouse (2013). Op. cit.; Tourish & Pinnington (2002). Op. cit.

59 Lee (2014). Op. cit.

60 Northouse (2013). Op. cit.; Rickards, T. and Clark, M. (2006), *Dilemmas of Leadership*. London, UK: Taylor & Francis; Yukl (1999). Op. cit.

61 Yukl (1999). Op. cit.

62 Yukl (1999). Op. cit.

63 Pearce, C.L. & Conger, J.A. (2003). All those years ago: The historical underpinnings of shared leadership. In C.L. Pearce and J.A. Conger (Eds), *Shared leadership: Reframing the hows and whys of leadership* (pp. 1–18). Thousand Oaks, CA: Sage.

64 Badaracco, J.L. (2001). We don't need another hero. *Harvard Business Review*, 79 (8), 120–126.

65 Leithwood, K., Day, C., Sammons, P., Harris, A. & Hopkins, D. (2006). *Successful school leadership: What it is and how it influences pupil learning*. Nottingham, UK: DfES Publications.

66 Bennett, N., Wise, C., Woods, P.A. & Harvey, J.A. (2003). *Distributed leadership* (p. 7). Nottingham, UK: National College of School Leadership.

67 Spillane, J.P. (2006). *Distributed leadership*. New York, NY: Wiley.

68 Leithwood, Day, Sammons, Harris & Hopkins (2006). Op. cit.

69 Spillane, J. & Diamond, J.B. (2007). *Distributed leadership in practice* (pp. 149–152). New York, NY: Teachers College Press.

70 Spillane (2006). Op. cit., p. 58.

71 Pearce, C. (2004). The future of leadership: Combining vertical and shared leadership to transform knowledge work. *Academy of Management Executive*, 18 (1), 47–57.

72 Bolden, R. (2011). Distributed leadership in organizations: A review of theory and research. *International Journal of Management Reviews*, 13 (3), 251–269.

73 Harris, A. (2013). Distributed leadership: Friend or foe? *Educational Management Administration & Leadership*, 41 (5), 545–554; Leithwood et al. (2006). Op. cit.

74 See: Graetz, F. (2000). Strategic change leadership. *Management Decisions*, 38 (8), 550–564; Iandoli, L. & Zollo, G. (2008). *Organisational Cognition and Learning*. New York, NY: Idea Group Incorporated.

75 See: Little, J.W. (1990). The persistence of privacy: Autonomy and initiative in teachers' professional relations. *Teachers College Record*, 91 (4), 509–536; Rosenholtz, S.J. (1989). *Teachers' workplace: The social organization of schools*. New York, NY: Longman.

76 See: Louis, K.S. & Marks, H. (1998). Does professional community affect the classroom? Teachers' work and student work in restructuring schools. *American Educational Research Journal, 33* (4), 757–798; Stoll, L. & Louis, K.S. (2007). *Professional learning communities.* New York, NY: Open University Press.

77 Mayrowetz, D. (2008). Making sense of distributed leadership: Exploring the multiple usages of the concept in the field. *Educational Administration Quarterly, 44* (3), 424–435.

78 See: Day, C., Sammons, P., Leithwood, K., Hopkins, D., Gu, Q., Brown, E. & Ahtaridou, E. (2011). *School leadership and student outcomes: Building and sustaining success.* Buckingham, UK: Open University Press; Leithwood, K., Mascall, B., Strauss, T., Sacks, R., Memon, N. & Yashkina (2007). Distributing leadership to make schools smarter: Taking ego out of the system. *Leadership and Policy Studies, 6* (1), 37–67; Leithwood, K. & Mascall, B. (2008). Collective leadership effects on student achievement. *Educational Administration Quarterly, 44* (4), 529–561.

79 Harris, A. (2011). Distributed leadership: Current evidence and future directions. *Journal of Management Development, 30* (10), 20–32; Leithwood & Mascall (2008). Op. cit.

80 Day, C., Sammons, P., Leithwood, K., Harris, A. & Hopkins. D. (2009). *The impact of school leadership on pupil outcomes: Final report.* Nottingham, UK: Department for Children, Schools and Families, as cited in Harris, A. (2009). Distributed leadership: What we know. In A. Harris (Ed.), *Distributed leadership: Different perspectives* (pp. 11–21). Dordrecht, Netherlands: Springer.

81 Day et al. (2009). Ibid.

82 Ban, Al-Ani, A.H. & Bligh, M.C. (2011). Collaborating with 'virtual strangers': Towards developing a framework for leadership in distributed teams. *Leadership, 7* (3), 219–249; Day et al. (2011). Op. cit.

83 Festinger, L., Schacter, S. & Back, K.W. (1950). *Social pressure in informal groups: A study of human factors in housing.* New York: NY: Harper; Heinicke, C.M. & Bales, R.F. (1953). Developmental trends in the structure of small groups. *Sociometry, 16* (1), 7–38.

84 Melnick, M.J. (1982). Six obstacles to effective team performance: Some small group considerations. *Journal of Sport Behavior, 5* (3), 114–123.

85 Storey, A. (2004). The problem of distributed leadership in schools. *School leadership & Management, 24* (3), 249–265; Timperley, H. (2005). Distributed leadership: Developing theory from practice. *Journal of Curriculum Studies, 37* (4), 395–420.

86 Hargreaves, A., Harris, A., Boyle, A., Ghent, K., Goodall, J., Gurn, A., McEwen, L., Reich, M. & Stone, J.C. (2010) *Performance beyond expectations.* London: National College for Leadership of Schools and Children's Services and Specialist Schools and Academies Trust.

87 Yukl, G. (2012), Effective leadership behaviors: What we know and what questions need more attention? *The Academy of Management Perspectives, 26* (4), 66–85.

88 See: Hartley D. (2010) Paradigms: How far does research in distributed leadership 'Stretch'? *Educational Management, Administration & Leadership, 38* (3), 271–285; Lumby, H. (2013). Distributed Leadership. The uses and abuses of power. *Educational Management Administration & Leadership, 41* (5), 581–597.

89 Lumby (2013). Ibid., p. 582.

90 Harris, A. & Spillane, J. (2008). Distributed leadership through the looking glass. *Management in Education, 22* (1), 31–34.

91 See: Gordon, R.D. (2010). Dispersed leadership: Exploring the impact of antecedent forms of power using a communicative framework. *Management Communication Quarterly, 24* (2), 260–287; Hartley, D. (2009). Education policy, distributed leadership and socio-cultural theory. *Educational Review, 61* (2), 139–150; Lumby (2013). Op. cit.

92 Rippin, A. (2007). Stitching up the leader: Empirically based reflections on leadership and gender. *Journal of Organizational Change Management, 20* (2), 209–226.

93 Lumby (2013). Op. cit.

94 See: Goldstein, J. (2004). Making sense of distributed leadership: The case of peer assistance and review. *Educational Evaluation and Policy Analysis, 26* (2), 173–197; Mitra, D.L. (2005).

Adults advising youth: Leading while getting out of the way. *Educational Administration Quarterly*, 41 (3), 520–553.

95 Sugrue, C. (2009). From heroes and heroines to hermaphrodites: Emasculation or emancipation of school leaders and leadership? *School Leadership and Management*, 29 (4), 353–371.

96 Grint, K. (2010). The sacred in leadership: Separation, sacrifice and silence. *Organization Studies*, 31 (1), 89–107.

97 Bolden (2011). Op. cit.

98 Barker, R. (2001). The nature of leadership. *Human Relations*, 54 (4), 469–494; Hosking, D.M. (1988). Organising, leadership and skillful process. *Journal of Management Studies*, 25 (2), 147–166; Uhl-Bien, M. (2006). Relational leadership theory: Exploring the social processes of leadership and organizing. *Leadership Quarterly*, 17 (6), 654–676.

99 Gronn, P. (2000). Distributed properties: A new architecture for leadership. *Educational Management Administration & Leadership*, 28 (3), 317–338.

100 Dansereau, F., Graen, G.B. & Haga,W.J. (1975). A vertical dyad linkage approach to leadership within formal organizations. *Organizational Behavior and Human Performance*, 13 (1), 46–78; Graen, G.B. & Cashman, J.F. (1975) A role-making model of leadership in formal organizations: A developmental approach. In J.G. Hunt & L.L. Larson (Eds), *Leadership frontiers* (pp. 143–165). Kent, OH: Kent State University Press.

101 Graen, G.B. & Scandura, T.A. (1987). Toward a psychology of dyadic organizing. *Research in Organizational Behavior*, 9, 175–208; Graen & Uhl-Bein (1995). Op. cit.; Schriesheim, C.A., Castro, S.L. & Cogliser, C.C. (1999). Leader–member exchange (LMX) research: A comprehensive review of theory, measurement, and data-analytic practices. *Leadership Quarterly*, 10 (1), 63–113.

102 Katz, D. & Kahn, R.L. (1978). *The social psychology of organizations*. New York, NY: John Wiley and Sons.

103 Gerstner, C.R. & Day, D.V. (1997). Meta-analytic review of leader-member exchange theory: Correlates and construct issues. *Journal of Applied Psychology*, 82 (6), 827–844.

104 Le Blanc, P.M. (1994) Leader's support: A study of the leader–member exchange model among nurses. Amsterdam, Netherlands: Thesis Publishers.

105 Graen, G.B. & Uhl-Bien, M. (1991a). The transformation of professionals into self-managing and partially self-designing contributions: Toward a theory of leader-making. *Journal of Management Systems*, 3 (3), 33–48; Graen, G.B. & Uhl-Bien, M. (1991b). Partnership-making applies equally well to teammate-sponsor teammate-competence network, and teammate-teammate relationships. *Journal of Management Systems*, 3 (3), 49–54.

106 Graen, B.G. & Uhl-Bien, M. (1995). Relationship-based approach to leadership. Development of leader-member exchange (LMX) theory of leadership over 25 years: Applying a multi-level multi-domain perspective. *The Leadership Quarterly*, 6 (2), 219–247.

107 Graen & Uhl-Bien (1995). Ibid.

108 Graen, G.B. (1976) Role making processes within complex organizations. In M.D. Dunnette (Ed.), *Handbook of industrial and organizational psychology* (pp. 1201–1245). Chicago, IL: Rand McNally.

109 See: Dockery, T.M. & Steiner, D.D. (1990) The role of initial interaction in leader–member exchange. *Group and Organization Studies*, 15 (4), 395–413; Liden, R.C., Wayne, S.J. & Stilwell, D. (1993). A longitudinal study on the early development of leader–member exchanges. *Journal of Applied Psychology*, 78 (4), 662–674; Wayne, S.J., Liden, R.C. & Sparrowe, R.T. (1994). Developing leader–member exchanges: The influence of gender and ingratiation. *The American Behavioral Scientist*, 37 (5), 697–714.

110 Graen, G.B., Dansereau, F., Minami, T. & Cashman, J. (1973). Leadership behaviors as cues to performance evaluation. *Academy of Management Journal*, 16 (4), 611–623; Graen, G.B. & Scandura, T.A. (1987). Toward a psychology of dyadic organizing. In B.M. Staw & L.L. Cummings (Eds), *Research in organizational behavior* (pp. 175–208). Greenwich, CT: JAI Press.

111 See: Graen & Scandura (1987). Op. cit.; Graen, G. (2006). Post Simon, March, Weick, and Graen: New leadership sharing as a key to understanding organizations. In G. Graen, & J.A. Graen (Eds), *Sharing network leadership*, 4 (pp. 269–279). Greenwich, CT: Information Age Publishing; Uhl-Bien, M. & Graen, G.B. (1993). Leadership-making in self-managing professional work teams: An empirical investigation. In K.E. Clark, M.B. Clark & D.P. Campbell (Eds), *The impact of leadership* (pp. 379–387). West Orange, NJ: Leadership Library of America.

112 Graen & Uhl-Bien (1995). Op. cit.

113 Bass, B.M. (1985). *Leadership and performance beyond expectations*. New York, NY: Free Press.

114 For a fuller discussion of these research obstacles, see: Gerstner, C.R. & Day, D.V. (1997). Meta-analytic review of leader-member exchange theory: Correlates and construct issues. *Journal of Applied Psychology*, 82 (6), 827–844.

115 See: Bauer, T.N., Erdogan, V., Liden, R.C. & Wayne, S.J. (2006). A longitudinal study of the moderating role of extraversion: Leader-member exchange, performance and turnover during new executive development. *Journal of Applied Psychology*, 91 (2), 298–310; Janssen. O. & Van Yperen, N.W. (2004). Employees' goal orientations, the quality of the leader-member exchange, and the outcomes of job performance and job satisfaction. *Academy of Management Journal*, 47 (3), 368–384.

116 Gerstner, C.R. & Day, D.V. (1997). Meta-analytic review of leader-member exchange theory: Correlates and construct issues. *Journal of Applied Psychology*, 82 (6), 827–844.

117 Wakabayashi, M. & Graen, G.B. (1984). The Japanese career progress study: A 7-year follow-up. *Journal of Applied Psychology*, 69 (4), 603–614.

118 Markham, S.E., Steven, E., Yammarino, F.J., Murry, W.D. & Palanski, M.E. (2010). Leader–member exchange, shared values, and performance agreement and levels of analysis do matter. *The Leadership Quarterly*, 21 (3): 469–480.

119 Ilies, R., Nahrgang, J.D. & Morgeson, F.P. (2007). Leader-member exchange and citizenship behaviors: A meta-analysis. *Journal of Applied Psychology*, 92 (1), 269–277.

120 Gertner & Day (1997). Op. cit.

121 Van Breukelen, W., Schyns, B. & LeBlanc, P. (2006). Leader-member exchange theory and research: Accomplishments and future challenges. *Leadership*, 2 (3), 295–316.

122 Schriesheim, C.A., Castro, S.L. & Cogliser, C.C. (1999). Leader–member exchange (LMX) research: A comprehensive review of theory, measurement, and data-analytic practices. *The Leadership Quarterly*, 10 (1), 63–113; Yammarino, F.J., Dionne, S.D., Chun, J.U. & Dansereau, F. (2005). Leadership and levels of analysis: A state-of-the-science review. *Leadership Quarterly*, 16 (6), 879–919.

123 Schriesheim, Castro & Cogliser (1999). Op. cit.

124 Van Breukelen, Schyns & LeBlanc (2006). Op. cit.

125 Yukl. G.A. (1994). *Leadership in organizations*, 3rd ed. Englewood Cliffs, NJ: Pearson/ Prentice Hall.

126 Van Breukelen, Schyns & LeBlanc (2006). Op. cit.

127 Cogliser, C.C. & Schreisheim, C.A. (2000). Exploring work unit context and leader-member exchange: A multi-level perspective. *Journal of Organizational Behavior*, 21 (5), 487–511.

128 Cogliser & Schreisheim (2000). Ibid.; Yukl, G. (2006). *Leadership in organizations*, 6th ed. Upper Saddle River, NJ: Prentice-Hall.

129 See: Brockner, J. & Grover, S. (1988). Predictors of survivors' job involvement following layoffs: A field study. *Journal of Applied Psychology*, 73 (3), 436–442; Lamertz, K. (2002). The social construction of fairness: Social influence and sense making in organizations. *Journal of Organizational Behavior*, 23 (1), 19–37; Masterson, S.S., Lewis, K., Goldman, B.M. & Taylor, M.S. (2000). Integrating justice and social exchange: The differing effects of fair procedures and treatment on work relationships. *Academy of Management Journal*, 43 (4), 738–748.

130 See: Hogg, M.A., Martin, R. & Weeden, K. (2003). Leader–member relations and social identity. In D. van Knippenberg & M.A. Hogg (Eds), *Leadership and power: Identity processes in groups and organizations* (pp. 18–33). London, UK: SAGE; Schriesheim, C.A., Castro, S.L. & Cogliser, C.C. (1999). Leader–member exchange (LMX) research: A comprehensive review of theory, measurement, and data-analytic practices. *The Leadership Quarterly*, 10 (1), 63–113.

131 Sullivan, D.M., Mitchell, M.S. & Uhl-Bien, M. (2003). The new conduct of business: How LMX can help capitalize on cultural diversity. In G.B. Graen (Ed.), *Dealing with diversity* (pp. 183–218). Greenwich, CT: Information Age Publishing.

132 Northouse, P.G. (2004). *Leadership: Theory and practice.* Thousand Oaks, CA: SAGE.

133 Van Breukelen, Schyns & LeBlanc (2006). Op. cit.

134 Schriesheim, Castro & Cogliser (1999). Op. cit.

135 Ilinitch, A.Y., D'Aveni, R.A. & Lewin, A.Y. (1996). New organizational forms and strategies for managing in hypercompetitive environments. *Organization Science*, 7 (3), 211–220.

136 Bettis, R.A. & Hitt, M.A. (1995). The new competitive landscape. *Strategic Management Journal*, 7 (13), 7–19; Boisot, M.H. (1998). *Knowledge assets: Securing competitive advantage in the information economy.* Oxford, UK: Oxford University Press.

137 Cilliers, P. (2001). Boundaries, hierarchies and networks in complex systems. *International Journal of Innovation Management*, 5 (2), 135–147; Marion, R. & Uhl-Bien, M. (2001). Leadership in complex organizations. *The Leadership Quarterly*, 12 (4), 389–418.

138 McKelvey, B. & Boisot, M.H. (2003). *Transcendental organizational foresight in nonlinear contexts.* Paper presented at the INSEAD Conference on Expanding Perspectives on Strategy Processes, Fontainebleau, France; Uhl-Bien, M., Marion, R. & McKelvey, B. (2007). Complexity leadership theory: Shifting leadership from the industrial age to the knowledge era. *The Leadership Quarterly*, 18 (4), 298–318.

139 Regine, B. & Lewin, R. (2000). Leading at the edge: How leaders influence complex systems. *Emergence: A Journal of Complexity Issues in Organizations and Management*, 2 (2), 5–23.

140 Homans, G.C. (1950). *The human group.* New York, NY: Harcourt, Brace and World; Roy, D. (1954). Efficiency and 'the fix': Informal intergroup relations in a piecework machine shop. *American Journal of Sociology*, 60 (3), 255–266.

141 Carley, K. & Hill, V. (2001). Structural change and learning within organizations. In A. Lomi & E.R. Larsen (Eds), *Dynamics of organizational societies* (pp. 63–92). Cambridge, MA: AAAI/MIT Press; Carley, K. & Lee, J.S. (1998). Dynamic organizations: Organizational adaptation in a changing environment. *Advances in Strategic Management: A Research Annual*, 15 (Special Issue), 269–297; Goodwin, B. (1994). *How the leopard changed its spots: The evolution of complexity.* New York, NY: Charles Scribner's Sons.

142 Dooley, K. (1996). Complex adaptive systems: A nominal definition. *The Chaos Network*, 8 (1), 2–3.

143 Marion, R. (1999). The edge of organization: Chaos and complexity theories of formal social organizations. Newbury Park, CA: Sage.

144 Lichtenstein, B., Uhl-Bien, M., Marion, R., Seers, A., Orton, D. & Schreiber, C. (2006). Complexity leadership theory: An interactive perspective on leading in complex adaptive systems. *Emergence: Complexity and Organization*, 8 (4), 2–12; Plowman, D.A., Silansky, S., Beck, L., Baker, K., Kulkarni, M. & Travis, D. (2007). The role of leadership in emergent, self-organization. *The Leadership Quarterly*, 18 (4), 341–356. Authors use the phrase "informal emergence" rather than "bottom up" behavior because they believe the latter is too suggestive of hierarchy.

145 Uhl-Bien, Marion & McKelvey (2007). Op. cit., p. 302.

146 Cilliers, P. (1998). *Complexity and postmodernism: Understanding complex systems.* London, UK: Routledge; Cillers uses the analogy that "a jumbo jet is *complicated* but mayonnaise is *complex.*"

147 Allen, W. (2013). *Complicated or complex—knowing the difference is important.* Retrieved from: http://learningforsustainability.net/sparksforchange/complicated-or-complex-knowing-the-difference-is-important-for-the-management-of-adaptive-systems/.

148 Hunt, J. (1999). Transformational/charismatic leadership's transformation of the field: A historical essay. *The Leadership Quarterly, 10* (2), 129–144; Osborn, R., Hunt, J.G. & Jauch, L.R. (2002). Toward a contextual theory of leadership. *The Leadership Quarterly, 13* (6), 797–837.

149 Cilliers (1998). Op. cit; Dooley (1996). Op. cit.; Hosking, D.M. (1988). Organizing, leadership and skillful process. *Journal of Management Studies, 25* (2), 147–166; Osborn, R., Hunt, J.G. & Jauch, L.R. (2002). Toward a contextual theory of leadership. *The Leadership Quarterly, 13* (6), 797–837.

150 Heifetz, R.A. (1994). *Leadership without easy answers.* Cambridge, MA: Harvard University Press; Heifetz, R.A. & Laurie, D.L. (2001). The work of leadership. *Harvard Business Review, 79* (11), 131–141.

151 Day, D.V. (2000). Leadership development: A review in context. The *Leadership Quarterly, 11* (4), 581–613.

152 Uhl-Bien, Marion & McKelvey (2007). Ibid.

153 Marion & Uhl-Bien (2007). Op. cit.; Schneider & Somers (2006). Op. cit.

154 Avolio, B.J., Walumbwa, F.O. & Weber, T.J. (2009). Leadership: Current theories, research, and future directions. *Annual Review of Psychology, 60* (1), 421–449.

155 Schneider & Somers (2006). Op. cit.

156 Montgomery, C.A., Wernerfelt, B. & Balakrishnan, S.V. (1989). Strategy content and the research process: A critique and commentary. *Strategic Management Journal, 10* (2), 189–197; Schneider & Somers (2006). Op. cit.

157 Horgan, J. (1995). From complexity to perplexity. *Scientific American, 272* (6), 104–109.

158 Sternman, J.D. & Wittenberg, J. (1999). Path dependence, competition, and succession in the dynamics of scientific revolution. *Organization Science, 10* (3), 322–341.

159 Goldstein, J. (1999). Emergence as a construct: History and issues. *Emergence, 1* (1), 49–72; Victor, B. & Stephens, C. (1994). The dark side of the new organizational forms: An editorial essay. *Organizational Science, 5* (4), 479–482; Osborn, R.N., Hunt, J.G. & Jauch, L.R. (2002). Toward a contextual theory of leadership. *The Leadership Quarterly, 13* (6), 797–837.

160 Wheatley, M. (1994). *Leadership and the new science.* San Francisco, CA: Berrett-Koehler.

161 Schneider & Somers (2007). Op. cit.

162 Yukl, G. (2012). Effective leadership behaviors: What we know and what questions need more attention? *The Academy of Management Perspectives, 26* (4), 66–85.

CHAPTER **4**

Motivating People to Accomplish Organizational Goals

GUIDING QUESTIONS

4.1 Explain how human motivation at work involves intrinsic, extrinsic, and contextual factors.

4.2 Describe how Abraham Maslow's needs hierarchy theory depicts employees' motivation and behaviors at work.

4.3 Discuss how Frederick Herzberg's motivation/hygiene theory portrays employees' motivation and behaviors at work.

4.4 Summarize how Douglas McGregor's Theory X and Theory Y help represent organizational leaders' views about employee motivation and behaviors at work.

4.5 Describe how David McClelland's acquired needs theory—for achievement, affiliation, and power—views employee motivation and behaviors at work.

4.6 Discuss how expectancy theory uses concepts of expectancy, instrumentality, and valence to explain motivation as a conscious and cognitive process.

4.7 Analyze how Albert Bandura's self-efficacy theory uses the interactions of cognition, behavior, and the environment to describe employee motivation and behaviors at work.

4.8 Trace how Edwin Locke and Gary Latham's goal setting theory uses goal commitment, feedback, task complexity, and personal goals to explain worker motivation at work.

2015 PROFESSIONAL STANDARDS FOR EDUCATIONAL LEADERS:
1, 2, 4, 5, 6, 7, 9, 10

CASE STUDY 4.1

A Case of Bait and Switch?

For 11 years, John Smith had been the principal of Tipton Middle School. He wanted to become a high school principal, but the Tipton High School principal did not plan to retire for another 15 years. Ambitious to move up, John applied to lead the prestigious Dandy High School two hours away. He applied in May, interviewed in June, and received the appointment at the June 30th school board meeting. Although the job search and appointment came late, John was excited; he submitted his resignation. The new contract started July 15 but did not list the school's name. It only mentioned "Principal in the Dandy County Public Schools" and the salary. After calling the central office, the human resources director told him that it was customary to place the position and salary in the contract, but not name the school. The director also told John that the Dandy superintendent would like to speak with him on July 15, at 9:00 a.m., before the general administrators' meeting at 10:00 a.m. The superintendent would then take John to the school and introduce him to everyone.

John knew that Dandy County had a residency requirement for its principals, so he put his house on the market and started packing. It was more expensive to live in suburban Dandy than in rural Tipton, but John thought the salary increase would take care of the higher cost of living. John got an all-cash contract offer on his home the next day—for much less than he wanted. He closed on the house the next week and then purchased a much more expensive and smaller home in Dandy, a mile away from the high school. With his new house closing at 4:00 p.m. on July 15, John was excited to get started.

On July 15, John arrived at the superintendent's office at 9:00 a.m., and the secretary escorted him in. The superintendent greeted John warmly and announced that he had a situation he needed to discuss. The superintendent told John that a bit of a shake up had occurred in administration since the June 30th board meeting. For legal reasons he could not discuss, he had reassigned John to Dandy Middle School as the principal. Although the middle school principal salary was about $20,000 lower than the high school salary, John would maintain the salary listed on the contract. John told the superintendent that he only applied for and accepted the job because he wanted to be a high school principal. The superintendent asked John if he still wanted the job and said in a rather stern voice that if he didn't want to come under the new conditions, they would accept his resignation.

At the general administrators' meeting, the superintendent announced John's appointment as the new principal of Dandy Middle School. But he did not hear a word that was said following that announcement. After the meeting, the superintendent drove John to the middle school and introduced him warmly to the staff. John was still numb. He walked into his new office and shut the door, left at 3:45 p.m., and arrived at the bank to close on his new, smaller, and more expensive home. After the closing, he walked through his new, empty home, and wished his Dad were still alive so he could ask for advice.

RUBRIC 4.1

Lens and/or factors to be considered in decision making	What are the factors at play in this case?	What steps should be considered in solving the problem?	What could have been done to avoid this dilemma?
The situation			
• The task	John's motivation and trust levels are low when he begins working in Dandy. His professional and financial commitment to Dandy may not be mutual.	John needs to discuss the situation with the superintendent or designee and make a decision about what action to take.	Dandy School Board officials should have kept John informed of the change in placement prior to his first day at work—so he could have planned accordingly.
• Personal abilities	Dandy school officials' actions show a low understanding of worker motivation. John's ability to make a good decision may be impaired.	John needs to speak with the superintendent to obtain a better understanding of the circumstances for the job change.	Even though the job search was late, Dandy officials should have been more transparent and shown appreciation for how the sudden position switch might affect John and his job performance.
• The school environment	Dandy Middle School may not have a principal for opening day or the new principal may not be motivated to do his best. This change will impact school climate.	Whatever the outcome, everyone needs to ensure that Dandy Middle School's climate and culture are not damaged.	The job search should have been started earlier so John could know his placement, make an informed decision, and begin to know his new school and faculty before teachers left for the summer.
	Look	Wider	
Organizational (i.e., the organizational goals, values, policies, culture)	Some dysfunction in the Dandy school system culture exists for this situation to have occurred.	Professional development for human resource personnel, and others on how motivation affects employee performance.	Dandy school officials need to operate with greater transparency and efficiency.
People (i.e., individuals with needs, beliefs, goals, relationships)	John came to Dandy County with a contract (albeit a psychological one), to be the high school principal. That was violated. The superintendent appears unwilling to discuss the matter beyond a vague mention of legal reasons.	Since John is now part of the Dandy school system, he is owed an honest explanation and sincere efforts to support his leadership within his school and district. John has two options: 1) check with own attorney to see if he has legal recourse; 2) accept situation and deal with it in a positive way.	Provide intensive and job-embedded professional development for all Dandy School District administrators and personnel about their roles in motivating—and demotivating—employees to work toward organizational goals.

continued . . .

Competing Interests			
(i.e., competing interests for power, influence, and resources)	Who became the high school principal? What were the competing interests that trumped John?	Find out what the problem is—and try to effectively resolve it.	
Tradition			
(i.e., school culture, rituals, meaning, heroes)	Dandy school officials may have a tradition of treating employees in this manner.	The school board should hire an expert to assess the district's climate and culture, educate them and central office about motivation and productivity, and develop and implement recommendations for improvement.	

OVERVIEW: LINKING EMPLOYEE NEEDS, BELIEFS, GOALS, AND PERFORMANCE

Twentieth century organizational leaders and industrial psychologists have tried to unravel the complexities of worker motivation and satisfaction. In the process, organizational thinking has shifting its focus—from rationality, structure, and control (without the complications of workers' needs or emotions)—to awareness that workers' feelings, beliefs, and perceptions bring an unavoidable irrationality and unexpected outcomes to organizational life. Frederick W. Taylor's scientific management pioneered the use of logically designed incentive systems as a way to motivate employees.[1] In the 1930s, the Hawthorne studies turned attention to how peer groups and supervisors impacted employees' performance and morale.[2] Since then, the hypothesized connections between employee motivation, satisfaction, and job performance has generated a high level of theoretical interest and research. Together, these help us identify and understand how employees' needs, beliefs, and goals affect human performance in organizations.

As a result, contemporary organizational and leadership theories all share a basic premise: people can be motivated to work more productively if the organization can fulfill certain socio-psychological needs. External political and economic influences including labor shortages, unionization, World War II, economic prosperity, and social science research findings contributed to this perspective. Now, leaders and administrators not only have responsibility for the visioning, planning, scheduling, and resources; they also must ensure the effective functioning of the workplace's social and individual systems. Understanding individual employees' needs, beliefs, and goals is essential if leaders are to identify appropriate ways to motivate better performance, higher satisfaction, and improved organizational outcomes.

DEFINING MOTIVATION

We all know what it feels like to be enthusiastic about engaging in an activity we really want to do—such as sports, art, music, or a hobby—that we do skillfully, attentively, and pleasurably. The passing hours can feel like minutes. Hard work feels like fun. Some call this "flow"[3] or being "in the zone"—a state of total concentration that allows our thoughts to run freely, easily, and creatively. We might say that we are motivated to perform this activity.

Motivation is the study of why people think and act as they do.[4] It is generally defined as an internal state that stimulates, directs, and maintains goal-directed behavior.[5] Motivation is what causes us to act, whether it is to make a sandwich or to read the newspaper. It involves the biological, emotional, social, cognitive, and contextual forces that activate behavior. Thus *motivation* is a psychological process that ensues from the interaction between the individual and the environment.[6] Context—the task itself, the situation, and the organizational culture—has the power to mediate opportunities for—and constraints against—employee behavior in organizations.

Motivation has three major components: *activation* (the decision to begin a behavior); *persistence* (the continued effort toward a goal despite obstacles in order to gain the desired outcome); and *intensity* (the concentration and vigor that goes into pursuing a goal). Motivation theories try to address these factors.

Several types of motivation help explain human behavior. *Intrinsic motivation* involves an individual's needs, interests, curiosity, and enjoyment. It is the natural tendency to seek and accept challenges as individuals pursue personal interests and use their capacities.[7] The activity, itself, is rewarding. In contrast, *extrinsic motivation* is a stimulus for doing an activity based on external incentives, rewards, pressures, and avoiding punishment. We work productively on the job to earn a salary, deserve a merit raise or a promotion, gain recognition and esteem, and to prevent a poor evaluation—even if we are not interested in the activity for its own sake. Combining intrinsic and extrinsic aspects, *work motivation* is a "set of energetic forces" that begins both inside and outside the person that initiates work-related behaviors and determines its form, direction, intensity, and duration.[8]

The main difference between intrinsic and extrinsic motivation is the person's reason for acting. Generally, a freely chosen purpose for action is intrinsic whereas an external pressure to act is extrinsic. But in work situations, intrinsic and extrinsic motives may blend. Teachers invest time and effort on a school improvement project that holds personal interest and because they believe the experience will benefit their students and help them grow professionally. It may even create the value-added that results in a desired promotion. In work environments, both intrinsic and extrinsic motivations support employee efforts and accomplishments. Accordingly, organizational leaders and managers must understand both aspects of motivation if they are to strengthen their employees' performance and achieve organizational goals.

MOTIVATION AND WORKER PSYCHOLOGY: NEEDS

Employee performance reflects both ability and motivation. Although environmental factors (such as the task itself, the situation, and the organizational culture) affect employee motivation and performance, the employee, as a distinct individual, brings internal factors—physiological and psychological needs—to the situation. These elements also influence how the worker will perceive and enact his/her job. Since motivation is an invisible, internal, and hypothetical construct, and we cannot see, touch, or measure it directly, we rely on established theories to help us understand and assess the ways motives express themselves in the workplace.[9] Abraham Maslow, Frederick Herzberg, Douglas McGregor, and David McClelland offer useful theoretical models of human needs as motivators.

Needs Hierarchy—Abraham H. Maslow

Abraham Maslow (1908–1970), one of the founders of humanistic psychology, studied self-actualizing people whom he admired. His models included Abraham Lincoln, Albert Einstein, and Eleanor Roosevelt. He investigated their frequent peak experiences, desires for creative work, and hopes for a better world.[10] Reacting against traditional behavioral psychology's view that human motivation is based solely on unmet basic needs and responses to external events, Maslow speculated that humans have inborn needs arranged in hierarchies of potency. Certain needs have priority over others; the appearance of one need usually depends on fairly well satisfying another, more basic need. He suggested five broad layers of need: physiological, safety, social, esteem, and self-actualization.[11]

Physiological Needs

These include human life's requirements for oxygen, water, protein, salt, sugar, calcium, and other vitamins and minerals. Additional physiological needs include getting enough activity and sleep, maintaining a pH balance and a body temperature near 98.6 degrees, and ridding oneself of wastes (such as CO_2, sweat, urine, and feces). Avoiding pain and having sex appear in this domain. A person who is extremely and chronically hungry or thirsty typically has no interest in anything but getting and consuming food and water.

Safety Needs

After individuals can regularly meet their physiological needs, safety and security needs become primary motives. The desire for order, structure, predictability, and limits may develop. Most Americans express safety needs by having a home, living in a secure neighborhood, having a steady job and a daily schedule, some money in the bank, life and medical insurance, and a good Individual Retirement Account.

Social Needs

When physiological and safety needs are largely met, individuals seek love and belonging. They usually want friends, a significant other, children, affectionate relationships, and membership in a community. Being a professional in a career fulfills part of this social need. Similarly, one aspect of individuals' sexual need is wanting love and affection, not simply physical arousal and release.

Esteem Needs

Maslow identified two types of esteem needs: lower and higher. The lower esteem needs include having others' respect, gaining status or prestige, recognition, reputation, appreciation, dignity, and perhaps, dominance. Higher esteem needs include the self-respect that comes from confidence, competence, achievement, mastery, independence, and freedom. Maslow considered the latter needs as "higher" because they did not depend on receiving them from others.

Self-actualization Needs

At Maslow's highest level, growth motivation takes priority. This stage reflects individuals' continuous desire to *self-actualize*: to fulfill potentials, to become the most complete person one can be. Self-actualizing behaviors include effectively using one's cognitive capacities (perceptual, intellectual, the desire to know and understand, and esthetic appreciation); being reality-centered (able to differentiate fake and dishonest from real and genuine); being problem-centered (actively find solutions to life's obstacles); able to separate means and ends (the journey can be as—or more—important than the outcomes); enjoying solitude as well as deep personal relationships with a few close family and friends; having autonomy (relatively independent of physical or social needs); and accepting of self, others, and nature (can be spontaneous and creative, and shows humility and respect toward others). At this stage, lower needs are largely met and the individual can fully pursue personal growth. Nonetheless, self-actualizers are not perfect; they can occasionally display the opposite of the qualities noted. Maslow suggests that only about two percent of the world's people are self-actualizing.[12]

Maslow saw the first four levels as *deficit needs* and the fifth level as *being needs*. Deficit needs are *survival needs*, essential to maintaining health and life. They hold our attention until they are satisfied. By contrast, being needs hold our attention without first feeling deprived. In his view, even love and esteem are essential to staying healthy. But under stressful conditions, or when the person perceives that survival is threatened, he or she can "regress" to a lower need level. For instance, when a teacher does not receive the desired promotion to department chair (esteem needs), he or she may seek friends with whom to commiserate and gain emotional support (safety and security needs). Likewise, an individual who experiences a significant problem when growing up—such as parents' divorce, serious illness, or death; frequent moves or homelessness; or economic or food insecurity—may have unmet survival, safety, security, and belonging needs that remain prominent throughout life. In addition, self-actualizers who do not fulfill their needs for meaningfulness, self-sufficiency, or other important values may develop depression, despair, alienation, and cynicism.[13]

Maslow observed that people's needs can be *relatively*—not 100 percent—satisfied before the next one emerges. In fact, most normal folks' basic needs are partially satisfied and partially dissatisfied. A satisfied deficit need is no longer a motivator. Maslow also believed that most behavior is multi-motivated, with several unmet needs acting simultaneously. Eating can be a necessity (physiological), an opportunity for gaining comfort (security), and an occasion for companionship (belonging). On the other hand, being needs tend to strengthen as a motivator as we fulfill them. At the same time, Maslow affirmed that biological, cultural, and situational factors—in addition to personal motives—can influence behavior. He came to believe that the needs hierarchy is not a rigid, fixed order. Rather, its sequence varies from person to person. Finally, Maslow concluded that much of what is wrong with the world is not the presence of bad people but people having unmet basic needs for survival, safety and security, esteem, love and belonging.[14]

At first glance, Maslow's theory connects to many of our own experiences and seems to have reasonable face validity; but investigators find it to be more useful than scientifically credible.[15] *Self-actualization* is a difficult construct to examine scientifically, and little research evidence exists to support its validity.[16] Of available studies, results are mixed: certain investigations support his concept,[17] some offer no support,[18] while a few refute the theory's claims of five distinct needs levels with a hierarchy of prepotency altogether.[19] In addition, research and theory in psychology find that a moderate amount of deprivation stimulates creative potential, keeps people motivated, is needed for healthy psychological development, and helps build a sense of competence needed for dealing with life's changes.[20]

As popular as Maslow's theory is in educational, clinical, and organizational settings, it has received much criticism.[21] Some psychologists argue that it has internal inconsistencies,[22] is reductionist (places too much faith in human biology), and incorrect.[23] Specifically, critics assert that certain people (such as Abe Lincoln and Eleanor Roosevelt, with very difficult childhoods) never fulfill their basis needs and yet become self-actualizing; Maslow downplays the role of environment and cultural in forming human personality and behavior; and he relies too heavily on Western and affluent cultures[24] (as well as American bias and elitism)[25] for his ideas about self-actualization and human development. In addition, naysayers accuse Maslow of using overstatement (i.e., simply because extreme deprivation is psychologically damaging does not mean that extreme ease of gratification is psychologically healthy)[26] or seeing self-actualization as a final stage in needs development rather than as an overriding "life force" motive in its own right.[27] Some conclude that Maslow's beliefs about an "intrinsic self" to be both naïve and harmful.[28] Critics also say Maslow's methodology—interviewing and studying a narrow sample of "successful" people and subjectively interpreting the findings as the basis for generating his theory—lacks empirical validation and critical evaluation.[29]

In fairness, Maslow never intended his theory to be accepted as "proven" but rather as a starting point for further investigation; and he often used criticism to rethink and revise his theory.[30] He saw himself as a pioneering psychologist who identified how meaning and purpose—not merely instinct or stimulus and response—motivated human life. His hierarchy offers a systematic way to think about the different needs that people have at any given time. Even Maslow's critics commend his theory's main outlines and recognize his serious scientific contribution to understanding individuals.[31] Just as Maslow concluded that we take our satisfied needs for granted, his motivation theory has become part of our contemporary culture.

Motivation/Hygiene Theory—Frederick Herzberg

In 1959, Frederick Herzberg (1923–2000), a Case Western Reserve University and medical school psychology professor and his colleagues, designed a two-factor theory of motivation: the motivation/hygiene theory. From his background in clinical psychology, Herzberg hypothesized that just as mental health and mental illness were two completely separate processes, job satisfaction contained two distinct processes. Certain job factors contribute to work satisfaction (motivation factors), and a separate list of factors contributes to work dissatisfaction (hygiene factors). Herzberg believed that Maslow's theory of personal growth and self-actualization helped explain employees' positive feelings about their jobs.[32] He made his theory measurable so it could be systematically researched, and he continued to extend and develop it.[33]

Herzberg proposed two psychological dimensions: satisfaction–no satisfaction, and dissatisfaction–no dissatisfaction. According to Herzberg, job satisfaction—or *motivation factors*—is the result of achievement, recognition, interesting work, increased responsibility, and advancement and/or learning. When present in a job, these intrinsic factors will satisfy the individual's needs related to personal growth and self-actualization. They will generate positive feelings and improved performance. The other dimension, job dissatisfaction—or *hygiene factors*—results from different features and describes the work context in which they are found. They include unfair company policies, incompetent or unfair supervision, poor interpersonal relations (especially with supervisors), unpleasant physical working conditions, threats to job status or security, and unsatisfactory salary or benefits. Motivator factors contribute to satisfaction–no satisfaction, and hygiene factors contribute to dissatisfaction–no dissatisfaction. Fulfilling hygiene needs can prevent dissatisfaction and poor performance, but only the satisfaction that results from motivation factors—the control and sense of meaningful achievement and personal growth—will bring the increased employee productivity. Herzberg argued that the most important difference between motivator and hygiene factors were that the motivator factors all involve psychological growth whereas the hygiene factors involve physical and psychological pain avoidance.

An application of Herzberg's theory—*job enrichment*—makes the work environment more meaningful and motivating by adding additional tasks to a job (horizontally) and requiring greater employee skill and judgment (vertically).[34] This approach has gained widespread popularity. In a 180-degree shift from the scientific management approach that produced simplified work tasks (and a reduced set of knowledge and skills to go with it), late twentieth century organizations endorsed job enrichment as a solution to the U.S.'s productivity problems.[35]

Research on Herzberg's dual-factor model has much support. His original study findings were consistent with his theory of motivators and hygiene factors[36]—although certain factors (such as salary) appeared to be both motivator and hygiene features.[37]

Additional studies partially support his two categories,[38] and strong correlations exist between the two-factor theory and research in intrinsic motivation.[39] Although research finds that employees who received job enrichment reported increases in job satisfaction and outperformed a control group on a variety of performance measures,[40] not all research supports the job enrichment theory.[41] Nonetheless, positive psychology studies in the 2000s—the study of positive human attributes and strengths—were consistent with the motivation-hygiene theory's basic tenets.[42]

Herzberg's critics take issue with several features of his theory and methodology.[43] They argue that Herzberg misinterpreted correlational data as causation, challenging his claim of identifying the "causes" of job satisfaction and dissatisfaction.[44] Overlapping factors as sources of satisfaction *and* dissatisfaction (such as salary, status, security, and interpersonal relationships) possibly negate the concept of a dual continuum.[45] Some believe that Herzberg's theory ignores the role of individual differences as a moderating variable,[46] while others object to his inconsistent use of terms.[47] Critics question the theory's generalizability, noting that Herzberg's research sample was predominantly white, male accountants and engineers in an era of heavy unionization, not representative of the range of occupational groups, individual diversity, and work environments that exist today.[48] Similarly, some contend that Herzberg's findings were artifacts of the particular research techniques.[49] In general, those investigations that replicated Herzberg's studies upheld the theory whereas those that used different methods tended not to support it.[50]

Although the dual-factor theory was never empirically validated or invalidated,[51] Herzberg's theory still has utility today. Many now regard the motivation/hygiene theory as an established and valid framework, a simple and practical paradigm that offers human resource professionals and organization leaders a model for promoting employee growth, development, and job satisfaction.

Theories X and Y—Douglas M. McGregor

Writing at a time when social science research was challenging traditional views about human nature in industrial organizations, Douglas M. McGregor (1906–1964), an MIT management professor, wrote *The Human Side of Enterprise* (1960).[52] McGregor asserted that organizational managers' assumptions about their employees' character— Theory X or Theory Y—influenced their choice of administrative behaviors. And, in a self-fulfilling cycle, employees responded accordingly.[53]

Managers who embrace Theory X (largely reflecting Scientific Management principles and Weber's idea of bureaucracy) assumes that the "average" person innately dislikes work, is lazy, untrustworthy, not very bright, lacks ambition, dislikes responsibility, is indifferent (or even resistant) to the organization's needs, and opposes change. As a result, the Theory X manager must rely on external control of workers' behaviors, using persuasion, rewards, or punishment to direct their actions and modify their behaviors to fit the organization's needs.

By comparison, those who adopt Theory Y (more in line with Follett, Mayo, Maslow, and Herzberg) depend mainly on workers' internal self-control and self-direction to guide their work behavior.[54] Theory Y asserts that spending physical and mental effort in work is natural as play or rest. Under proper conditions—such as serving objectives to which he or she is committed—the "average" person works hard, enjoys the work, is self-directed and self-controlled, often seeks to grow, accepts and seeks responsibility, and produces useful ideas and innovative solutions. Therefore, a managers' job is to create the conditions and practices that encourage workers to meet their own goals best by directing their efforts toward organizational goals. Theory Y management practices include job enrichment by reorganizing work to provide opportunities for satisfying social, esteem, and self-fulfillment needs, giving workers a voice in decisions that affect them, and including individual-generated goals and self-evaluations in performance appraisals.[55]

According to McGregor, human behavior in organizations is a result of the industrial organization's management philosophy, policy, and practices. To motivate workers, it is essential to consider their human needs. Using Maslow's five-level needs hierarchy of motivation, McGregor argued that when organization policies and practices deprive employees from meeting their social, esteem, or self-actualization needs, unproductive worker behaviors result. Thus, unwillingness to give more than minimal effort, hostility, resistance to change, and unwillingness to accept responsibilities at work are *symptoms* of employees' deprived social, egoistic, and growth needs. Good wages, generous fringe benefits, safe working conditions, and steady employment meet workers' physiological and safety needs. But without opportunities to meet their higher needs, people will feel deprived, and their actions on the job will reflect this.

Although Theory X/Y appears to have face validity and has become part of the leadership and management lexicon,[56] McGregor did not try to measure his constructs or conduct any research that directly tested his theory's validity.[57] He did, however, expect his work to generate scholarly interest and testable hypotheses.[58] Several research studies support Theory X/Y patterns and related employee outcomes (including health outcomes) and work culture qualities,[59] while other studies highlight positive parts of Theory X and criticize Theory Y's construct's incomplete theory of human motivation.[60]

Some critics question the relevance of McGregor's mid-twentieth century ideas about work motivation to the twenty-first century's uncertain work realities. Today's career paths, employees' sense of job security, job satisfaction, and the degree to which employees prefer security to creativity have markedly changed.[61] Critics also dispute a Theory X/Y based so closely on Maslow's needs hierarchy, a concept with its own theoretical and empirical challenges and that explains human—not *employee*—motivation.[62] Further, critics note that the theory may not be generalizable to other cultures;[63] it may even become less valid in the United States as American demographics and culture become increasingly diverse.[64] Likewise, critics point to Theory X/Y's misuse by managers who try to force fit Theory Y practices into a Theory X culture—a ploy that many employees see as dishonest and manipulative.[65] Arguing a different perspective, some assert that Theory X persists because it is appropriate for certain situations (i.e., emergencies), depends on the tasks to be performed (routine, detailed, bureaucratic), the subordinates to be managed (who prefer stable work environments and tasks), and the outcomes desired (adaptive rather than innovative); and certain people respond well to it.[66]

In McGregor's view, the difference between Theory X and Theory Y leadership behaviors is—"the difference between treating workers as children or treating them as mature adults."[67] Certain scholars view McGregor's Theory X and Y as one of the most important and influential theories in management and organizational behavior history.[68] Theory Y's optimistic view has become foundational to many principles of organizational development,[69] and its tenets remain a basic theory for explaining leadership and organizational values and practices. Building upon Maslow's notions, McGregor's Theory X/Y shows how organizational leaders can better motivate employees by respecting them for their innate capacities for responsibility, creativity, and personal growth and by shaping the conditions that encourage them to achieve the organization's goals. Although McGregor did not originate these ideas, he made them easy for practitioners to apply in their work settings.[70]

Acquired Needs Theory—David McClelland

David McClelland, (1917–1998), a Harvard University psychology professor, devoted his academic career to proposing and studying an acquired human needs theory. Building on Maslow's needs hierarchy, McClelland's 1961 book, *The Achieving Society*,[71] identified three motivators that he believed all people have as a result of their life experiences: a need for achievement (*n*Ach), a need for affiliation (*n*Aff), and a need for power (*n*Power). According to McClelland, all individuals possess a combination of these needs, and each need's strength acts as a motivator that leads a person to act in certain ways to satisfy it. McClelland pioneering work correlating *n*Ach with achievement or progress levels in several cultures and his finding that achievement behavior could be learned helped popularize his theory.[72]

As McClelland explained it, the *need for achievement—n*Ach—is an index of motivation, understood as a desire to excel for its own sake, for an inner feeling of personal improvement and accomplishment rather than for social recognition or prestige.[73] His research finds that individuals high in *n*Ach tend to act in certain ways. They prefer activities that involve skill and effort, provide moderate challenge and risk, present clear concrete performance feedback on how well they are doing, and offer opportunity to take personal responsibility for achieving the work goals. Individuals with high *n*Ach perform better at tasks in which they can measure their own progress. Societies in which members have a high *n*Ach have many entrepreneurs and high economic growth.

Similarly, people with a high need for affiliation—*n*Aff—tend to act in certain ways. They want to belong to the group; want to be liked and will often go along with group decisions; favor collaboration over competition; and dislike high risk or uncertainty.[74]

People with a high need for power—*n*Power—want to lead, influence, and control others; like to win arguments; enjoy competing and winning; and seek status and recognition.[75] McClelland identified two types of *n*Power—socialized power (i.e., influencing others for the sake of social, group, or organizational goals rather than aggrandizing oneself) and personal power (i.e., behavior that suggests personal dominance or aggression, such as fighting, sexual conquest, and excessive drug use).[76] When high *n*Power appears in a leadership motive pattern, individuals tend to have lower *n*Ach (so they can focus on positively influencing others' achievement rather than continually improving his/her own skills) and lower *n*Aff (making it easier for them to make difficult decisions for the good of the whole organization without undue concern about being disliked).[77] Maturity and a high degree of self-control (so as not to become authoritarian or aggressively self-serving) temper this leadership motive pattern.[78] Although both those with high *n*Ach and those with high *n*Power may produce "outstanding" work and may be consummate "achievers," people with strong *n*Power (such as military generals, politicians, and top executives) tend to be more involved in political life,[79] such as controlling communication channels up and down the organization. By contrast, those with high *n*Ach (such as business executives) may prefer to improve their own performance every day.[80]

In McClelland's view, these acquired needs are learned. All motives are personality factors learned at home through parents' early childrearing practices. Acquired needs exist regardless of culture or life experiences, and people's personalities and experiences influence which motivator is strongest. For instance, to learn the achievement motive, parents are warm, loving, encouraging, and flexible. They help their children set moderately high achievement goals.[81] As a result of this upbringing that also stresses independence and self-sufficiency, the individual's need for achievement remains a relatively stable predisposition throughout life.[82] In addition, certain religious and political ideologies reinforce the individualistic values in these childrearing practices. For example, mothers in the United States who have sons with high *n*Ach expect them to act in self-reliant ways at earlier ages than mothers of sons with low *n*Ach. Similarly, in test situations designed to observe parent-child interactions, parents of boys with high *n*Ach tended to set higher standards of excellence than parents of the "lows." McClelland also posits that adults can develop achievement motivation.[83]

Empirical studies on McClelland's three-part of needs theory offer extensive research support.[84] Certain studies do not, however—concluding instead that achievement is a multidimensional rather than a unitary construct.[85] Certain investigators suggest the need for further theory testing by "more objective" persons (than the constructs' originators).[86] Critics also fault McClelland's use of the Thematic Apperception Test for examining *n*Ach and other motives, citing its low reliability and methodological problems.[87]

Critics take issue with McClelland's concept of individual needs that work as independent motives to influence individuals' behaviors. They argue that needs for achievement, affiliation, and power, as constructs, are too inner-directed and would benefit from considering the roles of social interaction, the specific task, and contextual factors in influencing achievement.[88] Some contend that *n*Ach is too culture-, age-, and gender-bound and closely tied to the Protestant worth ethic to be universal and generalizable.[89] Certain critics suggest *n*Ach should be a developmental construct that takes different forms at different age levels.[90] This suggests that the quality is not childhood-based and stable but changes over time and situation.[91]

McClelland was one of the early advocates for considering employees' motivation. His insights about the achievement, affiliation, and power motives—that these are learned, and that people have and enact a mix of these characteristics—provides organizational leaders with an additional perspective about incentives that matter to its various members.

TABLE 4.1 Comparison of Needs Motivation Theories

Herzberg	Maslow (Being needs)	MacGregor	McClelland
Motivators for satisfaction	Self-Actualization Esteem Social	Theory Y motivators	nAchievement nPower nAffiliation
Hygiene prevent dissatisfaction	Safety Physiological (Deficit needs)	Theory X motivators	

Source: Leslie S. Kaplan and William A. Owings, 2017

Table 4.1 illustrates how McClelland's needs theory compares with Maslow, Herzberg, and MacGregor. Whereas Herzberg and MacGregor explicitly refer to Maslow's needs hierarchy as a reference point for their own needs theories, McClelland does not. One might assume that McClelland's needs for achievement, power, and affiliation might express human needs from any points on the needs scale.

REFLECTIONS AND RELEVANCE 4.1

Using the Needs Theories of Motivation

Maslow's five needs hierarchy, Herzberg's motivation/hygiene theory, McGregor's Theory X/Y, and McClelland's acquired needs theory all contribute to our understanding of human motivation in organizations.

Working in groups of four, discuss and answer the following questions. Then discuss the questions and answers as a class.

1. Identify one major idea *from each theorist* that you might use as a school leader to motivate your teachers, staff, and students—and give an example.
2. What human needs theorist, overall, do you think will influence your thinking and behavior the most as a leader who wants to motivate colleagues to achieve organizational goals? Explain how and why. Which theorist do you think will influence your thinking the least? Explain how and why.
3. What new insights, if any, have you gained from learning about these four needs theories?

MOTIVATION AND WORKER PSYCHOLOGY: BELIEFS

Although needs-based theories explain why a person must act, they do not explain why the person chooses specific actions to gain the desired outcomes. Unlike Maslow's, Herzberg's, McGregor's, and McClelland's *content* theories of motivation that focus on individuals' internal attributes (needs) as motivators, *process* theories of motivation—such as expectancy theory and self-efficacy theory—emphasize individual perceptions of the environment and the interactions that arise as a result of personal expectations. With belief theories, motivation can be understood as a conscious and cognitive process. Employees' beliefs about their abilities, their roles, their effectiveness in their assigned tasks, and the incentives they value receiving for performing well, all affect their impetus to work hard. Since expectancy theory and self-efficacy theory rely on intrinsic (i.e., individual's perceptions and beliefs) *and* extrinsic motivators (i.e., rewards, task difficulty relative to one's abilities) to explain workplace behavior, they offer a multifaceted approach to understanding employee motivation to do their jobs well.

Expectancy Theory—Victor H. Vroom, Lyman W. Porter & Edward E. Lawler

Expectancy theory has been called one of the most reliable and valid explanations of what motivates people to work.[92] It suggests that individuals, acting through self-interest, select action they perceive as maximizing their likelihood of attaining desirable outcomes. Victor H. Vroom (1932–), a Yale University School of Management professor who applied psychology to organizations, usually receives credit for developing the first complete version of expectancy theory for organizational settings.[93] Lyman W. Porter (1913–1990), an organizational psychology professor at University of California, Irvine and Edward E. Lawler III (1938–), a University of Southern California business professor and management researcher, built upon Vroom's concept to further develop the expectancy model.[94]

Expectancy theory rests on several basic assumptions:[95]

- People join organizations with expectations shaped by their needs, values, attitudes, personalities, abilities, goals, and past experiences. Each of these—along with environmental and situational factors (such as role perceptions)[96]—will influence how they react to the organization.
- Motivation is a conscious and cognitive process. Individuals make decisions about their own behaviors in organizations by using their capacities to think, reason, and anticipate the future.
- People want different things from the organization. These may include salary, job security, recognition, challenge, advancement, and growth.
- People choose among alternatives and behavior in ways that will optimize outcomes for themselves.

Expectancy theory proposes that the individual feels motivated to work when he or she perceives the following three conditions are present:[97]

1. *Expectancy*. Personally spending the effort will result in an acceptable level of performance. Effort and performance are related.
2. *Instrumentality*. The performance level achieved will result in a specific outcome for the individual. Good performances will be noticed and rewarded.

3. *Valence.* The outcome attained is personally valued. The person values the reward received to a certain extent.

These variables interact psychologically to create a motivational force that influences the employee to act in ways that bring pleasure and avoid pain. Any weakness in the links between expectancy and performance or between performance and outcome or in the degree of value the person attaches to the outcomes significantly affects the person's motivation. The person's motive strength is only as strong as its weakest link.

Figure 4.1 depicts Porter and Lawler's view of expectancy theory's relationship between work effort and employee satisfaction. When performance leads to rewards that the individual views as reasonable and desirable, they assume that high satisfaction will result.[98] The model suggests that the generally low performance-satisfaction link that appeared in earlier empirical studies may result from rewards not closely linked with performance.[99] This model does not account for all sources of employee satisfaction, however.

Although expectancy models have been the subject of much theoretical and research interest,[100] investigators disagree about the quality of the research and its findings. Some assert that the expectancy model has undergone rigorous empirical testing and deserves strong support.[101] Studies show that expectancy models can be used to fairly accurately predict choice of occupation, levels of job satisfaction, and levels of work effort.[102] Others, such as a 1996 meta-analysis of 77 studies covering nearly 30 years (1964–1990) of expectancy theory research on Vroom's work concludes that the model lacks validity and questions the earlier studies' methodology.[103]

Critics note that the expectancy model and its components are so complex and abstract, its terms so ambiguous (i.e., the many ways of defining "satisfaction" and "performance") and open to differing interpretations, that comparing or generalizing from empirical studies is problematic.[104] As a result, its practical usefulness is "questionable."[105] Others note that the theory is culture-bound, not relevant for non-United States populations.[106] Critics also challenge the theory for paying little

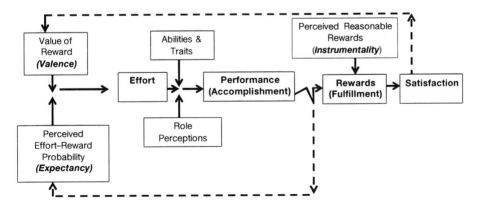

FIGURE 4.1 Expectancy Theory: Performance → Satisfaction

Source: Adapted from Pinder, C.C. (2008). The Porter-Lawler Model. *Work motivation in organizational behavior.* 2nd ed. (p. 373). New York, NY: Psychology Press.

attention to intrinsic rewards as motivators for doing a job well[107] and for not explaining how the relationships among expectancies, instrumentality, and valences occur.[108] In addition, skeptics question the theory's underlying assumptions,[109] its feasibility as a decision model,[110] and the absence of moderating variables (such as self-esteem).[111] They recommend that expectancy theory only be used as a within-person (rather than between persons) decision-making model or apply it at an organizational level.[112]

Despite the critics, expectancy theory has become a standard as a general framework for research in understanding employees' work motivation.[113] But even though the individual decision process it describes is probably accurate, the theory has little practical value as a predictor of employee work behavior. Nonetheless, organizational leaders benefit when they take the time to know each employee as an individual, learn the individual's reward preferences (valences), perceived skill levels and role options (instrumentalities), and outlooks about receiving meaningful "payoffs" in their organization (expectancies). In this way, leaders can identify more personalized incentives to motivate each employee to achieve desired organizational ends.

Self-Efficacy Theory—Albert Bandura

Albert Bandura (1925–), a Stanford University psychology professor, proposes that *self-efficacy*—how individuals' attitudes and expectations about their own ability to perform well in specific situations—helps them decide whether to engage in the activity and how much effort and persistence to use in the face of obstacles and unpleasant experiences.[114] In self-efficacy theory, cognition, behavior, and the environment interact and influence each other.

In Bandura's view, self-efficacy beliefs contribute to motivation in several ways. When confronted with obstacles or failure, people with self-doubts about their abilities—*low* self-efficacy—reduce their efforts or quickly give up. By contrast, those with strong beliefs in their capacities—*high* self-efficacy—put out greater effort when they do not master the challenge. A person with the same knowledge and skills may perform weakly, satisfactorily, or outstandingly depending on changes in their self-efficacy thinking.[115]

Additionally, people's self-efficacy—their belief that their competency can shape their environment and life path—influences their choices in interests, competencies, personal development, social networks, and careers.

Of course, expectations are not the only causes of behavior—nor do they produce the desired results—if the person's skills are not there. Given appropriate skills and adequate incentives, however, efficacy expectations are a major source of people's choice of pursuits, how much effort they will give, and how long they will stay with it if the situation becomes stressful. Notably, varied contextual factors—including the social situation, and specific circumstances—also influence the person's efficacy expectations.

Over time, people's self-efficacy judgments change as they gain new information and experiences from four information sources: mastery experiences (i.e., previously successful behavioral performances), modeling (i.e., observation of successful behavioral performance), verbal persuasion (i.e., convincing a person that he or she has the capability to perform a certain task), and physiological arousal (i.e., people's own anxiety and vulnerability to stress) at the time of the self-efficacy rating. The individual's cognitive appraisal and integration of these experiences determine their self-efficacy.[116] Mastery experiences are especially influential. Repeated successes raise expectations of, "I can do this!" Even occasional failures later are not likely to reduce the efficacy expectation: individuals can overcome their disappointing performances by a renewed effort and self-motivated persistence. Likewise, once established, strengthened self-efficacy tends to generalize to other situations in which the person had previous doubts about their own mastery—even if those activities are markedly different from those where they showed clear mastery. By contrast, repeated failures, especially happening early in the course of events, lower expectations for future successes. Teachers may not be ready to teach an intellectually rigorous curriculum, instruction, and assessment to every student until educators gain the necessary self-efficacy from seeing their own continuously improving and effective teaching practices.

Figure 4.2 depicts Bandura's view of how one's self-efficacy influences performance. The individual's self-appraisal influences one's choices of personal goals, effort, and persistence—along with one's knowledge and skills, and affected by the social situation and specific circumstances—leads to a performance. In turn, the feedback about how the individual perceives the causes of a successful or failing performance affects the person's analytical thinking about self-efficacy and later performances. Bandura believed that forethought included the person's expectancies and anticipated goals.[117]

A substantial body of research supports self-efficacy as a strong predictor of behavior.[118] This is especially true in educational settings: individual teachers' self-efficacy in instructional quality and effectiveness increases students' academic development;[119] faculty's collective efficacy in their instructional quality and students' academic progress strongly affects school culture;[120] and the lack of teachers' self-efficacy can harm students' self-efficacy and academic performance.[121] In non-education organizations, self-efficacy is associated with predicting and improving work-related performance in domains including learning and achievement,[122] adaptability to new technology;[123] enhanced self-efficacy increases performance,[124] and effective professional development methods.[125]

Critics of self-efficacy theory point to conceptual and methodological problems, arguing that Bandura's concept of efficacy is poorly defined, and the study methodology

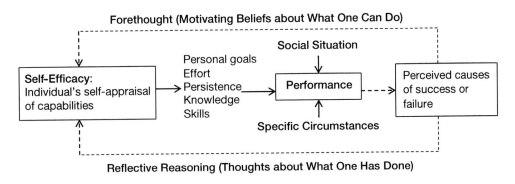

FIGURE 4.2 Albert Bandura's Model of Beliefs Motivating Behavior

Source: Adapted from Bandura, A. (1993). Perceived self-efficacy in cognitive development and functioning. *Educational Psychologist, 28* (2), 117–148 (Figure 8, p. 130).

is weak.[126] Social psychologists continue to debate the theorized relationship between self-efficacy and outcome expectancies: do they influence each other or does the causality only flow from self-efficacy to expected outcomes?[127] Since research appears to support both propositions, critics claim that it creates a "conceptual contradiction" that makes it difficult to design and enact interventions.[128]

Self-efficacy is an important factor in predicting and improving work performance in educational and other organizations.[129] People who think, with good reason, they can perform well on a task tend to do better than those who think they will fail. In addition, self-efficacy theory and its focus on cognitive processes underlying human motivation helps explain a variety of different motivation theories, including expectancy theory,[130] attribution theory,[131] and goal theory.[132] It is one of the bases underlying the success of schools' professional learning communities. As a motivation concept, its significance is well documented.

MOTIVATION AND WORKER PSYCHOLOGY: GOALS

During the 1950s and 1960s, before the insights from cognitive psychology changed how we understand human behavior, psychologists believed that "reinforcers" and "punishers" lying outside the person controlled his/her behavior. If the "motive" to act lay inside the person, psychologist's assumed the internal mechanisms were basically physiological or subconscious. Almost all agreed that introspection was not a valid method for understanding human motivation. T.A. Ryan (1970) proved to be an exception.[133] Ryan, a Cornell professor where Edwin Locke was studying for his graduate degree in industrial-organizational psychology, suggested that conscious goals affect behavior.[134] Since organizational psychologists are interested in being able to predict, explain, and influence employee performance on work-related tasks, focusing on the relationship between conscious performance goals and the level of task performance seemed like a good place to begin. And so Locke's dissertation started his development of goal setting theory.

Goal-Setting Theory—Edwin A. Locke and Gary P. Latham

Edwin A. Locke (1938–), a University of Maryland professor of leadership and motivation and his frequent collaborator, Gary P. Latham, a University of Toronto professor of organizational effectiveness, developed goal-setting theory. Interested in explaining why some people perform better on work tasks than others (apart from their knowledge and ability), Locke began by asking people what they were consciously trying to accomplish. What goals were they pursuing when they performed tasks? Locke and Latham reviewed evidence from many separate empirical studies[135] and continue to update and integrate goal setting theory with other theories.[136]

For Locke and Latham, a *goal* is what a person is consciously trying to accomplish, the object or aim of an action.[137] Internally, goals are ideas or desired outcomes. Externally, goals refer to the object or condition the person seeks, such as a certain job, performance level, or promotion. The idea guides action to achieve the object. In addition, goals have *two broad attributes*: *content* (the actual object sought) and *intensity* (the scope, focus, and complexity of the choice process). *Task specificity* (ranging on a continuum from "vague" to "specific") and *task difficulty* level (arrayed on a continuum from "easy" to "difficult" to "impossible") also affect goal setting.[138] *Difficulty* depends on the person's ability and experience to successfully complete the task, as well as its absolute complexity level. Goals that are both specific and difficult lead to the highest performance. Research supports these assertions.[139]

Goals affect performance through four mechanisms: directing attention, mobilizing effort, increasing persistence, and motivating strategy development.[140] First, goals direct a person's attention toward goal-relevant activities and away from goal-irrelevant activities. This effect occurs both cognitively and behaviorally.

Second, goals regulate effort and energy expenditure: high goals lead to greater effort than low goals (on simple lab-situated behaviors). Often, depending on deadlines, a trade-off occurs between intensity of effort and time: individuals may work faster and more intensely for a short period or work slower and less intensely for a long period.

Third, goals increase persistence of action or directed effort over time. The more the worker sees the goal as important and attainable, and the higher the worker's competence to do the task, the higher the persistence.

Fourth, goals influence the strategy one develops to attain their goals, including skill growth and creative problem solving. For example, when faced with task goals, people automatically use the knowledge and skills they have used before in similar situations. With new task goals, people engage in deliberate planning to develop the strategies to help them achieve their goal. And self-efficacy plays a role in goal setting: people with high self-efficacy are more likely to develop effective task strategies than are individuals with low self-efficacy.[141] Research supports these conclusions.[142] Specifically, empirical studies find that given sufficient ability and goal commitment, and the harder the goal, the higher the performance.

Locke and Latham also identified several moderators of goal setting: goal commitment, feedback, task complexity, and personal goals. *Goal commitment* is the strength of the person's determination to achieve the specific goal. The goal-performance relationship is strongest when people are dedicated to achieving their goals. This is especially key when goals are difficult because people will need high effort and face lower chances of success than with easy goals.[143]

Several factors facilitate goal commitment. First, goal commitment can be strengthened when individuals feel convinced of the goal's importance and its purpose or rationale (whether or not the goal was assigned or self-selected)[144] and feel certain that the goal is attainable (or at least make progress toward it). For instance, teachers who enter the profession with a sense of high purpose about their work's importance to American democracy, responsible citizenship, and their students' economic and social mobility are intrinsically motivated to the goal of ensuring each child's academic success and wellbeing.

Second, personal, self-set goals coinciding with prominent organizational goals also increase goal commitment.[145] When teachers working with colleagues in PLCs see themselves becoming more effective in fostering student learning, it reinforces their commitment to reaching the school's same goal.

Third, individuals increase their goal commitment when they feel self-efficacy. Employees gain self-efficacy through adequate training to increase mastery for success experiences, by finding role models, and by receiving persuasive communication that expresses believable confidence that the person can achieve the goal.[146] Self-efficacy influences the level of difficulty of the goal chosen or accepted, commitment to the goal, the individual's response to negative feedback or failure, and the choice of task strategies. In this way, ongoing professional development with direct application to classroom practices gives teachers occasion to practice their improving skills and see better student outcomes, heightening their confidence as effective educators.

Fourth, leadership can strengthen goal commitment.[147] As discussed in Chapter 3, transformational leaders raise the goal's importance to employees by helping them develop and express a shared, compelling vision, mission, and core values. Using inspiring messages, leaders frequently portray the goal as both desirable and attainable. As legitimate authority figures, leaders and managers can increase employees' efficacy through cognitive stimulation, acting as role models, expecting outstanding performance, delegating responsibility for key tasks, expressing genuine confidence in employees' capabilities, exerting reasonable pressure for performance, and building capacity through well-designed professional development.

In addition to goal commitment, feedback and task complexity also affect employees' goal setting. Employees increased their likelihood of setting goals when they receive specific feedback that reveals their progress in relation to their objectives. If employees do not know how well they are doing, they cannot adjust their efforts' level or direction to match what the goal requires. In schools, the daily formative data collecting and monitoring on student achievement give teachers essential information (feedback) about how well each student is mastering required curriculum objectives. These data help teachers plan instruction, reteaching, and extra tutoring. Likewise, task complexity plays a role in goal setting because more complex tasks require higher skill levels and work strategies (that not all employees assigned to the task may have). Research finds that when a complex task comes with a specific difficult *learning* goal (looking to improve employees' competence rather than compete on a *performance*), high goals lead to significantly higher performance on a complex task than does the general goal or urging people to "do their best."[148]

At the same time, goals are also a standard for judging employee satisfaction. Harder goals demand higher accomplishment in order to attain self-satisfaction than do easy goals. If a teacher is working toward a graduate degree in educational leadership, the person will not be satisfied unless he or she attains it—and the anticipated benefits in self-respect, salary, future job prospects, and life outcomes that come with it. To not attain the degree increases dissatisfaction. In experiments, the more goal successes one has, the higher one's satisfaction grows. And people with difficult goals produce more because they are dissatisfied when they produce less. Setting their satisfaction "bar" at a high level, they expect many psychological and practical results from setting and attaining high goals.

In Figure 4.3, Locke and Latham (1990) illustrate the factors that affect worker motivation. These include having high specific goals, high self-expectancy, mediated and moderated by several personal and contextual factors that lead to high performance,

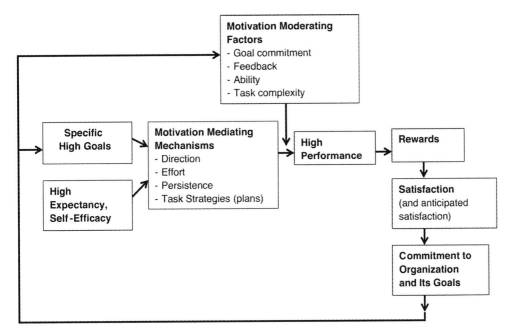

FIGURE 4.3 Goal Setting Theory: Motivation, High Performance, and Satisfaction

Source: Adapted from Locke, E.A. & Latham, G.P. (1990). Work motivation and satisfaction: Light at the end of the tunnel. *Psychological Science, 1* (4), 244.

rewards, satisfaction, and commitment to the organization and its goals, present and future.[149] Leaders play a major role in creating and maintaining this high performance cycle.

Lastly, Locke admits that goal setting can be dysfunctional. This occurs if goals are set for the wrong outcome or if a goal conflict exists. For example, if a person selects a specific, challenging goal for which he or she has no knowledge or expertise, he/she may not be able to identify useful work strategies. Demoralization and lower productivity may result. Similarly, goals that do not change even when relevant circumstances change may promote rigid and unproductive behaviors. For instance, teaching children to learn by rote for a factory economy does not prepare them to apply what they learn to solve problems and use critical thinking, skills essential for economic viability in today's knowledge-based economy. Persons may also use goals defensively, taking pride in their high aspirations without actually working to attain them.[150] For instance university professors who boast about their high number of "ABD" advisees (students who successfully complete "*A*ll *B*ut *D*issertation" for their Ph.D.) may point to their high expectations for graduate students' knowledge and performance. But the professors may not adequately be advising or teaching their doctoral students the knowledge, skills, and attitudes needed for success at this academic level.

Goals can also be misused by excessive risk taking. An ambitious principal who really wants to be a district superintendent may resign his or her position when invited for a superintendent job interview without having a signed contract for the desired position in hand. Goal setting may also increase stress, promote short-term thinking, and dishonesty.[151]

Studies on over 100 different tasks involving more than 40,000 participants in at least eight countries in laboratory and field situations find that setting a specific difficult goal leads to significant increases in employee productivity.[152] Goal setting studies also find links between goal setting and organizational profitability,[153] higher performance appraisals,[154] increased self-efficacy and self-regulation at work,[155] and establishment of a high-performance or high production cycle, rewards, high satisfaction, and high self-efficacy in perceived ability to meet future organizational challenges.[156] Goal setting has also been applied successfully in such domains as sports and health management and is deemed relevant to any self-directed activity.[157]

Early critics of goal setting theory point to gaps in theory development (some of which have since been addressed).[158] Some point to goal theory's harmful, unintended consequences.[159] Critical theorists take issue with its overly rational basis and argue it can only predict future outcomes in predictable and stable circumstances.[160] In response, Locke and Latham accuse critics of poor scholarship (such as using anecdotal evidence, citing unrepresentative studies, and misrepresentation) while admitting that goal setting, like any behavioral science technique, can be misused.[161]

Goal setting theory is arguably the most rigorously developed theory in organizational behavior.[162] It has practical applications, and it continues to mature. Goals are central or implicit variables in several theories of motivation in organizational behavior discussed in this chapter. Locke and Latham's focus on goals helped clarify and articulate its key role in employee choices, behaviors, and satisfaction.

REFLECTIONS AND RELEVANCE 4.2

Applying Belief and Goal-Setting Theories of Motivation

Expectancy, self-efficacy, and goal-setting theories all view motivation as a cognitive and conscious process. Working in groups of four, discuss and answer the questions below. When all groups have finished, discuss and answer the questions as a class.

1. Explain the specific aspects of expectancy, self-efficacy, and goal-setting theories that best explain the way you, as an individual, direct your career advancement. Illustrate with personal examples.
2. Identify which key ideas of each theory can help school leaders better understand and motivate their teachers, staff, and students to work toward attaining organizational goals. Give examples.
3. Which key ideas from these three motivation theories do you think will most influence your own leadership practice? Explain how and why.

IMPLICATIONS FOR EDUCATIONAL LEADERS

Rousing people to work vigorously and intelligently with others to achieve a common purpose is a key leadership challenge. Educators' personal needs, beliefs, and goals—interacting with the particular task, their skills, the specific situation, and the school environment—strongly influence how they think and act at work. The first step in motivating teachers is to build strong relationships with them as persons. Only by knowing each teacher and staff member as individuals can leaders address their needs, beliefs, and goals.

Addressing Relationships

It is not reasonable (or appropriate) to expect principals to develop deep, trusting, personal friendships with every teacher in their school. It is reasonable (and appropriate) to expect every principal or assistant principal to make certain that each teacher develops a mutually respectful and trusting working relationship with at least one of them.

Principals strengthen their teachers' work motivation when they establish a climate of respect for them as individuals with their own needs, beliefs, and goals. Only by knowing each teacher as a unique person can school leaders identify their needs, beliefs, and goals as they relate to increasing student learning and wellbeing. In this way, school leaders identify (and secure) the available incentives that mean the most to each teacher to incentivize their successful job performance. These mutually respectful relationships also permit mutual trust to develop—the assurance that each party will do as they say and follow through with their promises. Such practices strengthen the school's work climate in which all parties can feel safe, belonging, valued, and productive.

Addressing Needs

Different people want different things from their organizations. These may include an adequate salary, job security, collegiality, achievement, recognition, challenge, growth, and advancement. Although principals often lack the authority to raise salaries or to "hire and fire," they can create the conditions that encourage teachers to meet their own goals best by directing their efforts toward organizational goals. Leaders do this by providing opportunities for teachers to satisfy their affiliation and achievement needs by working with colleagues in an ethical professional community. Teachers can meet their growth needs with relevant and ongoing professional development and mentoring. Increasing competence brings teachers increased self-efficacy and the desire and persistence to take on important challenges. Similarly, leaders can give teachers a voice in decisions that affect them, recognize the learning curve necessary as teachers try out new practices and try on new beliefs.

Addressing Beliefs

Teachers' beliefs about their job's importance, their abilities to perform the job well, and the specific valued outcomes they expect to receive for doing so all impact on their work motivation. Again, school leaders can influence these. First, by articulating and repeatedly expressing an inspiring vision, an attainable mission, and core values needed to reach it, principals can strengthen teachers' beliefs about their work's significance and their own capacities to produce the desired results.

Second, principals strengthen teachers' beliefs about their own pedagogical competence—their self-efficacy—by providing ongoing opportunities to refine and extend their teaching effectiveness through reading, modeling, practice, observing others, giving and receiving feedback and encouragement. Their increasing confidence in their capacities to improve every student's learning will likely intensify teachers' attention and energies toward making it happen. Also, as legitimate authority figures, school leaders can increase teachers' self-efficacy by expecting outstanding performance, exerting reasonable pressure for accomplishing it, and delegating to them responsibility for key tasks that advance student outcomes.

Third, teachers' beliefs about what are "meaningful" rewards for performing well also motivate their impetus to work smartly. People choose among alternatives and behaviors—as swayed by environmental and situational factors—in ways that they think will bring them the maximum "payoff." When school leaders give each teacher the incentives that matter to them as individuals and consistently acknowledge their efforts and accomplishments, leaders strengthen the links between strong performance and desired outcomes.

Addressing Goals

A goal, what a person is trying to accomplish, directs attention and effort toward relevant activities, guides the choice of work strategies, and increases persistence to attain them. School leaders can strengthen teachers' goal commitment to increasing each student's academic success and wellbeing when they explain the school's objectives as highly desirable, realistically attainable, and adequately matched to the teachers' own capacities (and making certain, through professional development, that they do). Giving teachers occasions to set and meet their own professional goals within the organization and providing specific and timely feedback on their progress also helps them monitor their headway. When teachers can meet their personal, professional, and work goals at the same time, they increase their commitment to achieving them—and increase their satisfaction in doing so. Children, colleagues, and the larger community benefit.

NOTES

1 Taylor, F.W. (1911/1967), *Principles of scientific management*. New York, NY: Norton.
2 Roethlisberger, F.J. & Dickson, W.J. (1939/1956). *Management and the worker*. Cambridge, MA: Harvard University Press.
3 Csikszentmihalyi, M. (1990). *Flow: The psychology of optimal experience*. New York, NY: Harper and Row.
4 Graham, S. & Weiner, B. (1996). Theories and principles of motivation, In D. Berliner andR. Calfee (Eds), *Handbook of educational psychology* (pp. 63–84). New York, NY: Macmillan.
5 Hoy, W.K. & Miskel, C.F. (2013). *Educational administration. Theory, research, and practice*, 9th ed. (p. 170). New York, NY: McGraw-Hill.

6 Latham, G.P. & Pinder, C.C. (2005). Work motivation theory and research at the dawn of the twenty-first century. *Annual Review of Psychology, 56* (1), 485–516.

7 See: Deci, E. & Ryan, R.M. (1985). Intrinsic motivation and self-determination in human behavior. New York, NY: Plenum; Reeve, J., Deci, E. & Ryan, R.M. (2004). Self-determination theory: A dialectical framework for understanding the sociocultural influences on motivation and learning: Big theories revisited. (Vol 4, pp. 31–59). Greenwich, CT: Information Age Press.

8 Pinder C.C. (1998). *Work motivation in organizational behavior* (p. 11). Upper Saddle River, NJ: Prentice Hall.

9 Ambrose, M.L. & Kulik, C.T. (1999). Old friends, new faces: Motivation research in the 1990s. *Journal of Management, 25* (3), 231–292.

10 Hoffman, E. (2008). Abraham Maslow: A biographer's reflections. *Journal of Humanistic Psychology, 48* (4), 439–443.

11 Maslow, A.H. (1943). A theory of human motivation. *Psychological review, 50* (4), 370–396; Maslow, A.H. (1970). *Motivation and personality*, 2nd ed. New York, NY: Harper & Row; Maslow, A.H. (1968). *Towards a psychology of being*, 2nd ed. New York, NY: Harper & Row.

12 Maslow (1968). Ibid.

13 Boeree, D.G. (2006). Abraham Maslow (1908–1970). *Personality theories* (pp. 1–11). Retrieved from: www.social-psychology.de/do/pt_maslow.pdf.

14 Maslow, A.H. (1971). *The farthest reaches of human nature* (p. 300). New York, NY: Viking.

15 Arkes, H.R. & Garske, J.P. (1982). *Psychological theories of motivation* (p. 133). Monterey, CA: Brooks Cole.

16 Wahba, M.A. & Bridwell, L.G. (1973). Maslow reconsidered: A review of research on the need hierarchy theory. *Proceedings of the 33rd Annual Meeting of the Academy of Management*, 514–520.

17 See: Alderfer, C.P. (1969). An empirical test of a new theory of human needs. *Organizational Behavior and Human Performance, 4* (2), 142–175; Graham, W. & Balloun, J. (1973). An empirical test of Maslow's need hierarchy. *Journal of Humanistic Psychology, 13* (1), 97–108; Wuthnow, R. (1978). An empirical test of Maslow's theory of motivation. *Journal of Humanistic Psychology,18* (3), 75–77.

18 Lawler, E. & Suttle, J.L. (1972). A causal correlational test of the need hierarchy concept. *Organizational Behavior and Human Performance, 7* (2), 265–287; Miner, J.B. & Dachler, H.P. (1973). Personal attitudes and motivation. *Annual Review of Psychology, 24*, 379–402.

19 See: Hall, D.T. & Norigaim, K.E. (1968). An examination of Maslow's need hierarchy in an organizational setting. *Organizational Behavior and Human Performance, 3* (1), 12–35; Lawler, E.E. III & Suttle, J.L. (1972). A causal correlation test of the need hierarchy test. *Organizational Behavior and Human Performance, 7* (3), 265–287; Wahba M.A. & Bridwell, L.G. (1976). Maslow reconsidered: A review of research on the need hierarchy theory. *Organizational Behavior and Human Performance, 15* (2), 212–240.

20 See: Selye, H. (1974). *Stress without distress*. Philadelphia, PA: Lippencott; White, R. (1959). Motivation reconsidered: The concept of competence. *Psychological Review, 66* (5), 297–333.

21 For a detailed discussion of Maslow's theory's criticism, see: Neher, A. (1991). Maslow's theory of motivation: A critique. *Journal of Humanistic Psychology, 31* (3), 89–112.

22 Nehir (1991). Op. cit.; Smith, M.B. (1973). On self-actualization: A transambivalent examination of a focal theme in Maslow's psychology. *Journal of Humanistic Psychology, 13* (2), 17–33.

23 Geller, L. (1982). The failure of self-actualization theory. A critique of Carl Rogers and Abraham Maslow. *Journal of Humanistic Psychology, 22* (2), 56–73.

24 See: Daniels, M. (1982). The development of the concept of self-actualization in the writings of Abraham Maslow. *Current Psychological Reviews, 2* (1), 61–76; Geller, L. (1982). The failure of self-actualization theory. *Journal of Humanistic Psychology, 22* (2), 56–73;

Hofstede, G. (1980). Motivation, leadership, and organization: Do American theories apply abroad? *Organizational Dynamics, 9* (1), 42–63; Nehir (1991). Op. cit.; Pearson, E.M. & Podeschi, R.L. (1999). Humanism and individualism: Maslow and his critics. *Adult Education Quarterly, 50* (1), 41–55.

25 Buss, A.R. (1979). Humanistic psychology as liberal ideology: The socio-historical roots of Maslow's theory of self-actualization. *Journal of Humanistic Psychology, 193* (1), 43–55; Shaw, R. & Colimore, K. (1988). Humanistic psychology as ideology: An analysis of Maslow's contradictions. *Journal of Humanistic Psychology, 28* (3), 51–74.

26 Hoffman, E. (2008). Maslow in retrospect: Editorial board member assessments. *Journal of Humanistic Psychology, 48* (4), 456–457; Neher (1991) Op. cit.

27 Rennie, D.L. (2008). Two thoughts on Abraham Maslow. *Journal of Humanistic Psychology, 48* (4), 445–448; Nehir (1991) Op. cit.

28 Pearson, E.M. (1999). Humanism and individualism: Maslow and his critics. *Adult Education Quarterly, 50* (1), 41–56.

29 Neher (1991). Op. cit.; Seligman, M.E.P. & Csikszentmihalyi, M. (2000). Positive psychology: An introduction. *American Psychologist, 55* (1), 5–14.

30 Leontive, D.A. (2008). Maslow yesterday, today, and tomorrow. *Journal of Humanistic Psychology, 48*(4), 451–453; Maslow (1943). Op. cit.; Maslow, A. (1965). *Self-actualization and beyond.* Proceedings of the Conference on the Training of Counselors of Adults. May 22–28, 1965. Winchester, MA: New England board of Higher Education. ERIC. Retrieved from: http://eric.ed.gov/?id=ED012056.

31 Nahir (1991). Op. cit.

32 Herzberg, F., Mausner, B. & Snyderman, B.S. (1959). *The motivation to work.* New York, NY: Wiley.

33 Miner, J.B. (2015). Organizational behavior: Essential theories of motivation and leadership (pp. 61–74). New York, NY: Routledge.

34 Herzberg (1968/2003). One more time: How do you motivate employees? *Harvard Business Review, 81* (1), 87–96.

35 U.S. Department of Health, Education, and Welfare (1972). *Work in America.* Cambridge, MA: MIT Press.

36 Lodahl, T. (1964). Patterns of job attitudes in two assembly technologies. *Administrative Science Quarterly, 8* (4), 482–519; Schwab, D. & DeVitt, W. (1971). A test of the adequacy of the two factor theory as a predictor of self-report performance effects. *Personnel Psychology, 24*(2), 293–303.

37 Herzberg, Mausner & Snyderman (1959). Op. cit; In the studies, when salary was mentioned as a motivator, it was in relation to appreciation and recognition for a job well done—not as a factor, so researchers considered salary to primarily be a hygiene factor.

38 See: Bockman, V. (1971). The Herzberg controversy. *Personnel Psychology, 24* (2), 155–189; Schwab, D.P., DeVitt, H.W. & Cummings, L. (1971). A test of the adequacy of the two-factor theory as a predictor of self-report performance effects. *Personnel Psychology, 24* (2), 293–303; Bassett-Jones, N. & Lloyd, G.C. (2005). Does Herzberg's motivation theory have staying power? *Journal of Management Development, 24* (10), 929–943.

39 Sachau, D. (2007). Resurrecting the motivation-hygiene theory: Herzberg and the positive psychology movement. *Human Resource Development Review, 6* (4), 377–393.

40 See: Ford, R.N. (1973). Job enrichment lessons from AT&T. *Harvard Business Review, 51* (1), 96–106; Herzberg, F. & Zautra, A. (1976). Orthodox job enrichment: Measuring the quality in job satisfaction. *Personnel, 53* (5), 54–68.

41 See: Ewen, R., Smith, P., Hulin, C. & Locke, E. (1966). An empirical test of the Herzberg two-factor theory. *Journal of Applied Psychology, 50* (6), 544–550; Graen, G. (1966). Addendum to "An empirical test of the Herzberg two-factor theory." *Journal of Applied Psychology, 50* (6), 551–555; House, R. & Wigdor, L. (1967). Herzberg's dual-factor theory of job satisfaction and motivation: A review of the evidence and criticism. *Personnel Psychology, 20* (4), 369–389.

42 Seligman, M.E. & Csikszentmihalyi, M. (2000). Positive psychology: An introduction. *American Psychologist, 55* (1), 5–14.

43 For a thorough review of studies and criticism that refute Herzberg's theory, see: Stello, C.M. (2011). *Herzberg's two-factor theory of job satisfaction: An integrative literature review.* Department of Organizational Leadership, Policy, and Development, College of Education and Human Development, University of Minnesota. Retrieved from: www.cehd. umn.edu/olpd/research/studentconf/2011/stelloherzberg.pdf.

44 Farr, R. (1977). On the nature of attributional artifacts in qualitative research: Herzberg's two-factor theory of work motivation. *Journal of Occupational Psychology, 50* (1), 3–14.

45 See: Lindsay, C., Marks, E. & Gorlow, L. (1967). The Herzberg theory: A critique and reformulation. *Journal of Applied Psychology, 51* (4), 330–339; Maidani, E. (1991). Comparative study of Herzberg's two-factor theory of job satisfaction among public and private sectors. *Public Personnel Management, 20* (4), 441–448.

46 Gaziel, H. (1986). Correlates of job satisfaction: A study of the two factor theory in an educational setting. *The Journal of Psychology, 120* (6), 613–626.

47 King (1970). Op. cit.

48 Stello (2011). Op. cit.; Gibson, J.L., Ivancevich, J.M. & Donnelly, J.H. Jr. (1985). *Organizations: Behavior, structure, processes.* Plano, TX: Business Publication.

49 Herzberg used the critical incident method in which people have the tendency to give socially desirable responses and not of the underlying attitudinal and motivational facts. See: Wall, T. & Stephenson, G. (2007). Herzberg's two-factor theory of job attitudes: A critical evaluation and some fresh evidence. *Industrial Relations Journal, 1* (3), 41–65.

50 Bassett-Jones & Lloyd (2005). Op. cit.; Stello (2011). Op. cit.

51 Stello (2011). Op. cit.

52 McGregor, D. (1960). *The human side of enterprise.* New York, NY: McGraw-Hill.

53 McGregor uses the term "managers" to refer to managers of managers, an organizational leadership role. See McGregor (1960). Ibid, p. 55.

54 McGregor, D.M. (1957). The human side of enterprise. *Management Review, 46* (11), 22–28.

55 McGregor (1967). *The professional manager.* New York, NY: McGraw-Hill.

56 Kopelman, R.E., Prottas, D. & Falk, D.W. (2010). Construct validation of a Theory X/Y behavior scale. *Leadership and Organizational Development Journal, 31* (2), 120–135.

57 Miner, J.B. (2002). *Organizational behavior: Foundations, theories, and analyses.* New York, NY: Oxford University Press.

58 McGregor (1967). Op. cit., p. 55.

59 See: Balfour, D.L. & Marini, F. (1991). Child and adult, X and Y: Reflections on the process of public administration education, *Public Administration Review, 51* (6), 478–485; Larsson, J., Vinberg, S. & Wiklund, H. (2007). Leadership, quality, and healthy: Using McGregor's X and Y theory for analyzing values in relation to methodologies and outcomes. *Total Quality Management and Business Excellence, 18* (10), 1147–1168.

60 Bobic, M.P. & Davis, W.E. (2003). A kind word for Theory X: Or why so many newfangled management techniques quickly fail. *Journal of Public Administration Research & Theory, 13* (3), 239–265.

61 Bobic & Davis (2003). Ibid.

62 Bobic & Davis (2003). Op. cit.

63 Hofstede, G. (1987). The applicability of McGregor's theories in South East Asia. *Journal of Management Development, 6* (3), 9–18; Hofstede, G. (1994). Management scientists are human. *Management Science, 40* (1), 4–13.

64 Bobic & Davis (2003). Op. cit.

65 Heil, G., Bennis, W. & Stephens, D.C. (2000). *Douglas McGregor revisited: Managing the human side of the enterprise.* New York, NY: John Wiley and Sons.

66 Kirton, M.J. (1985). Adapters, innovators, and paradigm consistency. *Psychological Reports, 57* (2), 487–490.

67 McGregor (1957). Ibid., 27.

68 See: Bedeian, A.G. & Wren, D.A. (2001). Most influential management books of the 20th century. *Organizational Dynamics, 29* (3), 221–225; Carson, C.M. (2005). A historical view of Douglas McGregor's theory Y. *Management Decision, 43* (3), 450–460; Crainer, S. & Dearlove, D. (2006). The short history of great business ideas. *Business Strategy Review, 17* (3), 10–18.

69 Argyris, C. (1971). *Management and organizational development: The path from XA to YB.* New York, NY: McGraw-Hill; Friedlander, F. & Brown, L.D. (1977). Research on organization development: A synthesis and some implications. In W.W. Burke, (Ed.), *Current issues and strategies in organization development.* New York, NY: Human Science Press.

70 Carson, C.M (2005). A historical view of Douglas McGregor's theory Y. *Management Decision, 43* (3), 450–460.

71 McClelland, C.C. (1961). *The achieving society.* New York, NY: Free Press.

72 McClelland, D.C. & Winter, D. (1969). *Motivating economic achievement.* New York, NY: Free Press; Harrell, A.M. & Stahl, M.J. (1981). A behavioral decision theory approach for measuring McClelland's trichotomy of needs. *Journal of Applied Psychology, 66* (2), 242–247.

73 McClelland, D.C. (1966). The achievement motive in economic growth. In B.F. Hoselitz and W. E. Moore (Eds), *Industrialisation and society* (p. 76). New York, NY: UNESCO.

74 McClelland, D.C. (1965). Toward a theory of motive acquisition. *American Psychologist, 20* (5), 321–333.

75 McClelland, D.C. & Burnham, D.H. (1991). Good guys make bum bosses, In D.A. Kolb, I.M. Rubin, & J.S. Osland (Eds), *The organizational behavior reader,* 5th ed. (pp. 124–127). Englewood Cliffs, NJ: Prentice Hall.

76 McClelland, D.C. (1970). The two faces of power. *Journal of International Affairs, 24* (1), 29–47; McClelland, D.C. (1975). *Power: The inner experience.* New York, NY: Irvington.

77 McClelland, D.C. & Boyatzis, R.E. (1982). Leadership motive pattern and long-term success in management. *Journal of Applied Psychology, 67* (6), 737–743. The authors add that those with the leadership motive pattern also have other characteristics and values that make them effective in their organizational role; McClelland & Burnham (1976). Op. cit.

78 McClelland, D.C. & Burnham, D.H. (1976). Power is the great motivator. *Harvard Business Review, 25* (2), 159–166.

79 McClelland & Burnham (1976). Ibid.

80 McClelland (2001). Op. cit.

81 McClelland, D.C. (2001). The urge to achieve. In J.S. Osland, D.A. Kolb & I.M. Rubin (Eds), *The organizational behavior reader,* 7th ed., (pp. 94–96). Upper Saddle River, NJ: Prentice Hall.

82 Kagan, J. & Moss, H.A. (1962). *Birth to maturity.* New York, NY: Wiley.

83 McClelland (1961). Op. cit.; McClelland (1965). Op. cit.

84 Miner, J.B. (2015). *Organizational behavior: Essential theories of motivation and leadership* (p. 46). New York, NY: Routledge. Harrell, A.M. & Stahl, M.J. (1981). A behavioral decision theory approach for measuring McClelland's trichotomy of needs. *Journal of Applied Psychology, 66* (2), 242–247; McClelland & Boyatzis (1982). Op. cit.

85 Jackson, D.N., Ahmed, S.A. & Heapy, N.A. (1976). Is achievement a unitary concept? *Journal of Research in Personality, 10* (1), 1–21.

86 Erasmus, C.H. (1962). Book Review. *The achieving society. American Anthropologist, 64* (3), 622–625.

87 de Charms, R. (1958). A self-scored projective measure of achievement and affiliation motivation. *Journal of Consulting Psychology, 22* (3), 172; Reitman, W.R. & Atkinson, J.W. (1958). Some methodological problems in the use of thematic apperceptive measures of human motives. In J.W. Atkinson (Ed.), *Motives in fantasy, action, and society.* (pp. 664–683), Princeton, NJ: Van Nostrand.

88 Erasmus (1962). Ibid.; Maehr, M.L. & Nicholls, J.G. (1980). Culture and achievement motivation: A second look. In N. Warren (Ed.), *Studies in cross-cultural psychology*, 3. (pp. 192–326) New York, NY: Academic Press.
89 See: Atkinson, J.W. & Raynor, J.O. (1974). *Motivation and achievement*. New York, NY: Wiley; Triandis, H.C. (1994). Cross-cultural industrial and organizational psychology. In H.C. Triandis, M.D. Dunette & L.M. Hough. *Handbook of industrial and organizational psychology*, 2nd ed. Palo Alto, CA: Consulting Psychology Press; Wilken, P.H. (1979). *Entrepreneurship: A comparative and historical study*. Norwood, NJ: Ablex.
90 Maehr &Nicholls (1980). Op. cit.
91 See: Entwisle, D.R. (1972). To dispel fantasies about fantasy-based measures of achievement motivation. *Psychological Bulletin*, 77 (6), 377–391; Rauch, A. & Frese, M. (2000). Psychology approaches to entrepreneurial success: A general model and an overview of findings. In C.L. Cooper and I.T. Robertson (Eds), *International review of industrial and organisational psychology*. Chichester, UK: Wiley.
92 Hoy & Miskel (2013). Op. cit., p. 156.
93 Vroom, V.H. (1964). *Work and motivation*. New York, NY: Wiley.
94 Porter, L.W. & Lawler, E.F. (1968). *Managerial attitudes and performance*. Homewood, IL: Dorsey Press.
95 Vroom (1964). Op. cit.
96 Role perceptions are the kinds of activities and behaviors the individual believes he/she should do to perform his/her job successfully. Porter and Lawler (1968) added this dimension to expectancy theory.
97 Isaac, R.G., Zerbe, W.J. & Pitt, D.C. (2001). Leadership and motivation: The effective application of expectancy theory. *Journal of Managerial Issues*, 13 (2), 212–226.
98 Lawler, E.E. III (1987). Attitude surveys and job performance. *Personnel Administration*, 30 (5), 22–24; Porter, L.W. & Lawler, E.E. III (1986). What job attitudes tell about motivation. *Harvard Business Review*, 46 (January–February), 118–136; Porter & Lawler (1968). Op. cit.
99 Lawler, E.E. III & Porter, L.W. (1967). The effect of performance on job satisfaction. *Industrial Relations*, 7 (1), 20–28.
100 Van Eerde, W. & Thierry, H. (1996). Vroom's expectancy models and work-related criteria: A meta-analysis. *Journal of Applied Psychology*, 81 (5), 575–586.
101 See: Arnold, H.J. (1981). A test of the validity of the multiplicative hypotheses of expectancy-valence theories of work motivation. *Academy of Management Journal*, 24 (1), 128–141; Fudge, R.S. & Schlacter, J.L. (1999). Motivating employees to act ethically: An expectancy theory approach. *Journal of Business Ethics*, 18 (3), 295–304; Klein, H.J. (1991). Further evidence on the relationships between goal setting and expectancy theories. *Organizational Behavior and Human Decision Processes*, 49 (2), 230–257.
102 Ambrose, M.L. & Kulik, C.T. (1999). Old friends, new faces: Motivation research in the 1990s. *Journal of Management*, 25 (3), 231–292.
103 Van Eerde & Thierry (1996). Op. cit.
104 Lawler, E.E., III, & Suttle, J.L. (1973). Expectancy theory and job behavior. *Organizational Behavior and Human Performance*, 9 (3), 482–503.
105 Miner, J.B. (2003). The rated importance, scientific validity, and practical usefulness of organizational behavior theories: A quantitative review. *Academy of Management Learning & Education*, 2 (3), 250–268.
106 Hofstede (1980). Op. cit.
107 Deci, E.L. (1976). The hidden costs of rewards. *Organizational Dynamics*, 4 (3), 61–72.
108 Mitchell, T. R. (1974). Expectancy models of job satisfaction, occupational preference and effort: A theoretical, methodological, and empirical appraisal. *Psychological Bulletin*, 81 (12), 1053–1077.
109 Mitchell (1974). Ibid.
110 Mitchell (1974). Op. cit.

111 Korman, A.K. (1968). Task success, task popularity, and self-esteem as influences on task liking. *Journal of Applied Psychology, 52* (6), 484–490.

112 Ambrose & Kulik (1999). Op. cit.; Chen, M. & Miller, D. (1994). Competitive attack, retaliation, and performance: An expectancy-valence framework. *Strategic Management Journal, 15* (2), 85–102; Mitchell (1974). Op. cit.

113 Ambrose & Kulik (1999). Op. cit.

114 Bandura, A. (1977). Self-efficacy: Toward a unifying theory of behavioral change. *Psychological Review, 84* (2), 191–215.

115 Bandura, A. (1993). Perceived self-efficacy in cognitive development and functioning. *Educational Psychologist, 28* (2), 117–148.

116 Bandura, A. (1982). Self-efficacy mechanism in human agency. *American Psychologist, 37* (2), 122–147.

117 Bandura, A. (1993). Perceived self-efficacy in cognitive development and functioning. *Educational Psychologist, 28* (2), 117–148.

118 See: Holden, G. (1991). The relationship of self-efficacy appraisals to subsequent health related outcomes: A meta-analysis. *Social Work in Health Care, 16* (1), 53–93; Holden, G., Moncher, M.S., Schinke, S.P. & Barker, K.M. (1990). Self-efficacy of children and adolescents: A meta-analysis. *Psychological Reports, 66* (3), 1044–1046; Sadri, G. & Robertson, I.T. (1993). Self-efficacy and work related behavior: A review and meta-analysis. *Applied Psychology: An International Review, 42* (2), 139–152.

119 See: Ashton, P.T. & Webb, R.B. (1986). *Making a difference: Teachers' sense of efficacy and student achievement.* White Plains, NY: Longman; Gibson, S. & Dembo, M.H. (1984). Teacher efficacy: A construct validation. *Journal of Educational Psychology, 76* (4), 569–582; Woolfolk, A.E. & Hoy, W.K. (1990). Prospective teachers' sense of efficacy and belief about control. *Journal of Educational Psychology, 56* (3), 407–415.

120 See: Brookover, W.B., Beady, C., Flood, P., Schweitzer, J. & Wisenbaker, J. (1979). *School social systems and student achievement: Schools make a difference.* New York, NY: Prager; Good, T.L. & Brophy, J.E. (1986). Schools effects. In M.C. Wittrock (Ed.), *Handbook of research on teaching,* 3rd ed.,(pp. 570–602). New York, NY: McMillan; Rutter, M., Maughan, B., Mortimore, P., Ouston, J. & Smith, A. (1970). *Fifteen thousand hours: Secondary schools and their effects on children.* Cambridge, MA: Harvard University Press.

121 Midgley, C., Feldlaufer, H. & Eccles, J.S. (1989). Change in teacher efficacy and student self- and task-related beliefs in mathematics during the transition to junior high school. *Journal of Educational Psychology, 81* (2), 247–258.

122 Campbell, N.K. & Hackett, G. (1986). The effects of mathematics task performance on math self-efficacy and task interest. *Journal of Vocational Behavior, 28* (2), 149–162; Wood, R.E. & Locke, E.A. (1987). The relation of self-efficacy and grade goals to academic performance. *Educational and Psychological Measurement, 47* (4), 1013–1024.

123 Hill, T., Smith, N.D. & Mann, M.F. (1987). Role of efficacy expectations in predicting the decision to use advanced technologies. *Journal of Applied Psychology, 72* (2), 307–314.

124 Gist, M.E. (1989). The influence of training method on self-efficacy and idea generation among managers. *Personal Psychology, 42* (4), 787–805.

125 Frayne, C.A. & Latham, G.P. (1987). Application of social learning theory to employee self-management of attendance. *Journal of Applied Psychology, 72* (3), 387–392; Gist (1989). Op. cit.; Gist et al. (1989). Op. cit.

126 Williams, D.M. (2010). Outcome expectancy and self-efficacy: Theoretical implications of an unresolved contradiction. *Personality and Social Psychology Review, 14* (4), 417–425; Eastman, C. & Marzillier, J.S. (1984). Theoretical and methodological difficulties in Bandura's self-efficacy theory. *Cognitive Therapy and Research, 8* (3), 213–229.

127 Williams (2010). Op. cit.

128 Williams (2010). Op. cit.

129 Gist, M.E. (1987). Self-Efficacy: Implications for organizational behavior and human resource management. *Academy of Management Review*, 12 (3), 477–485; Gist, M.E. & Mitchell, T.R. (1992). Self-efficacy: A theoretical analysis of its determinants and malleability. *Academy of Management Review*, 17 (2), 183–211.

130 See: deVries, H., Dijkstra, M. & Kuhlman, P. (1988). Self-efficacy: The third factor besides attitude and subjective norm as a predictor of behavioral intentions. *Health Education Research*, 3 (3), 273–282; Madden, T.J., Ellen, P.S. & Ajzen, I. (1992). A comparison of the theory of planned behavior and the theory of reasoned action. *Personality and Social Psychology Bulletins*, 18 (1), 3–9.

131 Briefly, attribution theory focuses on how the ways individuals perceive the cause of their own or others' performance—as a function of ability, effort, task difficulty, or luck—influences their later choices and actions. See: Chwalisz, K.D., Altmaier, E.M. & Russell, D.W. (1992). Causal attributions, self-efficacy cognitions, and coping with stress. *Journal of Social and Clinical Psychology*, 11 (4), 377–400; Schunk, D.H. & Gunn, T.P. (1986). Self-efficacy and skill development: Influence of task strategies and attributions. *Journal of Educational Research*, 79 (4), 238–244.

132 Locke, E.A. & Latham, G.P. (1990). *A theory of goal setting and task performance.* Englewood Cliffs, NJ: Prentice-Hall.

133 Ryan, T.A. (1970). *Intentional behavior.* New York, NY: Ronald Press.

134 Locke, E.A. & Latham, G.P. (2002). Building a practically useful theory of goal setting and task motivation: A 35-year odyssey. *American Psychologist*, 57 (9), 705–717.

135 Latham & Pinder (2005). Op. cit.; Locke, E.A. & Latham, G.P. (2005). Goal setting theory: Theory building by induction. In K. Smith & M. Hitt (Eds), *Great minds in management.* New York, NY: Oxford University Press.

136 Locke, E.A. & Latham, B.P. (1990b). Work motivation and satisfaction: Light at the end of the tunnel. *Psychological Science*, 1 (4), 240–246.

137 Locke, E.A. (1968). Toward a theory of task motivation and incentives. *Organizational Behavior and Human Performance*, 3 (2), 157–189.

138 Latham, G.P. & Locke, E.A. (1991). Self-regulation through goal setting. *Organizational Behavior and Human Decision Processes*, 50 (2), 212–247.

139 Latham, B.P. & Yukl, G.A. (1975). A review of research on the application of goal setting in organizations. *Academy of Management Journal*, 18 (4), 824–845; Locke & Latham (1991). Op. cit.; Locke (1996). Op. cit.; Mento, A.J., Steel, R.P. & Karren, R.J. (1987). A meta-analytic study of the effects of goal setting on task performance: 1966–1984. *Organizational Behavior and Human Decision Processes*, 39 (1), 52–83.

140 Locke, E.A., Shaw, K.N., Saari, L.M. and Latham, G.P. (1981). Goal setting and task performance 1969–1980. *Psychological Bulletin*, 90 (1), 125–152.

141 See: Wood, R. & Locke, E. (1990). Goal setting and strategy effects on complex tasks. In B. Staw & L. Cummings (Eds), *Research in organizational behavior*, 12 (1), 73–109. Greenwich, CT: JAI Press; Latham, G.P. & Kinne, S.B. (1974). Improving job performance through training in goal setting. *Journal of Applied Psychology*, 59 (2), 187–191; Latham, G.P. & Baldes, J. (1975). The "practical significance" of Locke's theory of goal setting. *Journal of Applied Psychology*, 60 (1), 122–124.

142 See: Locke, E.A. & Latham, G.P. (2002). Building a practically useful theory of goal setting and task motivation: A 35-year odyssey. *American Psychologist*, 57 (9), 705–717; Latham & Yukl (1975). Op. cit.

143 Erez, M. & Zidon, I. (1984). Effects of goal acceptance on the relationship of goal setting and task performance. *Journal of Applied Psychology*, 69 (1), 69–78.

144 Latham, G.P., Erez, M. & Locke, E. (1988). Resolving scientific disputes by the joint design of crucial experiments by the antagonists: Application to the Erez–Latham dispute regarding participation in goal setting. *Journal of Applied Psychology*, 73 (4), 753–772.

145 Locke, E.A. (1991). The motivation sequence, the motivation hub and the motivation core. *Organizational Behavior and Human Decision Processes*, 50 (2), 288–299.

146 Bandura, A. (1997). *Self-efficacy: The exercise of control.* New York, NY: Freeman; White, S. & Locke, E. (2000). Problems with the Pygmalion effect and some proposed solutions. *Leadership Quarterly, 11* (3), 389–415.

147 Locke, E.A. & Associates (1991). *The essence of leadership.* New York, NY: Lexington (Macmillan).

148 Kanfer, R. & Ackerman, P.L. (1989). Motivation and cognitive abilities: An integrative aptitude treatment interaction approach to skill acquisition. *Journal of Applied Psychology, 74* (4), 657–690; Winters, D. & Latham, G. (1996). The effect of learning versus outcome goals on a simple versus a complex task. *Group and Organization Management, 21* (2), 236–250.

149 Locke & Latham (1990b). Op. cit.

150 Locke, E.A., Smith, K.G., Erez, M.E., Chah, D-Ok. & Shaffer, A. (1994). The effects of intra-individual goal conflict on performance. *Journal of Management, 20* (1), 67–91.

151 Locke, E.A. & Latham, G.P. (1984). *Goal setting: A motivational technique that works.* Englewood Cliffs, NJ: Prentice Hall.

152 See: Locke & Latham (1984). Ibid.; Latham, G.P. & Kinne, S.B. (1974). Improving job performance through training in goal setting. *Journal of Applied Psychology, 59* (2), 187–191; Latham, G.P. & Baldes, J. (1975). The "practical significance" of Locke's theory of goal setting. *Journal of Applied Psychology, 60* (1), 122–124.

153 Terpstra, D.E. & Rozell, E.J. (1994). The relationship of goal setting to organizational profitability. *Group and Organization Management, 19* (3), 285–294.

154 Latham, G.P., Mitchell, T.R. & Dossett, D.L. (1978). The importance of participative goal setting and anticipated rewards on goal difficulty and job performance. *Journal of Applied Psychology, 63* (2), 163–171; Brown, T.C. & Latham, G.P. (2000). The effects of goal setting and self-instruction training on the performance of unionized employees. *Industrial Relations, 55* (1), 80–94.

155 Frayne, C.A. & Latham, G.P. (1987). The application of social learning theory to employee self-management of attendance. *Journal of Applied Psychology, 72* (3), 387–392.

156 Locke, E.A. & Latham, G.P. (1990a). *A theory of goal setting and task performance.* Englewood Cliffs, NJ: Prentice Hall.

157 Locke & Latham (2002). Op. cit.

158 Latham & Yukl (1975). Op. cit.

159 Clegg, S. & Bailey, J.R. (Eds), (2008). *Goal-setting theory. International encyclopedia of organization studies* (pp. 580–583). Thousand Oaks, CA: Sage; Ordóñez, L., Schweitzer, M., Galinsky, A. & Bazerman, M. (2009). Goals gone wild: The systematic side effects of over-prescribing goal setting. *HBS Working Paper*, 09-983. Retrieved from: www.hbs.eduy/faulty/Publication%20Files/09-083.pdf. Negative consequences of goal setting include narrowing organization's focus that neglects important but non-specified goal areas (i.e., working for quarterly profits rather than long term sustainability), distorting risk preferences, increasing unethical behaviors, inhibiting learning, forming a culture of competition rather than cooperation (and resulting in lowered overall performance), and reducing intrinsic motivation.

160 Kayes, D.C. (2004). The 1996 Mt. Everest climbing disaster: The breakdown of learning in teams. *Human Relations, 57* (10), 1236–1284.

161 Locke, E.A. & Latham, G.P. (2009). Has goal setting gone wild, or have its attackers abandoned good scholarship? *Academy of Management Perspectives, 23* (1), 17–23.

162 Pinder, C. (1998). *Work motivation in organizational behavior.* Englewood Cliffs, NJ: Prentice Hall.

CHAPTER **5**

Leading Organizational Change/Organizational Learning

CASE STUDY 5.1

Too Many Suspensions. Why?

After eight years teaching at the 2,000 student Battendown Middle School, Ian Sutherland received an appointment as one of the five assistant principals. As a social studies teacher at Battendown, he had worked with the principal all these years, asking for leadership opportunities even before he entered the educational leadership program at the local university. During this time, Battendown Middle had contended with large numbers of discipline referrals—so many that the school board funded an additional assistant principal position primarily to deal with them. Ian's new job entailed dealing with discipline.

Ian and his principal sat down to talk about the new position. Both agreed that education's goal was to foster student intellectual and social development so they could become productive citizens—and helping students learn from their mistakes was an important part of that goal. Ian was to administer student discipline in a "fair and consistent manner in accordance with school and district policy" and, hopefully, students would gain a sense of responsibility and self discipline.

Soon Ian found himself doing little other than investigating discipline problems, suspending students, and meeting with parents of suspended students. In the first month of school, Ian suspended 62 students from school and placed another 31 students in in-school suspension. Ian was becoming disillusioned with his job. He knew educational leadership was about more than just suspending students and talking with parents about their children's misbehavior.

The next three months went along about the same—with just slight increases in the numbers of student discipline. Ian realized that at this current rate, by the end of the school year there would be almost 1,000 student suspensions in a 2,000 student middle school. That evening, Ian shared his frustration with his wife, Maria, a stellar MBA student at the local university. She had just finished a paper on Root Cause Analysis and asked what the breakdown on discipline referrals was—type of discipline infraction; which teacher made the referral; what grade level, gender, race, and achievement level of the student being suspended; number of repeat offenders; and the like. Ian responded that the school does not keep those kinds of records. Someone in the Central Office fills out the state and federal discipline summary data sheets. Maria said that Ian should know those statistics in order to better understand whether he was dealing with the cause or a symptom. Ian then knew what he had to do.

RUBRIC 5.1			
Lens and/or factors to be considered in decision making	What are the factors at play in this case?	What steps should be considered in solving the problem?	What could have been done to avoid this dilemma?
The situation			
• The task	Ian, a new AP, confronted with all discipline problems, is becoming overwhelmed. Over the years, the school has not identified and addressed the causes of improper student behavior.	Ian needs to collect data to determine who is being suspended, why, and from whom the referrals are coming. He needs to think of discipline in wider terms than student misbehavior.	Discipline information between the school and central office could have been shared. Student discipline not viewed as symptom—with need to identify and address their causes.
• Personal abilities	Ian accepted the job as a disciplinarian, but wants more job satisfaction than he is obtaining.	Does Ian have the time and ability to collect and analyze meaningful data? Can he reframe the discipline issue as symptoms for which he wants to find and address the causes?	Ian's graduate educational leadership program should have prepared him to use relevant data for making informed decisions and to think systemically about schools.
• The school environment	The school does not view student misbehavior as a response to problematic situations that need to be identified and fixed. They do not collect and analyze discipline data to inform thought and action.	Is the principal supportive of data collection and analysis by one of the APs? Can the principal reframe the situation to look for and address actual causes rather than punish symptoms?	The school system could have looked at causes and not just symptoms— single versus double loop learning. It needs to view problems holistically if it wants to effectively solve them.
	Look	Wider	
Organizational (i.e., the organizational goals, values, policies, culture)	The system is dealing with symptoms instead of the causes. The focus is on misbehavior, not effective teaching or school climate.	Ian needs to discuss the data collection and analysis issue with the principal, and they need to think more systemically for solutions.	The school and district may need to learn new ways of viewing (and responding to) discipline issues as instructional and climate issues.
People (i.e., individuals with needs, beliefs, goals, relationships)	Ian is a new AP in a new role—to deal with discipline. He had no useful mental model or role model for double-loop learning.	Ian and the principal both espouse a theory that differs from their theory-in-use.	Hiring a consultant to examine situation in its totality and give useful feedback might help change views and actions.

continued . . .

Competing Interests (i.e., competing interests for power, influence, and resources)	Not enough information. Are teachers referring students who are not academically successful with the current teaching practices?	Need more information.	Need more information.
Tradition (i.e., school culture, rituals, meaning, heroes)	The school has had a history of discipline problems and a culture that separates student behavior from teaching effectiveness and supportive school climate.	This one isolated case of dealing with symptoms versus causes may be wider than just with Ian. The school and district may not fully understand the link between teacher and student behaviors.	The school system could have had some deep conversations about problem solving and the interactions between teachers' and student behaviors. Needs assessments and professional development may be needed.

OVERVIEW: WHY CHANGE AND WHY IS IT DIFFICULT?

As the saying goes, "the only constant is change." *Change* is a process of altering, developing, or making something different from what is. Under enough external and internal pressures, organizations—including schools—either adapt to meet existing and coming realities, or they close up shop. They either adapt or die.

Change is people intensive. In organizations, change occurs in a context of human social interactions and collaborations that bring, modify, and sustain new perspectives and practices.[1] To deal successfully with change, organizations—that is, the people in them—must learn new ways to perceive, think, interpret, and respond to fast moving events affecting them. Change means learning. But most people will have to overcome their natural resistance to changes in habits or routines and cope with the insecurity that the unfamiliar and unknown bring if they are to improve their practices and outcomes.

Organization leaders play a significant role in guiding and managing this learning and changing process. The challenge for school leaders is to make change intentional. This means deliberately planning, directing, and establishing the conditions and situations that result in teacher learning and, in turn, new or higher outcomes for more students. This approach contrasts with unintentional change that appears randomly over time. This chapter will present models and perspectives to help future principals understand and lead change—and organizational learning—in their schools.

TWENTIETH CENTURY VIEWS: CHANGE AS ORGANIZATIONAL LEARNING

In the 1980s, scholars begin to understand *organizational change* as *organizational learning*. The discontinuities of an interdependent global economy, increased volatility, knowledge-intensive competition, technological innovations, and demographic changes sent long-standing organizations spinning.[2] Structures and rules that worked well enough in a stable environment no longer functioned well in a rapidly evolving one. Accordingly, scholars began shifting their organizational paradigm. From hierarchical and bureaucratic control of production and rigid boundaries, they now saw the need for supple learning organizations that would continuously adapt and solve problems through employee interactions around shared vision, culture, values, and information.

Learning can be understood as the ways organizations build, supplement, and organize knowledge and routines around their activities and within their cultures, adjusting and developing their employees' perspectives, knowledge, and skills.[3] Learning—its processes, outcomes, and essential role in facilitating adaptive change— gained appreciation as the key to competitiveness and organizational survival.[4] Leaders would have to build learning capacity within their organizations if they were to thrive in a highly competitive environment.

Many scholars have explored how leaders can leverage organizational change as a learning process. Kurt Lewin's descriptions of learning and the change processes, Chris Argyris's and Donald Schön's ideas about leadership, learning, and organizational change, Edgar Schein's concept of organizational culture, Peter Senge's ideas about the structures and strategies that leaders can use to maximize organizational learning, and complexity theory's concept of how organizations learn—all address how organizations can survive in a turbulent environment only if they—and their members—keep learning.

The Three-Stage Change Model—Kurt Lewin

A pioneer in change theory, Kurt Lewin (1890–1947) was a German-Jewish refugee scholar who fled Nazism to become a Cornell, University of Iowa, and MIT professor. As a social psychologist, Lewin greatly influenced thinking and research in organizational development. In his study of social conflict, group decision making, and democratic process, he conceived a theoretical framework to describe the change process and the motivation of change. Lewin believed that the key to resolving social conflict—and improve the human condition—was to facilitate planned change through learning, and help individuals understand and revise their perceptions of their world.[5]

Lewin's action research stressed that for change to be effective, it must occur at the group level, and it must be a participative and collaborative process.[6] His early studies included investigating ways to reduce violence between Catholic and Jewish teenage gangs and persuading American housewives to buy cheaper cuts of meat (namely, liver and kidneys) to avoid aggravating World War II shortages.[7] His findings strongly supported the use of group decision techniques to redefine members' cognitive standards (i.e., learn) about what is acceptable in motivating change.[8]

Believing that change and constancy are relative terms (differing only in the amount and type of change),[9] Lewin originated two theories to describe the change process: force field analysis and the three-stage change process. Lewin saw individual behavior as a function of the group environment, or "field." Any changes in behavior resulted from changes in the forces within the field. Accordingly, force field analysis of change posits that when the forces favoring change and those opposing change are in balance, the organization stays the same. In contrast, when forces driving and resisting change are not in balance, change can occur. This disequilibrium to drive change occurs either by adding forces favoring the desired change—or by weakening opposing forces against change. Eventually, a new equilibrium is established. In the former case, equilibrium occurs at a high-tension level; in the latter case, it happens at a low-tension level.[10] Since a group "forced" to change has the potential for aggressiveness, emotionality, and low constructiveness, Lewin advised that reducing resistance to change is preferable to increasing pressures to do so. Directly removing people who are resisting the change—or educating members through group discussions in which individuals experience others' views and begin to modify their own—can reduce resistance to change.[11]

For instance, a principal wants all students to have open access and academic supports to the most challenging courses (driving force). The teachers see no reason to change their practices: their school's achievement test scores are "the highest in the city" (restraining force). The principal reduces teachers' opposition to change by showing their students' scores falling far below those of the state and the nation. The teachers discuss these data and explain what these data mean to them and their students. Wanting their students to succeed wherever they choose to study, work, and live, the teachers decide to rethink their resistance to revising their academic access and support practices.

To address the concern that group changes might be unsustainable, Lewin buttressed his force field theory with a Three-Stage Change Management model, as depicted in Figure 5.1. Lewin believed that people's social habits thwart change. Therefore, preparing people in advance for the coming change is essential. In Stage One, a person's inner resistance—their personal defenses, group norms, or organizational culture[12]—

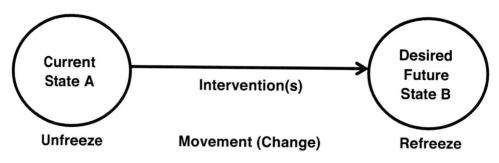

FIGURE 5.1 Kurt Lewin's Three-Stage Change Process.
Source: Adapted from Marshak, R.J. (1993). Lewin meets Confucius: A review of the organizational development model of change. *Journal of Applied Behavioral Science, 29* (4), 397.

must be *unfrozen*. Typically, learning occurs when group members have an experience that challenges their prior beliefs, creates "cognitive dissonance," and disrupts their satisfaction with the present situation. Members now perceive that the status quo is not working well, and they realize a "felt need"—an inner realization—to make a change. A high "felt need" facilitates change; a low one, inhibits it. In Stage Two, interventions are changes that help *move* or transition the group toward a desired future state by having them learn a new way of perceiving and acting in their world. Finally, in Stage Three, *refreezing* creates a new balance that reinforces and sustains the changes as a new status quo that withstands members' falling back to prior views and actions.

For Lewin, group learning was an essential part of organization change. Groups tend to hold on to their standards as a bulwark against change. If a member varies widely from the group's standard, others will likely ridicule, punish, and eventually, ostracize the "deviant" one. But if the group members themselves decide to modify their group standard, the changed behavior can be sustained, and the individual member can be expected to remain with the group. Thus, the process of *unfreezing* the existing level, *moving* to a new level, and *refreezing* group life at the new level generates an enduring and stable equilibrium that resists further change (until the next unfreezing).

Lewin investigated his own theories at work[13] and is credited with coining the term, "action research."[14] Some questioned whether this was "real" empirical or objective research.[15] Nonetheless, investigative findings have concluded that Lewin's force field analysis was valid within a limited scope of situations,[16] and field studies of organizational change confirmed the power of disconfirming messages to jump-start the change process.[17] Likewise, widespread support exists for an unlearning phase when individuals' (especially top managers') dominant beliefs and values are challenged.[18] A review of several decades of research evidence on organizational change concludes, "Lewin's approach is still relevant to the modern world."[19]

Lewin's change theory has received ample criticism. Critics argue that his concepts are too simplistic, mechanistic, and linear;[20] that his work is only relevant to small and isolated change projects and not to radical, transformational change;[21] that he ignores the role of power, politics, and conflict in organizations;[22] that he advocates top-down, management-driven change,[23] and that his model had questionable relevance for different cultures.[24] Lewin's defenders respond that these challenges are a narrow misreading of his work.[25] They point to substantial evidence in the social and physical sciences that supports his three-stage approach to change;[26] and they assert that Lewin recognized that any organization level could initiate change.[27] One reviewer argued that even Lewin's critics have drawn from his field theory and Three-Stage Change model to develop their own change paradigms.[28] Lastly, given Lewin's personal history as a Nazi refugee, it is not likely that he would ignore "political" issues in his professional life.[29]

Lewin saw learning and involvement as the key processes for achieving behavior change. His notions of planned change provide good theory and a generic blueprint for organizational development.[30] His groundbreaking ideas influenced the next generation of organizational scholars (including Chris Argyris, Donald Schön, and Edgar Schein, discussed in this chapter).

REFLECTIONS AND RELEVANCE 5.1

Lewin's force field analysis and Three-Stage Change management theory provide a blueprint for leading organizational learning and change.

As consultants to the local school board, you (this class) are hired to advise them on a change model and action plan for implementing a new program to the school district. (The new program can be one the class members are currently considering or implementing in their own schools. If no relevant project comes to mind, members can develop a plan for implementing interdisciplinary teams for grades 9 and 10 to help better transition middle school students to high school and prevent dropouts.)

Working in groups of four, apply Lewin's ideas to this consult. Develop and present a rationale for using his model with groups of educators and an action plan that includes descriptions of the activities you will use for unfreezing, movement, and refreezing. When your consulting group has completed the assignment, present your rationale and action plan to the school board (the rest of the class). Discuss your responses to this activity and its relevance to leading change in schools.

Leadership and Organizational Learning—Chris Argyris and Donald Schön

Chris Argyris (1923–2013), a Harvard University Graduate School of Business professor, added significantly to our understanding of how organization leaders enable change by facilitating organizational learning. To solve complex problems, leaders must be able to *learn*—to discover a problem, invent and implement solutions, and monitor the implementation's effectiveness—and continue to learn on the job. To help foster this behavior, Argyris and his colleague, Donald Schön (1930–1997), an MIT professor, developed a theory of action and model of learning to describe the way that organizations learn affects how they develop and adapt—or fail.

Theories of Action

Argyris and Schön argued that our culture socializes people to have mental maps that guide them in how to act in various situations.[31] Often operating beneath conscious awareness,[32] these mental maps—or microtheories of action—help people design and conduct their behaviors—including leadership and learning behaviors.[33]

But how people *actually* act in their personal and work lives—their *theories-in-use*—do not always match their "theory" (mental model) of how they *should* act in these types of situations—their *espoused theories*. Many of these theories of action are actually counterproductive to individual growth and organizational effectiveness. As a result of these faulty theories, organizations fail to adjust with changing circumstances and environments; and because they fail to adapt, organizations stagnate and deteriorate. Knowledge—or information that makes action effective—is needed to break out of this closed self-defeating cycle.

Theories-in-use can be inferred from watching a person's behaviors. Theories-in-use contain the person's assumptions about self, others, and the environment that the holder tries to satisfy in everyday life, and they suggest how the person will likely respond in an array of situations.

Theories-in-use have two main parts: governing variables and behavioral strategies. *Governing variables* are values that actors seek to satisfy. These include the underlying assumptions, values, and norms that the individual and/or to the organizational culture hold. These governing variables may specify the person's intended purpose, the desire to win (and not lose), and to not say or do anything that may generate colleagues' negative feelings. Or, in comparison, the governing variables may include the need to obtain and act on valid and useful information, make free and informed choices, and share power with competent and relevant others.[34] Each governing variable can be understood as a continuum with an acceptable range; a person's comfort level falls somewhere along the continuum, subjectively determined to not be too high or too low. Since any action may affect many governing variables, the person may have to trade off, meeting a more important value in exchange for not meeting a less important one.[35] For instance, a principal's governing variable affirms that parents and teachers must meet at school. But few parents actually attend PTA meetings or teacher conferences held there. Given this, the principal may want to rethink priorities and trade off meeting locations (such as, schedule meetings for local community centers or libraries closer to parents' homes) in exchange for increasing educator-parent contacts.

Behavioral strategies are the set of learned actions that people take to act upon their governing variables. These include deciding who defines the task, who is competent and relevant to participate in decision making or implementing the action, and who controls the environment. All human behavior is directed toward satisfying as many of these governing variables as possible.

A person's espoused theory and theory-in-use may not be congruent.[36] Hence the saying, "Do as I say, not as I do." For instance, a school counselor may believe that his philosophy of counseling (espoused theory) is to listen to students' concerns and not give advice. But when listening to a taped playback of a counseling interview, the counselor hears himself arguing with the student and telling him how to solve his problem (theory-in-use). According to Argyris, learning occurs when the espoused theory and theory-in-use match for the first time (and the actors recognize it as genuinely new).[37] Thus, in the next counseling session, if the counselor listens, it helps the student identify alternative solutions, discusses the pros and cons of each, and the student makes an informed decision, the counselor has aligned his theory-in-practice with his espoused theory (i.e., has learned a new, more effective behavior).

Although theories-in-use tend to be implicit, reflecting on the actions and their outcomes can make them explicit. This can be especially useful when the behavior does not produce the desired result, and the theory's adequacy or accuracy comes into question.[38] When this happens, people have two choices. Either they can look for another way (action theory) to reach the desired outcome that keeps the underlying values and norms unchanged. Or, they can rethink the appropriateness of their desired outcome, reflect on their values and norms (that is, the governing strategies and the social structure that created them), confront these in ways that are more congruent with their espoused values and theories, and learn from their errors. The first alternative is called single-loop learning. The second alternative is called double-loop learning. Reflective practice in organizations allows individuals, debriefing together, to revise their theories of action and their action strategies, discover what they did that encouraged or discouraged learning, and invent new strategies for learning.[39]

Models of Learning: Single- and Double-Loop

Argyris and Schön believed that organizational learning involves detecting and correcting a problem. *Single-loop learning* occurs when actors solve the problem by changing the action. *Double-loop learning* occurs when the actor changes the underlying governing assumptions and values that, in turn, lead to a change in action. Double-loop learning identifies the problem's root causes rather than simply treating its surface symptoms. Argyris and Schön asserted that only by addressing and modifying the organization's governing variables—such as its cultural norms, assumptions, and expectations—can substantial learning or meaningful change occur. Simply adding new programs and practices without first challenging and correcting the underlying assumptions, norms, and behaviors cannot improve outcomes.[40]

As Figure 5.2 illustrates, a continuous cycle in which the person or organization's *governing variables* (the person's intended goals, desires, values, and assumptions) lead to their choice of *action strategies* (the plans and sequences of moves that actors use to satisfying governing variables) that, in turn, lead to *consequences* (what occurs as a result of the action, intended or unintended, productive or unproductive).[41] The consequences of action depend on the actor's theory-in-use as well as those who receive the action.

As seen in Figure 5.2, in *single-loop learning*, people use a new action strategy that addresses the problem's symptoms within the same set of underlying assumptions and norms. Single-loop learning keeps the same governing variables instead of challenging

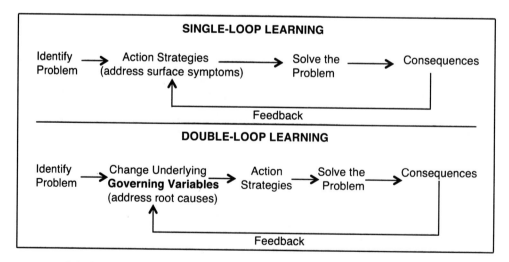

FIGURE 5.2 Single- and Double-loop Learning in Organizations.

Source: Based on Argyris, C., Putnam, R., & Smith, D.M. (1985). *Action science. Concepts, methods, and skills for research and intervention* (Chapter 3, pp. 80–102). San Francisco, CA: Jossey Bass.

them; feedback from consequences returns to the action strategies and not to the governing variables. The action may effectively resolve the problem. If it does not, the immediate problem may disappear but may reappear later, perhaps elsewhere and in another form. In contrast, with double-loop learning, feedback returns to the governing variables. Members publicly question the organization's norms, values, and assumptions. If found wanting, the governing variables can be changed and replaced by new, more appropriate beliefs and more effective behaviors.

Persistent errors in learning—problems that continue despite repeated attempts to fix them—are likely double-loop problems.[42] At such times, members must look closely at their personal, and the organization's, governing variables and question their meaning and worth to the present conditions, if they are to successfully solve today's problems (at least until circumstances change).

Argyris compared single- and double-loop learning to a household thermostat. A thermostat is programmed to turn up the temperature in a room when it gets colder and turn it down when the room gets too warm. A thermostat is single-loop learning when it follows its programming, received information about room temperature, and kicks "on" and "off" at the preset point, say 68 degrees. Double-loop learning occurs when the thermostat questions why it is programmed to turn on and off at 68 degrees, showing its capacity to detect error and question its own basic assumptions, norms, and goals.[43]

Organizational Learning

Argyris suggested that organizational learning (i.e., problem solving) can involve changing the governing variables. When assumptions and ideas are tested publicly—and are open to revision—leaders receive genuine feedback—despite the fact that others may feel uncomfortable, concerned that their own governing values are under threat. Similarly, intensive reflective practice, as part of double-loop learning, allows individuals to revise their theories of action and enact more appropriate, successful, and sustainable outcomes.[44]

For instance, English Department teachers had been "reserving" cafeteria seats for its members during faculty meetings. This practice annoyed teachers from other departments. When the irritated teachers complained, the principal replied with a single-loop strategy: "It's a big room. Sit somewhere else." In other words, change the behavior; don't challenge the underlying norms. Instead, if the principal had responded, "Let's open an inquiry and discuss interdepartmental concerns," the principal would be using a double-loop strategy aimed, first, at identifying and confronting underlying assumptions and norms and second, on adjusting behaviors. Now, the new governing norm can become: "No concern is off limits if it is addressed respectfully and openly." Rather than choose a different behavior within a given set of standards, let's choose among competing sets of standards.

Learning models are difficult to study empirically, as the lack of substantial research in this area would suggest.[45] However, research (usually qualitative field studies, simulations, and anecdotal evidence) finds that incremental (single-loop) and radical (double-loop) learning are meaningful concepts, and both learning types can strengthen organizational survival and prosperity under certain conditions.[46] But in different circumstances, they can also cause harm.[47] Studies also find that espoused theory of action based on single-loop learning is the most common model of action.[48]

Critics take issue with aspects of Argyris and Schön's conceptual work and research methodologies. Some consider their model simplistic.[49] Others assert that advocates of radical change neglect to identify what forms of change are associated with learning, or name the specific criteria for choosing one approach (single- or double-loop learning) over the other.[50] Certain critics observe that not all double-loop learning is a reliable or superior process for generating effective organizational knowledge,[51] citing the Chernobyl disaster as a case in point.[52] Some call Argyris and Schön's ideas naïve and idealistic for wanting to overcome and nullify organizations' political processes so that learning can occur, claiming that interactions among people and the meanings they produce are part of any organization.[53] Also, no evidence confirms that the double-loop learning process encourages challenging outdated norms and practices.[54]

Argyris and Schön's work has helped expand the view of organizational *change* to organizational *learning*—the process by which an organization evolves as a result of members' learning and new behaviors. Increasingly, many agree that organizational learning may be "the only sustainable competitive advantage"[55] in a rapidly changing environment. Likewise, scholars in a variety of independent disciplines concur that although the distinction between incremental (single-loop) and radical (double-loop) organizational learning is useful, both types can produce adaptive advantages—and dangers—for organizations.[56] And while the idea of leaders' agency to accurately assess, challenge, and constructively change their work environments to increase learning and generate improved outcomes is appealing, as Argyris acknowledged, "Learning to become aware of one's present theory-in-use and then altering it is a very difficult process."[57]

LEADING LEARNING AND CHANGE WITHIN AN ORGANIZATIONAL CULTURE

The 1930s Hawthorne Studies revealed the importance of norms, values, and social interactions in describing informal organizations' nature and functioning. The concept of organizational culture appeared in 1979,[58] borrowed from anthropology with its focus on symbolism, rituals, and shared norms and assumptions.[59] In the mid 1980s, Edgar Schein articulated a conceptual framework for analyzing, researching, and intervening in an organization's culture.[60] In 1990, Peter Senge popularized the concept of a learning organization and suggested ways to challenge outdated cultural assumptions. By late 1980s and early 1990s, culture became a popular subject in school research.[61] And from the mid 1990s into the twenty-first century, complexity theorists presented a theory of how organizations learn.

Organizational Culture—Edgar H. Schein

With his 1985 book, *Organizational Culture and Leadership*,[62] Edgar H. Schein (1928–), MIT Professor of Management Emeritus, is, arguably, the most influential theorist on organizational culture and learning. A social psychologist, Schein receives credit for inventing the term, "corporate culture."[63] He believed that today's rapid pace of change is creating thorny problems in economics, politics, and technology; and it requires rapid and complex learning. Unless organizations—that is, *the people in them*—can learn rapidly and shift their behaviors adaptively to the changing circumstances, their organizations will fail. Organizational culture plays a powerful role in whether or not this rapid adjustment and learning can occur. Schein's theory and research concludes that cultures—national, organization, and occupational— powerfully influence organizational performance.

Schein saw *culture* as a dynamic phenomenon—a pattern of shared basic assumptions that a group (or social units of any size) learned as it solved its internal and external problems.[64] These assumptions, beliefs, and solutions have worked well enough to be thought valid and taught to new members as the correct way to perceive, think, and feel in relation to those problems. Any social unit with a shared history will have evolved a culture. The culture's strength depends on how long it has existed, the stability of the group's membership, and the emotional intensity of their shared experiences. Yet, most people in a culture are not even aware of their own culture until they meet a different one.[65] According to Schein, change in culture occurs through cognitive restructuring, such as by redefining words to mean something other than what was assumed, interpreting concepts more broadly, or learning new standards of judgment and evaluation.[66]

Since the 1980s, *organizational culture* refers to the climate and practices that organizations develop around managing their people, or to the organization's espoused values and beliefs. Culture begins with leaders who enact their own values and assumptions on a group. If the group succeeds in achieving its goals, members take these values and assumptions for granted as the "right way" to do things. With ongoing reinforcement, these assumptions, values, and beliefs drop out of conscious awareness. As a result, much of what culture is lies below the surface, unconscious. As personality and character guide and limit an individual's thoughts and actions, culture's shared norms guide and constrain group members' actions. But as the environment changes and the group faces adaptive difficulties, some of its assumptions lose their validity. Whether a culture is "good" or "bad," "functional" or "ineffective" depends on the culture and its relationship to its environment.

Components of Organizational Culture

Organizational climate and culture are two separate but related constructs. Briefly, *climate*, a more specific construct, generally focuses on individual members' perceptions about a particular idea or thing (such as relational trust) whereas *culture* refers to members' more general assumptions, values, and behavior patterns.[67] According to Schein, climate is "a surface manifestation of culture."[68]

Research confirms the following characteristics of organizational culture:[69]

* *Observed behaviors*—what people do when they interact, such as their language, customs, and traditions.
* *Group norms*—informal customs for group behaviors, such as the group's standard for appropriate work attire.

- *Espoused values*—a group's publicly stated principles.
- *Formal philosophy*—the broad policies and ideological principles that guide a group's actions toward employees, customers, and stakeholders.
- *Rules of the game*—the unwritten guidelines for how to get along in the organization.
- *Climate*—the feeling the group and the facility's physical layout convey as they interact.
- *Embedded skills*—the group members' special competencies.
- *Habits of thinking*—members' mental models and shared cognitive frames that guide their perceptions, thought, and language, and that are taught to new members.
- *Shared meanings*—the emergent understandings that group members create as they interact.
- *Formal rituals and celebrations*—the ways the group celebrates important events or milestones.

These cultural elements—the repeated, tacit, shared ways of perceiving, thinking, and responding—operate as stabilizing forces in organizations. The group's beliefs and ethical rules remain conscious and clearly expressed because they serve the normative function of guiding members in how to behave in certain key situations and in educating new members on how to act. These norms include the level of resistance or acceptance to new learning and change.[70] A set of beliefs and values, embodied in an ideology or philosophy, can help members deal with the uncertainty of inherently uncontrollable or difficult events. Those who do not accept the culture risk being ostracized or ejected from the group.

Levels in Organizational Culture

Schein suggested that organizational culture appears on several levels, or at least to the degree by which the cultural phenomenon is visible to observers. Levels range from the very tangible and overt artifacts that one can see and touch, to the deeply embedded, unconscious basic assumptions that guide members' behavior. Schein observed that basic assumptions are similar to Argyris's theories-in-use and are difficult to change without double-loop learning.[71] The espoused beliefs, values, norms, and behavior rules that provide day-to-day operating principles that guide members' actions lie in between the artifacts and assumptions. Figure 5.3 illustrates Schein's view. Any group's culture can be studied at these three levels, but one must accurately understand the basic underlying assumptions before the artifacts or espoused values can be credibly interpreted.

For example, a school may prominently display their mascot, school colors, and photos of their multi-ethnic students working with their multi-ethnic teachers (artifacts). Their visibly posted mission statement (espoused beliefs and values) reads, "We Teach All Children," affirming their commitment to diversity. But if their deepest expectations (basic underlying assumptions) hold that since not all children are ready to learn the same challenging content and skills at the same time, and the school implements rigid academic tracking—rather than academic rigor *and* an array of academic and social supports—teachers may actually *prevent* all children from learning.

NO CONSCIOUS ⟵⟶ AWARENESS	SOME AWARENESS ⟵⟶ Expressed Beliefs, Values	VISIBLE ORGANIZATION Structure and Processes
(Taken-for-Granted) Underlying assumptions about: • Relationship to environment • Nature of relationships • Nature of reality	**(Meaning may be unclear)** Beliefs about: • Right/wrong • What will/won't work • Testable • Socially verifiable	**(May be hard to decode)** Tangible artifacts including: • Architecture, language, art, clothing, technology, observed rituals, mascots, office layouts, team colors

FIGURE 5.3 Edgar H. Schein's Continuum of Organizational Culture Awareness

Source: Based on Schein, E.H. (1990). Organizational culture. *American Psychologist*, 45 (2), 109–119.

Research and Criticism

The relationship between culture and implemented new behaviors has been challenging to investigate. Reasons for this include the multiple conceptualizations, dimensions, and divergent definitions of "culture" used;[72] the reliance on questionnaires, personality inventories, and case studies (that try to define, operationalize, and assess abstractions) to measure culture;[73] and the relative lack of empirical studies or mixed method approaches that could identify the limits of culture's influence.[74] One review found the ratio of experimental research to survey/case-study based research to be 1:10.[75] Nonetheless, studies of organizational culture find that organizations differ along lines of their dominant values—such as ideas of organizational innovation and change,[76] views on teamwork and collaboration for better decisions and outcomes,[77] sociability,[78] concern for people,[79] concern for hierarchy,[80] results orientation,[81] adaptability,[82] and others—that guide organizational behavior.[83] Studies confirm that although varied national cultures hold different values, they affirm Schein's three levels of culture as a common set of organizational assumptions.[84] Likewise, studies on technology and culture find that variations across cultural values may lead to differing perceptions and approaches to work design and practice.[85] Some suggest that a more complex conceptualization of culture—beyond examining the static influence of a few cultural elements in isolation from other culture elements and contextual variables—would bring a more accurate and complete understanding of organizational (and national) culture.[86]

Identifying weaknesses in Schein's culture concept, critics note that individual, group, and situational characteristics, alone or together, serve as moderating influences on organizational culture.[87] Similarly, subculture researchers contend that organizational culture is not unitary: professional subcultures,[88] an inter-connected managerial culture (the top-down view) and workplace culture (the members' view),[89] and the surrounding external environments[90] all influence an organization's culture. Others disagree with Schein's idea that culture's function is to maintain social structure.[91] One scholar considers Schein's conceptual model valid but criticizes his lack of process links between artifacts, values, and assumptions (i.e., what happens inside the arrows in his model, Figure 5.3) and suggests enlarging his theory to make it more dynamic.[92] At the same time, contingency theorists predict that not all values associated with culture have equal importance in implementing innovations:[93] cultures valuing organizational learning would need members to share values prizing collaboration, shared influence, and fact-based decision making.[94] One writer asserts that social anthropologists would find Schein's view that leaders create and manage (and if necessary, destroy) culture to control others as a means to achieve organizational goals to be "preposterous"—calling the notion "selective borrowing" from anthropology and sociology.[95]

Schein sees leadership and culture as two sides of the same coin. As culture defines the norms used to characterize leadership—setting unwritten guidelines for who gets promoted and who will gain followers—leaders' most important role is to create and manage culture.[96] When organizations lose their ability to constructively adapt to changing circumstances, leadership must step outside the culture that created it and begin to use a more flexible and appropriate change process. In Schein's view, the "ability to perceive the limitations in one's own culture and to evolve the culture adaptively is the essence and ultimate challenge of leadership."[97] And, if leaders "do not become conscious of the cultures in which they are embedded, those cultures will manage them."[98] Despite the real limits on leaders' authority to manage culture, they can still press the organizational culture in a desired direction. Finally, Schein advises leaders to find elements in their culture that are working and build on these to create new and more effective practices; it is easier to evolve a culture than to change it.

Learning Organizations—Peter Senge

Peter M. Senge, (1947–), a senior lecturer of MIT's Sloan School of Management and founder of the Society of Organizational Learning, popularized the concept of learning organizations. Senge believes that in a world of increasing interdependence and rapid change, high-performing organizations (including schools) are those that have the ability to learn and achieve sustained, improved performance over time.[99] Organizational learning is key to flexibility and competitive advantage in today's complex, fast moving environment. Since "organizations learn only through individuals who learn,"[100] sustained improvement depends on the rate of individual and organizational learning. Senge's learning organization creates a culture of learning, a community of learners, and ensures individual and group learning is a never-ending process of increasing organizational capacity.[101]

Although Senge and others have used the two terms—*organizational learning* (OL) and *learning organization* (LO)—interchangeably, the two separated conceptually in the mid-1990s. *Organizational learning*—the process by which shared understandings change[102]—became the broader, descriptive strand that addresses how individuals in the organization learn in ways that "may" result in behavior change. Its roots are in social and cognitive psychology. Argyris and Schön's single- and double-loop learning are examples of OL, and Senge built upon their ideas. *Learning organization*—where people at all levels are continually learning how to learn together in ways that expand their capacities to achieve the results they truly want—became a narrower, prescriptive strand with a strong practical focus on building an organization that learns and "must" result in behavior change. In either case, an organization's commitment and capacity for learning can be no stronger than that of its members.[103]

Change and Five Disciplines of Organizational Learning

Senge identified four challenges to initiating changes. First, a compelling case for change must exist. Time and help (second and third challenges) must be available to members during the change process. Lastly, as the perceived barriers to change are removed, no new problem takes their place.[104]

Next, Senge argued that since organizations are reflections of how we think and interact, and since interpersonal and cultural issues embedded in the current organization are the barriers that stymie most change efforts, the leaders' job is to help the organizational culture evolve so its members can learn new ways of perceiving and acting. Accordingly, Senge proposed five disciplines of organizational learning—personal mastery, shared vision, mental models, team learning, and systems thinking—that work as an ensemble to enable organization members to gain new ways of looking at the work, generate learning, and build the capacity for doing things in new improved ways.[105]

Personal mastery and shared vision represent ways to articulate individual and collective aspirations and use these to set a direction for organizational (school) improvement.[106] Leaders who want to build a shared vision need first to encourage members to develop their personal visions (personal mastery)—and then really listen to what they say.

Personal Mastery

Personal mastery is the individual's lifelong ability to develop his/her own capacity to learn (and, of course, the technical competencies to perform their jobs effectively). Since sustainable learning does not happen unless the learner's own intrinsic interest and curiosity ignites it, each organization member develops a coherent personal vision of what that individual deems most important. This personal vision focuses energies, develops patience, and encourages seeing current realities objectively and accurately. People with high levels of personal mastery—the vision and the capacity—can navigate the creative tension between their personal vision and reality. They can integrate reason and intuition, see their connectedness to the world, and learn to work with—rather than resist—the forces of change. In the process, people expand their ability to make better choices and achieve more of their desired outcomes.

Shared Vision

A *shared vision* is an idea or picture that aligns individual aspirations and goals with what the organization wants to accomplish. It builds a deep sense of common purpose, makes diverse organization activities coherent, and provides the focus and energy for learning. Members are excited about and committed to the shared vision because it reflects their own personal vision. With shared vision, "their company" becomes "our company," and employee commitment replaces compliance. Shared vision accelerates experimentation and learning, and new ways of thinking, and acting.

Building a shared vision includes involving reflective thinking, in-depth contemplation, dialog, and discussion of the members' mental models. Leaders initiate, model, and encourage this professional conversation during organizational planning.

Mental Models

Mental models are deeply held internal images, generalizations, and assumptions of how we *think* the world works. Frequently operating unconsciously and unavailable for examining or testing, mental models actively influence how we make sense of the world and how we act in it. Outdated mental models (such as Argyris's espoused theories) can impede learning and keep organization members using ineffective practices. When leaders and members use reflection and inquiry skills to identify and manage their mental models, they open their thinking to rigorous examination and testing. More accurate internal pictures and assumptions of how the world works expands their basic thinking and increases their own—and their organizations'—range of action.

Team Learning

Team learning is the discipline of group interaction. Using techniques like thoughtful *dialogue* (the free and creative exploration of complex and subtle issues from many viewpoints from which a new action may emerge) and skillful *discussion* (presenting and defending different viewpoints to find the one with the most benefit to supporting decision making now), small groups learn how to think more clearly and accurately, individually and collectively. By listening carefully to fully comprehend each other's meaning during inquiry and reflection, members learn from each other and create a group intelligence greater than the sum of individual members' knowledge. In addition, members come to see each other as colleagues (who may have different views), not as adversaries. And if teams learn, the organization learns.

Systems Thinking

Lastly, *systems thinking* is a conceptual framework that links all the other disciplines together into a coherent body of theory and practice. Thinking systemically helps organization members see the complex, interdependent forces and the multiple levels of explanation that exist in any complex situation that create and sustain "wicked" problems. Systems thinking helps clarify the "forest" from the "trees" and the processes of change (circles of causality) rather that in-this-moment snapshots (straight lines). Feedback—the reciprocal flow of influence—becomes an essential force in understanding the whole. With a systems perspective, it is possible to see that small, well-focused actions—leverage—can sometimes lead to significant, enduring improvements. For education, systems thinking includes the school, the district, the political bodies, local industries, the atmosphere and general health of the families, and individuals that comprise the systems' structure and behavior.

Research and Criticism

Research on Senge's five disciplines has been limited, but findings tend to support them as an effective means to prompt organizational change—despite their ambiguous terms (subject to multiple interpretations)[107] that make them difficult to operationalize. Senge's own studies rely on long-term community action research in realistic field settings[108] and present qualitative anecdotal data to confirm his theory's effectiveness.[109] An empirical study of employees in one organization using Senge's concepts found that team learning, shared vision, and systems thinking were valuable parts of a change effort but were insufficient as a total change methodology.[110] Researchers studying schools that used Senge's five disciplines found these elements inadequately implemented and with disappointing results.[111]

While giving Senge credit for popularizing the learning organization concept,[112] critics take issue with his theory, its omissions, and its implementation. Some assert that Senge's concepts are vague and not a coherent theory of systemic thinking.[113] Others question his omission of the ethical issues involved in setting "boundaries" within systems to make the problem-solving scale more manageable;[114] and his similar avoidance of discussing politics, knowledge-power,[115] and diversity in organizations.[116] Critics also fault Senge for using the terms "organization" and "community" inter-changeably (although they are sociologically different); for underestimating the pervasive power of traditional ownership and control in organizational life; and overestimating the power of formal rationality (dialogue, discussion, inquiry, and reflection) to resolve complex problems.[117] Likewise, critics assert that not all problems result from faulty perceptions, and incompatible rationalities; competing basic interests do exist. Finally, critics assert that his theory is difficult to put into practice.[118]

Ironically, Senge (1995) avowed that schools (as presently structured and governed) are "definitely not" learning organizations.[119] Nonetheless, he writes that principals with the greatest impact tend to see their roles as creating an environment where teachers

REFLECTIONS AND RELEVANCE 5.2

Peter Senge's Five Disciplines of Learning Organizations

Peter Senge theorized five disciplines of learning organizations—personal mastery, shared vision, mental models, team learning, and systems orientation—that enable organizations to learn and achieve sustainable improved performance over time.

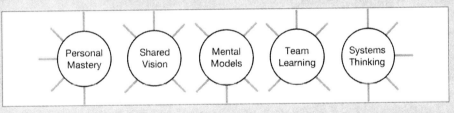

Working individually, reread the definitions for each of the five disciplines and determine what each discipline means to you. Complete the communications web graphic using words or phrases to describe your own views and values for "where you stand" in your own professional development on each discipline.

Then, working in pairs, share your perceptions of what the disciplines mean and where you personally stand on each. Then describe where your current school's culture stands on each. Discuss your findings as a class and consider the relationships between the presence of these five disciplines in your current school and the implications for leading change.

can continually learn. These leaders find teachers who are committed to doing things differently and want to work together to design an inclusive learning process. Similarly, superintendents find and support the principals who have this attitude. These are some of the building blocks for turning schools into "learning organizations."[120] Senge concludes that we can never transform our current system of organizational management until we transform our current system of education because they are the same system.[121]

REFLECTIONS AND RELEVANCE 5.3

Learning Organization, Levels of Culture, Single- and Double-Loop Learning

Chris Argyris and Donald Schön described how leaders can increase organizational learning. Edgar Schein posited that organizations contain three levels of culture that affect how organization members learn in response to changing circumstances. And Peter Senge articulated the five disciplines of a learning organization that create a culture of learning.

Working in groups of four, half the class will describe what a school's three levels of culture might contain or look like if the organizational culture welcomed organizational learning. The other half of the class will describe the three levels for a school culture that resists organizational learning. Each group will identify at least three to five specific artifacts, espoused beliefs and values, and basic underlying assumptions for their welcoming or resisting conditions. Decide where Senge's five disciplines—personal mastery, shared vision, mental models, team learning, and a systems orientation—might appear in an organization's culture. After completing this activity, the groups will present their findings to the rest of the class and discuss the following questions:

1. What artifacts might one observe in a school that infuses—or rejects—Senge's five disciplines of a learning organization?
2. What espoused beliefs and values typically reflect a school's culture that infuses—or rejects—Senge's five disciplines of a learning organization?
3. Name several basic underlying assumptions in a school that infuses—or rejects—Senge's five disciplines of a learning organization.
4. Explain how a school's culture affects its members' likelihood for using single- or double-loop learning strategies to solve problems?

COMPLEXITY THEORY, ORGANIZATIONAL LEARNING, AND CHANGE

According to Peter Senge, while people in organizations learn, organizations, not just individuals, can hold knowledge.[122] The ability to change rapidly and appropriately to environmental pressures is the core of an adaptive organization. The issue of creating, transferring, and diffusing organizational knowledge is essential to an organization's success. Complex systems *are* learning organizations. *Complexity research* can be understood as the study of learning and learning systems—including individuals, social groupings, bodies of knowledge, and cultures.[123] *Complexity theory* proposes a model of how cognition happens in human systems and how knowledge evolves in human organizations. It attempts to determine what happens at the interface between gaining information and generating knowledge—or how to create a learning organization.

As discussed in Chapter 3, complexity theory is the study of *emergent* order that arises in the interactions of many sub-systems or agents—in what are otherwise disorderly systems. Complexity's theory of knowledge in living systems is known as complex adaptive systems theory. *Complex adaptive systems* (CAS) are groups of independent, interconnected, and interactive agents, linked by multiple feedback loops, who share certain goals and operate in accord with individually and collectively held rules.[124] In CAS, *organizational knowledge* is the shared, unspoken, and explicit knowledge, common skills, expertise, and attitudes among people in an organization;[125] and *learning* is a dynamic social process. This is true in schools as in any organization. For example, teachers and students are embedded in an assortment of social, historical, and cultural systems—as well as with local, state, and federal mandates, norms, and expectations—all of which profoundly affect their actions and their learning.[126]

Focus on Human Interactions, Information Flow, and Change

Complexity theory focuses on the interactions of agents and sub-systems, not on individuals. Constantly adapting, the agents absorb information (learn) from their interactions with their internal and external environments. Small groups of people interact with a broader environment of competing ideas. Workgroups interact with other workgroups, linked by individuals who belong to many groups, by common tasks, and by their coordination within the larger enterprise. Change in one subsystem can result in changes in the others. The behavior of the whole comes from the interactions and interdependence of its subsystems, sometimes in unpredictable ways.[127] And because these interactions are nonlinear, their effects may be disproportionate to their cause. As one scholar observes, "A rolling pebble . . . can trigger an avalanche."[128] This occurs apart from any organizational structure—other than the mechanisms in place to ensure that ideas "stumble across one another."[129] Yet, in their capacity to select and self-organize, complex systems are adaptive.

From this interactive social process, insights arise, offering new ways of perceiving and understanding events and ideas and prompting new ways of behaving.[130] Innovations that lead to changes in knowledge and practice may be viewed as learning events.[131] These innovations allow the system to modify itself (or the environment) in response to disturbances that threaten the system's efficiency.[132] Looking simply at how *individuals* learn would miss these complex contextual learning factors,[133] especially when the focus is on the *knowledge producing system*.[134] Similarly, attention in complexity theory goes to shared/decentralized control, rather than to a particular top leader's actions. The system, itself, "decides" what is or is not acceptable.[135]

Complexity Leadership Theory (CLT)

When placed within a leadership context, complexity theory looks beyond the traditional bureaucratic top-down leadership hierarchy where all vision, inspiration, and change efforts begin at the top. Instead, CLT considers change as emergent, arising throughout the organization as people working on daily tasks confront—and overcome—problems. These working groups occurring throughout the organization are *complex adaptive systems*.

Complexity leadership theory (CLT) identifies three types of interacting leadership that all organizations need to link these complex adaptive systems and thereby ensure their continued successful adaptation to changing circumstances: administrative, adaptive, and enabling leadership.[136] *Administrative leadership* refers to persons in formal leadership and managerial positions who build vision, plan and coordinate activities, structure tasks, manage crises, and acquire resources to achieve goals. In schools, superintendents and principals use administrative leadership. *Adaptive leadership* is an informal, interacting dynamic among interdependent agents in the organization's social system that respond to struggles over conflicting needs, ideas, technologies, or preferences. Their interactions create alliances of people, ideas, and cooperative efforts to produce a useful outcome. In schools, assistant principals and teachers tend to enact adaptive leadership. *Enabling leadership*—positioned between administrative and adaptive leaders—helps these two roles function together. Enabling leaders effectively manage the productive tensions between the administrative and workgroup functions. Notably, by promoting the flow of knowledge and creativity from work groups' adaptive solutions into administrative structures, enabling leadership promotes a school's climate, structures, and conditions that allow informal leaders to solve problems and facilitates organizational learning. In schools, depending on how they perform their jobs, principals, assistant principals, and teachers can all function as enabling leaders. Figure 5.4 depicts the complexity leadership model.

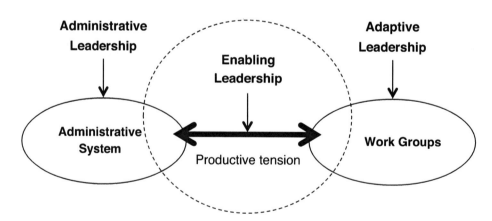

FIGURE 5.4 Complexity Leadership Model

Source: Based on Uhl-Bien, M., Marion, R. & McKelvey, B. (2007). Complexity leadership theory: Shifting leadership from the industrial age to the knowledge era. *The Leadership Quarterly, 18* (4), 298–318.

Research and Criticism

Complexity leadership theory's intricacy, ambiguity, and measurement challenges complicate its research. As a consequence, complexity leadership theory has not been widely researched,[137] those field studies conducted have failed to replicate prior findings,[138] and, therefore, CLT lacks a substantial research base to help it move from theory to practice.[139] Nonetheless, those studies that have been conducted (mainly case studies and computer modeling) suggest that integrating complexity theory perspectives on organization learning and change may help investigators better understand the non-linear organization change processes,[140] gain insights into organizational culture,[141] and be able to generate more effective strategies for coping in complex, turbulent environments.[142]

Critics of complexity leadership theory observe that although it stresses the importance of neighbor interactions to blend ideas and generate learning, the theory offers little generalizable advice on how to make this happen.[143] In addition, as with other forms of organizational or social change, critical theorists ask, "Who benefits?" and "Whose idea of change?"[144] Many conclude that if CLT is to advance beyond conceptual discussions, more substantive research is needed.[145]

Complexity leadership theory is systems thinking in practice.[146] Learning and organizational change from a CLT perspective sees webs of causation rather than simple, linear relationships. It describes how social interactions in small groups create knowledge and adaptive solutions to environmental changes across the organization, insights not available in traditional organization models.

By the late twentieth century, thinking and research on organizational change suggested that learning and change are not an on-and-off phenomenon. They are not episodic, discontinuous, or intermittent. Rather they are continuous, evolving, and

REFLECTIONS AND RELEVANCE 5.4

Complexity Leadership Theory and Learning Organizations

Complexity leadership theory describes how learning happens in human systems. Its main points include:

- The leadership focus is on social processes and interactions, not on individuals or formal positions.
- Leadership in organizations can be administrative, adaptive, and enabling.
- Innovations that lead to changes are learning events.
- The interactions are nonlinear, not direct cause and effect.
- Top-down leadership is less influential than decentralized or shared leadership.

Working in pairs, describe the types of CLT leadership you observe in your own school. Where and who enacts each type of CLT leadership? In what ways are you presently enacting an aspect of CLT leadership? How can school leaders foster CLT practices in their schools? Discuss your findings as a class.

incremental. Its effectiveness does not depend on the extent to which it is planned but on the ways information is shared and used. What is more, the change process is often spiral or open-ended rather than linear. The differences lie in the observers' orientation. From a distance, learning and change may appear episodic. Up close, learning and change tend to suggest ongoing adaptation and adjustment. As a result, *changing* rather than *change* might be the more appropriate term when considering organizational learning and the resulting behavior and outcome results.[147]

IMPLICATIONS FOR EDUCATIONAL LEADERS

In an era of rapid change, high performing organizations are those whose members have the ability to adapt quickly to shifting conditions, learn more effective responses, and achieve improved, sustained performance over time. Today's schools are dealing with changed expectations: that *every* student in increasingly diverse cohorts receive the academic preparation for economic survival and further education in an information dense, technology-infused environment. If education leaders are to guide and manage this change process, they must understand how to facilitate *organizational learning*— the dynamic social process by which the school evolves as the result of its members' acquiring new ways of understanding their milieu and new ways of acting in it (Senge's learning organization, complexity leadership theory).

Following are ideas that educational leaders can use to lead organizational learning and school improvement. These concepts work as an ensemble, enabling organization members to acquire new ways of interpreting events and responding to them. Although the sequence below suggests a logical linear process, the actual behaviors that facilitate organizational learning and change may occur simultaneously, overlapping and recurring (also complexity leadership theory).

Improvement Depends on Faculty Learning

Leaders and faculty must recognize that school improvement is as much about increasing teacher *learning* as it is about *change*. To solve complex problems, leaders must be able to *learn*—to identify a problem, invent and implement solutions, and monitor the implementation's effectiveness—and continue to learn on the job. Similarly, teachers must learn to rethink current assumptions and practices and learn more effective ways of interpreting and enacting their professional roles. Planning for change, therefore, requires preparing for extensive principal and teacher development using high quality adult learning practices. Importantly, group learning, using participative and collaborative processes, will be central if belief and behavior changes are to be widely supported and sustained (Lewin's Three-Stage Change model and Senge's team learning).

School Culture Affects Organizational Learning

Leaders' role is to help the organizational culture evolve (Schein). To do this, they need to recognize how national, school, and district cultures have their shared assumptions, norms, and expectations for thinking, and responding (Argyris and Schön's governing variables). But these "tried-and-true" solutions may no longer work well in the current environment. Many may even be counterproductive. Change in culture occurs through its members' *cognitive restructuring*—such as by redefining words or concepts to modify or expand their meaning and/or by presenting actual data that engenders members' "felt need" to do something differently. Accordingly, effective school leaders will help teacher groups publicly identify their mental models, shared assumptions, and norms, reflect on these and how they are practiced, discuss their present effectiveness, and revise or reinterpret, and apply them in more effective ways.

For this openness to occur, school leaders must first establish the conditions that support a culture of individual and group learning in their school. Here, adult learning becomes a never-ending process of increasing organizational capacity (Schein; Senge's learning organization). Such conditions include guaranteeing "safety" for faculty to publicly identify, test, and revise shared assumptions and norms; providing the space for teachers to try new approaches with realistic appreciation for their "learning curve;" and making time and help available to faculty and staff during the learning and change processes so the school culture may evolve.

In addition, establishing this new culture will include supporting teachers in developing their own individual goals (Senge's personal mastery) and aligning these with the organization's goals. This connection builds teacher commitment. Evolving the culture also entails developing a collective vision and an achievable mission (Senge's shared vision) for what teachers want to accomplish for their students (and for each other). Schein advises leaders to find elements in their culture that are working and build on these to create new and more effective practices; it is easier to evolve a culture than change it.

Change is a Process

Leading meaningful school improvement means understanding the change process and how leaders can plan for, direct, and manage the conditions and situations that result in adult learning and better outcomes for students. Educational leaders can plan and direct school improvement through three phases: Lewin's unfreezing, moving, and refreezing.

In *unfreezing*, leaders present a compelling case for change. They provide data and rationales to help teachers experience a "felt need," when they recognize and accept that what they are presently doing is not enough to achieve their goals. This tension between teachers' aspirations and their actual performance creates a willingness to consider and accept new approaches. However, for change to be effective, it must occur as a participative and collaborative group process. Group learning (Lewin; Senge's team learning) is an essential aspect of unfreezing: unless teachers' colleagues experience a "felt need" and agree to accept new approaches, any change will likely be superficial, sporadic, and short-lived. During this phase, leaders also will want to remove perceived barriers to change.

Moving involves teachers learning new ways of perceiving, thinking, and responding. It includes implementing, assessing, and refining approaches to generate improved student outcomes, in part, by using colleague, student, and leader feedback. During this stage, leaders will want to help faculty to reflect, challenge, and discuss assumptions or shared norms (Senge's mental models) and assess their effectiveness in the current environment. Likewise, problem solving by "tinkering around the edges" or making minor adjustments (Argyris and Schön's single-loop learning) and/or by challenging the underlying norms and standards before identifying an intervention (Argyris and Schön's double-loop learning) also occur during this phase. Innovations that lead to change in knowledge and practice may be viewed as learning events (complexity theory). *Refreezing* includes reinforcing the new behaviors with better outcomes and revising actions where needed, and stabilizing the change (until the next unfreezing).

Schools are Linked to Larger Systems

As part of planning for organizational learning, school leaders will want to assess the relationships between their school and the other schools in their district. The district—and its community—represents a larger system of complex, interdependent forces that affect the school's current problems. Awareness of these interdependences will help leaders identify supervisors and stakeholders whose approval and resources will be needed, as well as identify areas of potential resistance to address. Leaders can then work with all parties to recognize, understand, and accommodate the relevant factors and influences affecting their decisions.

Schools, like other complex organizations, either adapt to meet existing and coming realities, or they lose students, families, and teachers to competing education models. School leaders play an essential role in guiding and managing this learning and changing process.

NOTES

1 Ford, J.D. & Ford, L.W. (1995). The role of conversation in producing intentional change in organizations. *Academy of Management Review*, 20 (3), 541–570.
2 Daft, R.L. & Lewin, A.Y. (1993). Where are the theories for the "new" organizational forms? An editorial essay. *Organization Science*, 4 (4), i–vi (p. i).
3 Dodgson, M. (1993). Organizational learning: A review of some literatures. *Organization Studies*, 14 (3), 375–394.
4 Garratt, R. (1987). *The learning organization*. London, UK: Fontana/Collins; Peters, T. & Waterman, R. (1982). *In search of excellence: Lessons from America's best run companies*. New York, NY: Harper and Row; Senge, P. (1990b). The leader's new work: Building learning organizations. *Sloan Management Review*, 32 (1), 7–23.
5 Miner, J.B. (2005). From social psychology and personality theory. In K. Lewin (Ed.). *Organizational behavior I. Essential theories of motivation and leadership* (pp. 37–45). Armonk, NY: M.E. Sharpe.
6 Lewin, K. (1947b). Group decisions and social change. In T.M. Newcomb and E.L. Hartley (Eds), *Readings in Social Psychology* (pp. 197–211). New York, NY: Henry Holt.
7 Burnes, B. (2004). Kurt Lewin and the planned approach to change: A re-appraisal. *Journal of Management Studies*, 41 (6), 977–1002.
8 Lewin conducted similar experiments with sewing machine operators to study changes in productivity levels and the decision to eat whole wheat rather than white bread with students. See: Miner (2005). Op. cit.

9 Lewin, K. (1947a). Frontiers in group dynamics: Concept, method, and reality in social science, social equilibria, and social change. *Human Relations, 1* (5), 5–41.

10 Barker, R., Dembo, T. & Lewin, K. (1941). Frustration and regress: An experiment with young children. *Studies in Topological and Vector Psychology II.* University of Iowa Press.

11 Hendry, C. (1996). Understanding and creating whole organizational change through learning theory. *Human Relations, 49* (5), 621–641; Management & Business Studies Portal (n.d.). Kurt Lewin: Change management and group dynamics thinker. Retrieved from: www. mbsportal.bl.uk/taster/subjareas/busmanhist/mgmtthinkers/lewin.aspx.

12 Weick, K.E. & Quinn, R.E. (1999). Organizational change and development. *Annual Review of Psychology, 50* (1), 171–221.

13 See: Lewin (1947b). Op. cit.; Lewin, K. (1943). Forces behind food habits and methods of change. *Bulletin of the National Research Council, 109* (1), 35–65: Lewin, K. (1946). Action research and minority problems. *Journal of Social Issues, 2* (4), 34–46; Lewin, K., Lippitt, R. & White, R. (1939). Patterns of aggressive behavior in experimentally created "social climates." *Journal of Social Psychology, 10* (2), 271–299.

14 Smith, M.K. (2001). Kurt Lewin, groups, experiential learning and action research. *The encyclopedia of informal education.* Retrieved from: www.infed.org/thinkers/et-lewin.htm.

15 Smith (2001). Ibid., Stringer, E.T. (1999) *Action research*, 2nd ed. Thousand Oaks, CA: Sage.

16 Miner (2005). Op. cit.

17 Pedigrew, A.M. (1985). *The awakening giant.* Oxford, UK: Basil Blackwell; Tushman, M.L., Newman, W.H. & Romanelli, E. (1986). Convergence and upheaval: Managing the unsteady pace of organizational evolution. *California Management Review, 29* (1), 29–44.

18 Hedberg, B. (1981). How organizations learn and unlearn. In P.C. Nystrom & W.H. Starbuck (Eds), *A handbook of organizational design*, 1. (pp. 8–27). Oxford, UK: Oxford University Press; Nystrom, P. & Starbuck, W. (1984). To avoid organizational crises, unlearn. *Organizational Dynamics, 12* (4), 53–65.

19 Burnes (2004). Op. cit., p. 977.

20 See: Garvin, D.A. (1993). Building a learning organization. *Harvard Business Review, 71* (4), 78–91; Kanter, R.M., Stein, B.A. & Jick, T.D. (1992). *The challenge of organizational change.* New York, NY: Free Press; Pettigrew, A.M. (1990). Longitudinal field research on change: Theory and practice. *Organizational Science, 3* (1), 267–292; Wilson, D.C. (1992). *A strategy of change.* London, UK: Routledge.

21 See: Dawson, P. (1994). *Organizational change: A processual approach.* London, UK: Paul Chapman; Dunphy, D.D. & Stace, D.A. (1993). The strategic management of corporate change. *Human Relations, 46* (8), 903–918; Miller, D. & Fresen, P.H. (1984). *Organizations: A quantum view.* Englewood Cliffs, NJ: Prentice Hall.

22 Dawson (1992). Op. cit.; Hatch. M.J. (1997). *Organization theory: Modern, symbolic, and post-modern perspectives.* Oxford, UK: Oxford University Press; Pettigrew, A.M. (1980). The politics of organizational change. In N.B. Anderson (Ed.), *The human side of information processing.* (pp. 45–51). Amsterdam, Netherlands: North Holland; Wilson, D.C. (1992). *A strategy of change.* London, UK: Routledge.

23 Dawson (1994). Op. cit.; Kanter et al. (1992). Op. cit.; Wilson (1992). Op. cit.

24 Marshak, R.J. (1993). Lewin meets Confucius: A re-view of the OD model of change. *Journal of Applied Behavioral Science, 29* (4). 393–415.

25 Burnes (2004). Op. cit.

26 Elrod, P.D. & Tippett, D.D. (2002). The "Death Valley" of change. *Journal of Organizational Change Management, 15* (3), 273–291.

27 Lewin (1947b). Op. cit.; Bargal, D., Gold, M. & Lewi, M. (1992). The heritage of Kurt Lewin—Introduction. *Journal of Social Issues, 48* (2), 3–13.

28 Hendry, C. (1996). Understanding and creating whole organizational change through learning theory. *Human Relations, 49* (5), 621–641.

29 Burnes (2004). Op. cit.

30 Hendry (1996). Op. cit.; Weick, K.E. & Quinn, R.E. (1999). Organizational change and development. *Annual Review of Psychology, 50* (1), 361–386; Miner (2005). Op. cit.; Goldstein, J. (1993). Beyond Lewin's force field: A new model for organizational change interventions. *Advances in Organization Development, 2* (1), 72–88; Marshak (1993). Op. cit.

31 Argyris, C. & Schön, D. (1974). *Theory in practice: Increasing professional effectiveness,* San Francisco, CA: Jossey-Bass; Argyris (1976a). Op. cit.

32 Argyris, C. (1980) *Inner contradictions of rigorous research,* New York, NY: Academic Press; Argyris, C. (1976c). Theories of action that inhibit individual learning. *American Psychologist, 31* (9), 638–654.

33 Argyris, C. (1976a). Leadership, learning, and changing the status quo. *Organizational Dynamics, 4* (3), 29–43 (p. 29).

34 Argyris, C., Putnam, R. & McLain Smith, D. (1985). *Action science.* (pp. 80–102). San Francisco, CA: Jossey Bass Social and Behavioral Science Series. Retrieved from: www. actiondesign.com/assets/pdf/AScha3.pdf.

35 Argyris, Putnam & McLain Smith (1985). Ibid.

36 Argyris, C. (1976c). Theories of action that inhibit individual learning. *American Psychologist, 31* (9), 638–654.

37 Argyris, C. (1996). Crossroads–Unrecognized defenses of scholars: Impact on theory and research. *Organization Science, 7* (1), 79–87.

38 Schön, D.A. (1983). *The reflective practitioner.* Winston, NY: Basic Books; Schön, D.A. (1987). *Educating the reflective practitioner.* San Francisco, CA: Jossey Bass.

39 Argyris, D. & Schön, D. (1978). *Organizational learning.* London, UK: Addison-Wesley.

40 In later years (1996), Argyris acknowledged that his initial (1974) reasoning about double-loop learning's superiority over single-loop learning was flawed. Further study showed him that single-loop learning could also create "liberating alternatives." See: Argyris, C. (1996). Op. cit.

41 Argyris, C. & Schön, D. (1974). *Theory in practice.* San Francisco, CA: Jossey-Bass.

42 Argyris, Putnam & McLain Smith (1985). Op. cit.

43 Argyris, C. (2002). Double-loop learning, teaching, and research. *Academy of Management Learning & Education. 1* (2), 206–218.

44 Greenwood, J. (1998). The role of reflection in single and double loop learning. *Journal of Advanced Nursing, 27* (5), 1048–1053.

45 Miner, A.S. & Mezias, S.J. (1996). Ugly duckling no more: Pasts and futures of organizational learning research. *Organization Science, 7* (1), 88–99.

46 Miner & Mezias (1996). Ibid.

47 See: Abernathy, W.J. & Clark, K.B. (1988). Innovation: Mapping the winds of creative destruction. In M.L. Tushman & W.L. Moore (Eds), *Readings in the management of innovation,* 2nd ed. (pp. 25–36). Cambridge, MA: Ballinger; Anderson, P. & Tushman, M.L. (1990). Technical discontinuities and dominant designs: A cyclical model of technological change. *Administrative Science Quarterly, 35* (1), 604–633; Dewar, R.D. & Dutton, J.E. (1986). The adoption of radical and incremental innovations: An empirical analysis. *Management Science, 32* (11), 1422–1433; Ettlie, J.E., Bridges, W.P. & O'Keefe, R.D. (1984). Organization strategy and structural differences for radical versus incremental innovation. *Management Science, 30* (6), 682–695.

48 Argyris, C. (1976b). Single-loop and double-loop models in research on decision making. *Administrative Science Quarterly, 21* (3), 363–375; Argyris, C. (1969). The incompleteness of social psychology theory. *American Psychologist, 24* (10), 893–908; Argyris & Schön (1974). Op. cit.

49 deLodzia, G. (1977). Reviewed work: Increasing leadership effectiveness by Chris Argyris. *The Academy of Management Review, 2* (3), 508–510.

50 deLodzia (1977). Ibid.; Easterby-Smith, M. & Araujo, L. (1999). Organizational learning: Current debates and opportunities. In M. Easterby-Smith, J. Burgoyne & L. Araujo (Eds), *Organizational learning and the learning organization: Developments in theory and practice* (pp. 1–21). London, UK: Sage.

51 Blackman, D., Connelly, J. & Henderson, S. (2004). Does double loop learning create reliable knowledge? *The Learning Organization, 11* (1), 11–27.

52 The Chernobyl nuclear reactor accident in the former USSR occurred when engineers radically departed from existing operating parameters while experimenting with a new form of on-line refueling. Instead of a major scientific breakthrough, they created a deadly disaster.

53 Easterby & Araujo (1999). Op. cit.

54 Easterby & Araujo (1999). Op. cit.

55 Stata, R. (1989). Organizational learning—The key to management innovation. *Sloan Management Review, 30* (3), 63–74 (p. 64).

56 Miner & Mezias (1996). Op. cit.

57 Argyris (1976b). Op. cit.

58 Pettigrew, A. (1979). On studying organizational cultures. *Administrative Science Quarterly, 24* (4), 570–581.

59 Glisson, C. (2000). Organisational climate and culture. In R. Patti (Ed.), *The handbook of social welfare* (pp. 195–218). Thousand Oaks, CA: Sage; Ouchi, W. & Wilkins, A. (1985). Organizational culture. *Annual Review of Sociology, 11* (1), 457–483.

60 Hatch, M.J. (1993). The dynamics of organizational culture. *Academy of Management Review, 18* (4), 657–693; Maxwell, T. & Thomas, A. (1991). School climate and school culture. *Journal of Educational Administration, 29* (2), 72–83; Prosser, J. (1999). The evolution of school culture research. In J. Prosser (Ed.), *School culture* (pp. 1–14). London: Paul Chapman.

61 Maxwell & Thomas (1991). Op. cit.; Prosser (1999). Op. cit.

62 Schein, E.H. (1985). *Organizational culture and leadership*. San Francisco, CA: Jossey-Bass.

63 Foster, C. (n.d.). The theorists—Edgar H. Schein. Organisational Development. Retrieved from: http://organisationdevelopment.org/the-theorists-edgar-h-schein/.

64 Schein, E.H. (2004). *Organizational culture and leadership*, 3rd ed. San Francisco, CA: Jossey-Bass (pp. 88, 112).

65 Schein, E.H. (1996a). Culture: The missing concept in organization studies. *Administrative Science Quarterly, 41* (2), 229–240.

66 Schein E.H. (1996b). Kurt Lewin's change theory in the field and in the classroom: Notes toward a model of managed learning. *Systems Practice, 9* (1), 2–47.

67 Pettigrew. A.M. (1990). Organizational climate and culture: Two constructs in search of a role. In B. Schneider (Ed.), *Organizational climate and culture* (pp. 413–433). San Francisco, CA: Jossey-Bass, p. 416.

68 Schein (1990). Op. cit., p. 91.

69 See: Schein (2004). Op. cit., Exhibit 1.1, pp. 12–15.

70 Leung, K., Bhagat, R.S., Buchan, N.R., Erez, M. & Gibson, C.B. (2005). Culture and international business: Recent advances and their implications for future research. *Journal of International Business Studies, 36* (4), 357–378.

71 Argyris (1976a). Op. cit.; Argyris & Schön (1974). Op. cit.

72 See: Detert, J.R., Schroeder, R.G. & Mauriel, J.J. (2000). A framework for linking culture and improvement initiatives in organizations. *Academy of Management Review, 25* (4), 850–863; Leidner, D.E. & Kayworth, T. (2006). Review: A review of culture in information systems research: Toward a theory of information technology culture conflict. *MIS Quarterly, 30* (2), 357–399; Sackmann, S.A. (2002). Culture and sub-cultures: An analysis of organizational knowledge. *Administrative Science Quarterly, 37*, (1), 140–161.

73 Kluckhohn, F.R. & Strodtbeck, F.L. (1961). *Variations in value orientations*. New York, NY: Harper; England, G. (1975). *The manager and his values*. New York, NY: L Ballinger; Hall, E.T. (1966). *The hidden dimension*. New York, NY: Doubleday.

74 Leung et al. (2005). Op. cit.

75 Leung et al. (2005). Op. cit.

76 Denison, D. & Mishra, A. (1995). Toward a theory of organizational culture and effectiveness. *Organization Science*, 6 (2), 204–224; Gordon, G.G., & Cummins, W. (1979). *Managing management climate*. Lexington, MA: Lexington Book; Heck, R.H. & Marcoulides, G.A. (1996). School culture and performance: Testing the invariance of an organizational model. *School Effectiveness and School Improvement*, 7 (1): 76–95; Toole, J. (1996). *Professional work life of teachers*. Minneapolis, MN: University of Minnesota Compass Institute.

77 Denison, D.R. & Mishra. A.K. (1995). Toward a theory of organizational culture and effectiveness. *Organization Science*, 6 (2), 204–223; Kilmann, R.H., Saxton, M.J. & Serpa, R. (Eds*)*, *Gaining control of the corporate culture*. San Francisco, CA: Jossey-Bass; Sashkin, M. & Kiser, K.J. (1993). *Putting total quality management to work: What TQM means, how to use it, and how to sustain it over the long run*. San Francisco, CA: Berrett-Koehler.

78 Goffee, R. & Jones, G. (1966). What holds the modem company together? *Harvard Business Review*, 74 (6), 133–148.

79 Blake. D.R.S. & Mouton, J.S. (1964). *The managerial grid*. Houston, TX: Gulf Publishing.

80 Wilkins. A. & Ouchi, W.G. (1983). Efficient cultures: Exploring the relationship between culture and organizational performance. *Administrative Science Quarterly*, 28 (3), 468–481.

81 Hofstede. G. (1991). *Culture and organizations: Software of the mind*. London, UK: McGraw Hill.

82 Denison & Mishra (1995). Op. cit.

83 See Leidner & Kayworth (2006). Op. cit. for a table of researched organization and national culture values.

84 Kong, S-H. (2003). A portrait of Chinese enterprise through the lens of organizational culture, *Asian Academy of Management Journal*, 8 (1), 83–102.

85 See Leidner & Keyworth (2006). Op. cit.

86 Leung et al. (2005). Op. cit.

87 Leung et al. (2005). Op. cit.

88 Bloor, G. & Dawson, P. (1994). Understanding professional culture in organizational context. *Organization Studies*, 15 (2), 275–295.

89 Raz, A. (2002). *Emotions at work: Normative control, culture and organizations in Japan and America*. Cambridge, MA and London, UK: Harvard University Asia Center.

90 Firestone, W. & Louis, K. (1999). Schools as cultures. In J. Murphy & K. Louis (Eds), *Handbook of research on educational administration*, 2nd ed. (p. 297—322). San Francisco, CA: Jossey-Bass; Ott, J. (1989). *The organizational culture perspective*. Pacific Grove, CA: Brooks/Cole; Meyerson, D. & Martin, J. (1987). Cultural change: An integration of three views. *Journal of Management Studies* 24 (6), 623–648.

91 Feldman, M. (1991). The meanings of ambiguity: Learning from stories and metaphors. In P. Frost, L. Moore, M. Louis, C. Lundberg & J. Martin (Eds), *Reframing organizational culture*. (pp. 145–156). Newbury Park. CA: Sage; Martin. J. (1992). *Cultures in organizations: Three perspectives*. New York, NY: Oxford University Press; Meyerson, D. (1991a). "Normal" ambiguity? In P. Frost, L. Moore, M. Louis, C. Lundberg & J. Martin (Eds), *Reframing organizational culture*. (pp. 31–144). Newbury Park. CA: Sage; Meyerson, D. (1991b). Acknowledging and uncovering ambiguities in cultures. In P. Frost, L. Moore, M. Louis, C. Lundberg & I. Martin (Eds), *Reframing organizational culture*. (pp. 254–270). Newbury Park, CA: Sage.

92 Hatch (1993). Op. cit. Hatch suggests Schein explain how both stability and change can both be parts of the same processes to make his model more dynamic.

93 Lawrence, P. & Lorsch, J. (1967). *Organization and environment*. Boston, MA: Harvard University Press; Thompson, J.D. (1967). *Organizations in action; social science bases of administrative theory*. New York, NY: McGraw-Hill.

94 Fiol, C.M. & Lyles, M.A. (1985). Organizational learning. *Academy of Management Review*, *10* (4), 803–813; Schön, D.A. (1983). Organizational learning. In G. Morgan (Ed.), *Beyond method: Strategies for social research* (pp. 114–128). Newbury Park, CA: Sage.

95 Meek, V.L. (1988). Organizational culture: Origins and weaknesses. *Organization Studies*, *9* (4), 453–473.

96 Schein (2004). Op. cit.

97 Schein (2004). Op. cit., p. 2.

98 Schein (2004). Op. cit., p. 23.

99 Senge, P. & Sherman, J.D. (1992). Systems thinking and organizational learning: Acting locally and thinking globally in the organization of the future. *European Journal of Operational Research*, *59* (1), 137–150.

100 Senge, P. (1990a). *The fifth discipline* (p. 139). New York, NY: Doubleday.

101 Senge, P., Cambron-McCabe, L.T., Smith, B. & Dutton, J. (2012). Schools that learn (Updated and Revised). A fifth discipline fieldbook for educators, parents, and everyone who cares about education. New York, NY: Crown.

102 Senge (1990a). Op. cit.

103 Sun, P.Y.T. & Scott, J.L. (2003). Exploring the divide—Organizational learning and learning organization. *The Learning Organization*, *10* (4), 202–215.

104 Senge, P.M. (2007). Peter Michael Senge. *New Zealand: Open Future*. Retrieved from: www.openfuture.co.nz/petersenge.htm.

105 Senge, P.M. (1990b). The leader's new work: Building learning organizations. *Sloan Management Review*, *32* (1), 7–23; Senge, P.M. Kleiner, A., Roberts, C., Ross, R., Roth, G. & Smith, B. (1999). *The dance of change: The challenges to sustaining momentum in a learning organization*. New York, NY: Currency.

106 Senge et al. (2012). Op. cit.

107 Ortenblad, A. (2007). Senge's many faces: Problem or opportunity? *The Learning Organization*, *14* (2), 108–122.

108 Roth, G.L. & Senge, P.M. (1996). From theory to practice: Research territory, processes and structure at an organizational learning center. *Journal of Organizational Change Management*, *9* (1), 92–106.

109 Senge, P.M. & Scharmer, C. (2006). Community action research: Learning as a community of practitioners, consultants, and researchers. In P. Reason & H. Bradbury (Eds), *Handbook of action reach: Concise paperback edition*. (pp. 195–206). Thousand Oaks, CA: Sage.

110 Kiedrowski, P.J. (2006). Quantitative assessment of a Senge learning organization intervention. *The Learning Organization*, *13* (4), 369–383.

111 Shields, C. & Newton, E. (1994). Empowered leadership. *Journal of School Leadership*, *4* (2), 171–196; Isaacson, N. & Bamburg, J. (1992). Can schools become learning organizations? *Educational Leadership*, *50* (3), 42–44.

112 Zemke, R. (1999). Why organizations still aren't learning. *Training*, *18* (11), 40–45.

113 Flood, R.L. (1998). "Fifth discipline": Review and discussion. *Systemic Practice and action Research*, *11* (3), 259–273.

114 Sun & Scott (2003). Op. cit.

115 Knowledge-power is the belief that those in power determine what knowledge is valid, affecting factors including hierarchy, gender, race, and disability, a critical theory perspective. See: Fielding, M. (2001). Learning organization or learning community: A critique of Senge. *Reason in Practice*, *1* (2), 17–29.

116 Flood (1998). Op. cit.

117 Fielding (2001). Op. cit.

118 Ortenblad (2007). Op. cit.; Sun & Scott (2003). Op. cit.

119 O'Neil, J. (1995). On schools as learning organizations: A conversation with Peter Senge. *Educational Leadership*, *52* (7), 20–23. Senge has written *Schools that learn. A fifth discipline field book for educators* (updated and revised in 2012) from Crown Business, Random House, to help educators implement the disciplines into their schools.

120 O'Neil (1995). Op. cit.
121 Senge, P.M. (2006). *The fifth discipline. The art & practice of the learning organization.* Revised edition (p. xiii). New York, NY: Currency Doubleday.
122 Senge as cited in McElroy, M.W. (2000). Integrating complexity theory, knowledge management and organizational learning. *Journal of Knowledge Management,* 4 (3), 195–203.
123 Davis, B., Sumara, D. & Luce-Kapler, R. (2008). *Engaging minds: Changing teaching in complex times,* 2nd ed. New York, NY: Routledge.
124 Holland, J. (1995). *Hidden order: How adaptation builds complexity.* New York, NY: Addison-Wesley Publishing Company.
125 Marion, R. (2012). Leadership of creativity: Entity-based, collectivist, and complexity perspectives. In M. Mumford (Ed.), *Handbook of organizational creativity* (pp. 453–475). Amsterdam: Elsevier; Perry-Smith, J.E. & Shalley, C.E. (2003). The social side of creativity: A static and dynamic social network perspective. *Academy of Management Review,* 28 (1), 89–106.
126 See: Bowers, J., Cobb, P. & McClain, K. (1999). The evolution of mathematical practices: A case study. *Cognition and instruction* 17 (1), 25–64; Lave, J. & Wenger, E. (1991). *Situated learning: Legitimate peripheral participation.* New York, NY: Cambridge University Press; Cobb, P., Perlwitz, M. & Underwood, D. (1996). Constructivism and activity theory: A consideration of their similarities and differences as they related to mathematics education. In H. Mansfield, N.A. Pateman & N. Bednarz (Eds), *Mathematics for tomorrow's young children: International perspectives on curriculum.* Boston, MA: Kluwer Academic Publishing.
127 Larsen-Freeman, D. (1989). Pedagogical descriptions of language grammar. *Annual Review of Applied Linguistics* 10, 187–195 Cambridge, UK: Cambridge University Press.
128 Larsen-Freeman, D. (1997). Chaos/complexity science and second language acquisition. *Applied LInguistics,* 18 (2), 141–165.
129 Larsen-Freeman (1997). Ibid.
130 Marion, R. & Gonzales, L.D. (2014). *Leadership in education. Organizational theory for the practitioner,* 2nd ed. Long Grove, IL: Waveland Press, pp. 240–241.
131 McElroy (2000). Op. cit.
132 Fioretti, G. & B. Visser. (2004). A cognitive interpretation of organizational complexity. *Emergence: Complexity & Organizations, Special Double Issue,* 6 (1–2), 11–23 (p. 14); Mason, R. (2007). The external environment's effect on management and strategy. A complexity theory approach. *Management Decision,* 45 (1), 10–28 (p. 18).
133 Hurford, A. (2007). Complex systems as lenses on learning and teaching. Unpublished dissertation. Austin, TX: University of Texas. Retrieved from: www.lib.utexas.edu/etd/d/2007/hurforda33592/hurforda33592.pdf.
134 Larsen-Freeman (1997). Op. cit.
135 Larsen-Freeman (1997). Op. cit.
136 Uhl-Bien, M., Marion, R. & McKelvey (2007). Complexity leadership theory: Shifting leadership from the industrial age to the knowledge era. *The Leadership Quarterly,* 18 (4), 298–318; Reiter-Palmon, R. & Illies, J.J. (2004). Leadership and creativity: Understanding leadership from the creative problem-solving perspective. *The Leadership Quarterly,* 15, 55–77.
137 Mason, R. (2007). The external environment's effect on management and strategy. A complexity theory approach. *Management Decision,* 45 (1), 10–28.
138 Larsen-Freeman (1997). Op. cit.
139 Avolio, B.J., Walumbwa, F.O. & Weber, T.J. (2009). Leadership: Current theories, research, and future directions. *Annual Review of Psychology,* 60 (1), 421–449.
140 Styhre, A. (2002). Non-linear change in organizations: Organization change management informed by complexity theory. *Leadership & Organization Development Journal,* 23 (6), 343–351.

141 Frank, K.A. & Fahrbach, K. (1999). Organization culture as a complex system: Balance and information in models of influence and selection. *Organization Science*, *10* (3), 253–277.

142 Mason (2007). Op. cit.; White, L. (2000). Changing the "whole system" in the public sector. *Journal of Organizational Change Management*, *13* (2), 162–177.

143 Larsen-Freeman (1997). Op. cit.

144 Davis, B. & Sumara, D. (2008). Complexity as a theory of education. *Transnational Curriculum Inquiry*, *5* (2), 33–44. Retrieved from: http://ecs210.uregina.wikispaces.net/file/view/Complexity+as+a+Theory+of+Education.pdf.

145 Avolio, Walumbwa & Weber (2009). Op. cit.

146 McElroy (2000). Op. cit.

147 Weick & Quinn (1999). Op. cit.

CHAPTER 6

Managing Conflict for Organizational Effectiveness

CASE STUDY 6.1

Conflicting Stories

As an AP physics teacher at Battlefield High School for the last ten years, Glen Schultz was very popular with students and faculty alike. He finished a Leadership Preparation program at the local university and had just been appointed the new assistant principal at his school. Many of his close friends on the faculty were glad to have him there.

A conflict had been brewing over the last several years about grouping students for various high school courses. The school had various "tracks" for students. Students in the International Baccalaureate (IB) program and the Advanced Placement (AP) program had their own classes. The school also had an Honors program, "regular" classes, and remedial classes. Four years ago, a new principal was hired who firmly believed that all students should have a rigorous academic program. Part of the faculty agreed. But another part of the faculty believed that high achieving students should be grouped in classes to help "advanced" students reach their potential and the "slower" students grouped so teachers could help meet their learning needs. Before the principal ended the "regular" and remedial English classes, he provided affected teachers with professional development on how to engage and support students in a more challenging curriculum. The next year, student scores increased on the English state achievement tests—the only group in the school to see gains. The rest of the faculty expected the principal to end "regular" and remedial classes in other subject areas soon. Veteran teachers, who taught upper level classes, were apprehensive.

Glen had quietly sided with the teachers who wanted to maintain the student achievement grouping. But he did not openly support them while completing his leadership preparation program. Glen did not want to oppose the principal and possibly hurt his chances of moving into administration. On teachers' first day back for the new school year, the principal announced that the "regular" and remedial classes in the Social Studies department would end the following year. Teachers would have professional development during the current school year to prepare them to teach the honors curriculum to all non-IB or AP students. After the meeting, Glen's "friends" reminded him of his views and wanted him to side with them against the principal. Glen replied that he would talk with the principal and see what he could do—he still agreed with them.

The next day, another teacher group came to Glen's office. They had heard rumors that the detracking would not go forward as planned. This group, mostly newer faculty members, wanted the detracking plan to proceed. They liked it for two reasons. First, the average and "remedial" students were learning more; their test scores affirmed this. Second, as the newer teachers, they were generally assigned to the "lower level" classes until they gained seniority and became eligible to fill teaching vacancies in upper level courses as teacher turnover occurred. Unable to find fault in their reasoning, Glen told the group that he supported their ideas and would pass them along to the principal.

The next week, arguments broke out in the faculty workroom and lunchroom about the school's direction on detracking. At Thursday afternoon's faculty meeting, tensions and words grew heated. Both groups thought Glen supported their position. One person yelled, "Glen said he supported our position" while another retorted, "No, Glen supports us!" The principal glanced at Glen with a raised eyebrow.

Lens and/or factors to be considered in decision making	What are the factors at play in this case?	What steps should be considered in solving the problem?	What could have been done to avoid this dilemma?
The situation			
• The task	The principal was eliminating tracking in the social studies department. Glen told both groups what they wanted to hear.	Since Glen did not reinforce the principal's plan, he needs to make sure Glen clears this up with the faculty.	The principal could have shared and gained widespread faculty (and Glen's) support for his vision for all students' achievement earlier.
• Personal abilities	Glen did not understand his role as a school leader.	Glen needs to develop leadership maturity and fully support the principal's direction.	The principal could have met just with the teachers who taught the "honors" classes and informed them of pending changes.
• The school environment	The school's climate became fractured as tensions rose between teachers who did—and did not—support the change.	The principal could meet with the department, listen to the concerns, and provide the research and collegial support for the action.	The principal could have shared plans and research with the entire faculty to foster understanding of why the changes were being made.

RUBRIC 6.1

Look Wider

Lens and/or factors	What are the factors at play in this case?	What steps should be considered in solving the problem?	What could have been done to avoid this dilemma?
Organizational (i.e., the organizational goals, values, policies, culture)	This is a classic example of intragroup conflict exacerbated by the AP's leadership immaturity.	Recognize that focusing this conflict as internal (our school versus my department and theirs) may help. The principal could have laid out the plan to the faculty from the start with better communication.	From the onset, the principal could have developed a shared vision for the change with the leadership team and shared the test results of detracked English classes and the English teachers' experiences with the rest of the faculty.
People (i.e., individuals with needs, beliefs, goals, relationships)	The "veteran" teachers believe they earned the right to teach "upper level" classes. Newer teachers see the educational and personal value in detracking.	Recognize that opposition to changing the courses by those with competing interests may occur. Involve supportive parents and community in expressing high expectations for their children's learning.	Improved communication to develop a shared vision; impart colleagues' experiences with the change; the principal orients Glen to his new role with a more appropriate mental model before teachers return.

continued . . .

Competing Interests (i.e., competing interests for power, influence, and resources)	The two groups have competing interests in how classes are structured. Glen needs to resolve his role conflict and become an AP.	Share best practices with the faculty and explain with evidence and reason why this change is warranted.	If the school were having problems with teacher turnover, explaining the instructional and personnel advantages would help the faculty understand change value.
Tradition (i.e., school culture, rituals, meaning, heroes)	The principal was changing how classes were structured and how veteran and new teachers were treated.	Recognize that the change will impact how the school has operated for veteran teachers' benefit.	Consider—with faculty input—if the implementation should be done by department each year or on a larger scale.

OVERVIEW: WELL-MANAGED CONFLICT AS A KEY TO ORGANIZATIONAL EFFECTIVENESS

"Conflict is a stubborn fact of organizational life."[1] It is also one of the keys to effective organizational functioning.

Although most organizational leaders tend to view conflict as bad and something to be avoided or quickly resolved, in reality, conflict, well understood and managed, can have functional outcomes for organizations. Studies over the past two decades have examined and confirmed both the benefits of organizational conflict and the methods for facilitating productive conflict.[2]

Organizational conflict management is too expansive a topic to fit into one chapter. Our focus, therefore, will be to define *conflict* as it affects organizations, look at types of conflict that may appear in organizations, consider several evolving views on organizational conflict, and examine four influential theories about how conflict develops and affects organizational performance, and how organizations can manage it constructively. Examples will illustrate conflict in a school context. These perspectives add conceptual and practical dimensions that educational leaders can use to improve school outcomes.

UNDERSTANDING ORGANIZATIONAL CONFLICT

Conflict is a major organizational dynamic, either as a symptom, cause, or effect related to an organizational problem. Over the years, economists, socio-biologists, philosophers, political scientists, sociologists, psychologists, experts in international law, peace researchers, and theologians have each studied conflict as it relates to their discipline.[3] This extensive scope allows conflict study as a broad social phenomenon from interpersonal to international levels.

Defining Conflict

Morton Deutsch (1920–), the Columbia University social psychology professor and conflict resolution researcher, defined *conflict* as existing "whenever incompatible activities occur."[4] The incompatible actions—actual or perceived—prevent, obstruct, interfere with, injure, or in some way make the other person's action less likely or less effective. *Conflict in organizations* occurs when members engage in activities that are incompatible with those of their workplace colleagues, members of other workgroups, or unaffiliated persons who use their organization's services or products.[5]

Conflicts may arise from differences in information or beliefs; differing interests, desires, and values; a scarcity of desired resources (such as money, time, space, or position); or an interpersonal rivalry in which one person tries to "outdo or undo" the other. Most definitions of conflict agree that it results from incompatibility or opposition in goals, activities, or interaction among social entities.

Conflict is also a process. Scholars agree that conflict at any level shares a generic format, as Figure 6.1 illustrates. As with any social process, conflict has causes, a core series of steps, and results. The results or their effects feed back to influence the causes. This conflict cycle occurs within a context or environment, and the cycle will flow through several repetitions.[6]

In this conflict cycle, *causes* of conflict include individual characteristics (i.e., personality, values, commitment to one's position, stress, anger, and desire for autonomy); interpersonal factors (i.e., perceptions of the others' intentions and behaviors, misunderstandings, and distrust; communications; behaviors; structure, and prior interactions); and issues (i.e., complex or simple, multiple or few, vague or clear, principles, size, and whether the issue can be broken into smaller, more manageable parts). Research evidence, theory, and thoughtful observations support these conclusions.[7]

Likewise, conflict's *core processes* include the interpersonal behaviors and expressed emotions in which one or both disputants oppose the other's interests and goals. *Results* of conflict include effects that impact:

- *The individuals*—their emotions, tensions, anxiety, low job satisfaction, and reduced performance motivation or, at low conflict levels, stimulation and excitement.
- *Their relationships*—the perceptions leading to distrust of the other, misunderstandings, inability to see the other's perspective.

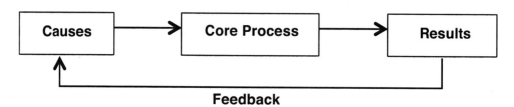

FIGURE 6.1 The Conflict Cycle

Source: Adapted from Wall, J.A., Jr. & Callister, R.R. (1995). Conflict and its management. *Journal of Management, 21* (3), 515–558 (p. 516).

- *Their communications*—interactions become more hostile, distorted, increased misunderstandings, avoidance, or increased contacts with those not directly involved.
- *Their behavior*—actions include avoidance, face saving tactics, venting emotions, confrontations, threats or physical force; with longer conflict, low commitment to decision implementation, increased absenteeism, more grievances, reduced productivity.
- *The organizational structure*—leadership shifts to more autocratic or authoritarian styles, decreased group interdependence and coordination.
- *The issues*—simple issues become complex, misunderstandings occur, and additional issues appear.
- *Other remaining residues*—including explicit or tacit agreements or deadlocks, tolerance of conflict and the opponent, resolving issues, and one or both sides gaining benefits.

The conflict cycles through these processes. Over time, its effects alter the original causes or generate new ones. Scholars conclude that theories of conflict appear to agree on these factors.[8]

Notably, incompatibilities, disagreement, or differences do not automatically lead to conflict. For conflict to happen or for members to become aware, it must exceed a certain intensity threshold—that is, reach the point at which the conflict is serious enough that it cannot be ignored. Individuals vary in their conflict awareness threshold; some feel it sooner than others.

Types of Conflict

Inside organizations, conflict may occur at different levels: intrapersonal, interpersonal, intragroup, and intergroup. *Intrapersonal conflict* occurs when an organization member is required to perform certain tasks and roles that do not match his/her expertise, interests, goals, and values. For instance, principals may expect teachers to serve as mentors to their students, encouraging students to openly say "what's on their mind." But teachers may feel very uncomfortable if pushed to act as "counselors," a professional role for which they are neither prepared nor qualified.

Interpersonal conflict occurs when two or more members of the same or different hierarchical levels or units have an incompatibility over a task, beliefs, or values. Two social studies teachers may disagree about the merits of tutoring low achieving students after school if the students have not prepared adequately or acted appropriately during the class.

In addition, *intragroup conflict* (or intradepartmental conflict) refers to incompatibility among members of a group or between two or more subgroups within a group in relation to its goals, tasks, procedures, or other factors. English department members may often argue about the merits of rigid tracking. Certain teachers may believe that heterogeneous mixing of students of varied abilities in high interest, high challenge, and high support classrooms is best for raising everyone's achievement. By contrast, several colleagues may believe that separating students by achievement allows teachers to better serve students' learning needs.

Finally, *intergroup conflict* (or interdepartmental conflict) recognizes incompatibility between two or more units or groups within an organization. Central office supervisors may schedule Parents Nights once each grading period, whereas principals and teachers would prefer them to occur once each semester.

Conflict may be actual or perceived. Misperceptions, misinformation, and the parties' own psychological states and personal values influence whether or not a conflict actually exists or whether parties only think it does. To illustrate this point, Deutsch offers an analogy of "pure conflict." Two starving men on a lifeboat have only enough food for one of them to survive. If one (or both) of the persons has social or religious values that celebrate "doing unto others" rather than self-preservation (i.e., such as the need to eat), no conflict may occur. Generally, *actual conflict* and its outcomes may be objectively observed, precisely measured, and rationally assessed for their quantifiable benefits or losses. In contrast, *perceived conflict* and outcomes are more difficult to observe, measure, or assess (except, perhaps, in a controlled laboratory situation).

Additionally, by its interdisciplinary nature, the field of conflict means different things to different people. The terms *conflict management* and *conflict resolution* are loosely used and interchangeable, often referring to the same strategies. Some scholars argue about whether one or another term suggests conflicts are bad for organizations and should be "resolved," or whether conflicts can be good for organizations and should be "managed" to create more beneficial outcomes.[9]

Nonetheless, contemporary conflict theory models tend to rest on three key assumptions. First, conflict begins from a variety of possible sources. Second, conflict follows a predictable course or pattern. And third, conflict is expressed in many ways, which can have both positive and negative consequences.[10] The theorists discussed in this chapter base their ideas on these three assumptions.

EVOLVING VIEWS ON ORGANIZATIONAL CONFLICT

Since the beginning of time, conflict has been a human dynamic. Yet over the centuries, theorists' beliefs about conflict have changed from perceiving it as a harmful force, an aberration to be avoided, to seeing it as a normal process with desirable outcomes.

The classical organization theorists—Frederick Taylor, Henri Fayol, and Max Weber—each assumed that conflict harmed organizational efficiency and should be minimized. Taylor argued that applying his scientific management principles would make labor-management conflict vanish. But he offered no suggestions for how managers might handle any hypothetical conflict in an organization. Although Fayol proposed broader and more systematic management approaches than Taylor, he also supposed that conflict harmed organizational effectiveness. He proposed organizational structures—such as hierarchy, rules and procedures, lines of authority, and division of labor—to limit members from participating in conflict. Likewise, Weber envisioned his bureaucracy with its efficiency anchored in well-defined authority, structure, rules, and procedures that would leave no room for conflict. Elton Mayo thought people in organizations brought irrational and conflictual elements into the work setting that would harm efficiency and proposed a human resources orientation to prevent or resolve these.

By comparison, Mary Parker Follett clearly recognized the value of constructive conflict in organizations, seeing it as a spur to individual and social progress. Follett advocated the need for a problem solving approach to handling discord—rather than using ineffective methods such as suppression, avoidance, dominance, or compromise.

While traditional organization theorists Taylor, Fayol, Weber, and Mayo each regarded conflict as anathema to organizational efficiency, their unique perspectives on organizations led to different solutions. Taylor, Fayol, and Weber tried to reduce conflict by adjusting the organization's technical-structural system whereas Mayo tried to minimize conflict by modifying its social system. Their approaches to reducing conflict strongly influenced organizational thinking during the early to mid-twentieth century. Follett, by comparison, saw merit in organizational conflict as a stimulus to improved effectiveness and innovation. Her work would influence contemporary thought about conflict in organizations.

Contemporary Views

In the 1960s, the American public churned over the Vietnam War, civil rights unrest, political assassinations, and the women's movement. These urgencies upended earlier views favoring societal stability and organizational harmony and prompted serious interest in conflict theory. During the late 1980s and early 1990s, investigations into how conflicts occurred in organizations became prominent. Now, conflict study became less about highly visible and public confrontations (such as strikes, walkouts, or firings) but rather recognized that most organizational conflict happens inevitably, informally, and often out of sight.[11]

Contemporary scholars see tension as normal, even desirable.[12] Some assert that an organization's goal is to design a system able to recognize and solve problems it confronts, not to achieve harmony.[13] They see conflict occurring between any groups in which the potential for inequality exists: unequal groups have competing values and goals. This ongoing intergroup friction creates the platform for unending change—in organizations and in society. Going further, some argue that conflict in organizations is unavoidable. Successful organizations actually build conflict management into their design.

In fact, scholars today propose a philosophy of organizational conflict that recognizes its necessity, encourages opposing viewpoints, defines conflict management to include stimulation as well as resolution methods, and considers conflict management to be a major leadership and administrative responsibility.[14] In this view, "Conflict becomes an instrument of social change and influence rather than a symptom of a breakdown in social relationships."[15] As a result, organizational conflict is now considered to be a reasonable, expected, and positive indicator of an effectively managed organization.

REFLECTIONS AND RELEVANCE 6.1

Conflict and You

Conflict is a reality of human society and rests on three assumptions. 1) It begins from a variety of sources; 2) It follows a predictable pattern or course; 3) It is expressed in a variety of ways and has both positive and negative outcomes.

What has been your personal experience with conflict? Thinking of a conflict that you experienced or observed at home or at work, answer the following questions and discuss your answers with a partner.

- Explain how you generally respond (thoughts and feelings) to observing or participating in conflict.
- Briefly describe a conflict you observed or experienced from start to finish.
- Identify its cause/s (issues, personality factors, environmental/situational conditions).
- Describe its core processes (individuals behaviors, expressed emotions).
- Identify its results—positive and/or negative for the issue, relationship, group or organization, others.

After the partners have finished, discuss your findings as a whole class.

CONFLICT THEORY

In the 1950s, Lewis Coser and Ralf Dahrendorf saw conflict's social benefits. Their contributions to conflict theory have become part of the shared fund of sociological knowledge.[16] Later in the century, Louis Pondy and Louis Kriesberg would identify the stages by which conflict developed. All four theorists believed that conflict could have mutually harmful or beneficial outcomes, depending on an array of factors.

Lewis A. Coser—Conflict can be Functional

Lewis A. Coser (1913–2003) is one of the earliest theorists to consider conflict's functional outcomes. Coser, a European political refugee from World War II, completed his Ph.D. dissertation in sociology at Columbia University. In his book, *The Functions of Social Conflict* (1956),[17] Coser argued that conflict is instinctual, found everywhere in human society. And human conflict is goal related, used to achieve desired ends. Accordingly, social conflict has productive potential: it provides the conditions for rational, conscious behavior.[18]

Coser defined *social conflict* as "the struggle over values or claims to status, power, and scarce resources in which the aims of conflict groups are not only to gain the desired values, but also to neutralize, injure, or eliminate rivals."[19] As he explained, any system implies an allocation of power, wealth, and status positions among certain individuals and subgroups. As a result, these individuals and subgroups have a vested interest in keeping this honor, wealth, and power; and they will actively resist attempts to lose it. At the same time, other like-minded individuals and subgroups may feel a sense of *relative deprivation*, having less of a desired resource in comparison to another person or group. To them, it appears that while certain people are doing better, they seem to be losing out. Since these dissatisfied people are not *absolutely deprived* (i.e., living well below the poverty line), they have the emotional and material resources available to involve themselves in conflict and social change. As dissatisfied individuals and groups agitate for their own larger share resources, those who hold "privileges" in the current system tend to see efforts to reallocate resources as an attack on the social order and on the system, itself.

Types of Functional Conflict

Coser proposed two types of functional conflict—internal and external. *Internal conflict* occurs between or among groups that operate in the same social system, and *external conflict* occurs outside the group. Coser believed that conflict within a group often helps to revitalize existing norms and contributes to forming new ones, allowing groups to adjust appropriately to new conditions. This ensures their continuance under changed circumstances. Internal conflict also provides a means to test the relative strength of opposing interests within the organization, offering a way to maintain or readjust the balance of power. Frequent, low-level conflict—where dissatisfied teachers and staff can express their grievances directly to their immediate supervisors and resolve the issues quickly—creates the moral and social structures that enable competing interests to work together: a highly functional result.

Nonetheless, Coser did not see all internal conflict as functional. Internal conflicts in which the contending parties no longer share the basic values upon which the group's legitimacy rests threaten to disrupt the group and be dysfunctional for the group's wellbeing. Further, he noted that unless a group's social structure showed flexibility, tolerated competing interests, and provided institutional ways for members to immediately and directly express their rival claims, it was more likely that internal conflict could tear the group apart. For example, initiating a major change in students' academic grouping, curriculum, instruction, or assessment without first developing a shared faculty vision and values to support this change, may lead to reluctant teacher compliance, and less than full cooperation in implementing it.

External conflict could also have functional outcomes. Generally speaking, as a group experiences external conflict, the boundaries around the group become stronger, its members experience more solidarity and camaraderie, the group uses power more efficiently, and it forms alliances with other groups. Members identify "insiders" and "outsiders." When schools' athletic teams compete, school-wide pep rallies with the marching band playing and cheerleaders yelling help generate the school spirit and reinforce group consciousness of "us" (School A) versus "them" (School B). Coser even claimed, "Groups may look for enemies to help maintain and/or increase internal cohesion."[20]

But, Coser challenged, external conflict did not always lead to functional outcomes, either to group cohesion or centralized control. Rather, external conflict could lead to the breakdown of social norms and values, not to group cohesion. If several School A students, in a misguided application of "school spirit," vandalized School B—with no discipline penalty for the perpetrators—other local students might see this as permission to vandalize other schools. In Coser's view, increased group cohesion in response to an external threat depended on meeting several preconditions: the group must exist—and see itself as a group—before external conflict begins, and the group must recognize the outside threat and perceive it as a menace to the whole group. In addition, Coser believed that non-violent conflicts did not need to lead to centralized control whereas violent conflicts—such as warfare—did.

Responding to Organizational Conflict

Coser proposed that conflict—whether internal or external—tends to be functional for a social structure *unless* no or insufficient avenues—either tolerance for competing viewpoints, or institutional means to express and resolve conflict—exist to express it. And although conflict could lead to mobilizing group members' energies in ways that inspire increased cohesion and (sometimes) centralization, if the group lacks the solidarity to begin with, outside conflict can make it disintegrate. This perspective has implications for successfully addressing organizational conflict.

Simply having different allocations of power, status, and resources within organizations does not, by itself, lead to conflict. But when certain groups within the organization compare their share of resources and feel deprived in comparison with others, *and question the legitimacy* of this distribution, discontent is likely to follow. If no institutionalized ways exist for those frustrated to express their grievances, they may find avenues outside the accepted organizational norms to bring change—either through enacting innovations that improve organizational practices or by openly rejecting the organization's goals in ways that may bring dysfunctional outcomes for the system.

In contrast, more elastic systems permit the open and direct expression of conflict within them. Members may adopt new patterns of behavior as they choose appropriate means for increasing their resources and rewards, and lessen their frustration. This allows the balance of power to shift without destroying the entire organization. Coser advocated for organizations to allow dissenting views—change—to be expressed in ways that benefitted (rather than fractured or destroyed) the organization. Figure 6.2 illustrates Coser's organizational conflict model that results in either functional or dysfunctional

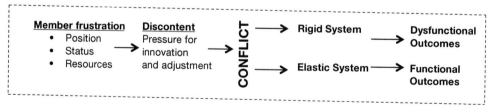

FIGURE 6.2 Coser's Organizational Conflict Model

Source: Based on Coser, L. (1956). *The functions of social conflict* (pp. 151–157). New York, NY: The Free Press.

outcomes, depending on the system's structures as rigid or elastic, and with porous boundaries that allow environmental influences to enter. Systems that tolerate competing views and have institutional means to express and resolve conflict tend to have more functional outcomes.

With an optimistic perspective, Coser asserted that organizational conflict applies pressure for innovation and adjustment, thereby preventing the system from calcifying. He saw the paradox of the human relations approach: denying or trying to reduce conflicts in the interests of industry may, inadvertently, generate dysfunctional outcomes by destroying an important stimulus—conflict—needed for technological innovation. Likewise, workers organized into unions virtually institutionalize conflict with management, exerting pressure on the decision makers to improve working conditions and benefits. For Coser, conflict in organizations made it possible for members to break free of "the eternal yesterday of precedent and tradition," overcome stifling routine and resistance to innovation, and become capable of creativity and renewal. At the same time, because conflict makes change possible, it threatens bureaucratic office holders (who may work harder to resist it).

Conflict and Violence

Coser believed that conflict could vary according to its level of violence. *Violence* is "the intentional use of physical force or power, threatened or actual, against oneself or another [or group] that either results in or has a high likelihood of resulting in injury, death, psychological harm, . . . or deprivation"[21] as a means to exercise control over another's actions. Although physical violence is not likely to result from teachers disagreeing with their administrators, aggressive behaviors are possible. Emotional harm, verbal abuse, or other form of injury or damage may also result. However, if people perceive conflict as a means to attain clearly articulated, rational goals, the conflict will tend to be less physically or verbally aggressive. For instance, a simple exchange—such as a teacher asking the principal for a different classroom next year—is low-level conflict. The principal assigns the teacher to the desired classroom (or the teacher accepts the principals' reasons why it cannot happen); no aggression occurs. Similarly, civil rights advocates often use passive resistance—such as simply sitting down where they are and refusing to get up and walk away when police request it—to achieve their goals. They suspect that physical violence will weaken public support for their legitimate claims. Likewise, goals about everyday concerns tend to generate less violence than goals that are larger than the group or daily concerns.

By comparison, conflict can be more violent when members have a strong emotional investment and transcendent goals. The more intensely the individuals feel about the contested issue, the higher their emotional engagement, and the greater the chances for behavioral acting out if the group feels threatened. For instance, a dozen teachers at risk for losing their jobs as the result of a district-wide reduction-in-force—who collectively fear their livelihood and profession may be taken unfairly—will have stronger emotions and more likelihood of disruption than if a dozen teachers are told they will be changing classrooms next year. The degree of emotional involvement and transcendent goals of the first group are substantially higher than those of the second, and members' responses may be quite different.

Research and Criticism

Despite conflict theory's popularity in the 1950s and 1960s, it largely lacked empirical research.[22] But available studies support many of Coser's assumptions. A 1976 review of empirical studies in anthropology, psychology, political science, and cross-cultural linkages supported Coser's view that external conflict increases group solidarity only under certain conditions—including the nature of the conflict and the nature of the group.[23] Additionally, substantial research supports Coser's belief that perceptions of group threat, arising from either actual or suspected competition for material or symbolic resources, are at least sufficient to produce dysfunctional consequences.[24]

Several critics have censured Coser's conflict theory for not fully abandoning the traditional sociological perspective that organizational conflict is harmful,[25] and thus presenting a distorted view of social reality.[26] Critics have also challenged Coser's conflict theory for not recognizing the possibility that group cohesion will only result after social conflict reaches a particular threshold,[27] for not considering possible negative outcomes of group cohesion (such as lowering the quality of leadership decision making with groupthink),[28] and for vagueness in other areas.[29]

In trying to demonstrate social conflict's positive outcomes, Coser departed from the traditional sociology view that organizations sought balance, valued consensus and harmony, and avoided conflict. In its place, he proposed a theory that social conflict, while divisive, also has integrating, stabilizing, and beneficial effects on organizations and social groups. He and Ralf Dahrendorf tried to balance consensus and stability in organizations with the realities of conflict and change.

Ralf Dahrendorf—Conditions that Facilitate Conflict

Ralf Dahrendorf (1929–2009), a German-British sociologist, scholar, and politician, also saw conflict as a normal part of how we structure society and create social order. His experiences as a high school student in Nazi Germany, sent to a concentration camp for distributing pamphlets opposing the regime, led him to champion social systems that recognized differing interests and aspirations, and put structures in place that allowed their expression.[30] In *Class and Conflict in Industrial Society* (1952),[31] Dahrendorf advanced a theory to understand conflict, its contributions to the social process, and its potential for progress.[32] Like Coser, he rejected sociology's prevailing view of idealized social cohesion and stability. Instead, he viewed conflict as social groups' struggles in response to specific social structures (such as positions within organizations), rather than as psychological (such as "aggressiveness"), or historical (such as African Americans versus whites in the United States) variables.[33]

Power, Authority, and Conflict

In Dahrendorf's conflict theory, power is the central feature of any society, and authority relations are the basis of social organization and conflict.[34] All social structures and organizations have hierarchical positions (and collectively, the group members who occupy them), with differing degrees of power and authority. *Power* could take the forms of brute force (i.e., physical strength or deadly weapons) or persuasion (i.e., requiring verbal and psychological skills); both are viewed as part of an individual's personality. In contrast, *authority*, the legitimate power to exercise control over other positions, resides in the position, not in the person. It is part of the institutional roles that manage social relations using binding and compulsory rules to achieve social order through legitimized power. And as occurs in any organizational hierarchy, some "command" and others "obey." For instance, teachers have authority over students; principals have authority over teachers; district superintendents have authority over principals. School boards have authority over superintendents. In addition, "ruling clusters" of roles that possess authority have an interest in preserving the status quo, while the "ruled clusters" without authority have an interest in redistributing power or clout and gaining more of the desired resources.

Situations involving authority relations contain differing sets of power interests— latent and manifest. *Latent interests* are those more or less unconscious concerns that belong to members with similar roles and expectations who are in loose association with each other but who share no special sense of group identity or mutual interest. American graduate students, in general, have only latent interests. By comparison, *manifest interests* are those conscious concerns that become clear and articulated when members with similar roles and expectations form an interest group defined by shared group identity and goals. For instance, when American graduate students in educational leadership realize that they must pass the SLLA (School Leaders' Licensure Assessment) to be eligible to apply for an assistant principal's or principal's position, their latent interests become manifest. With this shared goal of passing the SLLA clearly in mind, they may meet with graduate faculty to ensure that professors specifically teach the content to be assessed and provide SLLA preparation activities before taking the high stakes exam.

In organizations, when a group becomes aware of its objective interests (that is, when interests move from *latent* to *manifest*), groups engage in a contest—or conflict— with authority. Often, the resolution of this conflict involves redistributing authority (and the desirable resources that go with it) within the group, making conflict the source of social change in social systems. When educational leadership professors cede control of certain aspects of their curricula to meet graduate students' demands, authority for designing and enacting the prescribed program of study is redistributed.

In Dahrendorf's view, the continuity of social life occurs through authoritative power constraining its members through imposed norms and values, rather than by members forming a consensus around shared social beliefs.[35] In fact, social roles, norms, status positions, and values may reflect the interests of the society's most powerful and elite members rather than those of the middle or lower classes. As a result, norms always assume an aspect of power; they are negatively or positively enforced. In this regard, Dahrendorf defines his notion of conflict more narrowly than Coser.[36]

Organizational Conflict

While Dahrendorf's theory largely focuses on social class conflict, his ideas also relate to organizational conflict. In organizations, authority and power are not equally distributed. This divide allows members and management to categorize each other as "them" versus "us." These groups carry opposite latent interests that either want to preserve—or want to change—the status quo. Typically, those who support the status quo (usually, leaders and managers) and those who challenge it (usually, workers) organize themselves into like-minded interest groups, such as cliques, political parties or trade unions. They formulate their interests into specific programs and ideologies. Interest groups started in this way are in constant conflict, focused on either preserving or changing the status quo. Likewise, every form of social organization (including chess clubs, schools, churches, and industrial enterprises) contains opposing elements: stability and change, integration and conflict, function and dysfunction, consensus and constraint. To Dahrendorf, society is not an *ellipse* (a rounded entity that encloses all its elements) but rather a *hyperbola* (with the same foci as the ellipse but "open in many directions in a tension field of determining forces")[37]—that is, society is an open system.

Conditions that Facilitate Conflict

Dahrendorf identified three sets of conditions to be met if conflict is to occur: technical, political, and social. *Technical* conditions are those things that actually define a social group, without which a group cannot perform. These include committed members who lead the group, defining ideas or ideologies that differ from those in authority or power, and clear norms to guide behavior. *Political* conditions refer to the ability to meet and organize. Members need place and opportunity to gather, collect and review information, share concerns, and decide how to respond—in short, circumstances that allow an interest group to develop. *Social* conditions include communications (including speech, newspapers, U.S. Postal mail, email, and other Internet-based social media) and opportunities for individual and group mobility. The more effectively members can share information, the more likely they are to form interest groups.

But social conditions can also set limits on communication; communication channels must be available and reliable if an interest group is to develop. Search engines such as Google, listservs, social media like Twitter or Tumblr, and websites like Yahoo are structural Internet features that more predictably allow people to connect with each other than would relying on random, highly personal circumstances such as logging into an individual's Facebook page. Twenty-first century technical, political, and social conditions—the Internet and smart phones—allow jihadist groups to communicate and act upon their shared ideology across continents.

Conflict Violence and Intensity

These three conditions of organization—technical, political, and social—are related to conflict violence and conflict intensity. The more the group has met the technical, political, and social conditions, the more it has rational goals and uses reasonable means to achieve them, the less likely the conflict will be violent. Figure 6.3 depicts Dahrendorf's view of organizational conflict. When organizations provide a dissatisfied member (or members) with three conditions—technical, political, and social—they can form an interest group. And when they pursue rational goals using reasonable means, the resulting conflict tends to be low violence, and constructive resolution and functional organizational change become likely outcomes. Nonetheless, the resulting outcomes, over time, create the conditions for member dissatisfaction and the process continues.

Typically, physical violence among teachers and school leaders is rare. Rather, aggressiveness may appear as ostracism, verbal abuse, emotional/psychological injury, or material destruction rather than as physical battery. In addition, the more mobility from one group to another, and the presence of effective procedures for regulating

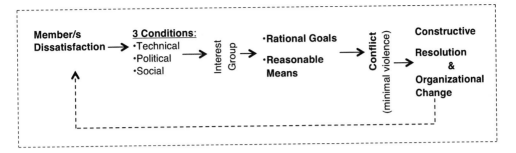

FIGURE 6.3 Dahrendorf's View of Organizational Conflict

Source: Based on Dahrendorf, R. (1958). Toward a theory of social conflict. *The Journal of Conflict Resolution, 2* (2), 170–183.

conflict—such as collective bargaining, arbitration, and due process—the less intense the conflict. For organizations, the presence of formal or informal norms and due process procedures to regulate conflict, the greater the likelihood that both parties will use them to resolve conflict constructively (and the less chance of aggression). This is especially true if both parties recognize the fundamental justice of the cause involved—even if they don't agree on the outcome—and are both well organized.[38] Eventually, the conflict—whatever its level of aggression—leads to changes in the organization's structure, in the involved groups' position, and in the dominant relations.[39]

Table 6.1 indicates Coser and Dahrendorf's areas of agreement on organizational conflict, the range of conflict behaviors, and the factors they see as increasing or decreasing functional or dysfunctional outcomes.

For Dahrendorf, conflict becomes institutionalized when new people hold authority positions and enforce different roles, norms, and values. Social mobility allows individuals to rise into authority positions. In turn, this sets up new structures of power, new grievances for people to form interest groups, and begin the conflict anew.

Research and Criticism

Research findings tend to support Dahrendorf's theory. It upholds the belief that workers without authority tend to perceive the authority structure as less legitimate than do workers who have authority.[40] Likewise, members of the authority class are *less likely* than the workers (without authority) to comply with or accept others' authority.[41] In fact, studies suggest that more divisions and conflict may exist *within* the authority class than *between* the authority and non-authority classes. In contrast, results from three different empirical studies challenge Dahrendorf's proposition that authority is a *dichotomy* (you either have authority or you don't). Rather, it appears to be a *continuum* (one has either more or less authority).[42] In a different vein, survey data from large national samples in the United States and Great Britain suggest the existence of two overlapping but distinct social stratification systems—one based on ownership of means of production and authority, and another based on education and occupational status—with important implications for employees' income, social class identification, and political views.[43] For the most part, researchers support Dahrendorf's concept of social conflict's presence in social relations despite their views that he oversimplifies the concept of legitimate power.[44]

TABLE 6.1 Coser and Dahrendorf on Organizational Conflict

Areas of Agreement	• Conflict is normal and potentially beneficial. • All social systems and organizations contain elements of stability and change, integration and conflict, function and dysfunction. • All systems allocate power/authority, wealth, and status to create "us" and "them." • Those with power/authority, wealth, and status resist efforts to change.
Range of Conflict Behaviors in Organizations	Mild & Functional (i.e., ostracism, criticism) to Increasingly Severe & Dysfunctional (i.e., verbal abuse, emotional harm, materials destruction, physical injury, death).
Functional Organizational Conflict Outcomes When . . .	• Conflict is a means to attain clearly articulated rational goals. • The organization has elastic system to permit open and direct expression of conflict. • The conflict allows the balance of power to shift resources without destroying the entire organization. • The organization's porous boundaries allow environmental influences to enter.

Dysfunctional Behaviors *Increase* as:	**Dysfunctional Behaviors** *Decrease* as:	**Dysfunctional Behaviors** *Increase* as:
Emotional involvement Transcendental goals Sense of deprivation Interest group ability to organize and communicate	Clearly stated rational goals Norms, procedures for resolving conflict	Interest group organization Social mobility
Increase	**Increase**	**Decrease**

Source: Based on: Allan, K. (2007). Conflict theory: Lewis Coser, Ralf Dahrendorf, and Randall Collins. *The social lens: An invitation to social and sociological theory.* 2nd ed. (pp. 211–241). Thousand Oaks, CA: Sage.

Scrutiny of Dahrendorf's work has been more theoretical than empirical.[45] Sociologists with differing orientations criticize his theory about conflict and authority.[46] Some find contradictions in his explanation of conflict,[47] observe that he does not identify the causal conditions under which authority relations are transformed into various kinds of conflict,[48] and argue against his equating social mobility with social change.[49] Additionally, certain critics believe his ideas about conflict's origins are too vague, with too many assumptions about "reality."[50] Some have questioned his theory's validity for other cultures.[51] While Dahrendorf's conflict theory offers insights into conflict's centrality in social life and organizations and has much empirical support, it never established itself as an enduring theory in the social sciences.[52]

Along with Coser, Dahrendorf introduced the idea of organizational conflict as a force for progress and change. He clearly identified the organizational conditions—technical, political, and social—that facilitate conflicts' functional outcomes. As one investigator concluded, "Dahrendorf's own work whatever its scientific validity . . . has performed a useful and welcome service" to understanding behavior in organizations.[53]

REFLECTIONS AND RELEVANCE 6.2

Organizational Conditions that De-Escalate Conflict

Coser, Dahrendorf, and Collins believed that certain conditions in organizations could de-escalate conflict and lead to more functional individual and organizational outcomes.

Working in groups of four, complete the table below for your own school worksites and/or school districts.

Conditions that De-Escalate Conflict and May Make it Functional	Describe processes, procedures, or other means by which your organization de-escalates conflict
Organization tolerates or accepts competing viewpoints and interests.	
Members can directly and verbally express their discontents and resolve competing claims.	
Formal and informal norms exist and operate about how to address frustrations.	
Formal grievance and due process procedures and protections exist and operate.	
Special office and expert personnel handle grievances and conflict.	
Members have social mobility: promotions, additional responsibilities, increases in status are available.	
Other.	

What means do your schools and districts use to de-escalate conflict? Which approaches seem to be the most—and least—effective? Which approaches seem to have the most functional—or dysfunctional—outcomes for your school or organization? As a class, discuss the types of conditions and practices that schools and districts can use to effectively de-escalate conflict and generate functional outcomes.

CONFLICT AND ORGANIZATIONAL PERFORMANCE

Organization theorists concur that a moderate amount of conflict is needed to attain an optimum organizational effectiveness.[54] As discussed in Chapter 5, the presence of tension and conflict seem to be essential qualities of learning organizations, needed to question, challenge, and improve the status quo. So if organizational conflict can have beneficial outcomes, contemporary organizations need to learn how to manage it—how to minimize conflict's dysfunctions and enhance its constructive functions—in ways that strengthen learning and organizational effectiveness.

As a field of study, research, and practice, conflict resolution/management began at the Cold War's height, in the 1940s–1960s.[55] Nuclear weapons made conflict between the superpowers a matter of life or death. National liberation struggles in Europe's African and Asian colonies, and civil rights and Vietnam War unrest in the United States all presented valid conflicts over real injustices. During the 1950s and 1960s, researchers looked at factors affecting the relations between potentially opposing groups. They asked how parties could prevent open fighting—or wage it constructively and solve it amicably. Since the mid-1980s, the increasing complexity of community, environmental, and socioeconomic conflicts—in which both sides hold high emotions and neither side is completely right or wrong—have made finding and maximizing mutual benefits the principle tool for managing contesting groups. By the early 1990s, the volume of conflict management research had grown so large that one set of investigators concluded "it virtually impossible" to write a comprehensive literature review.[56]

Louis Pondy and Louis Kriesberg each proposed process models of conflict that identified how it developed in stages. Both men stressed that conflict at all levels could have mutually harmful or mutually beneficial outcomes, depending on an array of factors.

Louis R. Pondy—Conflict Episode Theory

In his now classic 1967 article,[57] Louis R. Pondy (1938–1987), the late University of Illinois business professor, tried to synthesize the relationships among an organization's structural dimensions and employees' personality variables that affect conflict processes and outcomes. These he incorporated as elements of a "conflict episode." Although Pondy initially treated conflict as an "aberration," a breakdown in standard "harmonious" organizational processes, he later came to believe that organizational conflict was the norm; "harmony" was the anomaly.[58]

In his study of the conflict literature, Pondy identified three implicit orientations. First, each conflict relationship consists of an interlocking sequence of conflict episodes, each episode shows a pattern of development, and stable patterns appear across the conflict episodes. Second, conflict may be functional or dysfunctional for the individual and the organization. Third, conflict is closely and complexly tied to the organization's stability because it is a key factor in the feedback loops that characterize organizational behavior.[59]

Figure 6.4 illustrates Pondy's conflict episode theory. He proposed five sequential stages: (1) latent conflict (potential); (2) perceived conflict (awareness); (3) felt conflict

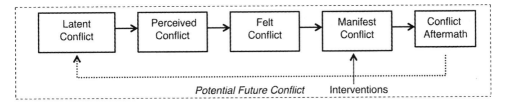

FIGURE 6.4 Pondy's Conflict Episode Theory

Source: Based on Pondy, L.R. (1967). Organizational conflict: Concepts and models. *Administrative Science Quarterly, 12* (2), 296–320.

(emotions); leading to (4) manifest conflict (behaviors); and (5) conflict aftermath (outcomes) that may feed back to create a new latent conflict.[60] These steps occur in an open environment that may impact the process. In his model, not every conflict episode necessarily passes through every stage. We'll consider each in turn.

Latent Conflict

Pondy identified three basic types of latent or potential conflict in organizations: competition for scarce resources, drives for autonomy, and divergent subunit goals. Competition forms the basis for conflict when parties' combined demands for resources exceed those available to the organization. Individuals' autonomy needs to establish the groundwork for conflict when one party either tries to exert control over some activity that the other party regards as his/her own territory, or seeks to insulate one's own goal pursuit from such control. And differing goals become a conflict source when two parties who must cooperate on a joint activity are unable to agree on what they should do or how to do it. A conflict situation may include two or more types of latent conflict at the same time, and they may be organizational or interpersonal.

Perceived Conflict

Persons become aware that conflict exists. One party recognizes that the other party wants to—or actually is—trying to block or stymie the first person's goal attainment. According to Pondy, misunderstandings may cause an individual to perceive conflict—suspect that the other is trying to prevent one's own goal attainment—even if no conditions of latent conflict exist.[61] These perceived conflicts may be resolved through more effective communication between and among relevant parties. But, Pondy added, if the parties' true positions *do* disagree, more open communication might actually intensify the conflict.

Felt Conflict

Parties become emotionally and consciously aware that a conflict exists. They feel stress, anxiety, and perhaps, hostility; and their heightened emotions alert them to the reality that conflict is about to occur. When individuals in organizations *personalize* the conflict (rather than make the conflict about the task), they experience strong emotions—often aggressive—about the issue and those involved in it, leading to dysfunctional outcomes.

Manifest (Overt) Conflict

Conflict becomes visible. Conflicting people overtly engage in verbal or physical behaviors that block another member's goal achievement. Since most organizational norms prohibit verbal and physical violence, people in organizations tend to express their anger more indirectly. For instance, yelling or insulting another (often accompanied by facial expressions and body postures to reinforce the persons' displeasure), forgetting to invite an adversary to a meeting, sabotage or coalition forming, withdrawal, and rigidly "working to the contract" to resist mistreatment by organizational superiors, are examples of organizational conflict behaviors. One must thoroughly understand an organization, its culture, work requirements, and expectations to be able to determine if a particular behavior or pattern of behavior is conflictual.

Pondy also concluded that an accumulation of conflict episodes leads to a *conflict relationship*, a gradual escalation to a state of disorder. This disorder may range in intensity and scope from a disagreement between colleagues to, in the extreme case, two nations at war. Notably, the parties involved may never perceive the potential conflict, or if they do perceive it, they may resolve the conflict before hostilities occur. Conflicts may develop and find resolution in a variety of ways.

Originally, Pondy suggested that conflict resolution interventions are best applied at the interfaces between perceived/felt and manifest conflict—to prevent conflicts that have reached awareness's of felt affect from erupting into uncooperative behaviors.[62] Later, he revised his model to offer five conflict resolution approaches to use during overt conflict, to resolve or minimize a dispute:[63]

Avoiding (lose/lose)

One or both sides recognize that a conflict exists but respond by withdrawing from or postponing the conflict. This is a relatively passive tactic and serves as a stopgap measure to buy time to decide how to best resolve the underlying problem. It is a useful approach to dealing with trivial issues or when conflict's potential disruption outweighs its benefits.

Accommodating (lose/win)

One side resolves the conflict by giving in to the other side at the cost of at least some of his/her own goals.[64] This is a rational approach if the other side has overwhelming power and the willingness to use it, if the relationship between the parties is more important than the specific issue of conflict, or if one side realizes it is wrong. Too much accommodation may lead to one feeling resentful or cheated.

Compromising (win/lose, win/lose)

Both sides gain and lose in order to resolve a conflict. Each party is partially satisfied and partially dissatisfied. In organizations, compromise is not necessarily good or bad. Because both sides need to "save face" and protect their relationship, the circumstances may work against allowing an obvious win/lose outcome. Compromising may be a useful approach when goals are important but not worth the effort or potential disruption of more assertive approaches.

Forcing (win/lose)

One or both sides aggressively tries to meet their own needs regardless of how it impacts the other side. This makes sense when the forcing side has superior power. But forcing brings problems: the loser feels humiliated, fails to achieve his/her desired outcome, and may respond with opposing force that jeopardizes the on-going relationship. Losing big could result in a huge struggle that ends in a stalemate (in which each party and the organization become losers) or a hollow victory (in which the winner sustains severe losses). Forcing may be a useful method when quick, decisive action is essential (i.e., emergencies) or on important issues where unpopular actions are needed (i.e., cost-cutting, enforcing unpopular rules, or discipline).

Collaborating (win/win)

One or both parties try to fully satisfy both parties' needs. This approach assumes that both sides have legitimate goals and creative problem solving skills. Looking below the surface dispute to identify the actual problem, redefining the situation, and finding an appropriate remedy can transform conflict into an opportunity for both sides to achieve their goals. Collaborating is useful when both sets of concerns are too essential to be compromised.

Skillful conflict resolution techniques—particularly collaboration and principled negotiation[65]—may be time consuming. But they may prevent conflict from escalating and preserve the relationships—and may also lead to improved organizational performance and outcomes.

Conflict Aftermath

According to Pondy, conflict outcomes may include increased, decreased, or stable organizational performance and results. A conflict episode that ends with each party genuinely satisfied with its resolution lays the basis for a more cooperative relationship. In contrast, if participants merely suppress but not resolve the conflict, or if they focus on latent conflicts not previously perceived and addressed, the latent conditions may be aggravated and erupt in more serious forms, until they are fixed or the relationship ends.

Pondy noted that the organization is not a closed system. The environment may ease the conditions of latent conflict and make more resources available. Or a changing environment may initiate new conflicts. Each conflict episode develops according to the complex combination of the effects from earlier conflict episodes and the environmental and situational influences of the current one. He also suggested that an optimal level of task conflict exists beyond or below which individual and group performance diminishes: too much conflict can produce low-quality outcomes when group members are performing non-routine tasks.[66]

Research and Criticism

Empirical studies support Pondy's notion that conflict can have both positive and negative outcomes (positive such as improving decision quality, strategic planning, and financial performance, and negative such as decreasing satisfaction and reducing productivity).[67] For example, studies find that conflict can be perceived and felt in different ways by different people experiencing the conflict episode;[68] integrative tactics of conflict resolution (win/win) resulted in greater member satisfaction, less feelings of inequity,[69] and higher quality solutions than with competitive strategies.[70] As the number of conflict episodes increase, feelings of equity and satisfaction decrease.[71] Studies have also found a curvilinear relationship between conflict and group performance on a task: the absence of conflict led to complacency, a moderate amount of conflict improved group performance, while high levels of conflict harmed group performance.[72] The type of task influences whether conflict helps, hinders, or has no significant impact on individual and group performance; and relationship conflict was harmful regardless of the type of task the group was performing. In short, the relationship between conflict and group performance is quite complex.

Some critics focused less on what Pondy proposed than on what he neglected to say. For instance, they noted that Pondy elaborated on conflict within the organization but did not address conflict between organizations.[73] Nor did he consider conflict's effects on third party co-workers.[74] Nor did he elaborate on the "manifest conflict" stage, leaving it for later investigators to do so.[75] Complexity theorists challenged Pondy's view on conflict episodes, asserting each could be unique, composed of different proportions of affective, cognitive, and process conflict;[76] and that many of these unique conflict episodes may occur at the same time (further complicating interventions for managing them).[77] Additionally, critics observed that Pondy's highly rational approach did not fit with those who advocated a non-rational (i.e., non-conscious, intuitive, or spontaneous) approach to conflict.[78]

Pondy's theory of conflict episodes provided a useful general direction upon which to build an integrative theory of conflict. His ideas—and the later research—contributed to a changing view of conflict in organizations. Conflict was a healthy process, not necessarily good or bad. Rather, it needed to be evaluated in terms of its functional or dysfunctional outcomes for individuals and organizations. As a result of Pondy's work, organizational practice moved away from conflict *resolution* (i.e., end conflict because it is always destructive) to conflict *management* (i.e., handle conflict wisely to

REFLECTIONS AND RELEVANCE 6.3

Applying Pondy's Conflict Episode Theory

Louis Pondy suggested that the conflict relationship was an interlocking series of conflict episodes. Using Figure 6.5 as a reference, work in groups of four to discuss what each step means. On the lines below each step, give details of what the conflict episode might look and sound like in school. Discuss your findings with the entire class.

Examples: Latent → Perceived → Felt → Manifest → Conflict
          Conflict   Conflict   Conflict   Conflict   Aftermath

_____   _____   _____   _____   _____

_____   _____   _____   _____   _____

gain organizational benefits) through negotiation, structural adaptation, and other types of intervention.[79]

Louis Kriesberg—Conflict Resolution Theory

A scholar and a practitioner, Louis Kriesberg (1926–), a Syracuse University Professor Emeritus of Sociology, is the founder/director emeritus of the Program on the Analysis and Resolution of Conflicts. His conflict resolution theory describes the stages of conflict and suggests how people can advance constructive conflicts that minimize violence, overcome antagonism, and generate mutually agreeable (win/win) and long-lasting solutions. His ideas on conflict resolution are in practice around the world.

Kriesberg defined *social conflicts* as existing when two or more persons or groups express the belief that they have incompatible objectives.[80] Defined in this way, Kriesberg stressed that many conflicts are not destructive, but are conducted according to shared rules adversaries regard as legitimate, such as with judicial proceedings and electoral politics. Citizens accept these legitimate conflicts as essential to society's wellbeing and to democracy, itself.[81]

As Kriesberg saw it, conflict was one aspect of a complex relationship between parties: it indicated a changing relationship marked by ongoing disagreement. The dispute may last an hour, a month, or years. But even as adversaries dispute, they may also be participating in agreeable and even cooperative interactions. How adversaries regard themselves and each other in their relationship and how they define the situation will influence how they define social conflict and how they interact with each other.[82] For instance, teachers of high school honors and AP courses may intensely disagree about the admissions criteria. Groups may advocate either for enrollment based on successfully completing prerequisites or for "open admissions" with extra academic support for interested but less able students. Knowing that they will continue to work together, colleagues are less likely to define their conflict in coercive, intractable, or violent terms.

The Conflict Resolution Cycle

Kriesberg's conflict resolution theory poses that conflict occurs in five major stages: (1) the underlying basis, (2) how the conflict emerges and manifests, (3) escalation and (4) de-escalation, and (5) its outcome or settlement.[83] Figure 6.5 shows this process. We will consider each stage in turn.

Bases

Social conflict's underlying causes include: (1) factors inside the adversaries, (2) inequalities between different categories or groups, and (3) features of social systems. First, factors inside the adversaries include personality, cultural patterns of aggression or rebellion, and political structures. Even-tempered department chairpersons in a school culture that stresses constructive problem solving are not likely to come to physical blows over serious disagreements in how to meet their interdependent responsibilities. Research does not support the view that any particular persons, groups, or countries are consistently more conflict-prone.[84]

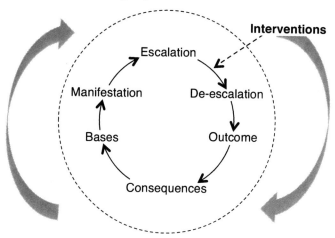

Economic, Political, Social, Cultural and Geographic Environments

FIGURE 6.5 Kriesberg's Conflict Cycle

Source: Adapted from Kriesberg, L. (2007). *Constructive conflicts: From escalation to resolution.* 3rd ed. (p. 23). New York, NY: Rowman & Littlefield.

Second, inequalities in political power, economic status, or religious or ideological conviction may be a source of underlying conflict between people or groups of differing categories. Teachers may clash with their school boards over wanting increased professional development opportunities or reimbursement for taking graduate education coursework. The evidence for such conflict sources is extensive.

Third, features of social systems within which the adversaries interact influence the sources of conflict. Systems lacking formal rules and means to resolve conflict effectively and those where employees are not interdependent tend to have more bases for conflict than systems with these. *Institutionalization* refers to the rules that every social system has for conducting disputes and formal procedures for accommodating differences among possible adversaries. Highly institutionalized procedures—such as open political systems, an independent judiciary, and due process procedures for worker grievances—provide viable ways to mutually accommodate inequalities and value differences without creating serious interpersonal or organizational divisions. For example, a teacher who believes he or she has been evaluated unfairly based on an "anonymous parent complaint" can try to resolve the issue with the evaluator and principal. If the teacher remains unsatisfied with the outcome, the school district has formal procedures to bring the concern "up the chain" for a fair and full inquiry and due process protections.

Similarly, *integration*—the degree of group or individuals' interdependence and the system's degree of consistency and equilibrium—fosters a high degree of mutual interdependence that limits the expression of hostility. Good working relationships between the counselors and academic departments helps design a master schedule with teaching assignments and class loads that teachers accept—reducing their possible dissatisfaction and conflict. In contrast, abrupt social change disturbs a group or society's equilibrium, generating the basis for conflict.[85] For instance, the recent cultural shift allowing transgender students to use restrooms that match their gender identity continues to roil communities despite administrative and legal rulings supporting it.

Further, Kriesberg posited that the bases that observers perceive to underlie the conflict will influence their choice of conflict resolution techniques. Those who believe that internal factors cause conflicts will try to get one or both parties to change. Those who believe that relational factors motivate the conflict tend to think that each party plays a role in instigating—and resolving—the discord. Those who stress systemic factors tend to look at the long term and contextual elements as the most promising avenues to lessen conflicts. Those who believe that all three factors stir conflict recognize that conflict can ensue from countless bases and may require varied interventions to reduce or end it. Importantly, Kriesberg saw conflicts as "always intermingled and interlocked;" every conflict has some objective, realistic basis.[86]

Manifestation

As parties interact and become aware that they are pursuing incompatible goals, three factors make it possible for overt conflict behavior to emerge: (1) the adversaries must have an idea of themselves as a collective entity with their own identity; (2) at least one of the adversaries must be dissatisfied with the current situation and recognize that their efforts can correct it; and (3) at least one adversary formulates a goal to remedy the grievance that requires changes from the other party. Research on collective behavior,[87] relative deprivation,[88] and resource mobilization[89] finds that all three factors prompt a conflict to emerge.

As adversaries interact, they become aware of their incompatible objectives: this friction helps them define themselves and each other. Whether or not one party tries to change an unsatisfactory situation depends, in part, on its leaders and members believing that they can fix the problem. Past experiences, traditions, and others' examples in similar conditions influence how they perceive their own capabilities as compared to those of their adversary. For instance, when teachers and parents find themselves at loggerheads over how to proceed with a failing student, they may invite an assistant principal and a counselor to join them in problem solving.

Once a conflict has emerged, the available options will influence how antagonists pursue their concerns. These alternatives depend, in part, on parties' past experience and knowledge as well as on the social context and each adversary's responsiveness to the other. Well-educated, socially influential parents unhappy with their schools' special education practices for their children with disabilities may advocate with their local school board for more inclusive practices supported by co-teaching. In contrast, less educated parents focused on earning a living to pay for rent and food may lack the information, time, and social/political entrée to advocate for their children's education.

Escalation

The conflict intensifies. Whatever the underlying cause, once parties begin to struggle against each other, the means of conducting the fight may grow in ways that move beyond the original conflict. Tactics become harsher, issues multiply, parties becoming increasingly absorbed in the effort, and goals shift from advancing one's interests to undermining or punishing the others.[90] As the conflict's intensity and scope increase, increasingly destructive behaviors—including violence—become possible. Escalation can produce actions in which the ends no longer justify the means.

Kriesberg theorized that within any adversary, cognitive and emotional processes and organizational developments either escalate or de-escalate a conflict. Cognitively, as a fight continues and the costs of waging it rise, parties tend to heighten the value of the fight's goal to justify the sacrifices already made. In contrast, if the costs of waging the fight become too high, parties may decide to devalue the goal. Strong emotions provide a motive for increasing their effort—or strong emotions may limit parties' abilities to notice any of their opponents' appeasing gestures (if offered). Similarly, crises tend to produce feelings of anxiety and surprise that often makes antagonists' thinking rigid, swaying them to pursue inappropriate polices (and reject more constructive or effective alternatives), and keep escalating the conflict.

Shifts within the organization can also escalate or de-escalate conflict. Rivalry for party (or academic department) leadership, for example, may increase or decrease conflict depending on the challenging rivals' strength from supporters. As the dispute continues, persons committed to the fight rise in influence while doubters are shunned. As people take sides, they reinforce the fight's intensity and scope. On the flip side, as the fight expands in scope and more people become involved, many of the new allies may have less commitment to the fight's goals than those initially in the struggle. Thus, newcomers may provide a moderating influence and a de-escalating force.

As the conflict continues, the structure of the relations between adversaries changes and may affect whether the conflict escalates or de-escalates. For instance, adversaries with a history of antagonism may want to "settle old scores," relations become polarized, communications become more difficult, awareness of common interests lessens, and the conflict escalates. In contrast, de-escalation occurs when the issues in dispute can be narrowed and separated into sub-issues whose gains and losses can be traded off against each other.[91]

De-escalation

The conflict intensity lessens. Kriesberg contended that since conflicts are inherent in social life, they should be viewed as opportunities to resolve problems and enact creative solutions. To do this, techniques such as negotiation and mediation can provide the structure and safety to move beyond arguing about positions and seek underlying interests, help transmit information not otherwise heard, suggest new options, build membership support for a proposed settlement, and facilitate opponents' recognition of each other's legitimate concerns.[92] Likewise, redefining a conflict as a "problem in need of a solution"—or as adversaries having a common enemy or a shared problem— is a useful de-escalation approach. Redefining allows parties to select a subset of issues that are open to settlement and relegate the more difficult ones for the future. This approach permits opponents to gain confidence and trust in each other as they successively (and successfully) begin to address their shared concerns.

Kriesberg asserted that the way each party responds to the other is one of the most basic conditions affecting whether a conflict escalates or de-escalates. Researchers disagree about whether a strong response—or an appeasing response—to an adversary's challenge limits or provokes escalation. Evidence exists to support each of these claims.[93] Overall, the data suggests that responses that are about at the level of the adversary's actions are most successful in limiting escalation.[94]

Kriesberg saw escalation and de-escalation explained by changes in the salience of a particular conflict, based on the assumption that every conflict is interlocked with many others. For example, the 2015 Black Lives Matter movement against police brutality toward African Americans is interconnected with centuries-long struggles for civil rights. It also converges and cuts across other critical conflicts of race, class, education, poverty, voting rights, wages, and criminal justice. When subgroups within each adversary unit find that they have common interests with others from different conflicts and join those struggles too, they spread their attention and efforts on more "causes," weakening the intensity and scope of their initial conflict (de-escalating). When Black Lives Matter advocates link forces with colleagues advocating for an increased minimum wage and voting rights, they weaken their relative commitment toward their first cause (and de-escalate the conflict).

Outcomes (Settlement)

Many factors affect a conflict's outcome. Conflict settlements have both *distributive* aspects (i.e., how much of what each adversary sought did each achieve at the other's expense?) and *joint* aspects (i.e., What were each adversaries' gains and losses?). Kriesberg identified three sets of factors that affect conflict outcomes: (1) the struggle's character; (2) external and general social forces over which the adversaries have little control; and (3) the way the adversaries end the conflict.[95]

First, the nature of the struggle itself affects the settlement. The more extreme one party's demands, the more likely they (and others) will view the struggle as a zero-sum fight: one party's gain equals the other party's loss. Similarly, the greater the size of the goal sought, the more resistance it stirs, and the more difficult it is to win the struggle. For instance, if one group seeks to completely displace their antagonists, the less likely their opponents will accept or give any new advantage to them. Research in this dimension is limited,[96] but findings suggest that violence (zero-sum) is often counter-productive whereas non-coercive inducements, rewards, and persuasion may be mutually beneficial.[97] Experimental findings suggest that one side consistently making concessions may not result in mutually beneficial outcomes.[98]

Second, social forces and contexts beyond the antagonists' control also affect outcomes. The struggle's economic, political, cultural, social, and geographic character places limits on the potential outcomes. Organizations have norms, rules, procedures, and grievance systems that spell out how people within them should handle conflict. As a result, settlements arising from worker-management strife are subject to conditions that neither the employers nor employees can change. For example, teachers' ability to bargain with school boards for improved salaries, benefits, and voice in decision making, is constrained by whether or not they are members of a union that can bargain collectively for them, the community and state's overall and current economic health, the monies available to direct toward teachers' salaries and benefits, and the availability of highly qualified and effective teachers in the labor market.

Third, how the conflict ends affects the conflict's settlement. Every dispute ends, even if the outcome becomes the basis for the next fight. The dispute may end implicitly: the opponents simply stop their conflict behavior and halt pursuit of contested goals. Or the conflict may end explicitly through direct or indirect negotiations with a clear resolution. The explicit end process may be institutionalized with many or few formal regulations about the procedures for resolving the struggle. Collective bargaining (where unions are involved), going to court, and voting are highly institutionalized procedures that our society offers for conflict management. Studies find that making high initial demands in bargaining for resolution seems to produce relatively higher gains, although it risks reaching no agreement.[99] Committing oneself to a bargaining position also seems to increase relative bargaining gains; the other side tends to believe that it must compromise if they are to reach an agreement. Research indicates that to facilitate reaching a win/win outcome, the adversaries must come to see themselves as facing a common problem (or sharing a common enemy)—and shift their attention to the conflicts they might be able to resolve to their mutual benefit—rather than first advocating for different sides of an issue and later finding a solution.[100]

Again, intermediaries can play key roles in helping end conflicts. They may impose or enforce a termination, serve as fact finders, and act as mediators. Studies indicate that the conflict's nature and its social environment can greatly limit mediators' effectiveness.[101] Certain conflicts only end when the warring parties decide, for their own reasons, to do so.

Research and Criticism

Kriesberg (2007b) cited research in sociology,[102] psychology,[103] social psychology,[104] analysis of non-violent action,[105] game theory,[106] peace research,[107] conflict management practices,[108] and conflict outcomes[109] (in international relations and domestic civil rights, interfaith, and ethnic conflicts), that support his conflict resolution theory regarding causes, escalation/de-escalation, and outcomes. Research on conflict resolution often focuses on the effectiveness of particular methods to limit, de-escalate, or end destructive conflicts.[110] At the same time, critics remind us that conflict knowledge—like most scientific knowledge—is based on an observed sample and measured at a specific time, in a certain context, and with imperfect instruments. This limits any study findings' generalizability and should be interpreted conservatively.[111]

Several critics call Kriesberg's conflict resolution theory a comprehensive and realistic approach that focuses on the relationships between people, personalizing and socializing the conflict perspective,[112] and avoids oversimplifying a highly complex phenomenon.[113] At the same time, critics fault Kriesberg's theory for making contradictory assumptions about human rationality and offering too many contributing factors at multiple levels of analysis (some with weak empirical support)—at the risk of losing the "forest for the trees" and overwhelming CR practitioners[114] (and graduate students). Some challenge Kriesberg's view that mediation should be used in tandem with other third party approaches to conflict resolution, preferring not to "blur responsibilities" or overload the dispute with third parties.[115]

Many of Kriesberg's ideas—especially the belief that adversaries can have win/win outcomes—have moved beyond academic interest and into the general public.

Understanding conflict's stages and processes and improving communication can help adversaries identify their common interests and values and look for ways to gain mutual benefits and reduce mutual losses. A variety of CR practices have become widely accepted strategies for managing conflicts. Knowing the theory, the conflict stages, and the related research offers insights to help organization leaders manage conflicts in their organizations.

REFLECTIONS AND RELEVANCE 6.4

Applying Louis Kriesberg's Conflict Resolution Cycle

Louis Kriesberg identified five steps in the conflict resolution cycle: bases (causes), manifestation (overt behaviors), escalation, de-escalation, and outcomes.

The class separates into five groups (or ten groups, if groups membership is larger than six). Group members will decide on which conflict resolution step they will focus on; every step in the conflict cycle must be the focus of at least one work group. Each group then will identify *at least five key points* about their selected step—and *what it might look and sound like if occurring in a school*—that will help education leaders lead conflict to functional outcomes. Groups will also discuss which conflict resolution approaches they see most often in use in their school—avoiding, accommodating, compromising, forcing, or collaborating. What happened, and how effective was this approach in producing functional outcomes? After the groups complete their task, they will report their findings to the whole class and discuss those aspects of Kriesberg's model that they believe will be most useful to school leadership practice.

IMPLICATIONS FOR EDUCATIONAL LEADERS

Wherever people interact, conflict is likely to appear. This is not necessarily a bad thing. Scholars agree that a moderate amount of conflict is needed to attain an optimum of organizational effectiveness. Of course, if not handled well, conflict can lead to dysfunctional outcomes, including job stress, burnout, and dissatisfaction; reduced communication between individuals and groups; a climate of distrust and suspicion, damaged relationships, increased resistance to change, and reduced organizational loyalty, commitment, and job performance. Since educational leaders are more successful when they learn how to recognize conflict and respond appropriately, this chapter offers four key take-aways.

Conflict is Normal and Universal

Conflict is part of all human relations. It is a regular aspect of how we structure society and create social order. Ralf Dahrendorf even claimed that democracy is about "organizing conflict and living with conflict." Since today's organizations are dealing with learning and continuous change to improve their performance—and employ people—it is essential that school leaders learn how to design effective strategies to recognize conflict, maximize its up-sides, and minimize its down-sides.

Conflict Can Be Functional

Conflict within a group can be an opportunity, not a threat. It stimulates innovation, creativity, and change; it improves organizational decision-making processes; and it identifies alternative solutions to problems. Conflict can enhance individual and group performance, providing occasions to articulate and clarify positions and view problems in fresh ways. Likewise, conflict can often help to revitalize exiting norms and contribute to forming new ones, allowing groups to adjust appropriately to current conditions and continue despite changed circumstances. The challenge for educational leaders is to make it so.

Conflict is a Dynamic Process

Conflict is an active sequence of events. Its pattern is relatively predictable. It begins from a variety of possible sources, follows a foreseeable course, expresses itself in many ways, and has both positive and negative outcomes. Although they have limited influence on others' personalities, when school leaders become aware of conflict between individuals or groups in the school, it is time to take practical action to recognize it, clarify it, understand it, and de-escalate it.

Reducing emotionally motivated behaviors and increasing rational goal-directed behaviors helps accomplish this. Serving as mediators or negotiators, school leaders can move conflicting parties beyond arguing to seek underlying interests. As neutral parties interested in finding workable solutions, they can help transmit information not otherwise heard, suggest new options, and build support for workable solutions. And they can redirect the blaming into solving the problem.

Mediating conflict begins by helping members clarify that the conflict is not the result of a misunderstanding. School leaders can help narrow the conflict's scope by breaking it into sub-issues that are open to settlement. Reframing the issue as a "problem in need of a solution" or as opponents having a shared problem can also deescalate the conflict. Postponing the secondary concerns until members can successfully address a mutual interest and develop trust and confidence in each other is another useful approach. And if school leaders cannot deal calmly and rationally with agitated individuals, or fluently apply these de-escalation techniques, they may want to obtain professional skills training in these areas—or engage a mutually trusted colleague (typically, an assistant principal, school counselor, department chair, or central office supervisor) who can.

As for the aftermath, finding a resolution that genuinely satisfies each party with a win/win outcome lays the groundwork for more cooperative and productive relationships. In contrast, if participants merely suppress but do not resolve the conflict, or if they focus on latent conflicts not previously perceived and addressed, the conflict may continue to burn in the same—or in different—forms.

School and Organizational Conditions can Facilitate Functional Conflict

Schools and districts usually have formal policies and informal norms that accept competing viewpoints and interests and provide institutional ways for members to express and resolve their concerns. They may be able to find a satisfactory resolution in their school. But if not, having formal grievance procedures and due process rights and protections offers a legitimate means for them to identify and effectively resolve conflicts. Likewise, school districts with permanent departments and specialized personnel to handle employee conflicts can make the conflicting parties' concessions become part of the organization. Also, organizations that offer social mobility—such as promotions, recognition, and opportunities for professional advancement—present avenues for members to gain greater resources, reducing potential conflict causes.

NOTES

1 Kolb, D.M. & Putnam, L.L. (1992). The multiple faces of conflict in organizations. *Journal of Organizational Behavior, 13* (3), 311–324.
2 See: Tjosvokd, D. (1991). Rights and responsibilities of dissent: Cooperative conflict. *Employee Responsibilities and Rights Journal, 4* (1), 13–23; Amason, A.C. & Schweiger, D.M. (1994). Resolving the paradox of conflict, strategic decision making, and organizational performance. *International Journal of Conflict Management, 5* (3), 239–253; Jehn, K.A. (1994). Enhancing effectiveness: An investigation of advantages and disadvantages of value-based intragroup conflict. *International Journal of Conflict Management, 4* (2), 223–238.
3 Rahim, M.A. (2011). *Managing conflict in organizations.* 4th ed. (p. 1). New Brunswick, NJ: Transaction Publishers.
4 Deutsch, M. (1969). Conflict: Productive and destructive. *Journal of Social Issues, 25* (1), 7–41 (p. 7).
5 Roloff, M.E. (1987). Communication and conflict. In C. R. Berger & S.H. Chaffee (Eds), *Handbook of communication science.* (pp. 484–534). Newbury Park, CA: Sage.
6 Wall, J.A. Jr. & Callister, R.R. (1995). Conflict and its management. *Journal of Management, 21* (3), 515–558.
7 Wall & Callister (1995). Ibid. See Wall & Callister for specific studies supporting the causes of conflict.
8 Baron, R.A. (1990). Conflict in organizations. In K.R. Murphy & F.E. Saal (Eds), *Psychology in organizations: Integrating science and practice.* (pp. 197–216). Hillsdale, NJ: Erlbaum; Mack, R.W. & Snyder, R.C. (1957). Analysis of social conflict: Toward an overview and synthesis. *Journal of Conflict Resolution, 1* (2), 212–248.
9 Rahim, M.A., Garrett, J.E. & Buntzman, G.F. (1992). Ethics of managing interpersonal conflict in organizations. *Journal of Business Ethics, 11* (5/6), 423–432.
10 Lewicki, R.J., Weiss, S.E. & Lewin, D. (1992). Models of conflict, negotiation, and third party intervention: A review and synthesis. *Journal of Organizational Behavior, 13* (3), 209–252.
11 Kolb, D.M. & Bartunek, J. (1992). Hidden conflict in organizations. Uncovering behind-the-scenes disputes. Beverly Hills, CA: Sage.
12 Litterer, J.A. (1966). Conflict in organization: A re-examination. *Academy of Management Journal, 9* (3), 178–186.
13 Whyte, W.H. (1967). Models for building and changing organizations. *Human Organizations, 26* (1), 22–31.

14 Robbins, S.P. (1974). *Managing organizational conflict: A nontraditional approach* (pp. 13–14). Englewood Cliffs, NJ: Prentice-Hall.

15 Nightingale, D. (1974). Conflict and conflict resolution. In G. Strouss, R.E. Miles, C.C. Snow & A.S. Tannenbaum (Eds), *Organizational behavior: Research and issues* (pp. 141–163). Madison, WI: Industrial Relations Research Association.

16 Oberschall, A. (1978). Theories of social conflict. *Annual Review of Sociology, 4* (1), 291–315.

17 Coser, L. (1956). *The functions of social conflict*. Glencoe, IL: Free Press. This book, based on his Ph.D. dissertation, was later named one of the best selling sociology books of the twentieth century.

18 Coser (1956). Ibid.; Coser, L.A. (1968). Conflict: III. Social aspects. In D.L. Sills (Ed.), *International encyclopedia of the social sciences, 3*. (pp. 232–236). New York, NY: Crowell Collier & Macmillan.

19 Coser, L.A. (1967). *Continuities in the study of social conflict* (p. 232). New York, NY: Free Press.

20 Coser (1956). Op. cit, p. 104; Stein, A.A. (1976). Conflict and cohesion. A review of the literature. *Journal of Conflict Resolution, 20* (1), 143–172.

21 World Health Organization (2016). *Definition and typology of violence*. Geneva, SW: Violence Prevention Alliance. Retrieved from: www.who.int/violenceprevention/approach/definition/en/.

22 Bernard, J. (1965). Some current conceptualization in the field of conflict. *American Journal of Sociology, 70* (4), 442–454; Horowitz, I.L. (1971). The treatment of conflict in sociological literature. *International Journal of Group Tensions, 1* (4), 350–363; Mullins, N.C. (1973). *Theories and theory groups in contemporary American sociology*. New York, NY: Harper & Row.

23 Stein, A.A. (1976). Conflict and cohesion. A review of the literature. *Journal of Conflict Resolution, 20* (1), 143–172.

24 Esses, V.M., Jackson, L.M. & Armstrong, T.L. (1998). Intergroup competition and attitudes toward immigrants and immigration: An instrumental model of group conflict. *Journal of Social Issues, 54* (4), 699–724; Taylor, D. M. & Moghaddam, F.M. (1987). *Theories of intergroup relations: International social psychological perspectives*. New York, NY: Praeger.

25 Sanderson, S.K. (2001). The evolution of human sociality: A Darwinian conflict perspective. New York, NY: Rowman & Littlefield; Turner, J.H. (1991). *The structure of sociological theory*, 5th ed. Belmont, CA: Wadsworth Publishing, p. 186.

26 Turner, J.H. (1975). A strategy for reformulating the dialectical and functional theories of conflict. *Social Forces, 53* (3), 433–444.

27 Dadrian, V.N. (1971). On the dual role of social conflict—An appraisal of Coser's theory. *International Journal of Group Tensions, 1* (4), 371–377.

28 Janis, I. (1972). *Victims of groupthink*. Boston, MA: Houghton Mifflin; Oberschall (1978). Op. cit.

29 Turner (1975). Op. cit.

30 Grimes, W. (2009, June 22). Ralf Dahrendorf, sociologist, dies at 80. *The New York Times*, A19. Retrieved from: www.nytimes.com/2009/06/22/world/europe/22dahrendorf.html?_r=0.

31 Dahrendorf, R. (1959). *Class and class conflict in industrial society*. Palo Alto, CA: Stanford University Press.

32 Dahrendorf, R. (1990). *The modern social conflict: An essay on the politics of liberty*. Berkeley and Los Angeles, CA: University of California Press.

33 Dahrendorf, R. (1958). Toward a theory of social conflict. *The Journal of Conflict Resolution, 2* (2), 170–183.

34 See: Allen, K. (2011). Conflict theory: Lewis Coser, Ralf Dahrendorf, and Randall Collins. In *The social lens: An invitation to social and sociological theory*, 2nd ed. (pp. 223–262). Thousand Oaks, CA: Sage.

35 Dahrendorf, R. (1968). *Essays in the theory of society*. London, UK: Routledge & Kegan Paul.

36 Allen (2011). Op. cit.

37 Dahrendorf (1958). Op. cit., p. 175.

38 Allen (2011). Op. cit. In contrast to factors that reduce the likelihood of conflict leading to violence, the larger the sense of relative deprivation, the more the likelihood of conflict.

39 Dahrendorf (1958). Op. cit.

40 Lopreato, J. (1968). Authority relations and class conflict. *Social Forces*, 47 (1), 70–79; Fox, W.S., Payne, D.E., Preist, T.B. & Philliber, W.W. (1977). Authority position, legitimacy of authority structure, and acquiescence to authored, *Social Forces*, 55 (4), 966–973.

41 Lopreato (1968). Op. cit.; Fox et al. (1977). Op. cit.

42 Lopreato (1968). Op. cit.; Fox et al. (1977). Op. cit.; Robinson, R.V. & Kelley, J. (1979). Class as conceived by Marx and Dahrendorf: Effects on income inequality and politics in the United States and Great Britain. *American Sociological Review*, 44 (1), 38–58.

43 Robinson & Kelley (1979). Ibid.

44 Lopreato (1968). Ibid.

45 Fox et al. (1977). Op. cit; Lopreato (1968). Op. cit.; Robinson & Kelley (1979). Op. cit.

46 Hazelrigg, L.E. (1972). Class, property, and authority: Dahrendorf's critique of Marx's theory of class. *Social Forces*, 50 (4), 473–487; Turner, J.H. (1973). From Utopia to where? A strategy for reformulating the Dahrendorf's conflict model. *Social Forces*, 52 (2), 236–244; Weingart, P. (1969). Beyond Parsons? A critique of Ralf Dahrendorf's conflict theory. *Social Forces*, 48 (2), 151–165.

47 Turner (1973). Op. cit.; Weingart (1969). Op. cit.

48 Turner (1973). Op. cit.

49 Weingart (1969). Op. cit.

50 Turner (1973). Op. cit.

51 Fox et. al. (1977). Op. cit.; Lopreato (1968). Op. cit.

52 Smelser, N.J. (2011). Ralf Dahrendorf. Biographical Memoirs. *Proceedings of the American Philosophical Society*, 155 (4), 465–469. Retrieved from: www.amphilsoc.org/sites/default/files/proceedings/1554sixDahrendorf.pdf.

53 Lopreato (1968). Op. cit., p. 77.

54 Rahim, M.A. (2002). Towards a theory of managing organizational conflict. *International Journal of Conflict Management*, 13 (3), 206–235.

55 Kriesberg, L. (2007b). The conflict resolution field. Origins, growth, and differentiation. In I.W. Zartman (Ed.), *Peacemaking in international conflict. Methods and techniques*. Revised edition. (pp. 25–60). Washington, DC: United States Institute of Peace.

56 Lewicki, Weiss & Lewin (1992). Op. cit.

57 Pondy, L.R. (1967). Organizational conflict: Concepts and models. *Administrative Science Quarterly*, 12 (2), 296–320.

58 Pondy, L.R. (1989b). Reflections on organizational conflict. *Journal of Organizational Change Management*, 2 (2), 94–98; Pondy, L.R. (1992). Reflections on organizational conflict. *Journal of Organizational Behavior*, 13 (3), 257–261.

59 Pondy, L.R. (1989a). Organizational conflict: Concepts and models. In H.J. Leavitt, L.R. Pondy & D.M. Boje (Eds), *Readings in managerial psychology*, 4th ed. (pp. 513–531). Chicago, IL: University of Chicago Press.

60 Pondy (1967). Op. cit.; Pondy (1989a). Op. cit.

61 Pondy believed that latent conflict may not reach the level of awareness because the individuals may block out mildly threatening conflicts and only recognize them when they become strong threats. Similarly, individuals focus their attention only on a few things at a time, not noticing latent conflicts until they grow into threats.

62 Pondy (1967). Op. cit., p. 304.

63 Carter, G.L. & Byrnes, J.F. (2006). *How to manage conflict in the organization*, 2nd ed. (Exhibit 1–2, Pondy's Revised Model of Conflict Dynamics, p. 8). New York, NY: American Management Association.

64 Some call this passive approach *appeasement*.

65 Briefly, *principled negotiation* includes: separating people from issues; focusing on interests, not positions; inventing options for mutual gain; using objective standards of fairness; having alternatives to a collaborative agreement; degree to which each party is knowledgeable; willingness to communicate. See: Fisher, R., Ury, W. & Patton, B. (2011). *Getting to yes. Negotiating agreement without giving in*, 3rd ed. New York, NY: Penguin Books.

66 Pondy (1967). Op. cit.

67 See: Gladstein, D.L. (1984). A model of task group effectiveness. *Administrative Science Quarterly, 29* (4), 499–517; Wall, V. & Nolan, L. (1986). Perceptions of inequity, satisfaction and conflict in task-oriented groups. *Human Relations, 39* (11), 1033–1052; Schwenk, C. & Cosier, R. (1993). Effects of consensus and devil's advocacy on strategic decision making. *Journal of Applied Social Psychology, 23* (2), 126–139.

68 Jehn, K.A. & Chatman, J.A. (2000). The influence of proportional and perceptual conflict composition on team performance. *International Journal of Conflict Management, 11* (1), 56–73.

69 Wall, V.D. Jr. & Nolan, L.L. (1986). Perceptions of inequity, satisfaction, and conflict in task-oriented groups. *Human Relations, 39* (11), 1033–1051.

70 Wall, V.D. Jr., Galanes, G.J. & Love, S. (1987). Small, task-oriented group conflict, conflict management, satisfaction, and decision quality. *Small Group Research 18* (1), 31–55.

71 Wall & Nolan (1986). Op. cit.

72 Jehn, K.A. (1995). A multimethod examination of benefits and detriments of intragroup conflict. *Administrative Science Quarterly, 40* (2), 256–282.

73 Gleiberman, A., Jeon, H.J. & Dant, R.P. (2012). *Conflict resolution through the principal's eyes: A preliminary propositional model.* Robert Mittelstaedt Doctoral Symposium, pp. 197–206. Retrieved from: http://cbatest40.unl.edu/academic-programs/departments/marketing/about/robert-mittelstaedt-doctoral-symposium/docs/2012_SymposiumProceedings.pdf#page=213.

74 Volkema, R.J., Farquhar, K. & Bergman, T.J. (1996). Third-party sensemaking in interpersonal conflicts at work: A theoretical framework. *Human Relations, 49* (11), 1437–1454.

75 Yasmi, Y., Schanz, H. & Salim, A. (2006). Manifestation of conflict escalation in natural resource management. *Environmental Science and Policy, 9* (6), 538–546.

76 Jehn & Chatman (2000). Op. cit.

77 Speakman, J. & Ryalis, L. (2010). A re-evaluation of conflict theory for the management of multiple, simultaneous conflict episodes. *Internal Journal of Conflict Management, 21* (2), 186–201.

78 See: Merry, S.E. & Silbey, S.S. (1984). What do plaintiffs want: Re-examining the concept of dispute. *Justice System Journal, 9* (2), 151–178; Martin, J. (1992). The suppression of gender conflict in organizations. In D.M. Kolb and J. Bartunek (Eds), *Hidden conflict in organizations: Uncovering behind-the-scenes disputes.* Beverly Hills, CA: Sage; Trice, H.M. (1984). Rites and ceremonials in organizational culture. In S.B. Bacharach, S.B. and S.M. Mitchell (Eds). *Perspectives on organizational sociology,* 4. Greenwich, CT: JAI Press.

79 Kolb, D.M. & Putnam, L.L. (1992). The multiple faces of conflict in organizations. *Journal of Organizational Behavior, 13* (3), 311–324.

80 Kriesberg, L. (2003). *Constructive conflicts: From escalation to resolution,* 2nd ed. Lanham, MD: Rowman and Littlefield.

81 Kriesberg, L. (2005). Nature, dynamics, and phases of intractability. In C.A. Crocker, F.O. Hampson, & P. Aall (Eds), *Grasping the nettle. Analyzing cases of intractable conflict.* (pp. 65–97). Washington, DC: United States Institute of Peace Press. Retrieved from: http://staff.maxwell.syr.edu/cgerard/Fundamentals%20of%20Conflict%20Resolution/Nature,%20Dynamics,%20and%20Phases%20of%20Intractability.pdf.

82 Kriesberg, L. (2007a). *Constructive conflicts: From escalation to resolution,* 3rd ed. New York, NY: Rowman and Littlefield.

83 Kriesberg, L. (1982). Social conflict theories and conflict resolution. *Peace & Change, 8* (2–3), 3–17.

84 Singer, J.D. (1981). Accounting for international war: The state of the discipline. *Journal of Peace Research, 18* (1), 1–18; Naroll, R., Bullough, V.L. & Naroll, F. (1974). *Military deterrence in history: A pilot cross-historical survey.* Albany, NY: State University of New York Press.

85 Johnson, C. (1966). *Revolutionary change.* Boston, MA: Little, Brown.

86 Kriesberg (1982). Op. cit., p. 5.

87 Turner, R.H. (1981). Collective behavior and resource mobilization as approaches to social movements: Issues and continuities. In L. Kriesberg (Ed.), *Research in social movements, conflicts and change,* 4. (pp. 1–24). Greenwich, CT: JAI Press.

88 Gurr, T.R. (1970). A comparative study of civil strife. In H.D. Graham & T.R. Gurr (Eds), *Violence in America: Historical and comparative perspectives.* (pp. 572–632). New York, NY: Bantam Books.

89 Oberschall, A. (1973). *Social conflict and social movements.* Englewood Cliffs, NJ: Prentice Hall; Tilly, C. (1978). *From mobilization to revolution.* Reading, MA: Addison-Wesley.

90 Pruitt, D.G. & Rubin, J.Z. (1994). *Social conflicts: Escalation, stalemate, and settlement.* 2nd ed. New York, NY: McGraw-Hill.

91 Fisher, R. (1964). Fractioning conflict. In R. Fisher (Ed.), *International conflict and behavioral science.* (pp. 91–109). New York, NY: Basic Books.

92 Kriesberg, L. (1991). Conflict resolution applications to peace studies. *Peace & Change, 16* (4), 400–417.

93 Morgan. W.R. (1970). Faculty mediation of student war protests. In J. Foster & D. Long (Eds), *Protest! Student activism in American.* (pp. 365–382). New York, NY: William Morrow and Co; Gurr (1970). Op. cit.; Kriesberg (1982). Op. cit.

94 Snyder, G.H. & Diesing, P. (1977). *Conflict among nations: Bargaining, decision making, and system structure in international crises.* Princeton, NJ: Princeton University Press.

95 Kriesberg (1982). Op. cit.

96 Gamson, W.A. (1975). *The strategy of social protest.* Homewood, IL: Dorsey.

97 Gamson (1975). Ibid. Taft, P. & Ross, P. (1969). American labor violence: Its causes, character and outcome. In H.D. Graham & T.R. Gurr (Eds), *Violence in America.* (pp. 281–395). New York, NY: Bantam Books.

98 Pruitt, D. & Lewis, S.A. (1977). The psychology of integrative bargaining. In D. Druckman (Ed.), *Negotiations.* Beverly Hills, CA: Sage.

99 Bartos, O.J. (1970). Determinants and consequences of toughness. In P.G. Swingle (Ed.), *The structure and conflict.* (pp. 45–68). New York, NY: Academic Press.

100 Fisher (1978). Op. cit.; Walton, R.E. & McKersie, R.B (1965). *A behavioral theory of labor negotiations: An analyses of a social interaction system.* New York, NY: McGraw-Hill; Kriesberg, L. (1981). Noncoercive inducements in U.S.–Soviet conflicts: Ending the occupation of Austria and nuclear weapons tests. *Journal of Political and Military Sociology, 9* (1), 1–16.

101 Kochan, T.A. & Jick, T. (1978). The public sector mediation process. A theory and empirical examination. *The Journal of Conflict Resolution, 22* (2), 209–240.

102 Coleman, J. (1957). *Community conflict.* New York, NY: Free Press; Coser, L. (1956). *The functions of social conflict.* New York, NY: Free Press; Sherif, M. (1966). *In common predicament.* Boston, MA: Houghton Mifflin.

103 Deutch, M. (1973). *The resolution of conflict: Constructive and destructive processes.* New Haven, CT: Yale University Press.

104 Brockner, J. & Rubin, J.Z. (1985). *Entrapment in escalating conflicts.* New York, NY: Springer-Verlag; Zartman, I.W. (Ed.). (1978). *The negotiation process: Theories and applications.* Beverly Hills, CA: Sage.

105 Sharp, G. (1973). *The politics of nonviolent action.* Boston, MA: Porter Sargent.

106 Rapoport, A. & Chammah, A.M. (1965). *The prisoner's dilemma: A study in conflict and cooperation.* Ann Arbor, MI: University of Michigan Press; Schelling, T. (1960). *The strategy of conflict.* Cambridge, MA: Harvard University Press; Snyder & Diesing (1977). Op. cit.

107 See: Stephenson, C.M. (1999). Peace studies: Overview. In L. Kirtz (Ed.), *Encyclopedia of violence, peace, and conflict, 2.* (pp. 809–820). San Diego, CA: Academic Press; Goldstein, J.S. & Freeman, J.R. (1990). *Three-way street: Strategic reciprocity in world politics.* Chicago, IL: University of Chicago Press.

108 See: Mitchell, C.R. & Webb, K. (1988). *New approaches to international mediation.* Westport, CT: Greenwood; Kressel, K. & Pruitt, D.G. (Eds) (1989). *Mediation research.* San Francisco, CA: Jossey-Bass; J. Bercovitch (Ed.). (1996). *Resolving international conflicts: The theory and practice of mediation.* Boulder, CO: Lunne Rienner.

109 See: Chufrin, G.I. & Saunders, H.H. (1993). A public peace process. *Negotiation Journal,* 9 (2), 155–177; Ray, L. (1982). The alternative dispute resolution movement. *Peace and Change, 8* (2/3), 117–128.

110 See: Cortright, D. & Lopez, G. (2002). *Sanctions and the search for security.* Boulder, CO: Lynne Rienner; Walter, B.F. & Snider, J. (Eds). (1999). *Civil wars, insecurity, and intervention.* New York, NY: Columbia University Press: O'Leary, R. & Bingham, L. (Eds). (2003). *The promise and performance of environmental conflict resolution.* Washington, DC: Resources for the Future Press.

111 Wall & Callister (1995). Op. cit.

112 Malan, J. (1999). Constructive conflicts: From escalation to resolution. Book Review. *African Journal on Conflict Resolution, 1* (1), 129–131; Maney, G.M. (2000). Reviewed work: *Constructive conflicts: From escalation to resolution.* By Louis Kreisberg. *Social Forces, 78* (3), 1181–1183.

113 Maney (2000). Ibid.

114 Maney (2000). Op. cit.

115 Wall, J.A. Jr., Stark, J.B. & Standifer, R.L. (2001). Mediation: A current review and theory development. *Journal of Conflict Resolution, 45* (3), 370–391.

CHAPTER 7

Communication in Organizations

GUIDING QUESTIONS

7.1 Identify the various intrapersonal, situational, and contextual factors that influence a message's meaning to a listener or observer.

7.2 Describe the major components of communication, and explain how they work together in a communicative event.

7.3 Recount the difficulties that leaders face in managing the information flows in their organizations.

7.4 Discuss how language's ambiguity can either benefit or hinder communication effectiveness in organizations.

7.5 Describe the cybernetic tradition's theory of communication's focus on interdependence, self-regulation, and control.

7.6 Explain the socio-psychological tradition's theory of communication as a social process of individuals' expression, interaction, and influence.

7.7 Discuss the sociocultural tradition's theory of people developing and maintaining society (and their personal identities) through shared beliefs.

7.8 Describe the critical theory tradition's view that in-groups can use communication to unfairly allocate power and privilege in a society or organization.

PROFESSIONAL STANDARDS FOR EDUCATIONAL LEADERS: 1, 5, 6, 8, 9

CASE STUDY 7.1

What Did You Say?

Erica Newbie became the new principal of the 800-student Poorhouse Middle School, a low-income and high-minority school in the inner city of a major metropolitan area. Ninety one percent of the students qualify for Free or Reduced-Price Lunch and 73 percent come from single parent households. Erica's previous principalship was in a wealthier, neighboring suburban area where she had "turned around" the school district's "high needs" middle school (22 percent qualified for FRPL and 18 percent came from a single parent household). She knew the importance of parental involvement in fostering student success. During her five years at the previous school, parent attendance at PTA meetings increased from virtually zero percent to more than 70 percent. She was determined to focus on parent involvement at Poorhouse and wanted to "turn around" her new school quickly in order to "save" more students.

Accordingly, on her first day, August 1, Erica sent emails home to parents, arranged to advertise the Back to School PTA meeting in the local paper three times each week, and placed 30 ads for the PTA meeting on the local PBS radio and TV stations. In front of the school, the billboard read, "Parents are Key in Their Child's Success: Come to the PTA Meeting on September 9!" Teachers sent a note home with their students on September 6 with a second reminder on September 8. Erica thought she had covered all the bases.

On September 9, only 14 parents appeared for the PTA meeting. Erica was stunned, then furious. Instead of thanking the parents who did attend, she criticized those who were absent, saying, "You coming out tonight shows that you care about your child's future. So many other parents couldn't find the time to get involved in their child's education. Don't they know how important school is? Don't they care? Don't they want their children to do well in school? I thank you for being concerned and loving parents."

The next day Poorhouse Middle started receiving irate and sometimes threatening calls from parents who would hang up as soon as they had their say. Comments like, "Who does Ms. Newbie think she is, saying I don't love my son?" "Ms. Newbie should go back to the burbs if that's what she thinks of us." Students also commented to her in the hallway, saying things like, "My momma is mad at you" and "My Dad wants to talk with you." Erica's cell phone vibrated with a text from the Superintendent wanting to see her after school let out that afternoon.

RUBRIC 7.1

Lens and/or factors to be considered in decision making	What are the factors at play in this case?	What steps should be considered in solving the problem?	What could have been done to avoid this dilemma?
The situation • The task	In Erica Newbie's rush to increase parental involvement at the school, she neglected to introduce herself and her vision appropriately to the community or show sensitivity to any demographic and cultural differences with her audience (with her misplaced criticism).	Erica should send the PTA a letter apologizing for her awkward start and asking for their help in scheduling visits to local churches and community centers where she can informally meet parents, listen to their concerns, and share her background and vision for their children's education.	Erica should have had enough self-awareness to recognize her disappointment at the low parent turnout and prevent this from affecting her message to parents. Plus, the meeting advertising may not have reached the intended audience.
• Personal abilities	Erica's lack of emotional intelligence prompted her to criticize parents inappropriately.	For Erica, professional development and mentoring around communication issues with diverse audiences.	Closer mentoring from the central office in communicating effectively with parents.
• The school environment	Erica's new school has a different demographic mix than her former school.	Erica needs to develop self-control and sensitivity to the audience.	See above.
	Look	Wider	
Organizational (i.e., the organizational goals, values, policies, culture)	Erica came to a school with vastly different demographics that she did not consider when planning her communication plan or statements.	An orientation for Erica to the school system's demographics and PD on dealing with education and poverty would be in order.	A required orientation for all new employees to the school system dealing with demographics and poverty would prevent many issues like this one.
People (i.e., individuals with needs, beliefs, goals, relationships)	In her rush to increase parental involvement, Erica forgot to consider some major elements of communication.	See above.	See above.
Competing Interests (i.e., competing interests for power, influence, and resources)	Parents heard the message that Erica did not believe they cared about their children's education.	Erica meant well but she insulted parents who may have been working two jobs, had no transportation, or could not afford a sitter. She needs to meet with parents at their convenience and reboot her introduction to them.	See above.

continued . . .

Tradition			
(i.e., school culture, rituals, meaning, heroes)	The school had a tradition of low or no parental participation in PTA meetings.	Erica has the right idea about increasing parental involvement, but she needs to find alternative ways to involve parents who may not be able to take time off work to attend evening meetings.	See above.

OVERVIEW: COMMUNICATION SKILLS CAN FACILITATE— OR UNDO—LEADERSHIP EFFECTIVENESS

Leadership depends on communication. In fact, J.W. Salacuse, Professor of Law and Diplomacy at Tufts University, asserts, "Communication is fundamental to building relationships and therefore to the ability to lead."[1] Language—the ability to communicate—is perhaps humanity's greatest accomplishment, making possible developments from relationships to civilization. But ineffective communication can cause innumerable problems—from arguments over a misunderstanding to world wars.

Communication is how the organization's work gets done. All organizations need to coordinate human activity: this requires exchanging information. Robust communication skills allow leaders to motivate others by communicating their vision, fostering a positive climate, building consensus, directing and coordinating work tasks, managing crises, and leading a community or an organization through change. Yet, despite its significance, only 51 percent of employees are satisfied with organizational communications.[2]

Eighty percent of people who fail at work do so because they do not relate well— do not *communicate* well—to other people.[3] An estimated one-third of all school principals leave their positions involuntarily.[4] Studies find the reason that most principals are demoted, dismissed, or counseled out of their positions is their failure to communicate in ways that build positive connections with teachers, parents, students, and colleagues.[5] In one state study, superintendents ranked principals' career-threatening skills deficiencies. "Works cooperatively with faculty and staff" headed the list.[6] Likewise, a 2007 National School Public Relations study of school superintendents found "The lack of communication and the failure to keep people informed" topped the factors affecting superintendents' failure.[7] Regardless of the organization's size or purposes, if the right people don't receive the right information at the right time in the right way, the enterprise falters.

Leading successful schools requires principals and teachers to speak, write, and behave in ways that influence others in ways we intend. Yet many factors—in our messages; in our teachers, parents, and students; in our school and community environments; and in ourselves—shape the messages we send and how others interpret them. Understanding the components of communication in organizations and the theories underlying their power to sway others to know and act as we intend—or that prevent them from doing so—is a key leadership skill.

DEFINING COMMUNICATION IN ORGANIZATIONS

Communication is the process of sending and receiving messages.[8] It is an activity by which two or more systems (usually people) exchange information.[9] These systems coexist in a larger environment. Exchanging information reduces uncertainty in the two systems' future behavior. Talking face-to-face, sending emails and texts, writing memos, conversing by telephone, participating in meetings, walking down the hall, and wearing professional attire are all forms of organizational communications. But communication is more than the transmitting of information from Person A to Person B.

Notably, "one cannot *not* communicate."[10] All aspects of human behavior—speaking and silence, gesturing and standing still—carry meaning for someone. Even conscious effort to not engage in communication shows itself as communicating something. Not receiving a birthday party invitation is a message. In reality, the speaker does not have total control of the message the listener receives. Rather, the listener, within the limits of cognitive capacity, determines what the message is and what it means to him or her. Misunderstandings often arise because of differences in past experiences, personal histories, and sometimes, in the language of the persons sending and receiving the information. These individual conditions color the understanding of what the message's words mean. The leadership challenge is to ensure that the message intended and sent is the message received and interpreted as intended.

Communication can be depicted graphically. Figure 7.1 illustrates how person-to-person communication occurs. Individuals are both senders and receivers.

Briefly, *senders* direct a *message* through a *channel* (the medium used to transmit the message) to a *receiver*, and the receiver's response sends *feedback* through a channel to the sender about whether or how well the receiver interpreted the message as intended. Several *contexts* also influenced the message: the larger environment, the particular situation, and the individuals' prior experiences and current thoughts and feelings—

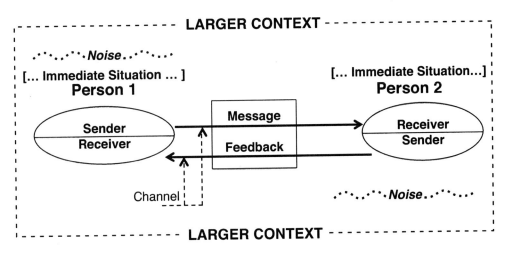

FIGURE 7.1 A Transmission Model of Communication

Source: Adapted from Clampitt, P.G. (2013). *Communicating for managerial effectiveness. Problems, strategies, solutions*. 5th ed. (p. 12). Thousand Oaks, CA: Sage.

including the relationship between sender and receiver. *Noise* is anything that interferes with the receiver hearing the message as the sender intended. In addition, the specific context makes certain interpretations more likely and others less likely. Sender and receiver may—or may not—understand the same larger and situational contexts in the same ways. And the personal experiences coloring the message interpretations are less likely to be shared. As a result, communication is complex. Content and context interact to produce meaning. Contexts may be both shared and individualistic, and messages may be interpreted accurately or inaccurately.

This transmission model of communication enjoys substantial research support.[11] Although late-twentieth-century critics challenged the transmission model as too individualistic (among other weaknesses), many argue that, at the very least, this model conceptualizes communication as a constitutive process that produces and reproduces shared meaning.[12]

REFLECTIONS AND RELEVANCE 7.1

What Messages are You Sending and Receiving?

Communication is how the organization's work gets done. Most educators have a routine that they follow once they arrive at their school for the day. First working alone and then sharing with a partner, reflect on your own typical first hour in the building. Identify all the ways—verbal (oral or written) and nonverbal—and the messages, that you communicate to others during your first hour at school.

- What messages are you intending to send?
- What channels are you using to send these messages?
- Who are your audiences (receivers)?
- What feedback are you receiving that your audience members are receiving your message as intended?
- What "noise" or factors in the immediate situation might interfere with others receiving your message as intended?
- Who in your audience might not be receiving the message you intend—and why not?
- Discuss your behavior and messages intended and sent during your first hour at work with your partner.

Feel free to add ideas to your own list. Then discuss your findings as a class. What messages do you as an education leader want to send to teachers, students, and staff every day from the moment you walk into the building—and by what channels can you effectively send them? By what feedback do you know if your messages are being received and interpreted as you intend? What "noise" or context factors can you control or at least influence? What messages or channels might you begin to use to better communicate with others in the school?

REFLECTIONS AND RELEVANCE 7.2

Controlling the Communication Event

You are a teacher. During a class change, you are walking from the office to your classroom when you see two seventh grade students pushing and shoving each other in the hall. Peers and classmates are gathering around them, yelling and cheering. Two teachers and an assistant principal are on the scene. The A.P. firmly directs the congregating students to move at once to their next period classrooms. With the teachers' active encouragement, the onlookers comply. When the crowd is gone, the A.P. tells the tussling students to stop their behavior immediately. Slowly, the pair complies, still glaring at each other. They walk with the A.P. to his office to debrief, contact parents, and receive any disciplinary consequence.

Working in groups of three or four, analyze this hall incident from a communication perspective. What was the A.P.'s communication strategy, and why did the intervention work? Identify the sender/s, the message/s, the channel/s, the receiver/s, the feedback, and the varied contexts (immediate situation, individuals' prior experiences and current thoughts and feelings, and the larger environment) that may have influenced the A.P.'s, the bystanders', and the aggressive students' thoughts and actions. Discuss as a class.

KEY ASPECTS OF COMMUNICATION IN ORGANIZATIONS

To paraphrase management guru Henry Mintzberg, organizational leaders do not leave meetings or hang up the telephone so they can get back to work. To a large degree, communication *is* their work.[13] Communication is the core of what leaders do and is central to their organization's effectiveness. Manager-watching studies show that they spend over 60 percent of their working time in scheduled and unscheduled meetings with others.[14] Most communication in organizations is face-to-face, generally related to tasks. Although typically brief, the interactions have enormous consequences for the organization's communication and cultural climate. Ample evidence suggests that organizations with effective communication strategies are successful while those with poor internal communication tend to struggle.[15]

In reviewing the literature, investigators find the advantages from high quality internal communications include: improved productivity, reduced absenteeism, higher quality of services and products, increased levels of innovation, fewer employee walkouts or strikes, and reduced costs.[16] A USA Gallup survey of over one million employees found a significant link between scores related to communication with managers and business performance, including increased employee retention, productivity and profitability, and customer satisfaction.[17] In contrast, a survey of 2,600 employees replied that a lack of communication from managers was the most demotivating aspect of their work, citing issues such as the complete lack of interaction, general absence of feedback, or meetings occurring "behind closed doors."[18] In short, school leaders who communicate effectively make their schools more successful.

Key Aspects of Organizational Communication

Organizations can be viewed as "collections of people trying to make sense of what is happening around them."[19] Talking to each other—communicating—about why others act as they do and what they think, is central to organizational life. Recognizing the components of human communication and their dynamics in helping us create meaning and purposeful action is a reasonable place to begin. As depicted in Figure 7.1, the major areas of organizational communication include:

Communicators

The people involved in communication have personal characteristics—such as age, gender, physique, disposition, attire, and emotional intelligence—that influence their actions and reactions to others' behaviors. *Emotional intelligence*[20] refers to the basic skills of social awareness and communication. It includes the ability to persuade and motive others, to empathize and build relationships, to handle one's own and others' emotions, to sensitively give open and honest feedback, to monitor one's own behavior, and to be keenly aware of organizational politics. Communicators also have personal histories and experiences that affect how they send, perceive, and interpret messages.

Messages

The signals and symbols we use to transmit what we mean in visual, auditory, tactile, or olfactory ways.[21] *Visual* messages include written communication and observed behaviors or visual cues. *Auditory* communication—that which we hear—may be face-to-face or technology mediated (such as by telephone). *Tactile* communication includes touch and bodily contact (such as handshakes, fist bumps, hugs and kisses). And *olfactory* messages include using perfumes, after-shave lotions, and other scents used to emit a pleasing aroma (and mask our natural body odors).

Nonverbal Communication

The visual ways that we use bodily activity to express information without using words merits special attention. Facial expressions, vocal cues, body gestures and movements, space, touch, and clothing are all forms of nonverbal communication. Even the amount of distance separating people in conversation or the amount of eye contact they make sends a nonverbal message (and the message's meaning varies from culture to culture). Facial mien—such as smiling or crying—and waving "Goodbye" are highly effective and universal means of conveying certain kinds of information.[22] In contrast, gesturing by joining thumb and forefinger to form a circle does not mean the same thing in all cultures. In the United States, it means, "OK"—a positive affirmation—whereas in

France and Belgium it means, "You are worth zero," and in Greece and Turkey it is an insulting, vulgar sexual invitation.[23]

How teachers and principals *say* something and how they *act* while saying it are as essential to the complete message—sometimes more so—as *what* they say. In the United States, telling a teacher, "Good job with that lesson" while looking away and frowning does not transmit the same message as delivering it with eye contact, a smile, and a handshake. Unless the verbal and nonverbal messages are *congruent*—that is, they convey the same message—the actual message remains open to question. Just because the principal announces to faculty that he or she has "an open door policy" does not mean the principal will make time to listen whenever a teacher appears in the office to share a concern.

Channel

Messages are conveyed through a *medium* and delivered through a *means*. The "mediums" include the visual, auditory, and olfactory channels. The "means" include face-to-face, telephone, written (through email, fax, text, website, U.S. Post, or newsletter), audio, or video. Skilled communicators choose and make optimum use of the channel deemed most appropriate to achieve the desired goal. Employees tend to prefer face-to-face communication with their administrators.[24]

Noise

The term used to describe anything that interferes with or distorts meanings and messages. Noise may include environmental factors (i.e., intrusive sounds, dim lighting, room temperature) that make people uncomfortable; psychological factors (i.e., personal biases, stereotypes, past experiences that affect how individuals interpret what a particular person is saying); and impairments (i.e., a physical, neurological, or psychiatric incapacity—such as loss of sight, hearing, or severe depression—that makes normal interaction channels difficult or impossible). Noise may also be semantic (when the actual meaning of what is being communicated becomes distorted as the result of language or cultural difference). In addition, demographic factors, particularly age and gender differences, have been found to have the potential to cause problems during social encounters. In our culture, for instance, a female may nod her head to indicate that she is listening (but not necessarily agreeing) whereas a male nodding his head tends to communicate agreement with what the speaker is saying.[25] Noise may also relate to the listeners' internal state at that particular time of day: teachers meeting immediately after students leave for the day are likely to be tired and hungry. Lastly, organizational "noise" (or barriers to communication) are those that the organization constructs, such as teachers on the same team who do not share the same planning period or overburdened assistant principals who do not have the time to visit classrooms frequently or give teachers' meaningful feedback on their teaching.

Feedback

Feedback is the verbal and nonverbal information we receive from others (as well as from ourselves by self-monitoring) in response to our actions, by which we can evaluate our performance. Feedback and knowledge of results have long been known as essential to effective human performance on any task. In fact, skilled communicators are high self-monitors, constantly analyzing and regulating their own behavior vis-à-vis others' responses. In organizations, feedback tends to flow mainly from persons in authority to their subordinates rather than the other way around.[26] Principals and assistant principals are responsible for observing and evaluating teachers. When upward feedback occurs, from teacher or staff to principal, it tends to be more positive than critical in nature.[27]

Because giving critical feedback upward (especially critical feedback about organizational goals and administrators' functioning) is essential to strong organizational performance, it deserves special attention.[28] When individuals with differing degrees of organizational power convey messages, extra dynamics often come into play. Realistically speaking, giving critical feedback upward tends to bring high risk and low rewards whereas articulating "good news" upward tends to bring low risk with high rewards.[29] Continually hearing the "rosy picture" can lead to principals (or other administrators) developing distorted perceptions of what is really occurring in their organizations. As a result, they may make inappropriate or harmful decisions. Studies have found the absence of critical upward communication to be a causal factor in organizational problems.[30] Investigators found repeated failures of critical upward communication at NASA helped explain many of its most high profile disasters, including the Columbia and Challenger tragedies. Although people are more likely to speak up when they believe that others will support them,[31] the failure to do so will discourage others from doing so. Looking more deeply, the absence of valued upward communication tends to reflect an organization that is hierarchical, punitive, and with a dysfunctional communication climate.[32]

Nonetheless, managers who actively seek out critical feedback find that it enhances their stature.[33] Researchers have argued that organizations should institutionalize critical upward communication, encouraging "devils' advocates" to criticize the "prevailing orthodoxy."[34] Of course, learning how to seek out and respond constructively to upward critical feedback may require special training in addition to a supportive organizational culture and climate. It must be remembered, however, that feedback always reflects the speaker's and the listener's position in complex social networks that influence their perceptions of reality. Information is always perceived and interpreted in idiosyncratic ways. Without an objective standard, determining feedback's accuracy is always complicated.

Context

Communication occurs within a particular situation and environment that influences behavior. A principal will act differently when talking to a teacher in the hall about an upset parent, as compared with discussing the parent's concern in the principal's office. The principal may also behave differently if speaking about the parent to a teacher whose husband is in the hospital. The specifics of each case play key roles in shaping the behavior.

Clearly, communication is so infused into organizational life that describing a school would be incomplete without considering the communication practices that occur within it. Understanding its parts and having the terms to describe them can help educational leaders become more aware of communication processes and identify where they are strong and where they need to grow.

Information Flow and Communication

Information in organizations can move in varied directions. Messages can move horizontally across similarly placed levels in the organizational chart, typically concerning work units' coordination. The social studies department chair can easily confer with the English department chair in the same building, or at other schools within the school district, to coordinate staff development or plan integrated curricular units. Information can flow vertically, upward and downward among people who are on different levels of authority within the organization. Assistant principals talk with teachers and principals speak with central office assistant superintendents. Most vertical communication in organizations tends to flow downward, especially in highly uncertain situations.[35] Similarly, cross-functional information can flow diagonally between individuals of different hierarchy levels. Principals can confer with custodians about becoming mentors to students, or secretaries can help teachers learn how to use the new copy machine. The receiving individual's mindset and the particular context in which the message is received influence the message's meanings. Speakers' organizational status also plays a role in influencing a message's meaning.

Organizational communication also flows vertically and horizontally through formal and informal channels. *Formal communication*—"official communication"—is what takes place within the well-known structure. These include the official bureaucratic management rules, policies, and work directions given orally, on paper, or electronically. Typically, formal information is collected and flows up to the top organization levels for leadership review and decision making, while directions flow down from the top to the worksite to implement. Formal communication can also flow horizontally, between two parts at the same level. *Informal communications*—the "grapevine"—are those messages that take place outside the formal communication channels. Coworkers interact socially to talk about their work and themselves. In this way, employees build social networks among organization members. Moreover, formal and informal communication channels operate at differing speeds. Formal communication tends to move slowly (it takes considerable time for all middle level administrators to read, revise, reread, and sign off), while informal communication tends to be very fast. According to scholars, informal communication in the organization is the second most frequently used channel; communication between the employee and his or her immediate supervisor is the most frequent.[36] Informal communications may occur inside or outside the workplace.

Recognizing the many directions in which organizational information flows, and the speed differentials between formal and informal communication, presents major challenges for school leaders. In reality, they cannot fully control the messages influencing thought and behavior in their schools.

Language is Ambiguous

Words can have a variety of meanings. One investigator concluded that more than 14,000 definitions exist for the 500 most frequently used words in the English language.[37] For instance, sprinters and politicians can *run* races (just different types), women can get *runs* in their leggings, and card sharks can have lucky *runs* of aces and kings. A *run* on a bank is bad whereas a home*run* at the baseball park is good. *Going to the bank* can suggest going to a financial institution or going fishing. Without a proper context, even simple everyday words can have unclear meanings.

Likewise, when communicating, the meaning is not just in the word but in the individuals' experiences with the word. Interpersonal interaction is inherently subtle, shaded, and indefinite in both form and content. Different people may interpret the same message differently. What a particular word means to one individual may not be what it means to another. No word has a meaning apart from the person using it and the context in which it is used. To a school custodian, an *evaluation* may signal the possible loss of employment whereas the principal may see an evaluation as an opportunity to demonstrate outstanding performance.

Ambiguity can also be a strategic tool. Many schools affirm the slogan, "Every child can learn." Does it mean that every child who attends this school can learn the required content and skills to high measurable standards? Does it mean the students—not the teachers—are responsible for student learning? Or is it just a throwaway line to keep up with the latest jargon? Without receiving more specifics, people read their own meaning into the statements. Because their private interpretations cannot be confirmed, the ambiguity leaves the speakers' options open. Educators can express their feelings ("I have some reservations about beginning this new reading program.") and later deny any specific interpretations should they arise ("You mean, are teachers are not competent to use it?").

Similarly, cognitive scientists theorize that ambiguity makes language more efficient.[38] Using findings from a 2012 study, they speculated that easy to pronounce, shorter words can be "reused" to mean different things, avoiding the need for a larger and more complex vocabulary. It is more efficient for listeners to infer certain things from the context that to have the speaker spend time on longer and more complicated statements.

Given language's inherent ambiguity, communicators can increase or decrease the probability that a word will receive the intended interpretation by providing an appropriate context. By stating their purpose in the context—to win an election or to make a deposit, for instance—increases the likelihood that the listener will interpret *run* and *bank* as the sender intended.

Language's ambiguity reflects its presence in an open system. Schools, as open systems, have permeable boundaries with other systems in their immediate and larger environments—socioeconomic, national culture, legal, physical, and demographic. Communication among organizational members using a common language creates the network that ties all subsystems to the larger systems, coordinates behavior, and makes it possible for the organization to share common assumptions and values, create an organizational identity and culture, and to achieve its goals. They also allow change to occur as members adapt to their shifting environment, even as organizations and environments change in response to these ongoing interactions.

REFLECTIONS AND RELEVANCE 7.3

Your school enrolls students from a highly diverse community. Working in small groups as a school leadership team, plan for the Annual Open House to welcome teachers, students, and parents to the new school year. The principal plans to greet everyone in a large common space, and teachers will meet in their classrooms with parents and students. Focusing on communication effectiveness, identify the factors that communicators need to consider to ensure that students and parents receive and interpret the school's message as intended using the guide below. Then discuss your findings as a class.

Communicative Factor	Plans, Ideas
1. What is the main *message* the school wants to send its teachers, staff, students, and parents?	
2. *Communicators*—who will be speaking? To be most effective what personal characteristics need to be seen and heard?	
3. *Messages*—What written, auditory, tactile, olfactory, and nonverbal communications do you prefer administrators, teachers and staff to send (and not send)? What should they avoid doing?	
4. *Noise*—What are the potential "noise" issues and what can you do to prevent (or at least, reduce) them?	
5. *Feedback*—What verbal and nonverbal feedback will you want during and after the event—and from whom—to help determine whether the intended message was received and interpreted correctly?	
6. *Context*—What will you do to ensure that the specific school settings used for the event reinforce the intended message?	
7. *Information flow*—Identify examples of formal, informal, vertical, horizontal, and diagonal information flow that may be observed at this event.	
8. *Ambiguity*—How might the principal or teachers use ambiguity as a strategic tool during the event?	

REFLECTIONS AND RELEVANCE 7.4

How Well Does Your Principal Communicate?

To a large degree, organizational leaders' work *is* communication. Using the template in Reflections and Relevance 7.3, observe and critique your own principal or other school leader as a communicator at a large meeting that includes teachers and parents. If possible, use an initial meeting, such as one welcoming teachers, parents, and students to a new school year or gathering to introduce an important issue. What are your principal's communication strengths (and what evidence can you identify to support this conclusion)? What do you see as your principal's communication weaknesses (and again, what evidence)?

COMMUNICATION THEORIES

Communication theories are concerned with how people create and share meaning with others. Theories can give orderly explanations of events, interactions, and processes that happen every day. They provide a thoughtful basis for thinking about and critically evaluating particular communicative acts and their practical implications. Studying theories and their supporting research can help clarify and improve one's own mental models and, ideally, one's own communication skills. As each theory has its insights and limitations, the more theories one knows, the more problem-solving options one gains.

As the focus of many different academic domains (including literature, rhetoric, cybernetics, psychology, social psychology and anthropology, and critical theory), communication theory includes multiple traditions. Each tradition responds to its particular eras, cultures, and social groups. And each tradition has different things to say about society, continuity and change, and the nature of communication.

The term *communication theory* did not receive wide usage until the 1940s.[39] Many scholars tended to ignore work published outside their own disciplinary or collegial boundaries. Until the late twentieth century, no canon, general theory, or even consensus existed on communication theory as a field. One analysis of seven communication theory textbooks identified 249 distinct "theories"; only 18 (7 percent) appeared in more than three textbooks.[40] Likewise, scholarship on communication theory continued within its separate domains, never reaching for more than the sum of its parts. As a result, little successful cross-fertilization occurred.[41]

Several communication theories hold relevance for educational leadership practice. Beginning with the end in mind, we will consider four separate communication theory traditions: cybernetics, socio-psychological, sociocultural, and critical theory.

Cybernetic Theory: Communication as Systems of Interacting Parts

Modern communication theory begins with the cybernetic tradition. *Cybernetics* is the science of how people, animals, and machines control and communicate information.[42] Theories in the cybernetics tradition—including systems theory, information science, cognitive and artificial intelligence, network analysis, functionalist social theory, interpersonal communication, and cybernetics—explain how physical, biological, social, and behavioral processes work. Stressing circular forces, cybernetics challenges the concept that one thing causes another in a linear manner. Figure 7.1, a transmission model in the cybernetic tradition, focuses on how things impact one another in a circular fashion, how systems' feedback loops can maintain stability and create change.

The cybernetic perspective theorizes communication as *information processing*—a complex system of interacting parts that influence each other and control the overall system's character. Feedback is the key that makes communication possible within a system. Communication's goal is to get the most information across with the least amount of interference. This information processing occurs in all types of complex systems—living or nonliving, macro or micro—enabling them to function (and, often, malfunction). Here, the system is more than the sum of its parts. Organizations are information-processing systems.[43] As with any organism, communication can facilitate both stability and change.

Coherence and consistence are key tenets of cybernetic communication theory. Using the transmission model, cybernetics views communication problems as breakdowns in the information flow resulting from noise, information overload, or a mismatch between structure and function. As resources for solving communications problems—for restoring coherence and consistency—this model offers an array of information-processing technologies and related methods of systems design and analysis, management, and in certain contexts, therapeutic intervention.

In the cybernetics' tradition, all systems are characterized by interdependence, self-regulation, and control. Like families, all systems are distinctive interdependent wholes distinguished by a pattern of relationships. Dependence on other parts of the system limits its independence. And a system cannot sustain itself without bringing in new resources (inputs). A system takes inputs from the environment, processes them, and creates outputs that return into the environment. The inputs and outputs may be tangible (such as a science project), energy (such as a marching band performance), or information (such as new knowledge and skills).

Similarly, systems are typified by self-regulation and control. Systems monitor, regulate, and control their outputs so they can remain stable and achieve goals. System controls can be relatively simple or highly complex. A home thermostat that regulates room temperatures according to a predetermined setting is a simple system, whereas a jet airplane is a highly complex system of interacting parts (in fact, systems within systems) that can take passengers, their baggage, and commercial cargo from their origin to their destination. Likewise, the human body is a highly complex set of interdependent, self-regulating, and controlling systems interacting with each other and with the individual's immediate and larger environments. By this reasoning, a school district with its central office and varied school sites is a school system with complex sets of interdependent entities. At the same time, systems in dynamic environments must be adaptable and capable of change.

Systems theorists are interested in the system's nature, functions, and how it is able to sustain and control itself over time. Complex systems contain series of feedback loops—*networks*—that connect its parts. Figure 7.2 portrays a simply cybernetic network. In this figure, the pluses (+) depict positive relationships and the minuses (–) depict negative relationships. In positive relationships, variables increase or decrease together. In negative relationships, they vary inversely: as one increases, the other decreases.

As indicated in Figure 7.2, many events influence the likelihood of a teacher receiving promotion to assistant principal. Promotion to department chair, leading a school improvement committee, and having access to child care and tuition reimbursement *increase* the likelihood of promotion to A.P. By contrast, getting sick and missing work, poorer performance, a less than fully supportive partner, and time on Facebook *decrease* the likelihood of promotion to A.P. Accordingly, in this graphic, some feedback network's loops are positive; others are negative.

Research and Criticism

Cybernetics theory researchers investigate how organizations evaluate, interpret, and retain messages in the system[44] and how information facilitates decision making during

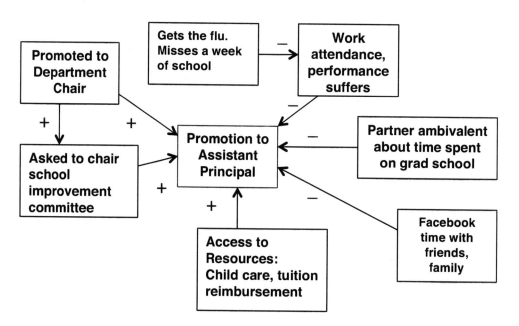

FIGURE 7.2 A Simple Cybernetic Network

Source: Based on Littlejohn, S. & Foss, K.A. (2011). *Theories of human communication*. 10th ed. (Chapter 3, pp. 43–78). Long Grove, IL: Waveland Press.

times of stable and unstable environments.[45] Despite their dryly-technical vocabulary, these studies hold implications for schools as organizations and for improving teaching and learning. For instance, studies find that when uncertainty and task complexity increase, the need for information processing increase. At these times, subsystems rely on horizontal (i.e., collegial and work group peers) rather than vertical (i.e., subordinate to superior in the organizational hierarchy) communication channels.[46] For instance, when the state issues new core subject mandates, English teachers are more likely to look to colleagues in the English and social studies departments for clarification before asking their administrators. Additionally, analysis of *cognitive load* in learning situations —the ability of humans to process only limited amounts of information at one time due to the information difficulty and outside distractors—can lead to instructional design that will generate gains in learning efficiency[47]—such as "chunking" information into meaningful parts for students to learn rather than presenting all the information at once.

Additionally, studies find that acquiring *schema* (i.e., cognitive constructs or mental models that organize information according to the way it will be taught) and *automatic processing* (i.e., using time and practice to allow cognitive processes to occur without conscious control) help prevent students' cognitive overload and facilitate learning.[48] For example, teachers who race to "cover the material" to prepare students for a major test may increase the amount of information *presented* but not necessarily increase the rate of information *transmitted*. Students can receive far more information than they can effectively process cognitively. In contrast, study participants receiving information with audio and related pictures—using multiple channel presentations (i.e., word with accompanying pictures)—learn more than participants using only one channel (i.e., of sound only or sound and unrelated pictures).[49] In cybernetic terms, "the human information processing system appears to function as a multiple-channel system until the system capacity overloads."[50]

Some critics consider cybernetic theory implausible, contesting the belief that the distinction between mind and matter is no more than the functional difference between software and hardware.[51] Similarly, critics challenge the cybernetics scholars' view that a message's meaning is irrelevant; its only value is to serve a communicative function such as feedback or reducing uncertainty.[52] Likewise, critics refute the notion that thought is simply information processing: to believe this is to affirm that individuals, groups, organizations, societies, robots, and artificial organisms all "think."[53] Critics also dispute the weak experimental designs of certain cybernetic studies[54] that lead to inconsistent findings and do not permit accurate interpretations or drawing conclusions for best practice. Taking the long view, cybernetics theory scholars suggest that theory-based research adds up over time.[55]

As a theory of communication, cybernetics offers both realistic and questionable ideas. Appealing to common sense, it presents a rational approach to everyday communication practice. It confronts the simplistic notions of linear cause and effect, noting that communication processes can be highly complex and subtle; it addresses communication breakdowns, stressing the problems of technical control, the complexity and unpredictability of feedback processes, and the probability that despite our best intentions, communicative acts will have unintended outcomes. Also, cybernetics emphasizes that the whole is greater than the sum of its parts; communicators must move beyond their individual perspectives to observe the broader, systemic communication processes; and individuals cannot be responsible for systemic outcomes that no single individual can control.[56]

Although cybernetic theories help understand relationships, they are less useful in understanding individual differences among system parts. The socio-psychological tradition offers a more practical perspective for comprehending individual people as communicators.

Socio-Psychological Theories: Communication as Interpersonal Influence

The socio-psychological tradition views communication as a function of the individuals' personalities interacting with their environments. Individuals' personalities (i.e., their temperaments, attitudes, intentions, emotional states, conscious thoughts, personality traits, unconscious conflicts, communication skills, and the socio-cultural system to which they belong) as modified by the immediate social context (including relationships, media technologies, institutions, and social culture) impact and shape the communication to produce a range of effects—cognitive, emotional, and behavioral. And although every personality is unique, personality in general is based on factors inherited and learned through the influences of home environment, societal culture, practice, and experience. Figure 7.3 illustrates the socio-psychological theory.

In this way, the socio-psychological communications theory explains the myriad of factors that impact why people behave as they do. Since human communication is complex and inherently vague, messages can have multiple meanings. Examples of poor communication—such as misunderstandings, misconceptions, noise, lack of attention, and confusion—may be due to the participants' personalities because the meanings are in the people, not in the messages.[57]

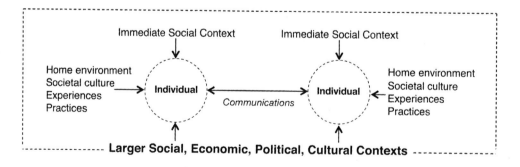

FIGURE 7.3 Socio-Psychological Communication Theory

Source: Based on Craig, R.T. (1999). Communication theory as a field. *Communication Theory, 9* (2), 119–161.

Socio-psychological tradition theorizes communication as expression, interaction, and influence—one of the main ways of affecting (and being affected by) others. A social process, communication may occur face-to-face or through technology from one-to-one, one-to-many, or many-to-many. In this view, one's personality or psychology will influence how people react to certain messages, accepting them or rejecting them, and how they communicate their own values. Careful, systematic observations can discover clear cause and effect relationships.

Additionally, this tradition asserts that communication occurs as the result of complementary processes that operate at the intrapersonal and interpersonal levels. At the *intrapersonal* level, communication involves processes that enable individuals to produce and comprehend messages. At the *interpersonal* level, communication involves processes that cause participants to simultaneously influence and be influenced by one another. These two sets of processes operate in concert. Communication occurs through symbols (i.e., words, such as, "Let's win this!") and signs (i.e., gesture, such as using ones index and middle fingers face out and with other fingers folded down to make a "V" for "victory"). Since any behavior, under the appropriate conditions, is potentially capable of conveying information, it becomes essential to distinguish between the communication behaviors that are most significant and those of little or no importance.

Several key ideas dominate the socio-psychological tradition: the value of empirical research in advancing knowledge about human communication; a cognitive orientation; the belief that internal human processes may be beyond our awareness; and the understanding of how the communication process develops and expresses itself. First, socio-psychologists believe that careful research can discover the universal mechanisms that govern human behavior. Accordingly, this tradition is most often linked with the "science" of communication research. Most studies center on persuasion and attitude change: message processing, how individuals plan message strategies, how receivers process message information, and messages' effects on individuals. *Trait theory*— identifying personality variables and communication tendencies—is a popular aspect of this socio-psychological approach.

Second, most socio-psychological theories have a cognitive orientation. Both the socio-psychological and cybernetic traditions see individuals as information processing systems.[58] The cognitive system's inputs (information) and outputs (plans and behaviors) and how these are represented cognitively are of special interest in both traditions. Cognitive mechanisms that serve attention, retention, inference, selection, motivation, planning, and strategizing also receive research interest.

Third, this tradition assumes that the human processing mechanisms are beyond our awareness. While persons may be conscious of specific aspects of the communication process—such as attention, memory, plans, and behaviors—the internal processes operate unseen and unknown. Communication scientists try to find and describe these systems.

Fourth, socio-psychologists are interested in how the human communication process develops and expresses itself. Can individual communication behavior be predicted? How does an individual account for, accommodate, and adapt to different communication situations? How is information assimilated, organized, and applied to form message strategies and plans? How is information integrated to form—and change—beliefs and attitudes? Investigators often use empirical studies to seek answers to these questions.

Research and Criticism

Extensive research in this tradition includes the relationship of nonverbal behavior and internal states,[59] and factors affecting the accuracy with which people can decode nonverbal behaviors.[60] Research findings support much of socio-psychological theory.[61] Studies conclude that individuals' predispositions shape their perceptions of reality;[62] individual differences affect their ability to encode or decode nonverbal information;[63] voice qualities are related to the speakers' affective state;[64] and much more.[65] Although research on how people socially construct meaning has had mixed findings,[66] results suggest that people do tend to take the intended meaning of utterances, shared mutual knowledge, and context factors into account when interpreting received messages.[67] And the extent that communicators are able to collaboratively and accurately gauge and negotiate a message's meaning can depend on their relative social organizational status.[68]

Critics of the socio-psychology communication theory tradition claim it over-emphasizes individualism, does not attend to larger social forces, and shows insensitivity to cultural differences.[69] Critics have also noted weaknesses in the research methodology of studies used to support this theory,[70] making it difficult to accurately understand what is occurring or to generalize to larger populations.[71] Critics observe, too, that this individualistic approach in behavioral and social sciences is typical of Western culture and thought since the eighteenth century and may not reflect communication processes in other cultures.[72]

The socio-psychological approach appeals to scientists and the general public because it seems believable and relevant. Intuitively, people understand that individual personalities and their immediate social situations affect how they communicate and how they react to others' communications with them. This tradition makes us more aware of how context factors—including social roles and relative status of speakers, time and place of interactions, formality, speech style, conversation topic, and actual circumstances—all affect how individuals send and interpret messages. At the same time, the socio-psychological theory strongly disputes the notion of humans as rational beings and questions personal autonomy and all unproven assumptions about the causes of human behavior that lack rigorous experimental evidence.[73]

Both the socio-psychological and sociocultural traditions in communication focus on the individual interacting with others. But the former places the individual in the foreground whereas the latter stresses social interactions.

Sociocultural Theory: Constructing and Maintaining Social Reality

Sociocultural theory of communication addresses the ways we develop our understandings, meanings, norms, roles, rituals, rules, and collective beliefs—even our personal identities—through our interactions in groups, communities, and cultures. This tradition theorizes *communication* as a symbolic process that produces and reproduces shared meanings, rituals, social structures, and sociocultural patterns through individuals interacting with language (oral, written, or kinesthetic). Language, numbers and arithmetic systems, music, and art are examples of symbolic tools that human cultures have created over time. These are passed down through generations, facilitating our relationship with the world. Humans apply these symbols to design practices, things, institutions, and a culture in which they can live together.[74] Using language to frame and communicate our thoughts and intentions through an array of media, we create, maintain, repair, and even transform our society. In brief, individuals are products of their sociocultural environments. Our everyday interactions depend on preexisting, shared cultural patterns and social structures. In this way, our daily behaviors largely "reproduce" the existing sociocultural order.[75] Figure 7.4 offers a graphic look at sociocultural theory of communications.

As Figure 7.4's arrows point in both directions and penetrate porous group boundaries, community, and larger social and cultural environments, people and their sociocultural environments reciprocally shape each other. The language we use from early childhood greatly influences how we perceive reality. For instance, the word b-l-u-e is not logically connected to the sky's color. We are able to see "blue" as a separate color in the electromagnetic wave spectrum because English language conventions determine that "blue" represents the color of the clear daytime sky. Not all languages and cultures recognize "blue" as we do. Our language shapes our world as we know it. And, unless our culture and language have a precise word for an event or object, it remains unnoticed to members of that culture. Again, the 50 definitions of snow reflect—and shape—the Eskimos' reality.

Similarly, although individuals process information cognitively, the categories that people use to do so are socially created. In sociocultural tradition, reality is not an objective set of arrangements outside of us. Rather we construct our reality through a process of communicating in groups, society, and culture. As a result, people together create the realities of their social groups, organizations, and cultures. Today's multiple

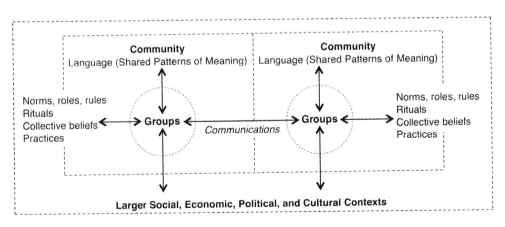

FIGURE 7.4 Sociocultural Theory of Communications

Source: Based on Craig, R.T. (1999). Communication theory as a field. *Communication Theory, 9* (2), 119–161.

media platforms, cable channels, and social networking sites make staying within one's "group" and "reality" easier. And since social interaction is a creative process that allows and even requires much improvisation, collectively and over the long term, it "produces" the very social order that makes interaction possible in the first place.[76]

Unlike the cybernetic tradition that looks at communication networks between and among people, sociocultural theories focus on the shared meanings and interpretations that people within the network construct, and their implications for societal and organizational life.[77] The sociocultural focus is not on transmitting information between individuals but on developing and maintaining society through shared beliefs. Some assert that a fully developed understanding of communication—and modern societies' existence—depends on incorporating both transmission and culture building forms.[78]

Many sociocultural theories study how interactions in social groups and cultures allow individuals to establish personal identities. They see identity as the fusion of the individual self with social, community, and cultural roles. For instance, a child's sense of self develops gradually by interacting with parents and family, experiencing the self through the expected reactions of others. Cooperative social activity becomes possible by anticipating others' attitudes and responses. A child living in northeast Chicago whose parents are well-educated professionals and who attends schools that encourage academic and social excellence will likely develop different personal aspirations, attitudes, and behaviors than might a child living in the New Orleans Ninth Ward whose high school-educated parents work full time in service industries and lack the hours and resources to supervise studying and school achievement.

Context is also very important in sociocultural theory. Symbols and words take on different meanings in different settings and in different situations. Sociocultural scholars focus on how individuals negotiate their identity from one situation to another, how community and culture form milieus for behaving and interpreting that behavior, and how different groups and cultures identify important symbols and assign their meaning.[79] Remember the varying interpretations for the symbol formed by joining thumb and forefinger to form a circle depending on whether one was in the United States, France, or Greece.

Culture refers not only to ethnic, national, or linguistic differences. Different organizations, professions, academic disciplines, gender, generation, religion, locality, social class, and political ideology each reflect unique cultural viewpoints. Conflict and misunderstandings increase when the meaning the actors ascribe to their practices and words differs from the meaning assigned to them by observers or participants, or when persons do not agree on what "common sense" is for a particular situation. For instance, principals and school counselors, both educators, will likely view "student con-fidentiality" differently according to their specialized professional preparation. Likewise, American liberals and libertarians see government's role differently. And when the social conditions leave members with few shared rituals, rules, or expectations, miscalculations, coordination difficulties, and discords increase.

Culture also impacts communication in organizations. Talk among co-workers transmits information. But it also establishes patterns of influence that affect who we are and what we do within the organization. Over time, these conversations give the organization a feel or character—a culture—that differs from that of other organizations.

These shared rules, norms, values, and practices are commonly accepted and used within that organization.

Recognizing this reality, sociocultural theory nurtures communicative practices that recognize cultural variety and relativity, value tolerance and understanding, and stress collective more than individual responsibility. This can be an especially useful insight for working with diverse school communities. Although parents and school personnel may want to advance each child's academic success and personal wellbeing, cross-community communication brings challenges in understanding the different language, norms, and rules. Since people interacting with language co-construct their own social realities, when their perceptual worlds collide, the sociocultural tradition's awareness of context and cultures' influence helps bridge the divide between "us" and "them." Leaders best span these differences—and create a more inclusive and caring school community—if they can identify shared values (such as cherishing children and their potential or being a good neighbor) and find a meaningful cooperative activity about which to communicate.

Additionally, sociocultural theory has much to say about problems stemming from technological change, breakdowns in traditional social orders, urbanization and mass society, bureaucratic rationalization, cultural fragmentation, and globalization. Their view is optimistic: as old interaction codes and media no longer function effectively in new contexts, the creative production of new meanings and new means of communication becomes possible.[80]

Research and Criticism

Sociocultural theory takes a skeptical view of empirical research. Since theorists believe that language constructs reality, whatever researchers "discover" is likely profoundly shaped by the culturally based interaction patterns they designed into the research protocol.[81] Nonetheless, sociocultural scholars do conduct studies to understand how people use language and other symbols in various settings while involved in normal daily activities.[82] We highlight a few here. Experiments confirm that the human mind is mediated by using symbolic tools or artifacts created by human culture over time, and as individuals mature in age and cognitive capacities, these language skills become increasingly sophisticated.[83] Younger children attempting highly complex tasks may require additional symbolic tools—more verbal direction and modeling, for example—to facilitate meaning.[84] Similarly, studies find that individuals who suffered cerebral damage from physical trauma, disease, or illness (such as a stroke) can improve their communication ability by using alternate means of communication such as writing or typing out letters to spell the words they want to say.[85] These studies not only validate part of the sociocultural communication theory but also help people recover from trauma.[86] In a different vein, several independently conducted empirical studies found that members of various national cultures share worldviews related to attitudes and behaviors, further confirming the shared patterns of meaning evident in sociocultural communication theory.[87] Investigations also conclude that social actors' "views" and "cultures"—the meaning they attach to words and events—generate empathies, alliances, confrontations, and conflict in varied social contexts, including large national politics, small local settings, and in large and small institutions.[88]

Meanwhile, critics of sociocultural research point to its methodological weaknesses. They note, for example, that investigators need to focus on more than a single moment of a process isolated from other moments—such as a single word. Instead, they should also consider the multiple dimensions of interactions—the social processes—that occur in a specific context.[89]

Sociocultural theory appeals to the well-accepted beliefs that individuals are products of their social environments; that groups develop their own norms, rituals, and worldviews; and that social change can be difficult and disruptive. It challenges the assumption of an "absolute reality," recognizing that individuals from different cultures (and subcultures) see and interpret the world differently. In an era of high student diversity, demographically shifting neighborhoods, and a globalized workplace, holding a sociocultural perspective on communications can give educators a heads-up to the possibilities of misunderstandings, and insights that help prevent these.

The critical tradition, discussed next, shares many of sociocultural theory's interests and assumptions, but it adds an important aspect. It moves thinking about communication from the descriptive to the judgmental.

The Critical Tradition: Communication as Power and Privilege

Critical studies of information, communication, and media analyze how in-groups use language to construct and reason about the world in ways to benefit certain societal interests and exploit others. This behavior contributes to unfair allocations of power and privilege in organizations and in society.

Many critical theory scholars assert that affluent or middle class people of Northern European heritage living in the United States often have the privilege and power to define what "normal" looks like in this country. All others are often marginalized. National origin, race, economic class, religion, gender, sexual orientation, and an array of other factors affect privilege and power. This is true of societies around the world.

The critical tradition has three core ideas. First, the current tacit systems of power structures and beliefs that guide society benefit certain interests and undermine others. The control of language perpetuates these power imbalances. For instance, organizational leaders and their media speak about current arrangements as natural "givens," relatively fixed entities rather than the results of organization leaders making many deliberate choices over time. Likewise, presenting management's interests as "everyone's interests" obscures the organization's specific power and control relationships, making it difficult for those without power to question their legitimacy.[90] These manipulative language practices disadvantage certain groups and make it difficult for members to understand and act on their own political interests.[91] Speaking for marginalized groups, critical theorists ask, for instance, who does and does not get to speak, what does and does not get said, and who stands to gain from a particular system?[92]

Second, finding and revealing oppressive social conditions and power arrangements —including the use of language to control or encourage free expression—is essential to promote a more equitable, freer, and more satisfying society for all its members. For instance, using the language of technocracy (i.e., the claimed "monopoly of expertise" based on specialization), organizational communications pretend to be neutral, impartial, and free from self-interested values and politics.[93] Expertise jargon is not neutral: it serves the interests of those with influence. Understanding the varied forms that oppression takes is essential to challenging and ending the false societal beliefs that keep people in place, and to taking corrective action. Accordingly, organizational leaders should communicate freely and interactively with members and stakeholders, use easily understood language, encourage good will, and present undistorted and well-grounded argument and dialog to actively achieve meaningful understanding (rather than unreflectively transmit "the company line").[94]

Third, theory requires action. Critical theories are normative and work to accomplish change in the society's conditions. Critical research intends to reveal the ways in which competing interests collide and how these conflicts are resolved to favor certain groups over others.[95]

Figure 7.5 illustrates critical theory's view of language distortions in organizations. Insiders, those with power, status, and influence control the organizational structures, norms, and decisions about what is and is not appropriate thought and behavior—and who does or does not have access to professional growth opportunities and upward mobility. These language distortions serve as a barrier to keep certain groups and individuals—and their ability to communicate ideas, norms, or leadership—outside the circle of power and influence.

Critical theory has many offshoots. Spanning ideas from Karl Marx to current theories of critical cultural, feminist theory, and related schools, critical theory approaches share a particular interest in how messages reinforce oppression in society. For instance, feminist studies scholars have analyzed, critiqued, and disputed assumptions about and experiences of males and females that infuse all aspects of life in efforts to achieve more equitable ways for women and men to conduct their home and work relationships. Similarly, postcolonial theories look at the process of "othering" that is responsible for creating stereotypes of nonwhite populations. Postmodernists question "established knowledge"—presented as "the way things are"—without also asking that the geographic, national, and historic links and omissions be made clear in discussions.

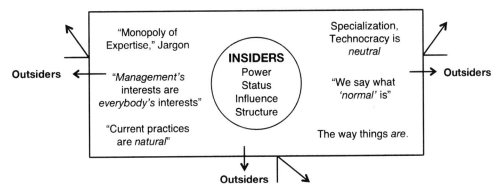

FIGURE 7.5 Critical Theory View of Communications in Organizations

Source: Based on Alvesson, M. & Deetz, S.A. (2006). Critical theory and postmodernism approaches to organizational studies. In S.R. Clegg, C. Hardy, T.B. Lawrence, & R. Nord (Eds), *The Sage handbook of organization studies* (pp. 255–283). Thousand Oaks, CA: Sage.

Research and Criticism

Insisting that knowledge is partisan and not "concrete truth," critical communication theorists tend to frown on empirical research. They argue that "traditional" communication scholars use narrow, value-laden definitions, and empirical methodologies that limit their studies' scope as a way to maintain control and stability of the political, economic, and social systems. These actions reduce the learning that could result from including wider perspectives.[96] Instead, critical communication theorists tend to rely on "rigorous" (critical) conceptual interpretive "essays" (i.e., interpretive research reports) from analyzing texts and recorded conversations. In this way, they believe that they gain insights into the organization's meaning structures and their connections to forces in the larger society that sustain them.

Nonetheless, empirical work on critical communication theory is increasing. These studies suggest how cultural-ideological control operates in relationship to all employees at varying management levels.[97] Several examples give an idea of their focus and outcomes. Studies draw attention to the role of management expertise leading to organizational members' passivity, how leaders mask ambiguity and contradictions, how they engineer values and definitions of reality, and how codes of money and formal power control the workplace experience, and tend to weaken low-level and other marginal groups' influence on the job.[98] Critical studies find that corporate culture communicates its norms and values throughout the organization with the effect of discouraging or denying opposing viewpoints from expression.[99] Organizations tend to use technical reasoning focused on control of means and ends (rather than using practical reasoning focused on understanding and shared decision making about the goals to be sought).[100] Studies also illustrate how the productive tension between technical control of the means and ends of goal achievement and humanistic factors such as creativity, variation, development, and meaningfulness[101] make human factors an afterthought to the efficient accomplishment of "rational" and "legitimate" corporate goals.[102] Gender bias in reasoning styles, asymmetrical social relations, and political priorities are also common research themes.[103]

Critics stress the need for critical communications schools to use empirical methods to investigate their ideas[104] and stop "politicizing" science and scholarship by hiding behind their rationale (or rationalization) that empirical data are constructions open to varying interpretations.[105] Just because data can be interpreted in various ways does not mean than empirical research is not worth doing.[106] Critics also fault critical scholars for making directive statements regarding what people *should* do (such as revolt or liberate themselves) while, at the same time, recognizing the problems with dominating beliefs and values (apart from their own).[107] Likewise, critics complain that critical communication theorists advance a universal normal standard for communication—rather than an objective, empirical one—despite normative standards' ties to local cultures and specific communication practices.[108] Finally, critics suggest that critical communication theorists not allow their own biases towards power, domination, and social imperfections to make their investigations less than fair minded.[109]

Critical communications theory draws attention to the social, historical, and political construction of knowledge, power, and social relations, and how each appears in contemporary organizations. It sees morally guided communicative reasoning—reflection, honest communications in open forums aimed at mutual understanding, rationality, and consensus—leading to individual autonomy, a social consensus, and constructive actions that better fulfill human needs. Its goal is to improve the world through social action, rather than to teach people to adapt to the world as it is.

REFLECTIONS AND RELEVANCE 7.5

Analyzing Cybernetic, Socio-psychological, Sociocultural, and Critical Theories of Communication

Each of the four theoretical traditions discussed offers a useful perspective on communication theory and practice. With the class separated into four (or more) groups, each group focusing on a different theoretical tradition and using the text as a resource, each group will answer the following questions for their selected theory tradition. When the groups have completed their analysis, they will report their findings to the entire class. Then, the class will discuss how they might use each theory tradition to improve communication when working as a teacher or educational leader.

1. Create a four to ten word phrase or slogan epitomizing the theory's main focus or meaning.
2. Write a brief statement encapsulating the theory's main idea.
3. Identify what this theory poses as the most important functions (or processes) in ensuring effective communication.
4. Specify the five most important factors (number one being the highest) of each of the following factors to this theory—information, network, system, personality, context, feedback, culture, interdependence, interaction, self-regulation, control, power, distortion, expertise—and explain your reasons.
5. Identify what this theory views as the main causes of miscommunication, misunderstandings, and conflict—and how to correct these.
6. Identify this theory's position on whether communication's message is an "objective reality" or "socially or individually constructed."
7. Identify the weaknesses of this theory as a guide for practical use.
8. Describe this theory's view of empirical research's value to validating it and expanding knowledge of how it works.
9. Explain the ways or situations in which this theory is likely to help you (or *not* help you) communicate more effectively with others as a teacher and school leader.

IMPLICATIONS FOR EDUCATIONAL LEADERS

Communication is a highly complex phenomenon. Many factors—in the persons, in the immediate situations, and in the larger environments—can *and do* interfere with the listeners' capacity to perceive and interpret the message the communicator intends. For teachers and school leaders, becoming a skilled communicator means being keenly aware of these influences and appreciating how they shape your own and your audience's understanding and responses. What follows are five key takeaways from communication theory to help sharpen your outlook and skills.

Message Content: Know What You Want to Say; Say and Do it Congruently

Interestingly, this chapter did not discuss *messages* apart from their function in a communicative episode (cybernetic theory). But for educational leaders, the message *content* is the essential core of any communication. When educators use language and other symbols to influence teachers, students, parents, and community members to think and act on specific goals, the message content must be deliberately tailored to facilitate understanding. And body language—voice quality, posture, physical gestures, facial expressions, and attire—need to reinforce (not undermine) this message. In addition, the communicator should explicitly invite audience members to ask for clarification and repetition, question the message, and expect meaningful and clear answers.

Personalities: The *Meaning* is in the *People*

Communication has no "absolute reality" apart from how people perceive it. Every person has unique characteristics—age, gender, cognitive capacity, emotional intelligence, communication skills, attitudes, intentions, unconscious conflicts, personal histories, professional experiences, and the sociocultural system to which he or she belongs—that affect how they perceive and construe messages (socio-psychological theory, sociocultural theory, critical theory). These personal traits, modified by the immediate social context, impact and shape their communication to produce a range of outcomes (cybernetic theory, socio-psychological theory, sociocultural theory, critical theory). Misunderstandings, misconceptions, and confusion often stem from factors in the communicator, in the audience, and in the immediate social situation that distort the intended meaning. Ultimately, the meaning of any communication is in the people, not in the messages. That is why continually receiving accurate and timely feedback on how the message is being received and interpreted is so essential to effective communication (cybernetic theory).

Audience: Persons and their Backgrounds Color the Message

Individuals are products of their sociocultural environments. Our society gives us language and, in turn, our language shapes our world as we know it. Even professions, academic disciplines, generational cohorts, and political ideologies reflect unique cultural viewpoints. Our everyday interactions depend on preexisting, shared cultural patterns and social structures (sociocultural theory). In today's diverse classrooms, children from varying regions within the United States learn together with students from wide-ranging national cultures, spoken languages, and religious traditions. They and their parents represent a wide array of educational, cultural, and linguistic customs. Without shared language, cultural patterns, and traditions, miscommunications and misunderstandings become more likely.

Just because no one asks questions does not mean that everyone understands or agrees. Beware of "false consensus" reached by administrative edict rather than by open discussion among all interested parties (critical theory). When education leaders address any students and parents, it is necessary to speak clearly, in easily understood, conversational words, free from expertise jargon, technical or legalistic language, or "education-ese" (sociocultural theory, critical theory). Likewise, all written material should have 100 percent correct spelling, grammar, and usage. This respectful expression (and the attitude of goodwill that goes with it) lessens the gap between "us" and "them" (sociocultural theory, critical theory). Leaders must also offer opportunities for parents and students to ask questions and discuss their concerns, and allow parents and students' views to influence outcomes (critical theory).

Regardless of audience size or format, from large groups to closed door IEP meetings, school leaders reduce the cultural and language loads when they use plain language, speak and act congruently, identify shared values (such as cherishing children and their potential or being a good neighbor), find a meaningful cooperative activity about which to communicate, and invite dialog and interactions (sociocultural theory, critical theory). Language can become a means to create an inclusive, caring, and supportive community rather than separating "us" from "them."

Context: "Noise" and Environment Shape the Message

Symbols and words take on different meanings in different settings and in different situations (cybernetic theory, socio-psychological theory, sociocultural theory, critical theory). The immediate social situation shades how the message will be received and interpreted. The context includes relationships, the social roles and relative status of the participants, the time and place of the interactions, the degree of formality or informality, the topic, and the actual circumstances—they all impact how messages are sent and interpreted.

The context also includes "noise" that interferes with or distorts meanings and messages (cybernetic theory). A room that is too small or too hot, ambient sounds, uncomfortable seats, the time of day, mixed with individuals' unique characteristics or physical impairments affect how and if listeners receive and interpret what is said as the communicator intended. Similarly, language and cultural differences as well as information overload can create "noise" that confuses listeners and distorts messages (socio-psychological theory, sociocultural theory, critical theory). Communicators need to ensure that the communicative environment is comfortable and not distracting for listeners/observers. Again, providing occasions for questions and feedback will help ensure that the messages intended and sent are the same as the messages received and interpreted (cybernetic theory, critical theory).

Feedback: The Essential Element to Effective Communication

Feedback and knowledge of results have long been known as essential to effective human performance in any task. An indispensable part of any communicative act, feedback provides the information by which we can evaluate (and improve) our performance (cybernetic theory).

Upward critical feedback from teachers and staff to principals—especially about organizational goals and the leader's performance—is particularly important (cybernetic theory, critical theory). But although such communication is fundamental to strong organizational performance, it is very difficult to obtain. In schools, since principals and teachers or staffs have different status and power, giving critical feedback upward tends to have high risk and low rewards. In contrast, expressing "good news" upward tends to bring low risk with high rewards (socio-psychological theory, sociocultural theory, critical theory). As a result, honest, specific, critical feedback tends not to happen. And, without this timely, accurate data, leaders may make inappropriate or harmful decisions (critical theory).

To encourage critical upward feedback, principals must first create the supportive school climate and culture that celebrates it (cybernetic theory, socio-psychological theory, sociocultural theory, critical theory). Those who risk disapproval (or worse) by volunteering critical feedback—especially if it is unpleasant for the school leader to hear—must receive sincere appreciation, not punishment, in return. In addition to explicitly asking for such feedback from trusted colleagues, the principal may want to appoint "red teams" to challenge tentative plans and "devil's advocates" to challenge the prevailing ideas, thereby institutionalizing critical upward communication. Of course, the feedback reflects the speakers' perceptions of reality (socio-psychological theory, sociocultural theory, critical theory), so identifying a trusted colleague with high situational awareness, a reliable and stable temperament, and good judgment makes sense. And, if the principal finds such a circumstance to be very uncomfortable, specialized training on how to seek out and respond constructively to upward critical feedback may be helpful.

Successful organizations and successful leaders depend on effective communication. Communication is basic to relationship building, vision sharing, direction setting, and activity coordinating. Communication is how the organization's work gets done. And it is the basis of the ability to lead.

NOTES

1 Salacuse, J.W. (2006). *Leading leaders* (p. 23). New York, NY: American Management Association.
2 Clampitt, P.G. (2013). *Communicating for managerial effectiveness. Problems, strategies, solutions*, 5th ed. (p. 7). Thousand Oaks, CA: Sage.
3 Bolton, R. (1979). *People skills. How to assert yourself, listen to others, and resolve conflicts* (p. 7). New York, NY: Simon & Schuster.
4 Davis, S.H. (1997). The principal's paradox: Remaining secure in a precarious position. *NASSP Bulletin*, 81 (592), 73–80.

5 Davis, S.H. (1998). Superintendents' perspectives on the involuntary departure of public school principals: The most frequent reasons why principals lose their jobs. *Educational Administration Quarterly, 34* (1), 58–90; Davis, S.H. (2000). Why principals lose their jobs: Comparing the perceptions of principals and superintendents, *Journal of School Leadership, 10* (1), 40–68; Bulach, C., Pickett, W. & Boothe, D. (1998). Mistakes educational leaders make. *Scholarsbank. Eric Digest, 122.* (EDO-EA-98-6). Retrieved from: https://scholarsbank. uoregon.edu/xmlui/bitstream/handle/1794/3345/digest122.pdf?sequence=1.

6 Matthews, D. (2002). Why principals fail and what we can learn from it. *Principal, 82* (1), 38–40.

7 Bagin, R. (2007). *How strong communications help superintendents get and keep their jobs.* Rockville, MD: National School Public Relations Association. Retrieved from: www. nspra.org/files/docs/strong_communication.pdf.

8 Heath, R. & Bryant, J. (2000). *Human communication theory and research: Concepts contexts, and challenges.* Mahwah, NJ: Lawrence Erlbaum Associates.

9 Barnett, G.A. (1997). Organizational communication systems: The traditional perspective. In L.O. Thayer and G.A. Barnett (Eds). *Organization-communication: The renaissance in system thinking* (p. 3). Greenwich, CT: Ablex Publishing.

10 Watzlawick, P., Beavin, J.H. & Jackson, D.D. (1967). *Pragmatics of human communication* (pp. 48–51). New York, NY: Macmillan. Gregory Bateson, the anthropologist, is often credited with this insight.

11 See: Carey, J.W. (1989). *Communication as culture. Essays on media and society.* Winchester, MA: Unwin Hyman; Deetz, S.A. (1994). Future of the discipline: The challenges, the research, and the social contribution. In S.A. Deetz (Ed.), *Communication yearbook 17.* (pp. 565–600). Thousand Oaks, CA: Sage; Rothenbuhler, E.W. (1998). *Ritual communication: From everyday conversation to mediated ceremony.* Thousand Oaks, CA: Sage; Shepherd, G.J. (1993). Building a discipline of communication. *Journal of Communication, 43* (3), 83–91.

12 Carey (1989). Op. cit.; Deetz (1994). Op. cit.; Shepherd (1993). Op. cit.

13 Mintzberg, H. (1989). *Mintzberg on management. Inside our strange world of organizations* (p. 18). New York, NY: The Free Press.

14 Schermerhorn, J.R. Jr. (1996), *The management and organizational behavior essentials.* New York, NY: John Wiley and Sons.

15 See: Pfeffer, J. (1994). *Competitive advantage through people: Unleashing the power of the workforce.* Boston, MA: Harvard Business School Press; Collins, J. & Porras , J. (2000). *Built to last: Successful habits of visionary companies.* 3rd ed. New York, NY: Random House; O'Reilly, C.O. III & Pfeffer, J. (2000). *Hidden value. How great companies achieve extraordinary results with ordinary people.* Boston, MA: Harvard Business School Press; Reichfield, F.F. (2001). *Loyalty rules! How today's leaders build lasting relationships.* Boston, MA: Harvard Business School Press.

16 Clampitt, P. & Downs, C. (1993). Employee perceptions for the relationship between communication and productivity: A field study. *Journal of Business Communication, 30* (1), 5–28.

17 Caulkin. S. (1998, April 19). How that pat on the head can mean money in the bank, *Observer: Work Section*, p. 1.

18 Reed Employment Services. (2002). Cited in D. Tourish & O. Hargie (Eds). (2004). *Key issues in organizational communication* (pp. 7–8). New York, NY: Routledge.

19 Weick, K. (2001). *Making sense of the organization* (p. 5). Oxford: Blackwell.

20 Goleman, D. (1995). *Emotional intelligence.* New York, NY: Bantam Books.

21 Hargie, O. & Dickson, D. (2004). *Skilled interpersonal communication: Research, theory, and practice,* 4th ed. London, UK: Routledge.

22 Ekman, P., Friesen, W.V., O'Sullivan, M., Diacoyanni-Tarlatziz, I., Krause, R., Pitcairn, T., Scherer, K., Chan, A., Heider, K., LeCompte, W.A., Ricci-Bitti, P.E. & Tomota, M. (1987). Universals and cultural differences in the judgments of facial expressions of emotions. *Journal of Personality and Social Psychology, 53* (4), 712–717.

23 Uyanne, M.C. & Oti, O.J. (2012). The influence of socio-cultural domains on communication. *African Research Review, 6* (4), 234–247.

24 Tourish, D. & Hargie, O. (1993). Don't you sometimes wish you were better informed? *Health Service Journal, 103* (5380), 28–29.

25 Stewart, J. & Logan, C. (1998). *Together: Communicating interpersonally*, 5th ed. New York, NY: McGraw-Hill.

26 Luthans, F. & Larsen, J. (1986). How managers really communicate. *Human Relations, 39* (3), 161–178.

27 Baron, R. (1996). "La vie en rose" revisited: Contrasting perceptions of informal upward feedback among managers and subordinates. *Management Communication Quarterly, 9* (3), 338–348.

28 Tourish, D. & Hargie, O. (2004). Motivating critical upward communication. In D. Tourish & O. Hargie (Eds). *Key issues in organizational communication* (pp. 188–204). New York, NY: Routledge.

29 Tourish, D. & Robson, P. (2006). Sensemaking and the distortion of critical upward communication in organizations. *Journal of Management Studies, 43* (4), 711–730.

30 Seeger, M. & Ulmer, R. (2003). Explaining Enron: Communication and responsible leadership. *Management Communication Quarterly, 17* (1), 58–84; Harrison, E. (1991). Strategic control at the CEO level. *Long Range Planning, 24* (3), 78–87; Wissema, H. (2002). Driving through red lights: How warning signals are missed or ignored. *Long Range Planning, 35* (5), 521–539.

31 Bowen, F. & Blackmon, K. (2003). Spirals of silence: The dynamic effects of diversity on organizational voice. *Journal of Management Studies, 40* (6), 1393–1417.

32 Tourish & Robson (2006). Op. cit.; Environments whose values and practices may not include supportiveness, participative decision making, and high levels of trust, confidence, and credibility, openness, and frankness. See: Redding, W. (1972). *Communication within the organization: An interpretive review of theory and research*. New York, NY: Industrial Communication Council.

33 Ashford, S. & Tsui, A. (1991). Self-regulation for managerial effectiveness: The role of active feedback seeking. *Academy of Management Journal, 34* (2), 251–280.

34 Wissema (2002). Op. cit., p. 522.

35 Hannaway, J. (1985). *Managers managing: The workings of an administrative system*. New York, NY: Oxford University Press.

36 Tubbs, S. & Moss, S. (2008). *Human communication: Principles and contexts*, 11th ed. Boston, MA: McGraw-Hill Higher Education, pp. 495–496.

37 Lutz, W. (1996). *The new doublespeak: Why no one knows what anyone's saying anymore* (p. 4). New York, NY: HarperCollins.

38 Finn, E. (2012, January 19). The advantage of ambiguity. *MIT News*. Retrieved from: http://news.mit.edu/2012/ambiguity-in-language-0119l; Piantadosi, S.T., Tily, H. & Gibson, E. (2012). The communicative function of ambiguity in language. *Cognition, 122* (3), 280–291.

39 Craig, R.T. & Muller, H.L. (Eds), (2007). *Theorizing communication: Readings across traditions* (p. xiv). Thousand Oaks, CA: Sage.

40 Anderson, J.A. (1996). *Communication theory. Epistemological foundations*. New York, NY: Guilford Press.

41 Craig, R.T. (1999). Communication theory as a field. *Communication Theory, 9* (2), 119–161; Rosengren, K.E. (1993). From field to frog ponds. *Journal of Communication, 43* (3), 6–17.

42 Cybernetics. Definition. *Merriam Webster Dictionary*. Retrieved from: www.merriam-webster.com/dictionary/cybernetics.

43 Putnam, L.L. (1982). Paradigms for organizational communication research: An overview and synthesis. *Western Journal of Speech Communication, 46* (2), 192–206.

44 See: Weick, K.E. (1979). *The social psychology of organizing*, 2nd ed. Reading, MA: Addison-Wesley; Bantz, C.R. & Smith, D.H. (1977). A critique and experimental test of Weick's model of organization. *Communication Monographs, 44* (3), 171–184; Putnam, L.L. & Sorenson, R.L. (1982). Equivocal messages in organizations. *Human Communication Research, 8* (2), 114–132.

45 Putnam (1982). Op. cit.

46 Tushman, M.L. (1978). Technical communication in R & D laboratories: The impact of project work characteristics. *Academy of Management Journal, 21* (4), 624–645.

47 Sweller, J. & Chandler, P. (1994). Why some material is difficult to learn. *Cognition and Instruction, 12* (3), 185–233.

48 Sweller & Chandler (1994). Ibid.

49 Hartman, F.R. (1961). Investigation of recognition learning under multiple-channel presentation and testing conditions. *AV Communication Review, 9* (1), 24–43; Severin, W.J. (1967a). Another look at cue summation. *AV Communication Review, 15* (4), 233–245; Severin, W.J. (1967b). The effectiveness of relevant pictures in multiple-channel communication. *AV Communication Review, 15* (4), 386–401.

50 Moore, D.M., Burton, J.K. & Myers, R.J. (2001) Multiple-channel communication: The theoretical and research foundations of multimedia. *The handbook of research for educational communications and technology*. (pp. 851–875). Bloomington, IN: Association for Educational Communications and Technology. Retrieved from: www.aect.org/edtech/ed1/29/.

51 Craig (1999). Op. cit.

52 Craig (1999). Op. cit.

53 Craig (1999). Op. cit.

54 Norberg, K. (1966). Visual perception theory and instructional communication. *AV Communication Review, 14* (3), 301–316; Smith, K.U. & Smith, M.F. (1966). *Cybernetic principles of learning and educational design*. (pp. 5–83). New York, NY: Holt, Rinehart and Winston.

55 Moore, Burton & Myers (2001). Op. cit.

56 Craig (1999). Op. cit.

57 Popescu, M. (2010). Psychology of communication—Between myth and reality. *International Journal of Academic Research in Accounting, Finance and Management Sciences, 2* (1), 321–325.

58 Shapiro, M.A., Hamilton, M.A., Lang, A. & Contractor, N.S. (2001). Information systems division: Intrapersonal meaning, attitude, and social systems. In W.B. Gudykunst (Ed.), *Communication yearbook 24*. (pp. 17–50).Thousand Oaks, CA: Sage.

59 See: Condon, W.S. (1980). The relation of interactional synchrony to cognitive and emotional processes. In M.R. Key (Ed.), *The relation of verbal and nonverbal behavior*. (pp. 49–65). The Hague, Netherlands: Mouton; Cosmides, L. (1983). Invariances in the acoustic expression of emotion in speech. *Journal of Experimental Psychology: Perception and Performance, 9* (6), 864–881; DePaulo, B.M., Kirkendol, S.E. & Tang, J.O. (1988). The motivational impairment effect in the communication of deception: Replications and extensions. *Journal of Nonverbal Behavior, 12* (3), 177–202; Kimble, C.E. & Seidel, S.D. (1991). Vocal signs of confidence. *Journal of Nonverbal Behavior, 15* (2), 99–105.

60 See: Archer, D. & Akert, R.M. (1977). Words and everything else: Verbal and nonverbal cues in social interpretation. *Journal of Personality and Social Psychology, 35* (6), 443–449; DePaulo, B.M., Rosenthal, R., Eisenstat, R.A., Rogers, A.L. & Finkelstein, S. (1978). Decoding discrepant nonverbal cues. *Journal of Personality and Social Psychology, 36* (3), 313–333; DePaulo, B.M., Rosenthal, R., Green, C.R. & Rosenkrantz, J. (1982). Diagnosing deceptive and mixed messages from verbal and nonverbal cues. *Journal of Personality and Social Psychology, 18* (5), 433–446; Scherer, K.R., Koivumaki, J. & Rosenthal, R. (1972). Minimal cues in the vocal communication of affect: Judging emotion from content-masked speech. *Journal of Psycholinguistic Research, 1* (3), 269–285.

61 Krauss, R.M. & Fussell, S.R. (1996). Social psychological models of interpersonal communication. In E.T. Higgins & A. Kruglanski (Eds), *Social psychology: Handbook of basic principles* (pp. 655–701). New York, NY: Guildford Press. Retrieved from: www.columbia.edu/~rmk7/PDF/Comm.pdf.

62 Donsbach (2005). Op. cit.

63 See: Archer & Akert (1977). Op. cit.; Cunningham, M.R. (1977). Personality and the structure of the nonverbal communication of emotion. *Journal of Personality*, 45 (4), 564–584; Morency, N. & Krauss, R.M. (1982). Components of nonverbal encoding and decoding skills in children. In R.E. Feldman (Ed.), *The development of nonverbal behavior* (pp. 181–199). New York, NY: Springer.

64 Cosmides (1993). Op. cit.; Scherer, K.R. (1986). Vocal affect expression: A review and a model for future research. *Psychological Bulletin*, 99 (2), 143–165; Williams, C.E. & Stevens, K.N. (1972). Emotions and speech: Some acoustical correlates. *Journal of the Acoustical Society of America*, 52, 233–248.

65 For a comprehensive discussion of communication research in the socio-psychology tradition, see Krauss & Fussell (1996). Op. cit.

66 See: Clark, H.H. (1979). Responding to indirect speech acts. *Cognitive Psychology*, 11 (4), 430–477; Clark, H.H. & Carlson, T.B. (1982). Hearers and speech acts. *Language*, 58 (2), 332–373; Clark, H.H. & Gerrig, R. (1983). Understanding old words with new meanings. *Journal of Verbal Learning and Verbal Behavior*, 22 (5), 591–608.

67 Krauss & Fussell (1996). Op. cit.

68 Sarangi, S.K., & Slembrouck, S. (1992). Non-cooperation in communication: A reassessment of Gricean pragmatics. *Journal of Pragmatics*, 17 (2), 117–154.

69 Littlejohn, S.W. & Foss, K.A. (Eds) (2009). *Encyclopedia of communication theory, 1* (p. 51). Thousand Oaks, CA: Sage.

70 Krauss & Fussell (1996). Op. cit.

71 Sarangi & Slembrouck (1992). Op. cit. Limitations include focusing on small behavior samples in laboratory settings and looking too narrowly at the immediate context without considering the wider context of social roles, time and place of interaction, formality, speech style, conversation topic, and actual circumstances—that also influence how messages are interpreted.

72 Littlejohn & Foss (2011). Op. cit.

73 Craig (1999). Op. cit.

74 Adam, G.S. (2009). Foreword. In Carey, J.W. (2009). *Communication as culture. Essays on media and society*. Revised edition. New York, NY: Routledge.

75 Craig, R.T. & Muller, H.L. (2007). The sociocultural tradition. In R.T. Craig and H.L. Muller (Eds), *Theorizing communication: Readings across traditions* (pp. 84, 365–377). Thousand Oaks, CA: Sage.

76 Craig & Muller (2007). Op. cit.

77 Munsayac, M. (n.d.). Organizational communication theories under the sociocultural tradition. Retrieved from: www.academia.edu/760713/Organizational_Communication_Theories_under_the_Sociocultural_Tradition.

78 Adam (2009). Op. cit.

79 Littlejohn & Foss (2011). Op. cit.

80 Craig (1999). Op. cit.

81 Littlejohn & Foss (2011). Op. cit.

82 Lantolf, J.P. (2000). *Sociocultural theory and second language learning*. New York, NY: Oxford University Press; Luria, A. (1979). *The making of mind* (p. 174). Cambridge, MA: Harvard University Press.

83 Vygotsky, L.S. (1987). As cited in Lantolf (2000). Op. cit., p. 3; Luria (1981). As cited in Lantolf (2000). Ibid., p. 4.

84 Wertsch, W.J. (1998). *Mind as action*. New York, NY: Oxford University Press.

85 Luria, A. (1973). *The working brain: An introduction to neuropsychology*. New York, NY: Basic Books.

86 Lantolf (2000). Op. cit.

87 See: Beck, D. & Cowan, C. (1996). *Spiral dynamics: Mastering values, leadership, and change*. Malden, MA: Blackwell; Wilbur, K. (2000). *A theory of everything: An integral vision for business, politics, science, and spirituality*. Boston, MA: Shambhala; Gebser, J. (1985). *The ever-present origin*. Athens, OH: Ohio University Press; Ray, P. & Anderson, S. (2000). *The cultural creatives*. New York, NY: Harmony Books; Inglehart, R. (1977). *The silent revolution: Changing values and political styles among western publics*. Princeton, NJ: Princeton University Press.

88 See: Bryk, A. (2000). *From tribal village to global village*. Stanford: Stanford University Press, CA; Gellner, E. (1983). *Nations and nationalisms*. Ithaca, NY: Cornell University Press; Mato, D. (1998a). The transnational making of representations of gender, ethnicity, and culture: Indigenous Peoples' Organizations at the Smithsonian Institution's Festival. *Cultural Studies*, 12 (2), 193–209; Mato, D. (1998b). Problems of social participation in Latin America in the age of globalization. In T. Jacobson & J. Servaes (Eds). *Theoretical approaches to participatory communication* (pp. 51–75). Cresskill, NJ: Hampton Press; Rappaport, J. (2005). *Intercultural utopias*. Durham, UK: Duke University Press.

89 Wertsch, J.V. (1995). The need for action in sociocultural research. In J.V. Wertsch, P. del Rio & A. Alvarez (Eds), *Sociocultural studies of mind* (pp. 56–75). New York, NY: Cambridge University Press; Leontieve, A.N. (1978). *Activity, consciousness, and personality*. Englewood Cliffs, NJ: Prentice Hall; Zinchenko, V. (1985). Vygotsky's ideas about units for the analysis of the mind. In J. Wertsch (Ed.), *Culture, communication, and cognition: Vygotskian perspectives* (pp. 94–118). New York, NY: Cambridge University Press.

90 Alvesson & Deetz (2006). Op. cit.

91 Alvesson, M. & Deetz, S.A. (2006). Critical theory and postmodernism approaches to organizational studies. In S.R. Clegg, C. Hardy, T.B. Lawrence & R. Nord (Eds). (2006). *The Sage handbook of organization studies* (pp. 255–283). Thousand Oaks, CA: Sage. Retrieved from: www.homeworkmarket.com/sites/default/files/qx/15/02/13/02/ot_required_reading_3_0.pdf.

92 Wander, P. (1996). Review essay: Marxism, post-colonialism, and rhetoric of contextualism. *Quarterly Journal of Speech*, 82 (4), 402–426.

93 Alvesson & Deetz (2006). Op. cit., p. 265.

94 Habermas, J. (1984). *The theory of communicative action. 1: Reasons and the rationalization of society*. Boston, MA: Beacon Press.

95 Wander (1996). Op. cit.

96 Hardt, H. (1992). *Critical communication studies. Communication, history, & theory in America* (p. xiv). New York, NY: Routledge.

97 Hodge, H., Kress, G. & Jones, G. (1979). The ideology of middle management. In R. Fowler, H. Hodge, G. Kress & T. Trew (Eds), *Language and control* (pp. 81–93). London, UK: Routledge and Kegan Paul; Czarniawska-Joerges, B. (1988). *Ideological control in nonideological organizations*. New York, NY: Praeger; Jackall, R. (1988). *Moral mazes*. New York, NY: Oxford University Press; Deetz, S. & Mumby, D. (1990). Power, discourse, and the workplace: Reclaiming the critical tradition in Communication studies in organizations. In J. Anderson (Ed.), *Communication yearbook 13*. (pp. 18–47). Newbury Park, CA: Sage; Alvesson, M. (2002a). *Understanding organizational culture*. London, UK: Sage.

98 Alvesson & Deetz (2006). Op. cit.

99 Jermier, J. (1985). When the sleeper wakes: A short story extending themes in radical organization theory. *Journal of Management*, 11 (2), 67–80; Rosen, M. (1985). You asked for it: Christmas at the bosses' expense. *Journal of Management Studies*, 25 (5), 463–480; Knights & Willmott (1987). Op. cit.; Mumby (1988). Op. cit.; Alvesson & Willmott (1996). Op. cit.; Alvesson (2002a). Op. cit.

100 Apel, K.O. (1979). *Toward a transformation of philosophy*. Translated by G. Adey and D. Frisby. London, UK: Routledge and Kegan Paul.

101 Sievers, B. (1986). Beyond the surrogate of motivation. *Organization Studies, 7* (4), 335–352; Alvesson, M. (1987). *Organizational theory and technocratic consciousness: Rationality, ideology, and quality of work*. Berlin & New York, NY: de Gruyter.

102 See: Mumby, D. (1988). *Communication and power in organizations: Discourse, ideology, and domination*. Norwood, NJ: Ablex; Fischer, F. (1990). *Technocracy and the politics of expertise*. Newbury Park, CA: Sage; Alvesson, M. & Wilmott, H. (1996). *Making sense of management: A critical analysis*, London, UK: Sage; M. Alvesson. & H. Wilmott (Eds). (2003). *Studying management critically*. London, UK: Sage.

103 Ferguson, K. (1984). The feminist case against bureaucracy. Philadelphia, PA: Temple University Press; Herhn, J. & Parkin, W. (1987). *'Sex' at 'work'. The power and paradox of organization sexuality*. Brighton, UK: Wheatsheaf Books Ltd.; Ashcraft, K.L. & Mumby, D.K. (2004). *Reworking gender: A feminist communicology of organization*. Thousand Oaks, CA: Sage.

104 See: Rosen (1985). Op. cit; Knights, D. & Willmott, H. (1987). Organizational culture as management strategy. *International Studies of Management and Organization, 17* (3), 40–63; Ashcraft, K.L. (1998). I wouldn't say I'm a feminist, but . . . Organizational micropractice and gender identity. *Management Communication Quarterly, 11* (4), 587–597.

105 Craig (1999). Op. cit.

106 Alvesson, M. (2002b). *Postmodernism and social research*. Buckingham, UK: Open University Press.

107 Deetz, S. (1992). *Democracy in the age of corporate colonization: Developments in communication and the politics of everyday life*. Albany, NY: State University of New York Press.

108 Craig (1999). Op. cit.

109 Alvesson & Deetz (2006). Op. cit.

CHAPTER 8

Building the Organization's Capacity

GUIDING QUESTIONS

8.1 Explain how building a school's organizational capacity is a long-term investment in people and their collective potential for growth and improved student outcomes.

8.2 Discuss the rationale and the ways that principals can indirectly impact student learning and achievement by focusing on creating the school conditions and structures that support teachers' capacity building.

8.3 Describe the factors that make effective professional learning communities different from how teachers work in traditional schools.

8.4 Clarify the ways that many teacher leadership roles are anchored in the school's professional community rather than in formal leadership positions.

8.5 Summarize the characteristics of potential teacher leaders.

8.6 Discuss the research-affirmed effects of teacher leadership on the teachers themselves, on their colleagues, and on student achievement.

8.7 Specify the cultural, intentional, and expertise conditions needed to build school capacity.

8.8 Explain Critical Race Theory's view that certain institutional factors in organizations deny opportunities to minority employees (and students).

PROFESSIONAL STANDARDS FOR EDUCATIONAL LEADERS:
1, 2, 3, 4, 5, 6, 7, 8, 9, 10

CASE STUDY 8.1

PLCs, Sure! (Psst!—What's a PLC?)

Rodney Johnson had just finished his doctoral program in educational leadership at the local state university. After 10 years of successful teaching and 3 years as a high school dean in charge of discipline in his large, urban school system, he was hired to be the Assistant Principal for Instruction in mid-sized, JFK Middle School in a rural school system. He thought that since he would be the only administrator with a doctorate, he would be able to advance quickly in the system. He wanted to be a principal or central office administrator in public schools before applying to become an assistant professor in higher education.

Rodney met with the principal, Mr. Yen, who told him the school had well-functioning Professional Learning Communities (PLCs) in place. Mr. Yen had come to the school four years earlier to improve student achievement, and the test scores, one measure of student achievement, had increased. Mr. Yen asked Rodney if he knew about PLCs but immediately caught himself and said, "Of course you do—you have your doctorate! I want you to head up our PLCs." Rodney just smiled, but really knew very little about PLCs.

As the school year got underway, Rodney started to learn the school's routines and how well everything seemed to work—much better than his last school. It was now time for him to conduct the first school-wide PLC meeting of the year. Rodney decided that he would use the PLCs' hour to share the latest research on teaching and learning with the groups. For an hour, he lectured to the teachers. Then he realized the time was over and thanked them all for coming. Rodney felt good about what he had done and thought teaching educators at his school would be good practice for when he made the move to higher education.

For the first semester, the PLC meetings followed the same lecture-centered agenda, and attendance slowly began to drop. By December, one-third of the group no longer attended the meetings. Results from the semester benchmark tests were sobering. The scores were 35 percent lower than the goal set at the end of last year. Mr. Yen called Rodney to his office, asking him to explain what had happened with the PLC members—they had been the driving force behind the test score improvements. Rodney told Mr. Yen that the group had been meeting weekly (or was it weakly?) all semester, but about a third had stopped coming. Mr. Yen called for a meeting of the PLC groups with Rodney.

As Mr. Yen began to chide the PLC's members who had stopped coming, one teacher offered, "Our PLCs used to discuss the instructional and individual issues we were having with students—how we might work with those who were having trouble with concepts. We now get a lecture from Dr. Johnson each week with no time to reflect on what we are doing and how we might be more effective with the students. We don't have our PLCs any longer—we have Education 301 with a wannabe professor."

Mr. Yen, with one eyebrow raised, turned and looked at Rodney.

RUBRIC 8.1			
Lens and/or factors to be considered in decision making	What are the factors at play in this case?	What steps should be considered in solving the problem?	What could have been done to avoid this dilemma?
The situation • The task	Rodney has been tasked with leading the PLCs and knows little about the concept or how they work.	Yen must clarify expectations for Rodney's role with PLCs so teacher leaders can continue PLC's successful practices.	Yen could have had Rodney observe PLCs in action and consulted with PLC teacher leaders about its best practices before taking a leadership role.
• Personal abilities	Unfamiliar with PLCs in concept or practice, Rodney also has weak understanding of effective instructional practices (lecturing for an hour?)	Rodney needs to admit his ignorance of PLCs to Yen, redefine his role, start observing PLCs in action, and read deeply about PLC concepts and practices.	Yen should not have assumed that Rodney had a thorough knowledge of PLCs. He should have asked more probing questions, clarified the AP's role, and overseen the transition.
• The school environment	JFK's PLCs have been working well, but teacher frustration is high with Rodney's failure to work the PLCs effectively.	Yen should meet with the PLCs and Rodney to redirect what had been a successful practice with good PLC teams.	In the interview or transition process Yen could have arranged for Rodney to interact with PLC teachers so the AP could start to learn the PLCs' practices and ethics.
Look		**Wider**	
Organizational (i.e., the organizational goals, values, policies, culture)	The school's PLCs had made good progress with improved teaching, learning, and test scores, but the new AP knew little about PLCs.	Yen needs to make certain all PLC members can continue in the pre-Rodney fashion, and Rodney can work with the PLC teams toward that end.	New leaders need help transitioning into a school and considering the school's culture, practices, and strengths.
People (i.e., individuals with needs, beliefs, goals, relationships)	Rodney's preoccupation with being an assistant professor prevents him from learning about PLCs and acting in ways to strengthen their impact.	Yen needs to make certain that PLC team members are back on track and that Rodney is prepared to work with them to achieve the school's goals.	Yen should have made certain Rodney understood the PLC's culture, practices, the value of teacher leadership, and that Rodney would continue these successful practices.

continued . . .

Competing Interests			
(i.e., competing interests for power, influence, and resources)	Rodney needs to address the school's present goals before addressing his own. Yen needs to make time to closely oversee the new AP's acculturation to the school.	Yen needs to help Rodney understand that his doctorate does not mean he knows everything he needs to know to be effective in this school or school system.	Yen should have monitored the PLC situation more closely as it had been key to JFK's improvement. Waiting until the semester benchmark test results arrived was too late.
Tradition			
(i.e., school culture, rituals, meaning, heroes)	Rodney has been brought into a role for which he was not prepared.	See above.	See above.

OVERVIEW: LEADERSHIP AS CAPACITY BUILDING

In today's organizations, many new hires want jobs with ample opportunities for professional learning and growth. Monique Valcour, an executive business coach and consultant, writes in *The Harvard Business Review* that job seekers from entry-level to executive are more interested in a potential job's opportunities for learning and development than in any other aspect. Why? Because they know that continuous learning is a key strategy for designing a sustainable career. Most of learning and development— as much as 90 percent—occurs on the job through new challenges and assignments, developmental feedback, conversations with colleagues and supervisors, and mentoring.[1]

A 2013 Gallup Organization report found that the vast majority of American workers (70 percent) were not expanding their knowledge and skills to reach their full potential.[2] But when employees feel that their employer cares about them and encourages them to make the most of their talents, employees are more likely to respond with increased discretionary effort, a stronger work ethic, and more enthusiasm and commitment.[3] In fact, the Gallup study found that when supervisors focus on employees' strengths or positive characteristics, almost two-thirds (61 percent) of these employees were actively and dedicatedly engaged in their work (twice the average of U.S. workers). This is noteworthy because employee engagement has a greater impact on work performance than do organizational policies and benefits.[4] Likewise, studies find that engaged workers apply their talents productively, improve their performance outcomes, and are less likely to become turnover statistics.[5]

This is no less true for schools. The best school leaders look for ways to focus their teachers' and staff's strengths, interests, and passions to create better outcomes for their students and more satisfying work lives for themselves.

As Peter Senge, author and senior lecturer at Massachusetts Institute of Technology observes, "[O]ver the long run, superior performance depends on superior learning."[6] Agreeing, Charlotte Danielson, author of the research-affirmed *Framework for Professional Practice*, notes, "High-level learning by students requires high-level instruction by their teachers."[7] Leadership is about contributing to others' learning and creating the opportunities for them to learn. So it makes sense that to nurture and develop students' knowledge and skills, we begin with developing their teachers' (and school leaders') capacity for superior performance.

DEFINING *ORGANIZATIONAL CAPACITY*

Generally, *capacity* refers to having the mental, emotional, or physical ability to accomplish a certain task.[8] In schools, *capacity building* is the process of developing the individual's or organization's ability to learn new ways of thinking and acting so they may make the changes required to improve learning for all students.[9] It is a long-term investment in people and their organizations' potential for growth.

For teachers, capacity building includes three broad areas: knowledge, craft skills, and dispositions.[10] *Knowledge* includes their subject matter and how to teach it to diverse learners, curriculum, and theories of learning, motivation, and assessment. *Craft skills* include planning, organizing, and arranging instruction; using instructional materials and technology; classroom management; monitoring and evaluating learning; and collaborating with colleagues, parents, community, and student support agencies to support student learning. *Dispositions* include beliefs, attitudes, values, and commitment —what teachers believe and care about. Effective teachers are committed to ensuring that each child learns to high levels, and they have confidence in their professional ability to make it happen.

In schools, *organizational capacity* refers to the entire faculty's collective competence to strengthen student performance in every classroom.[11] Teaching quality and teacher competence are enacted individually and as an organized, collective enterprise. The relationship between instructional quality and student achievement appears in Figure 8.1. Synthesizing prior research on school reform and educational change, the figure indicates student achievement most directly influenced by instructional quality. In turn, five key dimensions of capacity—(1) teachers' knowledge, skills, and dispositions; (2) principal leadership/distributed leadership; (3) program coherence; (4) professional community; and (5) technical resources—influence teachers' instructional quality. All five capacity dimensions are related, and each one has the potential to affect one or more of the others.[12] Through these links, the school's social resources—its professional community—become an educative engine for improved performance.[13] We will consider each dimension in turn.

- **Teachers' knowledge, skills, and dispositions.** These are the foundation of schools' organizational capacity. Every teacher is expected to be professionally competent in presenting an intellectually rigorous curriculum, pedagogy, assessment, and classroom management. Each must hold high expectations for each student's achievement. When referring to school capacity, the individual teachers' competence is exercised in an organized, collective endeavor.
- **Professional community.** A strong school-wide society of educators is characterized by shared goals for student learning and shared responsibility to reach them. It includes meaningful collaboration among faculty members and in-depth inquiry

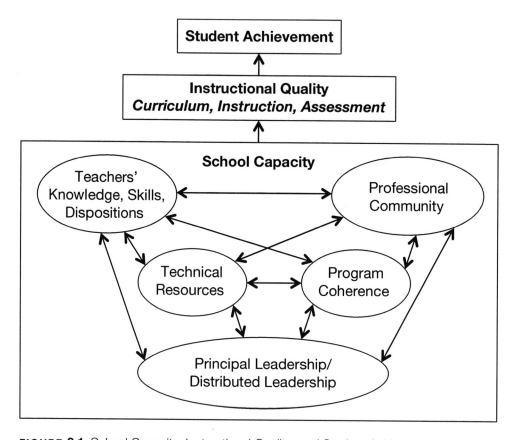

FIGURE 8.1 School Capacity, Instructional Quality, and Student Achievement

Source: Adapted from King, M.B. & Bouchard, K. (2011). The capacity to build organizational capacity in schools. *Journal of Educational Administration*, *49* (6), 653–669 (p. 655).

into assumptions, evidence, and alternative solutions to teaching and learning problems. Professional learning communities offer teachers occasions to influence their own work. Consensus exists that higher levels of professional community are linked to higher student achievement.[14]

- **Program coherence.** The extent to which a school's student and faculty programs are coordinated, aimed at clear learning goals, and sustained over time, is a measure of organizational integration. Programs that are unrelated to each other, that address only limited numbers of staff and students, or that end after a short time can weaken student and staff learning. Research suggests program coherence provides an important foundation for teaching quality and student achievement.[15]

- **Technical resources.** High quality curricula, books, and other instructional materials, laboratory equipment, computers with Internet connectivity, and sufficient workspace all contribute to student achievement. The more effectively teachers use these, the greater the benefit for students.

- **Effective school leadership.** At its core, leadership is about providing direction and exercising influence. Leaders establish the conditions that enable others to be effective. Effective educational leaders build teachers' capacity by offering intellectual stimulation, providing individualized support, presenting an appropriate professional model, and having strong, in-house opportunities for professional growth.[16] Leaders encourage their teachers to examine their assumptions about their work—consider the gaps between current and desired practices and outcomes —and rethink how they can perform their professional role. Effective education leaders also offer appropriate ways to show and monitor progress toward improvement. And they set an example with their own learning, consistent with the school's values and goals, strengthening others' beliefs about their capacities for change.[17]

Increasingly, effective school leadership includes both principals and teachers in collective, shared, or distributed leadership. As collaborative leaders, principals move from acting as a colleague in one context to being a formal leader in another. All leaders—formal and informal—focus on student learning.

At the same time, individual schools usually operate within a larger school district. Studies offer evidence that school district leadership and local school boards are essential to system-wide learning.[18] They can encourage and invest in learning throughout the system, or they can withhold support and funds, compromising a school's capacity to grow and improve. Addressing program coherence and technical resources requires principals to work with teachers and central office curriculum and technology administrators. As a result, wise principals extend their collaboration to the district superintendent and the central office personnel as allies and resources for capacity building.

REFLECTIONS AND RELEVANCE 8.1

Assessing Your Own Capacities for School Leadership

Building organizational capacity means increasing teachers' knowledge, skills, and dispositions, individually and collectively. As a future principal, in what areas do you need to increase your own professional capacities?

First working alone, review Figure 8.1, and identify the dimension of capacity in which you presently believe you have the most competence. Then rank order the remaining four dimensions according to how important you see capacity in each contributing to your school leadership effectiveness. After reflecting on the many school leadership responsibilities and challenges discussed here and in the previous seven chapters, select two areas/topics within each of your priorities in which you want to develop more knowledge, skills, and attitudes. Where and how might you learn these competencies? After you have completed this task, discuss your findings in groups of four and then with the whole class. What key capacities do most future principals want to develop and where will they find— or create—the opportunities to build them?

School leaders build their teachers'—and their schools'—capacity by integrating polices, strategies, resources, and other actions that develop their teachers. Fostering teachers' knowledge, skills, and competencies generates deeper motivation, commitment, shared identity, and new resources (time, ideas, materials) in ways that move the school (and school system) forward. When school leaders work to build their schools' collective capacity, they increase every educator's ability to learn from and with one another with the goal of improving learning. Although individual teachers can make a measurable difference with their own students, if the whole school is to make a positive difference for every student, the school ecology must evolve as a learning organization. As individuals learn and share knowledge with one another, the organization "learns."[19]

BUILDING ORGANIZATIONAL CAPACITY

An organization's ability to learn depends on the members' ability to learn. Improving teachers' knowledge, skills, and attitudes is a worthwhile investment. Research strongly supports the view that teachers have a powerful, direct effect on student learning;[20] and on the success of school reform initiatives.[21] Their effects on student learning have been found to be cumulative and long lasting.[22] At the same time, research affirms that principals indirectly influence student achievement by creating the conditions that actively foster learning.[23] Given this empirical backing, providing opportunities for teachers' professional learning, collaborative engagement, and informal leadership would seem a logical way to build individual and collective organizational capacity to positively impact student learning.

Leadership affects student achievement to the extent that it strengthens *professional community*—the special environment within which teachers work together to improve their practice and improve student learning. Classroom factors explain more than one-third of the variation in pupil achievement.[24] Empirical research evidence finds that promoting and participating in teacher learning and development, formally (in staff meetings and professional development) and informally (discussions about teaching pedagogy and specific teaching problems) is the school leadership behavior most strongly associated with positive student outcomes.[25] The other key leadership dimensions—shaping the culture and structures to support teaching and learning; establishing goals and expectations; providing resources aligned with instructional purposes; planning, coordinating, and evaluating teaching and the curriculum; and ensuring an orderly and supportive environment—serve this end.

Since school leadership is second only to classroom teaching as an in-school influence on student learning,[26] the more that school leaders focus their efforts and involvement on developing teachers' capacity for instructional effectiveness and leadership, the greater leaders' influence on student outcomes.

Leaders' Effects on Teachers' Instructional Capacity

Ironically, schools have not done a good job of providing for teacher learning. The teaching norms of isolation reflect their one-room-schoolhouse tradition. Accordingly, the most common form of professional development for teachers has been one-time, large group workshop events outside the classroom, sitting side-by-side with minimal interaction—and with little to no benefit for teachers looking to improve their practice. In contrast, recent evidence suggests that when professional development and teacher collaborative leadership are combined in mentoring, coaching, and study groups with attention focused on meeting individual teachers' professional needs in the classroom, the results are more likely to positively influence teaching practices.[27]

Figure 8.2 illustrates empirical findings on teachers' beliefs about their school leaders' impact on their capacity, motivation and commitment, and working conditions.[28] All three factors contribute to teachers' altered pedagogical practices and increased pupil learning and achievement. Teachers view their school leaders as having only a moderate influence on building their pedagogical capacities. But they see principals having a much greater influence on their motivation, commitment, and working conditions that impact their teaching performance. Teachers' beliefs about their capacity to use effective instructional strategies have the strongest influence on student learning and achievement.[29]

Figure 8.2 offers a key takeaway: Principals' attention to teachers' motivation, commitment, and working conditions can strongly influence teachers' confidence in having occasions to learn—and ability to implement—new and enhanced instructional practices that increase student learning and achievement. This is where professional learning communities have a role to play.

Professional Community and Teachers' Instructional Capacity

Professional learning communities (PLCs) rest on the idea of improving student learning by improving teacher practice. *PLCs are learning organizations in which small groups of teachers meet together regularly in collaborative teams with shared goals and work interdependently to improve achievement for each individual student they serve.*[30] In PLCs, every professional educator in the school engages with colleagues in the ongoing study and discussion of four essential questions that drive their work:[31]

School Leaders Have a...

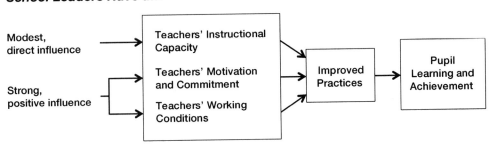

FIGURE 8.2 Effects of School Leadership on Teachers, Improved Practices, and Pupil Learning and Achievement

Source: Based on Leithwood, K., Day, C., Sammons, P., Harris, A., & Hopkins, D. (2006). *Seven strong claims about successful school leadership.* United Kingdom: National College for School Leadership. Retrieved from: http://dera.ioe.ac.uk/6967/1/download%3Fid%3D17387%26filename %3Dseven-claims-abo

1. What do we want each student to learn?
2. How will we know when each student has learned it?
3. How will we respond when a student experiences difficulty in learning?
4. How will we provide enrichment to those students who have demonstrated proficiency?

Answering the third and fourth questions distinguishes learning communities from traditional schools.[32] The staff responds promptly to struggling students as soon as they have difficulty learning by designing strategies to ensure that these students receive extra time and support needed to master the content. Similarly, teachers respond promptly to high achieving students who have demonstrated mastery of the content and would benefit from pursuing in depth an aspect of the content in which they have interest.

How PLCs Build Capacity

To build teacher capacity, PLCs begin with four main priorities: a focus on learning, collaborative culture, results, and providing timely, relevant information. Both teachers and students are learners. Working collaboratively, members engage in continuous and extensive conversations about intellectually rigorous and coherent systems of curriculum, instruction, assessment, and student development. Making their practice public, teachers share their ideas, materials, techniques, and talents. They develop shared norms and values about trust and children's (and their own) ability to learn. In the process, they create an inclusive and caring community, identify school priorities for using time and space, and specify how these factors can contribute to every student's learning and wellbeing. They continually gather data on student achievement and design common formative assessments. Teachers regularly visit each other's classrooms to observe colleagues trying out new approaches. And, they provide concrete, timely, relevant, and user-friendly feedback and assistance.

In collective inquiry, teachers analyze student work and develop a shared understanding of what high quality products are and look like. They identify students' common misunderstandings and determine which instructional strategies are—and are not—working. They develop culturally responsive practices to help every student succeed academically. Their goal is continuous refinement of their instructional practices, their success is judged by results (observed and measured student learning tied to curricular, district, and state goals) rather than by good intentions.

In PLCs, teacher learning and capacity building occur in four related ways. First, teachers gain ideas by reading and discussing relevant books and journal articles, viewing instructional videos of colleagues' teaching, personally observing effective classroom practices, or watching and critiquing expert presentations. Second, teachers transfer this information into their own classrooms by preparing and delivering lessons, materials, activities, and assessments with their students. Third, PLC members observe and reflect on the effects of these practices on student learning, asking (and answering, independently and with colleagues), "What worked?" "What is the evidence?" "What do I need to learn more deeply?" Fourth, PLC members meet with peers to discuss, problem solve, and create. They share what they have observed, how the students responded, and what they might want to fine-tune for the next use. In these ways, teachers work alone and together to increase their instructional capacities and improve student outcomes.

PLCs and Teacher, Student Outcomes

As a result of teachers actively participating in PLCs, students learn more. Research finds that well-developed PLCs have a positive impact on teaching practice and student learning beyond individual classrooms.[33] While most studies use teachers' perceptions to generate valid and useful data, several empirical studies also confirm this finding. In a 2008 literature review,[34] 11 empirical studies found changes in teaching practices, with five studies mentioning specific changes in teachers' classroom practices.[35] Teachers became more student-centered and developed stronger instructional norms. Collaboration, a focus on student learning, teacher authority (i.e., the ability of teachers to make decisions regarding both the processes of their learning communities and aspects of school governance), and continuous teacher learning appeared to promote the most changes in teaching practice.[36]

Specific successful PLC methods included focus on instructional techniques and how they impacted student learning. When PLCs maintained an intense and persistent focus on student learning, students showed gains from around 50 percent working at grade level or above to 75, 80, and 90 percent reaching proficiency on standardized state achievement tests (even after adjusting for grade level and student background). Their school's teaching culture also improved.[37] Notably, in PLCs where teachers collaborated but without structured work highly focused around student learning, similar gains were not evident. The review also documented that PLC's presence in a school contributed to higher levels of social support for achievement and higher levels of authentic pedagogy.[38] Other studies also affirm that professional community is a solid predictor of instructional practices that are strongly associated with student achievement;[39] school leadership and capacity building are mutually reinforcing.[40]

PLCs as Professional Development

Investigations on the characteristics of high quality professional development (PD) have generated a consensus around its content, context, and design.[41] Studies find the most useful professional development is sustained, job-embedded, and collaborative and emphasizes active hands-on teaching, assessment, observation, and reflection (rather than abstract discussions) with a focus on student learning. More specifically, research identifies regular peer observations of practice with feedback and assistance such as critical friends and videotaped lessons for peer review;[42] analysis of student work and student data;[43] and study groups[44] to increase student learning. But when PLCs combine all these practices, their impact on teacher capacities and student learning is stronger. These robust outcomes for high quality PD are especially true when PD is part of a school reform effort that links curriculum, assessment, and standards to intensive and sustained professional learning.[45]

The PLC model as professional development represents a major shift away from the traditional "sit-and-get" style in which consultants and university researchers not engaged in day-to-day teaching convey "knowledge *FOR* practice" to classroom teachers. By comparison, the PLC model is anchored in "knowledge *OF* practice" in which teachers treat their own classrooms and schools as sites for intentional investigation. In this context, teacher learning becomes a coherent, intensive, and constant part of a larger school ongoing reform effort. PLCs' rigorous, cumulative learning helps teachers develop the pedagogical skills to teach specific content and has strong, positive effects on practice.[46] Studies confirm that PLCs are working to shift teachers' habits of mind and create cultures of teaching that help educators improve teaching and learning in ways that boost their capacity as educators and student achievement.

REFLECTIONS AND RELEVANCE 8.2

Assessing Your Professional Learning Community

The principal of XYZ Middle School has hired your consulting group to visit *your* current school to assess your Professional Learning Community's *health* (how well are teachers working collaboratively and building their knowledge and skills in classroom practice?) and *effectiveness* (how well are students improving their learning and achievement?). Your consulting contract specifies four days of visiting PLCs in action, classroom visits, samples of student projects, formative and summative student assessments, and teacher, student, and parent interviews. On day 5, your team prepares your report and recommendations. You will need to get the maximum valid information in a very short time.

To prepare your consulting team, work in groups of four to:

1. Identify the five most important features of effective PLCs that you will look for—and how you will know when you see them.
2. Decide what data or artifacts you want to gather to inform your assessment:

    a. What specific evidence will you need if you are to determine the school's PLCs are functioning well (healthy)?
    b. What specific evidence will you need to suggest that the PLCs are *not* functioning well (not healthy)?
    c. What specific evidence will you need if you are to determine the school's PLCs are effective (in generating teacher growth, student achievement)?
    d. What specific evidence will you need to suggest that the PLCs are *not* effective?

After discussing these factors in your small groups—and applying them to each of your own school's PLC, share your ideas about evidence of PLC health and effectiveness with the entire class. Discuss the elements by which you know if a PLC is functioning effectively and successfully—or if it isn't.

BUILDING TEACHERS' LEADERSHIP CAPACITY

Many teachers are taking on school leadership roles. In a 2013 Metropolitan Life survey, 51 percent of teachers responded that they have leadership roles in their school (such as department chair or teacher mentor). Fifty-one percent also expressed interest in teaching part-time and combining additional responsibilities with their teaching assignment. Only 16 percent reported an interest in becoming a principal.[47]

Linda Lambert, Professor Emeritus at California State University, Hayward, defines *teacher leadership* as the specific roles and responsibilities in which the most effective teachers use their talents in the service of student and adult learning, collaboration, and school and system improvement.[48] Teacher leadership occurs in three main areas:[49]

Leadership of other teachers and students: Teachers can serve as facilitators, instructional coaches, mentors to other teachers, trainers, curriculum specialists, or union representatives. They can also create new instructional approaches and lead study groups.

Leadership of operational tasks: Teachers can serve as academic department heads, action researchers, and task force members to keep the school program organized and moving toward its goals.

Leadership through decision making or partnership: Teachers can assume leadership roles by serving on school improvement committees, initiating partnerships with business, higher education, and local educational agencies, the school districts, and parent-teacher-student associations.

Teacher leadership roles are anchored in the school's professional community rather than in formal leadership positions. Joseph Murphy, award-winning Vanderbilt University educational leadership professor, observed that school districts have struggled with little success to define a formal teacher role comparable to—but different than—the administrators' role. Consequently, rather than relying on a model of individual leadership in formal roles that focus on management and administrative responsibilities, teachers' pathways to leadership tend to include shared leadership and communities of practice, using informal roles that focus on instruction and learning. Rather than wield influence based on control, teacher leadership influence tends to be based on expertise and social capital. Instead of accountability to administrators and the bureaucratic hierarchy, teacher leaders tend to be accountable to their professional colleagues. Without leaving their classrooms, students, and pedagogy, teacher leadership expands its teaching role to include colleagues and develop deep and collaborative connections with them.[50] Table 8.1 compares traditional administrator leadership and evolving teacher leadership on several dimensions: role, nature of leadership, focus, influence, accountability, and relationship with the classroom.

Through their varied leadership roles, teachers translate school improvement into classroom practice, develop ownership of the changes they are working to make, and guide their colleagues toward shared goals. As key resources, teachers' expertise and knowledge of curriculum, instruction, assessment, and students' learning needs allow them to mediate between planning and realistic, successful practice. In these ways, teachers deepen and expand their involvement in teaching rather than leave their valued profession for what many view as an unsatisfying career change into school administration.

TABLE 8.1 Comparison of Administrator and Teacher Leadership

	Administrator (Traditional Role)	Teacher (Evolving Role)
Role	Formal position	Formal or informal position
Nature of leadership	Individual	Individual or shared
Focus	Set direction, plan, manage, control, coordinate school programs and operations	Facilitate teacher instruction and teacher/student learning; school decision making; lead operational tasks
Influence	Authority, control	Expertise, social capital
Accountability	To administrators, bureaucracy	To professional colleagues, students
Relationship with classroom	Indirect	Direct

Sources: Based on Lambert, L. (1998). *Building leadership capacity in schools*. Alexandria, VA: ASCD, pp. 3–4; and Murphy, J. (2005). *Connecting teacher leadership to school improvement*. Thousand Oaks, CA: Corwin.

IDENTIFYING TEACHER LEADERS

Teacher leaders are current or former teachers with significant instructional experience and reputations as excellent teachers. They are reflective, collaborative, demonstrate strong interpersonal skills, and hold their peers' respect. Their readiness to assume teacher leadership roles and responsibilities include:[51]

- Excellent professional teaching skills.
- Extensive knowledge of teaching and learning, curriculum, and content area.
- Clear and well developed personal philosophy of education.
- An interest in adult development.
- Location in a career stage that enables the person to give to others.
- Location in a personal life stage in which one has the time and energy to take on leadership responsibilities (suggesting highly competent midcareer and midlife individuals).
- Achievement and learning oriented, seek challenge and growth.

Briefly, potential teacher leaders are competent, credible, and approachable. They are willing to role model, take risks, and accept responsibility (although this orientation may create tensions with their colleagues and press the potential leaders to choose between their needs for achievement and affiliation). They are sensitive and receptive to others' ideas and emotions, and they display cognitive and emotional flexibility. They are also hardworking, able to manage their workload, and have strong organizational and administrative skills.[52] Perhaps most importantly, teacher leaders can use these qualities to help colleagues work collaboratively for results—improved professional practice, increased student learning outcomes, and continuous improvement. Their colleagues do not resent them; they "allow" these colleagues to be leaders.[53] Although principals can motivate staff and provide them with a supportive work environment, fellow teachers with current classroom credibility, willing to coach colleagues and offer positive peer pressure, have greater impact on teaching practice. What is more, studies have found that teachers' collaborative leadership leads to deeper and more lasting change.[54]

Effects of Teacher Leadership

The positive effects of teacher leadership appear in the teachers, their colleagues, and their students. They also appear in their relationships, classroom practices, and other school-level outcomes.

Impact on Teachers Themselves

Teacher leaders report that the experience helps them grow in leadership skills and organizational perspectives. Because their leadership role gives them more occasions to learn new information and behaviors, offers them more opportunities to observe and interact with other teachers around instructional practices, and involves them in research evaluating new instructional methods, some teacher leaders change their instructional practices. Depending on the nature of their leadership work, teachers identify increased motivation,[55] increased intellectual stimulation, reduced isolation, and reflection and analytics thinking about their practice (especially when given occasions to step back from intensive daily teaching).[56]

Not all teacher leadership experiences are positive, however. In studies from the 1990s, some teacher leaders have felt difficulty in switching roles between teacher and leader[57] and bore stress from juggling teaching and leading at the same time.[58] They have challenges with the fluctuating nature of their relationship with colleagues, especially when the links are more hierarchical and less horizontal, more professional and less social—relationships shifts that violate teachers' egalitarian professional norms.[59] As a result, teachers taking on leadership roles risked not leading well and potentially losing valued collegial friendships. Today, however, with teachers assuming more leadership responsibilities in instructional and organizational levels, teacher leadership is a more accepted aspect of education's culture.[60]

As the PLC investigations strongly suggest, teacher leadership in instructional areas appears to have the greater impact on colleagues and student achievement than does only participating in administrative decisions. Ample research supports the assertion that teacher leadership activities, especially in instructional areas, increase the likelihood of total school improvement.[61]

Overall, teachers have front-line familiarity with classroom issues and their school's culture. They understand the support they need to perform their jobs well. Their perspective can apprise administrators of daily realities, resulting in more situational awareness and more informed decisions. In these schools, who leads and who follows depends on the task, the problem, or the situation, not on who holds formal job titles.

Impact on Student Achievement

Until 2007, research on teacher leadership (in shared decision making with principals) and student achievement was limited, mostly descriptive, with generally unsupportive findings and methodological weaknesses that raised concerns about their validity.[62] Since then, investigations using more rigorous designs have identified more support for teacher leadership's impact on improving student learning outcomes.

Two related longitudinal studies, in 2007 and 2010, in 195 and 198 elementary schools, respectively, over four years found significant direct effects of shared leadership on change in the schools' academic capacity and indirect effects on student growth rates in math[63] and math and reading achievement.[64] A 2008 study from 90 elementary and secondary schools found that shared leadership explained a significant proportion of variation in student achievement across schools.[65] Another 2010 empirical investigation of school leadership and student achievement found that shared leadership was linked to student achievement indirectly, through its effects on teacher motivation and teachers' workplace settings (both factors that principals can influence).[66] The study also found that when principals and teachers share leadership, teachers' working relationships are stronger, and student achievement is higher, and no single pattern of leadership distribution was consistently linked to student learning. Moreover, expanding leadership to include teachers, parents, and district staff did not diminish perceptions of the principals' influence.[67]

Most importantly, studies affirm the view that school leadership has a greater influence on schools and students when it is widely distributed, and schools with the highest levels of student achievement attributed this to relatively high levels of leadership influence from an array of sources, especially teacher teams, parents, and students.[68]

Lastly, research finds that three interrelated capabilities—(1) deep leadership content knowledge, (2) used to solve school-based problems, (3) while building relational trust with colleagues, parents, and students—contribute to teacher leadership's positive outcomes.[69] In a meta-analysis of research on the direct and indirect effects of leadership on student outcomes, *instructional leadership* (i.e., leadership where the school's central focus on improving teaching and learning) has been found to be three to four times greater than *transformational leadership* (i.e., the leadership style where the leader works with employees to identify the need for change, a vision to guide the change, and inspires them to work together to make it happen).[70] The more leaders focus on their relationships, their work, and their skills in the core areas of teaching and learning, the greater their influence on student outcomes.

REFLECTIONS AND RELEVANCE 8.3

Building Your Teacher Leadership Capacities

Teacher leadership roles are anchored in the school's professional community.

You are interviewing for a position as a teacher leader in your school. Working in groups of four and taking turns role playing as interviewer, candidate, and two observing teachers, conduct a job interview including the following questions:

- What teacher leadership roles are you ready to accept—and how do you think they will help you build your leadership capacity?
- What personal and professional characteristics or qualities suggest that you are ready to accept a teacher leadership role in this school?
- What concerns do you have about accepting a teacher leadership role?
- In what ways does your current teaching or leadership position affect you, your colleagues, your students—and how do you know?
- What do you want from your principal and colleagues to help you grow in your leadership role?

After each role-play, observers will give feedback to the "candidate" about how to improve their responses. After the role plays, the class will discuss the experience and what they learned about themselves by participating in it.

CONDITIONS NEEDED TO BUILD SCHOOL CAPACITY

Principals wanting to build organizational capacity cannot simply direct teachers to set up and join PLCs—and then sit back and wait for student achievement to increase. For teachers' capacity to grow and positively impact students, the principal needs to ensure that certain basic structures are in place. First, the principal must create and sustain the school culture and conditions to support teacher and student learning. Second, the principal must develop a shared unity of purpose about the important problems the school faces. Third, the principal needs to hire educators who have (or can develop) the deep expertise in approaches to improving teaching, learning, and leading.[71] Let's consider each.

The Culture

Scholars and practitioners agree that school culture is a dominant influence on a school's ability to continuously improve.[72] For teachers to mature their capacities for instruction and leadership, the school culture must honor teachers for their expertise and willingness to share resources. It encourages and supports adults working together collaboratively in an open and trusting manner. The school creates a safe climate in which teachers can examine professional practices, take risks, try new approaches, admit mistakes, and voice constructive disagreements about the core issues of school improvement. In this environment, respecting each other as learners, teachers can work together to sharpen and expand their knowledge, skills, and dispositions in ways that better engage and advance even the most challenging students' learning.

In this context, principals' most important job is creating and sustaining the conditions that nurture professional community. Once the culture, organizational climate, and structural arrangements are in place, teachers can negotiate the norms and standards of daily practice without violating professional norms of equality and independence.[73]

Clearly, shaping school culture in this manner requires effective leadership, time, and attention.

Creating Needed Structures

Preparing a school to build teachers' professional capacities requires thoughtful preparation. This includes designing, using, and reinforcing the formal and informal structures to the school program that will aid teachers' ongoing learning. Structural changes such as creating regular, uninterrupted blocks of time for teacher-organized and led professional development; scheduling teachers with the same course assignments to common planning periods; and having teachers identify and schedule colleagues' presentations of "model lessons" as "best practices" build in occasions to strengthen and expand teachers' instructional repertoires. These structures and practices need time to take root and become "the way we do things around here." Research supports the view that providing time for teacher leaders to meet, plan, and discuss issues is essential to their success in building capacity.[74]

Defining the Principals' Role

Traditionally, principals had three main roles: managerial, political, and instructional. Typically, the first two took priority.[75] As a result, not every principal is comfortable moving from a bureaucratic mind-and-skill set to an instructional leader/change agent mind-and-skill set. Some principals may resist these shifted and expanded responsibilities —despite studies that find that "top-down," bureaucratic structures that tend to be effective in relatively stable environments with standard routines are actually counterproductive for today's schools.[76]

Likewise, principals who understand leadership as "heroic" or "the authority in charge" may be unwilling to share responsibility for instructional decisions with teachers and assistant principals. If their experiences had them "direct" teacher work, they may find it difficult to nurture and facilitate teachers as instructional and organizational leaders. Instead of the school having a few department chairpersons working on administrative tasks in their separate domains, principals who can accept their own revised leadership role can now have leadership cadres, groups of teacher leaders throughout the school who can participate in professional growth and school improvement activities, applying their expertise and interest in making decisions that affect them, their colleagues, and their students.

Notably, principals do not give up their power and control in distributed leadership situations; leadership in schools is not "all or nothing." With collaborative school leadership, principals keep their visioning, change agent, fiduciary, and bureaucratic responsibilities. They provide recurring occasions to help teachers and staff ask (and answer) the "right" questions and inform themselves with relevant data. Principals work with faculty to identify, learn, and practice the strategies for improved climate, teaching, and learning. This may mean "counseling out" and replacing those teachers who do not support the vision and who are unwilling to continue their professional learning, and hiring new educators who will enthusiastically carry out the school's goals. Principals also serve as a buffer between the school and the district office, protecting site-based initiatives.

Defining the Teachers' Role

Teachers may have similar role issues. Not every teacher wants to be a leader. For teachers who expect to close their classroom doors and teach their hearts out may find it unnerving to share their practice (and possible professional missteps) with colleagues. Without an established culture and climate of trust and continuous learning, giving critical feedback to colleagues may be as uncomfortable for certain teachers as receiving it. At the same time, teachers in traditional school cultures are used to knowing their specific curriculum, not the "big picture" of the school's overall direction. Plus, the traditional teacher norms of followership discourage them from accepting responsibilities outside the classroom.[77] Their egalitarian norm tends to portray the teacher who accepts a leadership role—instructional or otherwise—as "stepping out of line." This so-called "crab bucket culture"[78] (i.e., professional jealousy) reflects teachers' resentment of colleagues who appear to think themselves better that their peers. As crab catchers know, they do not have to put a lid on the bucket of caught crabs to keep them inside the pot; those already caught will reach up and drag others down should any try to climb out. Finally, teachers may become overwhelmed with the work expectations; planning and teaching well today and tomorrow are demanding and time consuming enough without the extra burdens of new initiatives, new collaborative work, and new knowledge and skills to master and put into practice.

In addition, the success of teacher leadership rests largely on their relationships with other educators in their school. Mutual trust and cooperation provide the necessary basis for satisfying professional connections and growth. Without trust and cooperation, it is difficult to initiate or keep the needed communication in which colleagues' activities become visible for observation and feedback. Likewise, teacher leaders need strong relationships with their principals. To do this, teacher leaders and principals should clarify their respective roles and working relationships. For example, teacher leaders may assume primary responsibility for leading (or co-leading) improvement in teaching and learning whereas principals assume primary responsibility for strategic leadership and aligning resources to support improvements in teaching and learning.

Unity of Purpose

Principals and teachers develop a sense of common intention, core values, and collective responsibility for improving student outcomes. This requires identifying and addressing the issues that interfere with every student learning. To develop a shared vision, they might ask: Are children from every demographic group achieving to high, measured levels and to state standards? Are teachers able to maintain safe, focused, caring, and inclusive classrooms so that every child can learn the required curriculum? Is the school's climate strong and positive enough so that every student feels valued and successful? Are discipline or attendance issues keeping certain students from learning apace with their peers? Are parents or guardians actively supporting their children's learning? Unless the school leaders and teachers can answer "Yes" to each of these questions (and back up their answers with credible data), they will not be able to accurately direct their improvement efforts.

Determining the school's primary focus requires collecting and analyzing data that regularly highlights progress toward the goals of improving teaching and learning and linking these with ongoing professional discussions about that progress. In these ways, teachers and leaders come to agree on their priorities, share norms about best practice, and hold each other accountable for results. Actively participating in this process develops a sense of ownership and commitment about the goals they want to reach, making follow through more likely. Similarly, they recognize that becoming a "great teacher" is a career-long enterprise and their professional obligation.

Need for Deep Expertise

Without sufficient numbers of skilled people to enact these cultural, structural, and pedagogical changes, capacity building cannot occur. In addition to providing PLCs to help expand teachers' instructional skills, school leaders can provide an array of opportunities for teachers to extend their leadership expertise. These include conversations, coaching, mentoring, networking, and new teacher induction.[79]

Conversations

By sharing ideas about teaching, learning, and leadership in one-on-one talks, principals can help teachers expand their knowledge beyond their immediate classrooms. Conducting dialogues about what the student data mean and discussing long-range improvement plans allow experienced school leaders to enlarge teachers' thinking about the whole school enterprise. Principals can "think out loud" to illustrate how they gather relevant information and make informed decisions about a wide array of educational issues. In this way, principals create a time and space for teachers to wrestle with thorny education concerns and school situations and to learn by example how leadership works.

Coaching

Principals coach teachers on practical leadership skills to improve their individual and organizational performance. Principals widen teachers' thinking when they help them try out new leadership strategies—such as how to plan and use a meeting agenda to facilitate a school improvement committee's discussions—and receive specific feedback on their effectiveness. The research literature on this type of coaching effectiveness is mixed. Most studies are anecdotal rather than empirical, and few empirical investigations meet standards of methodological reliability.[80]

Mentoring

Broader and more personal than coaching, mentoring is a personal/professional relationship directed at strengthening teachers' performance. The mentoring process includes coaching and feedback, modeling best practices, providing leadership experiences, planning the steps for career advancement, and taking part in leadership activities inside and outside the school. Again, investigations have concluded that mentoring as part of professional development for educational leaders was mixed, largely due to methodology limitations.[81]

Networking

Principals can encourage teachers to participate in professional groups and associations that help them develop their leadership thinking and skills. Offering a larger context for developing leadership, networking connects teachers with local, regional, and national associations, interest groups, and individuals. Networks view teachers as experts; create forums for sharing, dialog, and critique; invite teachers to accept responsibility for their own learning; and share opportunities for career advancement. They may provide professional standards to help direct and assess teachers' own teaching and leadership growth. Being part of a professional network situates learning in practice and relationships and strengthens teachers' professional identity. It is logical to assume that the impact of networking on teacher capacity depends on the duration, type, and quality of the networking relationship and practices.

New Teacher Induction

Helping beginning teachers start their career in a culture that supports adult learning and teacher leadership helps them envision the many roles available to them within education. When principals support new teachers with a clear, ongoing induction process and appropriate mentors, principals foster leadership in both newbies and veterans. Empirical studies of strong induction programs for beginning teachers find three positive sets of outcomes: increase in teacher commitment and retention, improved classroom teachers' instructional practices, and increased student achievement.[82]

Clearly, principals who want to build organizational capacity face a complex set of challenges. They must first work with others to establish an appropriate school culture, climate, and accommodating structures. Within teachers and staff, they must engender a unity of purpose, priorities, goals, and how they plan to make them a reality. Increasingly advanced levels of expertise in pedagogy and leadership will have to be fostered throughout the school. Doing all this takes a considerable investment of thought, planning, effort, and time. But as research strongly suggests, an investment in expanding teachers' capacities pays high dividends to teachers, their students, and their school.

REFLECTIONS AND RELEVANCE 8.4

Does Your School's Culture Support Capacity Building?

To build organizational capacity, principals must ensure that the school culture and structures are available to support teacher learning. Does your present school's culture support building your organization's capacity?

Working in pairs, answer "Yes" to any of the following questions, and give examples to illustrate your answer. After finishing, discuss as a class:
Does your schools' culture . . .

- Honor teachers for their expertise and willingness to share resources?

- Establish an environment of mutual respect, trust, and cooperation among educators?
- Create safe places for teachers to examine professional practice, take risks, try new approaches, admit mistakes and voice disagreements about school improvement?
- Provide structures and enough time for regular daily, weekly, or monthly scheduled occasions for teachers' collaborative work to expand and refine their instructional skills?
- Encourage your principal to become an instructional leader/change agent?
- Encourage teachers to accept leadership responsibilities outside their classroom and genuinely support them when they do?
- Facilitate hiring new teachers and administrators who share the school's goals and who want to continue their professional growth?
- Foster and reinforce the faculty's share purposes, values, and collective responsibility for improving student outcomes?
- Make data-informed decisions to support teacher and student learning?
- Provide varied one-on-one and group opportunities for teachers to deepen and expand their leadership knowledge, skills, and perspectives?

THEORIES OF CAPACITY BUILDING

Since the 1960s, scholars have asked why women and people of color are under-represented in organizational leadership positions as compared with their white, male colleagues. Critical race theorists have developed concepts to explain how this professional discrimination began and how it continues. In their view, such scholarship can lead to advocacy that affords women and minorities more opportunities for capacity building and organizational leadership.[83]

Critical Race Theory and Organizational Capacity Building

In 2008, Barack Obama shattered the political racial glass ceiling by becoming the 44th President of the United States. But his is a path that few can follow. At the highest levels of corporate America, diversity is lacking. In 1955, when *Fortune* magazine published its first list of the top 500 companies in the United States, every CEO on that list was a white male. As of March 2015, *Fortune* 500 companies had only four African American CEOs; just over 4 percent of top executives were African American, Asian, or Latin American.[84] In 2014 Wall Street, nearly two-thirds of entry-level bankers hired were white, and 78 percent were male. The same lack of diversity is true of some of America's best know companies—including Apple, Twitter, Facebook and Google.[85]

Why are so few women and minority leaders heading America's top companies? Ronald C. Parker, CEO of the Executive Leadership Council, responded that market globalization places more value on having international experience, and "Women and people of color aren't afforded those opportunities." Unconscious biases against those who don't look like a "typical" leader also make it difficult, he added.[86]

With its origins in the 1980s, critical race theory (CRT) is a movement fueled by scholar and political activists interested in studying and transforming the relationship among race, racism, and power.[87] CRT is also an analytical framework that looks at how culturally determined biases, infused throughout our American culture, undermine opportunities for certain groups to receive capacity building opportunities in organizations.

For CRT, *racism* is understood as "a system of ignorance, exploitation, and power used to oppress African Americans, Latinos, Asian Pacific Americans, Native Americans and other people on the basis of ethnicity, culture, mannerism, and skin color."[88] This definition makes three important points. First, one group deems itself superior to all others. Second, the superior group has the power to carry out the racist behavior. And third, racism benefits the superior group while it negatively affects the subordinate racial/ethnic groups.[89]

Similarly, CRT holds that race itself is a social construction that corresponds to no biological or genetic reality. Instead, races are categories that society invents, manipulates, and retires when convenient. Certain physical traits such as skin color, physique, or hair texture are only a very small part of genetic endowment and have little or nothing to do with distinctly human, higher-order traits such as personality, intelligence, and moral behavior. Nonetheless, CRT argues, in our society, every social indicator—from salary to life expectancy—reveals the advantages of being white.

CRT's Five Essential Themes

Supporting this conclusion, CRT advances five essential themes.[90] First, race and racism are widespread, permanent parts of ordinary daily life, and central factors in defining and explaining individuals' experiences.[91] It takes on institutional and individual forms, has conscious and unconscious elements, and makes a cumulative impact on both the individual and the group.[92] Race also intersects with other forms of subordination, including gender and class discrimination. Racism's end result: keeping minorities in subordinate positions.

Second, CRT challenges the dominant ideology for interpreting the world. It rejects West-European-Enlightenment claims of neutrality, objectivity, rationality, truth, and universality.[93] Instead, CRT asserts that socially powerful persons fabricate a reality to impose their view on the world in order to perpetuate their dominance. Thus, institutions are not race neutral, objective, meritocratic, or "colorblind." In CRT context, *colorblindness* can be understood as the beliefs and practices that everyone, regardless of skin pigment, should be treated the same to ensure equality. Racially colorblind people *pretend* that they do not see a person's race; they only see the person. Although commendable when a government decision maker refuses to go along with a local prejudice, colorblindness can be unreasonable when it does not consider individual differences or needs. Likewise, CRT argues that institutions use *colorblindness* and *post-racialism* (i.e., the belief that since the United States twice elected an African

American president, racism in this country no longer exists) to enforce exclusion based on "otherness." The result is to deny and minimize how organizations are reproducing the structure of racial power that exists in the larger society.

Similarly, CRT sees *meritocracy*—the belief that one achieves social and economic mobility mainly through individual effort and hard work, regardless of race, gender, socioeconomic status, or other social identity—as another source of society's racial power. Meritocracy defines how and to whom resources and opportunities will be distributed. In CRT's view, meritocracy is a storehouse of hidden, race-specific preferences for those who have the power to decide merit's meaning and consequences. Meritocracy determines who receives occasions for professional and societal mobility and who does not. The outcomes (i.e., the hiring decisions, or providing opportunities to grow, have influence, and rise professionally in the organization) are already rigged against those the decisions makers concur lack "merit." In CRT's view, meritocratic "neutral" policies help rationalize existing racial power and isolate, stigmatize, and ultimately suppress certain voices and ideas.[94]

Third, CRT fosters an overall commitment to social justice and the end of racism. It seeks to end the subordination of gender, class, and sexual orientation in private, organizational, and public life.[95] Actions for social justice work against "interest convergence"—the belief that Caucasian people will support racial justice only to the extent that they see something in it for themselves.[96] By keeping the status quo, white elites gain material benefits, working-class whites gain psychic benefits, and non-whites receive few to none.

Fourth, CRT recognizes the centrality of experiential knowledge as a valid knowledge source. Women and men of color's personal experiences are legitimate, appropriate, and essential data for scholarship, research, and teaching about racial subordination. In this way, women and people of color have high competence in matters that Caucasians are not likely to know or understand. Accordingly, CRT advocates that the lived experiences of peoples of color, in the form of storytelling, family histories, biographies, scenarios, parables, chronicles, and narratives, be used to inform more "objective" scholarship research.

Fifth, CRT champions an interdisciplinary perspective and methods to place race and racism in both historical and contemporary contexts. Many of CRT's basic insights and perspectives emerged from other disciplinary traditions—including education, sociology, psychology, political science, law, cultural studies, and philosophy. CRT represents an extension and deepening of critical theory. Over time, the CRT family tree expanded to include racialized experiences as women, Latinas/os, Native American, and Asian American communities' continuing search for a framework that addresses racism and oppression beyond black/white.[97] These dialogues reframe the conditions of racial power from a matter of individual prejudice or an outcome of social class to one of institutional bias.[98]

From these roots, CRT asserts that the United States has never been a colorblind society,[99] and skin color affects how people view their separate and interrelated worlds. This claim has research support. A longitudinal study of public opinion polls on racial/ethnic and social issues finds that African Americans, Latinos, and Caucasians have very different positions on an array of social issues.[100]

Research and Criticism

As discussed, research supports many of CRTs' assertions about institutional structures' negative outcomes for minorities. But critics take issue with the claim that *all* objective standards of factual accuracy, professional merit, or legal coherence are merely "social constructions" that white, heterosexual males use to exert power over others. Critics warn that an orientation that sees conspiracy in all laws and all modes of reasoning and CRT's censure—rather than logical argument—with those who disagree stifles free and reasonable debate about a social policy's reality or value.[101] Likewise, detractors challenge CRT's theory of knowledge and their celebration of the "authenticity" of one's racial or sexual group's experiences (often expressed through personalized story telling) as more valid than factual accuracy or logical consistency. Although personal stories may be qualitatively enlightening, they do not replace the professional's need for exhaustively researched and analytical manuscripts for law reviews or scholarly journals or to decide legal cases on constitutional rather than emotional grounds.[102] Plus, such authenticity makes it difficult to have open and structured conversations about these issues with others.[103] Overall, critics believe that although CRT's view has merit, it lacks balance, nuance, and neglects the factors that bind us.

REFLECTIONS AND RELEVANCE 8.5

Feminist and Critical Race Theory and Capacity Building

Critical race theorists' concepts explain their views about how organizations develop "objective," "neutral," and "meritocratic" structures, norms, and practices to unfairly distribute opportunities for professional growth and influence, limiting or denying them to women and people of color. Similar processes occur in schools to provide different quality educations to white children and children of color.

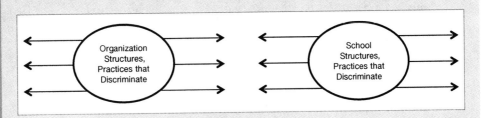

Working in pairs, complete the graphics above with examples of how these theorists see organizations (left graphic) and schools (right graphic) using unfair rules and practices to prevent women and people of color from having opportunities for capacity building and influence. When finished, discuss as a class.

Nonetheless, CRT heightens our awareness of racial issues and the experience of racism in our society and organizations. As an intellectual framework and social justice advocacy, CRT challenges the institutional structures—in corporations and schools—that unfairly distribute power, influence, and opportunities for advancement. Critical theorists work toward the elimination of oppression in all forms—race, class, and gender. In education, CRT insists that educators thoroughly investigate our nation's history while addressing our public schools' failure to adequately educate children of color. As our country becomes more diverse, identifying and developing each person's special gifts to their fullest brings benefits to each individual and to the entire society.

IMPLICATIONS FOR EDUCATIONAL LEADERS

Continuous learning is a key strategy for designing a sustainable career. By shaping a workplace environment that motivates and supports teacher learning, principals build organizational capacity so teachers can directly impact student learning. This chapter points to at least four ways that principals can build organizational capacity.

Foster Supportive School Culture and Structures

Leadership affects student achievement to the extent that it strengthens *professional community*—the special environment within which teachers work together to improve their practice and increase student learning. This means creating a school culture that respects teachers as learners and honors them for their expertise and willingness to share resources. Infused through all school activities, this culture provides the climate in which teachers can build the trust and mutual respect needed to work collegially to publicly identify and rethink their current assumptions, beliefs, and practices (as discussed in Chapter 3). They can try new approaches, admit and learn from mistakes. They can voice respectful disagreement about core school improvement issues. At the same time, this school culture promotes and reinforces the faculty's shared purposes, values, and collective responsibility for improving every student's outcomes. And it celebrates teachers' willingness to accept leadership responsibilities inside and outside their classrooms.

To make this happen, principals will want to put in place the formal and informal structures that uphold professional community. For instance, they can work with teachers to initiate PLCs. They can design the master schedule to provide dedicated time for daily or weekly (90-minutes) blocks for teachers to work collaboratively. Scheduling teachers who use the same curricula with common planning periods (and, ideally, adjacent to their lunch periods) also can facilitate teacher collaboration. Monthly grade level and faculty meetings can become forums for teachers to examine and discuss relevant journal articles or books and then consider its merits for their faculty and students. Such frequent, shared experiences can nurture collegiality, strengthen unity of purpose, and fortify the culture.

Make Professional Development Meaningful to Teachers

Effective professional development (PD) is central to effective teaching; it is not an "add-on." Researchers and practitioners agree: the most useful PD for teachers is sustained, job-embedded, and collaborative with a focus on student learning. It emphasizes active hands-on teaching, assessment, observation, and reflection (rather than "sit-and-listen" to abstract discussions or motivational speeches).

In PLCs, with mutually respectful and trusting environments, teachers can coach, mentor, and observe each other in daily practice. Combining lesson study, regular peer observations of teaching, with feedback about strengths, and collegial assistance in making needed improvements, well designed and led PLCs can profoundly impact teachers' knowledge, skills, and dispositions. Moreover, PLCs have measurable benefits for student learning. If school leaders provide sufficient rationale, resources, and time for teacher leaders to read, discuss, think, plan, and apply what they are learning, they can design (and lead) PLCs that work for their faculty.

Develop Comfort And Expertise in Today's Leadership Roles

At its heart, leadership is about providing direction and exercising influence. School leaders affect student achievement to the extent that they inspire teachers' motivation and commitment and establish the working conditions that enable teachers to improve their teaching and students' learning.

Some principals may have to shift their leadership thinking from the traditional administrative/managerial "*I'm in charge*," "*I have the answers*," and "*I will direct the work*" model to a more collaborative, "*We are in this together*" and "Let *us* learn *with* and *from* one another" model. Shared leadership with teachers for improving instruction brings more teacher efficacy and better student outcomes.

In this shared leadership role, principals keep their responsibility for developing a common purpose among their faculty and staff. Working with teachers to set a vision and develop a sense of mutual goals, values, and collective responsibilities for improving student learning remains a priority. It is this shared direction—and the process of continually defining and sustaining it throughout the educators' activities—that shapes and bolsters the culture that nurtures teacher and student learning.

Next, effective leadership means developing people. Principals recognize teachers with leadership potential, provide occasions for them to enact leadership, and offer guidance and constructive feedback on what these maturing teacher leaders do well and what skills they need to refine. Personally making time for one-on-one conversations, coaching, and mentoring relationships to deepen teachers' leadership perspectives, knowledge, and skills also builds teacher leadership capacity.

Teachers' pathways to increased responsibilities and influence tend to remain classroom connected. In addition to leading PLCs, teachers grow their leadership capacity when they work with building, district, and central office colleagues to review and ensure program coherence and to assess and update technical resources to supplement curriculum and instruction. With influence lying in their professional expertise and social capital, teachers remain collaboratively linked with—and accountable to—their professional colleagues and students as well as to their principals.

Importantly, the proverbial "buck" for school success still stops at the principal's desk. Only by focusing on developing individual, collective, and organizational capacity can principals ensure that every student, every year, works with motivated and effective teachers and leaders.

Remain Alert to Practices That Deny Capacity Building Opportunities

Despite their seeming neutrality, organizations often have formal policies and procedures, informal work practices and norms, and work patterns that limit opportunities for professional learning, career advancement, and power and influence for women, African American, Hispanic, and "other" persons deemed to be outside society's traditional mainstream. These organizational elements often reflect deeply embedded social biases and inaccurate beliefs about gender, class, racial/ethnic, and sexual orientations. School leaders are obliged to notice—*and challenge*—so-called "colorblind" or "meritocracy" policies and practices that unfairly distribute resources and rationalize existing gender and racial/ethnic power in their organization.

If as much as 90 percent of career learning and development occurs on the job, principals are well positioned to build organizational capacity when they understand its value to their school and the ways they can make it happen.

NOTES

1 Valcour, M. (2014, January 23). If you're not helping people develop, you're not management material. *Harvard Business Review.* Retrieved from: https://hbr.org/2014/01/if-youre-not-helping-people-develop-youre-not-management-material/.

2 Gallup. (2013). *State of the American workplace. Employee engagement insights for U.S. Business Leaders.* Washington, DC: Gallup. Retrieved from: www.ctdol.state.ct.us/osha/Breakfast/Archives/11-18-14/State_of_the_American_Workplace_Report_2013.pdf.

3 Sorenson, S. (2014, February 20). How employees' strengths make your company stronger. *Gallup Business Journal.* Retrieved from: www.gallup.com/businessjournal/167462/employees-strengths-company-stronger.aspx.

4 Gallup (2013). Op. cit.

5 Sorenson (2014, February 20). Op. cit.

6 Senge, P.M. (1990). The leader's new work: Building learning organizations. *Sloan Management Review, 32* (1). Reprint Series Retrieved from: www.simpsonexecutivecoaching.com/pdf/orglearning/leaders-new-work-building-learning-organizations-peter-senge.pdf.

7 Danielson, C. (2007). *Enhancing professional practice: A framework for teaching,* 2nd ed. Alexandria, VA: ASCD, p. 15.

8 Capacity. Merriam-Webster. Retrieved from: www.merriam-webster.com/dictionary/capacity.

9 Barnes, C. (2002). Standards reform in high-poverty schools: Managing conflict and building capacity. New York, NY: Teachers College Press; Cohen, D.K. & Ball, D.L. (1999). Instruction capacity and improvement. CPRE Research Report Series (RR-043). Philadelphia, PA: Consortium for Policy Research in Education, University of Pennsylvania.

10 McDiarmid, G.W. & Clevenger-Bright, M. (2008) Rethinking teacher capacity. In M. Cochran-Smith, S. Feiman-Nemser & D.J. McIntyre (Eds). *Handbook on research on teacher education. Enduring questions in changing contexts,* 3rd ed. (pp. 134–156). New York, NY: Routledge.

11 Newmann, F.M., King, M.B. & Youngs, P. (2000). Professional development that addresses school capacity: Lessons from urban elementary schools. *American Journal of Education*, *108* (4), pp. 259–299.

12 See: Bryk, A.S., Sebring, P.B., Allensworth, E., Luppescu, S. & Easton, J.Q. (2010). *Organizing schools for improvement: Lessons from Chicago*, University of Chicago Press, Chicago, IL; King, M.B. (2002). Professional development to promote school wide inquiry. *Teaching and Teacher Education*, *18* (3), 243–257; Newman et al. (2000). Op. cit.

13 King, M.B. & Bouchard, K. (2011). The capacity to build organizational capacity in schools. *Journal of Educational Administration*, *49* (6), 653–669.

14 Seashore Louis, K. & Marks, H.M. (1998). Does professional community affect the classroom? Teachers' work and student experiences in restructuring schools. *American Journal of Education*, *106* (4), 532–575.

15 See: Childress, S., Elmore, R.F., Grossman, A.S. & Johnson, S.M. (2007). *Managing school districts for high performance: Cases in public education leadership*. Cambridge, MA: Harvard Education Press; Newmann, F.M., Smith, B., Allensworth, E. & Bryk, A.S. (2001). Instructional program coherence: What it is and why it should guide school improvement policy. *Educational Evaluation and Policy Analysis*, *23* (4), 297–321.

16 Leithwood, K., Louis, K.S., Anderson, S. & Wahlstrom, K. (2004). *Review of research. How leadership influences student learning*. Center for Applied Research and Educational Improvement, University of Minnesota. Retrieved from: http://conservancy.umn.edu/bitstream/handle/11299/2035/CAREI%20ReviewofResearch%20How%20Leadership%20Influences.pdf?sequence=1&isAllowed=y.

17 Leithwood, K.A. & Riehl, C. (2003, Autumn). *What we know about successful school leadership*. A report by Division A of AERA, p. 6. Retrieved from: http://dcbsimpson.com/randd-leithwood-successful-leadership.pdf.

18 See: Datnow, A. (2005). The sustainability of comprehensive school reform models in changing district and state contexts. *Educational Administration Quarterly*, *41* (1), 121–153; Fullan, M. (2005). *Leadership and sustainability*. Thousand Oaks, CA: Corwin Press; Hightower, A., Knapp, M., Marsh, J. & McLaughlin, M. (2002). The district role in instructional renewal: Setting the stage for dialogue. In A. Hightower, M. Knapp, J. Marsh & M. McLaughlin (Eds), *School districts and instructional renewal* (pp. 193–201). New York, NY: Teachers College.

19 Senge, P. (1990). *The fifth discipline*. New York, NY: Doubleday.

20 See: Marzano, R., Pickering, D. & Pollock, J. (2001). *Classroom instruction that works*. Alexandria, VA: Association for Supervision and Curriculum Development; Williams, J.D., Friesen, S. & Milton, P. (2009). *What did you do in school today? Transforming classrooms through social, academic, and intellectual engagement*. (First National Report). Toronto: Canadian Education Association.

21 Dibbon, D., Galway, G. & Warren, P. (2012). Towards a better future for all. In G. Galway & D. Dibbon (Eds), *Education reform: From rhetoric to reality*. London, ON: Althouse Press; Knapp, M. (1997). Between systemic reform and the mathematics and science classroom: The dynamics of innovation, implementation, and professional learning. *Review of Educational Research*, *67* (2), 227–266.

22 See: Kain, J.F. (1998, October). *The impact of individual teachers and peers on individual student achievement*. Paper presented at the Association for Public Policy Analysis and Management 20th Annual Research Conference, New York; McCaffrey et al. (2003). Op. cit.; Bembry, K.L., Jordan, H.R., Gomez, E., Anderson, M.C. & Mendro, R.L. (1998). *Policy implications of long-term teacher effects on student achievement*. Paper presented at the 1998 Annual Meeting of the American Educational Research Association, San Diego, CA, April 1998. Retrieved from: www.dallasisd.org/cms/lib/TX01001475/Centricity/Shared/evalacct/research/articles/Bembry-Policy-Implications-of-Long-Term-Teacher-Effects-on-Student-Achievement-1998.pdf.

23 Leithwood, Louis, Anderson & Wahlstrom (2004). Op. cit.; Seashore-Louis, K, Leithwood, K., Wahlstrom, K. & Anderson, S.E. (2010). *Investigating the links to improved student learning. Final report of research findings.* New York, NY: The Wallace Foundation. Retrieved from: www.wallacefoundation.org/knowledge-center/school-leadership/key-research/Docu ments/Investigating-the-Links-to-Improved-Student-Learning.pdf.

24 Leithwood, K., Day, C., Sammons, P., Harris, A. & Hopkins, D. (2006). *Seven strong claims about successful school leadership.* United Kingdom: National College for School Leadership. Retrieved from: http://dera.ioe.ac.uk/6967/1/download%3Fid%3D17387%26filename%3D seven-claims-about-successful-school-leadership.pdf.

25 Robinson, V. (2007). The impact of leadership on student outcomes: Making sense of the evidence. *The Leadership Challenge—Improving learning in schools.* Auckland, New Zealand: Australian Council for Educational Research. Retrieved from: http://research.acer. edu.au/cgi/viewcontent.cgi?article=1006&context=research_conference_2007; Robinson, V.M.J., Lloyd, C.A. & Rowe, K.J. (2008). The impact of leadership on student outcomes: An analysis of the differential effects of leadership types. *Educational Administration Quarterly, 44* (5), 635–674. The effect sizes for instructional leadership on student outcomes were found, on average, to be three times larger, than the effect sizes for transformational leadership. The study limitations included a small number of published studies (22) and effect size statistics (12).

26 Leithwood, Day, Sammons, Harris & Hopkins (2006). Op. cit.

27 Garet, M., Porter, A., Desimone, L., Birman, B. & Suk Yoon, K. (2001). What makes professional development effective? Results from a national sample of teachers. *American Educational Research Journal, 38* (4), 915–945; Penuel, W., Fishman, B., Yamaguchi, R. & Gallagher, L. (2007). What makes professional development effective? Strategies that foster curriculum implementation. *American Educational Research Journal, 44* (4), 921–958.

28 Leithwood, Day, Sammons, Harris & Hopkins (2006). Op. cit.

29 Seashore-Louis, Leithwood, Wahlstrom & Anderson (2010). Op. cit.; Day, C., Stobart, G., Sammons, P., Kington, A. & Gu, Q. (2006). *Variations in teachers' work and lives and their effects on pupils: VITAE Report* (DfES Research Report 743), London, UK: Department for Education and Skills.

30 Brookhart, S. (2009). *Exploring formative feedback the professional learning community series.* Alexandria, VA: ASCD; Eaker, R., DuFour, R. & DuFour, R. (2002). *Getting started: Reculturing schools to become professional learning communities.* Bloomington, IN: Solution Tree.

31 DuFour, R., DuFour, R., Eaker, R. & Many, T. (2010). *Learning by doing: A handbook for professional learning communities at work.* Bloomington, IN: Solution Tree.

32 DuFour, DuFour, Eaker & Many (2010). Op. cit.

33 Vescio, V., Ross, D. & Adams, A. (2008). A review of research on the impact of professional learning communities on teaching practice and student learning. *Teaching and Teacher Education, 24* (1), 80–91; Darling-Hammond, L. & Richardson, N. (2009). Research review. Teacher learning: What matters? *How Teachers Learn, 66* (5), 46–53.

34 Vescio, Ross & Adams (2008). Ibid.

35 Dunne, F., Nave, B. & Lewis, A. (2000). Critical friends groups: Teachers helping teachers to improve student learning. *Phi Delta Kappa Research Bulletin, 28* (1), 9–12; Englert, C.S. & Tarrant, K.L. (1995). Creating collaborative cultures for educational change. *Remedial and Special Education, 16* (6), 325–336, 353; Hollins, E.R., McIntyre, L.R., DeBose, C., Hollins, K.S. & Towner, A. (2004). Promoting a self-sustaining learning community: Investigating an internal model for teacher development. *International Journal of Qualitative Studies in Education, 17* (2), 247–264; Louis, K.S. & Marks, H.M. (1998). Does professional learning community affect the classroom? Teachers' work and student experiences in restructuring schools. *American Journal of Education, 106* (4), 532–575; Strahan, D. (2003). Promoting a collaborative professional culture in three elementary schools that have beaten the odds. *The Elementary School Journal, 104* (2), 127–146.

36 See: Louis & Marks (1998). Op. cit.; Berry, B., Johnson, D. & Montgomery, D. (2005). The power of teacher leadership. *Educational Leadership*, 62 (5), 56–60; Bolam, R., McMahon, A., Stoll, L., Thomas, S., Wallace, M., Hawkey, K. & Greenwood, A. (2005). *Creating and sustaining professional learning communities. Research Report Number 637.* London, UK: General Teaching Council for England, Department for Education and Skills; Dunne, Nave, & Lewis (2000). Op. cit.; Supovitz, J.A. (2002). Developing communities of instructional practice. *Teachers College Record*, 104 (8), 1591–1626.

37 See: Berry, Johnson & Montgomery (2005). Op. cit.; Bolam, McMahon, Stoll, Thomas & Wallace (2005). Op. cit.; Hollins, McIntyre, DeBose, Hollins & Towner (2004). Op. cit.; Louis & Marks (1998). Op. cit.; Phillips, J. (2003). Powerful learning: Creating learning communities in urban school reform. *Journal of Curriculum and Supervision*, 18 (3), 240–258.

38 *Authentic pedagogy* was defined as emphasizing higher order thinking, the construction of meaning through conversation, and developing depth of knowledge beyond the classroom.

39 Seashore Louis, Leithwood, Wahlstrom & Anderson (2010). Op. cit.

40 Heck, R.H. & Hallinger, P. (2007). Assessing the contribution of distributed leadership to school improvement and growth in math achievement. *American Educational Research Journal*, 46 (3), 659–689.

41 Hawley, W.D. & Valli, L. (1999). The essentials of effective professional development: A new consensus. In L. Darling-Hammond & G. Sykes (Eds), *Teaching as the learning profession: Handbook for policy and practice* (pp. 127–150). San Francisco: Jossey-Bass; Darling-Hammond & Richardson (2009). Op. cit.

42 See: Hord, S. (1997). *Professional learning communities: Communities of continuous inquiry and improvement.* Austin, TX: Southwest Educational Development Laboratory; Sherin, M.G. (2004). New perspectives on the role of video in teacher education. In J. Brophy (Ed.), *Using video in teacher education: Advances in research on teaching*, 10 (1), 1–27. Oxford: Elsevier Press; Sato, M., Wei, R.C. & Darling-Hammond, L. (2008). Improving teachers' assessment practices through professional development: The case of National Board Certification. *American Educational Research Journal*, 45 (3), 669–700.

43 Strahan (2003). Op. cit.

44 Phillips (2003). Op. cit.

45 Darling-Hammond, L. & McLaughlin, M.W. (1995). Policies that support professional development in an era of reform. *Phi Delta Kappan*, 76 (8), 597–604.

46 Blank, R.K., de las Alas, N. & Smith, C. (2007). *Analysis of the quality of professional development programs for mathematics and science teachers.* Washington, DC: Council of Chief State School Officers; Wenglinsky, H. (2000). *How teaching matters: Bringing the classroom back into discussions of teacher quality.* Princeton, NY: Milken Family Foundation and Educational Testing Service.

47 Metropolitan Life Insurance Company (2013). *The MetLife survey of the American teacher: Challenges for school leadership.* New York, NY: MetLife. Retrieved from: www.metlife. com/assets/cao/foundation/MetLife-Teacher-Survey-2012.pdf.

48 Lambert, L. (1998). *Building leadership capacity in schools.* Alexandria, VA: ASCD, pp. 3–4.

49 Katzenmeyer, M. & Moller, G. (2009). *Awakening the sleeping giant: Helping teachers develop as leaders.* Thousand Oaks, CA: Corwin.

50 Murphy, J. (2005). *Connecting teacher leadership to school improvement.* Thousand Oaks, CA: Corwin.

51 Katzenmeyer & Moller (2009). Op. cit.

52 See: LeBlanc, P.R. & Shelton, M.M. (1997). Teacher leadership: The needs of teachers. *Action in Teacher Education*, 19 (1), 32–48; Lieberman, A., Saxl, E.R. & Miles, M.B. (2000). Teacher leadership: Ideology and practice. In *The Jossey-Bass reader on educational leadership* (pp. 339–345). San Francisco, CA: Jossey-Bass.

53 Danielson, C. (2006). *Teacher leadership that strengthens professional practice.* Alexandria, VA: ASCD.

54 See: Leithwood, K., Harris, A. & Strauss, T. (2010). *Leading school turnaround*. San Francisco, CA: Jossey-Bass; Leithwood, K., Patten, S. & Jantzi, D. (2010). Testing a conception of how school leadership influences student learning. *Educational Administration Quarterly*, 46 (5), 671–706; Lieberman, A. & Miller, L. (2004). *Teacher leadership*. San Francisco, CA: Jossey-Bass.

55 Smylie, M.A. (1994). Redesigning teachers' work: Connections to the classroom. In L. Darling-Hammond (Ed.), *Review of Research in Education*, 20, 129–177.

56 Porter, A.C. (1986). Teacher collaboration: New partnership to attack old problems. *Phi Delta Kappan*, 69 (2), 147–152.

57 LeBlanc & Shelton (1997). Op. cit.

58 Porter (1986). Op. cit.

59 See: Duke, D.L. (1994). Drift, detachment, and the need for teacher leadership. In D.R. Walling (Ed.), *Teachers as leaders: Perspectives on the professional development of teachers* (pp. 255–273). Bloomington, IN: Phi Delta Kappa Educational Foundation; Smylie, M.A. (1992). Teachers' reports of their interactions with teacher leaders concerning classroom instruction. *Elementary School Journal*, 93 (1), 85–98.

60 York-Barr, J. & Duke, K. (2004). What do we know about teacher leadership? Findings from two decades of scholarship. *Review of Educational Research*, 74 (3), 255–316.

61 See: DuFour, R., DuFour, R., Karhanek, G. & Eaker, R. (2010). *Raising the bar and closing the gap: Whatever it takes*. Bloomington, IN: Solution Tree; Leithwood, K., Harris, A. & Strauss, T. (2010). *Leading school turnaround*. San Francisco, CA: Jossey-Bass; Leithwood, Patten & Jantzi (2010). Op. cit.; Murphy (2005). Op. cit.; Smylie, M. (2010). *Continuous school improvement*. Thousand Oaks, CA: Corwin.

62 York-Barr & Duke (2004). Op. cit.; Heck, R.H. & Hallinger, P. (2007). Assessing the contribution of distributed leadership to school improvement and growth in math achievement. *American Educational Research Journal*, 46 (3), 659–689.

63 Heck & Hallinger (2007). Ibid.

64 Hallinger, P. & Heck, R. (2010). Collaborative leadership and school improvement: Understanding the impact on school capacity and student learning. *School Leadership and Management*, 30 (2), 95–110.

65 Leithwood, K. & Mascall, B. (2008). Collective leadership effects on student achievement. *Educational Administration Quarterly*, 44 (4), 529–561.

66 In this study, shared leadership included school and central office administrators, teacher leaders in formal positions, teacher grade level and department teams, certain individual teachers, certain individual parents, parent-teacher-student groups, and students.

67 Seashore-Louis, Leithwood, Wahlstrom & Anderson (2010). Op. cit.

68 Leithwood, K., Harris, A. & Hopkins, D. (2008). Seven strong claims about successful school leadership. *School Leadership and Management*, 28 (1), 27–42. Retrieved from: www.researchgate.net/profile/Alma_Harris/publication/251888122_Seven_strong_claims_about_successful_school_leadership/links/0deec5388768e8736d000000.pdf.

69 Robinson, V.J. (2010). From instructional leadership to leadership capabilities: Empirical findings and methodological challenges. Retrieved from: http://galileo.org/wp-content/uploads/2015/01/Robinson-2010-From-instructional-leadership-to-leadership-capabilities-Empirical-findings-and-methodological-challenges.pdf.

70 Robinson, V.M.J., Lloyd, C. & Rowe, K.J. (2008). The impact of leadership on student outcomes: An analysis of the differential effects of leadership type. *Educational Administration Quarterly*, 44 (5), 635–674.

71 Copland, M.A. (2003). Leadership of inquiry: Building and sustaining capacity for school improvement. *Educational Evaluation and Policy Analysis*, 25 (4), 375–395. Retrieved from: www.studentachievement.org/wp-content/uploads/Leadership-of-Inquiry-Copland.pdf.

72 See: Deal, T.E. & Peterson, K.D. (1998). *Shaping school culture: The heart of leadership*. San Francisco: Jossey-Bass; Fullan, M.G. (2001a). *Leading in a culture of change*. San

Francisco: Jossey-Bass; Fullan, M.G. (200lb). *The new meaning of educational change*, 3rd ed. New York, NY: Teachers College Press; York-Barr & Duke (2004). Op. cit.

73 Smylie, M.A. (1992). Teachers' reports of their interactions with teacher leaders concerning classroom instruction. *Elementary School Journal*, 93 (1), 85–98.

74 Ovando, M. (1994). *Effects of teacher leaders on their teaching practice*. Paper presented at the annual meeting of the University Council of Educational Administration, Philadelphia, PA; Louis, K.S., Kruse, S. & Raywid, M. (1996, May). Putting teachers at the center of reform: Learning schools and professional communities. *NASSP Bulletin*, 80 (580), 10–21.

75 Cuban, L. (1988). *The managerial imperative and the practice of leadership in schools*. Albany, NY: State University of New York Press.

76 Bryk, Sebring, Allensworth, Luppescu & Easton (2010). Op. cit.

77 Lieberman, A. & Miller, L. (1999). *Teachers: Transforming their world and their work*. New York, NY: Teachers College Press; Little, J.W. (1988). Assessing the prospects for teacher leadership. In A. Liebman (Ed.), *Building a professional culture in schools* (pp. 78–106). New York, NY: Teachers College Press; Moller, G. & Katzenmeyer, M. (1996). The promise of teacher leadership. *New Directions for School Leadership*, 1 (1), 1–17.

78 Duke (1994). Op. cit.

79 Owings, W.A. & Kaplan, L.S. (2012). *Leadership and organizational behavior. Theory into practice* (pp. 260–264). Upper Saddle River, NJ: Pearson.

80 Reeves, D. (2009). *Leading change in your school*. (pp. 72–74). Alexandria, VA: ASCD.

81 Daresh, J.C. (1995). Research based on mentoring for educational leaders: What do we know? *Journal of Educational Administration*, 33 (5), 6–16.

82 Ingersoll, R. & Strong, M. (2011). The impact of induction and mentoring programs for beginning teachers: A critical review of the research. *Review of Education Research*, 81 (2), 201–233.

83 A discussion of feminist theory and organizational capacity building appears on the book's companion website.

84 Berman (2015, February 2). Op. cit.

85 Wallace, G. (2014, October 1). Wall street still hires mostly white men. *CNN Money*. Retrieved from: http://money.cnn.com/2014/10/01/investing/wall-street-diversity-problem/ index.html?iid=EL. By contrast, the prison population is more than 60 percent racial and ethnic minorities. See: Racial disparity. (2016, January 20). The sentencing project. Research and advocacy for reform. Retrieved from: www.sentencingproject.org/template/page.cfm? id=122.

86 Berman (2015). Op. cit. The Executive Leadership Council is an organization that represents top black executives in the *Fortune 500* companies.

87 Delgado, R. & Stefancic, J. (2012). *Critical race theory. An introduction*. (2nd ed.) New York, NY: New York University Press; Litowitz, D.E. (1997). Some critical thoughts on critical race theory. *Notre Dame Law Review*, 72 (2), 503. CRT builds on the insights from the earlier movements—critical legal studies and radical feminism, from the American radical tradition (i.e., Frederick Douglass, W.E.B. DuBois, Cesar Chavez, Martin Luther King, Jr., and the 1960s and 1970s Black Power and Chicano movements), and from certain European philosophers and theorists.

88 Marable, M. (1992). *Black America* (p. 5). Westfield, NJ: Open Media.

89 Yosso T.J. & Solorzano, D.G. (2007). Conceptualizing a critical race theory in sociology. In M. Romero & E. Margolis. (Eds). *The Blackwell companion to social inequalities*. (pp. 117–146). Malden, MA: Blackwell Publishing.

90 Solorzano, D.G. (1997). Images and words that wound: Critical race theory, racial stereotyping, and teacher education. *Teacher Education Quarterly*, 24 (3), 5–19.

91 A discussion of critical race theory's views of institutionalized racism in schools appears in this book's companion website.

92 Davis, P. (1989). Law as microaggression. *Yale Law Journal, 98* (8), 1559–1577; Lawrence, C. (1987). The id, the ego, and equal protection: Reckoning with unconscious racism. *Stanford Law Review, 39* (2), 317–388.

93 Lynn, M. (1999). Toward a critical race pedagogy. A research note. *Urban Education, 33* (5), 606–626.

94 Crenshaw (2011). Op. cit.; Crenshaw, K. (1995). *Critical race theory: The key writings that formed the movement.* New York, NY: The New Press.

95 Matsuda, M. (1991). Voices of America: Accent, antidiscrimination law, and a jurisprudence for the last reconstruction. *Yale Law Journal, 100* (5), 1329–1407.

96 Brophy, A. (2008, May 11). Derrick Bell and James Madison on interest convergence. *Diverse: Issues in Higher Education.* Retrieved from: https://diverseeducation.wordpress.com/2008/05/11/derrick-bell-and-james-madison-on-interest-convergence/.

97 Ikemoto L. (1992). Furthering the inquiry: Race, class, and culture in the forced medical treatment of pregnant women. *Tennessee Law Review, 59* (3), 487–519; Chang, R. (1993). Toward an Asian American legal scholarship: Critical race theory, post-structuralism, and narrative space. *California Law Review, 81* (5), 1241–1323; Delgado, R. (1997). Rodrigo's fifteenth chronicle: Racial mixture, Latino-critical scholarship, and the black-white binary. *Texas Law Review, 75* (5), 1181–1201.

98 Crenshaw, K. (2011). Twenty years of critical race theory: Looking back to move forward. *Connecticut Law Review, 43 (5),* 1253–1352.

99 Gotanda, N. (1991). A critique of "Our constitution is color-blind." *Stanford Law Review, 44* (1), 1–68.

100 Bernstein, D. (2014, February19). "Entrenched anti-Semitic views" very rare among whites and Asian Americans, common among blacks, and Latinos. *The Washington Post.* Retrieved from: www.washingtonpost.com/news/volokh-conspiracy/wp/2014/02/19/entrenched-anti-semitic-views-very-rare-among-whites-and-asian-americans-common-among-blacks-and-latinos/; Gallup Editors. (2014, December 12). Gallup review: Black and white differences in views on race. *Gallup Politics.* Retrieved from: www.gallup.com/poll/180107/gallup-review-black-white-differences-views-race.aspx; Krogstad, J.M. (2015, February 27). *Hispanics more likely than whites to say global warming is caused by humans.* Pew Research Center. FactTank. Retrieved from: www.pewhispanic.org/2012/04/04/when-labels-dont-fit-hispanics-and-their-views-of-identity/.

101 Subotnik, D. (1998). What's wrong with critical race theory: Reopening the case for middle class values. *Cornell Journal of Law and Public Policy, 7* (3), 681–756.

102 Litowitz, D.F. (1999). Some critical thoughts on critical race theory. *Notre Dame Law Review, 72* (2), 503–529; Subotnik (1998). Op. cit.

103 Subotnik (1998). Op. cit.

Problem Solving and Decision Making

PROFESSIONAL STANDARDS FOR EDUCATIONAL LEADERS:
1, 2, 3, 5, 6, 8, 9, 10

CASE STUDY 9.1

Problem Solving Components in Altavista Schools

The Altavista City houses four Fortune 500 company headquarters and the state's flagship university. A white-collar population with a per capita income of $62,300 and a median home value of $415,000, it is the wealthiest locality with the highest property tax rate in the state. The school system is the pride of the city. At least 10 percent of the graduating class received acceptances to Ivy League schools, and more than 95 percent of seniors go on to higher education every year. The Talented and Gifted (TAG) program has won national awards, and every school has received Blue Ribbon Status awards from the U.S. Department of Education. Less than 1 percent of the students qualify for Free or Reduced-Price lunch, and fewer than 5 percent are eligible for special education services. Demographically, the school community is 97 percent White, 1 percent African American, 1 percent Asian, and 1 percent Hispanic.

Recently, another major corporation purchased the last large tract of land for business use. Instead of announcing a corporate headquarters, they revealed that they would build a chicken processing plant largely employing low skilled, minimum wage jobs. Since the locality had few applicants to fill the new jobs, the company offered transfers to employees in other locales. Many immigrant families moved into Altavista for the job opportunities and a "nicer" community for their children. Within a year, the school demographics changed to 82 percent White, 6 percent African American, 1 percent Asian, and 11 percent Hispanic with 10 percent eligible for Free or Reduced-Price Lunch and 9 percent eligible for special education services. Demand grew for special education teachers, alternative programs, and remedial classes—straining an increasingly tight city budget in an election year.

The School Board asked for increased financial support to meet these growing needs. But with the highest property tax rate in the state, and the City Council members reluctant to increase the tax rate, they passed a level-funded budget. The School Board needed to decide whether to cut services for existing programs to meet the changing needs. Teachers became increasingly anxious about what changes might take place. Some felt the City should not take resources away—or change—the award winning programs to accommodate the "new" students. Others believed they had a professional responsibility to meet the new students' needs. Meanwhile, opposition candidates announced their intention to run against the School Board members who had asked for an increased budget. Since the School Board was also an elected body, and all seven members were up for election in November, and the Superintendent's contract was up for renewal the following June, the School Board decided to appoint a committee to make recommendations to address this situation.

The Superintendent has tasked you with heading this committee. Define the problem variations, the mental models and context variables, and the individual differences involved in forming this committee, the problem solving process you propose to use, and your recommendation for addressing expenditures to the Superintendent.

RUBRIC 9.1			
Lens and/or factors to be considered in decision making	What are the factors at play in this case?	What steps should be considered in solving the problem?	What could have been done to avoid this dilemma?
The situation			
• The task	This is a wicked (ill-structured), complex, and dynamic problem. Its context includes social, historical, cultural, and political issues.	Define the problem, list the contextual variables, determine committee selection criteria, and generate a recommendation for the Superintendent.	Once district officials knew that a processing plant was coming, they should have anticipated the workforce related demographic changes in the student body and made plans accordingly.
• Personal abilities	Do you and your committee members have the perspective, openness to new ideas, access to relevant data, and influence skills to make meaningful and acceptable recommendations to the superintendent, school board, teachers, and community about reallocating funds?	What criteria should be used to select committee members and what constituencies should be considered? Will the committee chair be able to achieve consensus with a feasible solution?	District officials always need to closely monitor events in their local and wider communities for possible implications for their schools.
• The school environment	Teachers, proud of their schools' successes, are uncertain about possible changes and, possibly, whether they can succeed with these new students.	Teachers will need to expand their cultural awareness, expand their instructional repertoires, and learn how to build an inclusive school community.	Had the student demographics been anticipated, professional development activities and other program issues could have begun with the faculty.
Look	**Wider**		
Organizational (i.e., the organizational goals, values, policies, culture)	Organizational change due to changing demographics and finance constraints are shaping the issue. The district and schools will have to develop a more inclusive culture with instructional, curricular, and behavioral practices.	First, the committee members must represents all key stakeholders. Next, members will need to build consensus for a plan that will continue academic excellence while meeting the more diverse students' needs.	Better communication between the City and the School Board might have alerted the school to a potential issue sooner and initiated timely and thoughtful planning. On-going professional development for teachers and leaders to expand their capacities.

continued . . .

People			
(i.e., individuals with needs, beliefs, goals, relationships)	The school board, superintendent, and principals will have to decide whether and how to allocate resources without undermining programs that made the district strong. Teachers may need to develop additional classroom skills. Students and parents may have to adjust to include a new set of students.	All constituent groups need to be represented—City Council, School Board, educators (those who see the need to address new students' needs and those who want to continue tradition), parents (from both new and traditional groups), business, and local professors.	The school district could already have an advisory committee consisting of members from these representative groups working to advise the superintendent and board of relevant community and school concerns. The communication among these groups would already be in place.
Competing Interests			
(i.e., competing interests for power, influence, and resources)	School Board members have challengers in the next election if they support increased funding or reallocated resources to meet the demographic changes. Teachers will have to expand their awareness and instructional practices to help a wider array of students succeed.	Put open minded, influential representatives from various competing groups on the committee—including those who will implement changes—to review the situation, gather relevant data, and make appropriate recommendations to the superintendent.	Some teachers may resist changing their practices to help incoming students succeed. Principals and parents may see resource needs and allocations differently. New versus "old" parents may differ on how to reallocate resources, create a welcoming community for newcomers.
Tradition			
(i.e., school culture, rituals, meaning, heroes)	The school has a culture of high expectations for every student's academic success and well being. This culture needs to continue, but with additional academic and social supports for new students.	The district and schools can conduct orientations for new and current students and parents about the district's culture and everyone's role in supporting every child's ability to be successful in school.	The district could have been providing teachers with ongoing professional development about instructional and interpersonal practices to increase every student's learning.

OVERVIEW: DECISION MAKING IN ORGANIZATIONS

Albert Einstein, renowned theoretical physicist, once concluded, "If I were given one hour to save the planet, I would spend 59 minutes defining the problem and one minute resolving it." Likewise, Bernard Baruch, an American financier, philanthropist, and advisor to presidents Woodrow Wilson and Franklin D. Roosevelt, is said to have observed, "Whatever failures I have known, whatever errors I have committed, whatever follies I have witnessed in public and private life, have been the consequences of action without thought."[1] Learning how to solve problems effectively is an essential life skill. But, as these wise gentlemen remind us, before we can solve a problem successfully, we must first recognize and understand it.

In schools as in other organizations, the ability to solve the organization's problems with incisive, appropriate decisions is a key leadership competency. The current pace of educational change guarantees that school leaders will face an endless series of decisions. The increasing amounts of available, sophisticated data offer invaluable resources from which to identify problems and generate solutions. But, data can only inform, not drive, organizational decisions. Principals' and teachers' experiences, expertise, and understanding of the information—as well as awareness of countless factors beyond the data—are also critical to making decisions and solving problems.

Problem solving and decision making in schools is a time consuming, mentally rigorous, and emotionally exhausting process. What types of decisions do school leaders make? What factors do principals need to consider in problem solving? How does the decision model we learn in school fit with how people actually make decisions in the "real world"? Developing relevant mental models of the problem solving process—recognizing the components to consider, the social, environmental, and personal influences that affect the process and outcomes, and the types of thinking needed to find workable solutions—can help school leaders more confidently and skillfully address the array of issues they will confront in their leadership roles.

TYPES OF PROBLEMS IN SCHOOLS

Back in the day, when a sixth grader asked one of your authors, then a middle school assistant principal, "What is your job?" she replied, "To keep you safe and keep you learning." Although this simple, direct answer satisfied the student, it omits the immense set of complex arrangements, responsibilities, and problem solving for ideas, people, places, and things that make up school leadership.

The problems that principals face in school have changed over time. In 1940, teachers saw schools' most serious problems as children talking out of turn, chewing gum, making noise, and running in the halls.[2] More recently, surveys and national reports identify both familiar and new concerns, including lack of funding, poverty (a socioeconomic condition that heightens other risk factors that undermine children's school success),[3] effectively linking technology and education, and bullying.[4] And these serious problems do not begin to address the issues of increased accountability, educational standards, high stakes testing, and ensuring that every student is learning and academically successful. Then too, the "urgent but not important" day-to-day issues also compete for principals' attention: parents complain, teachers quarrel with department heads, and the bus garage calls at the last minute to cancel the day's field trip buses.

Although solving problems is arguably a school leader's most important cognitive activity, few principals actually learn how to solve school-based problems during their graduate programs. Those problems they do study tend to be well structured and fairly straightforward, very unlike those complex, poorly defined, and dynamic ones they find in their personal and professional lives.

9.1 REFLECTIONS AND RELEVANCE

The Top Five Problems in Your Current School

Today's schools are dealing with a wide scope of problems that interfere with student learning.

Working in groups of four, identify and briefly discuss the "Top 5" problems that your school is addressing in its efforts to educate every student. What problem or problems do you see in your school that is not currently noticed and addressed? When all groups have completed this task, work with the entire class to list all the "Top 5" most frequent problems your schools are addressing. What are the most difficult to resolve? What problems do you think your schools are overlooking? Who gets to decide what problems your school needs to address and what interventions to use? How does one become a member of this problem-identifying and decision-making group?

COMPONENTS OF PROBLEM SOLVING

Since Albert Einstein would spend his first 59 minutes defining the problem, it makes sense to first understand what a problem is and how to approach solving it. A *problem* is a matter or situation regarded as unwelcome or harmful that needs to be addressed and overcome.[5]

Because problems are not alike in content, form, or process, problem solving is not a uniform activity. Different types of problems require different types of solutions. Experienced problem solvers are successful because they recognize the type of problem they face and have an extensive range of solutions from which to draw. By contrast, novice problem solvers do not possess well-developed repertoires of conceptual problem models and cannot recognize problem types. As a result, they rely on general problem solving approaches, often with poor results.[6]

Likewise, individuals differ in their abilities and dispositions to solve problems. People vary in the types, amount, and complexity of the information they possess, in

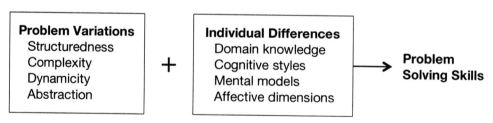

FIGURE 9.1 Components of Problem Solving Skills

Source: Based on Jonassen, D.H. (2000). Toward a design theory of problem solving. *Educational Technology Research and Development*, 48 (4), 63–85.

their cognitive styles, general problem solving strategies, self-confidence, and motivation or perseverance that influence the skills they bring to problem solving situations. David H. Jonassen (1947–2012), a University of Missouri information science professor, saw the ability to solve problems as a function of the problem's nature, how the problem is represented to the solver, and individual differences that mediate the process. Figure 9.1 illustrates this model.[7] Each of these factors will be discussed in turn.

Problem Variations

Problems vary in their nature. They may be clearly or poorly defined, routine or non-routine.[8] Problems also vary in the forms in which they appear and the knowledge and processes needed to solve them. They differ in complexity, from simple addition problems in elementary grades to complex social, economic, cultural, and political problems such as preventing civil wars. Intellectually, problems vary in at least four ways: structuredness, complexity, dynamicity, and context specificity or abstractness.[9] Each problem variation requires a different type of thinking.

Structuredness

Problems differ in how well they are configured, varying along a continuum from well structured to poorly structured. *Well-structured problems*, like those found in textbooks and in exams, are clearly defined, contain descriptions of all the relevant elements, and require applying a learned, limited, and known number of concepts, rules, and principles to a restricted problem situation. Here, (1) the problem solver sees all the problem elements; (2) solutions require a limited number of regular and well-defined rules and principles organized in predictive and prescriptive ways; and (3) the problems have knowable, comprehensible solutions. Solutions to well-structured problems are logical to the problem solver and have clear links between the nature of a problem and decision choices available.

In contrast, *ill-structured problems* (sometimes called "wicked problems") tend to appear in everyday and professional practice. They don't necessarily fit within one content domain. They contain elements that are unknown or unclear (or not known with any degree of confidence). They have multiple or no solutions, are open ended, and demand a high degree of judgment or personal beliefs in problem solving. They possess multiple criteria for evaluating solutions (so uncertainty exists about which concepts, rules, and principles are needed for the solution and how they are organized). Ill-structured problems also vary in the number of issues, functions, or variables involved; their degree of linkages; the nature of their functional relationships and stability over time; and how they are communicated to—and perceived by—problem solvers. As a result, their solutions are not predictable, convergent, or subject to a simple set of formal rules and principles. Because they are interdisciplinary, they may require the problem solver to integrate and apply concepts from several domains.

With the often ill-defined problems that we face in our homes and at work, the problem solver's challenge is to provide a structure where none is apparent. Contemporary research supports the view that well-structured and poorly structured problems tap different intellectual skills and thinking.[10]

Complexity

Problems vary in their intricacy. Problem solving complexity is a function of external factors, including the number of issues, functions, or variables the problem entails; the number of interactions and connections among these issues, functions, or variables; how clearly these variables are represented; and how consistently they behave over time.[11] Complexity also includes the problem's importance to the solver and the urgency or time frame within which it must be solved. Simple problems like those in textbooks typically have few variables. By comparison, complex problems may include many factors that interact in unpredictable ways. For instance, foreign policy issues tend to be complex and unpredictable. Problem difficulty is related to problem complexity.

Complex problems require more cognitive operations than simpler ones, placing a heavier cognitive load on the problem solver. Most textbook problems or graduate level simulations are well structured and relatively simple, with few variables to consider. In contrast, problems that appear in daily and professional life may be highly complex and ill structured, making heavier cognitive demands on the individual (and problem solving more difficult). This is why intensive, semester long or longer leadership internships with knowledgeable and involved, on-site mentors can prove invaluable learning experiences for future school leaders: the problems are authentic, ill structured, and often very complex. Ideally, experienced mentors help future leaders think through the problem, identify alternatives, and enact a workable solution.

Complexity and structure overlap. Ill-structured problems tend to be more complex, especially those that appear in everyday life—but they also may be quite simple. In turn, well-structured problems tend to be less complicated, but they can also be very complex. For instance, a social studies department whose members vigorously disagree about which textbook to adopt have a well-structured, complex problem. Deciding the date to hold the school's monthly fire drill is a well-structured, simple problem. In contrast, determining whether or not PTA embezzlement occurred at football games can be an ill-defined and complex problem.

Dynamicity

Problems may remain stable or may change over time. They vary in their stability or *dynamicity*. Problems may be dynamic because their conditions and contexts alter as time passes, and they become different problems. For example, a new principal brings to a school a fresh set of variables. Festering problems from the former principal's leadership style or ideas may end or reappear in new forms, and the new principal's personality and expectations for teachers may generate additional concerns.

Ill structured problems tend to be more dynamic than well-structured problems that tend to be static. The task environment and its factors shift with time. When the problem conditions change, the solver must continue to adapt his/her understanding of the problem while trying to find new solutions because the "tried-and-true" solutions may no longer work. For instance, smart phones complicate the process of keeping students' attention focused on their lessons because parents insist that safety requires their children keep their phones on their persons while at school. Two decades ago, personal cell phones were not widely available. By contrast, static problems have stable factors over time.

Context Specificity/Abstractness

Most contemporary research and theory in problem solving assert that problem-solving skills are domain and context specific; their solutions depend on having context or domain knowledge and cognitive operations specific to that domain.[12] Research finds that different graduate disciplines teach different forms of reasoning.[13] Graduate educational leadership students learn different types of problem solving for different circumstances and settings than do graduate mechanical engineers. And physicians preparing to work in an upscale Chicago hospital will learn different sets of diagnostic knowledge than a doctor planning to work in a Haitian clinic. Context also affects the types of social interactions and cognitive processing. Mathematicians solve problems differently from sociologists. Engineers at General Motors solve problems differently than shippers at Amazon. Different organizations have different structures, cultures, and sociological mixes. These factors all affect the kinds of problems that arise and how people solve them.

Context plays a larger role in real world problem solving than in textbook problems. For instance, middle school principals cannot ensure that students from different grade levels do not meet and socialize during lunch periods unless the schedules for grades six, seven, and eight (enforced by teachers' supervision) strictly control seventh and eighth graders' movements in the halls before and after grade six lunch periods.

Thus, problems within a domain or context vary in terms of their structuredness, complexity, and dynamicity. They also vary by their settings. Which set of conditions affect problems more—context or problem type—is not known.

Individual Differences

Individual differences mediate the ways people approach and conduct problem solving. A host of individual characteristics—familiarity, specific types of knowledge, cognitive styles, and affective dimensions—influence how a person solves problems.

Familiarity

Arguably, experience with the type of problem is the strongest predictor of problem solving ability. Those with understanding in a certain domain have better developed mental maps that they can apply more rapidly. This familiarity solving particular types of problems may not transfer to other kinds of problems, however. For instance, assistant principals with several years experience working with parents to resolve conflicts with teachers will likely work through these difficulties more quickly and successfully than a novice assistant principal. But the veteran AP may not be able to resolve as quickly an angry, tearful argument between two upset teachers. In addition, routine problems appear well structured to experienced problem solvers, and their skills are more easily transferable to new yet similar situations. By contrast, applying problem-solving skills to nonroutine situations takes more conscious attention and effort.

Knowledge

How much a person knows about the problematic issue is another strong predictor of successful problem solving. The more one knows about a certain subject or content (i.e., domain knowledge and skills), the better the individual can understand the problem and generate workable solutions. It is especially helpful when the person has integrated the domain knowledge, recognizing how different concepts within the topic relate to each other. Assistant principals who understand that middle school students typically care more about their friends' approval than their teachers' regard will discretely escort students from their classrooms to the APs' offices (or other safe and private location) before interviewing them about a disciplinary matter. Research suggests that this integrated knowledge may be a stronger predictor of problem solving than familiarity.[14]

Cognitive Styles

Individuals also vary in their patterns of thinking that control the ways they process and reason about information. Without getting into the cognitive psychology weeds, *cognitive controls*—such as whether the person tends to primarily focus on the immediate object or the surrounding environment, whether the person has the mental capacity or temperament to think about complex issues, and the individual's cognitive flexibility in juggling several ideas at once—all impact their problem solving effectiveness. Research finds that those who can look for clues in the environment (i.e., are field independent) are better problem solvers than those that focus only on the main object (i.e., field dependent).[15] It also seems logical that individuals with higher cognitive flexibility and cognitive complexity would be better problem solvers than others who prefer cognitive simplicity because the former can consider more alternatives at the same time and be more analytical with the facts at hand.[16]

Mental Models

Problem solving requires making a mental model or *representation* of the problem and its context. These mental models consist of various types of knowledge—including facts about the problem and its structure, how to perform tests and other problem solving activities, the problem's environment, and knowledge of how and when to use certain procedures. The problem's environment often contains social, historical, cultural influences, and other cues that may facilitate—or hinder—problem solving. Time is also a factor: Is the solution needed immediately or do problem solvers have time—and how much—to design and enact a workable solution?

Experienced problem solvers, familiar with how the predicament presents itself, can quickly integrate these different kinds of knowledge with their mental model of the problem. They separate the relevant from the irrelevant information in the context. They cognitively manipulate and test their models, trying out solutions in their minds before testing them in the real world. And they recognize that if problems differ in structure, complexity, and content, problem-solving processes must differ also. Of course, certain problems have no clear or easily identifiable path to their solution: educated guesses, trial-and-error, and intuitive judgments based on experience are needed to find workable answers.

Other Individual Differences

Although cognitive processes are necessary for problem solving, they are not sufficient. This is especially true for solving ill-structured, complex challenges. For these problems, individuals also need certain affective and motivational elements. A person's motivation to solve the problem—including interest in solving it, knowing how to solve it, having the self-confidence in their knowledge and skills to act intentionally, make choices, and exert effort and persistence in the face of obstacles or lack of quick success—come into play. Task persistence and effort are strong predictors of problem solving success. And as with most performances, a person's state characteristics—such as fatigue, anxiety, and stress—also affect their problem solving performance in a curvilinear fashion. Research suggests that perceived psychological stress and problem solving coping behaviors have an inverted-U-shaped relationship. Performance effectiveness has an optimum level of stress. As perceived stress goes up beyond a "moderate" level, "stress overload" develops, and problem-solving effectiveness goes down.[17]

Research and Criticism

Critics conclude that Jonassen supports his observations about problems and problem solving process with relevant literature.[18] At the same time, critics note that much of what Jonassen proposes about how to solve ill-structured problems has not been empirically validated—even though anecdotal evidence suggests that they work.[19] Nonetheless, Jonassen's clearly defined aspects of problems and variables used in the problem solving process provide a useful framework upon which to advance more thoughtful study of problem solving for leadership purposes.

9.2 REFLECTIONS AND RELEVANCE

Assessing Your Problem Solving Skills

Problems vary and so do individuals' abilities and dispositions to solve them. Review Figure 9.1, "Components of Problem Solving Skills" and the discussion of factors that follows. Then, working alone for approximately 10 minutes, recall a problem you recently solved or are still solving at your school. Assess yourself on the *problem variables* and *individual differences* on a scale from 1–5, 1 = needs growth, 5 = very competent. After the self-assessment, work in pairs to discuss your findings. Then, as a class, identify the range of problems and the variations and individual differences that you and your classmates are addressing at school. How, if at all, does the nature of problems and individual differences vary with the level of school in which you work? What does this self-assessment activity tell you about yourselves as problem solvers? What aspects do you want to improve, and how do you develop this capacity?

RATIONALITY AND DECISION MAKING

As generally understood, a person is *rational* to the extent that he or she chooses means effective to realize his or her goals.[20] *Reason* is the mind's power to think, understand, and infer, especially in orderly ways.[21] Problems are assumed to have single correct answers based on logical solutions. With cognitive learning theory, scholars came to see problem solving as a complex mental activity that included higher order thinking skills—such as visualization, association, abstraction, manipulation, reasoning, analysis, synthesis, evaluation, and generalization—each to be managed or coordinated.[22] As discussions of classical decision making, bounded rationality, and sensemaking will show, as the view of human rationality shifts, so do ideas of how people make decisions and solve problems.[23]

Classical Decision-Making Theory

During the 1960s and 1970s, investigators developed general models to explain problem-solving processes. These researchers assumed that one could use a simple, abstract, content-free, and decontextualized problem-solving paradigm that could transfer to any situation. Today, we know this as classical decision-making theory.

Assuming that decision makers act in a world of complete certainty, classical decision-making theory asserts that decision making should be completely rational and use optimizing steps to identify the best possible alternative to achieve the desired organizational goals. It contains the following sequential steps:

1. Identify the problem.
2. Establish goals and objectives.
3. Generate all possible alternatives.
4. Consider possible outcomes for each alternative.
5. Evaluate each alternative in terms of goals and objectives.
6. Choose the best alternative, that is, the one that maximizes the goals and objectives.
7. Implement and evaluate the decision.

Although still used in academic and corporate training settings, the classical decision-making model has come into disfavor. Late twentieth and early twenty-first century scholars identify several limits in its use for decision making and problem solving.[24] To begin, critics deem rationalistic models impractical: collecting, reviewing, and evaluating all the necessary data and weighing all the possible options to find an optimal solution is seldom plausible in terms of cost, time, and human capacity. Many find the model too narrow, lacking awareness of environmental, situational, political, or personal constraints that impact decision making. They censure its utopian, idealistic vision of decision making that ignores unintended consequences and does not mesh with how people actually decide. Likewise, the model's rigidity draws unrealistic separations between ends and means, values, and decisions, and facts and values. Critics also challenge its value bias, favoring rationality over other types of cognition. In fact, no consensus exists that rationality is a universal good. Nor can people even agree on its definition.[25]

Given these very real drawbacks, organizational thinkers designed alternatives to the classical decision model—options that included non-rational approaches. Chester Barnard, Herbert Simon, and Karl Weick would argue cogently that rationality in problem solving has its limits and offer decision makers alternate models or considerations that work within these real world constraints.[26]

Chester I. Barnard: Intuition in Decision Making

Chester I. Barnard (1886–1961), the American business executive who pioneered organizational theory and decision-making analysis, believed that non-conscious, intuitive processes played important parts in everyday organizational decisions. He likened management to "playing by ear."[27] Although first proposed in 1936, his ideas about intuition and non-rational decision making received little attention until rediscovered in the 1980s and 1990s.

Intuitions are "affectively charged judgments that arise through rapid, non-conscious, and holistic associations."[28] They are immediate cognitions without the use of conscious rational processes.[29] A study focus in philosophy, psychology, and management, intuiting processes information by making holistic associations, perceiving coherence (of pattern, meaning, or structure) among separate stimuli, and mapping these onto cognitive structures stored in long-term memory without conscious effort. This process permits rapid and accurate responses to highly demanding situations. Intuition also has strong, positive affective components, such as excitement, harmony, or "feelings of knowing" without rational analysis. Intuitions holistically "recognize" a solution and feel that it is the "right" one.

Concerned with the challenge of adjusting to changing circumstances, new kinds of work, and people and groups attaining common understanding, Barnard classified people's mental processes as logical and non-logical. *Logical processes* were "conscious thinking that could be expressed in words or reasoning." *Non-logical processes* were mental processes "not capable of being expressed in words."[30] Rather, they could only be known through judgment, decision, or action. Barnard understood intuition's vague feeling that certain things are relevant and others are not as the likely outcome of prior related experiences. This was implicit learning or tacit knowledge not yet articulated into conscious thought but inferred from behavior. Acknowledging logical reasoning's essential role in daily affairs, Barnard cautioned against over-emphasizing it at the expense of the non-logical (such as "intuition," "inspiration," "bright idea," "common sense," or "good judgment"). He believed that decision making required adapting to a complex concrete situation, most of which existed beyond the decision makers' ability to put into words.

To Barnard, intuition was basic to decision making and lay under nearly every aspect of it, even if decision makers often rationalized their decisions afterwards.[31] He saw intuition as "the invisible organic glue that bonds the various forms of

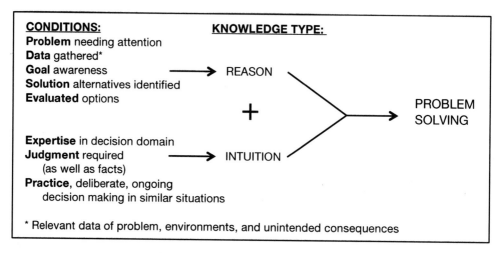

FIGURE 9.2 Types of Knowledge Needed for Effective Problem Solving
Source: Leslie S. Kaplan and William A. Owings, 2017

knowledge together," integrating thought and action in the knowledge discovery process.[32] Later studies would confirm that effective intuiting depends on several variables: (1) having expertise in the domain in which the decision will occur; (2) having a task requiring judgment (rather than more facts); and (3) having deliberate and ongoing practice making decisions in these types of situations.[33] Figure 9.2 presents a view of the conditions and types of knowing needed for effective problem solving.

Although a substantial body of research suggests that intuition is generally inferior to more rational models in decision making,[34] studies increasingly suggest that for certain people, under the appropriate conditions, intuition may be as good as—*or even better than*—other decision-making approaches.[35] Research findings also support Barnard's notion of intuition and non-logical processes' central role in organizational decision making.[36] Intuition in decision making may bring information not otherwise available through empirical inquiry alone. Studies find that within organizations, intuition may be vital to successfully completing highly complex tasks in a relatively short time[37] and may be especially needed in organizations involved in tumultuous environments.[38] Likewise, empirical neuroscience studies support the view that intuition can be considered as the subjective experience associated with the use of knowledge gained through implicit learning.[39]

Management scholars increasingly agree that both explicit behavior and implicit experience—linking intuition and reason—are essential for successful management decisions and actions. Real expertise—making rapid and accurate decisions in organizations—involves using both types of knowing.

9.3 REFLECTIONS AND RELEVANCE

Using Intuition in Decision Making

Chester Barnard cautioned against over-emphasizing logical reasoning at the expense of non-logical reasoning (such as intuition or inspiration).

In small groups, discuss a time when you used intuition to help solve a problem. As a class, discuss several examples of intuition. Under what conditions can you best use intuition? How might you effectively expand your intuition to solve problems?

Herbert Simon: Theory of Bounded Rationality

Herbert A. Simon (1916–2001), an American social scientist, synthesized his knowledge of political science, sociology, psychology, and anthropology into a key economic theory. Seeing decision making and rationality cutting across all social sciences, Simon wanted to understand both phenomena. But whereas economists traditionally saw decision making as perfect rationality encased in a formal mathematical structure, Simon used his social science insights to build a more general empirically grounded theory of human problem solving. These concepts would eventually win him the 1978 Nobel Prize for Economics. With his work, Simon moved decision making into an organizational context.

In the 1950s, Simon noted that economics tended to treat human behavior as rational, while psychology concerned itself with behavior's rational and irrational aspects. In economics, the "all-knowing" rational person always reaches the "best" decision that objectively delivers the "optimal" outcome but ignores contextual, social, or physiological limits on human cognition in decision making. Simon saw this economic view of human rationality as unrealistic. It made impractical demands of human's knowledge and cognitive capacities, and it poorly handled circumstances where uncertainty and unforeseen future events played major roles. Instead, Simon proposed replacing the classical model with insights from cognitive psychology, likening how an information processing system solves problems in ways similar to how the human brain solves problems. In cognitive psychology, the rational (but not all-knowing) person makes "good enough" decisions using a reasonable procedure in light of the available knowledge and means of assessing it.[40]

Simon saw *rationality* as "the set of skills or aptitudes we use to see if we can get from here to there—to find courses of action that will lead us to accomplish our goals."[41] People's rationality in decision making is the product of both their "inner environment" —their mental capacities and knowledge contents—and their "outer environment"— the world in which they act and which acts upon them.[42] Likewise, decisions are rational to the extent that they lead to obtaining their intended ends.

Simon likened classical models of rational choice to the visible tip of a very large iceberg.[43] An iceberg's mass lies largely unseen below the water's surface. Not observable are: a clear problem definition; all the relevant information; possible solutions and their likely outcomes; the range and content of the decision maker's values, preferences, and interests; and the present and future uncertainties in the environment. Since these factors can only be partially and imperfectly known, the resulting decision making is "incomplete, often inadequate ... based on uncertain information and partial ignorance," selective memory and perception. It usually ends with the discovery of available and satisfactory, not optimal, choices for action. With this analogy, Simon observed that rationality in decision making is intended—but not always—achieved. His behavioral theory of rational choice—*bounded rationality*—would reflect external social and environmental constraints and internal cognitive and emotional limits on human rationality.

Bounded Rationality

Using psychology as a starting point, Simon observed that people are goal oriented but often fail to achieve them because of environmental complexities and cognitive and emotional limitations. People have aspiration levels. They assess what the world is likely to provide in return for their efforts and what they can reasonably expect to achieve if they make good decisions and implement them well. In this way, people's aspiration levels adjust to realities based on their experiences (and those of others) about what is attainable. The realities of what ends are attainable become the main standard by which to judge whether a solution to a problem is satisfactory.[44]

Although organizations want its members to act in ways that help meet its goals, members' cognitive capacities, the available information, their values, and factors in the larger environment constrict their behaviors. Using decision premises and decision routines helps members bridge the gap between their own bounded rationality and the organization's reasonable needs to achieve its goals. Figure 9.3 depicts Simon's ideas about the personal, contextual, and organizational factors that impact decision making— bounded rationality, decision premises, and decision routines—to show organizations as decision-making systems. Although this depiction makes the process appear linear, in reality, the actual decision-making process is more like a cobweb than a straight line.[45]

In bounded rationality, Simon identified three categories of restrictions to a decision maker's cognitive capacities. These are mental skills, habits, and reflexes; the extent of

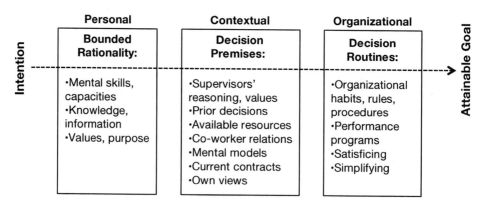

FIGURE 9.3 Simon's Organizationally Rational Behaviors

Source: Based on Simon, H.A. (1976). *Administrative behavior: A study of decision-making processes in administrative organizations*. 3rd ed. New York, NY: Free Press.

knowledge and information possessed; and values or conceptions of purpose which may differ from organizational goals[46] discussed above.

Decision Premises

Simon believed that organizations could alter the limits to its members' rationality by creating or changing the organizational context in which the decision making occurs. Organizations can control the *decision premises*—the guiding workplace norms that help individuals make decisions when they are uncertain about the information at hand or the "best practices" to address them.[47] Decision premises include the organization's or supervisor's reasoning of the facts and values for taking a certain action that steers the individual member's decision-making behavior (rather than the individual independently examining the actual decisions).[48] Prior decisions, available time and resources, social relations with co-workers, mental models, current contracts, views about a particular option's merit or value, and supervisors' directions also affect decision premises. Given the problem solver's cognitive back-and-forth among the problem representation, the relevant content knowledge, the situational factors, the decision makers' values, and the decision premises, decision making's cobweb nature appears.[49]

For instance, a principal wanting to schedule teacher observations for the school year will have decision premises including: legal and district deadlines for making employment decisions for teachers on continuing and annual contracts; the number of building administrators qualified to observe teachers using the district's performance rubric; and the amount of time required to use the performance rubric with high interrater reliability (so observers can generate valid and reliable reports). Most likely the school district also will have guidelines about keeping marginally effective teachers working at their best despite their lack of contract renewal.

Decision Routines, Satisficing, and Simplifying

Simon saw *decision routines*—performance programs, satisficing, and simplifying—as organizational habits, rules and procedures that members develop in response to recurring questions and that over time, become accepted practices. These behaviors become so familiar that members make them without consciously considering alternative actions. So engrained in organizational practice, decision routines become difficult to stop, even when conditions change; and what formerly worked no longer does.[50]

Simon introduced the *satisficing* and *simplifying* concepts to organizational decision making. *Satisficing* (a blend of *satisfying* and *sufficing*) means ending a search for solutions with a "satisfactory" or "good enough" option based on (the individual's and others') experiences about what is realistically attainable. This approach contrasts with an "optimizing" or "maximizing" search for an unattainable "best" solution. Simon believed that cognitive limits, environmental complexities, and time constraints restrict individuals' abilities to plan long behavior sequences. In addition, people make trade-offs among their values. As a result, people can make reasonably good choices with realistic amounts of calculation and using very incomplete information.[51]

For instance, a school district gave its high school textbook committee two months to recommend a book for course adoption. The committee reviewed two American History series, A and B. They compared and discussed A's and B's Tables of Contents, relative coverage of ten key topics, and supplemental resources. Although committee members preferred Series A, it cost twice as much as Series B (and would break the budget). So, they recommended Series B for adoption. Given their limited time, strict budget, and partial comparison of options, they satisficed: Series B would be "good enough" for their purposes.

Likewise, Simon saw organizational decision makers as *simplifying* the decision process by following decision routines and "rules of thumb" in problem solving to avoid uncertainty and reduce complexity in recurring situations. These performance programs are practices that had proven successful in the past. For example, when parents arrive to enroll their children in a new school, the school secretary greets them promptly and offers them a prescribed set of forms to complete. By restricting the range of available options, these decision routines greatly reduce the cognitive and information requirements for decision making.

Decision Making: Analytic and Intuitive

Simon believed that decision making requires both analytic and intuitive approaches to problem solving. Simon saw intuition as a sophisticated form of reasoning based on "chunking"[52] gained through years of relevant, job-specific experiences learning the task details of the work.[53] He stressed that although experts possess 50,000 chunks of information, they do not have world-class expertise in any domain with less than 10 years of intense application.[54] Given this, in ordinary situations, experts can be highly intuitive whereas in novel situations, their problem solving becomes more analytic. The effective organizational leader or administrator combines this formal and experiential knowledge and skills with the habit of applying them. Each approach enhances the effectiveness of the other.

Research and Criticism

Ample empirical studies in the laboratory, using computer models, and in the field, confirm that actual business decision making uses bounded rationality's assumptions.[55] Hundreds of studies in psychology and economics support the view that humans have limitations on their cognitive abilities to handle accurately large amounts of data.[56] Economists who include bounded rationality in their models have clear success in describing economic behavior beyond standard theory.[57] Likewise, many investigations using computers (to simulate human thinking) and experts (having substantial knowledge in particular domains thinking-out-loud about problem solving) confirm the steps in Simon's decision-making process.[58]

Nonetheless, Simon's ideas about bounded rationality have irritated critics. Simon's career, progressing from political science and through management theory, cognitive psychology, artificial intelligence, and economics, has prompted several scholars within these fields to label him a "heretic,"[59] call his ideas "naively simple,"[60] judge his contributions as "minor,"[61] and reject his portraying humans' behavior in what some see as a cold, one-dimensional manner.[62] While praising his theory as "realistic," they simultaneously fault it for promoting "making do" or "settling for less" strategies rather than search for more effective options.[63] In a different vein, some critics note that bounded rationality ignores emotion's role in decision making.[64] Feminist scholars challenge bounded rationality conceptually for its male-centered assumptions that favor rationality over affect, thereby excluding alternate ways of organizing data.[65] Despite these critiques,

9.4 REFLECTIONS AND RELEVANCE

Applying Simon's Theory of Bounded Rationality

Herbert Simon's bounded rationality concept theorizes that external (social and environmental) and internal (cognitive and emotional) constraints limit a person's ability to make rational decisions.

Working in small groups, recall or imagine a school-related problem. Then provide four examples—offering specific details—for each area of bounded rationality, writing specifics next to the asterisks under each category. Under Environmental, include at least two decision premises that affect your decision making in your problem situation. After all groups have finished, the class will discuss: What are the external (social and environmental, including decision premises) and internal (cognitive and emotional) factors that contribute to bounded rationality for school leaders? What are the merits and limitations of bounded rationality as a background to decision making for school leaders?

External Constraints		External Constraints *(Internal)*	
Social:	Environmental:	Cognitive:	Emotional:
•	•	•	•
•	•	•	•
•	•	•	•
•	•	•	•

today's economics, political science, and other disciplines have incorporated the bounded rationality concept and approaches.[66]

Simon's *bounded rationality* theory accepts limits on humans' abilities to comprehend and manipulate large amounts of information. He saw rationality in decision making as adaptive behavior that functioned within the constraints imposed by both the decision makers' capacities and the external situation. Using the bounded rationality theory, decision makers can look for satisfactory choices (instead of optimal ones) that permit organizational work to go forward.

SENSEMAKING AND DECISION MAKING

Since the 1980s and 1990s, many organizational scholars have suggested that decision making can also be understood as sensemaking. Karl E. Weick (1936–), a University of Michigan organizational theorist, is widely recognized as authoring the seminal book on sensemaking.[67] Over time, he continued to refine his ideas, and many others contributed to the sensemaking perspective.

Sensemaking literally means, making sense. It is a deliberate search for meaning as a way to deal with uncertainty. It involves turning unclear, unexpected, and confusing circumstances into a situation that is plainly understood in words that can serve as a catalyst to action.[68] Overwhelmingly, sensemaking focuses on analyzing the practical activities of real people engaged in concrete situations. An essential leadership behavior, sensemaking is especially important in dynamic and unstable contexts where leaders need to create and sustain coherent understanding, maintain relationships, and enable collective action to achieve organizational goals.[69]

Sensemaking is not a linear process. With sensemaking, people use partially overlapping processes to construct "realities" and then retrospectively make sense of them in a continuing back-and-forth of discovery and invention. In this way, sensemakers "actively author" the situations they are trying to understand.[70] Occurring largely through language and communication processes, sensemaking happens so subtly and quickly that it is easily taken for granted. So essential to organizational identity and functioning, it has been said that organizing is achieved to the extent that sensemaking is achieved.[71]

Figure 9.4 illustrates how the sensemaking perspective conceptualizes and defines sensemaking in organizations. As depicted here, sensemaking is an interactive process, with ambiguous trigger events (planned and unplanned, and major or minor) interacting

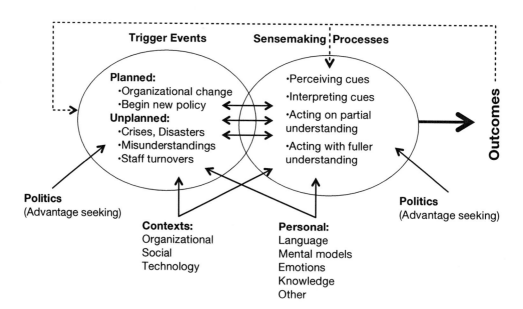

FIGURE 9.4 The Process of Making Sense

Source: Based on Sandberg, J. & Tsoukas, H. (2015). Making senses of the sensemaking perspective: Its constituents, limitations, and opportunities for further development. *Journal of Organizational Behavior, 36* (S1), p. S12.

with an array of sensemaking processes.[72] Everything is affected by impinging factors, including politics (advantage seeking), contexts (organizational, social, and technological), and personal (such as language, mental models, emotions, and knowledge). Through the sensemaking processes, decision makers arrive at outcomes, whose consequences then provide feedback that can influence later trigger events and sensemaking cues. We will consider each sensemaking process and factors influencing sensemaking in turn.

SENSEMAKING PROCESSES

Sensemaking processes begin when something unexpected or confusing happens to interrupt routine organizational activities. Then, people try to make sense of it so they can take plausible action to correct or integrate it into their ongoing work. The NASA Challenger disaster, for instance, triggered intensive sensemaking. After the fact, scientists identified a series of unexpected technical failures to help them explain what happened and provoke discussions about prevention. Much current research on how sensemaking occurs identifies three sets of interweaving processes: perceiving cues (noticing), making interpretations, and taking action.[73]

- **Perceiving cues (noticing)**. Individuals become aware of something amiss and begin to organize their experience by asking and answering: (1) "What happened/or is happening here?" and (2) "What does this event mean (and what should I do)?" Asking these questions brings an event into awareness, gives it a meaningful shape and structure that individuals hope is stable enough for them to act upon this meaning in the future.

  Next, the person identifies concrete salient cues in the environment to help structure the formless event into something that can be separated into meaningful chunks, labeled, or crudely categorized to make plausible action possible. Then the person looks for "reasons" that might help make sense of the event, using organizational frameworks (such as handbooks, Codes of Conduct, expectations, strategic or implementation plans, traditions, and acceptable justifications) as guides. If these "reasons" don't provide a plausible answer that allows the work to continue, sensemaking either identifies a substitute action or moves to further discussion.

  For example, while reviewing the semester's student achievement grades, an assistant principal finds that seventh grader, Tim, is failing every subject. Tim is a friendly, personable, and polite young man. Putting his concern into words, the AP asks, "Why is Tim failing?" "What does this mean, and what should we do to fix it?" In this way, the AP "regularizes" and simplifies the situation by classifying Tim's situation as serious lack of academic progress. To start finding the "reasons" why, the AP gathers Tim's past and current achievement, discipline, attendance, and health records.

- **Interpreting**. The person reflects back on past experiences and the present situation to find a meaningful, plausible pattern to explain what he or she sees and understands it to be. In our example, the AP reviews Tim's records and finds that Tim has average report card grades, average achievement test scores, no chronic health problems, and a referral-free discipline record. In Tim's attendance report, however, the AP notices 20 days of school missed during the first semester. Are Tim's excessive absences contributing to his academic failure? The report shows a 5-day absence in early October. The doctor's note is in the file, but the AP finds no other medical excuses or parent notes. What do Tim's parents think is happening? Have Tim's counselor and teachers noticed his absences, and what are they doing to address it so he can continue learning?

- **Enacting.** The person takes action, starting by communicating with others who share the same environment and work tasks. Sensemaking organizes the experience through communication. Talking with others makes tacit knowledge more public, clear, ordered, relevant, and usable to the situation at hand, forming the basis for action to address it.

  Continuing the example, the AP schedules a Student Assistance Team (SAT) meeting with Tim's school counselor, his core academic teachers, the school nurse, and the school psychologist. Together, they review and think through Tim's data. The members also discuss their anecdotal experiences with Tim and reflect on incidents with students in similar situations. Next, they summarize what they have noticed about Tim, develop a shared understanding of the problem and how they might address it, and identify who else needs to be involved. Then they plan their next steps.

Factors Influencing Sensemaking

Sensemaking is an interpretive process: people construct knowledge by how they perceive and define it. Reason, intuition, affect, and social context all play key roles. To a large degree, sensemaking is about the interaction of behavior and interpretation rather than the influence of conscious cognitive evaluation on choice.

- **Individual and collective factors.** Sensemaking operates at the individual and collective levels. Mentally filtering available clues and objective data through their prior experiences, personal biases, mental models, expectations, motivations, and feelings about similar situations, people alternate between reason and intuition, logic and emotions as they construct a plausible meaning to a novel circumstance.[74] As a result, individuals often see what they expect to see, see what they want to see,[75] or see the absence of what they expect to see because it deviates from the norm.[76] Organizational research supports the view that people's expectations and motives influence how they perceive events, which cues they notice, and how they construct their meaning.[77] Likewise, research supports the notion that rather than gather and weigh all available evidence before reaching a decision, individuals search for evidence that confirms or justifies their initial intuitions and preferences.[78]
- **Intuition, inference, and social context factors.** Intuition and social context also play essential roles in sensemaking. Intuitions—sometimes called "gut feelings"—are sudden, effortless, affect-based cognitive processes that allow individuals to

understand something immediately without the need for deliberate reasoning.[79] More holistic, associative, and faster than rational decision making, intuitive judgments about an issue happen without conscious awareness. Individuals infer that they must have reasoned in some logical and rational way to reach their assessment of the issue, even if they didn't. Organizational scholars recognize that persons often rationalize their actions—give explanations—by using acceptable accounts that keep their positive identity in their group.

In our example, the school counselor, with a professional background in counseling, adolescent psychology, and several years experiences working with maturing teenagers suddenly has a hunch: Tim's fear of failure may be keeping him home. If he fell behind in schoolwork after his initial 5-day illness and felt "dumb" in front of his peers when he returned to school, the counselor infers, he might have chosen to "save face" by avoiding the classroom and staying home. In Tim's view, better to look sick than stupid, the counselor proposes to the SAT members. This makes sense, and SAT members can plan their next steps to get Tim back to school. (Only Tim knows if they are right.)

Since our culture expects people to make decisions deliberately and thoughtfully, composing a rationale after-the-fact of how the person used logical analysis to make this decision boosts the person's and colleagues' confidence in the decision and allows the individual to be seen as acting appropriately according to society's norms. Rational descriptions of events are perceived as more credible than "It just came to me."[80]

In addition, social influences and shared mental models affect how individuals perceive, interpret, and act on issues. Research informs us that organizations strongly influence how their members behave and what they believe.[81] Those in positions of power or influence often shape what people accept or reject by controlling variables. These variables include: the cues highlighted or suppressed, who talks to whom, the criteria for plausible stories and permitted actions, which retrospective meanings are accepted or discredited, whether updating is encouraged or discouraged, and the standard of accuracy or plausibility to which speculations are held.[82]

Likewise, "social anchors"—certain persons in organizations who have influence—can help less experienced individuals understand confusing issues and help them test their interpretation of events. By sharing mental models with colleagues, organization members learn broader ways to understand the situation, helping others enlarge their perspective and interpretations of events.[83] With this enlarged cognitive framework, individuals can mentally construct an issue more comprehensively. Of course, the effects of using social anchors and mental models can be positive or negative, depending on the "role model's" perspective and skill sets. Turning to role models who have made corrupt behaviors "normal" parts of their repertoire can have harmful outcomes.

Sensemaking and Leadership

Sensemaking holds serious implications for leadership. Leaders—especially mid-level leaders like principals—help create meaning and purpose for their faculties, students, and communities. By drawing attention to key features (cues) of events, bracketing and interpreting what is happening, school leaders shape how people give them meaning. Then, leaders can offer options for acting on the cues by developing credible plans to move the organization beyond its current problems and toward where they want it to go. In this way, effective leaders become sensemakers and sensegivers. They help the group make events comprehensible, find a workable certainty, and guide how people understand themselves, their work, and their colleagues.[84]

Research and Criticism

Sensemaking research has followed many directions, including organizational change,[85] responses to crises,[86] forming organizational and professional cultures,[87] strategy,[88] organizational learning,[89] and creativity and innovation.[90] Research findings disagree about whether sensemaking is primarily a set of individual or collective processes,[91] whether it occurs moment-to-moment[92] or most notably in times of crisis or confusion,[93] whether it is largely reflective[94] or future oriented,[95] and whether individuals who in work teams tend to share understandings[96] or not.[97] Much of this disagreement comes from misunderstanding sensemaking as either/or rather than as more/less on a continuum, and as unique and linear rather than as integrated events. For instance, understanding creation, interpretation, and enactment as separate events is misleading. Sensemaking and action continuously interact, despite their frequent portrayal as occurring in a linear, step-by-step fashion.[98] Nonetheless, research supports sensemaking as a leadership behavior that influences others' understandings of issues. Findings include that organizational leaders at all levels have mental maps that they use for sensemaking activities;[99] politics and power influence sensemaking;[100] and the nature of sensemaking varies with the type of issue and situation.[101] Additionally, studies affirm sensemaking's pivotal role in organizational change;[102] detect the shifts in individuals' mental models during the change process;[103] and consider mid-level leaders' critical (and challenging) sensemaking and sensegiving roles as interpreters and "sellers" in implementing top-down organizational change.[104] Also, studies of sensemaking in crises or extreme situations observe that social structure and contexts have reciprocal relationships with sensemaking: each interacts with sensemaking, both influencing and being influenced by it.[105] These results suggest that managing change may be less about directing and controlling and more about facilitating mid-level leaders' sensemaking processes to ensure that top-level and mid-level interpretations align[106] and the changes are meaningful to organization members.

Sensemaking is not about "finding the truth" and "getting it right." Plausibility, rather than accuracy, drives it. In sensemaking, decision makers continually redraft an emerging story so that it becomes more comprehensive, includes more of the observed data, and stands more resiliently in the face of criticism. By making sense of the circumstances in ways that appear to move toward long-term goals—and improve the reasoning over time as supporting or discounting evidence appears—decision makers can solve problems effectively. This is how actual organizational problem solving works. At the same time, this plausibility rather than accuracy orientation places sensemaking in conflict with academic theories and administrative practices that assume only "accurate" perceptions increase decision quality and effective outcomes.

9.5 REFLECTIONS AND RELEVANCE

Using Sensemaking for Decision Making

Sensemaking is a set of partially overlapping processes that people use to give meaning (make sense of) confusing, unclear, or unexpected situations and then retroactively attribute reasoning to explain their conclusions or actions.

Work in groups of four, using a sensemaking process to solve the following situation:

> Dr. Owens began his principalship at 2200-student grades 9–12 Shenandoah County High School by reviewing the school's achievement data. Records for the past 15 years showed the following: a 13.8 percent student dropout rate (the highest in the state at the time; 15 percent of students were college bound; of the school's five guidance counselors, three were working with the college-bound students while two worked with all the others; the guidance director was close friends with many highly influential people in town. What is Dr. O to do to reduce the dropout rate?

After problem solving and decision making, refer to Figure 9.4 to identify where you used the sensemaking processes (perceiving cues, interpreting cues, acting on partial understanding, acting with fuller understanding), identify the personal, contextual, and political factors that affected your decision, and describe the (ideal) decision outcomes. As a class, discuss the merits and limitations of sensemaking as a decision-making approach for school leaders and individuals.

IMPLICATIONS FOR EDUCATIONAL LEADERS

This chapter's take-away—*if nothing else*—is that problem solving and decision making have many moving parts. To do it well involves skillfully juggling virtually countless variables, near and far, tangible and abstract, *all at the same time*. Plus, it means working within one's own cognitive, emotional, and physiological limits. In short, we all work within Herbert Simon's bounded rationality, looking for satisfactory choices that permit organizational work to go forward.

Since effective problem solving and decision making are key leadership competencies, developing useful mental models can help future principals act more competently and successfully. For school leaders, these mental models should include the following key ideas: (1) problems, individuals, and situations/environments differ; (2) decision making is a process; and (3) each decision model can add insights that improve school leaders' decision-making success.

Problems Differ

A problem's structure may be clearly or poorly defined; issues may be routine or non-routine, simple or complex, with few or many external factors to think through. Problems vary in the forms in which they appear and in the knowledge and processes needed to solve them. They may be urgent or "whenever." They may involve multidisciplinary and interlinked social, economic, cultural, and political dimensions. They may have multiple or no solutions and multiple or few criteria for evaluating them. Solving problems may require a high degree of judgment or personal beliefs—or none. Problems may be stable, or they may change over time. The intellectual skills and information needed to solve them may be general or domain and context specific. And each profession has its own way of solving problems. Understanding the general nature of problems is a logical place to begin to build familiarity and expertise in solving them.

Individuals Differ

Individuals vary in the types, amount, complexity, and information relevance they possess. They vary in their experiences and familiarity with the problem type or situation. They vary in their values and purpose, their interest in the problem, and their flexibility, temperament, and self-confidence in problem solving. They vary in their emotions at any particular time. Fatigue, anxiety, and stress also impact their problem solving performance. These individual factors influence the extent to which they gather information (and from which sources), how they interpret what they see or hear, the inferences they draw, the alternatives they consider, and those options they ultimately select. Even working within bounded rationality, not everyone is capable of collecting, reviewing, abstractly manipulating, and evaluating the reasonable amount of data necessary to generate a workable solution.

Recognizing these limiting realities and acting with self-awareness, school leaders can put themselves in the right frames of mind, body, and setting to increase the likelihood of making sound decisions. School leaders also benefit when they involve others—especially those with a personal stake *and* relevant expertise—in the decision-making process.[107] And, as Barnard, Simon, and Weick assert, school leaders make better decisions when they can access both their overt and tacit knowledge to solve problems. Ongoing learning and experiences help decision makers develop the analytic and intuitive approaches that lead to effective outcomes.

Situations and Environments Differ

Even familiar situations differ when they happen in unfamiliar settings. Moreover, the problem's environment often contains social, historical, cultural, political, and legal influences and other cues (such as decision premises) that may facilitate—or hinder—problem solving or successful enactment. Time brings another factor: is the solution needed right now or do problem solvers have time—and how much—to design a workable answer? Since all these variables impact decision making, they must be identified and considered as part of weighing alternative solutions.

Decision Making Is a Process

Regardless of the model, decision making typically follows a predictable format. These include: noticing or finding the problem; gathering, processing, and evaluating information and drawing conclusions; generating and elaborating alternative solutions; evaluating these solutions in relation to the specific situation and relevant environmental (contextual, social, legal, and political) concerns; choosing among the solutions; and implementing them. But given the problem solver's cognitive back-and-forth among the problem representation, the germane content knowledge and intuition, the decision maker's values, and the situational and environmental factors, decision making appears to be more of a cobweb than a straight line.

Decision models differ in how they address these steps and how they frame the larger environment. But, school leaders do not have to pick one best approach. Rather, they can select those insights they find useful from each model to more fully develop their own repertoire of effective decision-making approaches.

Constructing a Mental Model for Decision Making

To begin, the components of problem solving skills offers a scaffold for the various elements that impact a person's ability to successfully solve problems. This expands awareness of the scope of problem solving, highlighting the range of aspects decision makers will want to consider.

Simon's bounded rationality concept accepts that individual and external constraints on decision making exist. Effective decision makers make "good enough" (satisficing) decisions using reasonable procedures that allow the organization to move forward. Likewise, as Barnard, Simon, and Weick assert, reason and intuition, logical and non-logical processes are essential partners in successful decision making. Effective school leaders improve their decision-making capacities when then continually gain relevant experiences and knowledge so they may respond quickly and accurately in highly demanding situations.

As for sensemaking, it occurs naturally all the time—in planned events (such as major strategy sessions, organizational change activities, or figuring out how to begin a new work task), in unplanned situations (such as crises or misunderstandings), and in everything in between. From noticing errant cues to considering the individual and larger scale factors that impact decisions, sensemaking is integral to the decision process, regardless of the decision model used. By making circumstances meaningful in ways that move the organization toward its long-term goals—and improving solutions over time as supporting or discounting evidence appears—decision makers use sense-making to solve problems effectively.

NOTES

1 These iconic quotations attributed to Einstein and Baruch have become part of our common culture, frequently cited in business blogs and texts but not sourced to their original documents.

2 Kilpatrick, W. (1992). *Why Johnny can't tell right from wrong*. New York, NY: Simon & Schuster.

3 For a discussion of the poverty-based risk factors that harm children's school success, see: Owings, W.A. & Kaplan, L.S. (2013). Risk factors affecting school success. In *American public school finance*. (pp. 222–238). Belmont, CA: Wadsworth/Cengage Learning.

4 Chen, G. (2015, March 3). 10 major challenges facing public schools. *Public School Review*. Retrieved from: http://blogs.edweek.org/edweek/finding_common_ground/2014/01/10_critical_issues_facing_education.html?intc=main-mpsmvs; Mazzuca, J. (2002, December 3). Americans list biggest challenges of U.S. Schools. Gallup. Retrieved from: www.gallup.com/poll/7327/americans-list-biggest-challenges-us-schools.aspx.

5 Problem. *Merriam-Webster* online. Retrieved from: www.merriam-webster.com/dictionary/problem.

6 Mayer, R.E. (1992). *Thinking, problem solving, cognition*, 2nd ed. New York, NY: Freeman.

7 Jonassen, D.H. (2000). Toward a design theory of problem solving. *Educational Technology Research and Development, 48* (4), 63–85; Jonassen, D.H. (2004). *Learning how to solve problems. An instructional design guide* (pp.3–6). New York, NY: John Wiley & Sons; Jonassen, D.H. (2011). *Learning how to solve problems. An instructional design guide* (p. 6). New York, NY: Routledge.

8 Mayer, R.E. & Wittrock, M.C. (1996) Problem-solving transfer. In D.C. Berliner & R.C. Calfee (Eds), *Handbook of Educational Psychology* (pp. 47–62). New York, NY: Macmillan; Jonassen, D.H. (1997). Instructional design model for well-structured and ill-structured problem-solving learning outcomes. *Educational Technology Research and Development 45* (1), 65–95.

9 Jonassen (2004). Op. cit.; Jonassen, D.H. (1997). Instructional design model for well-structured and ill-structured problem-solving learning outcomes. *Educational Technology: Research and Development, 45* (1), 65–95.

10 Dunkle, M.E., Schraw, G. & Bendixen, L.D. (1995, April). *Cognitive processes in well-defined and ill-defined problem solving*. Paper presented at the annual meeting of the American Educational Research Association, San Francisco, CA; Hong, N.S., Jonassen, D.H. & McGee, S. (2003). Predictors of well-structured and ill-structured problem solving in an astronomy simulation. *Journal of Research in Science Teaching, 40* (1), 6–33; Cho, K.L. & Jonassen, D.H. (2002). The effects of argumentation scaffolds on argumentation and problem solving. *Educational Technology: Research and Development, 50* (3), 5–22.

11 Funke, J. (1991). Solving complex problems: Exploration and control of complex systems. In R. Sternberg & P.A. Frensch (Eds), *Complex problem solving: Principles and mechanisms* (pp. 185–222). Hillsdale, NJ: Lawrence Erlbaum Associates; English, L.D. (1998). Children's reasoning in solving relational problems of deduction. *Thinking and Reasoning, 4* (3), 249–281.

12 Mayer, R.E. (1992). *Thinking, problem solving, cognition*, 2nd ed. New York, NY: Freeman; Smith, M.U. (1991). A view from biology. In M.U. Smith (Ed.), *Toward a unified theory of problem solving* (pp. 1–20). Mahwah, N.J.: Erlbaum; Sternberg, R.J. & Frensch, P.A. (Eds). *Complex problem solving: Principles and mechanisms*. Mahwah, NJ: Erlbaum.

13 Lehman, D., Lempert, R. & Nisbett, R.E. (1988). The effects of graduate training on reasoning: Formal discipline and thinking about everyday life events. *Educational Psychologist, 43* (6), 431–442.

14 Robertson, W.C. (1990). Detection of cognitive structure with protocol data: Predicting performance on physics transfer problems. *Cognitive Science, 14* (2), 253–280; Gordon, S.E. & Gill, R.T. (1989). The formation and use of knowledge structures in problem solving domains. *Tech. Report AFOSR-88–0063*. Washington, DC: Bolling AFB; Jonassen (2000). Op. cit.

15 Davis, J.K. & Haueisen, W.C. (1976). Field independence and hypothesis testing. *Perceptual and Motor Skills, 43* (3), 763–769; Ronning, McCurdy & Ballinger (1984, January). Individual differences: A third component in problem solving instruction. *Journal of Research in Science Teaching, 21* (1), 71–82.

16 Stewin, L. & Anderson, C. (1974). Cognitive complexity as a determinant of information processing. *Alberta Journal of Educational Research*, 20 (3), 233–243.

17 Anderson, C.R. (1976). Coping behaviors as intervening mechanisms in the inverted-U stress-performance relationship. *Journal of Applied Psychology*, 61 (1), 30–34. Speculation suggests that motivation to solve a problem under high stress narrows the problem solver's perception to only very obvious clues, ignoring relevant information that may actually help performance. See: Vroom, V.H. (1964). *Work and motivation*. New York, NY: Wiley; Kahn, R.L. (1964). *Conflict and ambiguity: Studies in organizational roles and personal stress*. New York, NY: Wiley; Lazarus, R.S. (1966). *Psychological stress and the coping process*. New York, NY: McGraw-Hill.

18 Nordin, F. & Kowalkowski, C. (2010). Solutions offerings: A critical review and reconceptualization. *Journal of Service Management*, 21 (4), 441–459.

19 Ge, X. & Land, S.M. (2004). A conceptual framework for scaffolding ill-structured problem solving processes using question prompts and peer interactions. *Educational Technology Research and Development*, 52 (2), 5–22.

20 Goodin, R.E. (1976). *The politics of rational man* (p. 9). London, UK: Wiley.

21 Reason. Retrieved from: www.merriam-webster.com/dictionary/reason.

22 Garofalo, J. & Lester, F. (1985). Metacognition, cognitive monitoring, and mathematical performance. *Journal for Research in Mathematics Education*, 16 (3), 163–176.

23 A discussion of mixed scanning, incremental, and critical theory models of decision making appears on the book's companion website.

24 Novicevic, M.M., Hench, T.J. & Wren, D.A. (2002). "Playing by ear" . . . "in an incessant din of reasons": Chester Barnard and the history of intuition in management thought. *Management Decision*, 40 (10), 992–1002; Smith, G. & May D. (1980). The artificial debate between rationalist and incrementalist models of decision making. *Policy and Politics*, 8 (2), 147–161.

25 Simon, H.A. (1979). Rational decision making in business organizations. *The American Economic Review*, 69 (4), 493–513; March, J.G. (1994). *A primer on decision making. How decisions happen*. New York, NY: The Free Press.

26 Charles E. Lindblom's incremental model for problem solving, Amitai Etzioni's mixed scanning model for decision making, and critical theory's view of decision making—along with related research, criticism, and relevant learning activities—can be found on this book's companion website.

27 Chester I. Barnard, in a letter to A.A. Lowman, President, Northwestern Bell Telephone Company, March 23, 1939, as cited in Novicevic & Wren (2002). Ibid., p. 992.

28 Dane, E. & Pratt, M.G. (2007). Exploring intuition and its role in managerial decision making. *Academy of Management Review*, 32 (1), 33–54 (p. 40).

29 Cognition vs. Intuition—What's the difference? Retrieved from: http://wikidiff.com/intuition/cognition.

30 Barnard, C.I. (1968). *The functions of the executive*. 30th Anniversary ed. (p. 302). Cambridge, MA: Harvard University Press.

31 Barnard (1968). Ibid., pp. 302–305; Barnard, C.I. (1995). The significance of decisive behavior in social action: Notes on the nature of decision. *Journal of Management History*, 1 (4), 28–87.

32 Novocevic & Wren (2002). Op. cit., p. 998.

33 Dane & Pratt (2007). Op. cit.

34 See: Dawes, R.M., Faust, D. & Meehl, P.E. (1989). Clinical versus actuarial judgment. *Science*, 243 (4899), 1668–1674; Schoemaker, J.H . & Russo, J.E. (1993). A pyramid of decision approaches. *California Management Review*, 36 (1), 9–31.

35 Blattberg, R.C. & Hoch, S.J. (1990). Database models and managerial intuition: 50% model + 50% manager. *Management Science*, 36 (8), 887–899; Khatri, N. & Ng, H.A. (2000). The role of intuition in strategic decision making. *Human Relations*, 53 (1), 57–86.

36 Frederickson, J.W. (1985). Effects of decision making and organizational performance level on strategic decision processes. *Academy of Management Journal, 28* (4), 821–843; Burke, L.A. & Miller, M.K. (1999). Taking the mystery out of intuitive decision making. *Academy of Management Executive, 13* (4), 91–99; Osbeck, L.M. (1999). Conceptual problems in the development of psychological notion of "intuition." *Journal of the Theory of Social Behavior, 29* (3), 229–249.

37 Hayashi, A.M. (2001). When to trust your gut. *Harvard Business Review, 79* (2): 59–65; Isenberg (1984). Op. cit.; Shirley, D.A. & Langan-Fox, J. (1996). Intuition: A review of the literature. *Psychological Reports, 79* (2), 563–584.

38 Khatri, N. & Ng, H.A. (2000). The role of intuition in strategic decision making. *Human Relations, 53* (1), 57–86.

39 Lieberman, M.D. (2000). Intuition: A social cognitive neuroscience approach. *Psychological Bulletin, 126* (1), 109–137.

40 Simon, H.A. (1985). Human nature in politics: The dialogue of psychology with political science. *American Political Science Review, 79* (2), 293–304; Simon, H.A. (1986). Rationality in psychology and economics *Journal of Business, 59* (4), S209–S224.

41 Simon, H.A. (1987). Making management decisions: The role of intuition and emotion. *Academy of Management Executive, 1* (1): 57–64; Simon, H.A. (1993). Decision making: Rational, nonrational, and irrational. *Educational Administration Quarterly, 29* (3), 392–411 (p. 393).

42 Simon, H.A. (2000). Bounded rationality in social science: Today and tomorrow. *Mind and Society, 1* (1), 25–39.

43 Simon, H.A. (1978). Rational decision-making in business organizations. Nobel Memorial Lecture. Retrieved from: www.google.com/search?tbm=bks&hl=en&q=Shrivstava+1986+critical+theory+strategy#hl=en&q=Herbert+Simon+visible+tip+of+a+very+large+iceberg.

44 Simon, H.A. (1947). *Administrative behavior: A study of decision-making processes in administrative organization* (p. 241). New York, NY: Macmillan.

45 Swanson, R.A. (2003). Decision premises and their implications for developing decision-making expertise. *Advances in Developing Human Resources, 5* (4), 370–382.

46 Simon, H.A. (1976). *Administrative behavior: A study of decision-making processes in administrative organization.* 3rd ed. New York, NY; Free Press.

47 Swanson (2003). Op. cit.

48 Simon (1976). Op. cit., p. 133; Stewart, D.W. (1988). The decision premise: A basic tool for analyzing the ethical content of organizational behavior. *Public Administration Quarterly, 12* (3), 315–328.

49 Swanson (2003). Op. cit., p. 389.

50 Simon, H.A. (1945). *Administrative behavior.* New York, NY: Free Press; March, J.G. & Simon, H.A. (1958). *Organisations.* New York, NY: Wiley.

51 Simon, H.A. (1957). *Models of man: Social and rational.* New York, NY: Wiley; Simon, H.A. (1979). Rational decision making in business organizations. *The American Economic Review, 69* (4), 493–513; Simon (1945). Op. cit.

52 *Chunking* refers to grouping information together so it cognitively can be stored and remembered as a single concept. Simon, H.A. (1987). Making management decisions: The role of intuition and emotion. *Academy of Management Executive, 1* (1), 57–64 (p. 61).

53 Isenberg, D.J. (1984). How senior managers think. *Harvard Business Review, 63* (6), 81–90; Seebo, T.C. (1993). The value of experience and intuition. *Financial Management, 22* (1), 27.

54 Simon (1993). Op. cit.

55 See: Conlisk, J. (1996). Why Bounded Rationality? *Journal of Economic Literature, 34* (2): 669–700; Simon, H.A. & Trow, Observation of a business decision. *Journal of Business, 29* (4), 237–248, Chicago, IL: University of Chicago Press; Cyert, R.M., Feigenbaum, E.A. & March, J.G. (1959). Models in a behavioral theory of the firm. *Behavioral Science, 4* (2),

81–95; Swanson, R.A. (2003). Decision premises and their implications for developing decision-making expertise. *Advances in Developing Human Resources, 5* (4), 370–382.

56 See: Arkes, H.R. & Hammond, L. (1986). (Eds) *Judgment and decision making: An interdisciplinary reader*. Cambridge, UK: Cambridge University Press; Hogarth, R. (1980). *Judgment and choice: The psychology of decision*. New York, NY: Wiley; Payne, J.W., Bettman, J.R. & Johnson, E.J. (1992). Behavioral decision research: A constructive processing perspective. *Annual Review of Psychology, 43* (1), 87–131; Grether, D.M. & Plott, C.R. (1979). Economic theory of choice and the preference reversal phenomenon. *American Economic Review, 69* (4), 623–638.

57 Conlisk (1996). Op. cit.

58 Simon (1993). Op. cit.

59 See: Michie, D. (1980, August 22). Review of "Models of thought" by Herbert A. Simon. *Times Literary Supplement*, 942; Nicholson, T. & Abraham, P.L. (1978, October 30). Economics: Simon Says. *Newsweek*, 70; Roach, J.M. (1979). Simon says: Decision making is a "satisficing" experience. *Management Review* 68 (1), 8–17; Silk, L. (1978, November 9). Nobel winner's heretical views. *New York Times*, 53.

60 Kecney, R.L. & Raiffa, H. (1993). *Decisions with multiple objectives*. Cambridge, UK: Cambridge University Press.

61 Baumol, W.J. (1979). On the contributions of Herbert A. Simon to economics. *Scandinavian Journal of Economics, 81* (1), 74–82; Ando, A. (1979). On the contributions of Herbert A. Simon to economics. *Scandinavian Journal of Economics, 81* (1), 83–93.

62 Davis, C.R. (1996). The administrative rational model and public organizational theory. *Administration and Society, 28* (1), 39–60; Dennard, L.F. (1995). Neo-Darwinism and Simon's bureaucratic antihero. *Administration and Society, 26* (4), 464–487.

63 Forester, J. (1984). Bounded rationality and the politics of muddling through. *Public Administration Review, 44* (1), 23–31.

64 Hanoch, Y. (2002). "Neither an angel nor an ant": Emotion as an aid to bounded rationality. *Journal of Economic Psychology, 23* (1), 1–25.

65 Mumby, D.K. & Putnam, L.L. (1992). The politics of emotion: A feminist reading of bounded rationality. *Academy of Management Review, 17* (3), 465–486.

66 Sent, E-M. (2004). Behavioral economics: How psychology made its (limited) way back into economics. *History of Political Economy, 36* (4), 735–760.

67 Weick, K.E. (1995). *Sensemaking in organizations*, Thousand Oaks, CA: Sage.

68 Weick, K.E., Sutcliffe, K.M. & Obstfeld, D. (2005). Organizing and the process of sensemaking. *Organization Science, 16* (4), 409–421.

69 Weick, K.E. (1993). The collapse of sensemaking in organizations: The Mann Gulch disaster. *Administrative Science Quarterly, 38* (4), 628–652; Weick, K.E. (2001). *Making sense of the organization*. Oxford, UK: Blackwell.

70 Brown, A.D., Colville, I. & Pye, A. (2015). Making sense of sensemaking in organization studies. *Organization Studies, 36* (2), 267–277.

71 Sandberg, J. & Tsoukas, H. (2015). Making sense of the sensemaking perspective: Its constituents, limitations, and opportunities for further development. *Journal of Organizational Behavior, 36* (S1) S6–S32.

72 According to Sandberg & Tsoukas (2015). Ibid., triggering events for sensemaking occur on two parallel continua: from planned to unplanned and from major to minor.

73 Maitlis, S. & Christianson, M. (2014). Sensemaking in organizations: Taking stock and moving forward. *Academy of Management Annals, 8* (1), 57–125.

74 Sonenshein, S. (2007). The role of construction, intuition, and justification in responding to ethical issues at work: The sensemaking-intuition model. *Academy of Management Review, 32* (4), 1022–1040.

75 Sonenshein (2007). Ibid., p. 1029; Hastorf, A.H. & Cantril, H. (1954). They saw a game: A case study. *Journal of Abnormal and Social Psychology, 49* (1), 129–134.

76 Weick, Sutcliffe & Obstfeld (2005). Op. cit.

77 See: Ashforth, B.E. & Fried, Y. (1988). The mindlessness of organizational behaviors. *Human Relations, 41* (4), 305–329; Dearborn, D.C. & Simon, H. (1958). Selective perception: A note on the departmental identification of executives. *Sociometry, 21* (2), 140–144; Gioia, D.A. & Manz, C.C. (1985). Linking cognition and behavior: A script processing interpretation of vicarious learning. *Academy of Management Review, 10* (3), 527–539.

78 Baumeister, R. & Newman, L.S. (1994). Self-regulation of cognitive inference and decision processes. *Personality and Social Psychology Bulletin, 20* (1), 3–19.

79 Intuition. Google Dictionary. Retrieved from: www.google.com/search?tbm=bks&hl=en&q=Karl+WEick+bio#hl=en&q=intuition+definition.

80 Yukl, G., Guian, P.J. & Sottolano, D. (1995). Influence tactics used for different objectives with subordinates, peers, and superiors. *Group and Organization Management 20* (3), 272–297; Dutton, J.E. & Ashford, S.J. (1993). Selling issues to top management. *Academy of Management Review, 18* (3), 397–428.

81 Van Maanen, J. & Schein, E.H. (1979). Toward a theory of organizational socialization. *Research in Organizational Behavior, 1* (1): 209–264; Ashforth, B.E. & Anand, V. (2003). The normalization of corruption in organizations. *Research in Organizational Behavior, 25* (1), 1–52; Ashforth, B.E. & Mael, F. (1989). Social identity theory and the organization. *Academy of Management Review, 14* (1), 20–39.

82 Weick, Sutliffe & Obstfeld (2005). Op. cit.

83 Davis, M.H., Conklin, L., Smith, A. & Luce, C. (1996). Effect of perspective taking on the cognitive representation of persons: A merging of self and other. *Journal of Personality and Social Psychology, 70* (4), 713–726; Parker, S.K. & Axtell, C.M. (2001). Seeing another viewpoint: Antecedents and outcomes of employee perspective taking. *Academy of Management Journal, 44* (6), 1085–1100.

84 Marion, R. & Gonzalez, L.D. (2014). *Leadership in education. Organizational theory for the practitioner,* 2nd ed. Long Grove, IL: Waveland Press, pp. 223–225.

85 Balogun, J. & Johnson, G. (2004). Organizational restructuring and middle manager sensemaking. *Academy of Management Journal, 47* (4), 523–549; Balogun, J. & Johnson, G. (2005). From intended strategies to unintended outcomes: The impact of change recipient sensemaking. *Organization Studies, 26* (11), 1573–1601.

86 Colville, I., Pye, A. & Carter, M. (2013). Organizing to counter terrorism: Sensemaking amidst dynamic complexity. *Human Relations, 66* (9), 1201–1223.

87 Bloor, G. & Dawson, P. (1994). Understanding professional culture in organizational context. *Organization Studies, 15,* 275–295.

88 Pye, A.J. (1995). Strategy through dialogue and doing: A game of 'Mornington Crescent'? *Management Learning, 26* (4), 445–462.

89 Catino, M. & Patriotta, G. (2013). Learning from errors: Cognition, emotions and safety culture in the Italian air force. *Organization Studies, 34* (4), 437–467.

90 Drazin, R., Glynn, M.A. & Kazanjian, R.K. (1999). Multilevel theorizing about creativity in organizations: A sensemaking perspective. *Academy of Management Review, 24* (2), 286–307.

91 Maitlis & Christianson (2014). Op. cit.; Weick (1995). Op. cit.

92 Patriotta, G. & Brown, A.D. (2011). Sensemaking, metaphors and performance evaluation. *Scandinavian Journal of Management, 27* (1), 34–43.

93 Weick, Sutliffe & Obstfeld (2005). Op. cit.

94 Weick (1995). Op. cit.

95 Corley, K.G. & Gioia, D.A. (2011). Building theory about theory building: What constitutes a theoretical contribution? *Academy of Management Review, 36* (1), 12–32; Gioia, D.A. (2006). On Weick: An appreciation. *Organization Studies, 27* (11), 1709–1721; Ybema, S. (2010). Talk of change: Temporal contrasts and collective identities. *Organization Studies, 31* (4), 481–503.

96 Brown, J.S. & Duguid, P. (1998). Organizing knowledge. *California Management Review, 40* (3), 91–111.

97 Brown, A.D., Stacey, P. & Nandhakumar, J. (2008). Op. cit.

98 Sandberg & Tsoukas (2015). Op. cit.

99 See: Bougon, M., Weick, K. & Binkhorst, D. (1977). Cognition in organizations: An analysis of the Utrecht Jazz Orchestra. *Administrative Science Quarterly*, 22 (4), 606–639; Ford, I.D., Gadde, L-E., Håkansson, H. & Snehota, I. (2003). *Managing business relationships*. Chichester, UK: John Wiley & Sons.

100 See: Weber, K. & Glynn, M.A. (2006). Making sense with institutions: Context, thought and action in Karl Weick's theory. *Organization Studies*, 27 (11), 1639–1660; Vlaar, P.W., Van den Bosch, F.A. & Volberda, H.W. (2006). Coping with problems of understanding in interorganizational relationships: Using formalization as a means to make sense. *Organization Studies*, 27 (11), 1617–1638.

101 Gioia, D.A. & Chittipeddi, K. (1991). Sensemaking and sensegiving in strategic change initiation. *Strategic Management Journal*, 12 (6), 433–448; Gioia, D.A. & Thomas, J.B. (1996). Identity, image and issue interpretation: Sensemaking during strategic change in academia. *Administrative Science Quarterly*, 41 (3), 370–403; Bartunek, J., Krim, R., Necochea, R. & Humphries, M. (1999). Sensemaking, sensegiving, and leadership in strategic organizational development. In J. Wagner (Ed.), *Advances in qualitative organizational research*, 2 (1), 37–71. Greenwich, CT: JAI Press.

102 Isabella, L.A. (1990). Evolving interpretations as change unfolds: How managers construe key organizational events. *Academy of Management Journal*, 33 (1), 7–41; Gioia & Chittipeddi (1991). Op. cit.; Gioia & Thomas (1996). Op. cit.; Rouleau, L. (2005). Micro-practices of strategic sensemaking and sensegiving: How middle managers interpret and sell change every day. *Journal of Management Studies*, 42 (7), 1413–1441.

103 See: Balogun, J. & Johnson, J. (2004). Organizational restructuring and middle manager sensemaking. *Academy of Management Journal*, 47 (4), 523–549; Labianca, G., Gray, B., & Brass, D.J. (2000). A grounded model of organizational schema change during empowerment. *Organization Science*, 1 (1/2), 235–257.

104 See: Balogun, J. & Johnson, G. (2005). From intended strategies to unintended outcomes: The impact of change recipient sensemaking. *Organization Studies*, 26 (11), 1573–1601; Luscher, L.S. & Lewis, M.W. (2008). Organizational change and managerial sensemaking: Working through paradox. *Academy of Management Journal*, 51 (2), 221–240.

105 Weick (1993). Op. cit.; Weick, K.E. & Roberts, K.H. (1993). Collective mind in organizations: Heedful interrelating on flight decks. *Administrative Science Quarterly*, 38 (3), 357–381; Brown, A.D. (2000). Making sense of inquiry sensemaking. *Journal of Management Studies*, 37 (1), 45–75; Gephart, R.P. (1993). The textual approach: Risk and blame in disaster sensemaking. *Academy of Management Journal*, 36 (6), 1465–1514.

106 Balogun & Johnson (2005). Op. cit.

107 Bridges, E.M. (1967). A model for shared decision making in the school principalship. *Educational Administration Quarterly*, 3 (1), 49–61.

CHAPTER 10

Ethical Decision Making in Organizations

PROFESSIONAL STANDARDS FOR EDUCATIONAL LEADERS:
1, 2, 3, 6, 7, 9

CASE STUDY 10.1

Just a Small Favor to Ask

Karen Newcomer became the assistant elementary principal of Oakdale Elementary School on July 1 after having taught in the neighboring school district for 11 years. She was glad to become a part of the Oakdale community as she has several close family friends living there. On her first day of work, two of her Oakdale friends, the Oakdale PTSA President and Secretary, surprised her at the school. They came to take her out to lunch and celebrate her promotion to assistant principal and move to Oakdale. They left at 11:30 a.m. and went to Le Bernardin—an excellent and pricey four-star restaurant.

Karen's two friends paid for lunch. As they were leaving the restaurant, they had a little favor to ask. Karen replied, "Sure. What is it?" The two friends explained that their boys had been in the same class since kindergarten, and they wanted Karen to place them in the same class again for the coming school year in Mrs. Sterling's fifth grade class. Karen thought for a moment about her old school and how the administrators accommodated such requests from time to time. Karen replied, "Sure thing. I don't know of any reason why I can't take care of that."

When Karen returned to the school at 2:00 p.m., the principal looked up from his meeting with several staff members and gave Karen a scowling glance. Karen went back to her office and reviewed the school district's policy manual—something she meant to do before starting her new job. But with packing up at her old school and moving to the new school, she never got around to seeing if the new school's policies differed from the former school's. Her stomach knotted when she read the policy on parental requests for teacher placements.

According to the Oakdale policy, students were placed in classrooms based on their previous year teachers' recommendations and new grade levels, and parental requests would not be honored. Karen checked to see if the new placements had been made yet. She learned that the teachers met during the teacher work week after students left in June. Her two friends' children were not in the same class, and neither of them was placed in Mrs. Sterling's room.

Karen felt a pang of panic and wondered if anyone would find out if she adjusted the class lists. After all, sometimes it is easier to ask forgiveness than permission. Karen wondered if she should she tell her principal, but then she remembered his disapproving look after her long lunch. She wondered what her old friends and PTSA executives would think of her if she went back on her word. What should she do now?

RUBRIC 10.1			
Lens and/or factors to be considered in decision making	What are the factors at play in this case?	What steps should be considered in solving the problem?	What could have been done to avoid this dilemma?
The situation			
• The task	Karen made a commitment to her friends without knowing the new school's policies. Principal may disapprove of her long lunches.	Karen should have read and understood school policy before assuming the role.	Karen should not have committed to request without knowing the policy. Karen might have clarified principal's expectations for her summer work hours.
• Personal abilities	Karen's friendship with her two friends may have interfered with her decision making.	Does Karen have the ethical decision-making ability to tell her friends about the school policy?	Karen should have told friends that she would like to honor their request but would have to check with school policy.
• The school environment	The school environment supports rigid rules for student placement without regard for unusual situations.	Should Karen speak with the school counselor or the principal first?	Read the policy or make no promises until familiar with school's rules.
Look **Wider**			
Organizational (i.e., the organizational goals, values, policies, culture)	School policy versus what may have happened in past practice.	Talk with school counselor and principal.	Principal or central office should have orientation sessions for new administrators.
People (i.e., individuals with needs, beliefs, goals, relationships)	Karen's friends may have an ulterior motive beyond friendship.	Inform friends about policy.	Karen needs to clarify her ethical priorities— doing her job the right way over pleasing friends.
Competing Interests (i.e., competing interests for power, influence, and resources)	School policy about placement requests versus Karen's friendships; Karen's lunch hour versus principal's expectations.	Karen's first priority should be to follow policy about student placement, and know principal's expectations for summer lunch hour.	Find out expectations before inadvertently acting outside them.
Tradition (i.e., school culture, rituals, meaning, heroes)	School culture may be inflexible where flexibility might occasionally be needed.	Karen needs to learn more about the school before suggesting any changes.	Karen might have learned about the school traditions from friends and family living in the community.

OVERVIEW: WHY THE ATTENTION TO ETHICAL DECISION MAKING?

Over the past three decades, the general public's distrust of institutions has grown. A few examples explain why. In 2001, high-risk (fraudulent) accounting practices used to cover billions of dollars of debt from failed deals pushed Enron, the Houston energy giant, into sudden bankruptcy. The debacle lost billions of dollars in investments and retirement savings. In 2007, the subprime mortgage crisis jump-started the Great Recession with banks generating huge profits from slicing, dicing, packaging, and selling high-risk mortgages labeled as "Triple-A" safe. Because the banks were "too big to fail," taxpayers picked up the tab; millions of regular Americans lost their jobs and homes. In 2015, several former Atlanta educators were convicted of racketeering and faced jail time for their roles in a plan to inflate students' standardized test scores. These—and other cases—reflect organizations where leaders and subordinates acted unethically.

Also during this time, researchers in social psychology, organizational psychology, behavioral economics, and behavioral ethics developed and tested a variety of frameworks designed to explain why people make unethical decisions in the workplace.[1] Their conclusions: unethical decisions are not limited to "bad apples."[2] Otherwise "good people" can engage in unethical acts without awareness of their "offensive" character.[3] Factors in the issue, the individual, and the organization all affect (un)ethical decision making.

As organizations, schools also create countless occasions for decision makers to wrestle with ethical issues. How much weight should a principal give to an influential Dad who wants to handpick his child's teachers, despite the school's goal to give every child the opportunity to work with its most effective educators? Should principals assign highly effective, experienced teachers to classrooms with 12 high-powered achievers or to classrooms with 28 struggling students who need the most talented instructors to help them catch up and keep up with rigorous grade level work? These decisions—and others—may not make local headlines, but their impacts affect students' opportunities to learn what they need to advance academically and (eventually) economically and socially.

In this chapter, we will first consider James Rest's basic ethical decision-making theory that underpins many organizational ethics theories.[4] Next, we consider theoretical (and empirical) views about how factors in the issue, the individual, and the environment/context influence ethical decision making and behavior in organizations. A discussion of sensemaking-intuition theories of ethical decision making, dual process theory, and the theory of developing ethical expertise in the workplace follow. We conclude by discussing the implications for educational leadership of these ethical decision-making theories.

THE BASIC ETHICAL DECISION-MAKING PROCESS

People make decisions all the time. They make *ethical decisions* when they face a situation that requires a response or a solution that when performed freely, may harm or help others.[5] *Behavioral ethics* refers to the individual behavior judged according to generally accepted norms of moral or ethical conduct (the terms *moral* and *ethical* are commonly used interchangeably). The definition includes unethical behaviors (such as lying, cheating, and stealing), acts that reach a minimal moral standard and are not unethical (such as honesty or obeying the law), and actions that exceed moral minimums (such as charitable giving and "whistle blowing").[6] As leaders become aware of ethical situations and try to decide *and do* what is right and in the best interest of the organization, the people in it, and the larger community, they help shape their organization's climate and culture.

A Graphic Model of the Ethical Decision-Making Process

In the 1980s and 1990s, James Rest, Thomas Jones, and Linda Treviño introduced theoretical models of ethical decision making in organizations. Building upon rationalistic theories, each contributed to a fuller understanding of how individuals in organizations make and enact ethical decisions. Figure 10.1 integrates many of their ideas into a basic conceptual framework.

As Figure 10.1 illustrates, rationalist theorists (who believe that ethical decision making depends on logical, methodical, cognitive reasoning) see ethical decision making as a process, influenced by the ethical situation, characteristics of the ethical issue, individual variables, and environmental/contextual factors. In their views, ethical decisions stem from the individual's perception of a situation containing ethical issues (*ethical awareness*), the reasoning and judgment used to choose what to do in that circumstance (*ethical judgment*), deciding to enact the ethical decision (*ethical intent*), and performing the *ethical behavior*.[7] Although the process is largely a cognitive one,

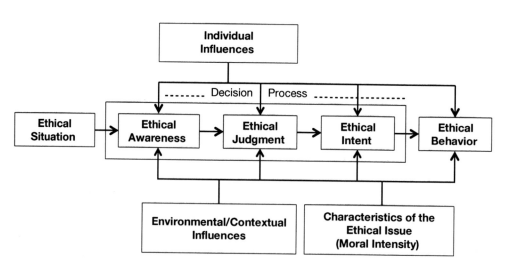

FIGURE 10.1 General Behavior Model for Ethical Decision Making.
Sources: Adapted from Wittmer, D.P. (2005). Developing a behavioral model for ethical decision making in organizations: Conceptual and empirical research. In H.G. Frederickson & R.K. Ghere (Eds), *Ethics in public management* (pp. 49–69, Figure 3.1, p. 54). Armonk, NY: M.E. Sharpe Inc.; Jones, T.M. (1991). Ethical decision making by individuals in organizations: An issue-contingent model. *Academy of Management Review, 16* (2), Figure 1, p. 370.

non-cognitive factors (such as personal experiences, education, emotions, and biases) and environmental factors inside and outside the organization (such as ethical climate, culture, and reward/punishment policies) also come into play. Using Figure 10.1 as a guide, we will discuss each factor in turn.

The Four-Steps Framework for Ethical Decision Making

James R. Rest (1941–1999), a University of Minnesota psychology professor and his colleagues, proposed that ethical decision making in organizations was a series of psychological steps. Integrating the theories and research on moral development and behavior from social, behavioral, psychoanalytic and cognitive perspectives, Rest argued that ethical judgment, although important, is not the only—or even the most important—influence on ethical decision making. The processes of establishing an ethical intent and engaging in ethical action were more important.[8]

Rest asserted that ethical decision making involves four distinct psychological processes: ethical sensitivity (awareness), ethical judgment, ethical motivation/intention, and ethical character/action. In Figure 10.1, these four steps appear as rectangles within the "Decision Process" and can be understood as described below—with related research findings:[9]

- **Ethical sensitivity (awareness).** *Ethical awareness* involves identifying an ethical issue. The person interprets the situation as containing an ethical problem or a relevant ethical standard or principle. The individual also recognizes that any decision or action in response to the circumstance has the potential to affect one's own or others' interests, wellbeing, or expectations.

  Identifying an issue as ethically important is an essential first step because it helps jump-start the ethical decision-making process, making acting ethically more likely. For instance, a principal realizes that creating the master schedule and assigning teachers to courses involves ethical issues related to equity, social justice, and creating meaningful learning opportunities for every student, as well as effective use of time and space. Research finds that ethical awareness is influenced by an array of factors in the issue, the person, and the environment.[10]

- **Ethical judgment.** Ethical judgment occurs once an individual becomes aware of an ethical issue and activates the assessing process. Here, the individual identifies the ethical course of action—what the "right" thing to do is. This step requires the person to reason through the alternative solutions, evaluate each one's possible outcomes, and decide which are ethically sound. Because ethical judgment depends on active and effective cognition, it makes sense that cognitive ethical development is strongly linked to age and education level.[11]

  Using ethical judgment, the principal creating the master schedule in the scenario above, weighs the options of teacher time, course assignments, student loads, and available rooms, and decides to create two sections of Algebra I with 15 students per class and one section of Math analysis with 30 students. In this way, struggling students have more opportunities for teachers to check their understanding and give prompt feedback to support their learning; the high achieving students need less individual teacher time in order to succeed.

- **Ethical intent.** The individual resolves to choose the ethical decision over a solution representing a different value—such as enhancing one's own interests or loyalty to a friend. A person's "sense of felt obligation" to act in a certain, principled way mediates the relationship between moral attitudes, judgments, and behaviors.[12] A teacher who knows ahead of time that he will be absent from his classroom and makes a mental note to prearrange his absence, secure a competent substitute, and prepare thoughtful lesson plans for use during his absence is acting with ethical intent. Researchers have found that ethical intent may be largely cognitive, but non-conscious; a more automatic, intuitive process based on individuals' mental maps[13] often influences the reasoning processes.[14]

- **Ethical behavior.** An individual performs the chosen ethical actions. As much a character component as a cognitive one, this step involves courage, skills, and determination to take the necessary steps to perform the ethical action despite obstacles. When the teacher in the above scenario actually informs the school secretary of the planned absence, secures (or arranges to secure) the competent substitute, and prepares useful lessons plans, he is enacting ethical behavior. Research supports the view that people with a greater sense of efficacy can initiate and maintain their intentions and translate them into action, even in the face of obstacles.[15]

Although these four steps are arranged logically, Rest posited that each step is separate and can affect the others. Failure at any phase can lead the person to not make or enact an ethical decision. For instance, the principal above may have strong moral judgment skills and is vocal about championing equity and social justice—and can clearly reason and evaluate alternative solutions—but will not be able to use them if he or she does not have the ethical sensitivity to recognize that building a master schedule contains a moral issue.

In the years since Rest's theory appeared, investigators have tested a wide assortment of concepts that influence this four-step process. Comprehensive reviews of the research on ethical decision making in organizations based on Rest's four-stage model generally support his framework's usefulness.[16]

REFLECTIONS AND RELEVANCE 10.1

Applying Rest's Framework

James Rest proposed an ethical decision-making framework that involves four distinct psychological processes: ethical sensitivity (awareness), ethical judgment, ethical motivation/intention, and ethical action.

In small groups of 3 or 4, construct a school-based situation—or use Case Study 10.1—in which an educator follows Rest's four steps in awareness, judgment, intent, and enacting an ethical decision. Present situations to class and discuss the usefulness and/or impracticality of using Rest's model for ethical decision making.

Issue Factors in Ethical Decision Making

Thomas M. Jones, Professor of Management at the University of Washington, built upon Rest's four-step model of ethical decision making in organizations. Jones proposed an issues-contingent theory in which the ethical issue's characteristics—its *moral intensity*—influence how the individual makes ethical decisions.

Jones defined *moral issues* as those decisions that an individual chooses to make that involve generating outcomes for others—ranging in a continuum from trivial to life ending. People may respond in different ways to ethical issues, he suggested, in a manner systematically related to the issue's specific characteristics. Ethical decision making, therefore, is contingent, depending on the moral issue itself as well as various factors in the individual and the environment.

Jones's primary interest was on qualities in the moral issue, itself—collectively called *moral intensity*—and how these characteristics affected ethical decision making.[17] Specifically, Jones's theory asserts that moral intensity has six dimensions representing every issue: size of consequences, social consensus, probability of effect, immediacy in time, proximity, and concentration of effect. These six aspects of moral intensity—all cognitive factors—impact each of Rest's four steps in the ethical decision-making process.

In Figure 10.1, moral intensity appears as "Characteristics of the Ethical Issue," influencing the four ethical decision steps. Let us consider these six characteristics in more detail.

- **Magnitude of consequences**: the sum total of the harms (or benefits) that the decision maker's actions do to victims (or beneficiaries). For instance, a behavior that harms 5,000 people is much larger than the same injury done to five people. An act that causes another person's death is of higher magnitude than an act that causes a broken bone. Most consequences in organizations do not reach a life-threatening or life-ending threshold.
- **Social consensus**: the extent of agreement among a social group that a proposed act is right or wrong. The group may be as large as the nation or as small as one's friendship circle. A strong social consensus or community standard that an act is ethically wrong increases its moral intensity. For instance, a human resources official who actively practiced his or her bias against hiring minority workers would likely receive social disapproval. But whereas legal decisions come with the clear weight of community consensus that this action is wrong, unethical decisions tend to lack such clear community norms and are more morally ambiguous.
- **Probability of effect**: the likelihood that the predicted consequences and the expected degree of benefit or harm will happen. Bad acts that are less likely to happen carry a lower probability of effect than bad acts that almost surely will cause much injury. For example, selling a gun to a person known to have served jail time for domestic violence has a greater chance of causing harm than selling the gun to a law-abiding citizen without prior violent behavior. Although individuals cannot accurately estimate these probabilities, their reasonable guesses may be enough to alert them to expect good or bad outcomes from their decisions.

- **Temporal immediacy:** the length of time between the action and its consequences. The shorter the time between the act and the outcome, the greater is its immediacy. For instance, changing the state teachers' retirement formula to increase employees' contributions and decrease employers' contributions to teacher pensions for all current and future employees to begin in five years has less temporal immediacy than changing the formula with everyone to begin after the start of the next school year. People tend to minimize events—discount the magnitude of consequences—that will happen far in the future.
- **Proximity:** the feeling of nearness (social, cultural, psychological, or physical) that the person making the ethical decision has to the individuals potentially affected by the consequences. People tend to care more about others to whom they feel close than they do about those who are far away or with whom they have no personal relationship. For instance, a reduction in force (RIF) in one's own school district has a greater proximity (physical, social, and psychological) than an RIF in another state. Research supports this concept.[18] Most principals and teachers have psychological—if not physical—proximity to their students, making protecting them from potential harm an ethical issue.
- **Concentration of effect:** an inverse function of the number of people affected by an act of a given magnitude. For instance, cheating 10 people out of $100 each has a more concentrated effect than cheating 100 people out of $10 each.

According to Jones, the vividness of a situation's moral intensity catches the decision maker's attention. Issues with high salience appear more extreme (greater magnitude of consequences), stand out (have higher concentration of effect), or involve others who are important or close (greater proximity) to the decision maker.[19] Issues with vividness are emotionally compelling, concrete, memory evoking, and close (socially, physically, culturally, psychologically proximate).[20] Social cognition research supports this view, suggesting that issues with high moral intensity are more vivid and salient and more likely to gain the individual's attention and be identified as ethical issues.[21]

Research supports many of Jones' ideas. Studies have found that social consensus,[22] magnitude of consequences,[23] probability of effect,[24] and proximity[25]—in combination or apart—are significant predictors of moral awareness, moral judgment, and moral intention.[26] In contrast, concentration of effect and temporal immediacy have been found to have little influence on the ethical decision-making process.[27]

REFLECTIONS AND RELEVANCE 10.2

Issue Factors in Ethical Decision Making

Thomas Jones proposed that ethical decision making depends on aspects of the moral issue as well as individual and environmental factors.

Working in pairs, identify a moral issue that you recently addressed. Then identify how the six dimensions of moral intensity in that situation impacted the ethical reasoning and decision of what action to take. When finished, discuss as a class.

- Magnitude of consequences
- Social consensus
- Probability of effect
- Temporal immediacy
- Proximity
- Concentration of effect

INDIVIDUAL FACTORS IN ETHICAL DECISION MAKING IN ORGANIZATIONS

Individual differences can strongly influence ethical decision making. The individual's ethical beliefs, cognitive capacity, emotions, education or training, and other variables have been found to shape whether and how individuals develop ethical awareness and whether and how they make and enact ethical decisions.[28] Figure 10.2 presents a model of individual factors in ethical decision making. Let's consider each in turn.

Cognitive Capacities and Ethical Decision Making

The ability to make ethical decisions rests, to a large degree, in an individual's cognitive capacities. To identify a situation's ethical implications, gather facts, and evaluate

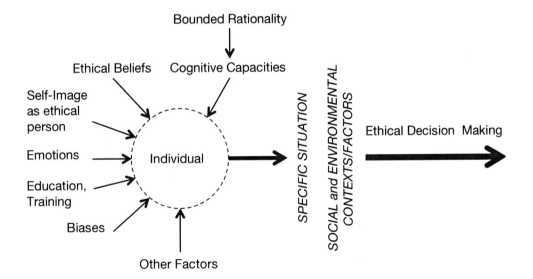

FIGURE 10.2 Individual Factors in Ethical Decision Making

Source: Based on Simon, H. (1991). Bounded rationality and organizational learning. *Organization Science*, 2 (1), 125–134; Reynolds, S.J. (2006). Moral awareness and ethical predispositions: Investigating the role of individual differences in the recognition of moral issues. *Journal of Applied Psychology*, 91 (1), 233–243.

alternate solutions' potential effectiveness and their ethical import requires a high level of abstract reasoning. It is not a surprise, therefore, that researchers generally find a positive relationship between an individual's cognitive moral development, ethical judgment, and ethical decision making.[29] But an individual's cognition is subject to many influences, including bounded rationality, biases, and emotions. These factors can restrain and weaken people's cognitive effectiveness, leaving room for other influences to enter ethical decision making.

Herbert A. Simon's *bounded rationality* concept asserts that individual decision making is constrained by the facts they have, the time available, and their own mental limits.[30] As a result, relying on individuals' cognition as the primary engine for ethical decision making in organizations is unrealistic.

Cognitive styles of problem solving and decision making—the characteristic ways one thinks—are another aspect of bounded rationality.[31] Individuals differ in their *cognitive complexity* (a measure of one's ability to assess multiple aspects of a problem situation) and in their *tolerance of ambiguity* (the degree of acceptance for dealing with uncertain situations). Similarly, personality traits, psychological needs, self concept, demographic factors, values, and one's memory of experiences all influence how an individual perceives, recognizes, and addresses an ethical dilemma and possible consequences. As a result, decision makers' actions may be more shaped by these internal dynamics than by the reality of the actual problem circumstances.[32]

Cognitive biases—the ways that people tend to misapply, ignore, or otherwise fail to use ethical awareness in decision making—can also constrain rational thinking. Negative outcomes for individuals, groups, and organizations may result. Limiting the number of alternative solutions considered before deciding how to act is an example of cognitive bias. Similarly, individuals may have a cognitive bias regarding who is "inside" or "outside" their group—based on personal prejudices and incorrect ideas about social groups. Research is consistent about who is considered to be "inside" or "outside" the moral community boundary in ethical situations: "Insiders" receive fair treatment. "Outsiders" do not.[33] As a result, out-group members are more likely to be harmed because they are excluded from ethical consideration. Given today's diversity in students, parents, and co-workers from varying cultural and geographic backgrounds, such "ethical exclusion" is highly problematic.

Individuals' Ethical Beliefs: "This is Who I Am"

Morality's motivating power is in its degree of integration with the self. If morality is central to a person's self-concept—"This is who I am"—failure to act ethically creates cognitive dissonance and emotional discomfort.[34] Not acting ethically becomes a betrayal of self. A teacher who stays most afternoons to work individually with struggling students because she wants to help them perform well in class is being true to who she sees herself as—a caring educator. Research finds that judgments that fit well with one's identity are shown to be more stable and lasting than judgments that are not in harmony with one's identity.[35]

Emotions in Ethical Decision Making

Emotion is an affective "feeling" state (usually positive or negative) that consists of a level of arousal (varying in intensity from mild to intense) that results from the appraisal of the initiating situation.[36] Until 2001, scholars of organizational ethics behavior generally assumed that emotions—positive or negative—had no place in a "rational" ethical decision-making process. Since then, researchers have found that emotion is intrinsic (and inevitable) to the process of making rational, ethical decisions, and attention to one's emotions may lead to better ethical decisions.[37]

Emotions influence cognitive processes. All stimuli evoke automatic affective evaluations that may strongly sway judgments and behaviors.[38] As a result, ethical situations and decisions are often affectively charged. Arguing that emotions are integral to rational decision making—and their effects may produce better or worse outcomes— Alice Gaudine and Linda Thorne, two Canadian ethics professors, hypothesize an affective relationship (with high or low arousal and positive or negative affect) to each of Rest's four steps in ethical decision making.[39] They suggest emotional arousal from awareness of a moral situation may even trigger the decision-making process. Ignoring these affective elements or assuming that they can be removed from making ethical decisions opens ethical reasoning to subjectivity, bias, and rationalization—and harmful outcomes. Likewise, people's aversion to the anxiety of uncertainty may lead them to avoid situations that contain an ethical dilemma or to choose the least-conflictual (and perhaps less effective) alternative solution.[40]

Fully discussing the research on emotion's influence on ethical decision making is beyond this chapter's scope. Nonetheless, the influence of affective processes on (un)ethical behaviors is complex and multiple, and their effects are likely to depend, in part, on the situational context.

REFLECTIONS AND RELEVANCE 10.3

Individual Factors in Ethical Decision Making

Individual differences can strongly influence ethical decision making. Who are you as an ethical decision maker? What has been the most difficult ethical decision you ever had to make?

Working individually, consider all the individual beliefs, cognitive, emotional, and additional factors that comprise you as an ethical decision maker. Identify several key words to describe yourself on each dimension and use these to create a word cloud, using letter size, shape, and color to illustrate their importance to you. Then working in small groups, introduce yourself to the others as you see yourself as an ethical decision maker, describing your most difficult ethical decision and your characteristics as an ethical decision maker. As a class, identify the most frequently used terms to describe this class as ethical decision makers. What types of ethical decisions do you observe in your present work setting?

ENVIRONMENTAL/CONTEXTUAL FACTORS IN ETHICAL DECISION MAKING

Making and acting upon ethical decisions are difficult enough when done alone. But organizational factors—bosses, colleagues, and clients; available opportunities; organizational culture; and situational variables—add extra layers of complications. Covertly or overtly, these factors affect the person's ability to reason and act ethically.

Investigators have found the following environmental variables related to ethical decision making in organizations:[41]

- **Codes of ethics.** Ethics codes typically spell out the organization's conduct standards, including the administration's core values and the types of ethical and legal issues employees are likely to face. Research on the impact of codes of ethics on organizational behavior has produced varied results. Although a 2010 meta-analytic review found no significant independent effect of codes of ethics on unethical choices,[42] research did find that employees' perceptions that the existing ethical code is enforced reduced unethical behavior. Ethical code enforcement is critical: data suggest that if employees cynically view the code of ethics as "only window dressing," increased unethical behavior may result. More positively, in 2012, the Ethics Resource Center found that formal comprehensive, multiple-part ethics programs are linked with a reduction in employees feeling pressure to compromise standards or to risk retaliation for reporting unethical behavior and increased reporting of misconduct.[43]

- **Ethical climate/culture.** *Ethical climate* is a shared perception among organization members about the criteria (such as kindness or principle) and focus (such as individual, group, community, or larger society) of ethical reasoning.[44] *Ethical culture* is an aspect of organizational culture that influences employees' ethical behavior through formal (e.g., rules and policies, performance management systems) and informal (e.g., norms, language, rituals) ethics-related organizational structures and systems.[45] Organizational climate and culture affect what behaviors are rewarded or disciplined. Members pay close attention. Research finds that organizational settings where the leadership, the reward system, and the cultural norms all supported ethical behavior had the largest negative influence on unethical conduct. In contrast, in organizations where these expectations were absent in leadership, rewards, and culture, a climate focused on self-interest exerted the most influence on unethical behavior.[46] Studies also affirm that subunits within an organization may create varied ethical culture and climate environments.[47] For instance, the Counseling and Social Studies Departments in the same school may operate by two very different sets of ethical rules and create two different ethical climates.

- **Organizational leadership influence.** As the organizations' authority figures, leaders have the power to get employees' attention and hold them accountable for meeting ethical standards. Employees tend to observe the standards their leaders set, express, and enact (or neglect to set, express, and enact). *Ethical leadership* can be defined as "the demonstration of normatively appropriate conduct through personal actions and interpersonal relationships, and the promotion of such conduct to followers through two-way communication, reinforcement, and decision-making."[48] Through their personal actions, interpersonal relationships, and promotion of such behavior in others, school leaders are their organization's ethical role models.[49] Studies find that ethical leadership behaviors have positive outcomes for employees and organizations. The more skilled the leader at communicating ethical awareness, ethical reasoning and judgment, and ethical actions, the more employees express ethical beliefs and see their organization as having an ethical climate.[50] Ethical leadership has also been found to reduce employees' inappropriate and unethical behavior.[51] Likewise, investigators found employees' perceptions of their supervisors' ethical leadership were linked with followers' willingness to report problems to management, to their dedication to the job, and to satisfaction with the supervisor.[52] Also, leadership influence on ethical behavior interacts with peer influence to impact ethical conduct: employees are more likely to feel safe reporting misconduct if they believe they have both their leaders' and their peers' support for doing so.[53] By contrast, leadership behaviors can also negatively effect employees' ethical behavior. Abuse by supervisors increases the likelihood of unethical behaviors by followers and lessens the likelihood that they will report misconduct.[54] And organizations characterized by strong expectations that members *obey* authority figures—a version of "do as I say, not as I do,"—have been found to have higher levels of unethical behavior than other organizations.[55]

- **Peer influence.** Since most employees work with other people, colleagues exert a potentially strong influence on ethical behavior. For better or worse, peers "help to establish a standard for ethical behavior through their actions or inaction."[56] Feeling psychologically close or connected to someone who acts either ethically (or unethically) can influence a colleague to move toward ethical (or unethical) attitudes and behaviors.[57] How peers speak about events at school—their use of ethical language—is one way that colleagues influence each other's moral awareness. Individuals who openly talk about ethics in organization are a good predictor of ethical conduct in that organization.[58] In contrast, "moral muteness" in organizations tends to support ethically problematic behavior.[59] A teacher who overhears coworkers complaining about certain "helicopter parents" might be less likely to join in if another colleague remarked, "Talking about children's private business is unprofessional!" This relationship between language and behavior is likely because of the language's impact on concept formation, employees' mental models, and moral awareness and decision making. Other studies support this view.[60]

- **Rewards and punishments.** Studies consistently (but not unanimously) find that unethical behavior tends to be more widespread in organizations that reward unethical behavior and less prevalent in organizations that punish it.[61] The relationship between ethical behavior and rewards is complex. For instance, individuals' expectations of fairness generate assumptions that ethical violators will be disciplined.[62] But when this expectation of fairness is not met, self-protective and possibly unethical behaviors may result. Studies show that weak punishments or sanctions—a mere "slap on the hand" for a highly disturbing offense—can generate more unethical behavior than having no sanctions at all.[63] Likewise, receiving economic incentives for "doing the right thing" can undermine individuals' motivation to engage in that behavior.[64]

- **Situational variables.** The situational factors that can contribute to unethical behaviors are too numerous to count. They include explicit, on-the-job pressures to act unethically, such as intense pressures to meet organizational goals[65] and role conflict (having a role with competing and contradictory expectations).[66] The Atlanta cheating scandal in which school administrators changed students' achievement test answers to raise schools' test scores is a case in point.

- **Additional environmental influences.** The research findings on organization size and ethical behavior are mixed; more studies are needed.[67] Besides the immediate context, more distant environmental elements also affect ethical decision making in organizations. These include: the governmental and legal environment (with their lawful requirements, judicial consequences, and strong social stigma that come from breaking them); the professional environment (such as ethical conduct codes affirmed in state or national licensing procedures and professional organizations); and personal environments (such as family and peer group norms and attitudes that affect the member's private life outside the organization).[68] School counselors, for instance, learn in their graduate programs that they must clearly advise all counselees at the first meeting that their relationship with the counselor is confidential *unless* the counselor has reason to believe the counselees intend to harm themselves or another. These and other variables affect how individuals perceive and act on workplace events that carry ethical dimensions.

Limitations of the Rationalistic Models

Although rational deliberation models have much empirical support, they have their weaknesses. First, critics argue that the research methodology is limiting, relying on an inadequate range of ethical frameworks, placing too much emphasis on deliberate ethical reasoning, and depending on oversimplified evidence.[69] Detractors also note that the rationalist models ignore the non-deliberative and non-conscious processes that often affect ethical behavior and behavior in general.[70] Evidence suggests that ethical judgment and behavior can occur *without* prior deliberative reasoning. Often, individuals cannot explain their reasons for their strong ethical responses.[71] And even if they can, their after-the-fact explanations do not prove that they engaged in ethical reasoning *before* their behavior.[72] Likewise, evidence suggests that individuals can make ethical judgments when under heavy *cognitive loads*—when they have to produce a large amount of mental activity and effort—as well as when they are not. Therefore, intentional deliberate thought is not always needed to form and enact ethical judgments.[73] Also, the fact that ethical judgments are closely linked to emotion suggests that conscious reasoning has its limits as initiator of actual ethical decision making and behavior.[74] Sometimes intuitive, emotional, and deliberate processes actually intertwine in the ethical decision-making process.[75]

Although rationalistic theories of ethical decision making in organizations and their research support have clarified how decision makers actually become aware of, think about, and act upon ethical issues, scholars recognize these theories' limitations. The idea of *sensemaking*—the process by which individuals living in a complex, dynamic world give meaning to their experiences—more fully expands our understanding of how people in organizations make ethical decisions.

REFLECTIONS AND RELEVANCE 10.4

Taking an Ethical Environmental Audit

Many environmental variables impact ethical decision making in organizations. You have been asked to conduct an Ethical Environment Audit for your school. First working alone and then in pairs, identify whether each of the factors is largely present or absent in your present workplace. Then identify the top three factors that most influence your own ethical conduct in your workplace. After pairs have finished, discuss as a class which school environmental factors school leaders can impact the most—and why.

Ethical Climate Factor	Presence in My School: Largely Present/Absent	Rank Order of Importance (1=highest)
Codes of ethics		
Ethical climate/culture		
Organizational leadership influence		
Peer influence		
Rewards and punishments		
Situational variables		
Organization size		
Additional factors:		

SENSEMAKING: MORAL INTUITION MODELS OF ETHICAL DECISION MAKING

Although behavioral ethicists initially theorized that ethical decision making in organizations was a deliberate, rational process, a rapidly expanding body of research has proposed the opposite: that ethical decision making is not always deliberative and rational. It can also be affective, intuitive, and impulsive. And like rational approaches, often open to error or situational influences.[76]

Moral intuition has been defined as "the sudden appearance in consciousness . . . of an evaluative feeling (like-dislike, good-bad) about a person or event without any conscious awareness of having gone through steps of weighting evidence, crafting evaluative arguments, or inferring a conclusion."[77] Some investigators consider the ethical decision-making process's underpinnings to be neurological[78] and affective.[79] Others view moral intuition as moral schema ("mental maps") or conceptually scripted responses that are so well learned that they become implicit, quickly accessible without deliberate thinking.[80] Many scholars support this view.[81]

The Sensemaking-Intuition Model of Ethical Decision Making in Organizations

In 2007, Scott Sonenshein, a management professor at Rice University, introduced the Sensemaking-Intuition Model (SIM) of ethical decision making in organizations. Sonenshein argues that issues are not inherently ethical or unethical. Rather, people in ambiguous and uncertain environments (typical of work organizations) do not so much make *rational* decisions as they make *sense* out of the stimuli that they face. That is, individuals socially construct ethical issues through a process of *sensemaking*—making quick intuitive judgments about ethical issues and then justifying their decisions to others.[82]

Figure 10.3 shows three phases of the sensemaking-intuition process of making ethical decisions in organizations: issue construction, intuitive-judgment, and explanation and justification. The SIM works as follows:[83]

- **Phase One: Issue Construction.** Individuals make their world meaningful to themselves in response to social stimuli in ambiguous and uncertain environments. When many interpretations of an event are possible, individuals become confused. They engage in sensemaking because they need a credible interpretation and some guidance as to how they should act. Both individuals and groups engage in sensemaking. For example, when Franklin High School's 3-year graduation ring contract with Custom Rings Company ended, principal Bill Allen sent requests to several ring companies for bids. He reviewed the offers and selected the company with the lowest bid. Three months later, he received a package containing a 16K gold Penn State ring inscribed with Bill's name and the year he earned his doctorate there. The enclosed card read, "With best wishes." Bill was puzzled. That afternoon, the English Department Chair stepped into Bill's office and asked, "Did you get the

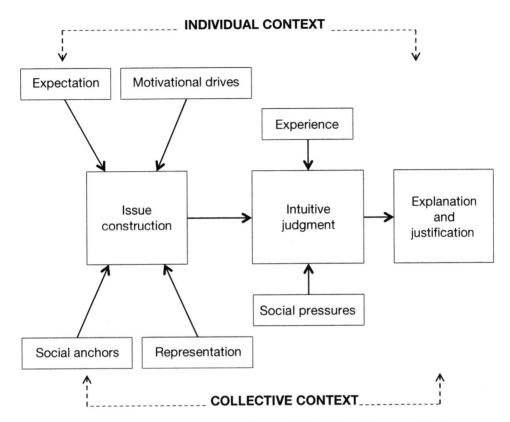

FIGURE 10.3 The Sensemaking–Intuition Model (SIM) of Ethical Decision Making

Source: Adapted from Sonenshein S. (2007). The role of construction, intuition, and justification in responding to ethical issues at work: the sensemaking-intuition model. *Academy of Management Review, 32* (4), 1028.

gift in the mail from my brother?" It seems the teacher's brother was the ring salesman with whom Bill signed the school's contract. Heart pounding, Bill instantly saw a conflict of interest. The salesman did not disclose that his brother was a faculty member. Could receiving the expensive ring be part of a plan to make it appear that Bill was taking a bribe in exchange for signing the contract? His discomfort alerted him to the reality that his situation was ethically fraught. What should he do?

Both individual and collective contexts affect sensemaking. At the individual level, social psychology[84] and organizational psychology[85] scholars support the idea that the person's expectations and past experiences powerfully influence how they perceive events. At the collective level, social anchors and representation will influence behavior. In Figure 10.3, *social anchors* refer to those persons in the individual's collegial or friendship network upon whom the individual may rely to get "a fresh set of eyes" to help expand the individual's thinking about what the situation means and how to address it. *Representation* refers to individuals having a mental model of how others see a situation. This conceptual image, often shared during informal conversations, gives individuals data and perspective about others' interpretations that can help broaden the person's own understanding of an event.

Continuing the scenario, as Bill anxiously debated what to do, he remembered something his father had always told him: "Don't do anything in private that you don't want to appear headlined in the *Baltimore Sun*." This maxim stayed with Bill, and he never would feel comfortable doing anything that he would not want printed in the newspaper.

- **Phase Two: Intuitive Judgment.** The process of constructing meaning ends (at least temporarily) when an individual reaches a credible interpretation. As soon as a person understands a situation as an ethical issue, the person instantly makes an *intuitive judgment*—an automatic, instantaneous reaction based on affect (a non-rational process)[86] of what is good or bad, right or wrong. These intuitions are influenced by individual-level factors (experience) and a collective-level factor (social pressure). As individuals gain experiences, they gradually learn how to handle certain situations, and they internalize these learnings into intuitions.[87] These non-rational factors include moral inclinations (such as sympathy, cooperation, conflict resolution, and mutual aid),[88] religious scruples,[89] emotions (such as anger, guilt, or shame), or a personal relationship with and feelings about the object of their ethical judgment.[90]

Bill had internalized his father's maxim; he sensed instantly that this situation was wrong. Bill identified alternatives. He could keep the ring or he could return it. He could pay the full retail price for it or pay only the salesman's wholesale cost. He could cancel the ring contract. Weighing the options, he believed it wrong to keep the expensive ring or to pay less than the full retail price. He could not return it without extra cost to the ring company because it was engraved with his name and graduation year; the company would have to reprocess it. He did not want to cancel the contract because students had already placed their ring orders. So he wrote a check to the salesperson for the full retail price and mailed it.

- **Phase Three: Explanation and Justification.** Because intuitions happen rapidly and below consciousness, individuals are often unaware of the process by which they reached a decision about an ethical issue. As a result, ethically compromised behavior often occurs unwittingly; the individuals do not always consciously recognize what they are doing because they are not using high levels of conscious thinking. Research suggests that individuals rarely change their minds from their initial responses to moral issues, even after being given new evidence and engaging in careful reasoning.[91] But they are aware of their reaction to an issue and their related actions. They explain and justify their reaction by looking back at themselves and ask, "Why did I react the way I did?"

Continuing Bill's story, after sending the full retail price check to purchase the ring, he informed the superintendent about the events and explained his actions to resolve the situation. Individuals often rationalize their actions after-the-fact by using socially constructed accounts that keep their favorable identity in the face of corrupt behavior. These explanations and justifications may include ethical reasoning—our American culture encourages individuals to use reasoning, rationality, and logic in response to moral issues. Because intuitive judgments happen so quickly and beneath awareness, individuals infer that they must have reasoned in some logical and rational way to reach their assessment of the issue, even if they didn't. They also justify their judgment in the same way, using tools of rational analysis after the fact. Research supports this view.[92]

In SIM, the three phases are related. Individuals construct ethical issues from equivocal and uncertain environments, develop intuitive judgments about their constructions, and explain and justify those reactions. The boundaries among these phases are somewhat fluid, however. Intuitions may emerge during any point of the process. In fact, the concept of sensemaking ends separations between cognition and action.[93]

Research and Criticism of Moral Intuition Models

Research shows that a large part of cognitive thought happens outside of consciousness.[94] Nonetheless, critics challenge both moral intuition theory's concepts and methodology[95] and reject the claim that deliberative reasoning is no more than a post-hoc rationalization for a gut reaction.[96] Critics argue that bursts of emotion are overvalued, and intuition can be flawed or wrong (as in a criminal mind).[97] They also make the case that even if a person's first responses to an ethical dilemma are intuitive, those intuitions are actually shaped and primed by the individual's prior learning and environmental factors that are both deliberative and inferential.[98] And, critics continue, rational deliberation still plays a role as individuals *reconsider* (rather than rationalize) their moral intuition-based judgment in light of other prior learning and influences.[99] In short, critics contend that intuitions are merely starting—and ending—points for rational deliberation.[100]

In turn, sensemaking theorists contend that their critics distort the meaning of moral intuitionist models, noting that these models do include various types of conscious reasoning. Intuition and reasoning—as well the individual's emotional assessments—are all types of cognition.[101] In the end, research supports aspects of each approach.

REFLECTIONS AND RELEVANCE 10.5

Using the Sensemaking-Intuition Model (SIM)

Sensemaking-intuition models of ethical decision making posit that under conditions of ambiguity and uncertainty, we do not so much *make* rational decisions as we *make sense* out of the stimuli that confront us.

Working in groups of four, apply the SIM approach to case study 10.1 (or any personal example of using intuition in making an ethical decision). Describe what Karen might have told herself as she used sensemaking to figure out the situation her friends' request created and what she should do:

- Phase 1: issue construction—relying on individual factors, social anchors, and representations;
- Phase 2: intuitive judgment—applying notions of right or wrong, good or bad; personal experiences; social pressure; and intuitions based on non-rational factors including intuitions, religious scruples, emotions, personal relationships and feelings about the object of her ethical judgment;
- Phase 3: explanation and justification—creating socially constructed accounts after the fact to explain what she did and why she did it.

After all groups are finished, discuss the usefulness of the SIM model as a descriptor of ethical decision making.

THE DUAL PROCESS APPROACH

Since both rationalist and sensemaking approaches to ethical decision making have theoretical, anecdotal, and research support, contemporary scholars are building a consensus around a "two-system" approach for ethical decision making. In this dual theory, both conscious deliberation and intuition contribute to effective ethical decisions and outcomes.[102]

Research shows that rational decision making and intuition may be more effective in certain situations than in others. Rational analysis may be more effective than intuition for tasks involving well-defined situations and definite objective criteria for success.[103] By contrast, intuition may be superior to rational analysis for judgments of tasks that involve "political, ethical, aesthetic, moral, or behavioral judgments" that lack objective criteria or visible solutions.[104] A novice principal may know that by policy, community members have 5 minutes to speak at school board meetings. By comparison, an experienced administrator who frequently attends school board meetings may recognize a change in a board member's behaviors when a difficult subject arises and intuit that the person is uncomfortable with the topic.

Likewise, research also finds that in unstable environments—when decision makers cannot depend on structured problems and "standard operating procedures"—intuitive decision making among executives results in greater organizational performance.[105] By its holistic associative nature, intuition may produce data that is not immediately available to conscious thinking and help integrate dissimilar elements of a problem into a coherent idea of how to move forward.[106] Research on intuition suggests that intuitions may have an advantage over rationality in circumstances that include the presence of positive moods,[107] stable individual differences in thinking styles,[108] and cultures that are accepting of ambiguity and chaos.[109]

Clearly, intuition can be a useful complement to rational thinking. In fact, some suggest that true expertise involves using both types of decision making.[110] In today's organizations, the ultimate skill may be the ability to alternate between the two. Although this *makes sense* anecdotally, empirical research in this area will be needed to determine whether this is so.

DEVELOPING ETHICAL EXPERTISE AT WORK

Just as people can develop expertise in sports, chess, or law, they can develop expertise in making ethical decisions. One might expect that as people gain more experience in life or the workplace, they become more able to make better ethical decisions. This is not necessarily the case. Research has found little agreement about the relationship between experience and ethical decision making in the workplace.[111] It could be that experience, alone, is not enough.

Constructing Complex Mental Models

From a workplace perspective, *ethical expertise* "is the degree to which one is knowledgeable about and skilled at applying moral values within a given work context"—an organization, an occupation, or a profession.[112] Ethical expertise can be learned (to varying extents) through experience, training, practice, and/or effort.

The more complex one's mental models, the more likely they will activate automatically when exposed to domain-related cues.[113] For instance, master teachers' cognitive schema makes them more likely to spot—and correctly interpret—classroom-related events than novice teachers who lack these experiences.[114] The novice may interpret two students talking to each other during a class assignment as cheating, while a master teacher may interpret this as students' desire for affiliation, peer support, and/or enacting cultural values. These divergent interpretations based on varying amounts of classroom experience and knowledge of students' background differences may lead to different teacher responses.

Likewise, the more complex an individuals' content-specific cognitive schema, the more those persons tend to perceive the ethical issues involved in the problems before them. These mental maps not only sensitize individuals to ethical problems. Persons are more likely to notice the problems' context and subtleties in ways that influence their ethical judgments. Research finds that experts' intuitive judgments tend to be both accurate and domain relevant.[115]

A Model: Developing Ethical Expertise at Work

Expertise research also suggests that expecting experience—by itself—to lead to ethical know-how is probably an oversimplification. Developing proficiency in a certain domain requires active participation and ample repetition over time with rapid and accurate feedback linked with a high degree of reflection, an essential component of learning.[116] Developing ethical decision-making expertise is no different.

As illustrated in Figure 10.4, Erik Dane and Scott Sonenshein, Rice University business professors, theorize that organization members gain ethical expertise to the extent that they actively and repeatedly engage with moral problems in the work setting. Ethical expertise grows as individuals participate in ethical decision making experiences in their organizations, receive high-quality social feedback, and reflect on this feedback. Let's consider their model:

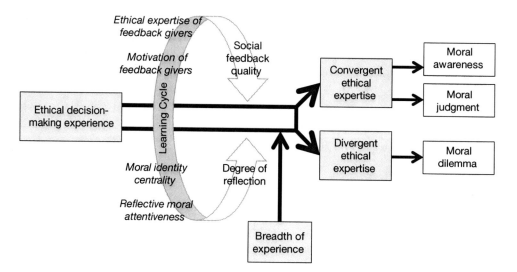

FIGURE 10.4 How Professionals Gain Ethical Expertise

Source: Adapted from Dane, E. & Sonenshein, S. (2015). On the role of experience in ethical decision making at work. An ethical expertise perspective. *Organizational Psychology Review, 5* (1), 79.

- **Ethical decision-making experience.** As organizational members engage with moral problems at work, they gain ethical decision-making experience.
- **The learning cycle.** Characteristics of the feedback givers (namely, their own ethical expertise and motivation for giving comment) and the decision makers (namely, their tendency to reflect seriously on decisions and experiences and the extent to which they value themselves as ethical people) contribute to the learning cycle. As a result, the social feedback's quality and the individual's degree of reflection on this feedback add to the individual's maturing ethical expertise. If the input or feedback disagrees with the individual's ideas or decisions so as to generate cognitive dissonance,[117] the individual is more likely to modify later decisions in ways that align with the organizationally "approved" solution. Cognitively, this adjusted view reflects an increased complexity of their context-specific mental maps. A novice A.P. may be confused when the principal asks a student to wear his T-shirt sporting a swastika inside out (or go home and change shirts). When the principal explains how a Nazi symbol was likely to disrupt the learning environment, the new A.P. rethinks his ideas about appropriate school attire.
- **Social feedback quality.** The feedback may vary in accuracy, precision, or general quality. Research suggests that feedback tends to be of higher quality when a person motivated to help others gives it (rather than being self-serving or ill-intentioned).[118] Receiving low-quality feedback can weaken the learning cycle and limit the development of ethical expertise. Dane and Sonenshein suggest that the quality of social feedback one receives is likely related to "the company one keeps at work."[119]
- **Degree of reflection.** Reflection involves thinking about prior events to gain insights or lessons. The relationship between ethical decision-making experience and the ethical expertise gained is probably stronger for individuals who spend time

reflecting about the moral problems they faced, the decisions they made in response, and how these decisions played out (successfully or unsuccessfully) within their work setting. These individuals are said to have a high degree of *reflective moral attentiveness*.[120] In contrast, those who do not reflect on these experiences and related feedback probably gain less ethical expertise; they have less reflective moral attentiveness. Scholars suggest that those who value themselves as highly ethical persons are strongly motivated to keep their decisions consistent with their moral identity.[121] They are likely to seriously reflect on their decisions and actions to ensure they are ethical.

- **Breadth of experience.** Experience is more than age, tenure, or opportunities for making ethical decisions. While research affirms that feedback[122] and reflection[123] help people identify an acceptable solution to an ethical problem (labeled in Figure 10.4 as *convergent ethical expertise*), feedback and reflection may also help individuals learn to think more flexibly about problems and generate unusual but effective solutions (labeled in Figure 10.4 as *divergent ethical expertise*).[124] Research indicates that individuals who think divergently tend to be persons who have gained experience in a variety of work settings, work units, and organizations and in a wide array of roles and tasks[125]—even in industries beyond the one where the current problem arose. Their experiences across varied domains that may differ significantly in their rules, principles, or norms, increase the flexibility in their mental models.[126] These individuals develop complex and flexible mental maps that allow them to work with and integrate moral values in innovative, differing, and effective ways.
- **Moral awareness, moral judgment, and moral dilemma.** According to Dane and Sonenshein's theory, convergent ethical expertise (in Figure 10.4, leading to moral awareness and moral judgment) reflects the rationalist perspective on ethical decision making whereas divergent ethical expertise (in Figure 10.4, leading to solving moral dilemmas) reflects the intuitionist viewpoint. *Convergent ethical expertise* permits identifying the appropriate solution to somewhat common ethical problems where identifying the appropriate rule or policy will be enough. *Divergent ethical expertise* permits the decision making to generate an innovative, novel, and effective solution for a more complex and unusual ethical situation where the rules are vague, ambiguous, or nonexistent.

Gaining Ethical Expertise

Not all types of expertise are the same. Ethical expertise differs from athletic expertise. First, proficiency in varied disciplines has different standards of effectiveness. Ethical expertise is tied to internal moral values whereas expertise in basketball is in overt measures of goals scored. Second, ethical expertise is gained differently than expertise in other areas. A hockey player can gain skill during mornings of repeated practice under the coach's observant eyes. In contrast, ethical decision making is job embedded, requiring real-time application along with high-quality feedback from many others within the organization. Social relationships at work may play a very influential role in developing its members' ethical expertise.

Likewise, experience is not a simple concept. Even when organizational members are similar in age, job, or organizational tenure, they may differ in the extent to which they have had ethical decision-making events. To gain ethical expertise, employees need multiple occasions to practice and perform ethical decision making: to engage with ethical dilemmas, to make ethical decisions, receive high quality feedback, and participate in intensive reflection about their thoughts, actions, and real world outcomes. Even organizational leaders with long-term tenure may not have had the experiences or learning opportunities to advance their own, their subordinates,' or their colleagues' ethical expertise.

The right learning experiences can help reduce the likelihood of making unethical decisions and actions. People's unethical decisions may have two causes: ignorance or bias. In the first instance, if members lack the knowledge and skills needed to make ethical choices, under the right conditions, they can develop the moral awareness and moral judgment needed to do so. In the second instance, if members hold implicit biases against particular demographic groups, individuals, or types of problem solving, these typically arise through rapid and automatic cognitive processes[127] and are not easily turned off. Despite this, in trusting and respectful environments, people can learn how to express these beliefs and open them to deliberate thought, inspection, and reflection. Ideally, each reason for making unethical decisions can be addressed through appropriate learning experiences, trusted competent feedback, and reflection.

Finally, knowing how to make ethical decisions is not the same as actually behaving ethically. Even when ethical expertise is present, ethical behavior is not a given. In certain situations, individuals with ethical expertise may feel obliged by economic or organization-wide events to act in ways that violate their organization's moral values for short-term gain rather than long-term sustainability. For instance, the former Atlanta Public Schools educators (mentioned earlier) chose to falsify their students' achievement test answers rather than identify struggling students who needed extra

REFLECTIONS AND RELEVANCE 10.6

Developing Ethical Expertise

Organizational members gain ethical expertise to the extent that they actively and repeatedly engage with ethical problems in work settings, make decisions, receive high quality social feedback, and reflect on it.

Working in groups of three or four, invent a school-based scenario in which educators can gain ethical expertise. Create a graphic to illustrate it, using every aspect of Figure 10.4 in the scenario. Consider school level, educator's role, time frame, and other persons who may be involved. Present and explain the graphic to the class. Discuss the extent to which each class member is developing his/her ethical expertise and the types of experiences they still need to enhance these insights and skills—and where, when, how will they get them in their current—or next—work setting?

time and teaching to improve their knowledge and skills. Additionally, high levels of physical exhaustion,[128] the lack of financial support[129] or moral courage,[130] or temptations that occur in "the heat of the moment"[131] may reduce the likelihood that people, including ethical experts, will choose the morally appropriate behaviors.

IMPLICATIONS FOR EDUCATIONAL LEADERS

Organizational leaders are essential to creating and sustaining a milieu in which members think and act ethically. School leaders can apply ethical decision-making theory and research in their roles as organizational models, as climate and culture builders, and as human capital developers.

School Leaders Are Organizational Role Models

Leaders are their organizations' ethical role models. Whether sitting behind a desk, walking the halls, or cheering for their school's team from the bleachers, educational leaders are always "on stage." Everyone in the school community listens and watches what school leaders say, do, and value. Through their personal actions and relationships, and by promoting such behavior in others, school leaders live out their expectations for ethical thought and action. The more skilled the leaders are in communicating ethical awareness, ethical reasoning and judgment, and ethical actions, the more employees will enact ethical practices. The attitude, "Do as I say (not as I do)" is a recipe for faculty and staff cynicism and inappropriate, unethical conduct.

As ethical role models, school leaders know themselves well. Since individual factors play major roles in ethical decision making, having insights into one's personality can improve educational leaders' own ethical conduct. What personal beliefs, philosophy of education, value orientations, problem solving styles, biases and preferences, and emotions affect their thinking and behavior? What worth does the educator place on his or her cognitive capacities and intuition (and emotions) as viable resources for decision making? Enhancing self-awareness calls for serious reflection and accurate feedback. The higher and more accurate the self-awareness, the higher the conscious control leaders will have over these personal dimensions during decision making—and the better the outcomes.

School Leaders Are Climate and Culture Builders

Although the terms are often used interchangeably, *culture* usually refers to the long-term, historically transmitted framework of cognitive beliefs, assumptions, unwritten rules, expectations, and practices. *Climate* typically refers to a more recent vintage of the same. These beliefs and norms affect the elements of school life: physical and psychological safety, how people treat each other, the intellectual atmosphere, rules and policies, traditions and routines, teaching and learning, and how members interpret events. By the consistency of their words and deeds in ethical situations, principals, assistant principals, and other school leaders can strongly influence their school's overall ethical climate.[132]

As the schools' authority figures, educational leaders have the power to gain employees' attention and hold them accountable for meeting ethical standards. The more skillfully educational leaders communicate—in words and deeds—their expectations for ethical awareness, ethical reasoning and judgment, and ethical actions, the more employees come to share and express these same ethical beliefs and behaviors. They view their organization as having an ethical climate. And if school leaders expect all faculty and staff to help create and sustain an ethical workplace, they must provide and identify many safe opportunities for faculty and staff to recognize and make ethical decisions, receive high quality social feedback, and engage in intensive reflection on their decisions. These actions further reinforce the school's ethical climate.

In addition, school leaders should become familiar with the environmental factors that inform ethical awareness and decision making in their organizations. The school or district may have codes of ethics that spell out the organization's core values and expected employee conduct in certain situations. School and district policies and guidelines may also clarify the expected decisions in routine recurring situations. Similarly, the community, the state education agency, and the relevant education professions may hold certain expectations for ethical behavior that need consideration. In contrast, the unfamiliar, uncertain, or ambiguous situations are those that may require school leaders to reflect on past experiences and use informed intuition and cognitive reasoning to help find appropriate—if novel—ethical solutions.

In organizations where the leadership, the reward (and punishment) system, and the climate and cultural norms all support ethical awareness, ethical decision making, and ethical behavior, people in the organization tend to act accordingly. Studies find that ethical leadership behaviors have positive outcomes for employees and organizations. The reverse is also true.

School Leaders Are Human Capital Developers

Human capital is a term that economists use when they refer to employees' knowledge, skills, and abilities that enhance their productivity and their motivations to apply their capacities to meet the organization's goals. Understanding and developing teachers' ethical decision making is another aspect of school leadership.

Teachers may be aware of overt ethical situations, those legally codified (such as sexual harassment, discrimination, and student confidentiality) or set by institutional policy (such as prohibiting teacher-student dating or academic dishonesty). But many novice and veteran teachers may not recognize the more subtle circumstances that hold ethical import—such as accepting gifts from students, not taking advantage of their power relationships over students, discussing students' personal business *only* with colleagues who do have an "educational need to know" (and then only in a private setting), or teaching a class when unprepared. Translating ethics or legal codes into actual day-to-day workplace behavior may not happen. For instance, commenting, "males are better than females at math" is both discriminatory and harassing! Clearly, many ambiguous situations remain about which to increase teachers' ethical awareness.

Since it is not always easy to recognize situations that carry moral consequences, educational leaders, teachers, and staff benefit when they can discuss ethical decision making in their work settings with respected colleagues, friends, and mentors. Together, in a psychologically safe environment, they can openly consider what they value as educators; what ethical decisions look like; the types of school-based circumstances that should prompt ethical awareness, decisions, and actions; and the merits and challenges of acting ethically. Increasing everyone's conscious awareness of ethical behavior is essential for making and enacting ethical decisions. What is more, receiving high quality input or feedback from a fresh set of *trusted* eyes can improve ethical awareness, decisions, and outcomes.

Faculty meetings, new teacher orientations, professional development activities, and grade level and department meetings can provide occasions to discuss possible ethical implications of various everyday situations: how to identify possible ethical situations; how to identify whom the decision will affect; and how to spot "right" and "wrong" alternative solutions (with likely consequences). Teachers can discuss and learn how to use their intuitions, emotions, and rational reasoning to recognize such situations and identify and enact reasonable and acceptable ethical solutions. They also can consider which persons in the school they trust enough to help them think through such dilemmas and offer high quality input and feedback.

During these conversations, teachers may express varying viewpoints; voices may rise, faces may redden, but these are positive signals that ethical issues matter to them. For school leaders, the goal is to make ethical issues and ethical decision making at school more visible, raise teachers' awareness of the ethical dilemmas existing all around them, and increase teachers' ethical expertise in awareness, decision making, and actions.

NOTES

1 For reviews of studies on organizational ethics, see: O'Fallon, M.J. & Butterfield, K.D. (2005). A review of the empirical ethical decision-making literature: 1996–2003. *Journal of Business Ethics, 59* (4), 375–413; Tenbrunsel, A.E. & Smith-Crowe, K. (2008). Ethical decision making: Where we've been and where we're going. *Academy of Management Annals, 2,* (1), 545–607; Kish-Gephart, J.J., Harrison, D.A. & Treviño, L.K. (2010). Bad apples, bad cases, and bad barrels: Metaanalytic evidence about sources of unethical decisions at work. *Journal of Applied Psychology, 95* (1), 1–31; Treviño, L.K., den Nieuwenboer, N.A. & Kish-Gephart, J.J. (2014). (Un)ethical behavior in organizations. *Annual Review of Psychology, 65* (1), 635–660; Treviño, L.K., Weaver, G.R. & Reynolds, S.J. (2006). Behavioral ethics in organizations: A review. *Journal of Management, 32* (6), 951–990.

2 Treviño, L.K. & Youngblood, S.A. (1990). Bad apples in bad barrels: A causal analysis of ethical decision making behavior. *Journal of Applied Psychology, 75* (4): 447–476.

3 See: Butterfield, K.D., Treviño, L.K. & Weaver, G.R. (2000). Moral awareness in business organizations: Influences of issue-related and social contest factors. *Human Relations, 53* (7), 981–1018; Dane, E. & Sonenshein, S. (2015). On the role of experience in ethical decision making at work. An ethical expertise perspective. *Organizational Psychology Review, 5* (1), 74–98; Treviño, Weaver & Reynolds (2006). Op. cit.; Treviño, den Nieuwenboer & Kish-Gephart (2014). Op. cit.

4 A discussion of Albert Bandura's social cognitive theory, the underpinnings of how people learn to behave and organizational ethics, appears on this book's companion website.

5 Velasquez, M.G. & Rostankowski, C. (1985). *Ethics: Theory and practice.* Englewood Cliffs, NJ: Prentice-Hall.

6 Treviño, Weaver & Reynolds (2006). Op. cit.

7 Wittmer, D.P. (2005). Developing a behavioral model for ethical decision making in organizations: Conceptual and empirical research. In H.G. Frederickson & R.K. Ghere (Eds). *Ethics in public management.* (pp. 49–69). Armonk, NY: M.E. Sharpe Inc. Rest actually used the term *moral,* but since the terms *ethical* and *moral* are interchangeable, Wittmer used the term *ethical.* Likewise, the authors of this book use the term *ethical* to maintain consistency for readers.

8 Rest, J.R. (1986). *Moral development: Advances in research and theory.* New York, NY: Praeger; Rest, J. (1994). Background: Theory and research. In J. Rest & D. Narvaez (Eds), *Moral development in the professions: Psychology and applied ethics* (pp. 1–26). New Jersey, NJ: Lawrence Erlbaum Associates, Inc.

9 Rest, J.R. (1984). The major components of morality. In J.R. Rest (Ed.), *Morality, moral behavior, and moral development* (pp. 24–38). New York, NY: John Wiley; Rest, J.R., Thoma, S. & Edwards, L. (1997). Designing and validating a measure of moral judgment: Stage preference and stage consistency approaches. *Journal of Educational Psychology, 89* (1), 5–28; Lincoln, S.H. & Holmes, E.K. (2011). Ethical decision making: A process influenced by moral intensity. *Journal of Healthcare, Science, and the Humanities, 1* (1), 55–69.

10 See: Butterfield, Treviño & Weaver (2000). Op. cit.; Reynolds, S.J. (2006). Moral awareness and ethical predispositions: Investigating the role of individual differences in the recognition of moral issues. *Journal of Applied Psychology, 91* (1), 233–243; Van Sandt, C.V., Shepard, J.M. & Zappe, S.M. (2006). An examination of the relationship between ethical work climate and moral awareness. *Journal of Business Ethics, 68* (4), 409–432.

11 Rest, J., Thoma, S.J., Moon, Y.L. & Getz, I. (1986). Different cultures, sexes, and religions. In J. Rest (Ed.), *Moral development: Advances in research and theory* (pp. 89–132). New York, NY: Praeger.

12 Eisenberg, N. (1986). *Altruistic emotion, cognition, and behavior.* Hillsdale, NJ: Lawrence Erlbaum, p. 206.

13 Narvaez, D. & Lapsley, D.K. (2005). The psychological foundations of everyday morality and moral expertise. In D.K. Lapsley & F.C. Power (Eds), *Character psychology and character education* (pp. 140–165). Notre Dame: University of Notre Dame Press.

14 See: Bergman, R. (2004). Identity as motivation: Toward a theory of the moral self. In D.K. Lapsley & D. Narvaez, (Eds), *Moral development, self and identity* (pp. 21–46). Mahwah, NJ: Lawrence Erlbaum; Blasi, A. (1999). Emotions and moral motivation. *Journal for the Theory of Social Behavior, 29* (1): 1–19; Blasi, A. (2005). Moral character: A psychological approach. In D.K. Lapsley & F.C. Power (Eds), *Character psychology and character education* (pp. 67–100). Notre Dame: University of Notre Dame Press.

15 Bandura, A. (1977). *Social learning theory.* New York, NY: General Learning Press; Mischel, W. & Mischel, H.N. (1976). A cognitive social learning approach to morality and self-regulation. In T. Likona (Ed.), *Moral development and behavior: Theory, research, and social issues* (pp. 84–107). New York, NY: Holt, Rinehart and Winston.

16 See: O'Fallon & Butterfield (2005). Op. cit.; Treviño et al. (2006). Op. cit.

17 Jones, T.M. (1991). Ethical decision making by individuals in organizations: An issue-contingent model. *Academy of Management Review, 16* (2), 366–395.

18 In a classic experiment, teachers were told to deliver what they thought were increasingly powerful shocks to a "learner" (an actor working with the researcher) when the "learner" did not answer certain questions correctly. The physically closer the teacher and "learner," the significantly less often the teachers were willing to administer the shocks. See: Milgram, S. (1974). *Obedience to authority.* New York, NY: Harper & Row.

19 Fiske, S.T. & Taylor, S.E. (1984). *Social cognition.* New York, NY: Random House.

20 Nisbett, R. & Ross, L. (1980). *Human inference: Strategies and shortcomings of social judgment.* Englewood Cliffs, NJ: Prentice-Hall.

21 Treviño, Weaver & Reynolds (2006). Op. cit.

22 See: Chia, A. & Mee, L. (2000). The effects of issue characteristics on the recognition of moral issues. *Journal of Business Ethics, 27* (3), 255–269; Barnett, T. (2001). Dimensions

of moral intensity and ethical decision making: An empirical study. *Journal of Applied Social Psychology, 31* (5), 1038–1057; Harrington, S. (1997). A test of a person issue contingent model of ethical decision making in organizations. *Journal of Business Ethics, 16* (4), 363–375; Singhapakdi, A., Vitell, S. & Kraft, K. (1996). Moral intensity and ethical decision-making of marketing professionals. *Journal of Business Research, 36* (3), 245–255.

23 Chia & Mee (2000). Op. cit.; Butterfield, Treviño & Weaver (2000). Op. cit.; Frey (2000). Op. cit.; Singhapakdi et al. (1996). Op. cit.

24 Lincoln & Holmes (2011). Op. cit.

25 Lincoln & Holmes (2011). Op. cit.

26 Morris, S. & McDonald, R. (1995). The role of moral intensity in moral judgments: An empirical investigation. *Journal of Business Ethics, 14* (9), 715–726; Singer, M. (1998). The role of subjective concerns and characteristics of the moral issue in moral considerations. *British Journal of Psychiatry, 89* (4), 663–679; Barnett, T. (2001). Dimensions of moral intensity and ethical decision making: An empirical study. *Journal of Applied Social Psychology, 31* (5), 1038–1057.

27 Barnett (2001). Op. cit.; Chia & Mee (2000). Op. cit.; Frey (2000). Op. cit.; Lincoln & Holmes (2011). Op. cit.

28 Reynolds (2006). Op. cit.

29 See, for example, Bass, K., Barnett. T. & Brown, G. (1999). Individual difference variables, ethical judgments, and ethical behavioral intentions. *Business Ethics Quarterly, 9* (2), 183–205; Cohen, J.R., Pant, L.W. & Sharp, D.J. (2001). An examination of differences in ethical-decision making between Canadian business students and accounting professionals, *Journal of Business Ethics, 30* (4), 319–336.

30 Simon, H. (1991). Bounded rationality and organizational learning. *Organization Science 2* (1): 125–134.

31 See: Benbasat, I. & Taylor, R.N. (1978). The impact of cognitive styles on information systems design. *Management Information Systems Quarterly, 2* (2), 43–54; Blaylock, B.K. & Rees, L.P. (1984). Cognitive style and the usefulness of information. *Decision Sciences, 15* (1), 74–91; Taggart, W. & Robey, D. (1981). Mind and managers: On the dual nature of human information processing and management. *Academy of Management Review 6* (2), 187–195.

32 Bommer, M., Gratto, C., Gravender, J. & Tuttle. M. (1987). A behavioral model of ethical and unethical decision making. *Journal of Business Ethics, 6* (4), 265–289.

33 Opotow, S. (1990). Moral exclusion and injustice: An introduction. *Journal of Social Issues, 46* (1), 1.

34 Blasi, A. (2004). Moral functioning: Moral understanding and personality. In D.K. Lapsley & D. Narvaez (Eds), *Moral development, self and identity* (pp. 335–348). Mahwah, NJ: Lawrence Erlbaum; Festinger, L.A. (1957). *A theory of cognitive dissonance.* Stanford, CA: Stanford University Press.

35 Bolton, L.E. & Reed A. II (2004). Sticky priors: The perseverance of identity effects on judgment. *Journal of Marketing Research, 41* (4): 397–441.

36 Russell, J.A. (2003). Core affect and the psychological construction of emotion. *Psychological Review, 110* (1), 145–172; Schachter, S. & Singer, J. (1962). Cognitive, social, and physiological determinants of emotional states. *Psychological Review, 69* (5), 379–399.

37 Gaudine, A. & Thorne, L. (2001). Emotion and ethical decision-making in organizations. *Journal of Business Ethics, 31* (2), 175–187; Etzioni, A. (1988). Normative-affective factors: Toward a new decision-making model. *Journal of Economic Psychology, 9* (2), 125–150.

38 Kahneman, D. (2003). A perspective on judgment and choice: Mapping bounded rationality. *American Psychologist, 58* (9), 697–720.

39 Gaudine & Thorne (2001). Op.cit.; Haidt, J. (2001). The emotional dog and its rational tail: A social intuitionist approach to moral judgment. *Psychological Review 108* (4), 814–834; Reynolds, S.J. (2006). A neurocognitive model of the ethical decision making process: Implications for study and practice. *Journal of Applied Psychology, 91* (4), 737–748; Krishnakumar, S. & Rymph, D. (2012). Uncomfortable ethical decisions: The role of

negative emotions and emotional intelligence in ethical decision-making. *Journal of Managerial Issues*, 24 (3), 321–344.

40 Rogerson, M.D., Gottlieb, M.C., Handelsman, M.M., Knapp, S. and Younggren, J. (2011). Nonrational processes in ethical decision making. *American Psychologist*, 66 (7), 614–623.

41 Treviño, den Nieuwenboer & Kish-Gephart (2014). Op. cit.

42 Kish-Gephart, Harrison & Trevino (2010). Op. cit.

43 Ethics Resource Center (2012). *2011 National Business Ethics Survey: Workplace Ethics in Transition*. Arlington, VA. Retrieved from: www.hreonline.com/pdfs/02012012Extra_Ethics Report.pdf.

44 Victor, B. & Cullen, J.B. (1988). The organizational bases of ethical work climates. *Administrative Science Quarterly*, 33 (1), 101–125.

45 Treviño, L.K. (1990). A cultural perspective on changing and developing organizational ethics. In R. Woodman and W. Passmore (Eds), *Research in organizational change and development*, 4 (pp. 195–230). Greenwhich, CT: JAI.

46 Treviño, L.K., Butterfield, K. & McCabe, D. (1998). The ethical context in organizations: Influences on employee attitudes and behaviors. *Business Ethics Quarterly*, 8 (3): 447–476; Martin K.D. & Cullen, J.B. (2006). Continuities and extensions of ethical climate theory: A meta-analytic review. *Journal of Business Ethics*, 69 (2), 175–194; Simha A. & Cullen, J.B. (2012). Ethical climates and their effects on organizational outcomes: Implications from the past and prophecies for the future. *Academy of Management Perspectives*, 26 (1), 20–34; Kish-Gephart et al. (2010). Op. cit.

47 Treviño, den Nieuwenboer & Kish-Gephart (2014). Op cit.

48 Brown, M., Treviño, L.K. & Harrison, D. (2005). Ethical leadership: A social learning perspective for construct development and testing. *Organizational Behavior and Human Decision Processes*, 97 (2), 117–134 (p. 120).

49 Treviño, L.K. & Brown, M.E. (2004). Managing to be ethical: Debunking five business ethics myths. *Academy of Management Executive*, 18 (2): 69–83.

50 Schminke, M., Ambrose, M.L. & Neubaum, D.O. (2005). The effect of leader moral development on ethical climate and employee attitudes. *Organizational Behavior and Human Decision Process*, 97 (2), 135–151.

51 Mayer, D.M., Kuenzi, M., Greenbaum, R., Bardes, M. & Salvador, R. (2009). How low does ethical leadership flow? Test of a trickle-down model. *Organizational Behavior and Human Decision Processes*, 108 (1), 1–113.

52 Brown et al. (2005). Op. cit.

53 Mayer, D.M., Nurmohamed, S., Treviño, L.K., Shapiro, D.L. & Schminke, M. (2013). Encouraging employees to report unethical conduct internally: It takes a village. *Organizational Behavior and Human Decision Processes*, 121, 89–103.

54 Hannah, S., Schaubroeck, J., Peng, C., Lord, R., Treviño, L.K. et al. (2013). Joint influences of individual and work unit abusive supervision on ethical intentions and behaviors: A moderated mediation model. *Journal of Applied Psychology*, 98 (4), 579–592.

55 Treviño et al. (1998, 1999). Op. cit.

56 Moore, C. & Gino, F. (2013). Ethically adrift: How others pull our moral compass from true north and how we can fix it. *Research in Organizational Behavior*, 33 (August), 53–77.

57 Gino, F. & Galinsky, A.D. (2012). Vicarious dishonesty: When psychological closeness creates distance from one's moral compass. *Organizational Behavior and Human Decision. Process*, 119 (1), 15–26.

58 Treviño et al. (1999). Op. cit.

59 Bird, F. (1996). *The muted conscience: Moral silence and the practice of ethics in business*. Westport, CT: Quorum Books.

60 Frank, R.H., Gilovic, T. & Regan, D.T. (1993). Does studying economics inhibit cooperation? *Journal of Economic Perspectives*, 7 (2), 159–171; Frank, R.H., Gilovic, T. & Regan, D.T. (1996). Do economists make bad citizens? *Journal of Economics Perspectives*, 10 (1): 187–192; Bandura (1999). Op. cit.

61 See: Ashkanasy, N.M., Windsor, C.A. & Treviño, L.K. (2006). Bad apples in bad barrels revisited: Cognitive moral development, just world beliefs, rewards, and ethical decision making. *Business Ethics Quarterly*, *16* (4), 449–474; Tenbrunsel, A.E. (1998). Misrepresentation and expectations of misrepresentation in an ethical dilemma: The role of incentives and temptation. *Academy of Management Journal*, *41* (3): 330–339; Trevino & Youngblood (1990). Op. cit.

62 See: Treviño, L.K. (1992). The social effects of punishment: A justice perspective. *Academy of Management Review*, *17* (4), 647–676; Treviño, L.K., & Ball, G.A. (1992). The social implications of punishing unethical behavior: Observers' cognitive and affective reactions. *Journal of Management*, *18* (4): 751–768.

63 Treviño, L.K., Weaver, G.R., Gibson, D.G. & Toffler, G.L. (1999). Managing ethics and legal compliance: What works and what hurts. *California Management*, *41* (2), 131–151.

64 Tenbrunsel, A.E. & Messick, D.M. (1999). Sanctioning systems, decision frames, and cooperation. *Administrative Science Quarterly*, *44* (4), 684–707.

65 Schweitzer, M.E., Ordóñez, L. & Douma, B. (2004). Goal setting as a motivator of unethical behavior. *Academy of Management Journal*, *47* (3), 422–432.

66 Grover, S. (1993). Why professionals lie: The impact of professional role conflict on reporting activity. *Organizational Behavior and Human Decision Processes*, *55* (2), 251–272; Grover, S. (1997). Lying in organizations: Theory, research and future directions. In R.A. Giacolone & J. Greenberg (Eds), *Antisocial behavior in organizations* (pp. 68–84). Thousand Oaks, CA: Sage.

67 O'Fallon & Butterfield (2005). Op. cit.; Treviño, Weaver & Reynolds (2006). Op. cit.

68 Bommer, Gratto, Gravender & Tuttle (1987). Op. cit.

69 Hogan, R., Johnson, J. & Emler, N. (1978). A socioanalytic theory of moral development. In W. Damon (Ed.), *New directions for child development*, *vol. 2* (pp. 1–18). San Francisco, CA: Jossey-Bass; Shweder, R., Mahapatra, M. & Miller, J. (1987). Culture and moral development. In J. Kagan & S. Lamm (Eds), *The emergence of morality in young children* (pp. 1–82). Chicago, IL: University of Chicago Press.

70 Bargh, J.A. & Chartrand, T.L. (1999). The unbearable automaticity of being. *American Psychologist*, *54* (7), 462–479; Chartrand, T.L. & Bargh, J.A. (2002). Nonconscious motivations: Their activation, operation, and consequences. In A. Tesser, D.A. Stapel & J.W. Wood (Eds), *Self and motivation: Emerging psychological perspectives* (pp. 13–41). Washington, DC: American Psychological Association; Haidt (2001). Op. cit.

71 Haidt (2001). Op. cit.

72 Reynolds, S.J. (2006). A neurocognitive model of the ethical decision-making process: Implications for study and practice. *Journal of Applied Psychology*, *91* (4), 737–748; Shweder, R., Mahapatra, M. & Miller, J. (1987). Culture and moral development. In J. Kagan & S. Lamm (Eds), *The emergence of morality in young children* (pp. 1–82). Chicago, IL: University of Chicago Press.

73 Greene, J.D., Morelli, S.A., Lowenberg, K., Nystrom, L.E. & Cohen, J.D. (2008). Cognitive load selectively interferes with utilitarian moral judgment. *Cognition*, *107* (3), 1144–1154.

74 Damasio, A.R. (1994). *Descartes' error: Emotion, reason, and the human brain*. New York, NY: Putnam; Greene, J.D., Nystrom, L.E., Engell, A.D., Darley, J.M. & Cohen, J.D. (2004). The neural bases of cognitive conflict and control in moral judgment. *Neuron*, *44* (2), 389–400.

75 Weaver, G.R., Reynolds, S.J. & Brown, M.E. (2014). Moral intuition. Connecting current knowledge to future organizational research and practice. *Journal of Management*, *40* (1), 100–129 (p. 101).

76 Weaver, Reynolds & Brown (2014). Ibid.

77 Haidt, J. & Bjorklund, F. (2008). Social intuitionists answer six questions about moral psychology. In W. Sinnott-Armstrong (Ed.), *Moral psychology, vol. 2: The cognitive science of morality: Intuition and diversity* (pp. 181–217). Cambridge, MA: Bradford Books.

78 See Greene, J. & Haidt, J. (2002). How (and where) does moral judgment work? *Trends in Cognitive Sciences*, 6 (12), 517–523; Lieberman, M.D. (2000.) Intuition: A social cognitive neuroscience approach. *Psychological Bulletin*, 126 (1), 109–137; Salvador, R. & Folger, R.G. (2009). Business ethics and the brain. *Business Ethics Quarterly*, 19 (1), 1–31.

79 See Damasio, A.R. (1994). *Descartes' error: Emotion, reason, and the human brain*. New York, NY: Putnam; Young, L. & Koenigs, M. (2007). Investigating emotion in moral cognition: A review of evidence from functional neuroimaging and neuropsychology. *British Medical Bulletin*, 84 (1), 69–79.

80 Lieberman (2000). Op. cit.; Narvaez, D., Lapsley, D.K., Hagele, S. & Lasky, B. (2006). Moral chronicity and social information processing: Tests of a social cognitive approach to the moral personality. *Journal of Research in Personality*, 40 (6), 966–985.

81 Haidt (2001). Op. cit.; Reynolds, S.J. (2006). A neurocognitive model of the ethical decision-making process: implications for study and practice. *Journal of Applied Psychology*, 91 (4), 737–748; Weaver, Reynolds & Brown (2014). Op. cit.

82 Sonenshein S. (2007). The role of construction, intuition, and justification in responding to ethical issues at work: The sensemaking-intuition model. *Academy of Management Review*, 32 (4), 1022–1040; Weaver, Reynolds & Brown (2014). Op. cit.

83 Sonenshein (2007). Op. cit.

84 Abelson, R.P. (1981). Psychological status of the script concept. *American Psychologist*, 36 (7), 715–729; Higgins, E.T. & Bargh, J.A. (1987). Social cognition and social perception. *Annual Review of Psychology*, 38 (1), 369–425.

85 Ashforth, B.E. & Fried, Y. (1988). The mindlessness of organizational behaviors. *Human Relations*, 41 (2), 305–329; Gioia, D.A. & Manz, C.C. (1985). Linking cognition and behavior: A script processing interpretation of vicarious learning. *Academy of Management Review*, 10 (3), 527–539.

86 Dane, E. & Pratt, M.G. (2007). Exploring intuition and its role in management decision making. *Academy of Management Review*, 32 (1), 33–54.

87 Reber, A.S. (1996). Implicit learning and tacit knowledge: An essay on the cognitive unconscious. Oxford, UK: Oxford University Press.

88 Margolis, J.D. (2004). Responsibility, inconsistency, and the paradoxes of morality in human nature: De Waal's window into business ethics. *Business Ethics Quarterly, Ruffin Series*, 4, 43–52.

89 Weaver, G.R. & Agle, B.R. (2002). Religiosity and ethical behavior in organizations: A symbolic interactionist perspective. *Academy of Management Review*, 27 (1), 77–97.

90 Krebs, D.L., Denton, E.A. & Wark, G. (1997). The forms and functions of real-life moral decision-making. *Journal of Moral Education*, 26 (2), 131–145.

91 Lord, C.G., Ross, L. & Lepper, M.R. (1979). Biased assimilation and attitude polarization: The effects of prior theories on subsequently considered evidence. *Journal of Personality and Social Psychology*, 37 (11), 2098–2109; Reynolds (2006). Op. cit.

92 Yukl, G., Guinan, P.J. & Sottolano, D. (1995). Influence tactics used for different objectives with subordinates, peers, and superiors. *Group and Organization Management*, 20 (3), 272–297; Dutton, J.E. & Ashford, S.J. 1993. Selling issues to top management. *Academy of Management Review*, 18 (3), 397–428.

93 Weick, K.E. (1979). *The social psychology of organizing*, 2nd ed. New York, NY: McGraw-Hill.

94 Bargh, J.A. (1996). Principles of automaticity. In E.T. Higgins & A. Kruglanski (Eds), *Social psychology: Handbook of basic principles* (pp. 169–183). New York, NY: Guilford Press; Bargh & Chartrand (1999). Op. cit.; Jacoby, L.L., Lindsay, D.S. & Toth, J.P. (1992). Unconscious influences revealed. *American Psychologist*, 47 (6), 802–809; Reber, A.S. (1992). An evolutionary context for the cognitive unconscious. *Philosophical Psychology*, 5 (1), 33–51.

95 Huebner, B., Dwyer, S. & Hauser, M. (2009). The role of emotion in moral psychology. *Trends in Cognitive Sciences*, 13 (1), 1–6; Pizarro, D., Inbar, Y. & Helion, C. (2011). On disgust and moral judgment. *Emotion Review*, 3 (3), 267–268.

96 Pizzaro, D.A. & Bloom, P. (2003). The intelligence of the moral intuitions: Comment on Haidt (2001). *Psychological Review, 110* (1), 193–196.

97 Narvaez, D. (n.d.). The social intuitionist model: Some counter-intuitions. Retrieved March 24, 2015 from: www3.nd.edu/~dnarvaez/documents/NarvaezresponsetoHaidtBjorklund.pdf.

98 Pizarro & Bloom (2003). Op. cit.; Turiel, E. (2006). Thought, emotions, and social interactional processes in moral development. In M. Killen & J.G. Smetana (Eds), *Handbook of moral development* (pp. 7–35). Mahwah, NJ: Lawrence Erlbaum.

99 Feinberg, M., Willer, R., Antonenko, O. & John, O.P. (2012). Liberating reason from the passions: Overriding intuitionist moral judgments through emotion reappraisal. *Psychological Science, 23* (7), 788–795; Monin, B., Pizarro, D.A. & Beer, J.S. (2007). Deciding versus reacting: Conceptions of moral judgment and the reason-affect debate. *Review of General Psychology, 11* (2), 99–111.

100 Feinberg et al. (2012). Op. cit.; Paxton, J.M., Ungar, L. & Greene, J.D. (2012). Reflection and reasoning in moral judgment. *Cognitive Science, 36*, 163–177.

101 Haidt (2010). Ibid.

102 See Gunia, B.C., Wang, L., Huang, L., Wang, J. & Murnighan, J.K. (2012). Contemplation and conversation: Subtle influences on moral decision making. *Academy of Management Journal, 55* (1), 13–33; Haidt, J. (2007). The new synthesis in moral psychology. *Science, 316* (5827), 998–1002.

103 MacGregor, D., Lichtenstein, S. & Slovic, P. (1988). Structuring knowledge retrieval: An analysis of decomposed quantitative judgments. *Organizational Behavior and Human Decision Processes, 42* (3), 303–323; McMackin, J. & Slovic, P. (2000). When does explicit justification impair decision making? *Applied Cognitive Psychology, 14* (6), 527–541

104 See: Haidt (2001). Op. cit.; Hammond, K.R., Hamm, R.M., Grassia, J. & Pearson, T. (1987). Direct comparison of the efficacy of intuitive and analytical cognition in expert judgment. *IEEE Transactions on Systems, Man, and Cybernetics, 17* (5), 753–770; Laughlin, P.R. & Ellis, A.L. (1986). Demonstrability and social combination processes on mathematical intellective tasks. *Journal of Experimental Social Psychology, 22* (3), 177–189.

105 Khatri, N. & Ng, H.A. (2000). The role of intuition in strategic decision making. *Human Relations, 53* (1), 57–86.

106 Shapiro, S. & Spence, M.T. (1997). Managerial intuition: A conceptual and operational framework. *Business Horizons, 40* (1), 63–68.

107 See: Bless, H., Bohner, G., Schwarz, N. & Strack, F. (1990). Mood and persuasion: A cognitive response analysis. *Personality and Social Psychology Bulletin, 16* (2), 331–345; Elsbach, K.D. & Barr, P.S. (1999). The effects of mood on individuals' use of structured decision protocols. *Organization Science, 10* (2), 181–198.

108 Briggs, K.C. & Myers, I.B. (1976). *Myers-Briggs type indicator*. Palo Alto, CA: Consulting Psychologists Press; Pacini, R. & Epstein, S. (1999). The relation of rational and experiential information processing styles to personality, basic beliefs, and the ratio-bias problem. *Journal of Personality and Social Psychology, 76* (6), 972–987.

109 Hofstede, G. (2001). *Culture's consequences*, 2nd ed. Thousand Oaks, CA: Sage; Cyert, R.M. & March, J.G. (1963). *A behavioral theory of the firm*. Englewood Cliffs, NJ: Prentice-Hall.

110 Simon, H.A. (1987). Making management decisions: The role of intuition and emotion. *Academy of Management Executive, 1* (1): 57–64.

111 Lee, T.W., Ferrell, L. & Mansfield, P. (2000). A review of empirical studies assessing ethical decision making in business. *Journal of Business Ethics, 25* (3), 185–204; O'Fallon & Butterfield (2005). Op. cit.

112 Dane & Sonenshein (2015). Op. cit., p. 77.

113 Lewandowsky, S., Little, D. & Kalish, M.L. (2007). Knowledge and expertise. In F.T. Durso (Ed.), *Handbook of applied cognition*, 2nd ed. (pp. 83–109). Chichester, UK: Wiley.

114 George, J.M. & Jones, G.R. (2001). Towards a process model of individual change in organizations. *Human Relations, 54* (4), 419–444.

115 Dane, E. & Pratt, M.G. (2007). Exploring intuition and its role in managerial decision making. *Academy of Management Review, 32* (1), 33–54.

116 Kahneman, D. & Klein, G. (2009). Conditions for intuitive expertise: A failure to disagree. *American Psychologist, 64* (6), 515–526.

117 *Cognitive dissonance* is the mental discomfort experienced by a person who is confronted with new information that conflicts with existing beliefs, ideas, or values.

118 De Dreu, C.K.W., Nijstad, B.A. & van Knippenberg, D. (2008). Motivated information processing in group judgment and decision making. *Personality and Social Psychology Review, 12* (1), 22–49.

119 Dane & Sonnenshein (2015). Op. cit., p. 83.

120 Reynolds, S.J. (2008). Moral attentiveness: Who pays attention to the moral aspects of life? *Journal of Applied Psychology, 93* (5), 1027–1041.

121 Aquino, K., Freeman, D., Reed, A., Lim, V.K.G. & Felps, W. (2009). Testing a social-cognitive model of moral behavior: The interactive influence of situations and moral identity centrality. *Journal of Personality and Social Psychology, 97* (1), 123–141; Mulder, L.B. & Aquino, K. (2013). The role of moral identity in the aftermath of dishonesty. *Organizational Behavior and Human Decision Processes, 121* (2), 219–230.

122 Lopes, L.L. & Oden, G.C. (1987). Distinguishing between random and nonrandom events. *Journal of Experimental Psychology: Learning, Memory, and Cognition, 13* (3), 392–400; Thompson, L. & DeHarpport, T. (1994). Social judgment, feedback, and interpersonal learning in negotiation. *Organizational Behavior and Human Decision Processes, 58* (3), 327–345.

123 Andrews, M. (1996). Using reflection to develop clinical expertise. *British Journal of Nursing, 5* (8), 508–513; Mamede, S. & Schmidt, H.G. (2004). The structure of reflective practice in medicine. *Medical Education, 38* (3), 302–308.

124 Memmert, D., Baker, J. & Bertsch, C. (2010). Play and practice in the development of sport-specific creativity in team ball sports. *High Ability Studies, 21* (1), 3–18.

125 Barnett, S. M. & Koslowski, B. (2002). Adaptive expertise: Effects of type of experience and the level of theoretical understanding it generates. *Thinking and Reasoning, 8* (4), 237–267; Kimball, D.R. & Holyoak, K.J. (2000). Transfer and expertise. In E. Tulving & F.I.M. Craik (Eds), *The Oxford handbook of memory* (pp. 109–122). New York, NY: Oxford University Press.

126 Dane, E. (2010). Reconsidering the trade-off between expertise and flexibility: A cognitive entrenchment perspective. *Academy of Management Review, 35* (4), 579–603.

127 Gawronski, B., Hofmann, W. & Wilbur, C.J. (2006). Are "implicit" attitudes unconscious? *Consciousness and Cognition, 15* (3), 485–499.

128 Barnes, C.M., Schaubroeck, J., Huth, M. & Ghumman, S. (2011). Lack of sleep and unethical conduct. *Organizational Behavior and Human Decision Processes, 115* (2), 169–180.

129 Sharma, E., Mazar, N., Alter, A.L. & Ariely, D. (2014). Financial deprivation selectively shifts moral standards and compromises moral decisions. *Organizational Behavior and Human Decision Processes, 123* (2), 90–100.

130 Sekerka, L.E., Bagozzi, R.P. & Charnigo, R. (2009). Facing ethical challenges in the workplace: Conceptualizing and measuring professional moral courage. *Journal of Business Ethics, 89* (4), 565–579.

131 Ariely, D. & Loewenstein, G. (2006). The heat of the moment: The effect of sexual arousal on sexual decision making. *Journal of Behavioral Decision Making, 19* (2), 87–98.

132 Since school culture is more deeply entrenched than climate, changing a school culture takes more sustained time, effort, and professional development than changing a school climate. See: Kaplan, L.S. & Owings, W.A. (2013). *Culture re-boot: Reinvigorating school culture to improve student outcomes.* Thousand Oaks, CA: Corwin.

Allocating Educational Resources

GUIDING QUESTIONS

11.1 Explain how ideas about education resource allocation have changed since the 1980s.

11.2 Identify the types of resources available to schools for instruction, and describe how they can work together to increase student learning.

11.3 Discuss how principals' priorities, beliefs, and constraints affect resource allocation.

11.4 Compare and contrast the traditional and learning-oriented perspectives on resource allocation for student learning.

11.5 Summarize the research findings and conclusions about the relationship between education funding—in total dollars and how monies are spent—and student achievement.

11.6 Discuss reasons why the relationship between school resource allocation efficiency and student performance outcomes is so contentious.

11.7 Describe how resource dependence theory depicts the ways school districts seek information and use influence strategies to decrease their environmental dependence for resources and to increase their control of allocation decisions.

CASE STUDY 11.1

It Was the Worst of Times. It was a Dickens of a Time

Danny Zuko had been appointed as the Principal of Rydell High School just as the Great Recession began. In April, as administrators were finalizing their budgets for the next school year, it was clear that the state and local education funding would be reduced. On Monday, Adam Arden, the superintendent, called key administrators together for a meeting and announced that each school's total budget (as well as the central office budget) would face an 8 percent reduction. That figure included personnel, maintenance and operations, and school administration—not just supplies. He gave the principals until Friday to decide the process they would use to cut their budgets and where the reductions would be.

Later that Monday, Danny met with his assistant principal, John Newton, to discuss the bleak scenario—reduction in force, larger class sizes, pay freezes, lost stipends, and more. After two days of haggling, Zuko and Newton could not figure the best way to cut 8 percent from Rydell's budget with the least adverse impact on student learning. On Wednesday, they invited Sid Calhoun, the bookkeeper, to work with them. Sid said that in his 20 years as bookkeeper, the school always had funds to increase budgets each year. He would simply add whatever percentage the school was going to receive to each department's previous year's budget. Sid suggested reducing each department's budget by 8 percent. They all agreed that across-the-board cuts were the fairest approach. They would send the recommendation to the Superintendent on Friday.

On Thursday afternoon, John met with the school leadership team (SLT) to announce the budget cuts and seek advice on how to inform the staff. Betty Channing, SLT Chair, was aghast. An 8 percent cut from every department's budget would upset teachers and hurt student learning! Trying to stay calm, she asked what alternative options the principal and AP had considered? Had they thought about resources other than money? Had the school system examined its staffing for redundancy such as teachers not teaching a full load and receiving assignments to administrative duties? Were teachers asked to teach additional sections for extra pay, when possible, instead of hiring new teachers? With challenges to current thinking in the air, other SLT members joined in. They asked if it were efficient to have two classes of French IV with a total of 21 students. Did it make sense for two middle schools to operate at half capacity? Could they be combined to save money? Could the parent and community supporters call their city council members and legislators, maybe rally at the state capital and county seat to advocate for a smaller cut to the education budget?

John left the SLT meeting and went immediately to speak with Zuko and tell him about the school leadership's concerns and ideas. Zuko thanked the AP and called the Superintendent.

RUBRIC 11.1

Lens and/or factors to be considered in decision making	What are the factors at play in this case?	What steps should be considered in solving the problem?	What could have been done to avoid this dilemma?
The situation			
• The task	With the Great Recession severely impacting the budget, the district is asking principals to cut 8 percent from their school's current year's budget for the coming year.	The superintendent and principals need to rethink how to address the 8 percent budget cut. They need to start at the district level, prioritize student learning, and consider more broadly than dollars. This may change amount to cut from each school's budget. Include the SLT in the planning process.	Prioritizing resources for good and bad times to protect student learning could have helped and should be an ongoing process.
• Personal abilities	The principal is finishing his first year at the school. He may lack experience or understanding about how to manage resources effectively and efficiently—or fully appreciate how his SLT can help.	All existing resources should be examined— finances, human capital, time, physical resources, information, instructional assets, parent and community resources, influence, and social and political resources.	The principal would have been better served by involving the SLT sooner. Collective information and wisdom can be an excellent resource.
• The school environment	The school may have been running on inertia. The coming crisis will test the collective ability in the school.	Making the SLT aware of the coming cuts and involving them in the information collecting and problem solving process may help to unify the staff toward a common vision of survival and protect student learning.	The problem hit most people unaware. Once the problem is manifested, dealing with all available resources makes for better decision-making outcomes.
Look	**Wider**		
Organizational (i.e., the organizational goals, values, policies, culture)	Survival, meeting student needs on a reduced budget, and conceptualizing resources beyond fiscal ones are at play. RIF policies will need to be examined.	At the central office and school levels, organizational and instructional priorities need to be determined. RIF policies need to be examined.	Avoiding the Great Recession is beyond the scope of a school system. Having a prioritized plan for resource allocation to prioritize student learning in good and bad fiscal times would be helpful.

continued . . .

People			
(i.e., individuals with needs, beliefs, goals, relationships)	People need to understand (and support) district and school priorities in cutting budgets. Also concerned about their own and colleagues' employment and financial security.	Staff members need to participate in providing ideas. Once decisions are made, human resource counselors need to be available for those who will be unemployed.	The district and each school could have developed a resource allocation plan prioritizing student learning for good and bad fiscal times.
Competing Interests			
(i.e., competing interests for power, influence, and resources)	Some people will look out for their own best interest (and their group's) versus what is best for the students. Parents may disagree about what is "best" for their students.	The students' academic success and well being—clearly and consensually defined—need to become a shared priority.	The superintendent, principals, teachers, and community could have generated and maintained a shared vision for student learning in difficult budget times.
Tradition			
(i.e., school culture, rituals, meaning, heroes)	Much of the existing culture could be jeopardized by the decision-making process and decision outcomes.	Providing for the academic success and well being of every student needs to be emphasized.	Having a tradition of meeting students' academic and well being needs and emphasizing that vision in good and bad fiscal times helps.

OVERVIEW: ENACTING EDUCATIONAL VALUES

At its core, when any school district makes decisions, it is choosing how to distribute (or redistribute) limited, often contested resources. School funding, school budgets, and resource allocations are ways that our communities enact their values for their children's future. In 2011–12, the United States spent over $620 billion on elementary and secondary schools, including an average $11,014 per student, for operating schools.[1]

In part, principals' impact on student achievement comes through their capacity to strategically seek, acquire, align, and manage the necessary resources to support teaching and learning. How superintendents and principals secure and target these resources to certain programs, structures, or materials, figuratively, "puts their money where their mouth is."

This chapter will consider the array of resources available to schools; the beliefs and priorities that impact resource allocation decisions; how school leaders can align school resources with teaching and learning; the research on the relationship between school funds and student achievement; efficiency's role in public schools securing and allocating resources; and insights from resource dependency theory that can help school leaders secure and allocate resources to support higher levels of student and teacher learning.[2]

ALLOCATING EDUCATIONAL RESOURCES

In education, *resource allocation* is the way in which school decision makers divide fiscal and non-fiscal assets between competing needs and spend them for education purposes. Typically, schools distribute these resources among functions such as instruction, school administration, student transportation, and physical plant operations and maintenance. Within each function, money is budgeted for expenditures such as salaries, benefits, professional development and materials. Studies find that most school district budgets spend at least 80 percent at school sites for such functions as instruction, school leadership, guidance and counseling services, supplies, and materials.[3] The remaining monies support the superintendent's office, insurance coverage, and other business and operating expenses. Because resources are usually limited while human wants and needs tend to be unlimited, and because any given resource may have many alternate uses, resource allocation becomes the focus of competing agendas.

Over the years, ideas about educational resources allocations have changed. A few decades ago, education supporters invested their political capital advocating for annual increases in per pupil dollars. Education leaders' responsibilities included balancing school and district budgets with the dollars available and correctly accounting for expenditures. Little attention went to how the resources aligned to teacher or student outcomes. Since the 1980s, the standards-based reform movement and school accountability expectations have profoundly transformed this situation. Now, educational leaders are answerable for improved student academic outcomes, not only accounting for incoming dollars. As a consequence, educational leaders now see resource allocation related to building high-performing systems that support every student's learning to high, measurable standards.

Today, developing and allocating resources to support improved teaching and learning are fundamental school leadership challenges. How well superintendents and principals assign, monitor, and assess their schools' resources—financial, human, material, and structural (time and space) and increasingly, how well they secure outside resources—contribute to schools' overall success. Governance issues concerning raising revenues and distributing educational resources play key roles in allocating assets to schools. The voting public, state legislatures, local school boards, superintendents, principals, and teachers' associations each offer guidance into how to assign resources and provide incentives to strongly and equitably support professional and student learning. Research also points to ways to get the most "bang" for the educational buck. But educational resources go well beyond dollars.

Types of Educational Resources

Dollars are necessary but not sufficient to operate successful schools or districts. In fact, the resources needed to fully support the education system are inherently complex. Educational leaders must be able to know how to allocate dollars into time and people; develop human capital; use intellectually rigorous and coherent systems of curriculum, instruction, and assessment; and provide incentives and supports for continuously improving classroom practice that directly impact student learning. Basic resources available to schools include:

- **Money:** Budgeting activities at several levels of the system, usually occurring in annual cycles, determine the amount of funds available to support education and how they are to be used. Most school funding comes from state, local, and federal governments through tax dollars, but it may also come from grants, with supplemental funds from private and public sources. No one level of the education system has complete control of the money's flow, distribution, and expenditure.

- **Human capital:** In economic terms, those are the individuals who the funds hire to do the education system's work. Each person brings a different level of motivation and expertise, developed over time through professional coursework and work/life experiences. In addition, teachers and principals must continually improve their capacity to increase student learning through job-embedded, ongoing, collaborative, and well-designed professional development activities targeted to teachers' and students' learning needs.

- **Time:** People's work together happens within an agreed upon time structure. People are assigned to tasks within blocks that allot hours within the day and across the year to different functions. Teaching and learning activities, collaborative planning, data collection and analysis, and viable professional development activities necessary to accomplish the schools' goals each require time. Some of the needed hours will be voluntary.

- **Physical resources:** Educators need material resources including clean, well-maintained, and well-lit school facilities, temperature-appropriate classrooms with comfortable desks and chairs, intellectually rigorous curricula with related materials, white boards, student-accessible computers (with suitable hardware and software), and daily supplies.

- **Information:** Planning and resource allocation decisions depend on decision makers having an array of relevant facts, knowledge of research-affirmed best practices, and other data if they are to make informed choices that move their organization toward achieving its goals. Information also includes specialized knowledge and personal familiarity with key players and how the system works. For example, the school district's lawyer, whose day job is at City Hall with the mayor, may have useful insider information to share in both arenas. Some assert that much of a superintendent's power comes from his or her position as a gatekeeper of information.[4]

- **Instructional assets:** Instructional resources can be conventional, personal, and environmental.[5] Conventional resources include teachers' formal qualifications, texts and supplementary materials, class size, time, facilities' upkeep, libraries, and laboratories. Each of these can make a difference in student learning. For instance, students in classes of 35 to 40 tend to have less access to teachers' time and expertise than do students in classes of 15–18 students. Pupils using up-to-date texts, e-texts, and on-line resources for science tend to have more current, interesting, and rigorous content than those relegated to using 20-year old books. Likewise, students whose teachers lack college majors and related pedagogy in their teaching content areas may not receive the clear, accurate explanations needed to correctly understand, remember, and apply the material.

Personal instructional resources include teachers' and students' knowledge, skills, and motivations that influence how they perceive and use the conventional resources. Teachers with low expectations for certain students' achievement may not actively challenge and reinforce their learning efforts. Likewise, students who think that intelligence is fixed—they are either smart or not—may not put the effort and persistence into expanding what they know and can do.

Similarly, environmental instructional resources such as leadership, academic press, and organizational structures impact whether and how teachers and students notice and use conventional or personal resources. Factors such as the school's social and professional organization—whether leaders cultivate an inclusive, caring, and supportive school community; whether the schools have viable professional learning communities to foster teachers' improved practices; whether the school's climate is free from distractions; and whether the daily bell schedule allows time for teachers to explain, model, and provide students with guided and independent practice (plus checks for understanding and ongoing feedback)—all influence how well teachers and students use the available resources.

How well teachers and students use these resources depends on the particular mix of conventional, personal, and environmental resources at hand and their inter-dependences. For instance, simply reducing class size from 50 to 25 students per teacher and providing the appropriate classrooms to do so (conventional resources) will not necessarily raise student achievement. For this to happen, the school needs a culture of learning and practices that continually upgrade teachers' professional knowledge and skills (environmental resources); a caring, inclusive, and supportive climate (environmental resources); teachers with high expectations and effective instructional repertoires to advance every student's learning and wellbeing (personal resources); an intellectually rigorous system of curriculum, instruction, and assessment (conventional resources); and students motivated to put in the time and effort to master the content (personal resources). In short, the instructional effects of conventional resources depend on how those who work in instruction use them and on the environments in which they work. Additional resources that lie outside teachers' and students' scope of practice, knowledge, norms, and incentives will have little measurable effect on learning.

- **Parents and community.** Parents and communities have assorted assets—in people, organizations, businesses, services, and funding possibilities—that can help motivate and buttress student learning. Researchers concur that increased parent and community involvement with students' learning increases their achievement and school success.[6]

Schools and districts also have less obvious resources available to them. Recognizing and wisely using these increases the range of assets available to underpin teaching and learning. These potent but less obvious resources include:

- **Influence.** Influence includes advantages that people use to sway others to act in certain ways. They include material assets, professional or "insider" knowledge, and positional and social authority that individuals can use to persuade another.[7]

- **Social resources.** These include allies, followers, and the potential to mobilize, motivate, or control others in the school or community. Social resources also involve personality factors (such as popularity, status, visibility, and perceived trustworthiness) and personal traits (such as having good "people skills"). For instance, a school board member may be a Garden Club participant along with the teachers' association leader; they might trade district-related information in exchange for each other's future backing.

- **Positional resources.** Individuals in certain posts in the organization have access to decision making, the authority to directly control others, and opportunities to access material resources and people networks, the political system, and the media. For example, because school counselors work daily with teachers and students (and consult with colleagues in other schools), counselors' position gives them the information, insight, experiences, and collaborative relationships needed to make informed suggestions for school districts wanting to develop social-emotional education components of school accountability to support student learning.

These varied resources are closely linked. They reciprocally impact and depend on the others to achieve their intended purposes. For instance, having sufficient monies and time without relevant materials and effective teachers cannot provide students with optimal learning opportunities. Similarly, a school full of enthusiastic, first and second-year teachers without the opportunities for ongoing collaboration and learning with effective mature colleagues lack regular occasions to improve classroom practices that increase student learning. Given the notable variations in schools' needs, capacities, and contexts, PreK-12 school leaders can better leverage the resources they do have if they strategically organize and assign their limited resources in ways that benefit student academic success and wellbeing.

Priorities, Beliefs, and Constraints in Allocating Educational Resources

Principals' resource allocation decisions reflect an array of priorities, beliefs, values, and constraints. Broadly, principals' priorities include the academic success and wellbeing of every student; building a school climate and culture that supports ethical behaviors, cultural responsiveness, high-quality teaching and learning, and continuous improvement; providing an appropriately rigorous curriculum, instruction, and assessment systems geared to state and local standards; shaping a decision-making process that includes input from teachers and other stakeholders (who have both high interest and relevant expertise in the issue under consideration); and engaging families and the community in meaningful ways that support student outcomes.

In addition, principals' and superintendents' beliefs about fairness also influence how they allocate resources. While they believe in equal treatment for individuals, they also recognize that students come to school with differing learning needs, family economic assets, and prior educational experiences. As a result, issues of equity and adequacy become critical concerns in allocating resources.

Briefly, *equality* is providing the same services to all students, regardless of their needs; *equity* is providing the services that students actually need to be successful; and *adequacy* involves giving students enough of what they need to succeed. If children with disabilities, children from poverty backgrounds, and children with limited English proficiency are to meet the same high academic performance standards as able, middle class, and affluent children, they will likely need additional resources of money, people, time, materials, and community assets than those allocated for their more affluent peers. As a fiscal concept, adequacy is value-based; people define it subjectively according to their experiences and opinions. The actual dollar amount for what funding is "adequate" remains unclear.

In fact, state courts have been trying for the past 30 years to determine what amount of state funding is "adequate" to ensure that schools can appropriately educate every student to high standards. Of the 50 states, 46 have seen lawsuits challenging state methods of funding public schools.[8] Adequacy litigation has consistently identified four educational goals that schools should achieve: 1) Prepare students to be citizens and economic participants in a democratic society; 2) Relate to contemporary (not outdated) educational needs; 3) Connect educational standards to more than a minimal level; and 4) Focus on providing opportunity rather than outcome.[9]

Constraints also play a key role in resource allocation decisions. These include: the school district's and the school's mission and vision; state and district requirements for staffing, academic standards, and accountability; teachers' and students' needs; organizational and legal restrictions; community needs and views; and the principals' own values and goals. Principals will want to conduct 360-degree environmental scans and detailed needs assessments in various areas of school life to generate the data, empirical and anecdotal, from which to make informed resource allocation choices. These choices must be aligned with school needs and operate within the relevant constraints.

For principals and superintendents, the implications are clear. School leaders cannot guarantee the academic and life success for every student. But educators can ensure that by allocating their resources fairly (in equitable and adequate ways), every student will have the welcoming learning environment, the academic press, and the array of academic and moral supports they need to learn and achieve to high standards.

REFLECTIONS AND RELEVANCE 11.1

Using School Resources to Improve Teaching and Learning

Developing and allocating resources to support improved teaching and learning are fundamental school leadership challenges.

Review the descriptions of each resource, and work in groups of three to create two Word Clouds using chart paper and colored markers. The first Word Cloud will depict the importance (amount and value to teaching and learning) of different resources in your school *as they presently exist.* For the second Word Cloud, depict *the way you think the resource priorities should be.* Make the resource of the largest size/amount and highest priority/value the largest. Make the resources with the least size/amount and lowest priority/value the smallest. Use color and designs to help illustrate meaning.

When the Word Clouds are completed, present them to the class and explain. As a class, discuss the relative importance of different education resources to teaching and learning. What differences in resource allocations do you see between the present image and how you think resource allocation should look? Which resources do you think are overvalued, undervalued, and why?

EVOLVING PERSPECTIVES ON FUNDING SCHOOLS FOR LEARNING

Over the years, the focus for allocating school resources has shifted from input-oriented compliance to outcome-oriented student learning. As compared with traditional funding systems, a learning-oriented system directs resources in ways that advance effective teaching and student learning. Accountability tracks whether and how educators use resources to support academic goals and holds educators and students answerable for their contributions to learning. This approach also supports a coherent instructional program, develops teachers' capacity to successfully instruct every student, uses compensation to incentivize strong classroom performance, and accounts for academic results. Unless resource management—that is, budgeting and spending directed into learning-related categories—has clear and transparent links to its student results, the resource effects on student learning remain uncertain.

The changing perspective between conventional and learning-oriented resource allocation represents a paradigm shift. In today's schools, managing education resources is about directly connecting funding to learning goals.

Theory of Action for School Resource Allocation

Once school leaders commit to learning-oriented improvements, they are obliged to work with other stakeholders' interests and constraints. Many of these are political: changing existing allocations has implications for those programs and persons currently receiving them. In conventional resourcing, "horse-trading" among competing interests occurs within the boundaries set by allocation parameters, including available funds for the year, filled and open positions in each school and across the district, and projected enrollment increases or decreases. By contrast, a learning-focused leadership theory of action prioritizes specific learning improvement goals and expresses a set of strategic actions that make achieving these goals more likely.

Figure 11.1 depicts this theory of action. By seeking and interpreting informa-tion (evidence) about learning needs, current programs, emerging conditions, and effects of earlier investments, leaders find more fully informed ways of developing and appraising allocation options. Although political constraints from existing allocation decisions and competing stakeholder interests continue, administrators try to balance vying interests. The learning-focused process gives voice to a potentially influential set of considerations. Student learning, strategies for addressing it, and evidence to inform resource allocation decisions become central discussion topics that might otherwise not be heard.

Since most resources arrive at the school through the district, learning focused resource allocation depends on instructional prioritizing and planning at the district level. Working with district officials, principals, teachers, and the community can identify goals and instructional priorities—such as improving graduation rates, retaining effective teachers, or starting a reading initiative for a certain group of students—to provide the framework for directing monies to learning ends. The best practice also encourages the district to create a multi-year financial plan with critical instructional goals prioritized and frequently reviewed.[10] In this way, leaders ensure that the stated goals remain relevant and funded. And rather than cutting around the margins (such as by reducing 10 percent from each budget category) when monies become tight, the priorities continue to receive funding.

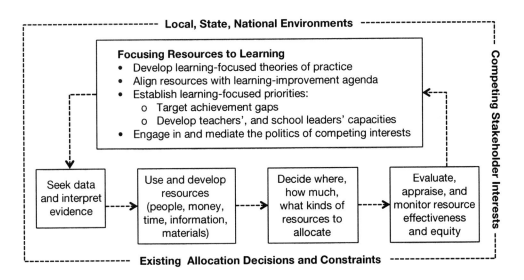

FIGURE 11.1 Learning-Focused Resource Allocation Cycle

Source: Based on Plecki, M.L. Alejano, C.R., Knapp, M.S., & Lochmiller, C.R. (2006). *Allocating resources and creating incentives to improve teaching and learning*. Seattle, WA: Center for the Study of Teaching and Policy, University of Washington. Retrieved from: https://depts. washington.edu/ctpmail/PDFs/Resources-Oct30.pdf or www.wallacefoundation.org/ knowledge-center/school-leadership/key-research/Documents/2-Allocating-Resources-and-Creating.pdf

To address competing interests, education leaders keep the focus on improved student learning. They invite multiple perspectives and contesting interests, especially those that value learning improvement. School leaders manage the deliberation process so that learning priorities and equity stay central to resource allocation decision making. They emphasize particular allocation outcomes, such as increasing every student's achievement and every teacher's improved practice. They guide the use of allotted resources, seeking and interpreting evidence about the allocation's uses and effects on achievement. In short, learning-oriented school leaders facilitate their school improvement cycle's culture of continuous improvement and feedback loops to support data-informed, learning-focused decisions about how to apportion resources and assess outcomes.

In addition, school leaders must work with an eye to existing and anticipated limitations—including the school, district, and state's financial conditions; the political considerations in local and state communities; district budget practices and earlier years' financial decisions; fixed or unanticipated costs for the physical plant (i.e., a leaky roof) or human resources (i.e., increased health care benefits' cost and current labor agreements); and conflicting parent and general public expectations (i.e., expanding the Advanced Placement options versus providing more courses for students completing industry certification). These constraints curtail school leaders' actions and prevent certain resource-related decisions that might be desirable.

In shifting paradigms, educators are deciding that since resources are precious and limited, they need to be strategically and deliberately focused on instructional priorities and student learning outcomes. A learning-oriented system for education resource allocation uses continuous instructional improvement to align and adapt resources to instructional and student needs. It creates transparency and flexibility to deliver resources to the teachers and students they intend to serve. As a system, it requires all parts to be present and working as intended.

RESEARCH ON MONEY AND STUDENT ACHIEVEMENT

Since the mid 1960s, policy makers, educators, economists, researchers, and the general public energetically have debated whether monies funding education made a measurable impact on student learning. Despite increasing revenues going to schools—largely for hiring additional teachers to meet student enrollment increases and to reduce class sizes, especially for students in grades 1–3 and students with learning needs—student achievement as measured by standardized tests appeared to be declining.[11]

The issues of money for schools have become highly politicized. Often, advocates base their arguments more on old data and ideology than on well-designed studies. Fortunately, numerous investigations have found overwhelming evidence that school funding—in total dollars and how moneys are spent—has a positive impact on student achievement.[12] Resources allocated toward instruction and effective teaching boost student learning and attainment. Understanding the argument and having "proof" that "money matters" when wisely spent can help school leaders better address their public's concern about funding education and accountability for public dollars.

In 1966, the U.S. Department of Education commissioned James S. Coleman, a University of Chicago sociologist, to assess whether children of different races, income groups, and national origins had equal educational opportunities in American public schools.[13] The Coleman Report concluded that overall, a weak association existed between school resources—such as school libraries, teachers' experience and education, expenditures, science labs, and other facilities—and schools' average student performance. Rather, Coleman and his colleagues determined that children's family's educational and social backgrounds—not their schools—were the most important determinants of children's academic success. Many took this to mean that schools did not "make a difference." In general, the scholarly community reaffirmed these findings.[14]

In the 1980s and 1990s, the Hoover Institution economist Eric Hanushek's econometric studies of school resources and student achievement supported this conclusion. Hanushek found no strong or consistent positive relationship between educational expenditures and student achievement.[15]

Other investigators drew a different conclusion: school resources can make a positive difference in student achievement. Larry Hedges, Rob Greenwald, and colleagues summarized a comprehensive collection of studies, including those that Hanushek examined.[16] Using improved meta-analytic methodology, Hedges and colleagues found that increasing education spending *did* result in higher achievement. And the relationship between expenditures and student outcomes had statistical and practical significance. *Money and how schools spend it are equally important*—and the link between money spent and student achievement is large enough to be educationally meaningful. They also found that school inputs such as adequate levels of expenditures per student; lower class sizes; teacher experience and high-quality preparation; and contemporary and well maintained buildings and facilities are positively related to student outcomes with effects consistently positive and large enough to be educationally important.[17] Similarly, other studies observed an economically efficient relation between educational inputs and student outcomes as long as the resources reach schools, classrooms, and students.[18]

Several noteworthy studies support this conclusion. An experimental study in Tennessee confirmed findings of a positive relationship between reduced class size in kindergarten through third grade and student outcomes.[19] Another investigation found that expenditures on instruction and reduced class size affected student achievement.[20] Likewise, many studies have identified significant relationships between teaching effectiveness and student achievement,[21] with effects that persist into adulthood.[22] One mid-1980s summary of the evidence on effective teaching (as measured by student gains on standardized tests) found that more effective teacher's instructional practices seemed significantly different than those of their less effective peers.[23] And a 2016 study of performance in disadvantaged urban schools estimated that a top teacher could, in one year, produce an added gain from students of one full year's worth of learning as compared to students working with a very ineffective teacher.[24]

Studies also find that school culture and school leaders and teachers' attitudes and behaviors can differentiate schools that are effective in increasing student learning and those that are not.[25] Another line of inquiry looking at the teacher and student interactions around specific content observed that instructional time was less important than the nature of academic tasks and teachers' instructional actions that mediated student learning.[26] Other studies conclude that student attributions about intelligence and learning—whether these were fixed or expandable through effort—play a key role in their classroom behaviors and learning.[27]

In 2016, Hanushek split the difference. Updating the Coleman Report's conclusions 50 years after its publication, Hanushek acknowledged that *how* schools spend their money is more important than *how much* is spent.[28] Schools that direct their resources wisely to instructional areas can make a positive increase in student achievement. Money, in and of itself without appropriate targeting to instruction and better teaching, is important but does not measurably impact student achievement.

Given these data, today's educators, policy makers, and investigators agree that resource effectiveness in increasing student learning depends largely on *how* schools use these resources in instruction. Instructional improvement will not necessarily happen simply by increasing the number of teachers, boosting teachers' salaries, or buying more books or computers. What teachers and students actually *do* with the allocated resources matters—*how* they use the resources in instruction—not merely if the resources are

---

REFLECTIONS AND RELEVANCE 11.2

Aligning School Resources for Student Learning

You (a central office Director of Curriculum and Instruction) and your partner (the district's Assessment Coordinator) work in a medium sized school district. Most of the district's students are achieving moderately well, but almost one-third are not reaching grade level proficiency as measured by achievement tests. One school piloted a professional learning community 3 years ago and now is seeing all students, including the traditionally lowest performers, making achievement gains. You and your colleague believe that using a student-oriented resource allocation model would improve teaching and increase student learning and achievement.

Prepare and deliver a 3-minute presentation to give to the superintendent, the district's finance director, and the school board on the reasons and evidence for recommending that the district move to a student learning-oriented resource allocation model rather than continue with the current compliance-oriented approach.

In your presentation, discuss:

- The evolving perspective on funding schools for learning
- Your rationale for proposing the student-oriented resource allocation approach
- The research on school funding and student achievement
- How the student learning orientation to resource allocation improves accountability
- Working with stakeholders who have competing interests

Create a graphic to help illustrate how this student-oriented resource allocation model would work and present your talk to your class.

present or absent. Providing schools with more funds without any change in practices is unlikely to lead to any systematic improvements in student outcomes. Rather, instructional improvement depends on improving student, teacher, and school leaders' skills and knowledge in using these resources for instruction, improving resources' usability, and enhancing conditions that enable resource use. Likewise, it depends on the principals' knowledge and skills in building and sustaining the vision and core values of high-quality education for every child; a learning environment of collective responsibility and academic press for every student's learning and wellbeing; enhancing the schools' academic organization; and fostering collegial relations that enable appropriate resource use by all members of the school community.

If schools are to accomplish the ambitious educational goals that communities hold for them, then school leaders can argue persuasively with plentiful evidence that intelligently targeting resources to specific instruction-related areas and monitoring their effectiveness can lead to gains in desired student outcomes.

EFFICIENCY IN SECURING AND ALLOCATING EDUCATIONAL RESOURCES

Since the Great Recession (2007–2009), limited resources are an education reality. Legislatures and mayors advise schools districts to stretch their "dwindling dollars" and "do more with less" by becoming more productive and efficient. At a time when public education expectations for every student's achievement have never been higher, education is competing with health care, public safety, and other community needs for a larger share of fewer available dollars.

Efficiency in public schools concerns itself with how much education or knowledge schools deliver (directly by teachers, indirectly by principals) to students—and how much students acquire—and at what cost.[29] School efficiency measures identify schools that get "the most bang for their educational buck." Typically, efficiency analyses using statistical models with large numbers of schools or districts are policy issues outside school leaders' wheelhouse. But the fact that resource allocation has an efficiency aspect deserves superintendents' and principals' attention. Communities expect their education leaders to be effective and efficient stewards of the public's education dollars. Especially at times of tight funding, educators must be able to show that they are improving student outcomes without substantially increasing costs.

Are Public Schools Using Their Resources Efficiently?

Determining *efficiency* is about evaluating how some organizational units achieve better or worse outcomes than others given comparable spending. In particular, *school allocation efficiency* considers the link between spending on schools and student performance outcomes. Performance outcomes may include measures such as the percent of students at each grade and in identified high school courses achieving "proficient" scores on standardized tests (disaggregated by race, ethnicity, free and reduced-price lunch, and other key variables); average daily attendance rates; percent of 12th grader graduating in four years; and total dollar amounts of grants awarded to the school.[30]

Basically, from an economists' viewpoint, an *inefficient* school has lower than expected outcomes with higher than expected spending. An *efficient* school generates higher than expected outcomes using lower than expected spending. Efficiency also assumes that public schools will not "rob Peter to pay Paul." Schools conduct their spending so no student's educational situation is made worse in order to improve another student's situation. Although most education leaders will not determine their school's efficiency statistically with mathematical equations, these concepts provide a normative frame for making resource acquisition and allocation decisions.

The issue of public school efficiency and productivity is highly contentious.[31] On one side of the controversy, policy makers assert that American public education suffers from *Baumol's*[32] *disease*—"the tendency of labor-intensive organizations to become more expensive over time but not any more productive."[33] They argue that if, on average, schools are producing only slightly better results than at earlier decades but at higher costs,[34] they are becoming less productive. To cure this "disease," economists suggest strategies to make schools more productive and efficient. These include: removing pay increments for teachers' experience or degree level; expanding the teacher work day and/or year with new duties (but without increasing salaries); removing class size mandates; adding performance pay based on student test score gains or teacher performance evaluations (without changing average salary levels); layoffs based solely on student test score results and not on teachers' seniority; and moving toward employee-funded defined contribution retirement plans (and away from defined benefit retirement plans).[35] Some of these "remedies" are already occurring.[36] These economists contend that current spending should be re-allocated to make each dollar spent on public education more productive and efficient.

In turn, other policy makers refute what they see as their opponents' over-simplifications and inaccuracies. They insist that educational spending has not risen markedly over the past few decades; rather, it has remained relatively constant.[37] Achievement test scores have not declined or remained flat as the numbers of teachers increased.[38] Therefore, education advocates claim, these productivity and efficiency proposals are "unwarranted and largely untested assumption[s]" that do not consider possible collateral damage to teaching and learning.[39]

Schools as Budget-Maximizing Bureaucracies

Traditional economists assume that private, profit-oriented businesses use budget-minimizing strategies to enhance efficiency and increase profits. By contrast, they assert that public organizations (such as schools) use budget-maximizing strategies because the incentives to minimize expenses are absent.[40] This perspective, *budget maximizing theory*,[41] describes key differences in how private and public organizations approach resource use.

Private business and public schools are different. For-profit businesses (such as Apple, Microsoft, or Mercedes Benz) and public bureaus (such as schools and legislatures) differ in their purposes, operations, underlying assumptions, and funding sources. For-profit businesses receive most of their revenues from consumer purchases. In comparison, public bureaus receive most of their revenues from taxing authorities. As a result, they lack the incentives to enact cost-effective behaviors.[42] And unlike for-profit businesses, schools supply services—that is, teaching and learning—whose value cannot be exchanged for money at a per-unit rate.[43]

These two dissimilar types of organizations also differ in their incentives toward efficiency. Unlike executives in private, for-profit businesses, public sector managers lack property rights or a profit motive in their organization's successful performance. And their recurring tax-supplied funding occurs without needing to satisfy individual consumers. As a result, public sector administrators do not have to generate cost-effective behaviors. Consequently, when traditional economists compare public schools with private, for-profit businesses, public schools districts appear as "economically inefficient" organizations.

Some economists speculate that given this lack of financial incentives to increase organizational efficiency, educators (and other public sector managers) try to maximize their own happiness and wellbeing by expanding their non-monetary benefits.[44] They may do this in three ways. First, they increase their budget size, scope of responsibility or ease of managing their unit as a way to gain higher prestige, enhance their public reputation, use patronage, or gain other privileges. People tend to perceive persons with larger agency budgets as more effective, more competent, and held in their bosses' higher regard than colleagues with flat or decreased resources. Second, education leaders who want employees to change their practices in order to achieve beneficial outcomes may seek budget increases to "buy" teachers' cooperation, responsiveness, and work effectiveness[45] (such as by sending teachers to professional conferences or hiring substitutes so they can participate in professional development during the school day).

Third, sponsors and top officials lack the time, information, staff, and comprehensive understanding of the organization's actual needs to monitor each step in the budget review process. Often, they let the budget increases slip by. The upshot: administrators enlarge their school or department's total budget during their tenure as an acceptable proxy for their enhanced personal value. With this budget maximizing strategy, theorists suggest, public school leaders' personal goals may take priority over the district's stated objectives. Inefficiency results (because compared to spending levels, their output is too low).[46]

Research and Criticism

Many studies affirm the conclusion that bureaucrats request moderate annual budget increases.[47] Studies also find that public bureaucrats tend to vote for political parties that favor state intervention,[48] and school superintendents hold tax rates as high as possible without having to obtain voter approval.[49] In a slightly different vein, studies find that civil servants tend to be "mission-minded"—committed to improving the quality of public services regardless of salary.[50] In fact, investigations observe little relation between growth of public bureaus and bureaucrats' salaries.[51] Nonetheless, legislators put budget controls into place because they believe that bureaus will always try to increase their budgets.[52]

At the same time, critics address several major concerns with this budget maximizing theory,[53] and these views have interest for educational leaders. First, although critics claim that the theory is slanted ideologically (towards a libertarian view of individual freedom, free markets, limited government, and peace),[54] other investigations have affirmed its validity and reliability.[55] Second, critics argue that the public bureau (i.e., public school) is not necessarily the only supplier of a service. But because public schools control about 90 percent of the PreK-12 education market, and have considerable support from state legislatures, taxpayers, and parents, public schools have sizeable sway over state education policy.[56] Third, it is difficult to determine the difference between public schools' current and optimum funding levels, in part, because economic

---

REFLECTIONS AND RELEVANCE 11.3

Efficiency in Securing and Allocating Educational Resources

School allocation efficiency looks at the link between spending on schools and student performance outcomes. Communities expect their education leaders to be effective and efficient stewards of public funds, and educators must be able to show that they are improving student outcomes without substantially increasing costs.

Your local school board's members include several business CEOs. Over the past few years, at budget approval time, the school board has expressed concerns to the superintendent about the district's rising education costs without a comparable gain in measured student achievement. This year, before administrators begin preparing their budget requests, the superintendent offers them guidance about how to proceed in this environment.

Working in groups of four, prepare the superintendent's 3–5 minute remarks to the district's administrators about the school board and community's concern for efficiency. Include in the presentation:

- The differences between efficient and inefficient schools and the community's and board's concern about rising school district budgets.
- The perils of district administrators and principals catching "Baumol's disease."
- The possible consequences to the district and employees should the community and board believe the district schools are inefficient.
- The need to avoid budget maximizing strategies and to find incentives that enhance administrators' esteem and reputation beyond larger budgets.

When the presentations are complete, each group will give this talk to the class. As a class, discuss the merits and downsides of considering this economic perspective when thinking about securing and allocating school resources.

researchers lack consensus about how to define an *optimum* level.[57] In the end, perhaps applying traditional economic (i.e., cost-minimizing) assumptions to public education funding and productivity/outcomes is more a political exercise than a logical one. When justifying taxpayer dollars for education, it helps to know the difference.

Reasonable and intelligent people will almost always agree that the amount of revenues available to a school affect its level of productivity.[58] Public school spending occurs in a sociopolitical environment of competing interests—political, organizational and personal—and limited resources. Despite the available research, examining the connections between effective spending, school characteristics, and student outcomes, making credible connections among these factors remains challenging. Nonetheless, understanding the efficiency concerns can help educators monitor their own actions as they advocate for—and allocate—resources to generate the maximum opportunities for student and school success.

RESOURCE DEPENDENCE THEORY AND RESOURCE ALLOCATION

In the 1970s, organizational theorists enlarged their focus on the environment. As they saw it, organizations' need for resources embeds them in networks of interdependencies and social relationships, situations and contexts that impact their abilities to secure and allocate resources. Drawing upon sociology and political science perspectives, resource dependence theory (RDT) views organizations as open systems, interdependent with their environments upon which they depend to provide *"critical" resources*—those essential for the organization to function—and to reduce or avoid uncertainty about being able to achieve their objectives.[59] With its 360-degree perspective and practical insights, RDT has become one of the most influential concepts in organizational theory and strategic management.[60]

RDT proposes that no organization is entirely self-sufficient, and resources are not always adequate, stable, or assured. Given this, organizations create various interdependent relationships, relying on internal and external coalitions of individuals and group stakeholders, to gain these essential resources so they can achieve their basic goals. But dependence is undesirable because it reduces the organization's range of choices in any given situation, threatening its stability and possibly its existence. Whoever controls these vital resources has the power over those actors who need them. The more crucial and scarce the resource, the greater the organization's dependence on the resource provider. Ultimately, the organizational leaders try to manage and strategically adapt to the requirements of external resource providers. Feedback from decisions and actions facilitates these interdependencies and affects the resource situation, the organization, and the demands of powerful groups.[61]

Since organizations interact through their people, the players' social influence and control of vital assets give them more or less clout to make decisions go according to their interests. This include choosing top administrative personnel (as those in power try to reproduce their views in important organization positions with folks like themselves). Those people, sub-units, or departments inside organizations who manage these important environmental dependencies (i.e., who have good relationships with the key players) and help the organization get what they need—such as central office finance directors—tend to hold more influence in decision making because of their essential role in ensuring organizational success and possibly, survival.[62]

For instance, governments are influential actors in obtaining and allocating resources for school districts. States and local governments typically each deliver about 44 percent of all elementary and secondary education funding; the federal government contributes about 12 percent of all direct expenditures.[63] In exchange for the funds, government regulations can "mandate" that school districts accept certain policies and decisions (or threaten to withdraw the resources). Imposed policies include teaching to state-approved K-12 academic content standards and assessing students' learning with state-mandated achievement tests. Organizations more dependent on government are likely to establish ongoing relationships with government officials to help the organization when relevant public policy issues arise. In this way, organizations can influence outcomes in favorable ways. Hence, many school districts have created legislative liaison positions. In addition, organizations moderately affected by governmental activities are likely to participate in collective organizations, such as the state and national educational associations or professional principals' associations to increase their influence on policy decisions.

RDT believes that by using their influence strategically, managers can reduce environmental uncertainty and dependence, increase their own control over resources, and reduce others' power over them.[64] RDT has administrators ascribe to three over-arching principles: continue their organization's survival; lessen the effects that external limitations create on in-house decision making; and maximize leaders' autonomy and discretion to enhance the organization's present and future adaptability.[65] One of the ways administrators minimize environmental dependencies is by constructing boards of directors[66]—similar to local school boards. As part of the organization and its environment, boards of directors maintain excellent relations with key external and internal stakeholders to ensure the resources flow into and from the organization and help the organization respond to external change. Here is where RDT has its largest research influence and its direct relevance for schools.

RESOURCE DEPENDENCE THEORY AND SCHOOLS

Like other boards of directors, a school board's size and composition enables the school district to minimize dependence and gain resources as the organization responds to external (and occasionally, internal) environmental conditions. Notably, board members bring four benefits to the school district:

1. Information in the form of advice and counsel;
2. Access to information channels between the organization and environment;
3. Preferential access to resources; and
4. Legitimacy.

Legitimacy, a political science term, is the social judgment that an organization is pursuing socially worthy goals in a socially acceptable manner.[67] Legitimacy justifies the organization's role in the social system, helps attract resources and constituents' continual support, and is, itself, a resource. Ample research supports these proposed benefits.[68] Typically, boards change their membership composition as the organization's environment changes, keeping the board's makeup (and accessible resources) matched to the schools' external needs.[69]

Typically, school district residents elect local school board members according to their important outside contacts, experiences, and knowledge. Board members derive their power and authority to make policy, to hire and fire the district superintendent, and to request funding for their district according to their state's constitution. In addition to setting a vision for the district, establishing standards, and assessing student learning outcomes, local school boards have a major responsibility for allocating resources to support district goals. Varied groups compete for available resources. Students and parents want specific programs. Communities want efficient use of taxpayer dollars and to prepare students to become the skilled employee base to attract new businesses. State and federal governments require students from every demographic to achieve well. And school district employees want job security, fair working conditions, reasonable salary and benefits, and opportunities for advancement. With responsibility to maintain fiscal solvency, school boards work with superintendents to decide whether and how to cut spending on teachers, staff, instructional programs, or facilities (without harming student achievement).

Figure 11.2 illustrates how external demands and resources and internal school district preferences become policy outcomes that affect resource allocations. School district agents—typically superintendents and school boards—can choose to accept, combine, reduce, or occasionally ignore external groups' inputs.[70] While teacher association representatives may *recommend* actions to the school board concerning salary or workplace issues, teachers' unions (operating in states that allow unions to have collective bargaining rights) actually *negotiate* with school boards or their designee (usually a central office administrator) on teacher employment terms and conditions. External actors—individuals, interest groups, or government officials—have or can secure resources, issue requests, and use influence strategies to accomplish their ends. Outcomes of the resource-seeking actions include board policies (including budgets, layoffs, facilities, district strategic plans, personnel assignments, and implementation plans for state and federal policy mandates), contracts, and administrator actions (including resource allocation decisions). All these exchanges occur within certain environments, institutional contexts, community structures, and public opinions that bring their own incentives and checks. The solid-line arrows in Figure 11.2 indicate that the actor is performing an action to affect another's behavior while the dotted-line arrows indicate internal school district members influencing each other's behaviors. Feedback from the outcomes returns to internal and external players to help them adapt their plans, actions, and future strategies to district decisions. As befitting an organization in an open system, the environmental factors, institutional context, community structure, and public opinion each influence the local school district, the individuals and interest groups, government policies, and school district outcomes.

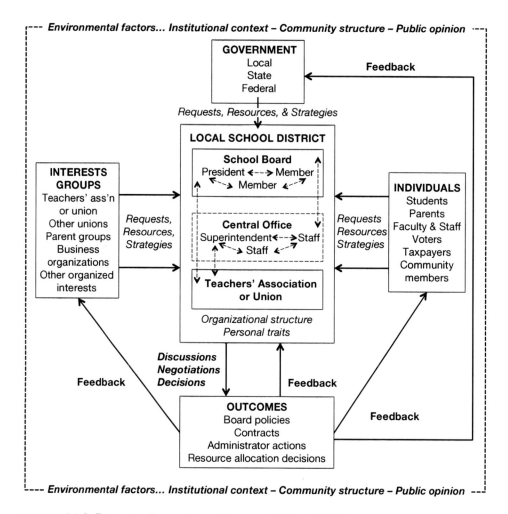

FIGURE 11.2 Resource Dependence Theory in School Districts

Source: Based on Zeehandelaar, D.B. (2012). *The local politics of education governance: Power and influence among school boards, superintendents, and teachers' unions.* (Unpublished doctoral dissertation). University of Southern California, Los Angeles, CA.

Pressures and constraints on school boards are many. For one thing, school districts cannot deficit-spend: they must balance their budgets within the limits of government categorical funding requirements. For another, their students must learn the knowledge and skills needed to meet state achievement benchmarks. Likewise, everyone—from superintendents to teacher associations, from union leaders to parents, community members, and business organizations—tries to protect their own priorities. They do this by influencing school board members' decisions about resource allocations. Inevitably, conflicting interests and scarce resources infuse the educational and resource decision-making process.[71]

Environmental factors. These affect the resources to which school agents have access, the influence strategies that leaders choose, and whether their leverage leads to resource allocation decisions that reflect their interests. The districts' demographics (i.e., students' and parents' ages, races and ethnicities, languages, religions, and education levels), community wealth, geographic size and location, and external policy mandates and laws limit or exclude certain resource availability and use while facilitating others. For example, the district residents' religious and cultural values may motivate conflicts with school boards about curriculum, instruction, spending or saving resources, and how districts should educate their children.[72] Federal and state laws issue strict compliance regulations about how schools are to educate students with disabilities. Likewise, large urban districts tend to have more active interests groups,[73] face more complex challenges, and use more restricted budgets than smaller, suburban, or rural counterparts.[74] And an aging population, increasing diversity, or decreasing wealth levels will also impact policy decisions on resource availability and allocations. As a result, some actors—depending on their external context factors—have a comparative advantage in securing resources and are more able to successfully leverage them.

Community structure. The existing relationship between the local political system and the public limits some influence strategies while fostering others. Since the public elects school board members, and the school board hires the superintendent, and interest groups are only as strong as their community backing, resource distribution is connected to the existing community makeup. The greater the resources an actor has, and the more accommodating the community is in allowing actors to leverage those resources, the more influence the actor will have.[75] Superintendents and school board members respond differently to board members in a community dominated by a few highly influential interest groups than in communities where many groups compete for clout. For instance, a school district located in a college town, where one-third of the school board members are professors at that college, will likely abide by these board members' preferences in curriculum decisions and hiring central office personnel (as long as the "preferred" candidate meets the minimum job requirements).

Public opinion and personal traits will also impact a school district's balance of influence and district leaders' decisions. If voters believe that their leaders share their values and goals, they tend to trust leaders' decisions without conflict.[76] By comparison, if district leaders suspect that the public does not agree with their values and goals, the leaders are more likely to accede to public demands (rather than challenge them) and possibly jeopardize the superintendent's tenure.[77] Similarly, personal traits—such as gender, education, family background, political ideology, religion and values, intelligence, honesty, open-mindedness, perceived alliances with favored groups, and motives for doing their job—affect actors' behaviors.[78] These traits may be influential because they are characteristics of that particular region's dominant societal culture or because they make the actor seem more trustworthy.[79] For example, if the area's influence leaders are its college professors, then actions of individuals with advanced professional degrees are more likely to influence board decision making than actions of individuals without them.

In-house context variables influence resource allocations, too. Organizational culture—such as the district's internal rules, norms, traditions, and values—limit certain actions while permitting or encouraging others.[80] These features give boards, super-intendents, and outside interests more or less leeway in how they distribute resources among internal actors. Successful transactions over resources fit within these existing traditions. For instance, certain historically conservative districts may keep large amounts of money in a "rainy day" reserve only to invest carefully in physical assets whereas other less conservative districts may prefer to keep minimal fiscal reserves and spend these on instructional programs and teachers' bonuses. Likewise, a school board member may successfully persuade an ambitious assistant superintendent to give the board member's son a high-level district job in exchange for the member's vote to promote the assistant to district superintendent when the position becomes vacant.

Influence strategies. As illustrated in Figure 11.2, internal and external actors use influence strategies to leverage their resources and motivate others to respond favorably to their demands.[81] *Influence strategies* are the deliberate use of a resource by one actor to persuade another to behave in a certain way. These influence strategies may be overt or covert. Overt, intentional, and visible influence strategies include bargaining, negotiating, collaborating, and accommodating as people act to secure their own and their groups' interests. Overt strategies may also involve using direct authority, making a decision for another person, or using coercion, persuasion, or force to compel another to make a particular decision. For instance, the principal has the authority to tell the guidance director to begin creating the next year's master schedule or which courses and rooms to assign to which teachers.

Covert, less visible influence strategies such as *constraints* are limitations that actors place on each other or on the situation. Working discretely behind-the-scenes, a person can use authority to limit the scope of decision making by setting the agenda (such as deciding what issues require a decision and which do not) and fixing the rules for participating in the process (such as who can attend, speak, and vote). In these situations, individuals use authority's influence to prevent others from making a decision. Influence can also be *manipulation*, when one person persuades another to act against his or her own interests or shapes the opposition's interests so that they are no longer in conflict. For example, superintendents can manipulate information by *filtering* it (i.e., strategically selecting what information to give) or *spinning* it (i.e., giving a slanted interpretation of information in order make a certain course of action seem favorable) in ways that sway the school board to accept his or her policy recommendations.[82]

Even the threat of action, explicit or tacit, is a potent influence strategy.[83] A large PTA membership has only potential influence until it chooses to mobilize members to endorse—or protest—a school board decision. The superintendent's concern about widespread parent action and its negative publicity can be as persuasive as an actual parent protest.

Boards, superintendents, and teacher unions face heavy public criticism for using authority or covert influence to put their own self-interest above the public good. Using money-saving tactics such as leaving educator positions vacant while raising class sizes (and accumulating unspent funds to use on the superintendent's "pet project"); imposing teacher and administrator (unpaid) "furloughs"; making curriculum decisions without teacher input; and having unidentified persons place glowing or critical stories about the school or district in the local media have an undue influence on resource allocations without increasing teaching effectiveness or student learning.[84]

RESEARCH AND CRITICISM

As a conceptual lens to explain organizations' behavior, resource dependence theory has strong empirical grounding: management decisions reflect internal and external influences, those who hold critical resources have power, and power influences behavior.[85] Likewise, differences in organizations' environments explain more of the variance in political behavior than individual differences can explain;[86] and environmental uncertainty triggers strategies to reduce it.[87] Meanwhile, the research on school board and district interactions around resource-seeking behaviors generally agrees that power (i.e., influence) is contested among school board, superintendents, teachers' unions, and the public; and each works to redistribute power and related resources—including financial capital, information, access to the decision-making processes, and internal allies, powerful interest groups, and broad constituent support—in their favor.[88] Additionally, a continual instability exists between lay control and professional expertise.[89] Board members and superintendents act within their existing spheres of influence to shape others' actions and to expand their own sphere,[90] a boundary increasingly blurred by districts' increasing complexity.[91] Likewise, board members and superintendents also juggle competing demands for resources to address student achievement, financial solvency, personal job security, and the organization's social acceptability or legality.[92] Community structure,[93] public opinion,[94] personal traits,[95] institutional context,[96] and influence strategies between the boards and superintendents[97] also play important roles in resource allocations. Studies also assert that the distribution of power to allocate resources favors the superintendent, within the limits allowed by the public, state and federal government, community demands, union collective bargaining agreements, and site-based management.[98]

Despite its research support, RDT faces conceptual challenges on aspects of more interest to political and social scientists than to educational leaders.[99] Critics note RDT's omissions, asserting that it does not consider an organization's historical, institutional, cultural, political, and transnational contexts;[100] does not clearly define the relationships shared between the environment and the organization;[101] ignores professional groups' cross-cutting linkages across the organization and in the external professional world;[102] omits the trust factor needed if organizations are to depend on stakeholders to help secure and allocate resources appropriately;[103] and doesn't clarify the types of dependencies between organizations and stakeholders.[104] Finally, RDT critics remind us that boards of directors' roles and characteristics vary widely among national cultures and within each country and organization.[105]

Managing the organization's environment is as important as managing the organization itself. Resource dependence theory's realistic and largely validated assumptions help organization leaders understand how organizations—such as school districts and schools—develop strategies to engage, manage, and perhaps shape—their environments as they secure and allocate essential resources.

REFLECTIONS AND RELEVANCE 11.4

Resource Dependence Theory and Resource Allocation

Resource dependence theory posits that since organizations depend on the outside environment to provide critical resources, administrators can reduce uncertainties and dependencies about securing and allocating these resources by using social relations and influence strategies.

Working in groups of four, discuss the following questions. Then bring the class together to discuss your findings.

[Note: Students might want to interview their principals or superintendents to find some of these answers and bring general observations—without "naming names"—to discuss at the next class. If so, all students from the same school or district should visit as a group to respect the superintendent or principals' time. Or, the professor can invite a current school administrator to visit this class and have class members interview this individual about RDT in action.]

1. What internal and external coalitions of individuals or group stakeholders hold considerable sway in your school district/school when it comes to securing resources or making resource allocation decisions?
2. Who are the most influential persons or departments inside and/or outside your school (or district) when it comes to securing resources or making resource allocation decisions?
3. Give examples of actions you have observed your school district superintendent or principal do to increase the school or district's "legitimacy" in the community.
4. Give examples of how you can, in your present position, use RDT to favorably influence internal and external stakeholders.
5. Identify several external constraints on your superintendent and/or principal's ability to secure or allocate resources.
6. Identify several in-house constraints on your superintendent and/or principal's ability to secure or allocate resources.
7. Identify several overt and covert influence strategies that you have observed or experienced as an educator. Describe the situation, the influence strategy, the outcome—and your personal and professional responses to its use.
8. Considering RDT, identify your own most valuable or essential resources as an educator. What can you do to increase or expand these?
9. Describe how can you use RDT in your present and future roles as an education leader.

IMPLICATIONS FOR EDUCATIONAL LEADERS

This chapter enhances school leaders' credibility as educators and accountability as responsible stewards of public dollars. Their mental models mature when they understand and act on the following conclusions: 1) Money matters in student achievement; 2) Essential education resources include more than dollars, teachers, and textbooks; 3) Targeting resources to learning-oriented activities improves student outcomes and accountability; 4) The schools' environments affect all these variables; and 5) School leaders' "people skills" can be a key resource that leverages student achievement goals from *potential* to *actual*.

Money Matters in Student Achievement

Despite rhetoric to the contrary, convincing evidence finds the link between money spent and student achievement is large enough to be educationally meaningful. But the money itself, while essential, is not sufficient to generate positive student results. Rather, *money in total dollars and how schools spend them* are equally important. Economists and education scholars agree: School funding specifically targeted toward effective teaching and learning favorably and measurably impacts student achievement.

Many studies have identified significant relationships between teaching effectiveness and student achievement, and these effects continue into adulthood. Notably, what teachers *do* with students in the classroom—how they *use* the instructional resources to design and interact with students around the academic tasks to mediate learning—is the means to successful results. With measurable and reportable outcomes, accountability is clear.

Essential School Resources are More Than Dollars, Teachers, and Textbooks

To generate the desired student outcomes, school leaders can draw on more than dollars and the teachers they hire or the books and computers they buy. Teachers and administrators' motivation, flexibility, knowledge, skills, values, priorities, and social and informational resources contribute to advancing each student's learning and wellbeing. Thoughtful investment in teachers' professional growth makes their skills available and renewable resources. In addition, assets stemming from personal attributes, environmental variables, parents and community qualities, and social and positional influence are resources that insightful school leaders can use strategically to improve teaching and student outcomes.

Information, itself, is a prized resource. Knowledge of research-based best practices for enhancing instructional effectiveness; specialized knowledge about ways to promote every student's academic progress and wellbeing; and personal familiarity with key players and how the school and community systems work can all be leveraged to benefit students. Such information enables leaders to make informed and coherent resource allocation decisions that move their schools forward.

Prioritize Learning-Focused Allocations

Resource allocations connect the means with their ends. Research evidence supports the link between resources directed to teaching and learning and improved student outcomes. A learning-oriented system for education resource allocation uses continuous instructional improvement to align and adapt assets to meet instructional goals. Gathering and interpreting evidence of student learning, identifying learners' needs, and assessing the effects of designated resources on student achievement gives school leaders the rationale and evidence to champion allocation options that favor student learning outcomes.

Of course, not everyone agrees about how to assign assets. To address competing interests, education leaders must make occasions to listen to those with varied viewpoints and try to reconcile these with improved teaching and learning outcomes. Likewise, leaders work with an eye to existing conditions and limitations that may prevent them from securing resources or making their preferred allocation decisions, and they adjust as necessary.

Remember the Environments

No organization is entirely self-sufficient. If schools are to function successfully, they need the right resources in the right amounts directed to the right activities. Schools rely on their internal and external environments to provide these. But resources are not always adequate, stable, or assured. Despite education leaders' apparent control, they are working in often unpredictable, varied, and changing contexts and situations (resource dependence theory).

To survive and thrive in such a dynamic setting, school leaders need a high degree of *situational awareness*[106]—the ongoing mindfulness of their immediate and wider environments. School leaders' situational awareness opens them to circumstances where they can identify and gain additional resources for their school—such as business summer internships for teachers or students or financial sponsorship for academic incentives. It can also help leaders spot occasions to generate community good will and get agreement for prioritizing resources for instructional ends. Situational awareness also heightens leaders' sensitivity to potential obstacles to securing or assigning resources that they can avoid or redirect. Managing the organization's environment is as important as managing the organization itself.

Environmental awareness also means recognizing that public schools vie for limited resources in a milieu of competing interests—political, organizational, and personal. Communities expect their education leaders to be effective and efficient with tax dollars. Determining *efficiency* in education is about evaluating how some schools achieve better or worse student performance outcomes than others given comparable spending. Of course, variables such as student demographics and community values also mediate between public schools' spending and learning outcomes. But as stewards of taxpayers' dollars, educators are obliged to show that they are improving student outcomes without substantially increasing costs (budget maximizing theory). Studies find an economically efficient relationship between educational inputs and student outcomes as long as the resources reach classrooms and students and are used appropriately. Given this, understanding the connections between school funding, budgets that prioritize effective teaching and student learning, and tying inputs to measurable and meaningful student outcomes can help school leaders justify their allocation decisions as efficient and effective means to maximize opportunities for student and school success.

Develop and Leverage Leaders' People Skills

Turning *potentials* into *actuals* also depends on school leaders' "people skills." Implicitly, this chapter suggests that successfully persuading others to provide resources, gaining supports for learning-focused allocation decisions, and motivating faculty and staff to continually enlarge their professional capacities builds upon many earlier pleasant and productive person-to-person exchanges. These so-called "soft skills" include awareness of self and others, having accurate empathy, speaking and listening effectively, and building relationships of trust, mutual respect, and productive interactions. School leaders' own personalities and personal characteristics—their reputations for competence, caring, and integrity; their approachability and friendliness; their ability to listen closely and speak effectively; their professional standing, perceived trustworthiness, and visibility in the school and community—can *become* invaluable resources. The same is true for any school members who engage with the public and need to gain their support.

Leveraging people skills enables school leaders to build wide-ranging relationships of shared interest in the academic success and wellbeing of every child. It helps them stay in touch with events, thinking, and undercurrents that could impact their school's effectiveness. The information and influence gained through these ongoing interactions make informed decisions possible. People skills also help school leaders expand the range of interested stakeholders who can accurately understand and appreciate what the schools do and what they need to improve teacher and student performance—and how to get them.

NOTES

1 National Center for Education Statistics (2015). *The condition of education 2015* (NCES 2015–144). *Public school expenditures*. Expenditures. Fast Facts. Washington, DC: U.S. Department of Education. Retrieved from: https://nces.ed.gov/fastfacts/display.asp?id=66.
2 A discussion of critical theory and resource allocation and a related learning activity appears on this book's companion website.
3 Odden, A.R. & Archibald, S. (2001). *Reallocating resources: How to boost student achievement without asking for more*. Thousand Oaks, CA: Corwin.
4 Pitner, N.J. & Ogawa, R.T. (1981). Organizational leadership: The case of the school superintendent. *Educational Administration Quarterly*, 17 (2), 45–65.
5 Cohen, D.K., Raudenbush, S.W. & Ball, D.L. (2003). Resources, instruction, and research. *Educational Evaluation and Policy Analysis*, 25 (2), 1–24.
6 Bryk, A. & Schneider, B. (2002). *Trust in schools: A core resource for improvement*. New York, NY: Russell Sage Foundation; Epstein, J. (2001). *School, family, and community partnerships: Preparing educators and improving schools*. Boulder, CO: Westview Press.

7 See: Bourdieu, P. (1986). The forms of capital. In J.E. Richardson (Ed.), *Handbook of theory of research for the sociology of education* (pp. 241–258). Westport, CT: Greenwood Press; Pfeffer, J. & Cialdini, R.B. (2003). Illusions of influence. In L.W. Porter, H.L. Angle & R.W. Allen (Eds), *Organizational influence processes* (pp. 59–73). New York, NY: M.E. Sharpe, Inc.

8 National Education Access Network. (2010). *Litigation.* New York, NY: Teachers College, Columbia University. Retrieved from: www.schoolfunding.info/litigation/litigation.php3; Harrison-Henderson, M. (2015, November 3). Mississippi's school funding challenge could be headed to court, no matter what voters decide. *HeckingerReport.org.* Retrieved from: http://hechingerreport.org/mississippis-school-funding-challenge-could-be-headed-to-court-no-matter-what-voters-decide/. The only states without funding adequacy litigation are Nevada, Utah, Hawaii, and Delaware.

9 Rebell, M.A. (2002). Education adequacy, democracy, and the courts. In T. Ready, E. Edley & C.E. Snow (Eds), *Achieving high educational standards for all: Conference summary* (pp. 218–268). Washington, DC: National Academy Press.

10 Superville, D.T. (2015, March 18). Districts expanding efforts to align budgets, academics. *Education Week, 34* (24), 1, 18.

11 Lips, D., Watkins, S.J. & Fleming. (2008, September 8). Does spending more on education improve academic achievement? *Backgrounder, 2179.* Washington, DC: The Heritage Foundation. Retrieved from: http://files.eric.ed.gov/fulltext/ED509499.pdf.

12 Hedges, L., Laine, R. & McLoughlin, M. (1994). Does money matter? A meta-analysis of studies of the effects of differential school inputs on student outcomes. *Educational Researcher, 23* (3), 5–14; Greenwald, R., Hedges, L.V. & Laine, R.D. (1996). The effect of school resources on student achievement. *Review of Educational Research, 66* (3), 361–396.

13 Coleman, J.S., Campbell, E.Q., Hobson, C.J., McPartland, J., Mood, A.M., Weinfeld, F.D. & York, R.L. (1966). *Equality of educational opportunity.* Washington, DC: U.S. Government Printing Office.

14 Cohen, Raudenbush & Ball (2003). Op. cit.; Jencks, C. (1972). *Inequality: A reassessment of the effect of family and schooling in America.* New York, NY: Basic Books.

15 Hanushek, E.A. (1986). The economics of schooling: Production and efficiency in public schools. *Journal of Economic Literature, 24* (3), 1141–1177; Hanushek, E.A. (1997). Assessing the effects of school resources on student performance: An update. *Educational Evaluation and Policy Analysis, 19* (2), 141–164.

16 Hedges, Laine & Greenwald (1994). Op. cit.; Greenwald, Hedges & Laine (1996). Op. cit.

17 Greenwald, Hedges & Laine (1996). Ibid; Hedges, L.V. & Greenwald, R. (1996). Have times changed? The relation between school resources and student performance. In G. Burtless (Ed.), *Does money matter? The effect of school resources on student achievement and adult success* (pp. 74–92). Washington, DC: Brookings Institution Press.

18 See: Cooper, B.S., Sarrel, R., Darvas, P., Alfano, F., Meier, E., Samuels, J. & Heinbuch, S. (1994). Making money matter in education: A micro-financial model for determining school-level allocations, efficiency, and productivity. *Journal of Education Finance, 20* (3), 66–87; Verstegen, D.A. & King, R.A. (1998). The relationship between school spending and student achievement: A review and analysis of 35 years of production function research. *Journal of Education Finance, 24* (4), 243–262.

19 Achilles, C.M., Harman, P. & Egelson, P. (1995). Using research results on class size to improve pupil achievement outcomes. *Research in the Schools, 2* (1), 23–30; Achilles, C.M. (2012). Class size policy: The STAR experiment and related class-size studies. *NCPEA Policy Brief, 1* (2). Ypsilanti, MI: National Council of Professors of Educational Administration.

20 Wenglinsky, H. (1997). *School district expenditures, school resources and student achievement: Modeling the production function.* Washington, DC: National Center for Education Statistics, Institute for Education Sciences. Retrieved from: https://nces.ed.gov/pubs98/dev97/98212h.asp.

21 See: Wright, S.P., Horn, S.P. & Sanders, W.L. (1997). Teacher and classroom context effects on student achievement: Implications for teacher evaluation. *Journal of Personnel Evaluation in Education, 11* (1), 57–67; Nye, B., Konstantopoulos, S.M. & Hedges, L.V. (2004). How large are teacher effects? *Educational Evaluation and Policy Analysis, 26* (3), 237–257.

22 Chetty, R., Friedman, J.N. & Rockoff, J.E. (2011). *The long-term impacts of teachers: Teacher value-added and student outcomes in adulthood.* NBER Working Paper 17699. Cambridge, MA: National Bureau of Economic Research. Retrieved from: http://standardized tests.procon.org/sourcefiles/the-long-term-impacts-of-teachers-teacher-value-added-and-student-outcomes-in-adulthood.pdf.

23 Brophy, J. & Good, T. (1986). Teacher behavior and student achievement. In M.C. Wittrock (Ed.), *Handbook of research on teaching,* 3rd ed. (pp. 328–375). New York, NY: Macmillan Publishing.

24 Hanushek, E.A. (2016, Spring). What matters for student achievement? *Education Next, 16* (2), 23–30. Retrieved from: http://hanushek.stanford.edu/sites/default/files/publications/Hanushek%202016%20EdNext%2016%282%29.pdf.

25 See: Edmonds, R. (1984). School effects and teacher effects. *Social Policy, 15* (2). 37–39; Edmonds, R. (1979). Effective schools for the urban poor. *Educational Leadership, 37* (1), 15–27; Rutter, M., Maughan B., Mortimore, P., Ousten, M. & Smith, A. (1979). *Fifteen thousand hours: Secondary schools and their effects on children.* Cambridge, MA: Harvard University Press.

26 Leinhardt, G., Zigmond, N. & Cooley, W. (1981). Reading instruction and its effects. *American Educational Research Journal, 18* (3), 343–361.

27 Dweck, C.S. (1986). Motivational processes affecting learning. *American Psychologist, 57* (5), 1179–1187; Dweck, C.S. (1988). Children's thinking about traits: Implications for judgments of the self and others. *Child Development, 69* (2), 391–403.

28 Hanushek (2016, Spring). Op. cit.

29 Rolle, A. (2003). Getting the biggest bang for the educational buck: An empirical analysis of public school corporations as budget-maximizing bureaus. In *Developments in school finance: 2001–02.* Fiscal proceedings from the annual state data conferences of July 2001 and July 2002 (pp. 27–36). Washington, DC: U.S. Department of Education, Institute of Education Sciences, NCES 2003–403. Retrieved from: http://nces.ed.gov/pubs2003/2003403.pdf#page=36.

30 Baker, B.D. & Welner, K.G. (2011, December). *Productivity research, the U.S. Department of Education, and high-quality evidence.* Boulder, CO: National Education Policy Center, University of Colorado Boulder.

31 Fortune, J.C. & O'Neil, J.S. (1994). Production-function analyses and the study of educational funding equity: A methodological critique. *Journal of Education Finance, 20* (1), 21–46.

32 William Baumol was a 1960s economist who observed that productivity—defined as the quantity of product per dollar expended—in the labor-intensive services sector lags behind manufacturing. Because labor-intensive services must compete with other parts of the economy for work, but it cannot cut staff without reducing output, costs constantly rise. The phenomenon of rising costs without corresponding output increases has been labeled *Baumol's cost disease.*

33 Hill, P. & Roza, M. (2010). *Curing Baumol's disease: In search of productivity gains in K-12 schooling.* Bothell, WA: Center on Reinventing Public Education, University of Washington, p. 1. Retrieved from: www.crpe.org/sites/default/files/whp_crpe1_baumols_jul10_0.pdf.

34 Higher costs include increases in educators' salaries and their health and pension benefits, increased numbers of employees including non-core teachers. See: Hill & Roza (2010). Ibid.

35 Petrilli, M. & Roza, M. (2011). *Stretching the school dollar: A brief for state policymakers.* Washington, DC: Thomas B. Fordham Institute. Retrieved from: http://edex.s3-us-west-2.amazonaws.com/publication/pdfs/20110106_STSD_PolicyBrief_8.pdf.

36 Chingos, M.M. (2014, June 5). Who profits from the master's degree pay bump for teachers? Brookings. Retrieved from: www.brookings.edu/research/papers/2014/06/05-masters-degree-pay-bump-chingos; Goldhaber, D. & Theobald, R. (2011). Managing the teacher workforce. *Education Next, 11* (4). Retrieved from: http://educationnext.org/managing-the-teacher-work force/; National Institute on Retirement Security. (2015, February). *Case studies of state pension plans that switched to defined contribution plans.* Washington, DC. Retrieved from: www.rsa-al.gov/uploads/files/Case_Studies_State_Pension_Plans_that_switched_to_DC_ Plans.pdf; Tuna, C. (2010, February 19). Fiscal woes push up class sizes. *The Wall Street Journal.* Retrieved from: www.wsj.com/articles/SB100014240527487043370045750600300 26160638.

37 Baker & Welner (2011). Op. cit., p. 16, Figure 1.

38 Since 1960, the increased number of teachers and their costs result from: inflation, increased school enrollments, the influx of students with special needs who required more intensive work with teachers, and the mandated reductions in class sizes. None of these categories are directly related to student instruction or achievement. Plus, NAEP scores have noticeably improved for each of the nation's commonly identified racial and ethnic subgroups over the past 35 years. See: Hanushek, E.A. & Rivkin, S.G. (1997). Understanding the twentieth century's growth in U.S. school spending. *Journal of Human Resources, 32* (1), 35–68; Barton, P.D. & Coley, R.J. (2010). *The Black–White achievement gap: When progress stopped.* Princeton, NJ: Educational Testing Service. Retrieved from: http://files.eric.ed.gov/ fulltext/ED511548.pdf.

39 Baker & Welner (2011). Op. cit.

40 Wildavsky, A. (1964). *The politics of the budgetary process.* Boston, MA: Little, Brown, and Company; Lynn, L.E. (1991). The budget-maximizing bureaucrat: Is there a case? In A. Blais & S. Dion (Eds), *The budget-maximizing bureaucrat: Appraisals and evidence* (pp. 59–84). Pittsburgh: University of Pittsburgh Press.

41 Niskanen, W.A. (1971). *Bureaucracy and representative government.* New York, NY: Aldine; Niskanen, W. (1975). Bureaucrats and politicians. *The Journal of Law and Economics 18* (3), 617–643.

42 Barnett, W.S. (1994). Obstacles and opportunities: Some simple economics of school finance reform. *Educational Policy, 8* (4), 436–452.

43 Mises, L. (1944). *Bureaucracy.* New Haven, CT: Yale University Press (pp. 47–49).

44 Niskanen, W.A. (1968). The peculiar economics of bureaucracy. *American Economic Review, 58* (2), 293–305; Niskanen, W.A. (1973). *Bureaucracy: Servant or master?* London, UK: The Institute of Economic Affairs.

45 Niskanen (1973). Ibid.

46 Niskanen (1968). Op. cit.; Niskanen (1971). Op. cit.; Niskanen (1975). Op. cit.

47 See: Bush, W.C. & Denzau, A.T. (1977). The voting behavior of bureaucrats and public sector growth. In T.E. Borcherding (Ed.), *Budgets and bureaucrats: The sources of government growth* (pp. 90–99). Durham, NC: Duke University Press; Lynn, L.E. (1991). The budget-maximizing bureaucrat: Is there a case? In A. Blais and S. Dion (Eds), *The budget-maximizing bureaucrat: Appraisals and evidence* (pp. 59–84). Pittsburgh, PA: University of Pittsburgh Press.

48 Blais, A. & Dion, S. (1991). Conclusions: Are bureaucrats budget maximizers? In A. Blais and S. Dion (Eds), *The budget-maximizing bureaucrat: Appraisals and evidence* (pp. 355–361). Pittsburgh, PA: University of Pittsburgh Press.

49 Kiewiet, D.R. (1991). Bureaucrats and budgetary outcomes: Quantitative analyses. In A. Blais and S. Dion (Eds), *The budget-maximizing bureaucrat: Appraisals and evidence* (pp. 143–174). Pittsburgh, PA: University of Pittsburgh Press.

50 Campbell, C. & Naulls, D. (1991). The limits of the budget-maximizing theory: Some evidence from officials' views of their roles and careers. In A. Blais & S. Dion (Eds), *The budget-maximizing bureaucrat: Appraisals and evidence* (pp. 85–118). Pittsburgh, PA: University of Pittsburgh Press.

51 Young, R.A. (1991). Budget size and bureaucratic careers. In A. Blais & S. Dion (Eds), *The budget-maximizing bureaucrat: Appraisals and evidence* (pp. 33–58). Pittsburgh, PA: University of Pittsburgh Press.

52 Aucoin, P. (1991). The politics and management of restraint budgeting. In A. Blais & S. Dion (Eds), *The budget-maximizing bureaucrat: Appraisals and evidence* (pp. 119–142). Pittsburgh, PA: University of Pittsburgh Press.

53 Campbell & Naulls (1991). Op. cit.; McNutt, P.A. (1996). *The economics of public choice.* Brookfield, VT: Edward Elgar; Stevens, J.B. (1993). *The economics of collective choice.* Boulder, CO: Westview.

54 One of its principal theorists, W.A. Niskanen, was associated with the CATO Institute, a libertarian-leaning think tank founded by Charles Koch.

55 Buchholz, T.G. (1990). *New ideas from dead economists: An introduction to modern economic thought.* New York, NY: Plume; Downs, A. (1998). *Political theory and public choice.* North Hampton, MA: Edward Elgar.

56 Jennings, J. (2013, March 28). Proportion of U.S. students in private schools is 10 percent and declining. The Blog. *Huffpost Politics.* Retrieved from: www.huffingtonpost.com/jack-jennings/proportion-of-us-students_b_2950948.html.

57 Rolle, A. (2004). An empirical discussion of public school districts as budget-maximizing agencies. *Journal of Education Finance, 29* (4), 277–297.

58 Alexander, K. (1998). Money matters: Commentary and analyses. *Journal of Education Finance, 24* (4), 237–242.

59 Pfeffer, J. & Salancik, G.R. (1978/2003). *The external control of organizations: A resource dependence perspective.* New York, NY: Harper & Row.

60 Hillman, A.J., Withers, M.C. & Collins, B.J. (2009). Resource dependence theory: A review. *Journal of Management, 35* (6), 1404–1427.

61 Aldrich, H.E. and Pfeffer, J. (1976). Environments of organizations. *Annual Review of Sociology, 2* (1), 79–105; Pfeffer, J. & Salancik, G.R. (1978/2003). *The external control of organizations: A resource dependence perspective.* New York, NY: Harper & Row; Thompson, J.D. (1967). *Organizations in action: Social science bases of administrative theory.* New York, NY: McGraw-Hill.

62 Salancik, G.R. & Pfeffer, J. (1974). The bases and use of power in organizational decision making: The case of a university. *Administrative Science Quarterly, 19* (4), 453–473; Salancik, G.R., Pfeffer, J. & Kelly, J.P. (1978). A contingency model of influence in organizational decision-making. *Pacific Sociological Review, 21* (2), 239–256; Pfeffer & Salancik (1978/2003). Op. cit.

63 Atlas. NewsAmerica (2015, June 29). Federal, state, and local K-12 school finance overview. *PreK-12 Financing Overview.* Retrieved from: http://atlas.newamerica.org/school-finance.

64 Pfeffer, J. (1987). A resource dependence perspective on interorganizational relations. In M.S. Mizruchi & M. Schwartz (Eds), *Intercorporate relations: The structural analysis of business* (pp. 22–55). Cambridge, UK: Cambridge University Press.

65 Benson, K.J. (1975). The interlocking network as a political economy. *Administrative Science Quarterly, 20* (2), 229–249; Pfeffer & Salancik (1978). Op. cit.; Silver, R.S. Conditions of autonomous action and performance. *Administration and Society 24* (4), 487–511.

66 Pfeffer & Salancik (1978/2003) suggest boards of directors as one of the actions that organizations can take to minimize environmental dependencies.

67 Pfeffer & Salancik (1978/2003). Op. cit. Like beauty, legitimacy rests in the eyes of the beholder.

68 See: Pfeffer & Salancik (1978/2003). Op. cit.; Luoma, P. & Goodstein, J. (1999). Stakeholders and corporate boards: Institutional influences on board composite and structure. *Academy of Management Journal, 4* (2), 553–563; Johnson, R.A. & Greening, D.W. (1999). The effects of corporate governance and institutional ownership types of corporate social performance. *Academy of Management Journal, 42* (5), 564–576.

69 Boeker, W. & Goodstein, J. (1991). Organizational performance and adaptation: Effects of environment and performance on changes in board composition. *Academy of Management Journal, 34* (4), 805–826; Pfeffer, J. (1972b). Size and composition of corporate boards of directors. *Administrative Science Quarterly, 17* (2), 218–229.

70 Iannaccone, L. & Lutz, F.W. (1970). *Politics, power and policy: The governing of local school districts.* Columbus, OH: Charles E. Merrill Publishing Company.

71 See: Alsbury, T.L. (2008). Hitting a moving target: How politics determines the changing roles of superintendents and school boards. In B.S. Cooper, J.G. Cibulka & L.D. Fusarelli (Eds), *Handbook of Education Politics and Policy* (pp. 126–147). New York, NY: Routledge; Berkman, M.B. & Plutzer, E. (2005). *Ten thousand democracies: Politics and public opinion in America's school districts.* Washington, DC: Georgetown University Press.

72 See: Banks, J.A. (1993). The canon debate, knowledge construction, and multicultural education. *Educational Researcher, 22* (5), 4–14; Loveless, T. (Ed.) (2002). *The great curriculum debate: How should we teach reading and math?* Washington, DC: Brookings; Cibulka, J.G. (1999). Ideological lenses for interpreting political and economic changes affecting schooling. In J. Murphy & K.S. Louis (Eds), *Handbook of research on educational administration,* 2nd ed. (pp. 163–192). San Francisco, CA: Jossey-Bass.

73 Hess, F.M. & Meeks, O. (2011). *Governance in the accountability era: The National School Boards Association,* The Thomas B. Fordham Institute, and the Iowa School Boards Foundation.

74 Grissom, J.A. (2010). The determinants of conflict on governing boards in public organizations: The case of California school boards. *Journal of Public Administration Research and Theory, 20* (3), 601–627.

75 Willower, D.J. (1991). Micropolitics and the sociology of school organizations. *Education and Urban Society, 23* (4), 442–454.

76 Iannaccone, L. & Lutz, F.W. (1970). *Politics, power and policy: The governing of local school districts.* Columbus, OH: Charles E. Merrill.

77 Eliot (1959). Op. cit.; Weiss, C.H. (1995). The four "I's" of school reform: How interests, ideology, information, and institution affect teachers and principals. *Harvard Educational Review, 65* (4), 571–593.

78 See: Levi, M. & Stoker, L. (2000). Political trust and trustworthiness. *Annual Review of Political Science, 3* (1), 475–507; Petersen, G.J. & Short, P.M. (2001). The school board president's perception of the district superintendent: Applying the lenses of social influence and social style. *Educational Administration Quarterly, 37* (4), 533–570.

79 Bourdieu, P. (1991). *Language and symbolic power* (Trans. G. Raymond & M. Adamson). Cambridge, UK: Polity Press.

80 See: Malen, B. (2006). Revisiting policy implementation as a political phenomenon: The case of reconstitution policies. In M.I. Honig (Ed.), *New directions in education policy implementation* (pp. 83–104). Albany, NY: State University of New York Press; March, J.G. & Simon, H.A. (1958). *Organizations.* New York, NY: John Wiley & Sons.

81 Zeehandelaar, D.B. (2012). *The local politics of education governance: Power and influence among school boards, superintendents, and teachers' unions.* (Unpublished doctoral dissertation) University of Southern California, Los Angeles, CA.

82 Zeehandelaar (2012). Ibid.

83 Bourdieu (1991). Op. cit.; Lukes, S. (1974, 2005). *Power: A radical view.* London, UK: Macmillan.

84 See: Chubb, J.E. & Moe, T.M. (1990). *Politics, markets, and America's schools.* Washington, DC: Brookings Institute; Goldstein, R.A. (2010). Imaging the frame: Media representations of teachers, their unions, NCLB, and education reform. *Educational Policy, 25* (4), 543–576.

85 See: Nienhüser, W. (2008). Resource dependence theory: How well does it explain behavior of organizations? *Management Revue, 19* (1/2), 9–32; Provan, K.G., Beyer, J.M. & Kruytbosch, C. (1980): Environmental linkages and power in resource-dependence

relations between organizations. *Administrative Science Quarterly, 25* (2), 200–225; Saidel, J.R. (1991). Resource interdependence: The relationship between state agencies and nonprofit organizations. *Public Administration Review, 51* (6), 543–553.

86 See: Lieberson, S. & O'Connor, J.F. (1972). Leadership and organizational performance: A study of large corporations. *American Sociological Review, 37* (2), 117–130; Salancik, G.R. & Pfeffer, J. (1977). Constraints on administrator discretion. The limited influence of mayors on city budgets. *Urban Affairs Quarterly, 12* (4), 475–498.

87 See: Pfeffer, J. (1972a). Merger as a response to organizational interdependence. *Administrative Science Quarterly, 17* (3), 382–394; Finkelstein, S. (1997). Interindustry merger patterns and resource dependence: A replication and extension of Pfeffer (1972a). *Strategic Management Journal, 18* (10), 787–810.

88 Mountford, M. (2008). Historical and current tensions among board-superintendent teams: Symptoms or cause? In T.L. Alsbury (Ed.), *The future of school board governance* (pp. 81–114). Lanham, MD: Rowman & Littlefield.

89 Tallerico, M. (1989). The dynamics of superintendent-school board relationships. *Urban Education, 24* (2), 215–232.

90 Marshall, C. & Mitchell, B.A. (1991). The assumptive worlds of fledgling administrators. *Education and Urban Society, 23* (4), 396–415.

91 Danzberger, J.P. & Usdan, M.D. (1994). Local education governance: Perspectives on problems and strategies for change. *Phi Delta Kappan, 75* (5), 366; Land, D. (2002). Local school boards under review: Their role and effectiveness in relation to students' academic achievement. *Review of Educational Research, 72* (2), 229–278.

92 Zeehandelaar (2012). Op. cit.

93 See: Bjork, L.G. & Gurley, D.K. (2005). Superintendent as educational statesman and political strategist. In L. G. Bjork & T.J. Kowalski (Eds), *The contemporary superintendent* (pp. 163–186). Thousand Oaks, CA: Corwin Press; Bjork, L.G., & Keedy, J.L. (2001). Politics and the superintendency in the USA: Restructuring in-service education. *Journal of In-Service Education, 27* (2), 275–302.

94 See: Greene, K.R. (1992). Models of school board policy-making. *Educational Administration Quarterly, 28* (2), 220–236; Hess (1999). *Spinning wheels.* Op. cit.; Iannaccone & Lutz (1970). Op. cit.

95 See: Zeigler, L.H., Jennings, M.K. & Peak, G.W. (1974). *Governing American schools: Political interaction in local school districts.* North Scituate, MA: Duxbury Press; Hess & Meeks (2011). Op. cit.; Petersen, G.J. & Short, P.M. (2001). The school board president's perception of the district superintendent: Applying the lenses of social influence and social style. *Educational Administration Quarterly, 37* (4), 533–570.

96 See: Boyd, W.L. (1976). The public, the professionals, and educational policy making: Who governs? *The Teachers College Record, 77* (4), 539–578; Greene (1991). Op. cit.; Zeigler et al. (1974). Op. cit.

97 See: Carter, G.G. & Cunningham, W.G. (1997). *The American school superintendent: Leading in an age of pressure.* San Francisco, CA: Jossey-Bass; Kowalski,T.J., McCord, R.S., Petersen, G.J., Young, I.P. & Ellerson, N.M. (2011). *The American school superintendent 2010 decennial study.* Lanham, MD: Rowman & Littlefield Publishing.

98 Boyd (1976). Op. cit.; Pitner & Ogawa (1981). Op. cit.; Kowalski et al. (2011). Op. cit.

99 Critics, for example, claim that organizations are more political, shaped by materialistic forces, and socially constructed, unlike how RDT sees them. See: Donaldson, L. (1995). *American anti-management theories of organizations.* Cambridge, UK: Cambridge University Press; Johnson, B.L. (1995). *Resource dependence theory: A political economy model of organizations.* ERIC Number ED387871. Retrieved from: http://files.eric.ed.gov/fulltext/ED387871.pdf; Clegg, S.R. & Rura-Polley, T. (1998). Jeffrey Pfeffer (1946–); Gerald R. Salancik (1943–96). In M. Warner (Ed.), *The IEBM handbook of management thinking.* (pp. 537–543). London, UK: International Thomson Business Press.

100 Walsh, J.P., Meyer, A.D. & Schoonhoven, C.B. (2006). A future for organization theory: Living in and living with changing organizations. *Organization Science, 17* (5), 657–671.

101 Johnson (1995). Op. cit.

102 Clarke, A.E. (1991). Social worlds/arenas theory as organizational theory. In A.L. Strauss & D.R. Maines (Eds), *Social organization and social process: Essays in honor of Anselm Strauss.* (pp, 119–158). New York, NY: Aldine de Gruyter.

103 Lamsa, A-M. & Pucetaite, R. (2006). Development of organizational trust among employees from a contextual perspective. *Business Ethics: A European Review, 15* (2), 130–141.

104 Frooman, J. (1999), Stakeholders influence strategies. *Academy of Management Review, 24* (2), 191–205.

105 Corbetta, G. & Salvato, C.A. (2004). The board of directors in family firms: One size fits all? *Family Business Review, 17* (2), 119–134.

106 In a meta-analysis of the school leadership research, 1978 to 2001, situational awareness had the highest statistically significant correlation with student achievement of the 21 specific types of school leader responsibilities. See: Marzano, R.J., Waters, T. & McNulty, B.A. (2005). *School leadership that works: From research to results.* Alexandria, VA: ASCD.

Index